P9-DGB-585

THE COMMENTARY READER

THE COMMENTARY READER

Two Decades of Articles and Stories

Edited by

NORMAN PODHORETZ

With an Introduction by Alfred Kazin

Atheneum New York

1966

Library of Congress catalog card number 66–16360
Published simultaneously in Canada by McClelland and Stewart Ltd.
Manufactured in the United States of America by H. Wolff, New York
Designed by Harry Ford
First Edition

IN MEMORIAM

ELLIOT E. COHEN

PREFACE

As has often been said by critics and admirers alike, *Commentary* is something of an anomaly. Subsidized by an organization with its own purposes to pursue, the magazine nevertheless enjoys complete editorial independence (which means simply that it is for the editors, and the editors alone, to decide what shall or shall not be published); a magazine with a special interest in problems of particular concern to Jews, it nevertheless deals regularly, and often preponderantly, with matters of the most general concern; a magazine for intellectuals, it nevertheless aims at being intelligible at all times to the "lay" reader; a magazine that aspires as far as possible to solidarity and scholarliness (what some would call "responsibility"), it nevertheless is at least sporadically hospitable to playfulness of mind and utopian speculation (what some would call "irresponsibility").

These apparent contradictions—and the list could easily be extended —were inherent in the enterprise from its very beginnings. *Commentary* was founded at the end of World War II by the American Jewish Committee "to meet the need for a journal of significant thought and opinion on Jewish affairs and contemporary issues." Sponsoring such a journal was, the Committee said, in line with its "general program to enlighten and clarify public opinion on problems of Jewish concern, to fight bigotry and protect human rights, and to promote Jewish cultural interest and creative achievement in America." Obviously, this abstract mandate might have been interpreted in any number of ways. The late Elliot E. Cohen, who was appointed editor of the new monthly and presided over it until his tragic death in 1959, chose to interpret it in the broadest possible sense. Thus the first issue of *Commentary* ever to appear (November 1945) included, along with essays on "The Spiritual Reconstruction of European Jewry" by the great historian Salo Baron and "On Being a Jewish Person" by the great theologian Franz Rosenzweig, a report by George Orwell on the British General Elections, a piece on the state of the theater by Louis Kronenberger, a short story by Paul Goodman, and reviews by Mary McCarthy (of Sophie Tucker's autobiography), the late Randall Jarrell (of a Canadian poet), and Harold Rosenberg (of a book by Thomas Mann).

And so it proceeded: a series on "The Crisis of the Individual" in which such figures as Reinhold Niebuhr and John Dewey participated, alternating with articles on "The Crisis in Palestine," Hasidism, anti-Semitism, Jewish music. In virtually every issue during the first few years there were contributions by as yet relatively obscure writers and critics like Saul Bellow, Hannah Arendt, James Baldwin, Alfred Kazin, Isaac Rosenfeld, Bernard Malamud, Irving Howe, and Nathan Glazer—some on "Jewish affairs," some on "contemporary issues," some on subjects that fell simultaneously into both categories. The result was that within an unusually short time Elliot Cohen (with the help of an extraordinarily gifted staff that included the late Robert Warshow, Nathan Glazer, Clement Greenberg, Irving Kristol, and later Martin Greenberg) succeeded in stamping the new magazine with an unmistakable identity which, with all the changes that were to take place in the next twenty years, would remain remarkably constant.

All good editors have a style, and it was the essence of Elliot Cohen's style that the magazine he produced should appear to be self-generated: no editor ever hid from his readers more insistently than he, and no "journal of opinion" ever came before the world with so chaste a presentation, chaste even in format and typography. When you looked at the cover of an issue of *Commentary* as edited by Elliot Cohen, you saw a quiet pattern of type that suggested homage to the classic virtues—order, harmony, balance, the whole taking precedence over the individual parts. No single article was ever featured, and the subject of each piece was always stressed above the name of its author, even when the author was a figure like Thomas Mann or John Dewey or Jean-Paul Sartre.

But the fact is that the impersonality of *Commentary*—as any of its contributors can testify—derived from a very powerful exertion of personality. At least half of the articles Elliot Cohen published were written only because he forced them into being. He was gifted with an uncanny sensitivity to what may be called the representative issues—that is, the problems preying on the minds of a great many people at any given moment, sometimes a touch below the level of awareness—and therefore he invariably knew where the relevant areas of discussion lay and by which writers they might be illuminated. Some editors (Robert Warshow was an example) are distinguished for their understanding of the peculiar talents of others, and they operate by helping a writer to realize his own intentions more perfectly. Elliot Cohen, on the other hand, was the kind of editor who works largely by feeding ideas to writers and by encouraging them to push harder and aim higher than they might otherwise have done. He was more concerned with broadening their intentions than with bringing the ideas they already had into full flower, and often he opened new worlds for them to explore, worlds of whose existence they had scarcely been conscious before. Given the energy and the skill with which he exercised this impulse to teach and guide and influence, virtually no article ever appeared in *Commentary* without some trace of his hand.

Commentary reflected the personality of Elliot Cohen in many other ways too. The great variety of subjects the magazine covered was not simply the mark of his limitless curiosity; it was—as Lionel Trilling once put it—a direct consequence of his refusal of intellectual "purity," a refusal to define himself by his exclusions and snobberies rather than by his passions and enthusiasms. To be sure, there was an ideological side to this refusal that several critics of *Commentary* found repugnant. These critics maintained that the widespread disillusionment with radicalism among intellectuals (Jewish intellectuals especially) had not, after all, changed the fact that American society was in its nature antagonistic to the values of a truly humane civilization, and they charged that the more "positive" relation to the culture implied by Elliot Cohen's stance was a species of "conformity." But the ideological issue mattered far less to the kind of magazine *Commentary* was than its critics (and perhaps even its editor) realized. What did matter was the unremitting monthly effort to create a magazine that would be simultaneously daring in conception and responsible in execution; a magazine that would look for a way of being both Jewish and non-parochial, of satisfying the requirements of the specialist as well as the needs of the literate reading public, of taking a stand against the decay of standards without falling victim to academicism, preciosity, or the spirit of coterie.

Those of us who have been charged with the responsibility for carrying on with *Commentary* since Elliot Cohen's death have continued to pursue these goals, and we have tried to remain true to the tradition of discourse he established—though it goes without saying that one can remain true to a tradition only by adapting it to changing circumstances. *Commentary* since 1960 has undergone several changes of format and several shifts in emphasis, but the aims of the magazine are much the same as they always were. *Commentary* today is less concerned than it used to be with the sociology of the American Jewish community, with the social sciences in general, with the character of the American middle class. It does, however, remain as interested as ever in the meaning of the Holocaust, the role of the United States in international affairs, the importance of ethnicity and religion in American life, the quality of contemporary culture, the problems of education, the elusive nature of Jewishness. It also remains committed to the idea that these varying preoccupations are all aspects of a single effort to make sense of the contemporary world. Lionel Trilling has said of Elliot Cohen that his "mind was dominated by his sense of the subtle interrelations that exist between the seemingly disparate parts of culture, and between the commonplaces of daily life and the most highly developed works of the human mind." This sense of things still lies behind the apparent anomaly that is *Commentary;* indeed, this sense of things *is Commentary.*

A word about the principle by which this book was put together. Limitations of space prohibited the inclusion of everything I would have wished to include, and consequently articles and stories have been omitted which had as good a claim to be included as those which eventually were included. So, too, many authors who were important contributors to the magazine are missing from this collection, usually because their pieces were rooted almost entirely in situations and problems which are no longer relevant or pressing. Because of these omissions, this volume does not provide a complete picture of the development of *Commentary* over the years, but it does, I hope, reflect the dominant concerns of the magazine in its first two decades. Each of the seven sections has been arranged chronologically, to give some rough notion of how a particular area of discussion was explored over time; and, with minor exceptions, none of the pieces has been altered (although, as is indicated in each case, a few titles have been changed). Thus, though not everything that has been characteristic of *Commentary* is reflected in this book, everything in this book is in some way characteristic of *Commentary.*

Thanks are due to Midge Decter, who aided in the agonizing job of making the selections; to my colleagues Theodore Solotaroff, Werner Dannhauser, and Marion Magid; to my secretary, Madeline Belkin; and above all to Ralph Samuel and the *Commentary* Publication Committee and John Slawson and the American Jewish Committee, whose generosity, boldness, and sympathy have made *Commentary* possible.

N. P.

CONTENTS

ALFRED KAZIN — *Introduction: The Jew as Modern American Writer* — xv

I THE HOLOCAUST AND AFTER

MARTIN GREENBERG — *The Common Man of the Nazis* — 3
IRVING KRISTOL — *The Nature of Nazism* — 11
SOLOMON F. BLOOM — *Dictator of the Lodz Ghetto* — 30
HANNAH ARENDT — *Germany—1950* — 49
HERBERT LUETHY — *Der Führer* — 61
THEODORE FRANKEL — *My Friend Paul* — 77
HAROLD ROSENBERG — *The Trial and Eichmann* — 98
TADEUSZ BOROWSKI — *This Way for the Gas* — 115

II EAST AND WEST

DAVID BERGELSON — *Story's End* — 129
LIONEL ABEL — *Art While Being Ruled* — 148
SIDNEY HOOK, H. STUART HUGHES, HANS J. MORGENTHAU, C. P. SNOW — *Western Values and Total War* — 159
OSCAR GASS — *China and the United States* — 200
GEORGE LICHTHEIM — *Reflections on Trotsky* — 240

III THE LIGHT OF HISTORY

ISAAC BABEL — *First Love* — 259

THEODOR H. GASTER	*The Passing of the Batlan*	265
MIDGE DECTER	*The Legacy of Henrietta Szold*	272
R. H. S. CROSSMAN	*Gentile Zionism and the Balfour Declaration*	284
ISAAC BASHEVIS SINGER	*Yentl the Yeshiva Boy*	295
DAVID DAICHES	*Presenting the Bible*	315
	IV GROUPS	
SAUL BELLOW	*Looking for Mr. Green*	335
BERNARD MALAMUD	*The Loan*	353
WALLACE MARKFIELD	*The Country of the Crazy Horse*	359
DAN JACOBSON	*The Example of Lipi Lippmann*	368
NORMAN PODHORETZ	*My Negro Problem—and Ours*	376
NATHAN GLAZER	*Negroes and Jews: The New Challenge to Pluralism*	388
MILTON HIMMELFARB	*How We Are*	399
BAYARD RUSTIN	*From Protest to Politics*	411
	V THOUGHT IN CRISIS	
CLEMENT GREENBERG	*The Plight of Our Culture*	425
EMIL L. FACKENHEIM	*The Dilemma of Liberal Judaism*	438
GERSHOM SCHOLEM	*Martin Buber's Hasidism*	451
LIONEL TRILLING	*Science, Literature, and Culture*	467
DAVID T. BAZELON	*The Paper Economy*	489
HENRY DAVID AIKEN	*The Revolt Against Ideology*	507
LESLIE H. FARBER	*"I'm Sorry, Dear"*	528
	VI WRITING	
EDMUND WILSON	*Paul Rosenfeld: Three Phases*	545
PHILIP RAHV	*Self-Definition in American Literature*	556
DWIGHT MACDONALD	*By Cozzens Possessed*	567
HENRY ROTH	*The Dun Dakotas*	586

IRVING HOWE — *A Yiddish "Modernist"* 589
PHILIP ROTH — *Writing American Fiction* 595
MARION MAGID — *The Innocence of Tennessee Williams* 610

VII THE AMERICAN PREDICAMENT

LESLIE A. FIEDLER — *Hiss, Chambers, and the Age of Innocence* 625
ROBERT WARSHOW — *The "Idealism" of Julius and Ethel Rosenberg* 642
JAMES BALDWIN — *Equal in Paris* 651
ISAAC ROSENFELD — *Life in Chicago* 664
NORMAN STEIN — *A Second Chance for Samson* 682
DANIEL BELL — *The Subversion of Collective Bargaining* 697
THEODORE SOLOTAROFF — *The Graduate Student: A Profile* 715
EDGAR Z. FRIEDENBERG — *The Gifted Student and His Enemies* 727
PAUL GOODMAN — *The Ineffectuality of Some Intelligent People* 740
WILLIAM PHILLIPS — *What Happened in the 30's* 752

INTRODUCTION

THE JEW AS MODERN AMERICAN WRITER

by Alfred Kazin

Emma Lazarus, who wrote those lines inscribed on the base of the Statue of Liberty ("Give me your tired, your poor . . . Your huddled masses, yearning to breathe free"), was the first Jew whom Ralph Waldo Emerson ever met. Emerson's daughter Ellen, an old Sunday-school teacher, noted how astonishing it was "to get at a real unconverted Jew (who had no objections to calling herself one, and talked freely about 'our Church' and 'we Jews'), and to hear how Old Testament sounds to her, and find she has been brought up to keep the Law, and the Feast of the Passover, and the day of Atonement. The interior view was more interesting than I could have imagined. She says her family are outlawed now, they no longer keep the Law, but Christian institutions don't interest her either."

Emma Lazarus had been sending Emerson her poems for years; he responded with uncertain praise, for they were excessively literary and understandably raised questions in the mind of so subtle a critic. But although she was not to become a consciously "Jewish" poet until the Russian pogroms aroused her, her being a Jew had certainly distinguished her in the literary world of Victorian America. She was that still exotic figure, that object of Christian curiosity, "the Jew"—and to descendants of the New England Puritans, straight out of their Bible.

Proust was to say that in every Jew "there is a prophet and a bounder." Emma Lazarus was still the "prophet" when she visited Concord. This was in 1876, when Jews in this country were getting known as "bounders." General Grant in a Civil War order had said "Jew" when he meant peddler, but impoverished farmers in the West now said "Jew" when they meant Wall Street financier. New England writers like James Russell Lowell and Henry Adams became obsessed with Jews and "the Jewish question" as soon as there were real Jews on the American scene. The "prophet" figure that literary New England had always known from books had become the "bounder"—and, worse, the ragged *shtetl* Jew whom

Adams examined with such loathing from a Russian railway car and in New York when he heard him speaking "a weird guttural Yiddish." Henry James, returning to his native downtown streets, announced that "the denizens of the New York Ghetto, heaped as thick as the splinters on the table of a glass-blower, had each, like the fine glass particle, his or her individual share of the whole hard glitter of Israel." The Jew in New York was an instance of alienness, an object to be studied. James would have been astonished to think of a writer coming out of this milieu. And, to do him justice, not many immigrant Jews saw themselves as writers in English. Henry Adams' sometime protégé, Bernard Berenson, who had come here from Lithuania, was to find himself only as an art historian in Italy.

William Dean Howells, now a Socialist in New York, praised Abraham Cahan's *Yekl: A Tale of the New York Ghetto*. But Howells was predisposed to Russian literature, Cahan was a "Russian" realist in English, and Howells, like so many Westerners enjoying or soon to enjoy New York's "Europeanness," was also a democratic idealist, naturally friendly to all these new peoples in New York. His friend Mark Twain said that Jews were members of the human race; "that is the worst you can say about them." But this easy Western humor was still very far from the creative equality that Jewish and non-Jewish writers were some day to feel. Mark Twain, like Maxim Gorky in Russia, protested against pogroms and was friendly to Jews; but as late as 1910, when he died, there was no significant type of the Jewish writer in this country. The older German-Jewish stock had produced many important scholars and publicists; it was to produce an original in Gertrude Stein. But the positive, creative role of the Jew as modern American, and above all as a modern American writer, was in the first years of this century being prepared not in the universities, not even in journalism, but in the vaudeville theaters, music halls, and burlesque houses where the pent-up eagerness of penniless immigrant youngsters met the raw urban scene on its own terms. It was not George Jean Nathan, Robert Nathan, or Ludwig Lewisohn any more than it was Arthur Krock, David Lawrence, Adolph Ochs, or Walter Lippmann who established the Jew in the national consciousness as a distinctly American figure; it was the Marx Brothers, Eddie Cantor, Al Jolson, Fannie Brice, George Gershwin. Jewish clowns, minstrels, song-writers helped to fit the Jew to America, and America to the Jew, with an élan that made for future creativity in literature as well as for the mass products of the "entertainment industry."

Proust, with his artist's disengagement from both "prophet" and "bounder"; Henry Adams, with his frivolous hatred of the immigrant ("five hundred thousand Jews in New York eating kosher, and saved from the drowning they deserve"), had never conceived of the Jew as a representative national entertainer. But in the naturalness and ease with which the Jewish vaudevillian put on blackface, used stereotypes, and ground out popular songs, in the avidity with which the public welcomed him, was the Jew's share in the common experience, the Jew's averageness and typicality, that were to make possible the Jew-as-writer in this country. In Western Europe, Jewish "notables" had been a handful—as odd as the occasional prime minister of Italy or Britain; in Eastern Europe, where the Jews were a mass, it was their very numbers that was so disturbing to anti-Semites in office, who even in Soviet Russia were to keep Jews down because the thought of too many Jews being allowed to exercise their talents at once could obviously be viewed as a threat to their own people. As Mikoyan was to say some years ago to a Jewish delegation, "We have our own cadres now." But in this country the very poverty and cultural rawness of the Jewish immigrant masses, the self-assertive egalitarianism of the general temper, and the naturalness with which different peoples could identify with each other in the unique halfway house that was New York (without New York it would no doubt all have been different, but without New York there would have been no immigrant epic, no America) gave individual performers the privilege of representing the popular mind. Never before had so numerous a mass of Jews been free citizens of the country in which they lived, and so close to the national life. And although many a genteel young literatus now analyzing Nathanael West and Saul Bellow shudders at his connection with Potash and Perlmutter, Eddie Cantor, and Fannie Brice, it is a fact that this "vulgar culture," proceeding merrily to the irreverent genius of the Marx Brothers (whose best movies were written by S. J. Perelman, the college chum and brother-in-law of Nathanael West), helped to found, as a natural habitat for the Jews in this country, the consciously grotesque style of parody that one finds in Perelman, West, Odets, Bellow, in many Broadway-Hollywood satirists, and even in an occasional literary critic, like Isaac Rosenfeld and Harold Rosenberg, impatient with the judicial tone that comes with the office. The Jewish writer, a late arrival in this country and admittedly of uncertain status, had to find his model in the majority culture, and although this had some depressing consequences in the mass, it was on the whole fortunate, for the sharply independent novelists, poets, and critics to come, that they were influenced more by the language of the street than by the stilted moralism that has always been a trap for the Jewish writer.

But of course the popular culture was invigorating and even liberating so long as it was one of many cultures operating simultaneously on the Jewish writer's mind. Ever since the legal emancipation of the Jews in Western Europe, there had been two principal cultures among the Jews—the orthodox, religious tradition, pursuing its own way often magnificently indifferent to the issues shaking European thought; and the newly secularistic culture of the "Jewish intellectuals," who found in the cause of "progressive humanity," in philosophic rationalism, in socialism, and cultural humanism, their sophisticated equivalent of Judaism. In Western Europe, for the most part, these two cultures no longer irritated each other. But among the Yiddish-speaking Jews of Eastern Europe, "enlightenment" did not appear until late in the 19th century; while in Western Europe the medieval ghettos were a barely tolerated memory, in Russia the Jewish Pale of Settlement, restricting most Jews to certain areas and restricting the intensity of their existence to the *shtetl* and its religious customs, remained a searing memory in the lives of immigrants and their children. The "dark" ages and the "modern" age, the ghetto and the revolutionary movement, persecution and free human development, were conjoined in the Jewish mind. The tension and ardor with which the two cultures of modern Jewry were related, in individual after individual, helps to explain the sudden flowering of painters among Russian Jews in the first years of this century, the extraordinary spiritual energy invested in the idea of socialism, the "twist" that Isaac Babel liked to give his Russian sentences, the general passion for "culture" and "cultural advancement," the revolutionary zeal with which former yeshiva boys turned political commissars spoke of the great new age of man.

Babel wrote of ex-seminarists riding away with the Red Cavalry from their "rotted" Bibles and Talmuds, Chagall's *rebbes* sprouted wings over the thatched roofs of Vitebsk and sang the joys of the flesh. The force of some immense personal transformation could be seen in the conscious energy of Trotsky's public role in the Russian Revolution. These revolutionaries, writers, scientists, painters were the "new men," the first mass secularists in the long religious history of the Jews, yet the zeal with which they engaged themselves to the "historic" task of desacralizing the European tradition often came from the profound history embedded in Judaism itself—it certainly did not come from the experience of Jews with other peoples in Eastern Europe. These "new men" had a vision of history that, as their critics were to tell them, was fanatically all of one piece, obstinately "Jewish" and "intellectual"—a vision in which some subtle purposiveness to history always managed to reassert itself in the face of repeated horrors. But what their critics could not recognize was that this obstinate quest for "meaning" was less a matter of conscious thought than a personal necessity, a requirement of survival, the historic circumstance that reasserted itself in case after case among the Jews, many of whom had good reason to believe that their lives were a triumph over every possible negation, and who, with the modesty of people for whom life itself is understandably the greatest good, found it easy to rejoice in the political and philosophical reasoning that assured them civic respect, civic peace, and the life of the mind.

"Excess of sorrow laughs," wrote Blake in *The Marriage of Heaven and Hell.* "Excess of joy weeps." For Jews in this country, who had triumphed over so much, remembered so much, were in such passionate relations with the two cultures—of religion and "modernity" that many believed in simultaneously—their conscious progress often became something legendary, a drama rooted in the existential fierceness of life lived and barely redeemed every single day. There was an intensity, a closeness to many conflicting emotions, that often seemed unaccountably excessive to other peoples. The need to explain himself to himself, to put his own house in order, was a basic drive behind many a Jewish writer. People to whom existence has often been a consciously fearful matter, who have lived at the crossroads between the cultures and on the threshold between life and death, naturally see existence as tension, issue, and drama, woven out of so many contradictions that only a work of art may appear to *hold* these conflicts, to compose them, to allow the human will some detachment. Surely never in history has a whole people had to endure such a purgation of emotions as took place at the Eichmann trial. It was this that led Harold Rosenberg to show the cruel dramatic necessity behind the trial—the need of the Jews to tell their story, to relive the unbearable, the inadmissible, the inexpressible. The Jew who has lived through the age of Hitler cannot even say, with Eliot, "After such knowledge, what forgiveness?" For he has to live with his knowledge if he is to live at all, and this "knowledge" enforces itself upon him as a fact both atrocious and dramatic, a mockery of the self-righteous Christianity that has always surrounded him, a parody of the Orthodox Judaism that has sought to justify the ways of God to man, a drama founded on the contrast between the victims and all those who remained spectators when the Jews were being slaughtered.

There are experiences so extreme that, after living them, one can do nothing with them *but* put them into words. There are experiences so terrible that one can finally do nothing with them but not forget them. This was already the case with many of the young Jewish writers just out of the city ghettos, who began to emerge in significant numbers only in the early 30's. Looking back on this emergence, one can see that it needed the peculiar crystallization of ancient experiences, and then the avidity with which young writers threw themselves on the American scene, to make possible that awareness of the Jew as a new force that one sees in such works of the 30's as Henry Roth's *Call It Sleep,* Michael Gold's *Jews Without Money,* Daniel Fuchs's *Summer in Williamsburg,* Albert Halper's *The Chute,* Odets' *Awake and Sing,* Meyer Levin's *The Old Bunch,* and even in West's *Miss Lonelyhearts,* whose hero is not named a Jew but who is haunted by the indiscriminate pity that was to mark the heroes of Bernard Malamud and Edward Wallant. In the 20's there had been several extraordinarily sensitive writers, notably Paul Rosenfeld and Waldo Frank, out of the older, German-Jewish stock; but on the whole, it needed the turbulent mixing of the ghetto and the depression to make possible the wild flurry of strong new novels and plays in the 30's.

Yet the social realists of the 30's were often boxed in, mentally, by the poverty and hopelessness of their upbringing and the bitterness, deprivations, and anti-Semitism of depression America. The extraordinary brevity of so many literary careers in America is a social fact that any account of the Jewish writer in America must contend with as an omen for the future. Although the aborted career is common enough in American writing and was particularly marked among writers of the 30's—many were shipwrecked by the failure of their political hopes, and many crippled as artists by the excessive effort it took to bring out their non-selling books—it is also a fact that writers from the "minorities" have a harder time getting started, and tend, as a group, to fade out more easily, than those writers from the older stocks whose literary culture was less deliberately won and is less self-conscious. A historian of the Negro novel in this country says that most Negroes who have published one book have never published another—and one might well wonder what, until the sudden fame of James Baldwin, would have induced any Negro writer in this country to keep at it except the necessity of telling his own story. Thinking of the family situation portrayed in *Call It Sleep*, one can see why, having written *that* up, to the vast indifference of the public in the 30's, the author should have felt that he was through. The real drama behind most Jewish novels and plays, even when they are topical and revolutionary in feeling, is the contrast between the hysterical tenderness of the Oedipal relation and the "world"; in the beginning there was the Jewish mother and her son, but the son grew up, he went out into the world, he became a writer. That was the beginning of his career and usually the end of the novel. Jews don't believe in original sin, but they certainly believe in the original love that they once knew in the *shtetl,* in the kitchen, in the Jewish household—and after *that* knowledge, what forgiveness? In this, at least, the sentimental author of *Jews Without Money* parallels the master of childhood in *Call It Sleep*.

What saved Jewish writing in America from its innate provincialism, what enabled it to survive the moral wreckage of the 30's, was the coming of the "intellectuals"—writers like Delmore Schwartz, Saul Bellow, Lionel Trilling, Karl Shapiro, Harold Rosenberg, Isaac Rosenfeld, Lionel Abel, Clement Greenberg, Bernard Malamud, Irving Howe, Philip Rahv, Leslie Fiedler, Robert Warshow, Paul Goodman, Norman Mailer, Philip Roth, William Phillips. It was these writers, and younger writers in their tradition, who made possible intellectual reviews like *Partisan Review* and serious, objective, unparochial magazines like *Commentary*—a magazine which has emphasized general issues and regularly included so many writers who are not Jews. *Commentary,* founded in November 1945, was hospitable to this new maturity and sophistication among Jewish writers in America; it established itself on the American scene easily, and with great naturalness, exactly in those years immediately after the war when American Jews began to publish imaginative works and intellectual studies of distinction—*Dangling Man, The Victim, The Middle of the Journey, The Liberal Imagination, Death of a Salesman, The Naked and the Dead, The World Is a Wedding, The Lonely Crowd, The Natural, The Adventures of Augie March, The Mirror and the Lamp, The Tradition of the New.*

Even a gifted writer outside this group, Salinger, contemptuous of its ideologies, was an "intellectual" writing about "intellectuals." Even a middlebrow sullenly critical of its preoccupations, Herman Wouk, did it the honor of "exposing" an intellectual in *The Caine Mutiny.* Whether they were novelists or just intellectual pundits at large, what these writers all had in common was the ascendancy of "modern literature," which has been more destructive of bourgeois standards than Marxism, was naturally international-minded, and in a culture bored with middle-class rhetoric upheld the primacy of intelligence and the freedom of the imagination. The heroes of these "intellectuals" were always Marx, Freud, Trotsky, Eliot, Joyce, Valéry; the "intellectuals" believed in the "great enlighteners," because their greatest freedom was to be enlighteners of all culture themselves, to be the instructors and illuminati of the modern spirit. Unlike so many earlier writers, who had only their hard story to tell and then departed, the Jewish "intellectuals" who emerged in the 40's found shelter under the wide wings of the "modern movement," and so showed an intellectual spirit that Jews had not always managed in the great world.

Commentary has, more than any other "Jewish" magazine known to me, been a symbol of and a home for this intellectual spirit. I remember that as the first issues began to appear at the end of that pivotal year of 1945, I was vaguely surprised that it dealt with so many general issues in so subtly critical and detached a fashion, regularly gave a forum to non-Jewish writers as well as to Jewish ones. Like many Jewish intellectuals of my time and place, brought up to revere the universalism of the Socialist ideal and of modern culture, I had equated "Jewish" magazines with a certain insularity of tone, subject matter, writers' names—with mediocrity. To be a "Jewish writer"—I knew several, and knew of many more, who indefatigably managed this by not being any particular kind of writer at all—was somehow to regress, to strike attitudes, to thwart the natural complexities of truth. There were just too many imprecisions and suppressions in the parochially satisfied "Jewish" writer. It was enough to be a Jew *and* a writer. "Jewish" magazines were not where literature could be found, and certainly not the great world. "Jewish" magazines worried over the writer's "negative" attitude toward his "Jewishness," nagged you like an old immigrant uncle who did not know how much resentment lay behind his "Jewishness."

But *Commentary,* to the grief of many intellectual guardians of the "Jewish" world, marked an end to that, which is why its interest for a large intellectual public has been so significant. It has always been natural for Protestant Americans to believe, in the words of John Jay Chapman, that "the heart of the world is Jewish." But after 1945 and the unparalleled, inexpressible martyrdom of the Jewish people in Europe, it was natural for non-Jews everywhere to believe, as Jews now had more reasons than ever to believe, that Jewish survival and Jewish self-determination related to everything in the world. The particular distinction of *Commentary* among Jewish magazines has been to articulate and to support this many-sided relatedness. As one can see from the extraordinary opening section of this anthology—"The Holocaust and After"—the Jewish writer after 1945 had particular reason to feel that this most terrible of all events in Jewish history bound him more closely to every fundamental question of human nature and historic failure involved in Europe's self-destruction. As the late Solomon Bloom showed in his detached and heart-rending study of Mordechai Chaim Rumkowski, the "Dictator of the Lodz Ghetto" who sent so many of his own people to death, the Jewish historian had materials more atrocious than any in modern literature for the recognition of how squalid and self-deluded human nature could be. Yet, as this anthology goes on to show, the Jewish art critic, essayist, economist, political observer, psychoanalyst, sociologist had only to take up aspects of contemporary experience in general to show the relevance to all this experience of his native, obstinate, questing spirit as a Jew. One can cite from this brilliant anthology, virtually at random, materials so various and fascinating as George Lichtheim's "Reflections on Trotsky," Hannah Arendt's stark notes on the German scene, David Daiches' examination of the new Biblical scholarship, Leslie Farber's " 'I'm Sorry, Dear.' " And where else would the non-Jewish writer and our common American problems come together so happily as in Dwight Macdonald's "By Cozzens Possessed," James Baldwin's "Equal In Paris," Edmund Wilson's "Paul Rosenfeld: Three Phases"?

Of course the prosperity that began with the war encouraged the new Jewish writers to feel that the country was theirs. Immediately after the war, indeed, some of them embraced this newfound land, their America, with an enthusiasm made slightly hysterical by the need to cast off Marxist ideology. Yet this new liveliness could be attributed in the greatest part to the closing up of a time-lag, to the sudden eruption of writers whose time had come—and who had often been brought up in old-fashioned ways that impressed the dizzyingly complex new world upon their minds with special vividness. Jean-Paul Sartre says in *Les Mots* of the grandfather who brought him up—"Between the first Russian Revolution and the first World War, fifteen years after Mallarmé's death . . . a man of the 19th century was foisting upon his grandson ideas that had been current under Louis Philippe. . . . Ought I to complain? . . . In our bustling societies, delays sometimes give a head start." Many a Jewish writer has been brought up on his grandfather's ideas, and now engages the last third of the 20th century with special eagerness. Generally speaking, the Jewish intellectuals who since the 40's have exercised so much influence on American culture started very far back. If the young man from the provinces, as Lionel Trilling named him, typifies the encounter with the great world in 19th-century novels, it was significantly the Jewish intellectual who was now to write the key book on Matthew Arnold, the definitive biographies of Henry Adams, Henry James, James Joyce, who was to become the theoretician of action painting, the most resourceful American novelist of the postwar period, the editor of the leading cultural review, the Reichian *enfant terrible* of the universities, the novelist of orgiastic high life in Palm Springs, Las Vegas, Hollywood, and the Waldorf Towers. Often enough graduates of the old revolutionary movement, with its intellectual ardor, its internationalism, its passion for political complexities, and its taste for action, these Jewish intellectuals combined an American belief in the "tradition of the new" with their own moral tradition and their passion for the Europe of the great thinkers, their driving personal ambition with the knowledge that they were exceptions, "survivors," as Moses Elkanah Herzog said, of the age that had seen their brethren slaughtered like cattle in the abattoirs that the Nazis had made of Eastern Europe. Just as it was Southern writers, with their knowledge of defeat and their instinctive irony, who in the 40's spoke to the chastened American mind, so it is Jewish writers who now represent to many Americans the unreality of their prosperity and the anxiety of their condition. In situations of inestimable complexity, requiring the most "sophisticated" and "expert" "analysis" of the "complex factors," it was often enough Jews, born and pushed to be intellectuals, who became the connoisseurs of the new chaos, the mental elite of the power age. Never was interpretation, explanation, commentary, a vital new *midrash,* so much needed as in the period, starting with the war, when the world was so much compressed and subtilized by the new technological revolution—and never were there so many Jewish intellectuals prepared to do the explaining. The ragged old "prophet" was not much in evidence, and the Jew-asbounder was not to be thought of, but the age of the intellectuals was in full swing.

All the writers were intellectuals now, the best writers as well as the most conformist—novelists like Saul Bellow and Norman Mailer dealt in the drama of concepts, had heroes who lived by concepts, and suffered for them. The world seemed suspended on concepts, and in the mass magazines as in the universities and publishing houses, a mass of indistinguishable sophisticates genuflected to the modern idols and talked the same textbook formulae about Joyce, James, Eliot, Faulkner, Picasso, Stravinsky. The Sunday book supplements were soon all as apocalyptic as a Jewish novelist after a divorce, and one could regularly read footnotes to the absurdity of the human condition, the death of tragedy, and the end of innocence by pseudo-serious minds who imitated Bellow, Mailer, Fiedler, Ginsberg, Goodman as humorlessly as teen-age girls copied hair styles from the magazines.

Definitely, it was now the thing to be Jewish. But in Western universities and small towns many a traditional novelist and professor of English felt out of it, and asked, with varying degrees of self-control, if there was no longer a good novel to be written about the frontier, about Main Street, about the good that was in marriage? Was it possible, these critics wondered aloud, that American life had become so deregionalized and lacking in local color that the big power units and the big cities had pre-empted the American scene, along with the supple Jewish intellectuals who were at home with them? Was it possible that Norman Mailer had become the representative American novelist?

It was entirely possible, and certainly the thought would not have astonished Mailer, just as the power of his example for other novelists did not astonish Saul Bellow. Whatever pain this ascendancy might cause to writers who felt out of it because they lived in Montana or in the wrong part of California, it was a fact that there were now Jewish novelists who, as writers, had mastered the complex resources of the modern novel, who wrote English lovingly, possessively, masterfully, for whom the language and the form, the intelligence of art, had become as natural a way of living as the Law had been to their grandfathers. Literature had indeed become their spiritual world, their essential personal salvation, in a world where all traditional markers were fast disappearing. But in the frothy turbulent "mix" of America in the 60's, with its glut, its power drives, its confusion of values, the Jewish writer found himself so much read, consulted, imitated, that he knew it would not be long before the reaction set in—and in fact the decorous plaint of the "Protestant minority" has been succeeded by crudely suggestive phrases about the "Jewish Establishment," the "O.K. writers and the Poor Goy," "The Jewish-American Push." Yet it is plainly a certain success that has been resented, not the Jew. And if the Jew has put his distinct mark on modern American writing, it is surely because, in a time when the old bourgeois certainties and humanist illusions have crumbled, the Jew is practiced in what James called "the imagination of disaster" and "does indeed see life as ferocious and sinister." The contemporary literary temper is saturnine, panicky, black in its humor but adroit in shifting the joke onto the shoulders of society. And the Jewish writer, with his natural interest in the social fact, has been particularly quick to show the lunacy and hollowness of so many present symbols of authority. Anxiety hangs like dry electricity in the atmosphere of modern American life, and the stimulus of this anxiety, with all its comic overtones, is the realized subject in the novels of Joseph Heller, Bruce Jay Friedman, Richard Stern, Jeremy Larner, the plays of Jack Gelber and Arthur Kopit. There is real madness to modern governments, modern war, modern moneymaking, advertising, science, and entertainment; this madness has been translated by many a Jewish writer into the country they live in, the time that offers them everything but hope. In a time of intoxicating prosperity, it has been natural for the Jewish writer to see how superficial society can be, how pretentious, atrocious, unstable —and comic. This, in a secular age when so many people believe in nothing but society's values, is the significance to literature of the Jewish writer's being a Jew.

I

THE HOLOCAUST AND AFTER

December 1946

Martin Greenberg

THE COMMON MAN OF THE NAZIS

The outbreak of the war put an end once and for all to the large but undistinguished body of anti-Nazi literature that flourished in the 30's. This literature was in its greater part directly influenced by the anti-Nazi bluster of Stalinism and the Stalinist popular front, and relied on the solidarity of the proletariat, both German and international, to bring about the downfall of Hitler. But the deployment of vast armies made it plain at last that the issue was to be settled otherwise.

Despite the fact that writers of considerable talent at one time or another contributed to it, this literature was a failure in every respect. And not the least of all its shortcomings was its curious inability to reckon seriously with its antagonist.

In André Malraux's *Days of Wrath,* in Ernst Toller's *Pastor Hall,* in *The Seventh Cross* by Anna Seghers, as well as in a host of lesser works, there is evident a strange unwillingness to permit the Nazi to enter the foreground of the story's consideration. (In *Watch on the Rhine,* by Lillian Hellman—which takes place on the Potomac, not the Rhine—there is not a single Nazi in the cast of the characters.) Usually the Nazi is only a slightly more precise detail in a generally vague and hostile background. The locus of the action is in the heroic agony of the protagonist—his suffering and his martyrdom, seen almost as predestined. A strange veil of indifference hangs between him and the world of the enemy's personality. His purpose is to suffer and endure in a kind of deliberate isolation, at least insofar as the Nazis are concerned, fortified by his faith in ultimate proletarian redemption.

The Nazi is ignored. Or if he is not entirely ignored, the most commonplace and venal motives are attributed to him. Occasionally—but not often—an obsessive, violent, and distraught inner world is hinted at, a world new and forbidding, but this rarely goes beyond having the Nazi character repeat by rote—but with the fervid accents of personal belief—the official ideological nonsense of Nazism.

This disdain of the Nazi, this lack of interest in him, wears the appearance of lofty moral superiority. Actually, it is not so. It is fear and ignorance, and a deliberate turning away from the incomprehensible and fearful.

The effect of such disdain, paradoxically, was not to detract from the conception of the strength of Nazism that prevails in these books. The world of Nazi power is their context, and although the Nazi man is ignored, Nazism, omnipresent and omnipotent, dominates the scene with a massive fatality.

The comparatively recent publication of two anti-Nazi works in German is the immediate occasion for this analysis. Bertolt Brecht's *Furcht und Elend des III. Reiches,* staged in this country as *The Private Life of the Master Race,* was written in 1938 and is an archetype of the literature of anti-Nazism. It is a dramatic spectacle in twenty-four scenes, and the whole is intended to provide a panorama of the "fear and misery" of life in every section of the Third Reich. Friedrich Torberg's *Mein Ist Die Rache,* not properly a part of this genre, but belonging to a later period, is a novelette about Jews in a German concentration camp, their gradual realization that the Nazi commandant intends their extermination as a group, and the—rather unreal—question as to whether vengeance is in their hands or in those of God.

Both Brecht and Torberg have experienced Nazism at first hand, and yet, as is invariably the case in the literary treatment of this subject, they fail to understand it imaginatively. There almost seems to be a law at work here. The more direct a writer's experience of Nazism, the less his imagination is able to comprehend it. Odets in *Till the Day I Die,* or Hollywood in a number of movies, although far removed in space from Nazi Germany, seemed better able to cope aesthetically with the Nazis, perhaps because, protected by an ocean, they were in a position to be more curious about the Nazis and less disdainful of them—that is, less afraid of them—as human beings.

This lack of imaginative understanding is, of course, a reflection of our general bafflement in the face of the phenomenon of Nazism. Nevertheless, one always hopes that playwrights and novelists will be able to by-pass the historical problem by a direct and intuitive grasp of the living reality. Brecht's play and Torberg's novelette, like the works of the others before them, disappoint such a hope. Nazism looms up monolithic and impenetrable in their pages, an impersonal, unassailable, and absolute force. There is no hint of its inner desperation and uncertainty; there is no hint of its violent contradictions, its frustrations, and its ambiguities.

Brecht consoles himself for this secret defeatism with a kind of grim, theoretical, surface cheerfulness: he assumes a catastrophic decline of the German standard of living under the Nazis, he assumes a sullen and intransigent proletariat, and he assumes certain laws of capitalist development, all of them together spelling the ultimate doom of the Third Reich.

Where Brecht draws his comfort from the commonplaces of the routine Marxian anti-fascism of the 30's, Torberg draws a colder and more uncertain comfort from the God of Israel.

The depersonalization of the Nazi man is the literary consequence of the impersonalization of Nazism. One thinks of no literary work that successfully portrays a Nazi *person*. In almost every case he is reduced to some absolute of inhumanity and functions in the story as a mechanical and abstract figure of speech. Or if some human weaknesses are conceded him—to indicate somehow that he is human after all—they are conceived in the most banal and cliché fashion, and no serious understanding of the Nazi is accomplished.

There prevailed in the 30's, to be sure, a general tendency to treat character impersonally as a consequence of the schematization of imaginative literature that the influence of Marxism had brought about. Literature was made to conform to the materialist interpretation of history; life was "reduced" to a bleak and arid class struggle, and humanity was "reduced" to a bleak—but sentimentalized—proletariat. The intelligentsia unburdened itself of its self-hatred by creating the proletarian hero—that rigid and lifeless figure whose every attribute implied a contemptuous dismissal of the "classless" and "disinterested" concerns of the intellectuals. It is amazing even to this day how negative and abstract was the literary conception of the worker, and how completely false. (Is this evidence of the restricted and doctrinal character of Marxism, and its inability to create a really universal attitude, heralding a new humanity and a new period in history? Does not socialism here have the suspicious appearance of a radical theory of the propertyless late middle class rather than of a tremendous social force destined to change the world?)

With the triumph of Hitler and the approach of the war, proletarian literature looked toward the international scene and transformed itself into "anti-fascist" literature. It was still the old morality literature, but one in which the Nazi conveniently played the role of the Devil, a role hitherto imperfectly fulfilled by "capitalist society."

The conversion of the Nazi into an abstraction is more surprising in Brecht's case. The Brecht who in the *Dreigroschenoper* was able to penetrate the essence of the big-city, industrial Common Man of capitalism with so exact an irony is here able to create only blank horrors, and this despite the fact that the Nazi Common Man was equally a child of the megalopolitan jungle Brecht knows so well.

One reason, perhaps, that Brecht's old irony failed to work against the

Nazis is that it was an irony aimed at urban and capitalist society—and the Nazis professed to be anti-capitalist, too, outdoing the Marxists, moreover, in condemning the perversions and degradations of modern urban life. The ideal human being in whose name they opposed the city was not the same ideal that the Marxists asserted—it was not the clear-eyed, square-hewn workingman of the city. It was the stolid, "wholesome," old-fashioned, rural petty-bourgeois. And here, precisely, was where pro-socialist propaganda fell into one of its subtlest, yet most damaging, ambiguities. Marx established as one of socialism's prime tasks the obliteration of the differences between town and country; yet socialism's whole quality has remained urban. The very word "socialism" summons up a vision of enormous vistas of shining concrete pavement and smoking factory-chimneys, of huge and smiling throngs of people passing by parks and cinemas —the décor of the rationalized megalopolis. Socialism came to be the world of large suburbs and long vacations. It came to represent a world new, mechanical, ingenious, full of "improvements." Socialism became Europe's version of an America purged of its imperfections.

The masses, however, have never been entirely urbanized. (The only entirely urbanized group in modern society is the Jews, whose metropolitan competence has always aroused the resentment of the Gentiles.) The memory of the countryside—from which they came originally—persists in the masses, together with a sentimental nostalgia for what now seems the stable, organic, and reasonably secure—if highly limited and somewhat boring—life they led there. This insipid nostalgia, this sentimentalization of rural life, has become one of the myths of urbanism. It is the plebeian version of the aristocratic Arcadia. The Nazis took advantage of this nostalgia in their attacks on modern industrial life, counterposing to the urban tradition of capitalism and socialism their rural ideal.

However, the human type the Nazis actually realized puzzled the anti-Nazis in a way that the merely reactionary Nazi rural ideal did not. Nazism succeeded in intimidating the world by more means than those of power politics and militarism. It reshaped the image of the masses into something inscrutable, threatening, and profoundly alien to traditional Western intelligence, so that it defied even the efforts of the artistic intelligence to assimilate it imaginatively.

It is the ordinary Nazi man, the mass man of the Nazi organizations, that constitutes the core of horror in the enigma of Nazism. The modern world expected the masses either to continue to suffer in traditional fashion, that is, to continue to exist at the sub-human level of life that generations of poverty impose, without ideas, without spirit, and without independence; or to become socialist, that is, to revolt against themselves, to revolt against the conditions of their existence and the limited type of humanity that such an existence thrusts upon them, in the interest of a superior and universal conception of humanity. Nazism, however, linked the spiritual poverty of the one role with the revolutionary dynamism of the other.

Hitler armed the German masses with a theory. Whereas socialism—and, indeed, all genuinely revolutionary mass movements—gave the masses a theory with which to transcend themselves, Nazism gave them a theory—racism—to confirm them in their mass nature. Their present spiritual status was given the primordial sanction of blood, and elevated to an eternal ideal. Within Germany, the racial class struggle replaced the economic class struggle, and the German masses, rather than striving to overcome their purely mass nature, strove to be purely German, i.e., they strove to realize more absolutely their present, mass self. In propagating the racial class struggle, Nazism made use of the revolutionary rhetoric of socialism so that it could masquerade as a revolution of the masses, and it further developed the masquerade by thrusting the economic class struggle outside the borders of the Reich into the realm of international power politics ("proletarian" vs. "capitalist" nations).

Once the power of the Nazi party was firmly established, it turned outside the borders of its country in classic German fashion to solve in an imperfect and debased fashion the problems that it could not solve at home. The national unification that Germany was never able to achieve by itself, it achieved belatedly in 1870 in a war against the French. It needed the First World War to accomplish—imperfectly—the democratic revolution it was unable to accomplish in 1848. And, finally, Germany needed the Nazi party and the Second World War to realize a corrupt and barbarous version of the socialist revolution that it had failed to achieve after 1918.

Nazism, from this point of view, is "kitsch" politics, and fully in the German political tradition. It wanted the emotional effect of a mass revolution without being able to summon up the inner historical strength that a mass revolution demands. The Nazis wanted the sensation of history without the risk and inner effort demanded by history.

For surely it is the case that Germany, the home of that Faustian spirit which worships most ardently at the altar of History, felt most grievously the lack of a history of its own. Germany never experienced an authentic Bastille Day, and the absence of such a historical experience condemned it to psychological and political immaturity, and to a political role in Europe incommensurate with its real strength. Nazism represents Germany's last desperate effort to dominate Europe without itself first submitting to the necessity of a democratic revolution.

In this last effort, Germany placed its fortunes in the hands of the plebs. The plebs, in the person of the Nazi party, were given political power in the hope that the masses might accomplish the conquest of Europe that the German ruling class was never able to accomplish on its own initiative.

Nazism is therefore political plebeianism—the attempt of the mob, armed with political power and a philosophy, to play a significant role in history. Incapable of accomplishing that other revolution which remains its country's only means of creating a real history, the German plebs poured all the frustrated passion of Germany's historical disappointment into an ersatz revolution against the Jews and the outside world. Who better than Hitler represents the passionate nothingness that is the political plebeian? Vulgar, ignorant, shrewd, brutal, and *empty*—that is the nature of the mass man, and he brings all these qualities with him into history on the rare occasion when his envious fanaticism is permitted to discover a purpose for itself, to patch together a theory out of its void, and to organize in its own image and its own right.

In no age have the "masses" made history. The mass, as mass, in an historical sense is literally nothing—the historical empty space in which events occur. In pre-history they did not exist—there were only families and tribes. In ancient civilizations they were almost completely ignored; the masses were simply a part of nature. When Roman society began to disintegrate, the threat that lay in the dead weight of the Roman masses finally won them a particular consideration—bread and circuses, the appropriate symbol of their spiritual and historical insufficiency. Under Christianity they were admitted into the human community, but their special nature was dissolved in the grandiose category of Christian humanity.

The various peasant revolts that have taken place in the history of Europe illustrate best of all the historical impotence of the masses. Many of these revolts achieved considerable initial success and conquered large reaches of territory but, unable to maintain themselves, were eventually put down, and events resumed their interrupted course almost as if nothing had happened. The peasants were unable to create or acquire an *idea* with which to challenge the idea of feudalism. They were unable, that is, to make history.

The West discovered the masses out of the same impulse that discovered America, and was amazed and repelled by their strangeness. Shakespeare's rude plebeians and ignorant mechanics are above all *curiosities* in their author's eyes. Shakespeare observes them with some of the same wonder with which Columbus observed the West Indian savages.

In our own day, the masses were observed minutely, and the horror of their lives was understood. They were understood, however, in their passive and suffering aspect, and they acquired real humanity and influenced history only insofar as they transcended the limitations of their mass nature in the revolutionary struggles for justice carried on by the egalitarian movements.

Under Nazism, the German masses abandoned this struggle for justice—and thus their humanity—without abandoning their resentful aggressiveness. In the place of the ideal of Socialist Man they substituted the Fanatic Plebeian. The plebeian *with an idea*—this is the creature that Brecht, Torberg, and the rest cannot understand. This is that "rough beast," that "shape with lion body and the head of a man" who, conceived in a time when "the best lack all conviction, while the worst are full of a passionate intensity . . . slouches toward Bethlehem to be born."

In Brecht, Malraux, Seghers, Toller, and Odets, the proletarian masses are counted on to destroy the power of the Nazis. When the course of events proved this expectation vain, this type of literature ceased to be written. In *Watch on the Rhine* (1941) already, there is no longer any talk of proletarian action. The hero is unpolitical—neither a Communist, Socialist, nor radical intellectual; he is simply an "anti-fascist" who was once an engineer. He returns to Germany at the end of the play to carry on the fight, but the fight is no longer the fight to rally the dispossessed (the Nazis had already done that), it is the guerrilla foray of an isolated individual. (Miss Hellman's sentimentalities are more hard-headed than her predecessors'—one has the right to expect that her hero later made contact with the O.S.S., served it well, and is now at least a technical adviser to the Allied Military Government.) In the case of Torberg, God replaces the proletariat. The genre of anti-Nazi literature is pretty well used up. The literature of "anti-fascism" had never been a literature of real struggle; now more than ever it becomes merely a literature of passivity.

Even while abandoning their faith in the masses, few of these writers suspected to what extent the envious and illiterate *Lumpenintellektuellen* had succeeded in creating a new type of mass man. The popular masses that had provided the great revolutions of the West with their social force had at last been halted in their progress toward universal democracy and a classless society. Whereas in France, England, and to a certain extent in America, where democratic revolutions had successfully taken place, this represented the *exhaustion* of a historical role, at least for a certain period, in Germany it represented the *frustration* of that role. The German masses, desperate in their necessity to act, and yet inwardly crippled by the long history of German political failure, squandered their energies on the gutter socialism of Hitler.

The sentimental plebeianism of the anti-Nazi writers blinded them to the aggressive plebeianism of the Nazis. Only the idea of socialism had united them with the masses, from whom they were otherwise entirely alienated. The failure of this idea severed the connection, and these writers have since then relapsed into an unenlightened disenchantment.

They, together with the entire anti-Nazi world, made the mistake of considering the Nazis merely reactionary. They failed to perceive—and did not wish to perceive—the significance of the fact that the Nazis had become the first to challenge traditional socialism's hold upon the masses. In the end the Nazi armies were defeated, not however by the embattled working class fighting in the name of humanity, not by the *enemies* of the Nazis, but by the mechanical and unenthusiastic mass armies of their *opponents*.

In the disintegration of Europe, in the utter collapse of all historical purpose, the void rose up in a frustrated and perverted effort to realize itself. The vision of doom that had secretly haunted the 19th century at last became reality. This reality the anti-Nazi writers persisted in ignoring. It is not so much their wrong politics that one finds most offensive—we can all be convicted of the same thing—it is not even their bad writing and false heroics. What is most appalling is their betrayal of the private vision of the artist. We do not demand of the artist that he be wiser than we are; we demand a simple kind of honesty that keeps him close and loyal to his intuitions. What is amazing in this literature is the complete absence of any intuitive sense of the quality of our age. One line of the poetry of Yeats, whom most of the anti-Nazi writers would consider "unenlightened"—although a good "private" poet—is weighted down with more reality than the whole body of anti-Nazi literature. An ultimate kind of corruption took place, and more talent than one generation can afford to waste was wasted.

September 1948

Irving Kristol

THE NATURE OF NAZISM

Before the war, discussion of the "nature of Nazism" threw up many intensely held and sharply conflicting viewpoints: Nazism was a disguised dictatorship of finance capitalism, it was a revolt of declassed intellectuals, it was a cover for a revived German militarism, it was a new kind of non-capitalist non-socialist social order, and so on. The debate was carried on with great acuity and on a very high level of subtlety. It must come as an unpleasant shock, therefore, to hear the distinguished British historian, H. R. Trevor-Roper, say in an aside that Rauschning's *Revolution of Nihilism*—that vulgar and sensational book authored by an ex-Nazi—has turned out to have been, on the whole, a reliable portrait of Nazism.

The Nazis, as they are revealed in postwar autopsies, had no economic, social, or political program. Or rather, they had a program with only two points. The first was a private point in the mind of Hitler: military expansion eastward, to carve out of Russia a huge province and re-enact the drama of the Teutonic Knights with a revised, happy ending. By the wealth and opportunities thereby obtained, he hoped to settle once and for all the possibility of, or the need for, Germany's ever having an internal politics of its own. All Germans would be completely involved in rule and exploitation, with the Nazis as overseers over sub-overseers.

The other point, the public and by far the more important one, was racism, i.e., anti-Semitism. Only a few contemporaries—Jacques Maritain, Maurice Samuel, Vladimir Jabotinsky, and some others—understood the true significance of anti-Semitism for the Nazis. The civilized world as a whole saw it simply as a nasty appeal to prejudice, a bit of dirty fighting on the part of unscrupulous politicians. They did not see that without anti-Semitism the Nazis could never have captured and maintained power. It was the one point in their entire system of double-talk that they really believed in (though it too was compounded of double-talk); it was the

Originally published as "What the Nazi Autopsies Show"

source of their special emotional dynamism and distinguished them from the other nationalist parties of Weimar Germany. Indeed, there was no Nazi ideology aside from anti-Jewish ideology: all the scientific, historical and sociological tomes of the Nazi academies had no other point of reference. Nazism existed to exclude the Jew, to hurt him, and even, if necessary, to be hurt by him, for that too set the seal on exclusion. Up until the very end, Hitler, Himmler, Goebbels, and Company maintained that the Third Reich was, quite literally, fighting a war to the death with international Jewry.

Nazi "theory" otherwise was a grab-bag of everything that sounded useful: Rosenberg's "Aryanism," Sombart's Prussian imperialism, Othmar Spann's "pure" fascism, Stefan George's aristocratism; it celebrated the purely subjective, the purely utilitarian, the "estrangement from the absolute" (Rosenberg). Nazi politics was the politics of the freebooter: its aim was absolute power in a period of social disintegration when established centers of authority had dissolved, and the masses of people lay passively awaiting violation. The essence of this attitude was best expressed by Ernst Juenger: "We find ourselves in the last phase of nihilism, characterized by the fact that while the creation of new systems and rules has already been carried far, the corresponding values have not become visible. . . . In such a situation, pain is the only standard that yields secure orientation."

The word "totalitarian" has obscured the nihilistic character of Nazi politics, since it seems to imply some sort of program for a drastic remaking of the social order.* We are still imbued with the rationalist political theory of the 18th century which ascribed to each government its "reason" and "purpose," and this has been strongly reinforced by Marxism with its theory of the state as an instrument to further the ends of the ruling class. Our concept of government, even "totalitarian" government, is still a positive one: the suggestion that a certain group rules because it has, by dint of violence and intrigue, successfully exercised an unbridled lust for power is regarded with suspicion, and searching parties continue to set out energetically to find out who is "really" pulling the strings and for what purpose.

* The application of the term "totalitarian" to both Stalin's Russia and Hitler's Germany seems to me a source of confusion. True, the effects of both systems on the free individual are similar. But in ideology, motives, and mainsprings of power, there is an essential difference between Communism and Nazism. Communism can claim a certain continuity with significant aspects of Western civilization—which may possibly make it a more profound and enduring menace to freedom and liberty. It has an elaborate ideology (Marxism) that claims absolute truth, and whose historical origin is linked to the flowering of "scientific" and "humanitarian" sentiments; thus, it has an initial appeal to "good" people. Furthermore, it receives constant encouragement from the present industrial society, with its twin drives toward a centralized "welfare state" and a "democratic" mass culture.

The Nazis, it is now clear, neither defended capitalism on principle nor destroyed it on principle. They were not interested in economic principles but in economic facts. Up to 1939 they wanted an economy that would keep the German people reasonably content and give them a chance to consolidate their position vis à vis the military, the civil administration, and the remnants of the democratic opposition. The bankers were able to give them this, so the bankers ran the economic system. When the needs of a two-front war became imperative, the bankers went out and the technocrats, led by Albert Speer, came in to mobilize for total war. When it was clear that the war was lost, the Nazis tried desperately to pull the entire German economy, including its very physical plant, down to ruin with them; that was the meaning, and the only meaning, of their "scorched earth" policy.

Burton Klein, in an article, "Germany's Preparation for War," in the March 1948 *American Economic Review,* demonstrates that, until 1939, Germany's "war economy" was a myth constructed mainly for foreign consumption. German aircraft production at the beginning of the war was about the same as Britain's while its rate of tank output was actually lower. When Hitler told the Reichstag and the world that he had spent ninety billion Reichsmarks for rearmament, it was a blatant lie—but the lie worked. When German troops were sent into the Rhineland (we learned at the Nuremberg trials), they had instructions to retire at the first sign of a French soldier; but the French were paralyzed by their "unpreparedness." Similarly, before Munich, the German generals, terrified at the prospect of war with England, drew up plans to assassinate Hitler and Himmler; when Chamberlain capitulated, Hitler's "infallibility" seemed more than enough to compensate for any military weakness.

The Germans did not have a war economy, partly because Hitler thought in terms of a blitzkreig and partly because Schacht, that "financial wizard," was a conservative economist who trembled at the thought of deficit financing and the specter of inflation. His recovery program consisted of public expenditures (covered mainly by taxation) coupled with strict wage and price controls to ensure greater employment and production rather than higher wages and prices. The program worked and the recovery was a real one for the German civilian: production of such civilian goods as autos, furniture, radios, etc., all rose considerably above the 1929 peak, while the share of national output directed toward rearming was not much higher than among the Western powers.

There was no mystery about German economics (though there was considerable mysterious talk about German economics). Economic recovery under the Nazis was the result of operations that any sensible and alert democratic government could have taken. That fact is, perhaps, the most poignant comment on the entire subject.

If "totalitarian economics" was a fabricated myth, then "totalitarian politics" was only slightly less so, on the evidence marshaled in *The Last Days of Hitler* by the Oxford historian and British Army Intelligence Officer, H. R. Trevor-Roper.

Nazi politics were not organized on any principle other than power. The questions of delegating authority and administering the functions of government were settled by a dog-fight among those who shared in the power. Writes Trevor-Roper: "Only policy, not administration, was effectively controlled from the center. . . . The structure of German politics and administration, instead of being, as the Nazis claimed, 'pyramidal' and 'monolithic' was, in fact, a confusion of private empires, private armies, and private intelligence services." (Of these latter, there were thirty competing organizations supplying the Foreign Ministry with information, almost all of it erroneous.) In turn, the leaders determining policy were themselves under a whole set of hidden and irresponsible influences. Who will ever be able to estimate the influence on world history of one Dr. Theodor Morrell, Hitler's personal physician, who made a fortune on quack patent medicines with which he systematically poisoned the *Führer?* Or of Himmler's astrologer, Wulf, or his masseur, Kersten—on whom he became more and more dependent?

The Nazi regime as described by Trevor-Roper, was—especially after 1941—a royal court rather than a government, with power concentrated in the hands of Hitler, and all the courtiers (Goering, Goebbels, Himmler, Bormann) intriguing for the succession. There is probably no more fantastic spectacle in all history than the one painted in brilliant detail in *The Last Days of Hitler:* the court in "session" in Hitler's bunker, Berlin burning and crumbling before their eyes, communications with the outside world practically shut off, the Russian armies in the suburbs, defeat a matter of days or hours, Hitler moving imaginary divisions on his military map—and all the Nazi leaders plotting furiously to be the heir to the power that they were sure Hitler would leave behind him! Each had his cabinet picked, posts allotted, and the terms of his "deal" with the Western powers worked out in detail.

With "statesmen" of this order at the top, it is no wonder that Nazi "totalitarianism" was not a very efficient affair. Samuel A. Goudsmit, an atomic scientist, tells in his book *Alsos* of the incredible disorganization of Nazi scientific research. ("Alsos" was the code name of the War Department mission that followed the army into Europe in search of evidence of Nazi preparations for atomic warfare.) There was no coordination between the different branches of the armed forces or between the armed forces and the universities. Party hacks who "did not believe in modern physics" because of its "Jewish-intellectual bias" were given posts of authority. German scientists were indiscriminately drafted while Hitler's favorite dancers and astrologers received exemptions. One discovery excited and frightened the Alsos mission: they found that the Auer chemical company was frantically acquiring thorium in occupied France and the Low Countries. But it turned out that all that Auer had in mind was to incorporate thorium in a new toothpaste with which it hoped to dazzle the market.

Yet, Nazi "totalitarianism" made one claim that was only too well founded: Hitler was Germany's *Führer* and his word was law. The longer we stare at Nazism the more our eyes focus on Hitler. He was its creator, his authority was supreme and unquestionable for every moment of its history; his notions and his whims dictated Nazi policy in every sphere; and there can be little doubt that his death would have been a death-blow to the regime itself. Hitler *was* Nazism. The war was *his* war—the generals and bankers were fearful and helpless. The extermination of the Jews was *his* project—as late as 1942, Goebbels was thinking of expelling them to Madagascar. The decision to fight to the bitter end, to see Germany forever destroyed rather than yield, was *his* decision. To the last second of his life, completely isolated in his Berlin bunker, every Nazi leader followed his wishes, or what they thought were his wishes.

Trevor-Roper sums this up:

> Liberal refugees, theoretical Marxists, despairing reactionaries have pretended, or persuaded themselves, that Hitler was himself only a pawn in a game which not he but some other politicians, or some more cosmic forces, were playing. It is a fundamental delusion. Whatever independent forces he may have used, whatever incidental support he may have borrowed, Hitler remained to the end the sole master of the movement which he had himself inspired and founded and which he was himself, by his personal leadership, to ruin. Neither Roehm nor Himmler, neither the army nor the Junkers, neither high finance nor heavy industry, ever controlled that demonic and disastrous genius, whatever assistance they may at times have given or received, with whatever hopes or credulities they may have solaced their misgivings, their frequent disappointments.

How and why this fussy, brutal, sentimental, hysterical, petty bourgeois could hypnotize his close associates, his followers, his party, and his nation is something a future biographer will have to work hard at to make clear to us. (Our contemporary biographers, like Konrad Heiden, have not, for all their good works, been successful in this respect.) The slow disappearance of the "great men" theory of history, ever since Carlyle, has not prepared us to cope with a phenomenon like Hitler. And it is more than likely that Carlyle himself would be at a loss—if not for words, then for an acceptable explanation. For the Nazis were in no sense "great men"; they were neither 20th-century Attilas nor Torquemadas nor Genghis Khans, and the more we ponder them the more incredible does the very fact of their leadership appear.

When one studies the case of The Nazi there comes a sickening emptiness of the stomach and a sense of bafflement. Can this be all? The disparity between the crime and the criminal is too monstrous.

We expect to find evil men, paragons of wickedness, slobbering, maniacal brutes; we are prepared to trace the lineaments of *The* Nazi on the face of every individual Nazi in order to define triumphantly the essential features of his character. But the Nazi leaders were not diabolists, they did not worship evil. For—greatest of ironies—the Nazis, like Adam and Eve before the fall, knew not of good and evil, and it is this cast of moral indifference that makes them appear so petty and colorless and superficial. The image of *The* Nazi is great and grotesque in our minds, but the Nazis in person turn out to be quite small and often ludicrous. That is what made the Nuremberg trials such a dismal affair. In the newsreel coverage of the trial we saw a harassed, uncomprehending crew of unshaven individuals—without dignity, fanaticism, obsessive hate, or the stature that large-scale wickedness often bestows. In comparison with John Dillinger, Hermann Goering looked like an indignant pickpocket. And to read through the proceedings of the trials, and to study the memoirs and diaries of the Nazi leaders that have recently been made available, only sharpens this impression of disproportion, and encourages the disorder of our sentiment.

For instance, in the light of his deeds it is hardly possible to think of the Nazi as pathetic; yet pathetic is the word that comes first to mind in reading the clumsy, coarsely written memoirs of Alfred Rosenberg, composed while awaiting trial in Nuremberg. The supreme ideologue of Nazism portrays himself for us as a superficial and simple-minded man, sincere in all his hypocrisies, a failure in Nazi politics, tearfully sentimental on his own account, an earnest philosophical quack. He had neither sufficient straightforward brutality nor sufficient political sense to secure a lasting position of authority in the Nazi movement. He was officially honored and respected as the author of the "Aryan bible," the bulky and unreadable *Myth of the Twentieth Century,* which sold over a million copies in Germany but which no one (including Hitler) read, and which was translated into only one foreign language—Japanese! Unofficially, he was despised by everyone (except Hitler—who thought him a loyal friend) and he had to sit fretfully and watch all the prerogatives of power snatched from his hands by Himmler, Bormann, and Goebbels.

Like Hitler, Rosenberg started out as a painter. But the artistic temperaments of the two men were of a different order. Hitler was a failure, a frustrated neurotic with a grudge against society. Rosenberg was, on his own level, quite successful; in a different era he would have been one of those banal painters of landscapes, member of a community art club, instructor in a small mediocre school, idolized by the mayor's wife, a cultural lion at civic tea parties. But the Russian and German revolutions cut off the roots that promised such a flowering; and his "philosophical ideas" (really puffed-up versions of his own rather primitive aesthetic doctrines) found a response in the hotbed of intellectual charlatanism that was postwar Munich; instead of the crank notions of the village aesthete (privately printed and distributed) they became the official "ideology" of a powerful nation.

In 1934, when Rosenberg was the Nazi spokesman in the Reichstag and elsewhere for "the suffering Germans in all foreign lands," his first collection of speeches and essays was published under the title of *Blood and Honor.* His publisher noted in a preface: "Born on January 12, 1893 in Reval (Esthonia), Alfred Rosenberg, as a Baltic German, lived through the sorrow and suffering of the *Auslanddeutschtums,* and then the Russian Revolution. In order to bring this suffering to the attention of all Germans, and in order to help guard against the Communist menace, he came to Germany at the end of 1917. . . ."

In his memoirs, Rosenberg gives a quite contrary picture. In the saccharine vocabulary of a slick-magazine, he recollects his "golden youth" when, as a "superior" German-speaking Balt he was able to combine daydreams of the Teutonic Knights with all the practical ease and advantages of a middle-class household in a Russia where pan-Slavism was only beginning to gnaw at a long tradition of tolerance for the Baltic Germans. He attended the Reval *gymnasium* where he was a model student, and where he was chosen *Klassenprimus* not for his scholarly record but for the good effect it might have on some of the more wayward students. Of his attitude toward his teachers Rosenberg writes: "When I was later active in Germany, I was astonished at the always erupting hostility toward teachers. This was freely and crassly expressed by many of my [party] comrades. . . . Of my teachers in Reval, I can speak only with the greatest respect." He also makes a point of the fact that there were Russian and Esthonian students among the Germanic majority, without the slightest hint of hostility or conflict.

It was Rosenberg's first wife, Hilda, who opened the door of European culture to him. Interested in Russian art, music, and ballet, she was the antithesis of the young, provincial *Baltdeutsch.* Under her influence he read Nietzsche (whose theatrical pathos disgusted him) and Tolstoy's *War and Peace* ("It made a very deep impression on me, and remains for me the great novel of European literature"). He continued his studies —architecture at the technical *Hochschule* in Riga—and his painting.

When he was able to see a display of early canvases by Picasso and Matisse, his reaction was: "Very bright: white, blue, rose, with many interesting shades, smoothly and ably painted; on the whole, however, superficial and sensational. This path does not lead to great art."

The years of war and revolution were comparatively placid for Rosenberg. He went to Moscow, boarded with a Russian family, studied, went to hear music at the Savoy, and passed his evenings in the coffee-houses on the Tverskaya. He read Houston Stewart Chamberlain with gusto, but the Russian revolution on which he became Germany's expert, passed him by at the time. Returning to Reval, he volunteered for the German army but was turned down because Esthonia was occupied territory; nor could he get permission to go to Germany. With time on his hands, he entered a competition sponsored by a furniture company to design the interior decoration of a living room. His two sketches won two second prizes.

Finally, in November 1918, Rosenberg was permitted to enter Germany. On this event he pontificates in his memoirs: "So I came to the Reich, originally a man given to art, philosophy, and history, who had never thought of mixing in politics. But I had observed the present, which was to become history."

Rosenberg's development as a successful Nazi followed the familiar pattern. Footloose and penniless in turbulent Munich, he gravitated toward the kindred souls who populated the Munich beerhall cellars: the White Russians, ex-officers, crackpot economic theorists—all those who ultimately coagulated into the NSDAP. His high-flown theories, especially his anti-Semitic ones, met with approval, and he turned out to be an industrious and prolific publicist.

But the high rank that Rosenberg attained in the Nazi hierarchy turned out to be a hollow success. The real politicians among the Nazis considered him a useful adjunct, but by no means indispensable and often very much of a nuisance. As early as 1925, Rosenberg whines, he could not get Hitler to take him along on his political tours. The founder and most renowned expositor of the theory of the master race was rudely shoved aside by political bosses who were ignorant of the essential polarity of Germanic and Greek art, and whose personal lives and financial dealings were not as impeccable as his, but who knew the business of party intrigue. As a result, Rosenberg adopted a protective ignorance, a careful "non-political" reaction to internal party happenings. (The fact that he was physically a coward was another motive.) Even while waiting for his trial at Nuremberg, he confessed ignorance as to what had really happened on the night of June 30, 1934 when Roehm and his cohorts were assassinated. His self-assumed ignorance was carried over to his job as Commissioner of Eastern Territories during the war: he left the liquidation of hundreds of thousands of Jews and Russians to his subordinates (appointed by the SS) who played the game of keeping him uninformed with a straight face. When conditions reached the point where it was impossible for him any longer to pretend, he protested to Hitler that the SS was overstepping its authority. Hitler soothed him, and the SS kept right on.

Rosenberg was no more swayed by humanitarian sympathies than the rest of his colleagues, and his criticism of the mass exterminations in the East was based partly on the grounds of political expediency (Goebbels shared his viewpoint on this matter), and partly on sheer exasperation at seeing all his powers successively appropriated; a bungler in every position that Hitler gave him, he was nonetheless anxious for political power. Brooding over his dispossession, he saw in it the corruption of Nazism from a high ideal to a coarse political dictatorship, in his own words, "the victory of sectarianism over the idea."

To Rosenberg, Goebbels was "a Mephistopheles." When Baldur von Schirach remarked that after all Goebbels was an artist too, Rosenberg retorted: "No, a *schmierant*." And in his memoirs, his vanity claimed its revenge on the brilliant and warped fanatic who usurped control of Nazi propaganda: "Hitler, of course, knew that I had a deeper understanding of art and culture than Goebbels, who was scarcely able to see beneath the surface." It is Goebbels whom Rosenberg blames for the anti-Jewish "excesses" and for having "linked art with propaganda." (!)

Similarly, Heinrich Himmler was for Rosenberg the "Gray Eminence" of the Third Reich. (Himmler had been born into a clerically-minded family and had revolted against political Catholicism; this only caused Rosenberg to remark bitterly: "A man can leave the Roman church ten times and still remain a Jesuit.") At length Rosenberg castigates Himmler for having absorbed all cultural institutions into the SS, for having brought the SS troops, in their brave obedience, into un-Germanic and horrible ways, and for having surrounded Hitler with satellites who fed him distorted versions of the true picture. In this, Rosenberg writes, he was ably abetted by Martin Bormann, the "mystery man" of the Third Reich. After 1941, Bormann, as Hitler's secretary, was the second most powerful man in Germany, the leader, in Rosenberg's words, of "the antechamber dictatorship"; yet he received very little publicity, his photo hardly ever appeared, his activities were barely mentioned in the press. "Bormann never uttered or defended a single idea. He led no men. He was the pure bureaucrat."

Those who are familiar with the history of revolutions will already have drawn the parallels. Trotsky on Stalin, Danton on Robespierre—always the same plaint of a revolution betrayed by willful and vicious men. But the French and Russian revolutions *were* predicated on an ideal, which was as genuine and widely felt as the degeneration that followed. Nazism had no ideal, only Rosenberg possessed one, the dupe of his own propaganda. And perhaps he didn't have one either; his revulsion can as well be interpreted as that of a cowardly man, rationalizing his resentment against those better fitted to rule in the Nazi machine. In any case, he has left us his word: "A great idea was misused by small men. . . . National Socialism was a European answer to a century's question. . . . National Socialism was finally misused and corrupted by men on whom its creator fatefully placed reliance."

But Rosenberg was too facile a philosopher to stop at mere disillusionment. The trouble with National Socialism, he came to realize in the last months of the war, was that it had "ideal" and "organization" but no "form." It is "form" that ensures the purity of "ideal" and "organization." He began to devise a scheme for a conservative republic that would prevent the emergence of a one-party dictatorship, and soon had turned out a volume on political theory, entitled *The Power of Form*. The work was destroyed in manuscript—and those who have looked into the *Myth of the Twentieth Century* will have few regrets.

It was inevitable that one of the Nazi leaders would reduce the inflated doctrine of "Aryanism" to its intellectual absurdity and prosaic brutality. This was Heinrich Himmler's task. Indeed, he took it so seriously and with such bloody consequences that Trevor-Roper refers to him as "the Great Inquisitor" of Nazism. However, Nazism was the kind of movement, and Himmler the kind of man, that could produce only a parody of a "Great Inquisitor." Hitler himself ridiculed Himmler's extravagant ideological pretensions,* while Speer regarded him as "half schoolmaster, half crank," and Rosenberg was appalled by his rigid application of Nazi dogma.

In his book *European Witness,* Stephen Spender remarks of the German that he "could not relate his own personality with his actions done in the name of duty." It is this gap between personality and duty which may help explain the picked *Einsatzgruppen*—for the most part educated men: doctors, lawyers, civil servants—who in cold blood exterminated several million people in Eastern Europe. And it helps us explain Himmler, a small, bespectacled, and mild bureaucrat whom his subordinates called, without irony, "gentle Heinrich," and who was a conscienceless murderer.

During the war, Himmler gave a speech to SS generals and police officials on concentration camps which reveals the mentality of the man:

* Hitler's attitude to "Aryanism" was a practical one: "Were it even proven that in the past there had been no Aryan race, it is for us to insist that such should exist in the future! For men of action that is the deciding standpoint." (*Mein Kampf*)

> It would be extremely instructive for every one . . . to inspect such a concentration camp. Once they have seen it, they are convinced that no one has been sent there unjustly; that it is the offal of criminals and freaks. . . . On the whole, education consists of discipline, never of any kind of instruction on an ideological basis, for the prisoners have for the most part slave-like souls. . . . Discipline means order. The order begins with these people living in clean barracks. Such a thing can really only be accomplished by us Germans, hardly another nation would be as human as we are. The laundry is frequently changed. The people are taught to wash themselves twice daily, and to use a toothbrush, a thing with which most of them have been unfamiliar.

It is almost incredible that Himmler actually believed all this. But he did believe it—and more. Himmler set the SS foreign intelligence section to studying Freemasonry and Rosicrucianism, the significance of the suppression of the harp in Ulster, and the inner meaning of Gothic spires and Eton top-hats. He was especially interested in runes (the still undeciphered script of the Norsemen), hoping to prove a link between the "Aryans" and the Japanese. On April 1, 1945—five weeks before the end of the war—he conceived of colonizing the Ukraine with a new religious sect thought up by his masseur.

In 1935, Himmler created the Ahnenerbe—the Academy of Ancestral Heritage—to propagate the truths of SS *Wissenschaft*. On one occasion during the war, when he was away at the front, he wrote the following letter (quoted by Goudsmit) to SS Colonel Sievers, head of the Ahnenerbe:

> In future weather researches, which we expect to carry out after the war by systematic organization of an immense number of single facts, I request you to take note of the following:
>
> The roots, or onions, of the meadow saffron are located at depths that vary from year to year. The deeper they are, the more severe the winter will be; the nearer they are to the surface, the milder the winter.
>
> This fact was called to my attention by the *Führer*.
>
> Heil Hitler!
> Himmler

It seems appropriate to point out here that Himmler was graduated from an agricultural academy.

Unfortunately, this buffoonery was not always so funny. Its logic led to the setting up of the "Applied War Research" department in the Ahnenerbe which was responsible for the grotesque and idiotic experiments on selected concentration camp inmates.

In the last months of the war, Himmler became concerned with his reputation as a butcher. He appointed a new Reich Commissioner for concentration camps, to reorganize them in a "humanistic spirit." He ordered an end to forced evacuation of the camps in the face of advancing Allied armies. Lest these acts be misunderstood, he spoke his mind to a Jewish Swedish representative on April 19, 1945: "They say that I am trying to forge an alibi. I need no alibi; I always did what seemed right for my people. It did not make me a rich man."

When Himmler heard that Hitler was doomed in Berlin, he decided that history had called him. In an interview with the Swedish Red Cross representative, Count Folke Bernadotte, he offered to surrender on the Western front and keep up the fight in the East until the Allies came to his assistance. As Bernadotte left, carrying these terms with him, Himmler began to worry whether he should shake hands or bow when he met Eisenhower. He drew up a new cabinet and chose a new name for his party. On May 5th, Himmler held his last staff conference in Flensburg; he had plans to set up a provisional government in Schleswig-Holstein. His one remaining problem, he said, was that he needed an interview with General Montgomery. When he was captured by the British, the shock of being treated like a criminal was too great, and he took poison.

Unlike Rosenberg and Himmler, Joseph Goebbels was not interested in any version of the Aryan myth. He was, on the other hand, very much interested in political myths as elaborated by Georges Sorel and Wilfred Pareto. The political myth was the form by which he molded the body politic to suit his "creative vision." Goebbels is on record as having said of Dostoevsky: "He writes because writing is still in the 19th century one of the possible modes of existence. The political solution was as yet unborn." Like so many Nazi leaders, Goebbels had tried to be an artist and (like them) had failed. He then set out to seek a "higher" artistry in politics.

In a suggestive chapter of his book, Stephen Spender discusses in detail Goebbels's novel *Michael,* published in 1929 when Goebbels was already on the road to his "political solution":

> Very little happens in *Michael.* The hero is a young student, his mind full of memories of 1918, who is supposed to be studying at Heidelberg. . . . He has love affairs and friendships. His relationship with people on whom he fastens his attention has two aspects. One is that others should believe in his own "demon," his genius. The other is that they are his opponents. These two

passionate impulses, together with his passionate nationalism, and a perpetual restless desire to transcend the narrow boundaries of his existence in postwar Germany on the wave of some tremendous emotion, leave him no room to be interested in human beings as human beings, and no room for self-criticism. Yet he has a great faith in himself, and if one asks how such a person can have such a faith, the answer is that the experience of constant turmoil gives him a convincing sense of the reality of his own existence, and it is this which he above all demands from life: to suffer, to be mad, to experience a sense of ecstasy.

Goebbels as a rebel was an aesthetic rebel, not against any specific iniquities of postwar Germany, but against life and society that conditions and limits the individual (especially the ugly, club-footed individual that was Goebbels); he was as pure an embodiment of Nietzscheanism as could be contrived. And just as Nietzscheanism had strong affinities with the *fin de siècle* aesthetic revolt against bourgeois society, so Goebbels seems to be in some sort of relationship with contemporary artists who revolt in disgust against their epoch and the people who inhabit it. There is, however, a decisive difference between Goebbels and such artists. Goebbels took a "political" solution (as Nietzsche did not); after all, to call a century a pigsty is one thing, to make it into a pigsty is another.

When Goebbels has his hero say: "Today we are all expressionists—men who want to make the world outside themselves take the form of their life within themselves," he expresses both his verbal affinity with the artist and his actual distance from him. For by the "world outside," the artist means the world of accomplished imagination, of paper and ink, bounded by the covers of a book: in creating this world, no matter how ugly, the artist may extend our understanding of human nature and possibilities. Goebbels, however, had in mind the world that bleeds—and a drop of blood is incommensurate with a bucketful of imagination.

Michael is full of the kind of ecstatic visions one might expect:

> I tear my heart out. What does a heart matter? I throw it into the storm of fire.
> I am a hero, a God, a Savior.
> I myself bleed. My arms hang down powerless.
> I have been hit.
> I become tired. I sink down.
> I lose consciousness.

By the time we meet Goebbels in his diaries, he has had considerable success in his "creative politics." He had, in the course of years, transformed Nazism from the ideological effervescence of a beer-hall into a working-class, "socialistic," anti-plutocratic movement that had swept the industrial Rhineland; he had created the *Führer* myth; he had organized Berlin into a Nazi stronghold; he had built the most effective propaganda machine the world had seen up to that time; he was one of the most powerful—and by far the most intelligent—of the rulers of Germany. The days of *Sturm und Drang* were a dim memory, replaced by factional scheming, managing a country at war, trying to produce a baby a year (his total was five, all given names beginning with H), and the innumerable other obligations of Nazi power.

Those who look into *The Goebbels Diaries* should know that what they are reading, though certainly written by Goebbels, is not a diary in the sense of something written in complete confidence and intimacy. That Goebbels kept a diary we know from many sources, aside from the inherent improbability of such a supreme egoist not taking advantage of the position history had accorded him. One of his subordinates, Rudolf Semmler, noted in *his* private diary: "For twenty years Goebbels has regularly and painstakingly kept a diary. Every day he spends an hour on this task. So far he has written twenty-three thick volumes in minute handwriting. Goebbels believes that one day this diary, read with the official archives, will provide one of the richest sources for the history of the Nazi party and Hitler's years of power."

Should these diaries ever turn up, there is no doubt that Goebbels' opinion would be vindicated. But these are not the diaries that make up the volume recently published. *The Goebbels Diaries* are excerpted from a typewritten manuscript of some seven hundred and fifty thousand words, covering nine and one-half months of the years 1942-43. They were obviously dictated to a professional typist—the lines were triple spaced and the margins wide—at a tremendous speed; one day's dictation went up to eighty-five typed pages! It is likely that they are a preliminary self-edited version of Goebbels' record which he was preparing to serve Germany and the world after Nazism's triumph; the various "indiscretions" that can be found would have been eventually eliminated to make up a document in conformity with the Nazi ideal, in such matters, of unmitigated dullness.

This helps explain why the *Diaries* are so exasperating and amorphous. They are neither an "inside story" of the Nazi regime nor of the Nazi mind; they provide only a few additional footnotes on well-worn themes.

The *Diaries* pay their respects to those anti-Nazis abroad who urged (unsuccessfully) that Allied propaganda seek to distinguish between the Nazis and the German people. For Lord Vansittart, Goebbels' discussion of the "anti-Hun" enthusiasm that he made fashionable among otherwise civilized intellectuals is sure to be unpleasant reading. At one point, Goebbels suggests the erection of a monument in Vansittart's honor, inscribed:

"To the Englishman who rendered the greatest service to the German cause during the war." In another entry, he writes: "A much more clever form of propaganda against the Reich has been proposed in the United States. The idea is not to go against the German people but against Nazism. I sense a certain danger. . . . I gave orders that the German press is not to publish or discuss turns of speech such as are being used increasingly in the American press."

That Goebbels was a pathological anti-Semite of the kind visible on the "lunatic fringe" of American politics is common knowledge, and the *Diaries* offer nothing to modify this notion. Nothing, that is, except a flashing, occasional—but groundless—doubt as to the ingenuousness of his opinions. When he writes indignantly: "They [the Jews] are now trying to stir up the entire world merely to incite public opinion against the National Socialist Reich and its anti-Semitic convictions," it would seem to have more the ring of hypocrisy than of pathology. Similarly, on May 11, 1942 he was moved to the following complaint: "There are still 40,000 Jews in Berlin and despite the heavy blows dealt them they are still insolent and aggressive"; the Jews referred to were half-Jews or Jewish women married to Christians, and they were all, with justification, in a state of near-death from fright. But there was no propagandistic point to be made by these fantastic statements. There is no explanation for them at all, except that Goebbels believed them; and the fact that he did believe them sets the stamp of authenticity upon his Nazism.

Goebbels is generally accounted as a "left-wing" Nazi, and if we keep in mind one qualification—that Goebbels would never allow a mere idea to stand between himself and an accretion of power—the label is correct. Goebbels' great contribution to Nazism had been to make it understandable and appealing to the urban working-class, and he personally held the military caste and the bourgeoisie in great contempt. In his diary we read: "Our prognosis regarding this war is surely right. It is being conducted by the capitalists of all countries against the German social commonwealth."

From the beginning, Goebbels demanded a "total war" which would concentrate all powers in the hands of a few Nazi rulers (including himself), and which would provide the opportunity for the annihilation of remnants of the old regime. As the end of the war drew close, when what he said could not possibly matter and when Hitler was sulking in his dugout, Goebbels had his day. Taking charge of Radio Berlin, he gave free vent to his radicalism, which turned out to be a radical nihilism. He created the specter of the Werewolves who would continue the fight for all time and under all conditions—at a moment when the leader of the Werewolves was negotiating a surrender to the British through the Danish underground movement.

He exulted at what Nazism had wrought: "Under the debris of our shattered cities, the last so-called achievements of the middle-class nineteenth century have been finally buried. . . . Together with the monuments of culture there crumble also the last obstacles to the fulfillment of our revolutionary task. Now that everything is in ruins we are forced to rebuild Europe. In the past, private possessions held us to bourgeois restraint. Now the bombs, instead of killing all Europeans, have only smashed the prison walls which held them captive."

No one paid any attention to these apocalyptic rantings, especially the Germans. But they inflated Goebbels' vanity and conscience (which, for him, were much the same thing) to a climax of dedication that saw him, alone among the top Nazis, remain loyal to his oath to die with Hitler, kill his wife and five children, and then commit suicide before he could be taken prisoner.

Even a casual glance over the members of the Nazi leadership corps will ascertain that it held no "well-balanced" individuals; in all of them there was an obvious psychic imbalance, an exaggeration of certain faculties and the atrophy of others, that was revealed in uncontrollable emotional drives, and a deteriorated sense of reality. It would seem from this that psychiatry is one discipline that might be appealed to in order to reach a true understanding of Nazism, and that the psychiatrist might be more helpful than the historian or the economist. But it does not turn out quite that way. Psychiatrists do find important things to say about the Nazi personality—but these point, not to the uniqueness of the Nazis, but to their psychological continuity with all of us who are not Nazis. We end up by knowing more about ourselves and about our potentialities for debasement, but little more about the Nazis.

This is the implicit point of *The Case of Rudolf Hess,* a report by the eight British and American psychiatrists who were in charge of Hess during his five-year imprisonment. It is a sober and unsensational work, in no way related to the wild incursions that psychiatrists so often make into politics and history. Dr. J. R. Rees, who edited the volume, does append a chapter in which he tries to probe into the specific German social background that produced Nazis; it is more scrupulous than the run of such attempts, though probably not less misleading.

Merely to look at the photograph of Hess on the dust cover gives rise to the belief that here at last we have the "real" Nazi; his heavy, beetled eyebrows, square jaw, and thin lips invoke images of cruelty and fanaticism. Just as Goebbels was the "public-relations man" and Goering the "military man," so Hess was the "party man" of Nazism. It is easy to imagine him as Professor Karl Haushofer's favorite student, studying geopolitics with passionate subjectivity; as leader of the SS, his every sinew taut with dogma; as Hitler's deputy, strutting across the platform at party ceremonies, his right arm forever stiffly upraised without apparent weariness.

Actually, however, by the time Hess flew to England, he had already lost his pre-eminent position in the Nazi movement. His colleagues regarded him as a "crackpot," and the SS came under the control of Himmler. It was only his past service and his loyalty to Hitler that kept Hess among the leadership, if only in appearance. He was given hard-luck cases to "fix" and uplifting speeches to make to fertile mothers.

Hess's sudden flight to England demonstrated that his fellow Nazis had not misjudged him. The purpose of this flight was exactly what Hess claimed it to be: he was shocked by the bombing of British women and children and was appalled by the prospect of a long and bloody war. His knowledge of British politics was a bundle of inaccurate clichés, and he was convinced that if he could pierce the curtain that Churchill had established around the King and his "court," he could persuade these latter to come to terms. That the third-ranking Nazi (on paper, anyway) should be so misinformed about the workings of the British government was in itself surprising. But a little probing by psychiatrists broke through the hard, stereotyped Nazi shell to the festering pulp beneath, and brought home to them the fact that they had a real "case" on their hands. Hess's pockets, when he parachuted into Scotland, bulged with homeopathic cures and quack medicines. He exhibited all the textbook neurotic symptoms: compulsive orderliness, tense secretiveness about his bowel movements, a fear of being passively conveyed in vehicles. He was an acute hypochondriac, a believer in "nature cures," and the victim of an immense persecution complex.

This persecution complex was at the basis of his anti-Semitism, which was really of classic dimensions. All during his imprisonment he complained of food poisoning, of being disturbed by strange noises at night, of torture at the hands of dentists and eye doctors. This he knew to be part of a world Jewish plot, whose power was due to the secret workings of "post-hypnotic suggestion" through which all the world's non-Jews were driven to self-destruction. When his attempted suicide (while in England) failed, he blamed the Jews for having incited him to the attempt because he had found out about their secret power of hypnosis. This Judaic post-hypnotic suggestion was produced by a secret chemical that was inserted into the world's food, and its consequences were manifold and subtle. Wrote Hess in his diary: "I could not foresee at this time that the Jews, in order to receive material for propaganda against Germany, would go so far as to bring the guards of German concentration camps, by use of the secret chemical, to treat the inmates as the OGPU did." Nor was this the limit of Jewish subtlety; Hess found occasion to complain that the Jews went so far as to put a poison into his food that actually made him feel better.

Hess's notorious amnesia, which at Nuremberg he claimed to have faked, was beyond doubt genuine, at least for the major portion of his imprisonment. It is catalogued by the psychiatrists as "hysterical amnesia" —a self-protective device against the impingement of the unpleasantness of the real world. Here are two summaries of Hess's psychic state:

> The paranoid features of his personality were clearly seen in egocentricity, based on a deep feeling of insecurity, a fear of being injured and attacked. The psychological interpretation of such an attitude is that the patient has severe uncertainty and conflict about his own value and acceptance by society. He clearly has no great confidence in the goodness of other people, and while withdrawing in one sense into his "self" he is always looking for an idealized person outside himself whom he might love and trust in order to assuage his loneliness. [Dr. Henry V. Dicks]

And:

> The findings . . . indicate that Hess suffers from a true psychoneurosis, primarily of the hysterical type which is grafted upon a basic paranoid personality. In other words, fundamentally Rudolf Hess is an introverted, shy, withdrawn, personality, who basically is suspicious of his environment and projects upon his surroundings concepts developing within himself. [Major Douglas Kelley]

It is something of a shock to a layman, after reading this case history, to find out that these psychiatrists did not at all consider Hess clinically insane or committable to an asylum. And it drives home the point that is suggested by the above two quotations: that Hess's psychic processes were not different in kind from those which might be discovered among French barbers, mid-Western university professors, or composers of letters-from-the-lovelorn in all lands. His unconscious faithfully adhered to the rules of the universal human unconscious, and we see that we are not entirely strangers to the twistings of his mind. If a list of his symptoms were clipped out and passed around as anonymous samples, they would arouse no special curiosity, so characteristic are they of what we have come to expect psychiatrists to dig up.

But where then does the Nazi come from? Dr. Rees, in his concluding chapter, attempts an answer. In effect what he says is that just these trite psychological derangements, when present in large numbers of people and spurred on by social and political institutions, make up Nazism. He writes: "The Nazi movement would seem to have been but a late and, as it were, caricatured expression of modes of behavior and aspiration which had been noted about the attitudes of the German elite long before the war of 1914-18. The outstanding among these were tendencies to exert power and domination, to have status and 'honor' . . . and a tendency to glorify mass movement as an expression of unity in subordination to a great leader figure." The patriarchal structure of the German family encouraged the growth of authoritarianism, at the same time that it left a potent residue of inferiority and resentment that sought outlet in a "scapegoat" complex.

This type of analysis is not exactly new—nor does it improve with age. Of course, German social history is extremely pertinent to the present, as is all history. But it is the specifics of pertinence that have to be isolated and demonstrated. That the German family was patriarchal at all is a moot point (there are sharp differences between Catholic and Protestant families as well as regional differences). And there were many Germans who were very sensitive with regard to status and honor, who enjoyed speaking of "fatherland," "duty," and "hard work" who never became Nazis. Indeed most of the conspirators against the Nazis were people of this kind (Goerdeler, Beck, Canaris, Gisevius, etc.), as are the members of the Social-Democratic, Communist, and Catholic center parties in that country today.

It is true that we cannot understand the present without understanding the past; but it does not follow that if we understand the past—or if we think we understand it—the present can be measured as a passive resultant. This sort of error—the "genetic fallacy"—is one that psychiatrists seem prone to commit by the very nature of their method, which works backward. A complete and detailed case history of Rudolf Hess would tell us much about him—but it would not tell us the full meaning of his becoming a Nazi. For intervening in the working out of his complexes there would be the act of moral choice; it is this act that makes of Hess a Nazi rather than, say, a "shy, withdrawn" librarian suspiciously guarding the books of some provincial library. Or, instead of a moral choice, a moral convulsion of the personality that set the line upon which Rudolf Hess walked through life while that distressed subconscious of his worked away in its "shy, withdrawn" depths.

The Nazis are human: that is what the psychiatrists tell us. We always knew that, though it does no harm to have it confirmed.

But the Nazis are also non-human: that is what we, their wounded fellow-creatures, have to tell the psychiatrists and ourselves, as we point to the incredible horrors they so calmly worked on the body and soul of mankind. And it is this very combination of the only-too-human and unimaginably-inhuman that makes the Nazis a persistent and nettling mystery for us.

Solomon F. Bloom

DICTATOR OF THE LODZ GHETTO

The Strange History of Mordechai Chaim Rumkowski

A few years ago a tremendous and extraordinary catastrophe struck the Jewish people. We are not in any danger of forgetting it, but rather of fearing to think about it and discounting it, as it were, as the consequence of one of the many "isms" that lie ready to hand: fascism, sadism, the-last-stage-of-capitalism, militarism gone mad, and so on. For our age abhors the unexplained event. Better a dozen theories than one obstreperous fact. We are in the way of killing true knowledge by premature understanding. Far from being comprehended, the Jewish catastrophe, and all the other Nazi horrors, bid fair to tease us out of thought, as the poet said, alas, of beauty and eternity.

These are matters of which it is important to know everything before concluding anything, not to speak of judging. And yet, the tragedy is unfamiliar to us in most of its crucial details. Particularly unfamiliar is the action and reaction of the Jews and their leaders on the spot. We have heard something, and not enough, of the resistance of various ghettos, and notably of the glorious rebellion of the Jews of Warsaw. But we have learned little of other, border-line cases, where resistance was mixed with a numb despair and a hope too long drawn out.

Such a case was that of the ghetto of the industrial city of Lodz, in Poland, which had the special misfortune to be ruled, from beginning to annihilation, by Mordechai Chaim Rumkowski.

It is easy to say, and yet both true and inadequate, that the meaning of Rumkowski's strange career lay in embodying the limitations of the societies it spanned, the Polish-Jewish community and the Nazi order. Otherwise an undistinguished man, he was able to do that in a drastic manner indeed.

Endowed with many incongruous abilities and propelled by overflowing passions, Rumkowski came naturally into a tense commerce with the world. He was already in his late fifties when he acted out his ambiguities in an almost adolescent pantomine. For many years he had sold insurance and managed a Jewish orphan asylum. Both occupations, pursued with conspicuous energy, merged in a continuous solicitation, whether of premiums or contributions, from the same wealthy citizens of Lodz. He practiced an all-too-familiar type of persuasion and salesmanship affected with a public interest.

Rumkowski found time also to become a character. He had made the easy discovery that many an enriched Jew—the industries of Lodz had grown phenomenally and raucously—lacked the courage of his accumulation and could be shouted out of his money. He became notorious for an impudent persistence that kept the orphanage in funds. When he did not play wrathful prophet to the rich, he paraded his love for children. The affection was as genuine as the parade: he was a widower with none of his own. He liked to surround himself with his charges, although he apparently drew the circle a bit close. It was whispered that he was guilty of familiarities with grown girls and women employed in the institution. There is even a report of a legal prosecution mysteriously dropped before it came to trial.

Certain it is that Rumkowski governed his institution with an ungloved iron hand, ignoring the wishes of contributors and coworkers alike. Money-raising tells for too much in the Jewish community, whether in Poland or the United States. Righteous table-thumping is always indulged. Nevertheless, Rumkowski could not go far in such a community as Lodz. His manners were rude and his learning nil. Despite the strength of his personality, he was condemned to a negligible influence, more annoying than pernicious.

The Nazis, however, tempted him with a vast opportunity. Lodz fell without a blow barely a week after the war broke out in September 1939. It was bound to be a city of special interest to Germany. With its twelve hundred enterprises and two million spindles, it had long been famous as the Manchester of the East. In a century, it had grown from a village to a city of nearly three-quarters of a million people, next to Warsaw the largest in the country. Here the Germans and the Jews repeated their traditional common role in Eastern Europe: they rather than the Poles had developed Lodz. In addition to nearly a quarter of a million Jews, the population included about ninety thousand Germans, the largest "Nordic" island in the Polish sea.

In Lodz as elsewhere, the Nazis invited the Jews to perpetrate their own spoliation and even immolation. This saved time, work, and money, and preserved "order," by reducing to a minimum the confrontation of tyrant with victim. Setting Jew against Jew created a diversion, degraded them, and confirmed the Nazis in their faith that man relishes bruality. The organized and autonomous community—complete, as everywhere in Eastern Europe, with powers of taxation, sanctions, and even political parties—was to carry out the commands of the conqueror. The community was organized democratically, but when the Nazis said community they meant the leader.

How they came to think that in Lodz the leader was Rumkowski is something of a mystery. He was a Zionist member of the elected council, and not an influential one. A month after the occupation, an officer burst into the council chamber and demanded to speak to the *"Aelteste der Juden,"* which was taken to mean the oldest member. Rumkowski, with his large head and white mane, was singled out, or he stepped forward. This account is probably folklore and contains more *Galgenhumor* than information. In *Hurban Lodz,* Israel Tabaksblatt, a survivor, reports the more likely version that Rumkowski intrigued behind the scenes for his elevation.

He was invested with a kind of *Führerschaft* but his powers did not reach their fullness until the Jews were shut off in a ghetto. For half a year the Nazis contented themselves with ordering them from the better streets, labeling them with the Star of David, displacing them in the better homes and businesses with *Volksgenossen* whose numbers were swollen by Baltic emigrants; drafting them for forced labor and engaging in rapine and shooting both organized and informal. This "liberal" regime came to an end in February 1940. First in Lodz and then in other cities—for the smaller towns were simply depopulated—the Germans revived the ghetto and degraded it to depths unplumbed in medieval days.

The Jews were driven from all parts of the city and herded into the Balut district in the north. Like all industrial centers, from Manchester to Pittsburgh, Lodz was overcrowded and jerry-built. A native writer has described it as "the most offensively ugly" of Polish cities and "most monstrously unhygienic," and a native poet was reduced to this apostrophe:

Let Sorrento, Ganges and Crimea
Exalted to the heavens be.
But give me Lodz: its very dirt
And smoke are sweeter far to me.

And nowhere was Lodz less lovely than in the slums of the Balut.

Thousands of Jews had somehow succeeded in fleeing the city, for the Nazi system took some time to jell, and the remaining 160,000 were pressed into 25,000 to 42,000 rooms—the estimates vary—or four to six in a room. The Germans then complained that the Ghetto was dirty. A sensitive police chief observed that "an indescribable odor" lay over the whole of it and that the Jews were covered with filth; he used a stronger word. Another official blamed the conditions on the *"niedrige Wohnkultur dieses Volkes."*

Characteristically, the Nazis approached the denouement of isolation only gradually, always encouraging the belief that the worst had come and gone, in order to forestall the resistance of flat despair. No hope abandon until it is too late. For a time, Poles were allowed into the Ghetto on business and Jews could leave during the day to work in the city. Then the gates were barred; nobody could come or go. The ten miles of wall and barbed wire which enclosed the Ghetto were patrolled night and day by soldiers. More than one Jew was killed, sometimes in sheer exuberance or jest, while merely passing along these walls. Only German guards and officials could penetrate hell and still emerge to purgatory.

In these forbidden precincts the authority of Rumkowski blossomed forth. He assumed the title of *Der Aelteste der Juden in Litzmannstadt-Getto* and the Polish title of *Prezes.* He received full power to maintain "an ordered social life." He alone was to maintain relations with German officials, and through them with the planet. He was to control the property of the Ghetto, judge and punish the inhabitants, and even execute them. Under this autocracy a shadow state arose with all the panoply of the real. The panoply plays here the role of the precise detail in *Gulliver's Travels:* it persuades us, for a moment, that the fantasy is true. But the meaning of Swift lies elsewhere, and so does that of Rumkowski's state.

It began with a budget rather than a social contract. Rumkowski levied a kind of single tax, making ordinary rent his fisc. But it appeared that too many of his subjects, bereft of jobs and incomes, were rather in need of relief themselves. Rumkowski thereupon ordered all currency and foreign remittances converted into his own fiat money, which became the only legal tender in the Ghetto. He decreed the sale of jewels, furs, and other valuables against the new paper. With some of the wealth —for most of it was siphoned off by the Nazis without any return—he imported food, doled out relief, bought raw materials, and organized an elaborate administrative apparatus. All the money issued by this state brought into being by the swastika was adorned wih the menorah and the star of David and bore the signature of Rumkowski, florid with curlicues.

After money, force. (How much simpler it is to organize a state than to improve a society!) Rumkowski recruited twelve hundred police, a corps of plain-clothesmen for investigations, confiscations, and secret arrests, and a private guard. His chief of police made himself notorious for cruelty and venality. Judges, jails, even corporal punishment, completed the scheme of coercion. The *Aelteste* reserved an "administrative" power of arrest, the right of seizure by direct oral command, and the right of grace and amnesty. His "monarchy" was not limited as far as the Ghetto was concerned. One might have said "empire," for he also controlled a "colony" of Gypsies doomed by the Germans to a speedy extermination.

At once more ornamental and useful was the Ghetto Post Office and its stamps. In its first year, it cleared 135,063 parcels from other parts of Poland and 14,299 from abroad, 64,049 incoming money orders worth 1,699,151 marks, 10,238 telegrams, and more than a million letters and cards. The mails were quite efficient, although there were occasions when the ruler had to acknowledge the receipt of whole carloads of parcels that the Germans whimsically kept for themselves. In compensation, Rumkowski let himself go philatelically. On one stamp, his white-aureoled and bespectacled image, softened by court artists, peers out of a star of David, imposed on a menorah. Or he surveys imperially the symbols of economic fertility: an industrial wheel against the background of smoking chimneys, a compass and carpenter's knife, and the all-important cotton bobbin.

The strongest arm of power, stronger than Jewish police and German Gestapo, was the control over food and jobs. "You can look into anything you wish and give your opinion, except the offices of food administration and personnel," Rumkowski warned his appointed council. "I alone will distribute food and name officials." Rations were lower and prices higher in the Ghetto than outside, although this was not entirely his fault, since the Germans paid him little for finished goods and charged him exorbitantly for imports. The Jews were exploited several times over. As a result, starvation was common and semi-starvation quite general. Their effect, as usual, was disease even more than hunger. Tabaksblatt remarks that "if any Ghetto Jew says that he ate his fill even once in those two years [of the "autonomous" state] he is lying." Both he and Dr. Albert Mazur, another survivor, mention cases where families concealed their dead in order to collect the extra ration. I spare the reader the details. (This practice was common in concentration camps: one lived off the dead, as it were.)

In a few years the Nazis could have killed all the Jews by this "cold" pogrom alone: but they were people in a hurry. A diary records that on July 5, 1942, 105 persons died and five were born: on the 27th the figures were 113 and zero. Even as the population was being reduced by mass deportation the death rate rose sharply—1940: 6,851; 1941: 11,437; 1942, 18,020.

The feeding of the Ghetto, such as it was, depended largely on its productiveness. Old industries were revived and new factories set up. One of the reasons why the Nazis tolerated the existence of the Ghetto as long as they did was their need for manufactures. Eventually most of the factories worked to supply the Wehrmacht. *"Unzere passport iz di arbeit,"* was one of Rumkowski's frequent slogans. He was proudest of his accomplishments in this field. The calendar printed in the Ghetto carefully records the anniversaries of the establishment of the various industries. The initial difficulties were indeed considerable: on the principle of grab rather than efficiency, the Nazis had removed the machines and tools of the Balut; the Ghetto contained too many unskilled persons; orders were at first few and raw materials lacking; exchange and barter trickled through sclerotic official arteries. In the first year, only fifteen to twenty per cent of the people could find work; the rest hungered on a sketchy relief. In the factory, as in the street, the iron hand ruled. The second issue of the *Getto Zeitung,* the official newspaper, announced plainly that "the Ghetto does not work by the clock." It did not.

What may have encouraged Rumkowski to believe, as he did, that he would be instrumental in saving a remnant of Polish Jewry was his ability to organize not only workshops but also hospitals and schools. He assembled medical personnel and supplies, although the German officials saw to it that his success here was tragically inadequate. They allowed him to improvise a whole school system. In the first spring, he gathered 7,366 boys and girls in primary schools, and 728 in secondary. The figures were doubled in the following year. The curriculum reflected the new conditions: religious instruction was strengthened, German could not be taught to the "inferior race," and Yiddish supplanted Polish, which had generally been the language of instruction, in the primary grades. The Ghetto was Jewish in a Yiddish sort of way, if one may say so. Rumkowski indulged the children with extra rations, sweets, and holiday gifts. His old professional interest stood him in good stead. The survivors concede quite generally that his devotion was authentic.

Such were the institutions of this crepuscular state. It was not precisely a Nazi state, for Jews cannot be brought to believe in invidious natural distinctions among themselves, and cannot make a virtue of brutality. But it resembled its progenitor in autocracy, servility, and corruption. The Nazi system bred a shrewd synthesis between systematic robbery as a matter of state policy and spontaneous rapine by subordinates and menials. A common interest made easy bedfellows of those two irreconcilable rivals of the manuals of political science: the individual and the state. Rumkowski appointed complaisant and self-seeking officials, and thus deprived the community of a responsible and competent public service. He showered them with opportunities for extortion and graft. Let no one think that there is no room in the shadow of death for accumulation and ostentation. Mammon long ago discovered that even Hell "wants not her hidden luster."

The members of the official apparatus ate well and concealed food for speculation and private security. Not a little was spoiled through too much prevision. There was no check over distribution—Rumkowski himself did not know how much came in or went out—with imaginable results. Money hoards have been uncovered. There are reports of orgies, both alimentary and sexual.

Rumkowski was wide open to the temptation of the flesh—that was an old story. Although during his "reign" he married a young woman of good family and half his age—a king must have a queen and if possible a dynasty—he was not averse to attending the inflammable festivities of his creatures. But, unlike them, he was not mercenary. He was captivated rather by the psychological and political perquisites of his strange and—he dared to think—promising role. Like all dictators he affected to despise politics, to love order, and to protect his loyal subjects. His favorite word was *ruh,* his goal *ruh in ghetto.* He was given to referring to "my children," "my workers," "my factories," and even "my Jews." He indulged the language of command. When nurses asked for a reduction of their inhuman working hours, he threatened to "crush" their "obstinacy." In decreeing shorter clothes for men to save material for patches, he announced that he "would carry out this plan of mine one hundred per cent and will not stop at anything, as is my custom." He meddled with religious rules: on calling on a bereaved man to return to his shop, he declared, with an unconscious pun, that "in these times it is permissible to sit *shiva* [seven mourning days] four days."

In tune with his times, Rumkowski encouraged a kind of *Führer* worship. The calendar of the Ghetto (printed incidentally on the back of advertising sheets for coffee, the original business of Hans Biebow, the *Leiter der Gettoverwaltung*) recorded only one historical date apart from the inauguration of industries—the birthday of the *Aelteste.* By an ironic chance, this fell on Purim, the festival of liberation from Haman. Rumkowski's concern for the young was effectively exploited by his political machine. On the eve of Rosh Hashanah 1942, he was presented with a large album, bound in hard wood and leather, containing the good wishes of the whole school system. The clear signatures of 14,587 pupils and 715 teachers, carefully numbered, may be read in the original copy now in the archives of the Yiddish Scientific Institute—Yivo—in New York. It is perhaps the most accurate roll of the martyrdom of the war. The list of each school is preceded by a prayer or verse, generally in Yiddish but occasionally in Hebrew or Polish. The parchment frontispiece hails Rumkowski as *Adonenu Ha-Nasi* (our lord, our prince), and praises him: *Atah Nasi deag lanu* (you, our prince, provide for us). I translate a few verses at random:

You lay down your life for us,
The end of your striving, we.

Stern of visage but mild of heart,
Your blood is shed for every child.

From purest well, the hearts of children,
Flow a thousand blessings upon your handsome head.

It was on his own *Getto Zeitung,* the only publication permitted to the community, that Rumkowski relied for the most Byzantine appreciation. The eighteen issues of this newspaper which appeared between June and September 1941 (they too can be read, in tiny photostatic reproductions, in the rich archives of the Yivo) present him as the model of an able and benevolent ruler: he feels "a sense of responsibility for everything that goes on in the Ghetto"; he is the only *kenner* of its problems; stern and just—the reporter does not envy the unfortunates who dare to lie to him—he unbends frequently; his countenance then becomes mild and genial, from his eyes "streams love," and a smile steals upon his lips; "it is then as if a familiar and quiet dove, gently flapping its wings, warms and cuddles its little ones. . . ."

Prose was not enough. In the very first issue of the *Zeitung,* L. Berman sang, significantly, the praise of "The Strong Arm":

Our President Rumkowski
Is blessed by the Lord above
Not alone with brains and talent
But with a firm and powerful arm.
Whether in offices or shops
Work is thorough, exemplary.
All is bound, all related
By the President's strong arm.
And at Dworska Number 20 [*the central office*]
Toil is always going on.
Whoever thinks of lying down
Feels the President's strong arm.
All the wilder elements
Have been put against the wall.
Peace and order reign in Ghetto
Only thanks to his strong arm.

But, again it was Rumkowski's love of children that touched most the laureate heart:

The President Rides Forth

Men and women, young and old,
Crowds gather here and there,
Everybody is pressing hard:
The President rides forth.
Now his fine gray-spotted horse
Suddenly comes to a halt,
And the mass is lighted up
By his head of silver hair.
All eyes and all hearts
Turn to him.
And the people strain and stretch
With petitions in their hands.
But the President is busy
And he sees no one now.
He has spied and stopped to chat
With a tiny child of seven.

Engulfed by adulation, Rumkowski took to posturing. He affected the flowing cloak, shining boots, the imperious cane. The same gray horse always drew his carriage. On the first Rosh Hashanah in the Ghetto, in 1940, he went to the synagogue in state, clad in a long white cloak, adorned by a hand-worked silver collar, similar to the Talith Hatorah, and crowned with a blue and white hat with eight points. He was accompanied by a suite of higher officials; crowds and police lined the streets and inclined in a *Gut Yom Tov,* occasionally sardonic, as he passed them in review. His court artists portrayed him throwing his cloak protectingly over the children of the Ghetto, who look up adoringly to him, or brooding over the problems of the Ghetto in the dead of night.

When everyone rested he alone waked, worked, endlessly planned. He felt lonely and unappreciated. "I am ever disturbed in my work," he announced plaintively. The poet's petitioners were a nuisance to his hero. Vulgar milling has "a bad effect upon a man who works hard and has little time to rest." He thundered that he would disregard such petitions even if, in a moment of weakness, he accepted them. They must be dropped in a special box at his office. "The Lord knows that I would like to please everyone but where shall I get the means? I know very well that many people abuse my affection for children—they are the only ones who never disturb me in my work—and some people smuggle petitions through them. I will put an end to that too."

Now and then, the abnormality implicit here would break through with violent clarity. As the Jews were driven from Lodz to the Balut, he is said to have sat in his office contemplating the possible titles he might assume as the chief of the new Ghetto. He yielded to sudden passions. He might berate people in the streets, or apply his cane, or, again, order a beard which displeased him summarily cut. He once struck a physician. Just as suddenly he might become overcheerful and ebullient and ooze goodwill. He might break out in song. Sometimes contrition seized him. He showed up at a gathering of physicians and their families, uninvited and unwelcome, and proceeded to justify his rule: They say I am a dictator; that is not true; my ambition is to save a remnant and future Jewry will be beholden to me; only history will be able to judge my work which, in perspective, will be shown to have been beneficent. And so forth.

The story of Rumkowski's state is not of course the whole story of the Ghetto. His policy, or any other, could not hope to exhaust society. Through the crevices of his obscurantist despotism, spontaneous effort burst in all its forms: reading circles, recitations, amateur theatricals, little orchestras, lectures, literary evenings.

And as the desert hath green spots, the sea
Small islands scattered amid stormy waves,
So that disastrous period did not want
Bright sprinklings of all human excellence.

Incredible as it may seem, literary and other artistic production went on, although the results disappeared with their creators. A few pieces remain. For example, some verses of the sensitive Hasidic poet S. Shayevich, from which I quote:

The Lord has showered even us with gentle hand:
A double gift—
The death-decree and spring.
The garden blooms, and the sun shines.
And the slaughterer slaughters. . . .

But we crave no recompense or mercy.
For when you slay a man
You slay his God as well.

Nothing could stifle Jewish humor and ridicule. Deportation orders were "invitations to a wedding" (*chasene kartlech*); as the Eastern front drew near, it seemed that "help is behind your back, death in front of your nose." The story goes that once in performing a marriage, for which he bestowed an extra ration of food, Rumkowski put the usual question, "Do you love her" and the swift reply came: "Meantime I am hungry. . . ."

At first, Rumkowski hoped to secure the support of intellectuals. He was soon disillusioned. The more decent elements waged an unremitting warfare, necessarily muffled and in the end hopeless, against his machine. Satirical poems and songs were circulated clandestinely, and political sketches shown. In turn, as I. Spiegel, one of the few surviving writers, puts it, Rumkowski "did everything he could to break the writer's pen and the painter's palette." He censored plays and vaudeville acts, denied writers precious paper and ink, withdrew the rations of some, and spied upon others. The Germans finished the job. When Rumkowski approved the production of a play—its name was, of all things, *Es vet sein besser!*—the Germans dispersed the audience. Along with virtually everything else, they confiscated the musical instruments of the Ghetto. Occasionally the strains of an illegal violin wafted through the night and made dictators uneasy.

Political work was more dangerous, for politics naturally meant opposition. Unfortunately, the various parties were unable to merge their energies. The Zionist factions cooperated to further cultural, athletic, and economic activity; indeed they pointed the way to Rumkowski in reconstructing life in the Ghetto. Another coalition, that of the Left, was weaker: even the Communists were divided. And little wonder, for the inauguration of the Ghetto fell in the period of the notorious pact of friendship between the Soviet Union and Nazi Germany, when, in Molotov's words, Nazism was "a matter of taste." His taste.

Moreover, Rumkowski handled the opposition with ferocity. He censored mail and controlled the printing press. He did not hesitate to ask the Germans to send troops into the Ghetto to shoot down demonstrators, for in the early days there were not wanting both strikes and public demonstrations of protest. Fishermen, butchers, and coachmen particularly distinguished themselves in challenging his police, and Rumkowski visited upon them a refinement of revenge. He thrust the "Three F's" (*fisher, fleisher, fuhrmenner*) into the first batch of deportees demanded by the Nazis; later, when women were deported, he argued persuasively that unattached persons be given "preference," and their widows—for the men were of course never heard of again—were thereupon shipped out. And finally, when the Nazis asked for children, the orphans of the "Three F's" were given the same "preference" on the same grounds.

Such methods went far to paralyze the will to resist. But there were still other factors than the Rumkowski machine that prevented Lodz from repeating the rebellions in Warsaw, Vilna, and elsewhere. The Ghetto there was more tightly sealed, and it proved impossible to obtain the necessary weapons. The Jews were surrounded by Germans as well as Poles and this rendered communication with the outside world most difficult. Two messengers sent to Warsaw for help in the winter of 1942-3 never returned.

Of daring there was plenty. There were explosions of individuals who met outrage with a desperate and lonely violence. With a quieter courage, people in their thousands—distinguished and ordinary—refused to break down morally, whatever the provocation. Simply to persist in remaining human exacted the highest act of faith. There were Orthodox Jews who would not touch "unclean" food and so invited a double doom. Although it smelled of death to own a radio or repeat its reports, hundreds of people joined to spread news in concentric waves every day. The radio was the only hint that the world still existed. The *Getto Zeitung* carried only local news. "It was through radio reports that the Ghetto heard of the mass butchery of the Jews of Cracow, Lublin, Warsaw, and other cities; it was through radio reports that they bewailed their own deported families, which perished in Kolo, Khelmno, and other places." In 1941 twelve men were arrested, but radio reports continued to be spread. Finally, on the eve of the final liquidation of the community in 1944, a young scoundrel led the Gestapo to the secret radios. One of their owners, Nathan Widavsky, a leading Zionist who was acquainted with the underground activists, took his life by painful poisoning, lest he break under torture and reveal their identities. The informer was later beaten to death by Jews in a concentration camp, the common destination of good and bad.

These were but the incidental expenses of Rumkowski's brittle glory. The higher price was exacted by the Nazis. His authority was distinctly delegated, delegated on a leash. Dictator of the community, he was a slave to his masters, as they were to theirs. For police matters he was responsible to the Gestapo and its counterpart for criminal work, the equally ill-famed Kripo. For economic and general administrative matters he was responsible to Hans Biebow, who became German *Leiter der Gettoverwaltung* upon the establishment of the closed quarter. Biebow had been recommended highly as a Nazi of spotless faith, and found the grinding of Jews much more lucrative than the coffee business in which he had been engaged for eighteen years. He was executed, for his myriad crimes, by an Allied court in 1947.

But Rumkowski was not only a subordinate executive, he was also, inescapably, a Jew, and no Nazi was so low as to owe him deference. This was brought home to him early in his "reign." The Nazis, with that cynical adherence to legality which was their concession to German propriety, had told Rumkowski to secure a council to advise and assist him. Of course there was no question of election. Rumkowski simply informed the nineteen members of their appointment. They were abler men and better regarded than himself. Before long, they were summoned to the Gestapo and beaten, tortured, and blackmailed. Rumkowski, who always had physical courage, rushed to protect them. Sovereignty was quickly abashed. The troopers fell upon him too, and the Polish Mayor of Lodz barely rescued his life. The council disappeared *spurlos* and Rumkowski appointed another, remarking significantly that "acceptance of the mandate is compulsory." On a later occasion, when he was well established and fat with power, he was invited to Biebow's house, where the German master, in his cups, beat him, apparently for the fun of it. This incident was confirmed to me by the young physician, now in America, who treated Rumkowski's wounds after the "audience."

The real tribute the Germans exacted was more tangible than dignity. It was property, men for work, and men for the death machines. Rumkowski had to help the Germans squeeze out the valuables of the community. Thousands were sent off to toil—on private as well as public enterprises, under murderous conditions—and never to return. German employers paid 0.70 Reichsmarks a day per slave to a special account of the *German* administration of the Ghetto. It was from this account that the henchmen were paid for snatching other Jews for extermination.

Even before the Ghetto was set up the Germans made a demand for twenty-five thousand people. Lodz was shocked and Rumkowski protested that it was impossible to organize so large an evacuation. He compromised by giving up social "surplusage." Some five to six thousand dependent persons were sent off.

Lodz soon learned to be less sensitive and Rumkowski less independent. About a year after the Ghetto was sealed off, deportation began in earnest. The Nazis asked for ten thousand men to work, so they said, in the Fatherland. Volunteering was tried and failed. Rumkowski then discovered that there were too many dishonest people about: *thousands* of persons were seized for theft! (It was on this occasion that he threw in the "Three F's," for good measure.) He boasted before a meeting of factory managers that he could have "bought off many of the ten thousand. But I did not want to do it. Not at all. Let them be an example to other thieves." Then the Germans seized fifty-seven mentally ill people; in that case, they said plainly they would do away with them as "unnecessary burdens."

Still the Jews were encouraged to believe that the worst was over. Like all civilized people, they discounted atrocity stories. Lodz evidently was to be spared—otherwise why would the Germans pour Jews *into* Lodz? In the fall of 1941, about eighteen thousand Jews arrived from nearby towns: twelve smaller communities were thus liquidated. At the same time, 19,980 refugees, better dressed and including many eminent men, were brought from abroad, principally from Berlin, Vienna, and Prague. But reason quailed before Nazi method. Importation, it turned out, was merely a step toward re-deportation; repeated deportations were an inexpensive form of extermination. Dumped into an already teeming Ghetto, the refugees lived, or rather died, under incredibly difficult circumstances. For example, of the 2,651 persons brought in from nearby Vlotzlavek, only 347 eventually survived. In the following spring, the foreign Jews were ordered re-deported, with the exception of the holders of the German Iron Cross and other small categories. They were allowed to take with them bundles of 12½ kilograms, after having brought fifty kilograms. In a matter of six months the score for these foreign Jews stood:

Originally arrived	19,980
Died in Lodz	6,247
Left in Lodz	3,206
Remainder, deported again	10,527

Half of the refugees were thus disposed of.

But that was not enough. The importation of German Jews had meantime been made the excuse for the deportation of natives, for, it was carefully explained—how the Nazis liked to give reasons!—the population of the Ghetto must remain fixed. Was it not already uncomfortably crowded? They therefore demanded the surrender of an equivalent number, in batches of one thousand a day. A conference was called in the Ghetto. Some speakers argued that only the old and very young be delivered: the others stood a better chance to maintain the Ghetto. Others said that the delicate ages were unfit to support the trials which deportation portended. It was decided to send whole families, so as to promote mutual assistance. Dying people, and sometimes even dead, were thrown into the trucks, to make up the figure. "Fooled the Germans!" Then it was noticed that the Germans weren't keeping count at all! Panic seized the Ghetto. The Nazis desisted, but they had sent out almost double the number of foreign refugees. Perhaps sixty thousand people—one-third of the Ghetto—had gone. But where? One of the later refugees brought a letter from the rabbi of Grabow, which is near Lodz:

Grabow, 19 January, 1942

Dearest:

I have received your letter of November 8. I did not wish to answer your questions about the other towns, because there were various reports about them. But, to our misfortune, we know everything now. There was an eyewitness here today, who was there himself, in Hell. The place is the village of Khelmo, near Dombie, and all the Jews are buried there in the forest called

Lubow. That is what has happened to the Jews of Koyl, Dombie, Klodeve, and Isbik-Koyavsky. Thousands of Gypsies from Lodz were also brought there and suffered the same fate. Since last week, thousands of Jews from Lodz are arriving there. All these people are being killed by gas poisoning and also by shooting.

The heart turns to stone, the eyes well up. Don't think this is written by a madman. It is the bitter, outrageous truth. Tear your clothes, Son of Man, throw yourself on the ground, run into the streets, and cry or laugh from sheer madness. Perhaps He Whose Name is Hallowed will come to our help and save the remnant. Help, Creator!

Write whether you know of this.

I. Sillman

"And He shall save a remnant"! Did Rumkowski believe it? He was after all in the best position to suspect, if not to know, the worst. Yet his ambition, to the end, seemed tied to the possibility that his realm would be preserved. The miscalculation was astronomical. The fact is that the end of the Ghetto had been determined *before* its birth. The very secret order of *Regierungs-praesident* Uebelhor of Kalis, dated December 10, 1939 and circulated only among twelve carefully specified German commands, characterized its establishment as a "transitional measure." "I reserve the precise time, and the means," he declared, "by which the Ghetto, and thereby the city of Lodz, will be cleared of Jews. In any case, our final aim must be to burn out this pesthole."

Not the wishes of a Rumkowski alone, but even those of the local German officials were quite irrelevant. It was to their material interest to continue the Ghetto as a source of further profit. But the fate of Lodz, as of the rest of Jewry, lay all the time in the lap of the government at Berlin. And that government, apart from its quite adequate malevolence, was swayed only by the fortunes of war. And the worse the war went for Hitler, the worse it was for the Jews. From 1942 on, Mars no longer smiled on his favorite. Russia was half-occupied but not at all conquered. The United States was straining its vast energies in the production of war supplies. Germany was entering her fourth year of war, and her industrial stocks were running low. It was decided to turn the Ghetto into a work camp consisting only of adults and so use its manpower more fully. Overwork and semi-starvation would eventually dispose of this labor force automatically, and the momentary aim of exploitation would converge upon the initial, and final, aim of annihilation. The two ends would meet in one.

The first hint of trouble came in April 1942 when "declassed" persons were registered for work, on pain of losing their rations. Thousands of men and women were driven into the shops. Then came the order that all children from five to twelve, and the aged and ailing, must also register—it could hardly be for work. Only a few showed up. Rumkowski threateningly ordered speed. He promised the firemen to spare their families if they would help to round up the youngsters. It was not enough. Rumkowski never avoided responsibility: he placed himself at the head of troops of children and led them to the registration office and thence to the railroad station. They were shipped off. Since Rumkowski truly loved the young, this was the most tragic day in his life, but he was no man to be broken by tragedy, even his own.

But the numbers were reckoned as too slight for the Nazi maw. A more peremptory order came that all children must be given up at once. No reason was given. Fantastic rumors gained credence: they were to be put out to pasture and their blood saved up for wounded German soldiers; they would be raised as "kosher Aryans." Everything seemed possible except only the inevitable. The Jews were badly in need of a St. Tertullian to teach them how to believe the incredible.

Anticipating trouble, Rumkowski called a meeting of the parents. He and his henchmen appealed to their selfishness: many times in Jewish history it had been necessary to sacrifice a part of the people in order to save the rest; such a time had now come; unless the children were given up, everyone else would perish; children could be replaced, but adults . . . ; mothers, give up your children, and we will save the Ghetto.

A wail went up from a thousand hearts. Israel wept.

No children were given up. At last, in the fourth week of August 1944 the impatient Germans ordered everybody indoors, cordoned off block after block, and, going from house to house, chased the people into the street. They seized the young, the old, the sick, the ailing, the weak, and pushed them or threw them—frequently literally—into carts and trucks. And off! In orphanages children huddled together crying *"Mir viln nisht shtarbn"* ("We don't want to die"), and their chorus echoed far behind the speeding trucks. Even the trained snatchers quailed before this massacre of innocents, and Biebow had to order not only special pay, but also extra liquor and cigarettes in order to maintain morale.

The raids of that week netted some fifteen thousand souls, among them several thousand children. Why would anyone bother to keep a precise count? The population of the Ghetto dropped to about seventy thousand, all of whom were *arbeitsfähig,* or nearly all, for a few children were saved by falsely raising their ages and, to make the deception plausible, putting them to especially hard work. We have photographs of children handling smiths' tools which seem heavier than themselves. Soon ninety-five per cent of the people were working—the ideal of full employment. Additional factories opened. Production hummed. The remnant worked for the Wehrmacht, which was in retreat—and so was the remnant.

The mask of "autonomy" was taken off. The post office with its stamps and parcels, the now superfluous schools, the emptied hospitals and orphanages and convalescent homes, were closed one by one. At the same time, a revolution from above deprived Rumkowski of two of the greatest sources of his power. Where the opposition had failed, a clique of creatures of the Germans succeeded. The German and the Jewish head of the Ghetto had never got along well—to the credit of both. Biebow did not trust Rumkowski and Rumkowski could hardly relish the humiliations visited upon him by Biebow. The *Leiter* seized the occasion of the liquidation of the "superfluous" Jews to weaken the authority of the *Aelteste;* he could not dismiss him since the appointment of Rumkowski had been made by superior authorities. The supervision of the factories and the distribution of food—and these, apart from police, were virtually all the "government" a labor camp needed—were turned over, the one to Aaron Jacobovich, a relatively innocuous but narrow-visioned functionary, and the other to David Gertler. Before the war, Gertler had moved on the fringes of the underworld, and then he had snuggled into the congruent graces of the Gestapo. His end was highly characteristic of the regime which had exalted him. One day he was sauntering on a street in the Ghetto, coatless and hatless: an automobile drew up, he was bundled in and whisked off. His successor was quite fittingly the man who had engineered the conspiracy against Rumkowski, one David Marek.

But the *Aelteste* retained the titular leadership. Neither the Jewish nor the German administration could do without him. They soon had need of all his abilities. The revolution had not improved conditions in the Ghetto and the war was going from bad to worse for the Germans. The workers were driven harder and fed more lightly than ever. On much smaller bread rations than the Polish workers just outside, in the city, they produced two-thirds more. German officials reported that many Jews "literally collapsed at their work benches from sheer exhaustion." Rive Kwiatowsky, in stark verse, summed up the life of the Ghetto as thousands of feet dragging corpses to factories.

Restlessness grew. It was apparently becoming more difficult to manage the camp. Informal "literary" circles dared to assume concrete organization. Rumkowski was moved to protest that the Germans were not accorded the customary deference. He commanded that the workers must rise from their benches upon the appearance of a uniform or, as the Russian Jew of old used to say, a *knepl,* and must not sit down again until all the uniforms had filed in and a factory hand, previously designated for this purpose, had given the order *"Wiederarbeiten!"* In the street, Jewish police and firemen must spring to attention upon passing a German military or even a civil official, Jewish civilians must bare their heads, women bow. The "sharpest penalties" were threatened for keeping hands in pockets or cigarette in mouth while saluting.

It was evidently getting dark. By the middle of 1944 the tide of war had turned decisively. The Germans were speeding out of Russia and the Anglo-Americans were fighting on the continent. In August came the order to liquidate the remainder of the Jews and to raze the Ghetto. Intent, as always, on performing outrage quietly and inexpensively, the Germans again called for volunteers. Rumkowski arranged a mass meeting and Biebow himself addressed it. He told the Jews that their destination was Germany, and assured them, on the word of honor of a German official, that there they would find work and good treatment. "Pack up your things," he concluded, "and present yourselves" at the railroad station. Few responded.

It was Rumkowski's turn. In repeated proclamations he insisted that it was to the interest of the Jews themselves to cooperate freely. Pressure, and force, had nevertheless to be invoked. In factory after factory, the workers were told to show up in a body, with their families. The recalcitrants—and there were many, for Rumkowski had to issue order after order to the same factories—were hunted down in their homes and the homes of friends. Those who concealed themselves and anybody who helped them were to be executed. Finally section after section of the Ghetto was blocked off and cleared.

Every day, in the months of August and September 1944, long trains of packed and sealed freight cars pulled out of the railway station of Lodz and headed for extermination camps, mostly for Auschwitz. After a few days of dragging and shunting they arrived, by design, in the dead of night. The doors were unsealed and the Jews—leaving many dead of suffocation, starvation, and disease behind them—descended. They were immediately divided into two long files. Feeling their arms and muscles and tapping their chests, Nazi troopers hustled the weak into the line that led, in a matter of days, to gas and fire. Of the healthy, in the second line, many were also destroyed in the camps, more or less at random, but others found their way to labor camps, there to die more slowly from overwork and inhuman treatment. The rare survivors belonged largely to this more fortunate file.

Back in the Ghetto, several hundred men were left to gather up, for the Germans, the few remaining valuables and then to destroy the houses. Another group of a few hundred people managed to conceal themselves underground. Several weeks later an informer led the Nazis to the hideout, but it was too late. The order to present themselves for another "registration" was disobeyed. The Russian armies were approaching and German discipline collapsed. When the Russians marched in, twelve hundred-odd people greeted them, the remnant of nearly a quarter-million Jews of the great industrial city of Lodz, the Manchester of the East.

And Rumkowski?

One day, during the final liquidation, he was standing on the station platform overseeing the loading of cars. A German official, reading from a list of deportees, summoned Rumkowski's brother to enter the train. The Jewish dictator asked that he be allowed to stay.

The official refused curtly but invited Rumkowski to go along, if he wished. Rumkowski joined his brother on the train. That is one version of his end. Another is that the Nazi command gave him a sealed letter addressed to the chief of the camp of destination and assured him that he would of course receive special treatment.

When the transport arrived at the death camp, Rumkowski and his family were the first to be thrust into the gas chamber.

October 1950

Hannah Arendt

GERMANY–1950

In less than six years Germany laid waste the moral structure of Western society, committing crimes that nobody would have believed possible, while her conquerors buried in rubble the visible marks of more than a thousand years of German history. Then into this devastated land, truncated by the Oder-Neisse borderline and hardly able to sustain its demoralized and exhausted population, streamed millions of people from the Eastern provinces, from the Balkans and from Eastern Europe, adding to the general picture of catastrophe the peculiarly modern touches of physical homelessness, social rootlessness, and political rightlessness. The wisdom of Allied policy in expelling all German-speaking minorities from non-German countries—as though there was not enough homelessness in the world already— may be doubted. But the fact is that European peoples who had experienced the murderous demographic politics of Germany during the war were seized with horror, even more than with wrath, at the very idea of having to live together with Germans in the same territory.

The sight of Germany's destroyed cities and the knowledge of German concentration and extermination camps have covered Europe with a cloud of melancholy. Together, they have made the memory of the last war more poignant and more persistent, the fear of future wars more actual. Not the "German problem," insofar as it is a national one within the comity of European nations, but the *nightmare* of Germany in its physical, moral, and political ruin has become almost as decisive an element in the general atmosphere of European life as the Communist movements.

But nowhere is this nightmare of destruction and horror less felt and less talked about than in Germany itself. A lack of response is evident everywhere, and it is difficult to say whether this signifies a half-con-

Originally published as "The Aftermath of Nazi Rule"

cious refusal to yield to grief or a genuine inability to feel. Amid the ruins, Germans mail each other picture postcards still showing the cathedrals and market places, the public buildings and bridges that no longer exist. And the indifference with which they walk through the rubble has its exact counterpart in the absence of mourning for the dead, or in the apathy with which they react, or rather fail to react, to the fate of the refugees in their midst. This general lack of emotion, at any rate this apparent heartlessness, sometimes covered over with cheap sentimentality, is only the most conspicuous outward symptom of a deep-rooted, stubborn, and at times vicious refusal to face and come to terms with what really happened.

Indifference, and the irritation that comes when indifference is challenged, can be tested on many intellectual levels. The most obvious experiment is to state *expressis verbis* what the other fellow has noticed from the beginning of the conversation, namely, that you are a Jew. This is usually followed by a little embarrassed pause; and then comes—not a personal question, such as "Where did you go after you left Germany?"; no sign of sympathy, such as "What happened to your family?"—but a deluge of stories about how Germans have suffered (true enough, of course, but beside the point); and if the object of this little experiment happens to be educated and intelligent, he will proceed to draw up a balance between German suffering and the suffering of others, the implication being that one side cancels the other and we may as well proceed to a more promising topic of conversion. Similarly evasive is the standard reaction to the ruins. When there is any overt reaction at all, it consists of a sigh followed by the half-rhetorical, half-wistful question, "Why must mankind always wage wars?" The average German looks for the causes of the last war not in the acts of the Nazi regime, but in the events that led to the expulsion of Adam and Eve from Paradise.

Such an escape from reality is also, of course, an escape from responsibility. In this the Germans are not alone; all the peoples of Western Europe have developed the habit of blaming their misfortunes on some force out of their reach: it may be America and the Atlantic Pact today, the legacy of Nazi occupation tomorrow, and history in general every day of the week. But this attitude is more pronounced in Germany, where the temptation to blame everything under the sun on the occupying powers is difficult to resist: in the British zone everything is blamed on British fear of German competition; in the French zone on French nationalism; and in the American zone, where things are better in every respect, on American ignorance of the European mentality. The complaints are only natural, and they all contain a kernel of truth; but behind them is a stubborn unwillingness to make use of the many possibilities left to German initiative. This is perhaps most clearly revealed in the German newspapers, which express all their convictions in a carefully cultivated style of *Schadenfreude,* malicious joy in ruination. It is as though the Germans, denied the power to rule the world, had fallen in love with impotence as such, and now find a positive pleasure in contemplating international tensions and the unavoidable mistakes that occur in the business of governing, regardless of the possible consequences for themselves. Fear of Russian aggression does not necessarily result in an unequivocal pro-American attitude, but often leads to a determined neutrality, as though it were as absurd to take sides in the conflict as it would be to take sides in an earthquake. The awareness that neutrality will not change one's fate makes it in turn impossible to translate this mood into a rational policy, and the mood itself, by its very irrationality, becames even more bitter.

But, whether faced or evaded, the realities of Nazi crimes, of war and defeat, still visibly dominate the whole fabric of German life, and the Germans have developed various devices for dodging their shocking impact.

The reality of the death-factories is transformed into a mere potentiality: Germans did only what others are capable of doing (with many illustrative examples, of course) or what others will do in the near future; therefore, anybody who brings up this topic is *ipso facto* suspected of self-righteousness. In this context, Allied policy in Germany is frequently explained as a campaign of successful revenge, even though it later turns out that the German who offers this interpretation is quite aware that most of the things he complains of were either the immediate consequence of the lost war or happened outside the will and control of the Western powers. But the insistence that there must be a careful scheme of revenge serves as a consoling argument, demonstrating the equal sinfulness of all men.

The reality of the destruction that surrounds every German is dissolved into a reflective but not very deep-rooted self-pity, easily dissipated when ugly little one-story structures that might have been imported from some Main Street in America spring up on some of the great avenues to conceal fragmentarily the grimness of the landscape, and to offer an abundance of provincial elegance in super-modern display windows. In France and Great Britain, people feel a greater sadness about the relatively few landmarks destroyed in the war than the Germans do for all their lost treasures together. The boastful hope is expressed in Germany that the country will become the "most modern" in Europe; yet it is mere talk, and some person who has just voiced that hope will insist a few minutes later, at another turn in the conversation, that the next war will do to all European cities what this one did to Germany's—which of course is possible, but signifies again only the transformation of reality into potentiality. The undertone of satisfaction that one often detects in the Germans' talk about the next war expresses no sinister renewal of German plans of conquest, as so many observers have maintained, but is only another device for escaping reality: in an eventual equality of destruction, the German situation would lose its acuteness.

But perhaps the most striking and frightening aspect of the German flight from reality is the habit of treating facts as though they were mere opinions. For example, the question of who started the last war, by no means a hotly debated issue, is answered by a surprising variety of opinions. An otherwise quite normally intelligent woman in Southern Germany told me that the Russians had begun the war with an attack on Danzig; this is only the crudest of many examples. Nor is this transformation of facts into opinions restricted to the war question; in all fields there is a kind of gentlemen's agreement by which everyone has a right to his ignorance under the pretext that everyone has a right to his opinion—and behind this is the tacit assumption that opinions really do not matter. This is a very serious thing, not only because it often makes discussion so hopeless (one does not ordinarily carry a reference library along everywhere), but primarily because the average German honestly believes this free-for-all, this nihilistic relativity about facts, to be the essence of democracy. In fact, of course, it is a legacy of the Nazi regime.

The lies of totalitarian propaganda are distinguished from the normal lying of non-totalitarian regimes in times of emergency by their consistent denial of the importance of facts in general: all facts can be changed and all lies can be made true. The Nazi impress on the German mind consists primarily in a conditioning whereby reality has ceased to be the sum total of hard inescapable facts and has become a conglomeration of ever-changing events and slogans in which a thing can be true today and false tomorrow. This conditioning may be precisely one of the reasons for the surprisingly few traces of any lasting Nazi indoctrination, as well as for an equally surprising lack of interest in the refuting of Nazi doctrines. What one is up against is not indoctrination but the incapacity or unwillingness to distinguish altogether between fact and opinion. A discussion about the events of the Spanish Civil War will be conducted on the same level as a discussion of the theoretical merits and shortcomings of democracy.

Thus the problem at the German universities is not so much to reintroduce freedom to teach as to reestablish honest research, to confront the student with an unbiased account of what actually happened, and to eliminate the teachers who have become incapable of doing so. The danger to German academic life is not only from those who hold that freedom of speech should be exchanged for a dictatorship in which a single unfounded, irresponsible opinion would acquire a monopoly over all others, but equally from those who ignore facts and reality and establish their private opinions, not necessarily as the only right ones, but as opinions that are as justified as others.

The unreality and irrelevance of most of these opinions, as compared with the grim relevance of the experience of those who hold them, is sharply underlined by their having been formed before 1933. There is an almost instinctive urge to take refuge in the thoughts and ideas one held before anything compromising had happened. The result is that while Germany has changed beyond recognition—physically and psychologically —people talk and behave superficially as though absolutely nothing had happened since 1932. The authors of the few really important books written in Germany since 1933 or published since 1945 were already famous twenty and twenty-five years ago. The younger generation seems to be petrified, inarticulate, incapable of consistent thought.

A young German art historian, guiding his audience among the masterpieces of the Berlin Museum, which had been sent on tour through several American cities, pointed to the Ancient Egyptian statue of Nefertiti as the sculpture "for which the whole world envies us," and then proceeded to say (a) that even the Americans had not "dared" to carry this "symbol of the Berlin collections" to the United States, and (b) that because of the "intervention of the Americans," the British did not "dare" to carry the Nefertiti to the British Museum. The two contradictory attitudes to the Americans were separated by only a single sentence: the speaker, devoid of convictions, was merely groping automatically among the clichés with which his mind was furnished to find the one that might fit the occasion. The clichés have more often an old-fashioned nationalistic than an outspoken Nazi tone, but in any case one seeks in vain to discover behind them a consistent point of view, be it even a bad one.

With the downfall of Nazism, the Germans found themselves again exposed to facts and reality. But the experience of totalitarianism has robbed them of all spontaneous speech and comprehension, so that now, having no official line to guide them, they are, as it were, speechless, incapable of articulating thoughts and adequately expressing their feelings. The intellectual atmosphere is clouded with vague pointless generalities, with opinions formed long before the events they are supposed to fit actually happened; one is oppressed by a kind of pervasive public stupidity which cannot be trusted to judge correctly the most elementary events, and which, for example, makes it possible for a newspaper to complain, "The world at large once again deserted us"—a statement comparable for blind self-centeredness to the remark Ernst Juenger in his war diaries (*Strahlungen,* 1949) tells of having overheard in a conversation about Russian prisoners assigned to work near Hannover: "It seems there are scoundrels among them. They steal food from the dogs." As Juenger observes, "One often has the impression that the German middle classes are possessed by the devil."

The rapidity with which, after the currency reform, everyday life in Germany returned to normal and reconstruction began in all fields, has become the talk of Europe. Without a doubt, people nowhere work so hard and long as in Germany. It is a well-known fact that Germans have for generations been overfond of working; and their present industriousness seems at first glance to give substance to the opinion that Germany is still potentially the most dangerous European nation. There are, moreover, many strong incentives for work. Unemployment is rampant and the position of the trade unions is so weak that compensation for overtime is not even demanded by the workers, who frequently refuse to report it to the unions; the housing situation is worse than the many new buildings would seem to indicate: business and office buildings for the great industrial and insurance companies have an unquestioned priority over dwelling units, and the result is that people prefer going to work on Saturdays and even Sundays to staying at home in overcrowded apartments. In rebuilding, as in almost all areas of German life, everything is done (often in a most spectacular way) to restore a facsimile of pre-war economic and industrial conditions, and very little is done for the welfare of the masses of the people.

Yet none of these facts can explain the atmosphere of feverish busyness on the one hand and the comparatively mediocre production on the other. Beneath the surface, the German attitude to work has undergone a deep change. The old virtue of seeking excellence in the finished product, no matter what the working conditions, has yielded to a mere blind need to keep busy, a greedy craving for something to do every moment of the day. Watching the Germans busily stumble through the ruins of a thousand years of their own history, shrugging their shoulders at the destroyed landmarks or resentful when reminded of the deeds of horror that haunt the whole surrounding world, one comes to realize that busyness has become their chief defense against reality. And one wants to cry out: But this is not real—real are the ruins, real are the past horrors, real are the dead whom you have forgotten. But they are living ghosts, whom speech and argument, the glance of human eyes and the mourning of human hearts, no longer touch.

There are, of course, many Germans whom this description does not fit. Above all, there is Berlin, whose people, in the midst of the most horrible physical destruction, have remained intact. I do not know why this should be so, but customs, manners, speech, approaches to people, are in the smallest details so absolutely different from everything one sees and has to face in the rest of Germany, that Berlin is almost like another country. There is hardly any resentment in Berlin against the victors and apparently never was; while the first saturation bombings from England were pulverizing the city, Berliners are reported to have crawled out of their cellars and, seeing one block after another gone, remarked: "Well, if the Tommies mean to keep this up, they'll soon have to bring their own houses with them." There is no embarrassment and no guilt-feeling, but frank and detailed recital of what happened to Berlin's Jews at the beginning of the war. Most important of all, in Berlin the people still actively hate Hitler, and even though they have more reason than other Germans to feel themselves pawns in international politics, they do not feel impotent but are convinced that their attitudes count for something; given half a chance, they will at least sell their lives dear.

The Berliners work just as hard as other people in Germany, but they are less busy, they will take time to show one around the ruins and will somewhat solemnly recite the names of the streets that are gone. It is hard to believe, but it seems there is something in the Berliners' claim that Hitler never entirely succeeded in conquering them. They are remarkably well-informed and have kept their sense of humor and their characteristically ironical friendliness. The only change in the people—apart from their having become somewhat sadder and less ready for laughter—is that "Red Berlin" is now violently anti-Communist. But here again there is an important difference between Berlin and the rest of Germany: only Berliners take the trouble to point out clearly the similarities between Hitler and Stalin, and only Berliners bother to tell you that they are of course not against the Russian people—a sentiment all the more remarkable if one remembers what happened to the Berliners, many of whom had welcomed the Red Army as the true liberator, during the first months of occupation, and what is still happening to them in the Eastern sector.

Berlin is an exception, but unfortunately not a very important one. For the city is hermetically sealed off and has little intercourse with the rest of the country, except that one meets people everywhere who because of the uncertainty there left Berlin for the Western zones and now complain bitterly of their loneliness and disgust. Indeed, there are quite a number of Germans who are "different"; but they use up their energy in efforts to penetrate the stifling atmosphere that surrounds them, and remain completely isolated. In a way these people are today worse off psychologically than in the worst years of Hitler's terror. In the last years of the war, there did exist a vague comradeship of opposition among all who for one reason or another were against the regime. Together they hoped for the day of defeat, and since—apart from the few well-known exceptions—they had no real intention of doing anything to hasten that day, they could enjoy the charm of a half-imaginary rebellion. The very danger involved in even the mere thought of opposition created a sentiment of solidarity all the more consoling because it could express itself only in such intangible gestures of emotion as a glance or a handclasp, which assumed a significance out of all proportion. The emergence from this overheated intimacy of danger into the crude egotism and spreading shallowness of postwar life has been a truly heartbreaking experience for many people. (It may be remarked that today in the Eastern zone, with its police regime, this time almost universally detested by the population, an even stronger atmosphere of comradeship, intimacy, and half-spoken sign language prevails than under the Nazis, so that it is often precisely the best elements in the Eastern zone who find it difficult to make up their minds to move to the West.)

II

Perhaps the saddest part of a sad story is the failure of the three devices used by the Western Allies to solve the moral, economic, and political problem of Germany. Denazification, revival of free enterprise, and federalization are certainly not the cause of present conditions in Germany, but they have helped to conceal and thus to perpetuate moral confusion, economic chaos, social injustice, and political impotence.

Denazification rested on the assumption that there were objective criteria not only for clear-cut distinction between Nazis and non-Nazis, but for the whole Nazi hierarchy ranging from little sympathizer to war criminal. From the beginning, the whole system, based upon length of party membership, ranks and offices held, date of first entrance, etc., was very complicated, and involved almost everyone. The very few who had been able to keep alive outside the stream of life in Hitler Germany were exempt, and of course rightly so; but they were joined by a number of very different characters who had been lucky or cautious or influential enough to avoid the many annoyances of party membership: men who had actually been prominent in Nazi Germany but now were not required to go through the denazification process. Some of these gentlemen, mostly of the upper middle classes, have by now established open contact with their less fortunate colleagues, jailed for some war crime. This they do partly to seek advice in economic and industrial matters, but also because they have at last become bored with hypocrisy. The injustices of the denazification system were simple and monotonous: the city-employed garbage collector, who under Hitler had to become a party member or look for another job, was caught in the denazification net, while his superiors either went scot-free because they knew how to manage these matters, or else suffered the same penalty as he: to them, of course, a much less serious matter.

Worse than these daily injustices was the fact that the system, devised to draw clear moral and political distinctions in the chaos of a completely disorganized people, actually tended to blur even the few genuine distinctions that had survived the Nazi regime. Active opponents to the regime naturally had to enter a Nazi organization in order to camouflage their illegal activities, and these members of such resistance movement as had existed in Germany were caught in the same net as their enemies, to the great pleasure of the latter. In theory, it was possible to present proofs of anti-Nazi activity; but not only was it difficult to convince occupation officers without the slightest experience of the intricacies of a terror regime; there was also the danger that the applicant might compromise himself in the eyes of the authorities, who were, after all, primarily interested in peace and order, by showing too convincingly that he had been capable of independent thought and rebellious action.

It is doubtful, however, that the denazification program has stifled new political formations in Germany that might conceivably have grown out of the resistance to Nazism, since the resistance movement itself had so very little vitality in the first place. But there is no doubt that denazification has created an unwholesome new community of interest among the more-or-less compromised, those who for opportunistic reasons had become more-or-less convinced Nazis. This powerful group of slightly dubious characters excludes both those who kept their integrity and those who participated in any resounding way in the Nazi movement. It would be inaccurate in either case to think of exclusion as based on specific political convictions; the elimination of confirmed anti-Nazis does not prove the others to be confirmed Nazis, and the elimination of "famous" Nazis does not mean that the others hate Nazism. It is simply that the denazification program has been a direct threat to livelihood and existence, and the majority have tried to relieve the pressure by a system of mutual assurance that the whole thing need not be taken too seriously. Such assurance can be gained only from those who are as much and as little compromised as oneself. Those who became Nazis out of conviction as well as those who kept their integrity are felt to constitute an alien and threatening element, partly because they cannot be frightened by their past, but also because their very existence is living testimony that something really serious happened, that some decisive act was committed. Thus it has come about that not only the active Nazis but the convinced anti-Nazis are excluded from positions of power and influence in Germany today; this is the most significant symptom of the German intelligentsia's unwillingness to take its own past seriously or to shoulder the burden of responsibility bequeathed to it by the Hitler regime.

The community of interest that exists among the more-or-less compromised is further strengthened by the general German—but not only German!—attitude to official questionnaires. In contrast to Anglo-Saxon and American habits, Europeans do not always believe in telling the absolute truth when an official body asks embarrassing questions. In countries whose legal system does not allow one to give testimony in one's own cause, lying is considered no great sin if the truth happens to prejudice one's chances. Thus for many Germans there is a discrepancy between their answers to military government questionnaires and the truth as known to their neighbors; and so the bonds of duplicity are strengthened.

Yet it was not even conscious dishonesty that defeated the denazification program. A great number of Germans, especially among the more educated, apparently are no longer capable of telling the truth even if they want to. All those who became Nazis after 1933 yielded to some kind of pressure, which ranged from the crude threat to life and livelihood, to various considerations of career, to reflections about the "irresistible stream of history." In the cases of physical or economic pressure, there should have been the possibility of mental reservation, of acquiring with cynicism that absolutely necessary membership card. But, curiously, it seems that very few Germans were capable of such healthy cynicism; what bothered them was not the membership card but the mental reservation, so that they often ended by adding to their enforced enrollment the necessary convictions, in order to shed the burden of duplicity. Today, they have a certain inclination to remember only the initial pressure, which was real enough; from their belated inner adjustment to Nazi doctrines, dictated by conscience, they have drawn the half-conscious conclusion that it was their conscience itself that betrayed them—an experience that does not exactly promote moral improvement.

Certainly the impact of an everyday life wholly permeated by Nazi doctrines and practices was not easy to resist. The position of an anti-Nazi resembled that of a normal person who happens to be thrown into an insane asylum where all the inmates have exactly the same delusion: it becomes difficult under such circumstances to trust one's own senses. And there was the continual added strain of behaving according to the rules of the insane environment, which after all was the only tangible reality, in which a man could never afford to lose his sense of direction. This demanded an ever-present awareness of one's whole existence, an attention that could never relax into the automatic reactions we all use to cope with the many daily situations. The absence of such automatic reactions is the chief element in the anxiety of maladjustment; and although, objectively speaking, maladjustment in Nazi society signified mental normality, the strain of maladjustment on the individual was just as great as in a normal society.

The deep moral confusion in Germany today, which has grown out of this Nazi-fabricated confusion of truth with reality, is more than amorality and has deeper causes than mere wickedness. The so-called "good Germans" are often as misled in their moral judgments of themselves and others as those who simply refuse to recognize that anything wrong or out of the ordinary was done by Germany at all. Quite a number of Germans who are even somewhat over-emphatic about German guilt in general and their own guilt in particular become curiously confused if they are forced to articulate their opinions; they may make a mountain out of some irrelevant molehill, while some real enormity escapes their notice altogether. One variation of this confusion is that Germans who confess their own guilt are in many cases altogether innocent in the ordinary, down-to-earth sense, whereas those who are guilty of something real have the calmest consciences in the world. The recently published postwar diary of Knut Hamsun, which has found a large and enthusiastic audience in Germany, gives testimony on the highest level to this horrible innocence that transforms itself into a persecution complex when confronted with the judgment of a morally intact world.

Ernst Juenger's war diaries offer perhaps the best and most honest evidence of the tremendous difficulties the individual encounters in keeping himself and his standards of truth and morality intact in a world where truth and morality have lost all visible expression. Despite the undeniable influence of Juenger's earlier writings on certain members of the Nazi intelligentsia, he was an active anti-Nazi from the first to the last day of the regime, proving that the somewhat old-fashioned notion of honor, once current in the Prussian officer corps, was quite sufficient for individual resistance. Yet even this unquestionable integrity has a hollow ring; it is as though morality had ceased to work and had become an empty shell into which the person who has to live, function, and survive all day long, retires for the night and solitude only. Day and night become nightmares of each other. The moral judgment, reserved for the night, is a nightmare of fear of being discovered by day; and the life of the day is a nightmare of horror in the betrayal of the intact conscience that functions only by night.

In view of the very complicated moral situation of the country at the close of the war, it is not surprising that American denazification policy failed in its initial effort to arouse the conscience of the German people to the enormity of the crimes committed in their name and under conditions of organized complicity. And even this initial effort, beset by many mistakes due to ignorance of the circumstances of the Nazi system, quickly came into conflict with American plans for the reconstruction of Germany. To be sure, this is a sad story which is not made less sad by the realization that the Allied powers had very little choice and that even the best conceivable denazification program would hardly have achieved better results. The truth of the matter is that only a revolution could have denazified Germany—the outbreak of the German people's spontaneous wrath against all those they knew to be prominent members of the Nazi regime. Uncontrolled and bloody as such an uprising might have been, it certainly would have followed better standards of justice than a paper procedure. But the revolution did not come to pass, and not primarily because it was difficult to organize under the eyes of four foreign armies. It is only too likely that not a single soldier, German or foreign, would have been needed to shield the real culprits from the wrath of the people. This wrath does not exist today, and apparently it has never existed.

February 1954

Herbert Luethy

DER FÜHRER

Is the abomination that was Adolf Hitler ripe for the judgment of history?

For the moment, the stream of material on him, mostly cheap journalism and gossip, that began pouring forth in Germany after 1945, seems to be drying up; even the most sensational "memoirs" are almost all behind us. And now we have two serious, painstaking, and richly documented biographies issued almost simultaneously, one by an Oxford historian, Alan Bullock (*Hitler: A Study in Tyranny*), and the other by two Germans, Walter Görlitz and H. A. Quint (*Adolf Hitler: Eine Biographie*). It is a curious experience to read both books together. The same facts and actions are presented, from the same sources, and they lead to the same ineluctable "moral." Yet the tone and attitude of the two books could not be more different.

Not surprisingly, the Oxford historian maintains a detachment of which Hitler's German biographers are incapable. His book, for this reason, has a precision and unity which their flickering, indistinct, and somewhat lurid portrait lacks. The ghost of the *"Führer"* still haunts Görlitz and Quint—and they shudder at it in a curious way. We seem to hear them exclaiming at each new turn of events: "What a monster!" or: "Still—what a man!" The exclamation marks they punctuate every second or third sentence with make them sound as if they were trying to make sure the reader felt the "appropriate" emotions. "He opened his heart to no one! Even now there was no friend to whom he trusted himself unreservedly, there was no woman who could have boasted that she ruled him. He feared nothing so much as that. He hid his innermost mystery in absolute darkness until his death!"

Yet in their style and attitude, as well as in their susceptibility to dime-novel "demonism," Görlitz and Quint are unquestionably closer to

Originally published as "The Wretched Little Demon That Was Hitler"

Hitler than Bullock. This may make their book not only more palatable to German readers but, in an odd, ambiguous way, truer to life insofar as it more closely reflects the atmosphere in which Hitler himself moved. The way Bullock writes about Hitler is perhaps not really possible yet for Germans living in Germany. It's the way a historian would write about Tutankhamen or Nebuchadnezzar—testing his data by traditional standards of evidence, refraining almost completely from judgments, and, above all, trying always to distinguish between opinion and fact—which the two German biographers tend constantly to jumble.

Darkness lies over the first thirty years of Hitler's life, for which we have only a few raw, impersonal facts and some thin, late, and contradictory legends, in part constructed by Hitler himself and in part dutifully propagated by others; but Bullock gives objectively both the darkness and the legends, even down to the unlikeliest minutiae. Hitler tells in *Mein Kampf* how as a little boy in Leonding he was always the leader when playing at war with the other boys, and a few old neighbors are supposed later—decades after the event, when Hitler was already great and powerful and such memories were worth their weight in gold—to have confirmed this. "Yes, we remember. What a daredevil that Hitler was!" Was he really? Görlitz and Quint write: "On the hill opposite the Leonding church, and in the meadow behind the family house, the village children played at Boers and Englishmen. Hitler led the Boers, and the English were beaten!" Bullock notes dryly: "He has been described as the natural leader of the children in their games—which may or may not be true." This is the difference between a history and a biographical novel.

There are even more significant differences between the two books. Every time the Nazis perpetrate a crime, Görlitz and Quint fall prey to tormenting doubts: did the *"Führer"* himself know about it? The Reichstag fire, for instance—it came at just the right time, a real gift from the gods, it was exploited "with lightning swiftness" to suspend all constitutional freedoms and create an atmosphere of terror. The official explanation of the new Nazi regime, that it was a Communist plot, was a fabrication from beginning to end, but *concocted with genius,* according to Görlitz and Quint, who also write that "the suspicion exists" that the SA "had a hand in the game," and even raise the "insoluble question, still, of when Goering noticed that not everything about this act of arson was open and aboveboard . . . something that the party state could naturally never admit!" So Görlitz and Quint are left *in doubt.* The Nazi putsch in Austria and the murder of Chancellor Dollfuss? Hitler "dissociated himself" from these acts "in the sharpest possible manner"—"lightning quick." The mass murders of June 30, 1934? In this exceptional case, to be sure, Hitler himself led a murder squad, but "Hitler sincerely believed then, we must grant him, that the SA intended a putsch." This "we must grant him" is worth a whole library.

There is no question here, however, of special pleading. That it was the spirit of Hitler himself that engulfed Germany, and later Europe, is stressed over and over by the two German authors—but we have been transported imperceptibly from the level of personality to that of "spirit," where things are less crude and no longer reek of blood. And if the source and origin of these events is historically perfectly clear, Görlitz and Quint are nevertheless quite right from a legal point of view: there is no documentary evidence—it was in every case carefully destroyed, the witnesses, most of them, along with it—and throughout his life Hitler trusted himself just as little to paper as he did to any human being. Nothing can be proved about Hitler, for good or for evil, from his birth to his death.

Nothing personal can be proved against him—and nothing personally meaningful either. He spoke in clichés and "eternal verities," literally "like a book," always alone, always holding a pose—before conversational partners as before audiences. The man who stamped his image on a whole epoch—an epoch that resembled him anyhow—had no image himself: only a mask, stuck together out of a mustache and a forelock, which he hid in his hands whenever he laughed, because laughter did not fit with the stance of wild energy that he maintained so fiercely. The poor devil from Leonding, the unsuccessful high school student of Linz, the unsuccessful bohemian of Vienna, down and out, without home or family, without profession or calling, and soon, indeed, stateless, without wife, sweetheart, friend, or comrade, finally rose in the world: through politics, the ideal vocation of the vocationless, of the man who concerns himself with what does not concern him, and can devote unlimited time to it because he himself has nothing that concerns him personally; who, for lack of a destiny of his own, becomes the master of the destiny of his society, and who can wrap himself so tightly in a pose because he possesses nothing else. And yet, on the heights of power, Hitler remained the same poor devil. In the very center of mighty events set in motion from that center itself, there stood a being of almost inconceivable spiritual, moral, and human inferiority.

It is understandable enough that Hitler's political opponents should always have seen him, until it was too late, as a mere tool, whether of the Reichswehr, the Junkers, or heavy industry. It was an error; he was no tool, even if his entire career is unthinkable without the scheming officers of the post-1918 German army, who set him loose on Germany as a nationalist agitator and information agent; or without the dark ferment of Bavarian conspiracies, beer-hall putschists, vigilante tribunals, and the *Freikorps;* or without the protection and complicity of highly placed "nationalist" politicians, from the Munich police commissioner and a Bavarian minister of justice to the Ludendorff clique and the "black Reichswehr," under whose protection this promoter of riots, organizer of meeting-hall brawls, and putschist, who did not even become a German citizen until 1932, remained safe from punishment or deportation; or without the Kahrs, Thyssens, Hugenbergs, and Papens, who thought they could use him as a "drummer boy."

But not only Hitler's enemies, also those who came to terms with him made the mistake of regarding him as a mere tool. "The history of Hitler is the history of his underestimation," observes Veit Valentin, in his *History of the Germans*—and he is quoted approvingly by Görlitz and Quint. They seek to avoid that error.

But what was it that was underestimated in Hitler? Wherein did his power lie? "Every single one of his ideas," Bullock notes, "from the exaltation of the heroic leader, the racial myth, anti-Semitism, the community of the *Volk*, and the attack on the intellect, to the idea of a ruling elite, the subordination of the individual and the doctrine that might is right, is to be found in anti-rational and racist writers (not only in Germany but also in France and other European countries) during the hundred years which separate the Romantic movement from the foundation of the Third Reich. By 1914 they had become the stale commonplaces of radical anti-Semitic and pan-German journalism and café-talk in every city in Central Europe. . . .

"Hitler's originality lay not in his ideas, but in the terrifyingly literal way in which he set to work to translate fantasy into reality, and his unequaled grasp of the means by which to do this. To read Hitler's table talk at his headquarters in 1941-1942 is to feel continual astonishment at the lack of magnanimity and wisdom in his conversation, the main qualities of which were cunning and brutality, a cocksure ignorance and an ineradicable vulgarity. Yet this vulgarity of mind, like the insignificance of his appearance, the badly fitting raincoat and the lock of hair plastered over his forehead, was perfectly compatible with brilliant political gifts. Accustomed to associate such gifts with the qualities of intellect which a Napoleon or a Bismarck possessed, or with the strength of character of a Cromwell or a Lincoln, we are astonished and offended by this combination. Yet to underestimate Hitler as a politician, to dismiss him as an hysterical demagogue, is to make precisely the mistake that so many Germans made in the early 1930's."

The danger of underestimating him no longer seems very great. Even those who once found this black-haired apostle of the blond Aryan hero comic have long since stopped laughing. "If you would see his monument, look around." And, all things considered, it was not primarily an error of underestimation that the German people committed as regards

Hitler. On the contrary. The problem Hitler's German biographers struggle with is quite different: how to reconcile the gravity, the catastrophic magnitude of the events, with the vulgar mediocrity of the individual who initiated them; and, if not to explain this, at least to make it conceivable how a great and civilized nation could identify itself with a spiritually and morally retarded being. Their constant harping on the necessity of taking Hitler seriously is the measure of their failure in this. What kind of biography is it that halts its narrative every few pages to insist that there really is something to the man it depicts, even if it is impossible to discern just what it is?

Often the effort to "take Hitler seriously" becomes grotesque. Thus Görlitz and Quint say, in connection with Hitler's early rejection of Marx and Marxism, that he had undoubtedly read not Marx himself but, at most, "pamphlets about or against Marxism." But a few pages later—after voicing their own commonplace notions about the place of Marxism in the philosophy of history—they note ponderously that "Hitler, however, rejected it [Marxism] not so much from the standpoint of pure historical theory as from that of racism, as 'Jewish science.' . . . By so doing, he, unquestionably one of the most important of anti-Marxists, turned the tables on it, and in exchange made the racial interpretation of history by his own act a universally valid absolute." The reader groans at this point. All this man, who was "unquestionably" one of the most important of anti-Marxists, knew about Karl Marx, that great and genuinely difficult thinker, he knew by hearsay—that is, that he was a Jew. And he "refuted" the Marxist analysis of society and its critique of history with "Death to the Jew!"—"not so much," therefore, "from the standpoint of pure historical theory." The superstition that tremendous historical events have to have spiritual, high-minded causes—that a man who greatly affected the destiny of nations must needs himself be great—here reaches its ultimate effect in a monstrous confusion of values and categories.

What seems to be the insuperable difficulty incurred by both these conscientious biographies of Hitler is to find the category of historical greatness into which to fit him. "Greatness" itself is unquestionable, for Hitler's "greatness" left as its monument one of the greatest shambles in history; nothing more is required to put a man in the schoolbooks, and a great deal has gone into history, from the arsonist of Ephesus to the Capitoline geese. Moreover, Hitler's public role is well known, the available sources for the history of National Socialism are richer than those for most other epochs of history. But this contributes very little to his personal biography; in the face of "Hitler the man," the verifiable sources dry up, the image grows cloudy, all the outlines of an articulated personality disappear. How every reality of Hitler, the man, resists all efforts to lend him greatness!

The greatest advantage these new biographies of Hitler have over the one written by Konrad Heiden in the 1930's, which still has its value today and is hardly surpassed for the period it covers, is in their last chapters, which cover events Heiden did not yet have the chance to observe. In Bullock's book, the last chapter is entitled "The Emperor Without His Clothes," and tells about the madhouse that was Hitler's bunker in April 1945: the widening gap between Hitler's private world and reality; his last months as Supreme War Commander; his operations with phantom armies; his wild commands, issued into the void, for offensives, dismissals, death sentences; his insane outbursts against anyone who wanted to halt the collective suicide of Germany. Long before this, Hitler had uttered the following sentence (variations of which recur over and over in his conversation) in his last public speech in Munich on November 9, 1943—a sentence hurriedly expunged from the official versions: "I will not mourn for the German people if they fail this test. . . ."

This, its final stage, made his whole career all the more inconceivable. How did this mythomaniac acquire the power to force his delusions on reality for so many years, and make a whole nation follow him so obediently into the abyss?

Bullock finds Hitler's place in history "alongside Attila the Hun, the barbarian king who was surnamed not the Great, but the Scourge of God," and Görlitz and Quint, with the cautious reservation that "it is not for us to make the final historical judgment," come to the same conclusion. But this all too convenient parallel can, at best, do justice only to the external scale of the catastrophe, not to Hitler's personality. Whatever he was, there was nothing primitive, natural, or elemental about him, nothing of the uncomplicated barbarism of a nomad chief. To see him as a wild, unchained force of nature is to fall for his own pose. This "Scourge of God" fell upon Europe not out of the steppes but from the Viennese gutter.

What is missing from both biographies is the peculiar, penetrating smell—"demoniacally" thrilling to some, repellent to others—that the whole Nazi movement exhaled in the years of its ascendancy. No one thinks of the category "genius" in connection with Attila or Genghis Khan; with Hitler it is impossible to avoid the word, which in almost every language other than German can denote the bad as well as the good, the highest as well as the lowest spirit that can possess men—or swine. And unsatisfactory as is that demonology which takes over the task of explaining what the rational understanding still cannot, it unquestionably comes closer to the phenomenon of Hitler than the notion of barbarism. "Schicklgruber, possessed by demons"—as unspeakably vulgar as it sounds, that is the correct starting point. Not Attila, but the villain of a *Dracula*-type thriller best approximates Hitler as a historical figure; his band of "old fighters"—that chosen collection of pederasts, drug addicts, rowdies, crackpots, and criminals—belong with some nest of vampires rather than a barbarian horde.

Historians do not want to descend to the level of popular magazines, of scandal and sensation; they are used to other references. But how else can they reach Adolf Hitler's level? It is hard for history to move on a higher plane than its subject, and everything private in Hitler's life is doubtful, sordid, or disreputable.

The problem presents itself on the first page of every biography of Hitler. "On the 6th of June, 1876, there appeared before the notary in Weitra-an-der-Lainsitz, in the department of Gmund in Lower Austria, an eighty-four-year-old former miller named Johann Georg Hiedler, who, in the presence of three witnesses . . . declared that the customs officer Alois Schicklgruber, born out of wedlock on June 17, 1837, in Strones, to the serving-maid Anna Maria Schicklgruber, whom he [Hiedler] had married in 1842, was his own and the said serving-maid's natural son. . . ." Alois Schicklgruber was forty years old, had already been married and divorced, and had two children by his cook when he was thus legitimized. Johann Hiedler had married Alois' mother thirty-five years before, but had not bothered then to recognize his illegimate son, and never bothered about him after his wife's death five years later. Furthermore, he, Hiedler, dropped out of sight during the intervening thirty years. It was the sort of thing that often happened among peasants.

Alan Bullock tactfully ignores the whole thing: what has it got to do with the case? Yet it is pertinent that the apostle of the myth of race, who made blood origin the sole criterion of humanity, did not really know who his own grandfather was. It is equally pertinent that the son of the Jewish family in Graz by whom Anna Maria Schicklgruber was employed at the time of her confinement contributed to the support of her son Alois for twenty years—the Alois who was Hitler's father, and whom Hitler hated with a hatred he could not hide even in *Mein Kampf,* with a hatred that led him to rebel against all authority, all discipline, and every ordered way of life, and decided him upon his abortive "artistic career." And it is also pertinent that a ragged Viennese postcard-painter, Adolf Hitler, in an old, black, knee-length coat a second-hand dealer had given him, with long black hair and sparse unshaven beard, really looked exactly the way he later, in *Mein Kampf,* described "the Jew in a caftan" whose sight had such a traumatic effect upon him. Those who have tried to come to grips with Hitler's "doctrine" were long ago struck by the fact that he always projected his own image upon those he hated and excoriated. We will build no theory on this, and we also prefer to leave his hidden origins hidden.

But what's the use, then, of the genealogical tables that Görlitz and Quint print, only, finally, to "concede" what is obvious anyway, that "in Adolf Hitler's physiognomy very little of German ancestry is to be seen"? This is taking a tone too lofty for the subject. The *homo alpinus,* with his black lock of hair over a slanting forehead, flanked by his little Mephisto Goebbels, as herald of the Nordic hero—only naked horror blinds us to the ludicrousness of this burlesque-hall act. Does *everything* about Hitler really have to be "taken seriously" because his Reich cost twenty-five million lives?

But we do not need gossip, revelations, or explanations of the "Geli Raubal affair," or the intimate diaries of Eva Braun, to clear up Hitler's case. His true, authorized, and incontestable portrait was painted by himself in *Mein Kampf* and no biography, however painstaking and conscientious, can replace the reading of that book for anyone seeking to grasp his personality. *Mein Kampf,* which was once thrust into almost every German's hands, seems to have been read by few, and to the end by even fewer.

That the book teems with gross untruths and even worse half-truths does not prevent it from mirroring the spiritual personality of its author with alarming if involuntary truthfulness. Nor does it matter that it depicts the external circumstances of Hitler's career with vague, obliterating, or self-glorifying strokes—about the first thirty years of his life Hitler juggled with one contradictory and obviously untenable version after another, until in the *Reichshandbuch der Deutschen Gesellschaft* the notice he himself wrote states that, as the "descendant of an Austrian family of finance officials," he "devoted himself to architecture" during his youth in Vienna, and in 1912 moved to Munich "in order to find a wider field for his political activity." Even the style, decked out with stilted flourishes and padded with verbiage, distends itself as it spreads its sorry "world view," like a peacock's tail, over 800 pages. But the spirit expressed in this ideological portrait of himself is his own, unmistakable amid all the rubbish.

Many of the questions that his biographers wrestle with disappear as soon as we go to *Mein Kampf*. All the deliberations and conjectures about his education, the "enormous reading" of his bohemian period in Vienna, then become meaningless. Did he read Nietzsche, Schopenhauer, Mommsen, Le Bon, Gobineau, Chamberlain, Haeckel? We do not know; Hitler himself avoided every mention of the names of all the authors he supposedly had read. The few shopworn quotations from great writers that sprinkle his writings and speeches were on every tongue, and could have come to him at fourth or fifth hand. He took from everything—as he noted complacently—what suited him.

As sole "philosophic" foundation, sufficient alike for stockbreeding, the animal kingdom, and the life of nations, he had a primitive biological Darwinism, expressed in pseudo-scientific vulgarizations. He showed an abysmal lack of understanding of anything having to do with society, morality, government, civilization, or religion—in short, of anything human higher than the pack. His knowledge of the world was that of a village grumbler whose information was all got from the local newspaper. And under all this there lay an arbitrary belief in force such as required no extensive reading to attain—but with which one could go far. This is the whole intellectually graspable content of Hitler's picture of the world.

For long stretches that picture is nothing but the blustering of a barroom debater who knows how to do everything better because he doesn't know how to do anything. Yet, though—or precisely because—Hitler had little systematic understanding of any question involving factors more complicated than those of force or cunning, ideas occurred to him such as seldom occur to serious statesmen and diplomats because they are excluded by experience or respect for the rules of the game. The Gordian knot and Columbus' egg are standing examples of the fact that the simplest solution of a difficult problem is always by force and cunning—stand an egg on end by breaking it, and untie a knot by cutting it. It is not a difficult trick, anybody can do it; but it is successful because nobody else does do it. However, such success seldom outlasts the effect of its surprise. Adolf Hitler went from one stupendous triumph to another, making German and then world history, until all the eggs were broken and all the knots cut—then, to his amazement, the others, "those idiots," turned and fought.

But it was not in his methods, which others had discovered and practiced before him, that Hitler's originality lay; rather in the "demonic possessedness" with which, a nonentity out of nothingness, he began his mad career, swept millions along with him, and landed them and himself in utter catastrophe. Barroom debaters, even the brawling kind, do not usually have anything demonic about them, and are generally burdened with private lives that limit the time available for world conquest. This political tub-thumping, even though Hitler obviously takes it very seriously himself, is still mere frosting, like the pseudo-scientific learning that pornographic literature used to dress itself up in—and which was likewise often taken very seriously by the pornographers themselves. What is really and truly "demonic" about Hitler's wild, bloated effusions is not his political "views," his "world-historical" ruminations, or his nationalism, his arrogance, and his belief in force: but rather a reek of obscenity, of degenerate and perverted lewdness, that almost hits the reader of *Mein Kampf* in the face.

When Hitler starts talking about "race" and "blood" every attempt at even the most primitive kind of rational argument ends, and he lapses into the language of sexual hallucination. To each his own: French literature has the Marquis de Sade; German literature, *Mein Kampf*. Its obsessive theme is embodied in the image of the black-haired demon and the blond virgin—the repressed wish-fulfillment dream of an unhappy adolescence. This nightmare of sex became the fixed point around which Hitler's image of the world revolved. His sick imagination saw nothing else during his years in Vienna; later, the nightmare spread to become a glacial cap of madness covering the whole world.

One would have to quote endlessly from Hitler's remarks on syphilis, education, the tasks of the racist state, to grasp the whole clinical picture. He was a sick man for whom woman and sex remained always in the realm of sinful fantasy. If you want to find out Hitler's "mystery" or his wretched "demon," here it is, drawn by Hitler himself.

Hitler's central political idea is a vulgar rationalization of a sexual hallucination, an insane vision in which history, politics, and "the life struggle of races" unroll in images of copulation, promiscuity, blood defilement, natural selection, cross-breeding, bastardization, rape, and abduction—world history as a sexual orgy in which filthy and diabolic subhumans lie in wait for blond maidens.

Hitler was thirty-five when he dictated *Mein Kampf*. When his "Table Talk" * was recorded, he was over fifty, the absolute dictator and supreme war commander of a country he had led into a war against the whole world—and yet nothing had really changed. True, the need to rationalize had now become dominant, and the telegraphic style in which his party comrade, Dr. Picker, recorded his utterances makes it impossible to taste the full flavor of his fantasies. But more than ever is human history seen in the context of a Darwinian animal world. "In reply to an objection by Reich Press Chief Dietrich, the *Führer* said: 'What is true of the wild horses is true of every community of living creatures that wishes to maintain itself in the world. If there is no bellwether the community is dissolved, atomized—everything comes to an end. It is for this reason that the apes, for example, trampled outsiders to death as aliens. And what is valid for the apes must be even more valid for human beings.'"

Hitler notes with satisfaction that the "quality" of the children around Berchtesgaden had already "improved" substantially thanks to the "blood-freshening" activities of a division of the SS stationed there, who "take their task of bringing children into the world as a racial duty." "It is a practice which must be followed; to those districts in which a tendency toward degeneracy is apparent, we must send a body of elite

* *Hitler's Secret Conversations, 1941-1944,* with an Introductory Essay by H. R. Trevor-Roper. This selection overlaps with, but is somewhat different from that published in the original German.

troops, and in ten or twenty years' time the bloodstock will be improved out of all recognition." "In life, battle and love go hand in hand, and the inhibited little bourgeois must be content with the crumbs which remain." On the other hand, he noted with regret that the northern French had been perceptibly "Nordicized" by the occupation of their territory by German soldiers during the First World War; precious German blood should not be injected into alien races and allowed to filter up into their "leadership strata." This was the level on which things were discussed at Hitler's headquarters; ideas that should have remained lavatory jokes parade as eternal truths and divine revelation.

The fantasies of *Mein Kampf* had by now hardened into a systematic delirium. The "Table Talk" fully confirms what Rauschning, ten years before, had reported of Hitler's "secret teachings" about the "breeding of the superman." Publicly, Hitler had always spoken as if he considered the German people "Aryan," but within the circle of his worshippers he revealed the dark secret that the "Aryan" no longer existed—or perhaps not yet; he would have to be created by Hitler's personal intervention in a bungled Creation; state-directed biological mutations, "forced breeding," as animal-breeder Darré said, would be necessary. Their "Nordic essence" was to be extracted from the European peoples that lent themselves to the process. Eastern Europe and Russia were to be excluded from this forced "upward breeding," and illiteracy, plague, and poverty were to kill off superfluous slave populations to make room for the brave new asphalt world of the Nordic race. This was the deeper meaning, which Hitler alone perceived, of a war that was to mark a turning point in world history.

The sources from which Hitler drew the materials for this monstrous structure lie in the past, and they have been distorted almost beyond recognition. All of German Romanticism, with its "instinctive" and "blood" definitions of race, nation, and culture—a whole tradition of operatic Germanness—emptied itself into this spiritual swamp.

Nor did these pathological fantasies remain mere theory; in Auschwitz and Maidanek the "final solution of the Jewish question" was "achieved" in millionfold murder. The euthanasia program for the extermination of the mentally ill, and of "inferior" human specimens in general, was set in motion by Hitler's decree on the first day of the war; in the conquered territories of the East the *Einsatzgruppen* set out to exterminate or tread down "slave peoples" with systematic brutality. The Race and Resettlement Bureau of the SS catalogued with pedantic minuteness the breeding value (estimated down to decimal points) of hundreds of thousands of "resettled" people who were to be employed for racial breeding in the "German resettlement area"; in Poland, Holland, and Norway the rounding up had already begun of those whose blood was considered suitable for the same purpose in Himmler's proposed new German cities. Never did lunacy become world history on such a scale.

Hitler's early life was that of a lonely, orphaned, unhappy, rootless man, unsuccessful in every human sphere, who had never found a single healthy or genuine human contact, or a task or milieu of his own; who, in his own growing isolation from humanity, refused, out of anxiety, to show himself to anyone except in the pose of a lonely and misunderstood genius. This panicky refusal to meet anyone on an equal plane without posturing, his systematic avoidance of all confrontation, discussion, examination, or self-examination, the flight from himself into an unreal world of uninterrupted monologues where he could hide his inner emptiness—all this remained with Hitler until the end of his life.

He had thanked God on his knees for the coming of war in 1914, but here, too, the political reasons he cites are grotesque and twisted rationalizations of a purely personal joy in the arrival of a "mass experience" that would at last give his life some meaning. But even this "mass experience" remained as inwardly empty as the clichés to which his description of this "greatest and most unforgettable time of my earthly life," beside which "everything in the past was reduced to mere nothingness," are limited. In the trenches too he sat apart, as once he had sat "somewhere apart," as he himself said, among the Viennese building workers at the midday break. The other soldiers had homes, families, wives, wrote and received letters, yearned for their old lives—he had no one, and his outburst of rage in *Mein Kampf* against the "foolish letters of the German women" which "demoralized the front," "this poison manufactured by thoughtless wives at home," is laden with hate and envy. For him—homeless, without real education or calling, without a goal—civilian life meant a return to nothingness. What was he good for? In ordinary times, perhaps, he could have become preacher of some eccentric sect (even in his last years, between critical military decisions, he would long-windedly lecture his entourage on vegetarianism, the harmfulness of alcohol and tobacco, and Hörbiger's theories about the glacial age). But these were not ordinary times. The age of the scabrous bohemian hero had dawned, the age of the *ratés,* of the failures.

In the slowly dissolving German army in post-Armistice Munich, commanded by Republic-hating officers who were later to make up the *Freikorps,* all the irreconcilables, at odds with God and the world and thirsting for national revenge, tried to scrape along in a provisional military life. Here the discharged Adolf Hitler, who did not know what was to become of him, likewise nursed his resentment and despair. In a course on "national thinking" organized on the initiative of Captain Roehm, he found his political finishing school; one need look no further for the sources of his "doctrines," even if he himself, in *Mein Kampf,* dates his political enlightenment a decade or two back. Here, in the company of men of like fate and outlook, he acquired the whole arsenal of nationalist slogans he was to draw on for the rest of his career: the "stab-in-the-back" lie, the betrayal by the "Jewish-Marxist November criminals," the "shame of Versailles," "racial thinking"—the whole set of inflammatory platitudes of the extreme German Right.

In this hothouse atmosphere his hour ripened. At last, in a discussion in which "one of the participants thought it necessary to break a lance for the Jews," the spirit came upon him, and "aroused," he uttered aloud that hatred of the Jewish "corrupter of the people" which had fermented within him for so long. The audience, the atmosphere, the theme—everything came together. What was lowest in him poured forth, and it spoke to what was lowest in his listeners; the contact was made—he was a speaker! His talent had been discovered. "The result . . . was that I was assigned, a few days later, to serve as a so-called 'educational officer' with a Munich regiment."

In his capacity as nationalist propagandist among troops, and as "information agent" for what was to become the "Black Reichswehr," he was sent as a political observer to a meeting of the newly founded German Workers party, one of the extremist nationalist organizations then springing up like mushrooms from the soil of Munich, and with his oratorical conquest of its seven members, Hitler began his conquest of the world. The remaining twenty years of his life were to be one long monologue before a slowly swelling audience, a monologue half-German, screaming, inarticulate, but aimed unerringly at every evil instinct in his fellow men. With jubilation, he noted the effect of his first public speech before an audience of one hundred and eleven people: "What I had before simply felt internally, without knowing it in any way, had now been proved by reality: I could speak! After thirty minutes the people in the little room had been electrified. . . ."

From this to the mass frenzies of Nuremberg, the rest of Hitler's career is one single, continuous intensification of this orgy of mass oratory, the first and only form of human contact he had ever known, and to which, when he had once tasted it, he returned obsessively like an addict to his drug. He had nothing but his burning hatred and his pathological obsessions, but it was clear now that this was enough to bring under his spell hundreds, then thousands, then hundreds of thousands of others who likewise possessed nothing else. He, who possessed no one, could possess masses; he, who could not deal with his fellow man as an individual, could "electrify" him as part of a crowd, dehumanize him, work him up into raving excitement and (in his own words) "forward-driving hysteria."

The mass meeting became the realization of his fantasies, the witches' sabbath over which he ruled, released at last from the inner prison of his individuality and carried away by the mass delirium he himself evoked. The first audiences he addressed had been composed only of men; now the women came, too, the elderly, "motherly friends" who introduced the unmannerly "little wolf" to society, the hysterical hero-worshippers who instinctively divined the little boy imprisoned within the great man; the "convulsion squad" of the mass meetings, whom his presence sent into hysterical fits.

What Hitler said hardly mattered and he learned quickly, indeed, to alter his rationalizations according to his audience. A torrent of pathologically erotic hatred, with dark affect-laden verbal symbols—"disgrace," "blood," "shame," "Jew," "race," "sin"—washed over his audience and transformed it into a mass bereft of its senses.

He talked himself into fame, he talked himself into power, he talked himself into war, and he talked himself into disaster. Did he know what he was doing? Nowhere can it be shown that his political aims, his ideas about the future, consisted of anything but the marching, the *heil*ing, the flags and the torches of the huge crowds straining up to him. And as the last event in the program of delirium, there came the vision of a collectively organized procreation of the Nordic superman out of test tubes of sacred blood, a vision embodied in the elite columns of the SS as they marched in to the strains of *Parsifal*. His speeches during the second half of the war, with Germany already on the slope of catastrophe, show an absolute incapacity to see the world war he had called down upon Germany in any other perspective but that of his early struggles and oratorical triumphs, the meeting-hall brawls and the election campaigns in which he by fanatical energy—ten or more election speeches a day—had first shown his power.

Just as all the terms he, and his admirers, found for his special talent for mass suggestion—sleepwalking, hypnosis, animal magnetism—point toward the realm of hysteria, so his career, magnified by the power he wielded, reminds one of a hysterical woman who, having once discovered she could always get her way by nervous attacks and fits of screaming, forever afterward responds to all contradiction or resistance with a nervous collapse. Hitler's tantrums were worked up and heightened systematically once experience had demonstrated their effect; they were synthetic, consciously induced. The fit of rage was turned on and off at will, the rug-chewing became an instrument to be manipulated, a weapon in the struggle for power within the party, a diplomatic arm, finally a weapon to be used in the supreme direction of war—and even in the disastrous last months of his life, he found that these fits of rage which no one dared contradict could make possible, if not the impossible, then at least the insane. (What he spoke came to pass: the national revolution, the

Greater German Reich, the subjugation of Europe, the pogroms, the massacres, the downfall of the world—the world around him became putty in his hands, and confirmed his madness.) Perhaps Hitler's real biography is nothing but this single, endless, obsessive monologue, a waking dream outside real life, and outside what had hitherto been called history. When he was not making a speech he fell back into a brooding half-sleep, abandoned by the demon, incapable of action or decision, buried in himself—*post coitum triste*. Perhaps that discrepancy with which his biographers struggle—between the monstrous shadow he cast over world history and the person that produced it—is nothing but the discrepancy between a medium's state of excitement and his relapse into the apathy of his own insignificant individuality.

But here the problem of Hitler ends, and becomes the problem of the materials out of which he built his empire.

Hitler did not create the "mass soul" that gave itself up to him; it fell to him because he was made in its image. Certainly, all the external conditions for this explosion of failure, rootlessness, and long-fermented hatred were already present in Germany and Germans: the collapse of the Kaiser's Reich, the great lie of the "stab in the back" that from the beginning poisoned the development of the Weimar Republic, the smoldering atmosphere of chauvinist conspiracy, the inflation, the declassing of the middle classes, the Great Depression and its despair, the secret jockeying for power amid political chaos. These are recorded in both biographies with great and depressing conscientiousness. As Bullock rightly points out in his "Epilogue": "Hitler, indeed, was a European, no less than a German phenomenon. The conditions and the state of mind which he exploited, the *malaise* of which he was the symptom, were not confined to one country, although they were more strongly marked in Germany than anywhere else. . . . He was in revolt against 'the System' not just in Germany but in Europe, against that liberal bourgeois order, symbolized for him in the Vienna which had once rejected him. To destroy this was his mission, the mission in which he never ceased to believe; and in this, the most deeply felt of his purposes, he did not fail. . . ."

European in this sense all the epiphenomena of the Third Reich—the crisis of society and civilization, the "masses," the total state, the nihilism—certainly were. Nonetheless, it would be idle to attempt to argue away the unmistakable *Germanness* of the phenomenon of Adolf Hitler and of the specific spirit he stamped on his Reich, that sick, obscene savagery which had no parallel in Fascism, Bolshevism, or any of the other totalitarian movements. The foul instincts that Hitler's blood cult conjured to the surface rose from the depths of a sour, spectral, airless, brooding psyche, and that psyche was an aspect peculiar to the "German nature" to which Hitler could appeal with such murderous success—an aspect the rest of the world viewed with startled incomprehension.

The Third Reich contained other impulses besides this nightmare. Once set in motion, it had the force to move unswervingly to a repetition, ten times as disastrous, of the First World War—but it was not in this that the ghastly originality of Hitler's Third Reich lay. The elevation of certain depraved fantasies—diseased products of a sick mind such as could conceive Auschwitz, Maidanek, and the human stock-breeding files of the Bureau of Race and Resettlement—into the official philosophy of a civilized nation: this was what was original and unique in Hitler's achievement. It was this that marked an absolute zero in human history, far below all barbarism, below all horrors and crimes of war and revolution, below Stalin's slave camps. The nightmare has vanished, but who can wonder that its neighbors and witnesses still feel the horror of it in their bones?

Translated from the German by Irving Pfefferblit

Theodore Frankel

MY FRIEND PAUL

One Who Survived

Looking at Paul Weiss, one would never suspect that only twelve years have passed since he came out of Buchenwald. He seems younger than his thirty years, and with his fair skin, blond hair, blue eyes set deeply beneath a broad, low forehead, his straight nose and slightly prognathous jaw, he is often taken for an Irishman—so long as he keeps quiet.

I have known Paul (this, incidentally, is not his real name) since he came to this country in 1949 and I believe I have become his friend, or as much of one as he will let an American be. But then I, being a *Yecke,* a Jew born and raised in Germany, don't count in Paul's eyes as a real American.

Part of Paul's difficulty in making friends with Americans, Jewish or Gentile, lies in his struggle with the English language. For a man so eloquent in his native tongue, descending to the low intellectual level imposed upon him by a limited English vocabulary is galling indeed. Most of his friends are Polish Jews like himself and with them he speaks a Polish whose purity of accent and wealth of vocabulary are remarkable and rare. And his Yiddish, which he uses with me, spiked with frequent Russian and Polish curses, technical terms in German, and American slang, is no less rich and fluent. But Paul's difficulties are not confined to the English language. Observing him over the years, I have been disturbed by his inability and, yes, his unwillingness to come to terms with America.

More than seven years have passed since Paul came to this country and he is still drifting from temporary job to temporary job, from one furnished room to another, while his only real friends are still those few of his fellow refugees who can be seen hanging around The Senator Cafeteria on Broadway and 96th Street. He shows no sign of settling down; the mere mention of marriage makes him shudder.

As I have said, I met Paul when he first arrived in this country, and very soon he became a special problem to me. As the years slipped by for him, their waste somehow became a challenge for me: his difficulty in finding himself in America was a reproach to me, who had had such an easy time of it, his lostness was a threat to my new and tender roots. I brooded over these things for a long time, and there was even a period in my life when the only thing that mattered deeply to me was to understand Paul, to know all about him, to account for every minute of his past, indeed to reach a point where I could quite literally put myself in his place and make his memories my own. Even while this was happening I realized that Paul himself—much as I liked and esteemed him—was merely serving as a focus for those dark, unquiet feelings I carried with me for having been saved when those I loved most had died in the very camps Paul had been in.

Of course, Paul's life did not furnish me with my catharsis—how could it? But those endless conversations we had, those interminable monologues of his, gradually yielded, if not the full understanding, then at least the intimation, the aura of a fate that might, but for exceptional good luck, have been my own.

When I wanted to see Paul, I would go up to The Senator Cafeteria, where I was sure to find him, in one of those small clusters of men who stand day and night in front of the place, or else sit inside or divert themselves in the poolroom above. After disengaging him from his friends, I would sit down with him to a piece of Danish and a cup of coffee, amid the familiar noises of the cafeteria—the voices of the customers ordering their meals, the clatter of the chefs at the range, the squeal of the busboys' carts, the hum of conversation, and the steady knocking of heavy silverware on heavy crockery. From time to time Paul would wave to a passing friend, then he would settle back, bite into his Danish, and tell me about the night in Auschwitz when the Germans gassed five thousand Gypsies to make room for new inmates.

The beginnings of Paul's life were completely unremarkable. He was born and raised in a middle-sized Polish town, the spoiled younger son of a Jewish shopkeeper. He has mentioned his father only once to me, saying that he had great handle-bar mustaches, but he often speaks of his mother and he has shown me photographs which portray her as a dignified matron with unusually piercing eyes. *"A sheyne yidene,"* Paul affectionately calls her. I have also seen snapshots of Paul himself, first at ten, in his new knickers, smiling as only a mother's favorite does, and again at the age of fourteen, in a cape dramatically flung over his shoulder. At school he was known for his astounding memory, his ability as a storyteller, and his frequent absences. Among his friends he was admired for his precocious skill at billiards.

When he was fourteen the Germans came, at sixteen he was taken to a work camp, and from there to a succession of work and concentration camps until, early in 1945, he reached the notorious "Little Camp," a subdivision of the huge Buchenwald camp. Naturally, there are no pictures of Paul at that time, yet from the movies taken when the camp was liberated in April 1945, we know exactly what Paul must have looked like. Who can ever forget those living skeletons propped up against the heaps of the dead?

There is a description by a French student, quoted in Reitlinger's *The Final Solution,* of the arrival of a transport from Auschwitz at Buchenwald, possibly the very transport of which Paul was a part. The writer does not mention that the prisoners, many of whom had been driven halfway across Europe on foot or in open cattle cars, frequently had to lie for as many as three days and three nights in the open plain around the camp, struggling to keep awake in the snow and the bitter cold, until they were admitted. But he does tell us what their arrival in camp was like: "Sometimes under the pressure of blows they would suddenly break into movement like a herd of cattle, jostling each other. It was impossible to extract from their lips their names, much less the date of birth. Kindness itself had not the power to make them speak. They would only look at you with a long expressionless stare. If they tried to answer, their tongues could not reach their dried-up palate to make a sound. One was aware of a poisonous breath appearing to come from entrails already in a state of decomposition. That was what the transport was like in the winter 1944-45, that winter when death achieved the prodigious figure of 13,000 detainees in the last three months before our liberation."

I once asked Paul how it felt to be in a concentration camp, but he did not understand quite what I meant. He has no impulse toward introspection: he has spent far too much time looking only at the man opposite on whose reaction his very life might depend to have cultivated any interest in his own responses to experience. Trying a different tack, I then asked Paul to reconstruct for me the routine of an average day in Buchenwald, trusting to his phenomenal memory to dredge up the details of a moment now more than eleven years gone. With the skill of a born raconteur he began by sketching in the background: the biting cold of that February 1945, the emaciated internees in their thin prison pajamas, the barbed wire and the watch towers surrounding the camp, the frozen mud and the physical desolation within. Finally he described the seventeen "temporary" wooden structures that comprised the Little Camp which was by then overflowing with prisoners who had been evacuated from the camps in Poland and Austria already overrun by the Russians.

These barracks, located directly off the *Appell Platz,* were a hell compared to which the regular concentration camp at Buchenwald seemed but a mild purgatory. The buildings, unheated and inadequately lit, were divided lengthwise into two equal parts by a low wall, about two feet high. On either side of this barrier there ran a narrow corridor, the only free space in the room. The rest of the cabin was jammed tight with three- and four-decker wooden bunks (the infamous *"boxen"*) on the bare boards of which the prisoners were packed, usually ten to twelve to each deck, so tight they all had to sleep on the same side without ever being able to turn over. "Still," Paul told me, "we warmed each other that way, except when the man next to you died during the night, which happened quite often. And though we were all hardly more than skeletons, our cumulative weight became so great at times that the *boxen* would sink right through the floor."

A typical day in Buchenwald began, according to Paul, at six in the morning with a blast of whistles over the loudspeaker system. A minute later the *Stubendienst* (orderlies in charge of the barracks; these soft jobs almost invariably went to German prisoners) began to drive the inmates off the bunks with shouts of *"Aufstehen! Aufstehen!"* This was no easy matter, a handful of men hustling two thousand exhausted creatures out of bed and into the bitter winter darkness, and every morning there were a good many who could not, or would not, get off the bunks. Many were dead, many more were too weak to move, and still more pretended to be even weaker than they actually were for fear of what the day had in store. These "simulators" rarely had any luck because the *Stubendienst* were experts at distinguishing among the various degrees of exhaustion, and they forced everyone who could at all move to line up outside the barracks in columns of four. There the prisoners stood, dressed only in their gray-blue cotton pajamas, caps made of the same material, and wooden Dutch cloppers—the only clothing they possessed. At the command they began to move slowly, their shoes crunching the snow, to a barracks two hundred yards down the road. "We must have been quite a sight," Paul recalls now. "Like a parade of walking skeletons. And how we must have stunk! In all those months we never changed or washed our clothes once. There was no soap. And anyhow, who cared?"

The destination of their morning march was the wash barracks, another wooden structure, which was unheated and completely empty except for two or three water pipes and a trough below them running down the center of the building. These pipes were perforated; ice-cold water came spouting out of the holes and was drawn off into the trough. The prisoners lined up on both sides of the pipes, removed their pajama tops and washed themselves in the icy water. Neither soap nor towels were available and each man dried himself as best he could. Then the shivering men were marched back to the barracks for breakfast.

Now it may be significant that in the matter of breakfast Paul's memory, usually capable of total recall, is more than a little hazy, and that at various times he has told me several different versions of how the meal was arranged. But after checking with his friends, he settled definitely on this one: from the wash barracks the prisoners were marched back into their own barracks, where they lay down on their bunks again. Then the *Blockälteste* (the official barracks boss—again, in most cases a German prisoner) came along and distributed the morning's ration in a manner grimly reminiscent of feeding at the zoo.

There were groans and moaning and arguments as the well-fed and warmly dressed *Blockälteste* strode down the corridor through the offal, the filth, and the stench, thrusting the ration into the bunks, where it was grasped by desperate hands. The ration consisted of a quarter of a loaf of bread and a pat of margarine. The procedure for distributing the coffee was even more grotesque. A huge pot filled with a lukewarm, muddy liquid (burnt chickory, mostly) was wheeled or carried down the aisle. Since the prisoners were lying down twelve deep parallel to the wall and corridor, those next to the wall had to crawl—cup in one hand and bread clutched in the other—over the bodies of their fellows, stretch their cups over the edge of the bunk, get them filled, and crawl back again. A few remembering that their portion of bread would have to tide them over until night, would hide it on their persons and just drink the coffee. The great majority, however, gobbled down their ration immediately, for the possession of bread, in however small a quantity, was an open invitation to thievery. The Russian prisoners of war, who were relative latecomers to the camps and therefore healthier than the rest, were particularly feared in this respect. They were known to work in gangs, and in the dim twilight of the barracks or out in the yard they stole the bread or took it by force.

Since the Little Camp was not a regular concentration camp, the prisoners were not assigned permanent jobs—at least not in the last months of the war—but were ordinarily left to their own devices for the rest of the day.

In bad weather they lay on their bunks or walked up and down the corridor in the barracks; when the sun shone and it was a little warmer, they wandered around the yard. Small groups of friends, people from the same town or province, relatives however distant, stood and walked together, talked and looked for friends among new arrivals. According to Paul, the Jewish prisoners seldom made friends with non-Jews and never trusted them entirely.

Paul himself had been officially passing for a non-Jew long before he got to Buchenwald; nonetheless he kept to the company of other Jews.

He would not have survived without them. On the long trek from Auschwitz to Buchenwald there were many times when he wanted to lie down in the snow and die, but his friends would not let him. On other occasions during the march when he felt stronger, he in turn would encourage them to go on. In the camps, too, they helped each other as much as they could. "Wherever I went," Paul says again and again, "whatever camp I was sent to, I found *yidn* and *chaverim*."

This trust and dependence on fellow Jews has never left Paul; it is even reflected in the way he talks. For instance, whenever he mentions a Gentile he will say: *yener Polack* or *yener Deitsh* ("that Pole" or "that German"), rarely giving the person's name, even when he knows it; but he always speaks of a Jew by name and always specifies exactly how he is related to him: "So-and-so, my father's cousin's oldest son," or "So-and-so, an uncle of a classmate of mine," or simply, *"A kollege"* (a buddy). It is also very important to Paul that he should be surrounded by trusted friends. Again and again he will mention people, Jews and occasionally a Gentile who saved his life, and say: "Ha, he was my best friend." Or after telling a particularly exciting story in which he figured prominently, and seeing his audience impressed, he will laugh in triumph: *"Du halst fun mir, eh, kollegele?"*—"I'm O.K., eh, pal?"

Not much could be done in the Little Camp to fill the time between morning and evening meals. There was almost no "organizing," no possibility of getting additional food or clothing from the SS guards through bribery, because there was nothing left to bribe with. The day was one unending wait filled with hunger pains and endless shuffling in the dirty yard or the cavernous barracks. Death and the stench of death were everywhere: death by starvation and death by burning, death by scientific injection and death by murder for a piece of bread, death by old age and death by disease.

Sometimes, when new transports arrived, frostbite cases by the score lay screaming in the yard and those who were walking outside stepped heedlessly over their writhing bodies. The fires of life were almost extinguished and there seems to have taken place a lowering of awareness that made most things bearable and blotted out perception of the rest.

H. G. Adler in his monumental book *Theresienstadt* comments on this particular aspect of concentration camp life: "Reality was, quite literally, unhinged [*ver-rückt*]. Nothing in it corresponded to what reality had been. . . . It became unreal and ghostly. It was perceived as a deception, hallucination, dream, as the monstrosities of a sick imagination. . . . One was confused and oneself confounded the confusion. This went so far that the existence of reality was not accepted; it had decomposed into an impossibility, a non-reality. The extent of this process, as a collective phenomenon, is without parallel in the written history of man."

For Paul, too, his life in Buchenwald remains indistinct. A kind of haze has settled over even his extraordinary memory, and simple facts (like the routine at breakfast) are always sliding away from him, to be recaptured only by checking with his friends. There are also vast areas of life in Buchenwald of which he is totally ignorant. To this day he and his friends know almost nothing about the bitter struggle for supremacy between political and criminal prisoners. Though these struggles took place behind the scenes and in the regular camp, their outcome often affected the lives of Paul and his fellow prisoners in the Little Camp. Nor does he know anything about the homosexuality so widespread in some camps. "Maybe it was going on in the regular camp," he says. "We in the Little Camp were too weak to think about sex. All we were interested in was a loaf of bread."

Waiting became the major reality in those last months before liberation. One waited to be fed or to be called to the gates or to be killed. Congregated in small groups, the prisoners filled the long day with talk. What did they talk about? First and foremost: bread. It is curious that neither Paul nor his friends remember talking about any other food. There was no craving for liquor: only the dream of cramming a whole loaf of bread down one's gullet, not to have to share it with anybody else, but to gulp it down, all of it, at one crack. And then another loaf and another.

When the talk was not of bread, it had to do with the future. None of the prisoners seems ever to have speculated about what he would do next year or five years hence—only about what the Germans would do to him before the war was over. As the signs of Germany's defeat multiplied—and on this the grapevine was extremely accurate—the tension and fear became greater. The prisoners could not believe that the Germans would let them survive to testify about the camps.

Feeding for the second and last time began early in the afternoon. It took place in a barracks which for some reason was called *"Das Kino,"* the "Cinema." The lines began to form as early as eleven o'clock in the morning, but most prisoners tried to hold out until a little later. By three o'clock, rain or shine, hail or snow, the lines seemed a thousand deep, but they moved quite rapidly. The "Cinema" looked like prisoners' messes everywhere; long tables and low benches, and up front the distributing line. The privileged German prisoners in charge of serving the food had the process worked out with the proverbial efficiency of Germans. One ladled out the lukewarm soup—mostly potato, pea, or turnip—another doled out a piece of bread, sometimes with ersatz jam, and the third marked the prisoners' food cards to make sure that nobody cheated. A man whose food card had been lost or stolen was in desperate straits. The prisoners ate their meals either in the hall or in the yard, and there again the danger of stealing was great.

The final and the most feared event of the day was the evening roll call. Every single inmate—in some camps even the day's dead—had to be present and accounted for. In the Little Camp the prisoners lined up four deep in front of their barracks and waited to be counted, first by the *Blockälteste* and then by the SS man in charge. Quite often, while the SS man was busy with another barrack, the *Blockälteste* would put his "men" through an exercise, *"Mützen ab, Mützen auf!* [caps off, caps on!]" and drill them till they did it smartly. Ordinarily the roll call took two hours and, coming at the end of the day, the long wait in the bitter cold was an ordeal. But if even a single prisoner could not be accounted for, either because he had escaped or—and this occurred more frequently—because he had died somewhere unnoticed, the whole camp would be kept on its feet until the missing man was found, occasionally as much as four and six hours later. At long last the inmates were permitted to return to their barracks. Sometimes, Paul says, it was only by mustering his last reserves of strength that he finally managed to crawl up with the others into his bunk, twelve to a board, squeezed tight and all lying on the same side together, waiting.

Waiting for his friends in a small café on Munich's Mehlstrasse a year later, in February 1946, Paul was slowly and a little noisily consuming a *Schillerlocke* and a *café au lait*. Pictures taken at the time show that he was still a little haggard, but his hair, which had been kept shorn for the last four years, was now long in the German fashion, his eyes looked large and clear, and his complexion was soft, almost boyish. He wore a stylish gray leather coat, his elegantly cut suit cost $100, his custom-tailored shirt was of imported English linen, and his cuff links solid gold. A diamond ring glittered on his pinkie and a fat Havana cigar in his mouth; he was, in short, the very picture of a successful petty black-marketeer at the tender age of twenty-one.

After the Americans liberated Buchenwald in the spring of 1945, Paul had stayed around the camp for a while, slowly building up his strength on good American food and the foundations of his fortune on American cigarettes which the soldiers gave him either as a gift or in return for the eggs which he regularly "requisitioned" from nearby German farms. By July of 1945 he was strong enough and had enough cigarettes, then worth their weight in gold, to leave camp, and along with a friend he set out for a *hachsharah* (a settlement to train prospective emigrants for life on an Israeli kibbutz) that had been established near Fulda. (Going to Israel was then every liberated Jewish prisoner's first idea.)

The trip was an exhilarating experience. For the first time in four years Paul moved as a free man, and for the first time in rather more than four years he could acknowledge himself a Jew. "You know," Paul said, when he told me about this episode, "I was not much of a Jew at home and in most ways I was not much more of one when I came out of the camps. I was no more religious, I was no more nationalistic or anything like that. But after all those years when I had to deny my Jewishness, it was wonderful to be able to say I am a Jew. And it was wonderful to see other Jews walking free and upright, to find out that there were still some who had survived, because for all we knew everybody might have been killed. In those first days, whenever Jews met on the street, even if they did not know each other, it was like a holiday. We used to go up to each other and ask: *'Amcho?' Amcho* means God's people, Israel. I hadn't heard the phrase used this way before, but suddenly, after the war, it had become a password for us, and all over Germany you could hear it: *'Amcho, amcho.'*"

Paul never got to Fulda and the *hachsharah*. On the way he ran into a couple of friends who were going to Munich for purposes of "business," and he decided to follow them instead. Once there, he stayed for good. "Oi," he sighs now in reminiscence, "you cannot imagine how well we lived in Germany in those days. You had to be crazy to go and dig ditches in Israel or to learn a trade with a German who made you work ten hours a day and paid a few lousy pennies. And who wanted to be in Poland and work for the Communists in a *kolkhoz?* I went back to my home town Kielce in 1946. Our house was destroyed, my parents were dead, only a handful of Jews had returned from the camps.

"And what do you think those Polacks had done? That Easter they had spread a rumor that the Jews had slaughtered two Christian children for Passover and then they went and had themselves a regular old-fashioned pogrom. A mob finished off anyone Hitler hadn't killed. Luckily, for business purposes I was passing as a non-Jew. Brother, I sold the wagonload of leather that I'd managed to get over the border on false papers, picked up a load of sugar, and made tracks back to Germany.

"Now those Germans—you can't imagine how timid and good they were in those days. We got everything from them, food, housing—and that wasn't easy to get with everything in ruins—whatever we needed. Once I was traveling to Frankfurt to see a friend and the conductor came over and asked for my ticket. 'I paid already,' I answered. 'Let's see your ticket,' he said. I didn't say a word, I just rolled up my sleeve and showed him the number they had tattooed on me in Auschwitz. He walked away, fast. And then I started hollering at him, oh, did I give it to him. But," Paul adds, "who needed their charity? There was plenty of money to be made."

The source of this money was, of course, the black market, which in those days spanned the entire Continent and whose capital was Munich.

There you could buy and sell—at a profit—what all Europe demanded: bread and liquor, clothes and typewriters, paper and saccharine, genuine dollars and false ones, faked papers and real diamonds. From Munich's Mehlstrasse the trade routes ran to French, Dutch, and Belgian ports in the west, to Switzerland, Italy, and possibly North Africa in the south, and, finding little difficulty in penetrating the Iron Curtain, to the satellite countries in the east.

However deplorable such a situation may have been, the development of a black market was inevitable in postwar Europe with its ghastly scarcities, the disruption of established trade routes, the breakdown of currencies, and the complete absence of governmental authority. But what gave the European black market in those years its special character was the presence, in the midst of the ruined Continent, of the immensely rich, the fantastically opulent American army, laden down—or so it seemed to the starving Europeans—with food, cigarettes, and hard currency. Given the fact that Europe had a large supply of some things the Americans were interested in, notably women, a good deal of exchanging was bound to take place, and the conduits through which ran this golden stream were provided by an army of black-marketeers recruited from all the dispossessed elements in Europe and including, alas, a sizable contingent from the concentration camps. The latter had, in fact, a considerable advantage over their competitors, their survival in camp having depended only too often on their skill in evasion and bribery. In addition, being homeless, they were highly mobile, almost without exception multilingual, and possessed of a thorough (and hard earned) knowledge of several countries. They enjoyed excellent connections (some antedating the war), previous business experience, and all the advantages of belonging to a marked group—solidarity, favorable credit conditions, and up-to-the minute inside information.

The dollar trade was the mainstay and basis of all other black market operations, and Paul soon became active in it. He took a room in a small town half an hour by train from Munich, and, his pockets crammed with German marks, would go to the nearby American base on the last day of every month, when the troops were paid; sometimes he made the trip more often than that. American personnel stationed abroad were paid in scrip, a currency issued by the army which could legally be used only in the PX. The soldiers, eager to entertain their Frauleins in German bars and night clubs, were willing to buy marks at a considerable discount, say at 65 per cent of what a regular dollar would bring in the market.

Paul was soon well known as a seller of German money and able to find steady customers, so that (working at night) he usually managed to get rid of his marks, no matter how great the quantity, in less than half an hour. The following day, he would sleep late and then consume a substantial breakfast served by his landlady, after which, his wallet bulging with American scrip, he would board a train at eleven o'clock and reach the Mehlstrasse by noon. The Mehlstrasse was as well organized as the New York Commodity Exchange, and considerably more flexible. To the uninitiated it might have looked like nothing more remarkable than a street filled with small groups of exceptionally well dressed DP's who were always standing around arguing, talking, or just waiting; but Paul knew that every corner, every café, was the post of a specialized trading interest, and if he had, say, a good diamond to sell, he would be able to get his price from one group and then buy perhaps a load of flour from another located nearby.

The minute Paul reached the Mehlstrasse, he would grab the first passer-by and ask, *"Was kosten Weiche?"* (What's the price on the dollar?—Dollar bills being known as *Weiche,* "soft money," to distinguish them from the "hard" twenty-dollar gold coins for which there was also quite a demand at one time). If Paul was satisfied with the going rate of exchange on the market he would sell his scrip for dollars, usually at not too large a profit, and then, when he felt the price was right, he would exchange his dollars for German marks and start the circle all over again.

Meanwhile the people who had bought Paul's scrip were forced to travel a somewhat more circuitous route to profit by their dollars. They could neither use the scrip themselves nor redeem it with the American authorities. Because of these difficulties, the usual practice was to work with a high American officer who, for a large rake-off, would pay for the scrip in travelers' checks. Since German banks possessed no foreign currency, the travelers' checks had to be collected into a pool and sent by courier to Switzerland, where they were redeemed—legally and in full—in American dollars. From Switzerland the golden stream of U.S. currency flowed back again to Munich, and the circle began anew.

After getting rid of his scrip, Paul would settle back to his *Schillerlocken* and his *café au lait,* talk, play cards, billiards, or table tennis, kibitz and wait. Wait for what? For business, gossip, pleasure, or for nothing in particular; it did not really matter. He was well fed, he had plenty of money, and he was surrounded by his friends.

The world of the Mehlstrasse in those days was fascinating to watch. There were small fly-by-night operators like Paul and his friends, and there were the big guns who had the capital to buy truckloads of American cigarettes that had been sent over for sale in Austria, divert them to Munich, and fix the police all along the line. There were confidence men, and there were fixers with connections in the police and the customs. There were thieves, hold-up men, and informers, along with two distinct types of gangsters: the so-called *"Blattes,"* wily veterans in crime who had served time in all prisons of Europe and were famous for their past exploits, as well as the new men, the *"postavchiki,"* who made up in daring what they lacked in experience. There were the indispensable forgers, men who could duplicate with equal facility Polish and Russian passports, British transit permits, American military passes, German ration books, and French automobile licenses. There were hordes of deserters from all armies, and there were armies of prostitutes. And all this pullulated in one vast buzzing heap, eating, drinking, making merry and, for a change, watching others starve.

There were many in those years who starved. One of them was Paul's landlord, a former SS man. For him Paul had devised a special kind of humiliation. He remembered how the SS guards in the concentration camps had taken pleasure in grinding their cigarette butts under their heels and then watching the prisoners dig them out of the dirt. Now, seeing his landlord's greedy look when he smoked, Paul, in turn, took care always to step on his butt. "Still," he says, "I did not smoke them down the way the Germans did and I just stepped on them lightly, I did not grind them under my heel. Also, I walked around with an obsession in those days. Whenever I passed a bakery I had to buy two or three loaves of fresh bread which I could never eat. So I'd give them to the landlady."

But most of the hungry people were those who failed for one reason or another to profit from the black market, or who, on principle, would have nothing to do with it. There were very few of the latter, however, and Paul, remembering the frozen-faced British majors, the high-spirited American colonels, the morose Germans with whom he did business, doubts if there were any at all. Paul is indulgent on this matter; he does not blame the Germans, because they were hungry, and as for the Americans, the English, the French, and the Russians, did not the spoils belong to the victor? He has never volunteered an alibi for himself.

Paul has literally hundreds of stories about life in Munich and every time I hear them they become more elaborate and exciting. His favorite, here cut down to manageable size, concerns the great typewriter "action." It begins with his buddy Shloime "Greps" returning from Paris with the hot news that there was an enormous demand for second-hand typewriters in France (new typewriters could not be obtained anywhere, even on the black market) and that the prices were sky-high owing to the French tariff on German machines. Paul understood immediately that Shloime wanted to smuggle the machines across the German border, and when he heard that Shloime had "found" an old route the Resistance had used to smuggle refugees out of Germany, he declared himself willing to sink capital and time into the enterprise.

The first thing was to get the typewriters. There were none in the

Mehlstrasse and so the two boys—they were hardly twenty-one—began systematically combing Munich for machines. Their best bet, they found, were stores which had sold typewriters before the war and now had switched to other lines. "At first," Paul recalls, "nobody would admit to having typewriters. If they did, we could just have plunked down our marks and walked away with the machines. Don't worry, those Germans were sly, all right. So we let them know we knew the ropes. If the owner was interested he'd turn to his wife and say, 'So, *Muttchen,* what do you think?' and she'd answer, *"Ach ja, Vati,* maybe the *Herr Professor* from across the street would be interested. What are the *Herren* offering? The *Herr Professor* is very partial to coffee.' Then we knew we were in, because for genuine coffee, *Bohnenkaffee,* and for real butter those Germans would sell their souls, not to mention their typewriters. When we came back the following day, sure enough, there'd be our machine. Sometimes it was as good as new, you could see it had lain in the store's cellar all through the war; and sometimes it looked pretty beat up and I guess it really came from the *Herr Professor* across the street. It made no difference to us. We gave them about twenty dollars worth of coffee we had gotten in the Mehlstrasse and beat it."

When they had collected a dozen machines, Paul and his friend would crate them in wooden boxes and send them as baggage by rail to a German town near the French border. Boarding the same train, they would claim the "baggage" on arrival and leave it with a friendly hotel owner. In the evening, as soon as it was dark enough, they would hire a truck and transport the stuff to a farm situated very close to the border. There, in the farmer's barn, they would uncrate the machines and put them into rucksacks. At eleven o'clock Shloime and Paul would each strap a rucksack on his back and another on his chest, with a third to be carried by hand. The farmer and one of his friends would then guide them through the woods and over the border, sometimes even carrying the third rucksack for them. On the French side they would leave the machines with another farmer and repeat the trip, bringing across the other six machines. By then it was usually five in the morning and daylight would be approaching.

They would pay the farmers off with flour, about ten or fifteen pounds to each, and start walking to the nearest railroad station. From there they would take the train to Saarbrücken, soon come to terms with a customer, hire another truck, pick up the merchandise, and make the final delivery. Their profits generally amounted to $300, paid in legal U.S. tender. Then with this money they would buy French cognac and smuggle it back to Munich.

"Brother," says Paul gleefully, "we had them coming and going. But remember, it was not always so easy. One time the border patrol saw us and started shooting. *Mame zisse,* I thought my last moment had come. The farmers, those cowards, took off like hares while we were weighed down with those damned machines. Boy, we lay there in that dark forest and prayed for all we were worth while the bullets flew past us. Luckily, the patrol had no dogs with them and couldn't find us."

For a while business flourished and Paul and Shloime had to take in four partners, each of whom specialized in a different phase of the enterprise. In the end two of the gang were caught and put in jail for six months. Paul, who had retired from the actual smuggling before that, now decided to leave the business for good, but not before salvaging as much as he could of the last, unsuccessful shipment of thirty typewriters. These, his connections had told him, had been shipped back by the French to Munich. With extreme trepidation he walked one day into the railroad station to claim his crates. But when the clerk asked him to wait a minute, he smelled a rat, walked quietly to the men's room, dove out of the window, and ran home as fast as his legs could carry him. There was now only one way of recovering the typewriters: to contact the police fixer—quite a job in itself, involving numerous intermediaries and mysterious telephone calls—and to make a deal with him. The fixer's terms were stiff: a fifty-fifty split. To this day Paul gets mad when he talks about that part of it, but then he resigns himself once more. "A choice I had?" he asks rhetorically. "Listen, when those guys get you, you have to pay through the nose. But it was worth it. Imagine, this guy took me right to police headquarters and two cops in uniform brought out my crates and loaded them straight on the truck. Yes, that's how we did business in Munich in those days," and he throws his head back and cackles gleefully.

Play, if one takes Paul's word for it, was only a little less sensational than business. "Listen," he once told me, "when we came back from a trip we lived like kings. We went to the finest night clubs, the Regina Palast, Deutsches Theater, and ate caviar and drank champagne. We were the biggest sports in town and doormen and headwaiters couldn't do enough for us."

After one listens to Paul's big stories, the photographs he offers in evidence come as a distinct disappointment. True, the studio portraits show his good profile and display him carefully posed, gazing soulfully into the distance, but the snapshots are less impressive. Is this anxious little huddle of boys really the intrepid band of smugglers, is this mean-looking little sharpie really the legendary Shloime "Greps"? And Paul himself, how small he seems against the giant ruins of the destroyed city! And when I press for details in his stories, Paul will admit, though reluctantly, that the daily routine was by and large pretty prosaic, while some of his friends will declare roundly that it could become quite dull and that their entertainment, and their occupation, for weeks on end consisted of nothing but billiards, table tennis, and cards. There was a great deal of nervous drinking, especially during the later years, when the black market became more hazardous and the German police and the American CIC more efficient. Life was then one unending round of killing time, hanging around street corners, sitting in cafés or poolrooms, waiting for business. There was always room for business, even at night in the night clubs.

But however important business was, and the things its profits bought, there was one thing more important, the only one, I sometimes get the impression, that really mattered: the fact that the boys always worked together. Again and again this note of solidarity, of unquestioned loyalty is sounded in the stories. Jasha, one of Paul's oldest friends, once said to me, "I always want to be surrounded with Jews; let me be with Chaim, Shmiel, and Yankel, and I'll be happy." And Paul, in one of his rare introspective moods, explained. "You must understand that when we left Buchenwald we were just like a bunch of sheep. We had been told for so long what to do, we just could not do anything individually, we had to do everything together. And remember, too, we had nobody else, no parents, no family, no country even, just each other, and we stuck together in good times as we had in bad. And one more thing: remember we were still surrounded by Germans and what they had done was always with us. We did business with them, we lived in their houses, but we never trusted them and they never liked us. It was like being on an island by ourselves. Some of the boys fell in love with German girls and married them, but I never could forget that the only people I belonged to were those guys in the Mehlstrasse." Thus the years from 1945 to 1949.

Today Paul is still waiting and he is still with his friends. One can see them, when the weather is good, standing in small groups on Broadway and 96th Street, talking volubly in Polish and Yiddish, or silently watching the stream of humanity push past them day and night. Their world is bounded by the cafeteria, the poolroom upstairs, the Chinese restaurant on the next block, and the nearby hotels where they take furnished rooms by the week. Since they came to this country in 1949—about the time when the black market declined—their mode of living has not changed essentially; a certain number may have settled down to steady jobs and marriage—indeed quite a few had done so earlier in Germany—but there remains a small hard core whose roots are sunk into 96th Street and nowhere else.

When Paul arrived here at the age of twenty-four, very little of his European "earnings" was left. His education had ended when he was fourteen, he had no skill of any kind, and he knew only a hundred or so

English words, picked up largely in his dealings with the American troops. Most of the older immigrants coming over with him were content to take jobs as stock clerks, machine operators, and the like, hoping to work themselves up as so many had done before them; but unlike them, Paul had never held a steady job or known responsibility. Nor had his life been one to encourage the habit of planning in advance. Having always lived for the day, he now lacked the patience and foresight to endure a dull and badly paid job for the sake of possible future advancement.

It is unlikely that these considerations presented themselves to Paul as clearly as this; most probably, he simply drifted along with his friends, just as he had done in Munich, and took up the kind of employment that they had found most congenial—working in the Jewish resort hotels of Lakewood, the Catskills, and lately, Florida. Paul started in as a busboy, but when he grew used to the work and picked up enough English, he became a full-fledged waiter. And a waiter he has continued to be and apparently will remain. Off season he returns to 96th Street.

And so his life has taken on a curiously split character; each half has its own locus, its own routine and, above all, its own sense of time, so disparate and so peculiar to itself that the two spheres do not seem to touch except in the singular personality which shuttles to and fro between them.

Away from 96th Street, up in the resorts of the Catskills or down in the hotels of Lakewood during the winter, the work is back-breaking and nerve-racking, the food for the help by and large of inferior quality, the living conditions callously sub-standard, and time itself brutally chopped into pieces by the meat-cleaver hands of the kitchen clock.

Paul is up at seven amid a crowd of weary and sullen waiters, in some hotels squeezed ten to fourteen into a dormitory room jammed with double-decker beds, a few closets, an abundance of trunks, and heaps of soiled underwear and comic books. His working day begins at eight when the dining room opens for breakfast, and rarely ends before nine at night. He may get out for some fresh air between breakfast and lunch, though frequently he does not. He is free for three hours between lunch and supper, but all the rest of the time—seven days a week for more than ten weeks—he is working, often at top speed and to the point of physical and nervous exhaustion.

To and fro he runs, lugging the monstrously heavy trays, the sweat pouring over his face, out of the air-conditioned dining room and into the broiling kitchen filled with hurrying, screaming waiters, himself screaming at the cooks, fellow waiters, busboys; always hustling, dodging trays, picking up food, and racing out of the pandemonium back into the dining room, dishing out the food, apologizing to guests when the kitchen has run out of certain items. Almost all waiters are tense while they work, but Paul always hovers on the edge of panic. His eyes bulge, he mutters to himself while he runs along, he forgets orders and rushes back to the kitchen like a man possessed. If traffic gets too busy and he has to wait in line for soup or meat, he is apt to lose his head and to push aside whoever is in front of him. Then there are noisy arguments, recriminations, and, when everything has cooled down, apologies.

Paul's free time is limited. In the afternoon he goes down to the hotel swimming pool for an hour, but stays out of the water. Not a good swimmer, he is too vain to be seen doing anything at which he does not excel. He sits around for a while, exposes his flabby, oil-smeared body to the sun, and then gets a nap. At night many of the younger waiters go dancing in the "casino," as the entertainment and dance halls belonging to the hotels are called, but Paul is usually too spent and prefers to drive into town with a couple of like-minded boys for a hot pastrami sandwich and a cup of tea. The ensuing bull session concerns girls, sports, jazz, and the dining room. Paul is an expert on all these topics and ever since he acquired some fluency in English he has invariably monopolized the conversation. He simply out-shouts and out-talks his companions. But what really gets the other fellows to listen is a certain caustic quality in his speech, a sharpness of wit still not quite perfectly translated into English, and the habit of putting his audience on the defensive by a series of sweeping attacks on American mores.

In the end, however, the conversation always returns to the dining room. At that hour of the night weary waiters, waitresses, and busboys sit in snack bars, all-night diners, and restaurants all over the mountains and tell each other the troubles of their day. The air is full of smoke and of "so I says to him" and "he says to me" and round and round it goes, over and over again. But they never tire of it. When Paul and his friends have gotten everything out of their system, they leave the waitress a disproportionately large tip and go back to their dormitories; sometimes they fall asleep immediately, but at other times dice and poker games are on in the hotel, and their uneasy sleep will be disturbed by bright lights and loud arguments.

This, however, is only one side of Paul's life, the side in which he is not truly himself, or only intermittently so—panicking in the kitchen, hustling customers, or soliloquizing at night. His real life begins with his return to the city, when he blossoms once again into a personality, when he is once again a *mentsh*. His first appearance on 96th Street would be worthy of an actor. He'll quietly approach a gossiping group, give the man nearest him a resounding whack on the shoulder, and start cursing him in Yiddish and Polish. *"Behemeh!"* he'll scream, *"meese chaye,"* and launch into a stream of oaths which are accepted in the spirit offered, a virtuoso performance expression the joy of return and fraternal solidarity. Then he will flash a roll of several hundred dollars and drag somebody down to Phil Kronfeld's to help him choose a new winter wardrobe.

Paul loves company and he will give anything to be admired; what better opportunity to satisfy both these needs than when buying several hundred dollars worth of sharp clothing? Round and round he'll turn in front of the haberdasher's triple mirrors, stretch out his chin, admire himself front, side, and back, and spend a fortune. He will buy flashy sport jackets costing \$75 each, Italian silk suits at \$150, shoes at \$30 a pair, custom-tailored shirts, hand-painted ties, cashmere overcoats setting him back, as he would say, "two yards" (\$200).

On the other hand, he is not particularly concerned about his lodgings and he may float around for several weeks, spending a few days with a relative in Brooklyn, a fortnight with some friends in the Bronx, or, if he finds travel companions but not otherwise, he may go to Miami for a month. After a while, he usually settles with a friend into a furnished room in one of the hotels around 96th Street, and there spends the time between working seasons.

Paul's life in New York, freed from the tyranny of the kitchen clock, is deliberately sluggish and aimless. Appointments are made for "sometime in the afternoon" or "after supper" and the place is left equally vague, "around 96th," or "ask anybody, they'll tell you where I am."

Paul and his friends seldom go to sleep before two or three in the morning, and rarely get up before noon. Then they will make themselves coffee on a hot plate in their rooms, and spend the next few hours reading magazines. At about three o'clock they begin flocking to the cafeteria from hotel rooms and furnished apartments all over the neighborhood. They may go upstairs to the poolroom and while away the afternoon kibitzing or playing pocket billiards. Paul playing pool is quite a different person from the panicky dervish of the Catskill kitchens. Impeccably dressed, he makes the very picture of a gentleman sportsman. When he picks up the cue stick reserved especially for him, the noisy, dingy poolroom with its green tables and cold fluorescent lights, the cries of the players and the clack-clack of the balls, even the chatter of his partner, all fall away into silence. He inclines his head, squints his eyes, and bends slowly over the table; suddenly his stick darts out with lightning speed, the ball shoots forward like a bullet, hits another ball, and drops it into a pocket. Point!

The afternoon passes and then the evening and nothing really happens. When not playing billiards or ping pong (a game at which he is also a near master) Paul sits around kibitzing. When he gets hungry he goes down to the cafeteria or to the Chinese restaurant down the street.

At night in warm weather he'll stand outside with his *landsleit,* but he is too nervous to stay put for long, and sooner or later he will take one of the boys by the arm and walk him along Broadway. Paul suffers from insomnia, and these nocturnal wanderings can last till three in the morning.

At 1 or 2 A.M., when The Senator closes, those of the gang not otherwise engaged move across the street to one of the all-night cafeterias, filled at that hour with shabbily dressed men and women without a place to sleep, elderly insomniacs, quiet drunks, and tired street walkers. Paul does not bother much with the latter, although he knows a great number of them by name and is as knowledgeable about their various specialties as he is about everything else. By and large, Paul is wary of women; sometimes he goes to one of the German clubs in Yorkville where he can sit down, have a beer, and ask a girl to have a drink with him. He stays away from American girls, though; he does not trust them and apparently has never known one for whom he could feel any affection. For that matter, he seems not to have had any special feelings for his German girls either; in fact, it is remarkable how few his flesh-and-blood loyalties really are.

There is his dead brother's German wife, now living in Brooklyn, to whom he is very devoted—and there are the boys on 96th Street. But even on 96th Street Paul's attachment is more to the group as a whole than to any one individual. To be sure, at a given time he will be on particularly good terms with one fellow, room and work with him, but the friendship will rarely outlast the year. In a relatively short time they will have got on each other's nerves, and the following year Paul will have a new best buddy. The same seems to hold true for the others of the group; its composition may change, relations within it be upset, yet the group as a whole maintains its coherence.

Withal, it is a very matter-of-fact and unsentimental association and one whose members are singularly devoid of illusions about one another. It is based to a large extent on practical considerations. Whether one of the boys is looking for several thousand dollars for a business venture or a couple of bucks for the week; whether he needs a job or a room, witnesses for his naturalization, advice on compensation claims against the German government, or information on business conditions in Europe, he will find them on 96th Street. But apart from this and apart from the social aspect of it, the pleasure of talking in one's native tongue to friends beset by the same problems; apart from their need to belong somewhere, and apart from the habit of so many years, what binds these men together ultimately are the memories and, perhaps more importantly, the attitudes of the time when they stood all alone against a world which had marked them for destruction, when there was nobody, neither family nor society, who could help them, and when all they had were those who now stand next to them on 96th Street—or, more precisely, those others like them who died on the way.

In the years that have passed since that time the world has changed, but they cannot believe that it has. Is it any wonder that their first impulse is to distrust, that they always expect the worse, that they are never entirely at ease with a Gentile, and remain suspicious of American Jews so determinedly integrated in non-Jewish life? Perhaps if Paul and his friends had been thrown individually into the "melting pot," their need to belong would have broken down the barriers inside them, and they might at least have become part of the American Jewish community. As it was, they brought over a ready-made community of their own, *eigene mentshen,* and so had no need to make the effort of reaching across, or the readiness to grow into those new attachments of family and community which would have enabled them to achieve more normal lives. And so it is their ultimate misfortune that the finest thing they have ever experienced, their solidarity, should stand between themselves and growth and maturity.

Now their solidarity, too, is turning sour and sterile, and they constantly bicker with one another. Their present life lacks not only the great and tragic quality which it had in camp, but also the excitement, however spurious, it had in Munich, and it has now degenerated into purposeless waiting, discontent, and fear of the future. What will become of them, what will they be ten, twenty years from now? They don't know, and there is nothing, they feel, that they can do about it.

And yet, for all the emptiness, Broadway and 96th Street is where the only roots they have in this world are found, and so it is on 96th Street that they are most content. Some of the boys have gone back to Europe, but their letters are not sufficiently enticing to tempt the others to follow. There is a great deal of talk on 96th Street about the good old days in Munich and quite a lot of grumbling about the hardships of life in America, but never any spontaneous mention of the concentration camps. When I asked him about this the other day, Paul said, "I no longer think of all that as having really happened, or if it did, that it happened to me. I just can't realize any more that it was really I in that long march to Buchenwald who licked the sooty water off a locomotive to quench my thirst. It seems like something that happened to somebody else."

To see what 96th Street means to them one need only watch Paul after a season in the Catskills as he settles down in the car carrying him home. He turns on the radio and leans forward eagerly. The strong, sad rhythm of jazz floods the car and Paul in a slightly hoarse voice sings the blues along with Count Basie, with the Duke, with King Cole, with the great Satchmo. "April in Paris," the announcer says and Paul closes his eyes, claps his hands and sways from side to side. "One mo' time," he croaks, anticipating the frayed voice in the radio, "one mo' time." Soon, soon, he'll be back with the boys, all together, waiting.

November 1961

Harold Rosenberg

THE TRIAL AND EICHMANN

"In this harsh world draw thy breath in pain to tell my story," the dying Hamlet begged his friend Horatio. Telling can, apparently, require a sacrifice—in Hamlet's view, the supreme sacrifice of remaining alive. Why tell it then? What good will it do? It is a shocking story; to repeat it can only induce bad dreams, particularly in the few survivors of the bloody tragedy. Also, the story is confused and points to no edifying conclusion. For Horatio to accede to Hamlet's appeal, the passion of the friend and the poet must overcome the impulse of the man to seek relief from the past in oblivion.

Human beings, we assume, are entitled to peace of mind, and this privilege ought to be surrendered only if it can be demonstrated that the recalling of miseries will serve some useful purpose—that of social therapy perhaps, or of patriotism, or of progress toward a better world. Thus press reports of the trial of "The Attorney General versus Adolf, the son of Adolf Karl Eichmann" concluded their horrid accounts by arguing apologetically that virtuous ends might be furthered: "It is hoped," ran the refrain, "that bringing these evils to light will prevent anything like them from ever happening again." Dr. Servatius, chief attorney for the defense, asked in his summation that the case be determined in such a way as to "serve as a warning signpost for history" and a contribution to the cause of peace.

But suppose the justification for the telling were inadequate or even absurd? Can one really believe that the Trial of Eichmann will deter mass murderers in the future, or that it will advance international relations? Suppose the only predictable result of recalling the shootings, hangings, and gassings is to arouse fright in the susceptible and to perpetuate in Jews the memory of injuries suffered? To weigh the narration of "The Final Solution of the Jewish Problem" in terms of its probable effects is all but to argue for its suppression. And it is a fact that prominent among those who condemned in advance the proceedings in Jerusalem were representatives of mental health and social amelioration. But even among the supporters of the Trial, who dared squarely to represent the dead? Who dared to assert that the story of their sufferings must be recounted regardless of consequences? Yet is not the right of the victim to have his story told an absolute right?

The Trial undertook the function of tragic poetry, that of making the pathetic and terrifying past live again in the mind. But it had to carry out this function on a world stage ruled by the utilitarian code. One read in the press immediately after Eichmann's capture that, despite international law, he was to be tried in Israel in order to satisfy popular passion there, particularly among the ex-Europeans whose families had perished in the murder program. This was held to be objectionable. In our culture, conditioned by psychiatry to seek "action outlets" for emotions (in disregard of such "outlets" as hearing and contemplating recognized by other societies), the excitement in Israel over the trapped Nazi raised the specter of pathological fixation, vendetta, lynching. What were the enraged Israelis going to do to Eichmann to avenge themselves for the Jewish blood shed by the Nazis? Sermons and warnings poured out from partisans of forgiveness, legality, and scientific objectivity. With the liberal world demanding, "Say what for, or convict yourselves of Nazi-like barbarism," Ben Gurion replied that revenge was out of the question and that the purpose of the Trial was to alert mankind to the dangers of anti-Semitism. Others suggested that the Trial aimed at stimulating Israeli patriotism by reminding the new generation that their fathers could go to their deaths unresisting in a despairing failure of will, but that national independence had brought them the spirit and the means to fight back. With statements like these in mind, Dr. Servatius was able at the end of the Trial to characterize it as a "political case."

Yet all these useful and forward-looking motives, not altogether free of false notes, were but a rationalistic disguise for the irresistible demand for a tragic retelling by multitudes inconceivably brought into the psychic unity of an antique folk by an inconceivable blow, their not-to-be-denied poetic passion to hear related, and before the whole of humanity, the terrible fate of their stricken relatives and ancestors. The Trial was a way of giving public shape to a tormenting memory.

But the need forced upon it to justify itself in terms of its effects was bound to lead to distortions. It is a few of these distortions that I wish to discuss here, it being understood that no criticism is intended of any of the officials concerned with the case; for not only were they under the outside pressure to have the Trial "make sense"; they were obliged also, as we shall see, to participate in incongruities by the legal situation itself.

Had the Eichmann Trial been "a political case," or *only* a political case, it should have been conducted quite differently. Compared, for example, with other show trials of our time, such as the Moscow Trials or the Hiss Case, it reveals few signs of belonging to the same species. In these, the political message was *the* point, and every bit of evidence concerning the guilt of the defendant was organized to hammer that message home. Different as were the procedures of the Soviet People's Courts from those of courts ruled by the Bill of Rights, the offenses charged in each were presented in such a way as to appear less important in themselves than as symbols of conspiracies involving thousands of active, shadowy culprits not present in the courtroom. The trial in each of these cases was a cautionary parable hitting at these hidden enemies; hence it was not necessary that the misconduct alleged should possess the gravity of ordinary crime. Thus the Russians visibly fabricated fables out of police-inspired "confessions"; while our own federal prosecutor, overleaping the statute of limitations in order to reach into a previous decade, won a verdict of perjury by presenting proof of espionage comprising old typewriters, Persian rugs, prothonotary warblers, pumpkins, and other fanciful cuttings from the world between everyday life and mystery literature.

In Jerusalem, by contrast, the actual past was everything, beyond any lesson, and masses of fact were piled into the record for no other reason than that there were people to recount them. Once the testimony concerning the anguish of the Jews began, all forms, whether required for legally upholding an indictment or for "setting signposts for history," became obstacles in the way of the narrative impulse. Everyone with a personal or group tragedy to relate had to be given his day in court as in some vast collective dirge. For almost two months, the defendant and the world heard from individuals escaped from the grave about fathers and mothers, graybeards, adolescents, babies, starved, beaten to death, strangled, machine-gunned, gassed, burned. One who had been a boy in Auschwitz had to tell how children had been selected by height for the gas chambers. The gruesome humor of the Nazis was not forgotten—the gas chamber with a sign on it with the name of a Jewish foundation and bearing a copper Star of David—nor the gratuitous sadism of SS officers. Public-relations strategists everywhere, watching the reaction of the German press, the liberal press, the lunatic-fringe press, listening to their neighbors, studying interviews with men and women on the street, cried out: Too much, too much—the mind of the audience is becoming dulled, the horrors are losing their effect. And still another witness, one who had crawled out from under a heap of corpses, had to tell how the victims had been forced to lay themselves head to foot one on top of the other before being shot. . . .

Most of this testimony may have been legally admissible as bearing on the *corpus delicti* of the total Nazi crime but seemed subject to question when not tied to the part in it of the defendant's Department of Jewish Affairs. Counsel for the defense, however, shrewdly allowing himself to be swept by the current of dreadful recollections, rarely raised an objection. Would not the emotional catharsis eventually brought on by this awfulness have a calming, if not exhausting, effect likely to improve his client's chances? Those who feared "emotionalism" at the Trial showed less understanding than Dr. Servatius of the route by which man achieves the distance necessary for fairness toward enemies. Interruptions came largely from the bench, which numerous times rebuked the Attorney General for letting his witnesses run on, though it, too, made no serious effort to choke off the flow.

But there was a contrast even more decisive than a hunger for fact between the Trial in Jerusalem and those in Moscow and New York. In each of the last, the trial *marked the beginning of a new course:* in Moscow the liquidation of the Old Bolsheviks and the tightening of Stalin's dictatorship; in the United States the initiation of militant anti-Communism, with the repentant ex-Communist in the vanguard. These trials were properly termed "political cases" in that the trial itself was a political act producing political consequences. But what could the Eichmann Trial initiate? Of what new course could it mark the beginning? The Eichmann case looked to the past, not to the future. It was the conclusion of the first phase of a process of tragic recollection, and of refining the recollection, that will last as long as there are Jews. As such, it was beyond politics and had no need of justification by a "message."

"It is not an individual that is in the dock at this historical trial—" said Ben Gurion, "and not the Nazi regime alone—but anti-Semitism throughout history." How could supplying Eichmann with a platform on which to maintain that one could collaborate in the murder of millions of Jews *without being an anti-Semite* contribute to a verdict against anti-Semitism? And if it was not an individual who was in the dock, why was the Trial, as we shall observe later, all but scuttled in the attempt to prove Eichmann a "fiend"? These questions touch the root of confusion in the prosecution's case.

It might be contended, of course, that Eichmann in stubbornly denying anti-Semitic feelings was lying or insisting on a private definition of anti-Semitism. But in either event he was the wrong man for the kind of case outlined by Ben Gurion and set forth in the indictment. In such a case the defendant should serve as a clear example and not have to be tied to the issue by argument. One who could be linked to anti-Semitism only by overcoming his objections is scarcely a good specimen of the Jew-baiter throughout the ages. Shout at Eichmann though he might, the

Prosecutor could not establish that the defendant was falsifying the way he felt about Jews or that what he did feel fell into the generally recognized category of anti-Semitism. Yes, he believed that the Jews were "enemies of the Reich," and such a belief is, of course, typical of "patriotic" anti-Semites; but he believed in the Jew-as-enemy in a kind of abstract, theological way, like a member of a cult speculating on the nature of things. The real question was how one passed from anti-Semitism of this sort to murder, and the answer to this question is not to be found in anti-Semitism itself. In regard to Eichmann, it was to be found in the Nazi outlook, which contained a principle separate from and far worse than anti-Semitism, a principle by which the poison of anti-Semitism itself was made more virulent. Perhaps under the guidance of this Nazi principle one could, as Eichmann declared, feel personally friendly toward the Jews and still be their murderer. Not through fear of disobeying orders, as Eichmann kept trying to explain, but through a peculiar giddiness that began in a half-acceptance of the vicious absurdities contained in the Nazi interpretation of history and grew with each of Hitler's victories into a permanent lightmindedness and sense of magical rightness that was able to respond to any proposal, and the more outrageous the better, "Well, let's try it." At any rate, the substance of Eichmann's testimony was that all his actions flowed from his membership in the party and the SS, and though the Prosecutor did his utmost to prove actual personal hatred of Jews, his success on this score was doubtful and the anti-Semitic lesson weakened to that extent.

But if the Trial did not expose the special Nazi mania so deadly to Jews as well as to anyone upon whom it happened to light, neither did it warn very effectively against the ordinary anti-Semitism of which the Nazis made such effective use in Germany and wherever else they could find it. If anti-Semitism was on trial in Jerusalem, why was it not identified, and with enough emphasis to capture the notice of the world press, in its connection with the activities of Eichmann's Department of Jewish Affairs, as exemplified by the betrayal and murder of Jews by non-police and non-party anti-Semites in Germany, as well as in Poland, Czechoslovakia, Hungary? The infamous Wansee Conference called by Heydrich in January 1942, to organize the material and technical means to put to death the eleven million Jews spread throughout the nations of Europe, was attended by representatives of major organs of the German state, including the Reich Minister of the Interior, the State Secretary in charge of the Four Year Plan, the Reich Minister of Justice, the Under Secretary of Foreign Affairs. The measures for annihilation proposed and accepted at the Conference affected industry, transportation, civilian agencies of government. Heydrich, in opening the Conference, followed the reasoning and even the phraseology of the order issued earlier by Goering which authorized the Final Solution as "a complement to" previous "solutions" for eliminating the Jews from German living space through violence, economic strangulation, forced emigration, and evacuation. In other words, the promulgators of the murder plan made clear that physically exterminating the Jews was but an extension of the anti-Semitic measures already operating in every phase of German life, and that the new conspiracy counted on the general anti-Semitism that had made those measures effective, as a readiness for murder. This, in fact, it turned out to be. Since the magnitude of the plan made secrecy impossible, once the wheels had began to turn, persons controlling German industries, social institutions, and armed forces became, through their anti-Semitism or their tolerance of it, conscious accomplices of Hitler's crimes; whether in the last degree or a lesser one was a matter to be determined individually.

What more could be asked for a Trial intended to warn the world against anti-Semitism than this opportunity to expose the exact link between the respectable anti-Semite and the concentration-camp brute? Not in Eichmann's anti-Semitism but in the anti-Semitism of the sober German man of affairs lay the potential warning of the Trial. No doubt many of the citizens of the Third Reich had conceived their anti-Semitism as an "innocent" dislike of Jews, as do others like them today. The Final Solution proved that the Jew-baiter of any variety exposes himself to being implicated in the criminality and madness of others. Ought not an edifying Trial have made every effort to demonstrate this once and for all by showing how representative types of "mere" anti-Semites were drawn step by step into the program of skull-bashings and gassings? The Prosecutor in his opening remarks did refer to "the germ of anti-Semitism" among the Germans which Hitler "stimulated and transformed." But if there was evidence at the Trial that aimed over Eichmann's head at his collaborators in the societies where he functioned, the press seems to have missed it.

Nor did the Trial devote much attention to exposing the usefulness of anti-Semitism to the Nazis, both in building their own power and in destroying that of rival organizations and states. Certainly, one of the best ways of warning the world against anti-Semitism is to demonstrate its workings as a dangerous weapon. Eichmann himself is a model of how the myth of the enemy-Jew can be used to transform the ordinary man of present-day society into a menace to *all* his neighbors. Do patriots everywhere know enough about how the persecution of the Jews in Germany and later in the occupied countries contributed to terrorizing the populations, splitting apart individuals and groups, arousing the meanest and most dishonest impulses, pulverizing trust and personal dignity, and finally forcing people to follow their masters into the abyss by making them partners in unspeakable crimes? The career of Eichmann made the Trial a potential showcase for anti-Semitic demoralization: fearful of being mistaken for a Jew, he seeks protection in his Nazi uniform; clinging to the enemy-Jew idea, he is forced to overcome habits of politeness and neighborliness; once in power he begins to give vent to a criminal opportunism that causes him to alternate between megalomania and envy of those above him. "Is this the type of citizen you desire?" the Trial should have asked the nations. But though this characterization in no way diminished Eichmann's guilt, the Prosecutor, more deeply involved in the tactics of a criminal case than a political one, would have none of it.

Finally, if the mission of the Trial was to convict anti-Semitism, how could it have failed to post before the world the contrasting fates of the countries in which the Final Solution was aided by native Jew-haters—i.e., Germany, Poland, Hungary, Czechoslovakia—and those in which it met the obstacle of human solidarity—Denmark, Holland, Italy, Bulgaria, France? Should not everyone have been awakened to it as an outstanding fact of our time that the nations poisoned by anti-Semitism proved less fortunate in regard to their own freedom than those whose citizens saved their Jewish compatriots from the transports? Wasn't this meaning of Eichmann's experience in various countries worth highlighting?

As the first collective confrontation of the Nazi outrage, the Trial of Eichmann represents a recovery of the Jews from the shock of the death camps, a recovery that took fifteen years and which is still by no means complete (though let no one believe that it could be hastened by silence). Only across a distance of time could the epic accounting begin. It is already difficult to recall how little we knew before the Trial of what had been done to the Jews of Europe. It is not that the facts of the persecution were unavailable; most of the information elicited in Jerusalem had been brought to the surface by the numerous War Crimes tribunals and investigating commissions, and by reports, memoirs, and survivors' accounts. As early as 1952, Gerald Reitlinger's *The Final Solution* had organized into sequence the various phases of the annihilation program and the horrors visited upon different groups of victims. Yet it is questionable that much of this growing body of knowledge entered the general consciousness or even that of many Jews. Even today the Nazi conspiracy is rarely grasped in the various stages and objectives through which it developed as the leaders reacted to world events and tested how far the conscience of a civilization would allow itself to be outraged. For most who lived through this period, the Nuremburg Laws, asphyxiation buses, rabbis scrubbing pavements, boycotts, death marches, the Crystal Night atrocities, gas chambers, are all jumbled together in a vague hurt as of a bruise received in the dark. One still meets people who speak of six million *German* Jews killed. Perhaps no crime in history has been better documented or more vaguely apprehended.

One reason for our ignorance lies in the character and interests of our "communications" media, a subject we cannot enter into here. Another reason lies within ourselves, in the nature of our ideas and of our way of understanding large public occurrences. The scientific temper of our time has so accustomed us to generalize about "forces" and "trends" that we pay little attention to the events themselves, has so accustomed us to look behind the happening for its cause that we give scant notice to the human actors engaged in the doing. The deadliest foe is dissolved into an abstraction; he becomes an instance or a symptom.

But the unfolding of a crime cannot be grasped except through the actions of the perpetrator of the crime. Without Iago, the tragedy of Othello disintegrates into a dream of jealousy. In the absence of the enemy whose complex of assaults was in fact a single continuing attack, the tragedy of the Jews lacked coherence as well as particularity—those shot on the Polish border, gassed at Belsen, seemed, as Dr. Servatius was to suggest they were, but war victims of a different kind. The ordeal of the Jews was fully exposed with the opening of the death camps, but to absorb this knowledge into our experience it was necessary that we confront the image of the assassin and the motive and method of his attack. Only the presence of the enemy could bring all these disparate acts into focus as a thrust against the Jews which they were all but powerless to resist.

One knew, of course, that the ones most directly responsible were Hitler, Himmler, Goering, Heydrich. But when one tried to fix these figures at the center of the fury, they failed somehow to stay in place, less perhaps because they were already dead by the time the entire scale of their deed had risen to view than because killing Jews was only a fraction of their crimes; carried back to the masters of the Reich, the sufferings of the Jews blended with those of the Czechs, the Poles, the Russians, indeed masses of injured throughout the world.

With the seizure of Eichmann there appeared suddenly a living protagonist for *this* crime, a man bound to the misery of the Jews as his specialty, his sole reason for being. The chief of the Department of Jewish Affairs, Sec. IV B4 of the combined Gestapo and SS, was particularly and totally identified with the murder plan in that he had no other role, no status nor stature apart from this single function, that of ferrying Jews to their deaths. Even his comparatively low rank, of which he tried to make so much at his Trial as proving his lack of authority to initiate or avoid decisions, stood as a mark of his complete association with the Jews, in that it reflected the Nazi contempt for them—the power of life and death over the Jews could be put into the hands of a mere lieutenant colonel. With Eichmann in his cage in Jerusalem it was possible for the first time to visualize the massacres that had taken place across the face of Eastern Europe not as disconnected atrocities, like outbursts of violence in an insane asylum, but as a planned and centralized undertaking aimed at the annihilation of all Jews. By his presence, Eichmann removed the crime from the madhouse and situated it in history. Unlike other pogroms, the German atrocity now became part of the chronicle of a great nation, memorable to its members as well as to the Jews.

The Trial was thus a re-enactment of the transports and the camps that brought face to face the main characters of the tragedy. As a medium of dramatic narration, however, a trial has basic shortcomings. These were exaggerated in the unprecedented case of the six million. Characteristics of the judicial form hampered the public telling of the story of the Jews, at the same time that they favored the strategy of the defendant in reducing his culpability to the vanishing point.

The question-and-answer form of a trial examination breaks into fragments the events described by the witness. In the Eichmann case, witnesses were allowed to speak with a minimum of interruption from counsel. But as against this advantage, no witness for the prosecution actually had more than a tiny bit to tell about the gigantic offensive by which he had been overtaken. Nor was any order possible in the series of testimonies by survivors that would fill out the shape of the whole offense. Moreover, of the story received in fragments, the press communicated still smaller fragments, indeed only the minutest samples. Thus once again the world saw a splatter of atrocities but without an active human center. For the first time more than a passing glimpse was gained of the dreadful fate that befell the Jews of Europe, and this was the great contribution of the Trial. But what led to this fate, both in regard to the events that brought it about and the persons in various degrees responsible for it, was still left largely to conjecture.

Another handicap of court procedure is that the bench, unlike the poet or story-teller in his recapture of the specific emotional quality of the event recounted, does its best to bleach out the human coloration of incidents as an impediment to impartial judgment. Like other scientific approaches, the law exaggerates the *neutrality* of what is done: a witness may testify that he saw *X* climb a wall and enter a window but not that he was convinced that *X* intended to rob the apartment—which makes the activity of the robber identical with that of a householder who has lost his key. The law all but invites an Eichmann to describe himself as a "transport officer." No doubt, there is an "objective" ingredient in the actions of men, and it is possible that sequences of actions can organize themselves apart from human intention to bring about a catastrophe. The Greek theater, which emphasized the *fatality* of disaster, compensated for this emphasis by the protests and outcries of the Chorus. In the Eichmann case, the calm of judicial procedure often led to offense, if not outrage; and something comparable to the Greek Chorus was spontaneously brought into being in Jerusalem by survivors of the camps who sprang up in the gallery from time to time to hurl curses at the defendant seated in his block of ice—but these were hastily ejected from the courtroom to quiet the seas of rage, frustration, and anguish that welled up underneath it.

But while order could be restored, the court had no way of rectifying the imbalance between what was being said by the defense and what had been done in the camps. Instead of the grief and horror appropriate to the narration of tragic happenings, the law court establishes an atmosphere of discussion. A trial implies a contest; the very word "defendant" contains the thought that a defense is possible. This in a way regularizes the offense of the accused—even if he is found guilty, it will be within a category of crime known to the law and accepted by it as possessing precedents. As a defendant, Eichmann, had, by definition, a "case."

In keeping with this legal assumption that Eichmann's guilt was a subject of debate, things were discussed that are not discussable. For instance, wasn't it to the advantage of the Jews to be delivered to the gas chambers more efficiently? "It cannot be denied," the defendant testified, "that this orderliness [which he had introduced into the deportations and which speeded them up] was to some extent to the benefit of the people who were deported." Given Eichmann's admissions both before and during the Trial, the reasonable examination of his behavior and motives put things in a grotesque light, as if the judges, the Prosecutor, the spectators, had by their mere presence agreed to cooperate with the defense in respecting its monstrous hypotheses. A kind of black humor was thus precipitated at which one could not allow oneself to laugh. At this Trial, the verdict of which was bound to be incongruous—"how punish one man for six million dead?"—every analytical statement tended to turn into a ridiculous statement and a new insult to any sense of a human order. Taking advantage to the limit of his legal privilege of minimizing his guilt by surgically separating his segment of the action from the whole—"Killing is one thing, but transportation is something else. I had nothing to do with killing"—Eichmann barely stops short of justifying his Gestapo: since he had not personally initiated the Gestapo program, he did no wrong in carrying it out. Here the terminology of debate produces unspeakable assumptions as in a dialogue between dope addicts. Defending his delivery of the Jews to the hangman as conducted in good taste and implying no enmity to Jews, Eichmann takes for granted his right to dispose of Jews by calling attention to ways worse than his of exercising this right, i.e., by brutes and sadists. On testimony as to his having beaten a Vienna community leader, he excuses himself for having lost his temper and enters into a dissertation on his customary gentlemanly manners—until one almost forgets what an infinite grievance and humiliation it was that any Jew, just because he was a Jew, should even have had to talk to this individual. But if for the hunter of women and babies to describe himself, and be described by a respected lawyer, as merely "arranging timetables" is an insane contention, the insanity is not in Eichmann but in the logic of normal trial procedure when applied in this case.

The necessary coolness of a courtroom favored Eichmann—I even venture to propose that counting in advance on the neutral style of the law (duplicated in that creation of law, bureaucracy) contributed to the formation of his character as a Nazi. Was not the detached perspective toward his own part in the Final Solution suggested to him early in his career by the fearful prospect of one day being brought to trial? Detachment and "correctness" constituted his anticipatory defense and made up the "legal personality" that he would present before the bar. "He always told me," testified his friend Dieter Wisliceny, long before Eichmann was caught, "that the most important thing was to be covered at all times by one's superiors. He shunned all personal responsibility and took care to shelter behind his superiors . . . and to inveigle them into accepting liability for all his actions." This Nazi conducted his life of villainy along the lines of the plea he would make years later in the Jerusalem courtroom. In William Shirer's account of Hitler's moves until his assault on Poland, the *Führer*'s entire strategy pivots on preparing points of retreat and disavowal should the policeman's club rap on the door. In Israel, as earlier in the Weimar Republic, the law was confounded by a new problem: that of dealing with a defendant who as part of his preparation for his crime has penetrated the limitations of legal theory in regard to actions inspired by ideological combines, limitations based on the need of the court to define separately the offense of each person brought before it, unless the court itself is prepared to commit itself ideologically by a verdict of criminal conspiracy against the agents of a particular movement.

One of the extreme distortions of the Eichmann Trial was that it presented to the world only the courtroom identity which Eichmann had created over the years for just this courtroom situation, and which he had refined to the utmost in his long months of imprisonment. The self-fascinated ego he had disclosed in Argentina to the Dutch journalist Sassen was kept off the stage. So, too, was one of the conditions that directly contributed to making the murder program possible: the waves of egotistical afflatus that carried the Nazis and Germans of all classes from peak to peak of brutal arrogance after Hitler had begun his triumphal march across Europe. Here again the "Chorus" supplied a correction more revealing than hours of cross-examination to Eichmann's carefully constructed image of the little clerk checking his memos: "But you should have seen him in his SS uniform," cried a voice from the gallery.

To Eichmann, playing the part of defendant supplied a degree of safety and assurance he could obtain in no other way. The longer the Trial went on, the farther removed he became from the reality of his acts, and the more *"unschuldig"* he grew in his own eyes—toward the end he was threatening to wreck the Trial by confessing at random if the Prosecutor pressed him too hard on points that did not coincide with the image he chose to present. In court Eichmann no longer had to reflect on what he had done. He had only to strengthen the defense he had chosen from among those made available by the legal tradition, that of having acted within an unbreakable chain of causes or under the direction of a superior will.

The Trial was held in order to tell the story of the Jews of Europe. But Eichmann passionately desired to tell *his* story—we know that in 1956, no longer able to endure his incognito, he told at length the tale of his life to a stranger he met in a Buenos Aires bar. One may conjecture that being captured by the Israelis was to Eichmann a mixed misfortune. True, his life was put in danger; in return he was given the opportunity to become one of the most memorable figures of this century. What could have meant more to this *"kleiner Mann"* who, above all else, found his anonymity intolerable?

Also, what better moment could have been chosen for Eichmann? Had he been brought to the dock at Nuremberg, he would have been overshadowed by scores of offenders far above him in rank and interest: Reich Marshals, propagandists, diplomats, slave-labor industrialists—gentlemen who spoke in much the same style as Eichmann and even at times looked like him. In my files, for instance, I find a clipping from the New York *Times* dated January 4, 1946, which contains a photograph of a Major General of Police named Otto Ohlendorf testifying before a War Crimes court. Allow for the fifteen years that have elapsed and this youthful-looking man with his earphones is as much like Eichmann as would be two cadets or seminarians. As to manner and character, the *Times* reporter supplied the following:

> The 90,000 lives that Ohlendorf confessed taking at Adolf Hitler's command seemed to rest easily on his conscience. He talked in a matter-of-fact tone, admitting each mass killing as calmly as if the victims had been cattle or sheep. Yet in appearance he is not particularly brutal or inhuman, looking more like a somewhat humorless shoe salesman one might meet anywhere. . . . Ohlendorf

> described the manner in which Jews were rounded up and killed as a man might describe an ordinary business transaction.

When the world had major generals like these to observe, why should it have paid attention to a mere lieutenant colonel?

By 1961, however, the star performers of Nazi frightfulness had vanished, while mankind, after a decade and a half of respite, was prepared to endure a review of the past. Best of all for Eichmann, he was to be tried in Israel—for only among Jews was he first in importance and certain of recognition in the full scope of his former power.

But Eichmann's outlook for immortality was imperiled by one possibility: that the Prosecutor would rest his case after establishing Eichmann's function as the head of the Department of Jewish Affairs and the steps he had taken to carry out that function. By the precedent of Nuremberg, an accomplice in mass murder may earn a capital sentence, though his deeds had been performed in obedience to orders. There would not be much satisfaction for Eichmann in a trial that condemned him for his exact part in the complex of decisions and measures constituting the Final Solution. In a case along such lines he would be liable to maximum punishment yet without being relieved of his anonymity.

Eichmann was, however, able to head off such a trial by the confessions in his preliminary examination. Given his willingness to admit his role in the murder operation, it was plain that an indictment restricted to Eichmann's part in the Final Solution would be met by a plea of guilty—in that event, there would be no trial and the value of Eichmann's capture would be vitiated. There could be a trial only if Eichmann were charged with personal guilt over and above actions incontestably related to his Gestapo functions. In sum, the condition of the trial was that Eichmann's personality should be made central to the question of his guilt.

With this kind of charge Eichmann was prepared to cope. Having mounted the world stage, he would now defend himself, like Hitler before him, as the little man, the put-upon "front soldier," the honest victim of unfair dislike—specifically, in this instance, the "link in the sausage," the "cog in the machine." Seen abstractly—that is, apart from the murder apparatus into which Eichmann had been feeding bodies—this was a defense which the contemporary world could thoroughly appreciate. The Nazi mind is nothing if not "modern"; the strength of Hitler's movement lay in its keenness regarding the perversities of present-day experience and its cynicism in making use of them. Chief among these common perversities is the sense of loss of self and responsibility that comes from functioning in a large organization. Eichmann's defense was designed to appeal to the universal appreciation of the plight of the organization man. Who cannot grasp that one in the middle of a chain of command—a link in the sausage—simply passes down orders he receives from above, without having the power to alter their content or to influence their ultimate effect? Everyone in an organization is in a sense nothing but a "traffic officer," while the directors at the top reach decisions that reflect a collective mind separate from that of each. It is the fictitious being of the corporation that acts, while all the persons in the company are innocent. And this plea of immunity through the corporation is one that sits very well in legal logic; for the corporation, too, like the government bureau, is the creature of the law itself; it is a "fictitious legal entity," set up precisely to supply immunity to the individuals who manipulate its levers. It is not thinkable to be the dispatcher of human shipments to death factories, but by analogy with the clean hands of the office man in charge of shipping fish fertilizer or veal carcasses, it *is* thinkable.

With the cog idea Eichmann was able to play the Nazi double game of the servile hero. He was a nobody acting under orders, but this nobody had to be able, in order to do his gruesome duty, to conquer the creature in himself, with its sentiments, its weaknesses. Eichmann tells how he faltered at the sight of the "fountain of blood," but that had he been ordered to do so, he would have slain his own father. Thus the "cog" becomes the protagonist of an ethical drama, overcoming in anguish his excess of human feeling; in the end he is, in his own eyes, a noble warrior deserving sympathy for his conflicts and sufferings. In sum, Eichmann's defense exemplifies the chicanery of *protected* viciousness with which the Nazis allured the leaders of Germany's industry and armed forces—through the Nazi concept of the cog they would even be able to avoid responsibility for the Nazis.

A cog cannot, of course, be concerned with suffering inflicted by the machine of which it is a part. Eichmann's defense endeavored to associate him with the literary image of an inquisitor so "abstract" that the screams of the victims could not break through his absorption with his gears and timetables. Such an abstract man, however, is authentic only if he also purges himself of any sensitivity to his own pain, like the officer of Kafka's *The Penal Colony* who throws himself into the lethal machine out of fidelity to his idea. But what of a "cog" that is infinitely concerned with staying alive? What of this dedicated agent of death who suddenly shows so much respect for his own mere existence? The efforts pursued by Eichmann following the end of the war to save his skin destroy any credibility that might attach itself to the image of the unwilling slave of orders from above. He executed those orders because he benefited from executing them—his lust to survive belies any surrender of self to the "machine," any transcendence into impersonality. His behavior after the Nazi collapse demonstrates that, like most of his fellow criminals, he gave himself to the *Führer* and the party not as a religious convert gives himself to his cult but as a swindler assumes the discipline of the band. Eichmann in court thus personifies the fraudulence of Nazi alienation. His enterprising self-defense, proving that he committed his crimes for his own advantage, makes him personally guilty of the death of each human being he delivered to the executioner.

Eichmann's distortion of the relation between the individual and the organization and between the follower and his cult gives his defense its typical Nazi character. It is a defense that arises from the very heart of the present-day social juggling with responsibility which the Nazis had translated into the political principle of the all-responsible *Führer* and the strategy of bureaucratic disavowal. Through Hitler, a party and a nation of innocents were created by drawing all into the corporation (all, that is, who were to be allowed to survive). Except for Hitler himself, each of these corporate limbs or organization men could claim before the bar of liberal jurisprudence that as a man he was something other than his actions and opposed to them. In contrast to the necessity imposed upon his behavior by the organization,* his freedom was private, inward, and intangible, and by the preferences of this inner state he would demand to be judged.

Thus to convict Eichmann *totally,* Prosecutor Hausner strove to "restore," as a New York *Times* headline put it, "the arch-killer," to prove Eichmann subjectively an enemy of the Jews, one animated by "bottomless hatred" and "murderous fury" and still devoid of remorse;† while Judge Landau asked Dr. Servatius during the latter's summation: "Do we have anything in the testimony of the accused . . . which shows that he revolted internally against the extermination orders?" But suppose he had "revolted internally" while still continuing to send Jews to the ovens? He did revolt, Dr. Servatius replied, but he was powerless to make his objections manifest. So the issue seemed unresolved—in contrast to the electrical monopoly cases in which the U. S. Federal Judge indignantly cast aside evidence regarding the personal good character of the defendants, as well as the defense of orders from above. For unless the law judges according to the actions of the defendant it risks losing itself in the metaphysics of doing versus being. In the Eichmann Trial, perhaps out of excessive sensitivity to the coercion of individuals by

* It will be recalled that one of the dramatic moments of the Trial came when Eichmann stepped out of his glass cage to defend himself with—an organization chart.

† Hausner's complaint in his summation that Eichmann showed no remorse indicated that the Prosecutor either failed or refused to understand Eichmann's defense: since according to this defense no harm had emanated from Eichmann as a person, but only passed through him as a "link," he had nothing to regret, except perhaps having been imposed upon by the Nazi "error."

impersonal forces, what the defendant had *not* done was allowed to become part of the proceedings, as Hitler had been allowed by the democratic world to talk about not invading Czechoslovakia after he had delivered his ultimatum. But except for being the executive in charge of the Gestapo's Jew-killing department—how careful he was to distinguish the responsibility of this department from that of the Wehrmacht and the Foreign Office!—Eichmann was "a man like everyone else."

By the conditions of his Trial, Eichmann had to be allowed to compete with the survivors in their telling of the story of the Jews of Europe. He had to be allowed his defense, deceitful, absurd, and outrageous as it was. The issue of his subjective guilt was, however, a distraction that ought to have been reduced to a minimum. Why should this self-styled nobody who had hurled into silence so many of the subtlest and most humane intellects of Europe have been permitted to elaborate on each trait of his character, his opinions on all sorts of matters, including Kant's categorical imperative, and his conception of himself as Pontius Pilate and as a "romantic," his reaction to his wife's reading the Bible, his drinking of mare's milk and *schnapps?* One question would have sufficed to complete the formulation of his culpability: "Weren't you the head of Sec. IV B4 of RSHA charged with the extermination of the Jews of Europe, and did you not carry out the function assigned to you to the best of your ability?" Any intimation that one could be *more* guilty than Eichmann after his admission that "I knew that some of the Jews would be exterminated" revealed an intrinsic confusion of values. Regardless of the verdict, the Trial should have affirmed in the most positive terms that absolutely nothing could weigh a hair's-breadth in the guilt of one who had performed with efficiency and zeal the job of deliberately sending innocent men, women, and children to be tortured, shot, and gassed.

Unfortunately, the Israeli Attorney General accepted with the zeal of a courtroom David the challenge of Eichmann to prove his inner viciousness as well as the criminality of his deeds. The world looked to the testimony of Eichmann not for an image of the Fiend but for a clearer and more detailed delineation of the evolution of the Nazi murder plan out of programs of discrimination and expulsion, for information on where the action of the Final Solution began and what each category of its executants had added to it in practice. Instead of light on these matters, it got Eichmann's contest with the Prosecutor, as Mr. Hausner strove by cross-examination, in which shouts of "liar" and heavy sarcasm were met by sour rage, to "break down" the defendant as in an ordinary case of manslaughter or burglary. For twenty-five days the stage was surrendered to this tournament. In the interval the anguish of Auschwitz and Maidanek was forced into the background. Yet in the end the Attorney General, for all his oratory about Eichmann's murdering with "fervor and insatiable lust," was compelled to fall back on the irrefutable charge of his being "involved in a conspiracy to commit crimes against the Jewish people and against humanity . . . and occupying a central position in this conspiracy in its executive stage."

While the story of the mass victim had been shredded into bits by courtroom procedure, the defense was able from first to last to maintain a single, continuing impression: that of the embattled prisoner parrying endless confrontations and questions with itemized explanations of his lack of responsibility. By the time the cross-examination was over, each molecule of the enormous crime had been funneled through Eichmann into a void. Even his style of speech had been used to veil the atrocious reality which the Trial had attempted to communicate: "He seemed," wrote Lawrence Fellows in the *Times,* "to be avoiding wherever possible the use of words like Jews, death, concentration camps. His testimony was shot through with mention of superior orders, and it was immersed in the special jargon of bureaucracy." Eichmann's weeks on the stand had the effect not of breaking him down but of breaking down in the mind of the world audience the outlines, traced with such difficulty, of the Final Solution as a conspiracy of murderous men, and transforming it into an *impersonal process.* Not only was the form of events lost but even their chronology. "Mr. Hausner," Presiding Judge Landau objected at one point, "we discussed Holland and France last week and now we have come back to them again."

Thus there was presented in Jerusalem an indispensable account of the tragedy of the Jews in this era, but it was an account marred in the telling and needing to be gone over and interpreted again and again.

Tadeusz Borowski

THIS WAY FOR THE GAS

A Story

Everybody is naked in the camp. Though the delousing is finished and our clothes are back from the tanks of the Ozone-2 that efficiently kills lice in clothing and humans in ovens. The heat is unbearable. The camp has been sealed off tight so that not a single prisoner, not one solitary louse, can get through the gate. All day long thousands of naked people drag themselves over the paths or lie against the walls and on the roof ledges. The women's camp is being deloused and twenty-eight thousand women have been stripped naked and chased out of their barracks. They are standing together in the yard nearby.

The heat rises, the hours are endless. There have been no new transports for several days. We are without even our usual distraction; the wide roads leading to the crematories are empty.

Several of us sit on the top bunk. We dangle our legs and slice the neat loaves of crisp, crumbly bread. It is a little coarse to the taste, the kind that stays fresh for weeks. Sent all the way from Warsaw; only a week ago my mother held this white bread in her hands . . . dear God, dear God. . . .

We unwrap the bacon, the onion, we open a can of condensed milk. Henri, the fat Frenchman, dreams out loud about French wine brought in with the transports from Strasbourg, Paris, Marseille. The sweat streams down his body.

"Listen, *mon ami,* next time we go on the loading ramp, I'll bring you real champagne. I bet you never had any, what?"

"No, but you can't smuggle it through the gate, so stop kidding. Better try and get me some shoes, the perforated kind, you know, with a double sole, and that shirt you promised a while back."

"Patience, patience, when the new transports come in, I'll bring all you want. We'll be going on the ramp again."

"And what if there aren't any more oven transports?" I say spitefully.

"Can't you see how fast things are thawing out around here—unlimited packages, no more beatings? You write letters home even. . . . All kinds of talk is going around and, dammit, they'll run out of people!"

"Stop talking nonsense." Henri's serious fat face moves rhythmically, his mouth is filled with sardines. We have been friends for a long time but I don't know his last name. "Stop talking nonsense," he repeats, swallowing hard. "They can't run out of people; we'll starve to death in this blasted camp. All of us live on what they bring."

"Not all. We have our packages. . . ."

"Yes, you and your friend and ten other friends of yours. You Poles get packages. But what about us and the Jews and the Russkis? And if we had no food, no supplies from the transports, you think you could eat those packages of yours in peace? We wouldn't let you!"

"You would, you'd starve to death like the Greeks. Around here, whoever has grub, has strength."

"Anyway, you have enough, we have enough, so why argue?"

Right, why argue. They have enough, I have enough, we eat together and we sleep on the same bunks. Henri slices the bread, he makes a tomato salad. It tastes good with mustard. Below us, the naked miserable creatures drenched in sweat plod along the narrow aisles and crowd into the lower bunks in eights and tens. They are naked and thin, stink of sweat and excrement, their cheeks are hollow. Directly underneath me, in the lowest bunk, is a rabbi; he has covered his head with a rag and is reading from a Hebrew prayer book (there's no shortage of this type of literature). He is wailing, loudly and monotonously.

"Couldn't he be shut up? He's been hollering as though he'd caught God himself by the feet."

"I don't feel like moving. Let him holler, he'll go to the oven that much sooner."

"Religion is the opium of the people," Henri, who is a Communist and a rentier, says sententiously. "If they didn't believe in God and eternal life, they'd have torn down the crematories long ago."

"Why don't you do it then?" The question is a rhetorical one, which the Frenchman ignores. "Idiot," he says and stuffs tomato in his mouth.

Suddenly there's a commotion over by the entrance. Below us, they scurry in fright to their bunks. Our block leader walks in with a serious expression on his face.

"Canada*! *Antreten!* Hurry up! A transport is coming!"

"Good God!" yells Henri, jumping down. He swallows the tomato,

* The name (because Canada was supposed to be the land of great riches) used by the camp inmates to designate the storehouses where valuables taken from gassed prisoners were kept; the word was also used for inmates employed around this activity.—Ed.

grabs his coat, shouts *"Raus"* to the prisoners in the lower bunks, and runs to the door. The Canada men are leaving for the loading ramp.

"Henri, the shoes!" I call after him.

"Keine Angst!" he shouts back.

I proceed to put away the food. I tie a piece of rope around the suitcase, pull on my trousers, and scramble down. In the doorway I bump into Henri.

"Allez, allez, vite, vite!"

"Was ist los?"

"Want to come to the ramp with us?"

"Sure, why not?"

"Come along then, take your coat. They're short a few men. I've already spoken to the kapo," and he pushes me through the door.

We line up, someone takes our numbers, someone up ahead calls "March, march," and now we are running toward the gate, accompanied by shouts of a multilingual crowd that is already being pushed back to the barracks. Not everybody has the privilege of going on the ramp. We've almost reached the gate. *Links, zwei, drei, vier! Muetzen ab!* Erect, arms stretched stiffly down our hips, we pass through the gate briskly, smartly, almost gracefully. A sleepy SS man holding a large pad phlegmatically checks us off, marking each five men with a wave of his arm.

"Hundert!" he calls after we have all passed.

"Stimmt!" comes a hoarse shout from out front.

We march rapidly, almost at a run. All around there are guards, young men with machine guns. We pass some deserted barracks, and a clump of unfamiliar green, apple and pear trees. We burst on to the highway, and now we have arrived. A couple of yards more; there, surrounded by trees, is the ramp.

A cheerful little station, typical of many such provincial railroad stops: a small square, framed by tall chestnuts and paved with yellow gravel. Over to the side, by the road, stands a wooden shed; further along are large stacks of old rails, logs, bricks. This is where they do the loading for Birkenau: the supplies for construction in the camp, and the people for the gas ovens.

Now the guards are being posted along the rails, on the logs, in the green shade of the Silesian chestnuts, forming a tight circle around the ramp. They wipe the sweat from their faces and drink from their canteens. It is unbearably hot, the sun stands motionless at its zenith.

"Disperse!"

We sit down in the narrow streaks of shade alongside the stacked rails. The hungry Greeks (several of them managed to come along, God only knows how) hunt under the rails. Someone finds a few pieces of mildewed bread, someone else a few half-rotten sardines. They eat.

"Schweinedreck," spits a young, tall guard with corn-colored hair and dreamy blue eyes, "soon you'll have so much food to stuff in your guts, you'll burst." He adjusts his gun, wipes his face with a handkerchief.

"Now you be careful," Henri says to me. "Don't take any money, they might be checking. Anyway, who the hell needs money, we have enough to eat. Don't take suits, either, or they'll think you plan to escape. Just get a shirt, a silk one, with a collar. And an undershirt. And if you find something to drink, don't bother calling me. I can manage for myself, but you watch your step or they'll let you have it."

"They'll beat us?"

"Sure thing. You have to have eyes in your back. *Arschaugen."*

"Was wir arbeiten?" ask the Greeks nervously, chewing on the moldy bits of bread.

"Niks. Transport kommen, alles Krematorium, compris?"

"Alles verstehen," they answer in crematory Esperanto.

In the meantime the ramp has become more and more bustling, more and more noisy. The crews are divided into those who will open and unload the arriving freight cars and those who are to stay by the wooden steps. Motorcycles drive up, delivering SS officers, bemedaled, glittering with brass, beefy men with highly polished boots and shiny, brutal faces. Some carry briefcases, others hold thin, flexible whips. They greet each other raising an arm, Roman fashion, then shake hands cordially. Some stroll over the ramp; the silver squares glitter on their collars, the bamboo whips snap impatiently.

We lie against the rails and gaze listlessly at the men in their green uniforms, at the green trees, and at the church steeple which is visible from the distant village.

"The transport is coming," somebody says. We rise expectantly. Around the bend, one after another, the cattle cars begin rolling in: the train backs up, a conductor leans out, waves his arm, blows a whistle. The locomotive whistles back loudly, puffs, the train rolls slowly in along the ramp. Through the tiny barred windows, pale, wilted, exhausted human faces appear, tangled hair, terrified women, unshaven men. They gaze at the station in silence as the train slowly passes. But suddenly inside the cars something begins stirring and pounding.

"Water! Air!" come the monotonous, despairing cries.

Faces push at the windows, lips gasp desperately for air. The pressing faces draw a few breaths, then disappear; others come and disappear. The cries and moans get louder.

A man in a green uniform covered with more glitter than any of the others jerks up his head, his lips twist in disgust. He inhales deeply, then with a rapid gesture throws the cigarette away and signals to the guard. Slowly the guard removes the machine gun from his shoulder, aims, sends a series of shots across the train. All is quiet now. Meantime the trucks have arrived, steps are being drawn up, and Canada men stand ready at the train exits. The SS officer with the briefcase raises his hand:

"Whoever takes gold or anything besides food will be shot for stealing the property of the Reich. Understand? *Verstanden?"*

"Jawohl!" we answer unevenly, but eagerly.

"Also los! Begin!"

The bolts crack, the doors open. A wave of fresh air pours into the train. People . . . inhumanly cramped, buried under a terrifying amount of luggage, trunks, suitcases, packages, cases, bundles of every kind (they have brought everything that had been their past and was to start their future). They have been packed into a monstrous heap, have fainted from heat, have suffocated, trampled each other. Now they cluster at the open doors, breathing like fish cast out on the beach.

"Attention, get out. Take your luggage. Take everything. All the stuff must be piled up by the exits. Your coats too. It's summer. March to the left. Understand?"

"Sir, what's going to happen to us?" they jump down on to the gravel, anxious, worn out.

"Where are you from?"

"Sosnowiec, Bedzin, sir. What's going to happen to us?" They repeat the question stubbornly, gazing into our tired eyes.

"I don't know, I don't understand Polish." It's the concentration camp law that those going to their death must be deceived up to the end. This is the only permitted form of charity.

The heat has increased. The sun is directly over our heads, the white-hot sky quivers, the air vibrates, an occasional breeze feels like a sizzling, molten gust. Our lips are parched, the mouth fills with the salty taste of blood. The body is weak and heavy from lying in the sun. Water!

A huge, multicolored wave of people, loaded down with luggage, pours from the train like a wide river that tries to find a new bed. But before they have a chance to come to, before they can inhale some fresh air and look at the sky, bundles are already being snatched out of their hands, coats are pulled off their backs, women's purses and umbrellas are taken away from them.

"But sir, it's for the sun, I cannot. . . ."

"Verboten," one of us barks through clenched teeth, hissing sharply. There's an SS man standing behind one's back, calm, controlled, correct.

"Meine Herrschaften, ladies and gentlemen, don't throw your things around, please. Show some good will," he says kindly; his hands nervously play with the slender whip.

"Certainly, certainly," many voices answer, and now they walk alongside the train a little more cheerfully. A woman bends quickly to pick up a purse. The whip flies, the woman cries out, stumbles and falls under the feet of the surging crowd. A child behind her screams: *"Mamele!"*—a very small girl with tangled black curls.

The heaps grow. Suitcases, bundles, blankets, coats, pocketbooks that open as they fall, spilling coins, gold, watches; mountains of bread pile up at the exits, jars of marmalades, jams; masses of meat, sausages; sugar spills on the gravel. Trucks, loaded with people, start up with a deafening roar amidst the wailing and screaming of women separated from their children and the stupefied silence of the men left behind. They are the ones who had been ordered to step to the right—they are the healthy and the young who will go to the camp. In the end they will not escape the gas ovens, only first they must work.

Trucks go and come, without interruption, as on a monstrous belt. A Red Cross van goes back and forth incessantly: it transports gas, the gas that will kill these people.

The Canada men working at the trucks are not able to stop for a moment even to catch their breath. They push those going to the ovens up the steps, pack them in tightly, sixty in each truck, more or less. A young, clean-shaven gentleman, an SS man with a notebook in his hand, stands on the side; every truck gets one mark in the notebook. When sixteen trucks have gone, it makes one thousand, more or less. The gentleman is calm, precise. No truck can leave without his signal and a mark in his notebook: *Ordnung muss sein*. The marks grow into thousands, the thousands into entire transports; later the transports will be described in a word: "from Salonika," "from Strasbourg," "from Rotterdam." This one will be "Sosnowiec-Bedzin."

The train has been unloaded. A thin, pock-marked SS man composedly peers inside, shakes his head in disgust and motions toward us.

"Rein. Clean this up!"

We climb inside. Scattered in corners among human excrement and lost wrist watches lie smothered, trampled, squashed babies, naked little monsters with huge heads and blown-up bellies. We carry them out like chickens, holding several in each hand.

"Don't take them to the truck, pass them to the women," says the SS man lighting a cigarette. His lighter isn't working properly, he is preoccupied with fixing it.

"Take them, for God's sake!" I blow up when the women run from me in horror, hiding their heads between their shoulders. The name of God sounds strangely pointless, since the babies will go with the women on the trucks, all will go, without exception. We know what will happen, and we look at each other with hate and horror.

"So, you don't want to take them?" says the pock-marked SS man with a note of surprise and reproach in his voice, and he reaches for his revolver.

"You mustn't shoot, I'll carry them." A tall, gray-haired woman takes the little corpses out of my hands and for an instant looks straight into my eyes. "My child, my child," she whispers, and smiles. Then she walks away, stumbling on the gravel. I lean against the side of the train. I am terribly tired. Someone pulls at my sleeve.

"En avant, to the rails, come on!" I look up, but the face swims before my eyes, dissolves, huge and transparent, melts into the motionless trees and the churning crowd. . . . I blink rapidly: Henri.

"Listen, Henri, are we good people?"

"That's stupid, why do you ask?"

"You see, my friend, you see, I am furious, unreasonably furious at these people—that I must be here because of them. I don't feel any pity for them, I'm not sorry that they're going to the gas. Damn them all! I could throw myself at them with my fists. It must be pathological, I can't understand. . . ."

"Ah, on the contrary, it is natural, foreseen, calculated. This job exhausts you, you rebel against it—and the easiest way to relieve your hate is to turn against someone weaker. Why, I'd even call it healthy. It's simple logic, *compris?"* He seats himself comfortably against the heap of rails. "Look at the Greeks, they know how to make the most of it! They stuff their bellies with anything they can lay their hands on; one has just consumed a whole jar of marmalade."

"Swine! Tomorrow half of them will die of the shits."

"Swine? You've been hungry."

"Swine!" I say again furiously. I close my eyes. The air is filled with ghastly noises, the earth trembles under me, I can feel a sticky moisture on my eyelids. My throat is utterly dry. The morbid procession streams on and on—trucks growl like mad dogs. I shut my eyes tight, but I can still see corpses dragged out of cars, trampled infants, cripples piled on top of the dead, wave after wave of people . . . freight cars roll in, the heaps of clothes, suitcases, and bundles grow, people get out, look at the sun, take a few breaths, beg for water, walk to the trucks, drive away. And again freight cars pull in, again people. . . . The scenes become confused in my mind; I am not sure whether all this is happening, or whether I am dreaming. There's humming inside my head, I feel that I must vomit.

Henri touches my arm. "Don't sleep, we must load up the loot."

Now all the people are gone. In the distance, the last few trucks roll along the road in clouds of dust, the train has left, several SS men promenade stiffly along the ramp, the silver glitters on their uniforms. Their boots shine, their red, beefy faces shine.

We start loading the loot. We lift heavy trunks, toss them up with an effort into the trucks. There they are arranged in stacks, packed tightly. One of the trunks falls open, suits, shirts, books drop out on the ground. . . . I pick up a small, heavy package. I unwrap it: gold, about two handfuls; bracelets, rings, pins, diamonds.

"Gib hier," calmly says an SS man holding up his briefcase full of gold and colored foreign currency. The gold will go to the Reich.

It is hot, terribly hot. Our throats are dry, every word hurts. Oh, anything for a drink of water! Faster, faster, let's get it over with so we can rest. At last we are done, all the trucks have gone. Now we quickly clean up the remaining transport dirt, "so there'll be no traces left of the *Schweinerei."* But just as the last truck disappears behind the trees and we go—finally!—to rest in the shade, a shrill whistle sounds over the bend. Slowly, terribly slowly, the train rolls in, the engine answers with a deafening shriek; weary, pale faces at the windows, flat, as though cut out of paper, with huge, feverishly burning eyes. Already trucks are pulling up, already the calm gentleman with the notebook is here, and SS men emerge from their canteen carrying briefcases for the gold and money. We open the train doors.

It is impossible to control oneself any longer. Brutally we yank suitcases from people's hands, impatiently pull off their coats. Go on, go on, vanish. They go, they vanish. Men, women, children. Some of them know.

Here's a woman—she walks quickly, but tries to appear calm. A small child, with a pink cherub's face, runs behind her and unable to catch up stretches out his little hands and cries: "Mummy! Mummy!"

"Pick up your child, woman!"

"Sir, it's not my child, it's not mine!" she shouts hysterically and runs on, covering her face with her hands. She wants to hide, she wants to get to those who will not ride the trucks, those who will go on foot, those who will live. She is young, healthy, good looking, she wants to stay alive. But the child runs after her, wailing very loudly: "Mummy, mummy, don't run away!"

"It's not mine, not mine, no!"

But she is already caught by Andrei, a sailor from Sebastopol. His eyes are glazed from vodka and the heat. With one powerful blow he knocks her off her feet, then seizes the falling woman by the hair and drags her up again. His face is distorted with fury.

"Ah you, bloody Jewess! So you're running away from your own child! I'll fix you, you whore!" His big arm chokes her, he lifts her in the air and tosses her up on the truck like a heavy sack of grain. "Here! Take this with you, bitch!" and he throws the child at her feet.

"Gut gemacht, good work, that's the way to deal with unnatural

mothers," says the SS man standing at the foot of the truck. *"Gut, gut Ruski."*

"Shut your mouth," growls Andrei through clenched teeth and walks away. From under a pile of rags he pulls out a canteen, unscrews it, takes a few deep swallows, passes it to me. The strong alcohol burns the throat. My head swims, my legs are shaky, again I feel like throwing up.

And suddenly, above the teeming crowd pushing forward like a river driven by an unseen power, there appears a girl. She hops lightly from the train onto the gravel, looks around inquiringly, like one who is very much surprised at something. Her soft, blond hair has fallen on her shoulders in a torrent, she throws it back impatiently. With an automatic gesture she pulls her hands along her blouse, casually straightens her skirt. She stands this way for an instant, then her gaze leaves the crowd and glides along our faces, as though searching for someone. Unconsciously I continue to stare at her until our eyes meet.

"Listen, listen, tell me, where are they taking us?"

I look at her. Here, standing before me, is a girl—a girl with enchanting blond hair, with beautiful breasts, in a little cotton blouse, with a wise, mature look in her eyes. She stands here, looking straight into my face, waiting. And over there is the gas oven: communal death, disgusting and ugly. And over there is the concentration camp: the shaved head, the heavy Soviet trousers in sweltering weather, the sickening, stale odor of dirty, damp female bodies, the animal hunger, the inhuman labor, and later the same gas oven, only an even more hideous, more terrible death. . . .

"Why did she bring it, they'll take it away from her anyway," I think to myself, noticing a lovely gold watch on her delicate wrist.

"Listen, tell me?" she repeats.

I do not answer. Her lips tighten. "I know," she says with a shade of proud contempt in her voice, tossing back her head; she walks resolutely toward the trucks. Someone tries to stop her; boldly she pushes him aside and runs up the steps. I can only catch in the distance a glimpse of her blond hair as it flies in the breeze.

I go back inside the train, I carry out babies, I unload luggage. I touch corpses, but I can't overcome the mounting, uncontrollable terror. I try to run away from them, but they are everywhere: lined up on the gravel, on the cement edge of the ramp, inside the freight cars. Infants, hideous naked women, men twisted by convulsions. I escape as far as I can go, but immediately a whip falls across my back. Out of the side of my eye I can see an SS man, swearing profusely. I stagger forward and run, lose myself in the Canada group. Now, at last, again we can rest against the stack of rails. The sun has leaned deeply over the horizon and is illuminating the ramp with a reddish glow. In the silence that settles over nature at this time of day, the human cries and groans seem to rise ever more loudly to the sky.

Only from this distance can one have a full view of the inferno on the teeming ramp. There are two human beings who have fallen to the ground locked in a last desperate embrace. The man has dug into the woman's flesh and holds on to her clothing with his teeth. She shouts hysterically, swears, cries, until at last a large boot comes down over her throat and she is silent. They are pulled apart and dragged like animals to the truck. Here are four Canada men, carrying a corpse: a huge, swollen female body. Swearing, wet from strain, they kick out of the way some stray children who have been running all over the ramp and howling like dogs. The men pick the children up by the collars, heads, arms, and toss them on the heaps in the trucks. They collect big swollen puffed-up corpses from all over the ramp, pile on top of them the invalids, the semi-smothered, the sick, the unconscious. The mountain of corpses seethes, howls, groans. The driver starts the motor, the truck begins rolling.

"Halt! Halt!" yells an SS man. "Stop, damn you!" An old gentleman, dressed in tails and wearing a band on his arm, is being dragged toward the truck. His head knocks against the gravel and stones, he groans and wails monotonously and continually: *"Ich will mit dem Herrn Kommendanten sprechen*—I wish to speak with the commander. . . ." With senile stubbornness, he keeps repeating this all the way. Tossed up on the truck, trampled by others, choked, he moans still: *"Ich will mit dem. . . ."*

"Quiet, old man!" shouts a young SS man, laughing loudly. "In half an hour you'll be talking to the highest commander! Only don't forget to say *Heil Hitler* to him!"

Others are carrying a little girl without a leg; they hold her by the arms and the one remaining leg. Tears are running down her face, she whispers softly: "Sir, it hurts, it hurts. . . ." They throw her on the truck, on top of the corpses. She will be burned alive with them.

The evening has arrived, cool and clear. We lie against the rails—it is incredibly quiet.

"Did you get the shoes?" asks Henri.

"No."

"Why?"

"My God, man, I've enough, absolutely enough!"

"Already? After a first transport? Just think, I . . . since Christmas, at least a million people have passed through my hands. The worst are the transports from around Paris: one always meets friends."

"And what do you tell them?"

"That they're going to have a bath, and then we'll meet at the camp.

What would you tell them?"

I do not answer. We drink coffee mixed with alcohol.

"Henri, what are we waiting for?"

"There'll be another transport."

"When it comes, I'm not going to unload it. I can't take any more."

"It's gotten you down, what? Nice Canada?" Henri grins amiably and disappears in the dark. In a moment he is back. "All right. Just sit here quietly. I'll try to find you your shoes."

"Don't bother me about the shoes." I want to sleep. The night is dark.

Again there's a whistle, another transport. Freight cars emerge from the darkness into a small circle of light on the ramp. Somewhere the trucks are growling. They back up to the steps, black, ghostlike. *Wasser! Luft!* The same all over again, like a late showing of the same film: a series of shots, the train is silent. But now a small girl leans out from a window and, losing her balance, falls over on the sand. She lies for a moment without moving and then rises and begins walking around in a circle, faster and faster, waving her stiff arms, breathing spasmodically and howling in a thin voice. She has lost her mind in the crowded train. This is hard on the nerves, so an SS man runs up and kicks her between the shoulders with his large boot. She falls. Holding her down with his foot he draws out a revolver, shoots once, then the second time: she remains on the ground kicking the dirt with her feet until she stiffens. The train doors are being opened.

Again I stand at the exits. A warm, sickening smell gushes from the inside. The mountain of people filling the cars almost to the ceiling is motionless, horribly tangled, but still steaming.

"Ausladen!" comes the voice of an SS man who has walked into the circle of light. "Why are you standing like sheep? Start unloading!" His whip flies and falls on our backs. I seize the hand of a corpse: the fingers close tightly around mine. I pull back with a scream and stagger away. My heart pounds, jumps up to my throat. I can no longer control the nausea. Hunched under the train I begin to vomit. Then, like a man drunk, I weave over to the stack of rails.

I lie against the cool, kind metal and dream about returning to the camp to be with my friends who are not going to the gas ovens tonight. The lights on the ramp flicker with a spectral glow, the people walk on and on, endlessly, swarming, stupefied, anxious. They believe that now they must face a new life in the camp, and they prepare themselves emotionally for a hard struggle ahead. They don't know that in just a few moments they will die, that the gold, money, and diamonds which they have so prudently hidden in their clothing and on their bodies is now useless to them.

It is almost finished. The dead are being cleared off the ramp and loaded into the last truck. Canada men, carrying heavy loads of bread, marmalade, sugar, etc. are lining up to go. For a few days the whole camp will live on this transport. For a few days the whole camp will talk about the "Sosnowiec-Bedzin." The "Sosnowiec-Bedzin" has been a good, rich transport.

The stars are already beginning to pale as we walk back to the camp. The sky becomes translucent and lifts higher over our heads—it is getting light.

Great columns of smoke rise from the crematories and merge up above into a huge black river which very slowly floats through the sky over Birkenau and disappears beyond the forests in the direction of Trzebinia. The "Sosnowiec-Bedzin" transport is already burning.

We pass an SS detachment marching with machine guns to change guard. They step briskly, evenly, shoulder to shoulder, one mass, one will. *"Und morgen die ganze Welt. . ."* they sing at the top of their voices.

"Rechts ran! To the right march!" comes a command from up ahead. We move out of their way.

Translated from the Polish by Barbara Vedder

II

EAST AND WEST

May 1960

David Bergelson

STORY'S END

A Story

This new room—I got it through the State Housing Agency—will be my salvation. I feel it in every bone of my body—here's where I write my first strong, solid piece.

Material? The fascinating apartment itself.

I'm tremendously excited. Now I stop being a beginner and make a name for myself.

I felt it the very day I moved in. I inspected every nook and cranny of the apartment. Everywhere I smelt a special odor, the perfume peculiar to a certain kind of woman. I began trying to track down the source of that odor. I caught a glimpse of my neighbors on either side. What a piece of luck! Fellow novices, what fools you are! No writer springs full-grown from Minerva's forehead. It's simple: to begin, dig up good material. Meet life face to face—the way I'm doing in this apartment.

The first person I became acquainted with was Eli Krisman. He's a compositor in a printing shop. He calls himself a Communist, but I don't believe him. If it was up to me, I might let him be a candidate for the party—or perhaps not even that. At any rate, he talks to me about Communism as though it were a matter of habit—he's really indifferent. There's a red Japanese fan hanging on the wall of his room, framed by a pair of mandolins and a guitar. The point about Krisman is that he's a fanatic about cleanliness. He spends his day off polishing his shoes, for no good reason that I can make out.

Here's how I'll start my story:

"He acts exactly like a married man without a wife."

My other neighbor (in the room on my right) is a very fat, smallish, pale young fellow. His face has the yellowish color of white bread that has risen satisfactorily after being well kneaded—the consistency of noodle dough. You might put his age at anywhere between nineteen and thirty-three. His name is Jonah Maskileyson—a name as pimply as his face.

I find him very suspect. He seldom steps out of his room. On the other side of the wall between our rooms, I often hear him pulling some very heavy object out from under his bed. He opens it, removes something, puts it back. Then he walks around his room, very deliberately. I need only cough or take one step for Maskileyson to grow frightened. He quickly pushes the heavy object back under his bed and then is very quiet for a while, as though out of breath.

Once I met him in the hall afterward, and asked him where he hailed from. He turned bashful. It was a long time before he could answer. Finally, he smiled, and said: "But where should I hail from? Begging your pardon, I'm from Priluk."

I didn't understand the necessity for the smile. As for his "begging your pardon," I was reminded of an old woman I once heard say, "Tt-tt, the bus, begging your pardon, has already left."

But my main subject will be the young woman who used to own this apartment. Everything about her—her body, her face—is sinful. At a guess, she's thirty-two.

She lives in the room to the left of mine, down the hall. The hall is dark. Suddenly, you go down two unexpected steps. You feel your way. There's a heavy cloth drape hanging in front of her door—either green or blue, it's so dark, you can barely see.

And then, all at once, you smell it: the odor of perfume, powder, all kinds of cosmetics. It sets you thinking of a pretty woman, a glorious rendezvous. Drape, perfume, darkness, all hint at the creature comforts waiting on the other side of the door.

The door opens.

Your first view: Persian rugs. Low, soft, upholstered furniture. Gobelins on the wall. Japanese screens around the wide, wide bed. White fur.

Then your eyes roam about. You see varicolored silk pillows. Pillows on the sofas and on the big soft chairs. Pillows everywhere.

And in a corner, a dazzling pair of high-heeled slippers, very pointed. Also, the strings of a discarded corset.

In the opposite corner, the slender figure of the landlady, sitting.

There's something wrong about her: the scar on her neck—short but quite deep. It could be the vestige of a childhood operation. Or it could be a memento from the time one of her lovers attacked her with a knife. (I really am not obliged to wrack my brains over *that.*) But after I return to my room, the one thing I remember is the scar—it's a warning not to confuse her with any other woman. Afterward, I remember the rest of her.

There's a black spot at the left corner of her wide, blood-red, sweet-tooth lips. The rouged spots on her cheeks, looking as though she'd been pinched. The nose with a slight hook—the hook belongs. Long gold rings in the bold red lobes of her ears. And, most important of all: long-lashed eyes. You imagine they must be black and very sad until you look closely and perceive they're really dark blue and very jolly.

I've been living here a few days.

I walk the streets aimlessly; I'm very busy. Suddenly I recall her slender, arched figure, her bare arms as she moves through the apartment in a loose house dress. I have a strong impulse to return to my room. I remember the goings-on in the evening, the shady characters who visit her till late at night—there are still shady characters around, though the Reds have been in power several years*—and I'm happy to be in a position to write about it. (That is to say, to fight it.) I go home eager to take pen in hand and write.

My first meeting with the landlady (it was in the dark hall). She opened her door and stood there, introducing herself. An odd kind of silent introduction. But it made much more of an impression than the more talkative kind.

She threw me a look that produced two sensations: first, a stirring in my groin. Second, the feeling that I'm missing something. What it is exactly I don't know, but I'm certain about it. There's something missing in my life.

The same day (a second encounter). Another glance, more familiar this time. I list my thoughts again: I'm still young. I have black satin eyes. I'm wearing a black satin pleated jacket. I'm a beginning writer with leftist sympathies. I side with the Reds. I must contribute to Soviet literature a piece of writing that's true, straight from life. Everything I see here I'll use to illuminate my new piece.

What is more: if necessary, I'll report everything I know to the proper authorities.

From that point on, I began to listen avidly to every conversation on the other side of the thin wall separating our rooms. I learned a great deal.

II

The landlady has a deaf, old father—he used to own a five-story house. He lives somewhere three or four streets away. The boarders call him "old Zabarski." He's husky, gray-haired, well dressed, just the way you would picture an old absentee landlord. (Interesting speculation: how does a man like this get along under the Reds?) His deafness—the wads of cotton in both ears—seems deliberately put on to increase his importance. As though he has the right to insist that everyone speak very loud to him, not because he's deaf, but because he used to own a five-story

* This story was originally published in Kiev in 1927.—Ed.

house, and is still a somebody.

Every morning—the city still damp with the shadowy, lingering coolness of night—he comes to receive a report from his daughter. She serves as his go-between on his various affairs. He rings the front doorbell three times—that's the signal it's him coming, old Zabarski himself.

I open my door a crack and see Krisman, the sleepy compositor, who has to get out of bed and let the old man in. Krisman holds up his falling pants with one hand, a nasty expression on his face. His other hand is busy scratching the back of his neck, and he looks as though he's about to punch the old man. But it doesn't seem to bother old Zabarski at all. He says politely, with vast dignity, "Thank you very much."

A second later he has slipped through the heavy cloth drape into his daughter's room.

I sit up in bed, mouth open and sleepy eyes shut, and, leaning against the wall, listen.

"I propositioned him," Sonia Zabarski shouts into the old man's deaf ear. "It was dangerous. I said to him, 'You've got a chance to be rich . . . perfectly legal.' "

Silence. . . . The old man must be taking snuff.

"Well?" he asks.

"He's young!" the landlady shouts louder. "A *spez*—a technician but no Communist. Has just been on the job for a month. He doesn't take money."

Four such mornings . . . five . . . six. . . . It's clear now how the old man gets along. He's an "operator." Uses his daughter to "build up contacts" among technicians. Where money isn't inducement enough, his daughter offers her body.

What a way to make a living!

Lying in bed, I yawn and fall asleep thinking of the material I shall write up. Fine material. In the darkling interval between waking and sleeping I remember Sonia Zabarski—young, pretty, a good figure. She was born to please herself and to please others. No one is fool enough to admit it, but everyone dreams of just that. She has a habit of not locking the bathroom door from the inside when she's washing in the morning. Once, not realizing she was there, I opened the door. She was half-naked. She didn't even apologize. Startled, I stepped back. There was a brief meeting of our eyes—hers seemed to ask whether I had seen . . . ? and whether I really . . . ?

Pooh! The devil take her!

I decide that the first thing to do is to describe deaf old Zabarski arriving every morning to receive an accounting from his daughter.

This is the way I'll begin:

"The sun came up late over the great city. Above the high, many-storied walls, triangular patches of sky looked down, seeming higher and bluer than the sky."

I am pleased with the beginning—particularly the triangular patches of sky. Eyes shut, I lie there seeing those clouds.

"Blue like zinc. . . ."

Now I'm sure I'm going to become a writer with a big name.

At last—a beginner no longer!

I am beside myself with joy. My thoughts run away with me. Suddenly I catch myself in the middle of a chapter quite different from what I had intended:

"A young, very pretty woman in a long fur coat is walking down the street. It is the beginning of winter, the first snow is falling. Sonia Zabarski (surprisingly, not yet in jail!) is walking the length of the city park to keep a rendezvous with a tall young official. Unable to seduce him for her father's black-market activities, she has fallen in love with him. She waits some time for him to appear, and begins to lose hope. . . ."

And the young official is really myself. Why me of all people? For no good reason. I think it a pity that anyone else should be the official.

So I fall asleep with an odd sweet-and-sour feeling, a young man whom a pretty woman has fallen in love with because she can't seduce him for her father's crooked affairs.

Out of pity for her, I finally do turn up in the city park, appearing from a side street.

Around nine o'clock, when I got up and began to dress, I remembered how considerate I was in the story. Yawning, I thought about the government, how badly it needs fellow-traveling young writers like myself to help end corruption.

Still plenty of corruption.

A chat with Maskileyson, the boyish-looking pimply fellow to my right. We were standing near his door.

I found out that the landlady's husband, a Red Army doctor, has left her. "About a year and a half ago, or more," the boy-man drawls.

I listened with assumed indifference, as though it didn't matter to me one way or another. After a moment's silence, "But still," I asked, "she stays on here as the wife of a Red Army man?"

"Yes . . . she's still here."

And his chubby cheeks grimaced cautiously, like a bashful child. Meaning, he wondered also but was too quiet a person to say anything.

It turned out that once, when the housing office tried to move her out of her big room into a smaller one, she made a tremendous fuss. She located several influentials, and was finally allowed to stay. Incidentally, the compositor—Eli Krisman—he helped her too.

I (prudently), "Why?"

He didn't reply. But the muscles around his fleshy nose quivered in the direction of a half-smile. The implication being: "For her good deeds!"

Another chat with Maskileyson. It has to do with the noisy crowds—mostly men—in the landlady's room till late at night. But there are also occasions when they come singly—quietly, almost secretly. For these visits she dresses very simply, very correct. Afterward, she'll brag to the boarders.

"You know who was to see me?" She mentions a name.

"For instance," I asked. "Whose name?"

"For instance," repeats the boy-man. "Names out of a hat."

It's a shame: Maskileyson doesn't seem to be involved in her affairs. Anyway, it turns out there isn't much material in him. All he does is sit in his room all day. He's waiting for a visa from his brother in Argentina. The heavy object he's always dragging out from under his bed is nothing but a common ordinary suitcase, where his things have lain packed for over a year. He has an old, worn-out student's hat with a broken lacquered visor in it. He bought the cap from an ex-student very cheap, because it's not worn nowadays—the way officer's epaulets are out of fashion. Another thing he keeps in the suitcase is an eighth-grade diploma he received when the revolution broke out. Getting the diploma came very hard (he says so himself), because ever since he was a child he's had a thick skull. Besides, his father died when he was young. His mother was always chiding him:

"Your cousins have no trouble at all. They go through the *gymnasium,* on to the university, and get it over with. All the time you're forever studying, but nothing ever comes of it."

And when he finally did get his diploma, his mother was dead, there was a revolution, and a fellow like him—a man with an eighth-grade *gymnasium* diploma—wasn't worth much any more in this country. On the other hand, a diploma was still a valuable thing to have in Argentina—that's what his brother wrote, the one who was supposed to send him a visa.

Obviously, to pass the time the boy locks his door and opens the suitcase.

Once, when we were the only ones in the apartment, I looked through his keyhole to see what he was doing.

He was staring at the diploma. He stared a long time. Then he folded it with care, gingerly took his student's cap out of the suitcase and, just as gingerly, as though it were made of glass, put it on. Then, slowly and carefully, he walked back and forth through the room. Obviously, he is very depressed because no one in our country cares about his having a diploma. When he receives the visa from his brother, he'll begin feeling like a somebody again. And the moment he crosses the Soviet border, he'll put his cap on. . . . Let the whole world know him for what he is!

Here's something perplexing: why did the landlady give an idiot like this a room in her apartment—and why has she kept him on for over a year?

The answer is: (1) Old Zabarski visits her on business every morning; (2) there are criminal doings in her apartment; (3) actually, her room is the base for a gang of criminals.

So it pays the landlady to board her rooms out to idiots who have no idea what's happening under their nose.

Then where do I fit in—a young leftist writer—just a beginner, to be sure, but still loyal to the Red government? In Moscow they're sweating trying to find out what's wrong, why every step comes so hard—while here, in the very apartment I live in, technicians are being bribed over my landlady's body. I've a bee in my bonnet to use this as material for a story. But why don't I simply report it all to the proper authorities instead?

The only reason is that I don't have the facts, not yet. I still don't know who's in my landlady's gang. First I must learn all their secrets, catch her and her whole gang, red-handed.

III

My ear grows sharper every day. Not a rustle of her well-shaped body escapes me. No one has asked me to do it? What of that? It's my duty, isn't it?

Quiet. Two o'clock in the afternoon. I hear from the other side of the wall a small, light cough—the kind of cough only exceptionally pretty women produce, as though to tell you: "I'm at home . . . in my room."

After the cough, silence again. I strain my ears. Another rustle. Very low, coming from the Persian rug on the floor. She must be putting on her slippers. I imagine her doing it in my room; she wouldn't be bashful, because she's become very familiar with me. I can almost see her in the act: the lines of her bent, sitting figure, the shape of her folded legs, the way she slips a slender foot into the slippers, very light, because that's the way she is. And the swift movement of her fingers—long, restless fingers with gleaming, manicured nails, so long they droop and spread at the tips, like shoulder blades.

She coughs again. "Here I am."

I pace my room, sniffing the odor of perfume and powder. I'm slightly unhappy about her going out in her best clothes, leaving the whole apartment empty for several hours. On the other hand . . . I'm sure it doesn't matter, her pleasing me so much as a woman. To the contrary. There's no law against my acting like a man, is there? As a matter of fact, it encourages me to follow the dictates of my conscience. If necessary, I'll hand her in. I'll just write a letter to the proper authorities:

"In apartment number blank, house number blank, street such and such, in the room across the way from mine, every night this is what has been going on." And I'll go into details. Then I'll sign my name—they can take it any way they wish, but I'll listen to the voice of my conscience.

That's positive.

So there is no reason for me to be afraid because the landlady is trying so hard to get on intimate terms with me.

Not by accident does she leave the door of the washroom ajar every morning while she's washing. Who but me would she expect to meet there, when she and I are usually the only ones in the apartment at that hour?

Once, when she was done with her toilet, she sauntered through the whole apartment, looking into all the boarders' rooms—in her role of landlady, ostensibly. She came to my room.

"Ah!" she marveled. "You home? I thought you weren't in. None of the others are."

As she spoke she looked me straight in the eyes with a friendly half-smile, as though to say: "What pretty satiny eyes you have. . . . I like you, but you're a kind of clumsy oaf, young fellow. You have no idea how to behave when you've a landlady like me and none of the other boarders is home."

Then, as though to give me some inkling of what a young fellow like myself might expect from a landlady like her, standing close to me in the doorway, she stretched her arms over her head, in a kind of early morning yawn.

Her breasts curved out round and full, her whole body straining, as after light calisthenics.

She seemed to be waiting for a reply. When I said nothing, she glanced around my room. Actually she was more interested in looking at me than at my room.

"Both your windows are bare," she said. "We'll have to find you some curtains. Coming into the courtyard in the evening, one can see everything that's going on in your room. I've been thinking of it."

Now, what did she mean by that?

She'd been thinking of me. (That's the first thing.) And then, the idea had entered her head that a young fellow like me—things might be going on in my room at night that people outside in the courtyard ought not to be witnessing. As for her, she was no puritan—she'd put up curtains for me.

I lost my tongue. Why didn't I say, "It really doesn't matter. It doesn't make the slightest difference to me whether I have curtains or not"?

I was so sorry not to have spoken that after she had gone I left the house. I went out for some fresh air—it was stifling there.

I wondered whether I was running a slight fever. The people I passed in the street looked different somehow, as though their landlady had visited each of them that morning with the offer to put up curtains in their room.

A few days later I came into my room after a walk to find freshly starched curtains hanging over both windows. Clean, snug, long curtains. They gave the whole room a new, comfortable line. The landlady's odor lay in their pleats. The moment I entered, I smelled her perfume. As though she had sprinkled it everywhere—on the pillows tumbled on the made bed, on the four chairs next to the wall, the small couch with its hollow mattress. Everything in the room gave me a sense of well-being.

The chest in the corner, the paper on the small covered table that serves as my desk, seemed to be waiting quietly to rebuke me. "You fool, you're too late. You should have come earlier."

I had the sensation of being a happy newlywed. And to someone so light.

The apartment was silent—apparently no one was at home.

I don't know how long I paced my room. Finally, fatigued as though I had been to a noisy wedding, I lay down on the small couch to rest in the room's luxury. I was tired, the way you feel after a hot bath. My whole body wanted to lie there forever. My eyes shut of their own accord, to see the scene I was writing close up.

". . . How different Sonia Zabarski looks, seen from a distance. Everything about her has changed, even her walk. Her face, slightly drawn, has become even lovelier through suffering. The eyes under her long eyelashes, once so blue and jolly, are darker now, almost black, and very sad. She broke off with her deaf old father a long time ago. He doesn't come to see her any more—the fact is, Sonia Zabarski has few visitors nowadays. For she's in love with a tall young official—he's a famous author. He emerges from a side street to meet her in the city park."

At that point the thoughts and feelings linking me with reality ceased. I couldn't bear to leave the spot in the city park where I was meeting her.

I fell asleep with a sense of ease and sweetness, unaware that my cheek pressing hard against the pillow was turning red. I don't know how long my sleep lasted. I remember being annoyed at a disturbing sound that kept trying to pull me out of bed.

Slender, light fingers were knocking at my door. I sensed their slenderness sight unseen. With a dying heart, I sat up and listened. The fingers knocked again.

"Come in!"

The landlady stood in the doorway. She wasn't sad and she wasn't crying. Her blue eyes, smiling at me with sinful charm, preceded her into the room.

"You poor thing," she laughed at me for being so sleepy, so lost-looking, and at my red, creased cheek.

"Poor, poor thing. . . . Woke you up, did I? I've come to borrow your table and chairs. I'm having company tonight. A lot of people."

Of course. It would never dawn on the landlady to repent and become a woman of suffering. Never occurred to her that the proper thing to do was to break with her deaf old father and the rest of the gang, forbid them to enter her room.

The boarders always lent her chairs and tables when she had a party. Her jolly eyes rested on mine: Would I be less obliging than the other boarders?

I lost my self-control. My only thought was that I was completely unlike her gang—I wasn't just an ordinary young writer . . . not nowadays with the Red government in power. Our country had too many dirty corners to sweep out.

So I was unhappy at not having refused the curtains when she offered them. But now, because I was still sleepy; because I didn't know what to tell her about the table and chairs; because I lost my self-control under her friendly glance—now, all unexpectedly, I blurted out what I should have said when she asked me about the curtains: "It doesn't matter . . . all the same to me."

And then, independent of my mind, my legs began to move about the room. But she was overjoyed and never paid the slightest attention to my reply.

She began carrying the chairs out, one after another. It wasn't until all the chairs were moved, and the bare walls were staring complainingly at me for not having defended them from this attack, that I realized how foolish my "it's all the same to me" had been.

Her gang would be sitting on my chairs tonight. It would look as though I was helping them.

Now all that was left to move was my writing table. It wasn't very big, but it was awkward. She attacked it from various sides, pulling it in to her so that it pressed against her belly, the two far legs hanging off the ground. Her face turned red, and she fell to laughing. Finally, she gave me a questioning, happy look.

"Well? Are you a gentleman or not? What about it, friend?"

I don't remember how it happened but I, who was never much of an athlete, suddenly was possessed of the strength of Hercules. A few minutes later, when I was myself again, it was all over and done with. I, quiet unassuming Baru, a young writer who considered himself ready to give his life for the Red government if need be—bent over double, had carried into my landlady's room on my back the very table on which it was my duty to write the whole truth about her to the proper authorities.

Breathing hard with the exertion and excitement, I stood on the Persian rug next to the table in her room. The door was shut tight (it may have been locked), and the landlady was obviously pleased—because I had acted the gentleman, and because I had stayed and we were alone in her room. She came over, eyes smiling, and stood in front of me, her arms at her side, shoulders slightly slumped, breasts curving round and full toward me.

Something I had never expected occurred. I think more than anything it was the scar on her neck that upset me. . . . My knees began to tremble and I fell into her arms.

All the time I lay there I never stopped wondering how everything about her was much more delicious, much more sinful, than I had imagined it would be, glimpsing her half-naked in the bathroom, or hearing her cough from the other side of the wall.

At last, her voice, tinged with sleepy weariness, awakened me. "Well, young fellow, that's enough for you. Enough for the first time."

I could see she had no regrets. In fact, she looked quite content. From that I gathered that nothing bad had happened, and that I had nothing to regret either.

But there was no time for regrets, anyway. Someone had been ringing the front doorbell for some time, very hard. The landlady was standing at the mirror.

"Go," she said, fixing my hair with quick fingers.

I remained standing in front of her.

"Go away!" she pushed me with her knee. "Off with you! Quick!"

IV

I paced my room, aware that I had lost something but not sure exactly what it was.

I heard the landlady shouting into her father's deaf ear. "Did you fetch the wine? Put it in that corner. Get more. They'll all be here. Tonight. They'll be drinking. Tell Leov to come too. I'll introduce him to the V.P.—the way he works, 1-2-3—there's a man for you!"

She was shouting louder than usual. Obviously, she felt freer than she had yesterday—there was no longer anyone to be afraid of in the apartment.

Pacing back and forth as I listened to her loud voice, I discovered I was dissatisfied with myself—with what had happened in the landlady's room, with my fatigued body. It berated me:

"You've slipped badly, haven't you? No more clean conscience for you. You're one of her gang now, no better than somebody called Leov, no better than that V.P.—the one who works 1-2-3. Why did you have to do it?"

On the other hand, reason came to my moral defense.

"It makes no difference. There's no law against enjoying your landlady's body, so long as you haven't committed a crime because of it. And you haven't. The way you feel about her, and her deaf father, and the whole gang that's going to get drunk at her place tonight—the way you feel about them hasn't changed a whit.

"If necessary, you're still ready to write to the proper authorities about the whole kit and caboodle, sometime. And not sometime in the distant future, either, but right now. This evening, in fact."

To prove to my body that it's all wrong about me, I begin composing the letter in my head:

"For three weeks I've been living in apartment number. . . ."

No, better tell it exactly.

"Today is exactly seventeen days since I began living in this apartment. It used to belong to a Mrs. Sonia Zabarski, who still lives here. She purports to be the wife of a Red Army doctor, but actually the abovementioned husband left her a long time ago—probably for good reason. The fact is, he threw her over."

My body is calm now, convinced it was badly mistaken about me—I'm not sparing the landlady at all, though I'm quite fond of her. In fact, you might say I'm passionately in love with her. The devil! I'd be a criminal not to turn her in. Because a criminal is what she is.

It's foolish of me, but she's the only thing I can think of.

Listen here! If you're to be honest, be honest. Here's pen and ink. Act calmly—there's no hurry. But act.

I settled down at the window sill, pleased at my coolness as I began writing.

"Today is exactly seventeen days. . . ."

I write with decisions, at great length. The light's been on in my room for some time, but I don't remember having noticed it was growing dark and having put the light on. I keep writing, slowly, deliberately, like a man of decision.

The front doorbell rings festively. The landlady's guests are beginning to arrive. Somebody's in her room. I can hear her voice. The newcomer's footsteps are firm, young, happy, jangling like spurs. Suddenly it grows quiet there.

I sit where I am, dying, and listen intently. She's alone there with somebody. They're kissing.

"A gang of criminals," I resume writing. "Imagine: catching this gang means uncovering a vast network of huge illegal activity throughout the country. The chief agent, Sonia Zabarski, has seduced many honest young people who could have been very useful to the country's new order."

I rise and pace about again, thinking. "My God, I could have been seduced too!"

The doorbell rings again and again. Apparently, the guests are arriving in two's and three's. They're coming on business.

"Listen, comrade," somebody repeats for the hundredth time, like a religious chant, "back home where I come from in Deep Russia. . . ."

I move around my room, glad it's all over now, and I've signed it. All there, lying snug in my breast pocket. Clear evidence that I'm not in the least involved in what's happening on the other side of the wall.

I listen to the happy, self-satisfied murmur. As though sin is the only thing that counts in this world—everything else is dirt.

For me as a writer. . . . I mean, for the big piece I've begun writing, it certainly would be very useful now if I could be there and have a look at those miserable people—learn to know them, as individuals.

I keep thinking of that after I put out the light in my room the better to hear in the dark.

"These people—put them all together and they make up the criminal world. But each of them has a face of his own, his own nose, eyes—and his own heart. To write about them properly, you have to be with them, just for a short time at any rate. Just one evening, be one of them, go to the landlady's party with them, share their feelings: 'She has set the table, put out the wine, dressed up, just for me.' "

All at once I forgot what I had in my breast pocket. I hurried to the small, broken-down couch in the darkness; there was a rushing in my heart. It spread to my chest. After all, nothing like that had ever happened to me before. Like being married to her, that Sonia Zabarski. For I'm a pure young man. This kind of relationship with a woman stirs me deeply. Afterward, there's an emptiness.

Why do we have to feel so empty afterward?

I've forgotten the half-drunk murmur on the other side of the wall. I don't know how long I lay like that, angry at myself. Suddenly I sat up—there was a rustle at my door. I felt lively again, as though a lost happiness were returning.

The landlady's perfumed, made-up, frightfully busy head popped through the open door.

"You here?" she threw the words rapidly at me in the darkness. "Darling, do get dressed, get out of bed, come and meet everybody."

So she hadn't forgotten.

"Well, what's up?" A few minutes later, she bent her head down to mine again. "You coming?"

And she fled back to her guests.

It doesn't seem to make any difference to me. I stride through the room, thinking about many things, but mostly about my story:

"She is walking alongside the city park, waiting for someone, with a feeling of great pain, deep suffering, immense regret. . . ."

But I need an ending. Everything you write has to have an ending.

She hadn't forgotten.

She sticks her head into my room again. This time she looks quickly around, to make sure there's no one here with me. Shutting the door behind her, she hurries to the window sill. She's all dressed up, and smells of happiness, good times, weddings.

Taking me by the hand, she stands there for a while, without words, facing me. My knees tremble again, and the same thing happens as before. Again I am amazed that everything about her is so much more sinful and sweeter than I had imagined it would be.

"Well, young fellow," the landlady wakes me with a low whisper.

And she flies back to her guests.

I look after her, suddenly realizing my misfortune.

Look here: this piece I've been writing is in very bad shape. There's no ending. I've been stuck at the same passage for more than a week. The story hasn't moved; she's still standing in the city park as the first snow falls. I have no idea what to write next.

Maybe it would be a good idea to go to her room now. "To go or not to go, that is the question."

Very possibly, if I do go and see her gang face to face, the ending will come to me.

I begin dressing, slowly and deliberately, deciding, once and for all, that I'm not going for my own sake, but for my story.

I have to go.

V

The heavy drape hung before the landlady's room, as usual.

It was lively in there; you could hear the whiskey-and-cake noise.

I bumped into two of the guests in the hall, one a very young man in an army uniform, the older man a civilian.

The soldier pulls the civilian aside to register a complaint.

"Listen, brother, I don't like it here. What did you drag me into?" He lets out a string of curses, ending with the word "Scum!" Then breaking free of the civilian's grasping hand, he leaves.

"He'll be back," someone consoles the civilian, "Don't you worry. He'll be back."

With mixed feelings, I slip my hand behind the drape and find the doorknob. I don't care for the civilian who has stayed on, and I like the young soldier who spat as he left. I gather that I'm not the only one in the same situation. That is to say, there are other honest people trapped like me.

But, once I open the door and see what a good time people are having in the brightly lit room, I forget both feelings.

The holiday lights, and the flowers, and the variety of food, and wine bottles tall and short, catch my eye. But the landlady is more beguiling than they—her eyes nod shiningly toward me, offering the protection of their long lashes.

She introduces me to her guests, holding my arm with her left hand, firm and warm, as though I were a rare object belonging to her. What does she want to use me for?

Two young women, shoulders and arms bared, gauge me with their eyes during the introductions. They smile envious congratulations at the landlady. "Excellent!" their eyes approve. "Where did you pick up this wonderful buy?"

They seem to know all about us. . . . The landlady must have been bragging. And, much as they guess, they suspect even more.

But I haven't the time for regrets—I'm too pleased with how all this is going to look in my story. There's no longer the slightest doubt in my mind that I was right to come; my piece would have been no good if I hadn't. It doesn't matter now that everybody here considers me one of them. For a brief moment I wonder what is going to happen.

There are a great many people in the room, many curious things are going on that a writer can't help observing with interest. For example, the civilian from the hall—he has the face of an ex-police chief—is far gone already, slobbering over the two women I'd been introduced to; however hard I look at them, all I can see is bare shoulders and backs.

Suddenly I grow frightened. Is someone calling me? But when I turn around, I see that the landlady is calling somebody else; she's just smiling at me.

Nodding just the slightest bit toward the three people standing near me, like the smart girl she is, she conveys her meaning: her affairs are progressing.

One of the three is a small, fat man with a yellow, well-combed beard. He's freshly shaven and all dressed up, like an elderly bridegroom at his second wedding. He keeps looking at the big cigar he's smoking with an expression that says: "I'm big and rich, too." He gestures with reserve, befitting a man who doesn't want to strain himself, talking carefully to the young people who sit facing him. Every new subject he introduces with "Listen, comrades. Back home where I come from, in Deep Russia. . . ."

This must be the V.P., the one the landlady shouted about in her father's deaf ear: "1-2-3. What a man!"

Apparently, he's the hub of all the landlady's business, because she rarely steps away from his chair. Every once in a while she bends over to stroke his hand and smile, whispering nice things in his ear. She forces him to pay attention to her, with the constant reminder that what's really important is not the consignment of fats the two young men are selling him, but the landlady herself. He's getting her pretty face and fine figure very cheap.

My mind is occupied with the thought that I'll have to change the V.P. in my story. I don't like him—he's a little too short. But my thoughts are interrupted; somebody has been persistently ringing the hall bell, very hard and angrily.

The landlady runs out, half-frightened, to see who it is. When she returns, it's obvious she's been quarreling. "Nothing . . . just a neighbor, first floor front. A drunk . . . always beating his wife." She's angry. "He's not satisfied that I pay rent by the month. He'd have me pay for every extra guest. The devil with him! Krisman will be coming home soon. He's on the house committee."

When did the room become so noisy and jolly all at once? When did they finish their business?

The landlady drank with everybody at the table, first the whole company, then with each guest separately. She had to run out and see who was at the door and whether Krisman had come home yet. Krisman's room was empty, but she returned carrying the two mandolins and guitar from his wall.

Two women began strumming the mandolins.

A mouth opened and a throat burst into song.

A pair of lips parted for a kiss.

And voices quite naturally grew louder, everybody talking at once.

A drunk tried to show how steady his hand was. Much to his surprise, it didn't work, and a bottle of red wine spilled on the white tablecloth. It crashed into some glasses and broke a dish with a loud clatter. Everyone at the table began to feel that there was no more need for the decencies; they had been broken too.

Now everybody began drinking heavily, to spite their own bad manners. And of them all, I was the worst offender.

I was still sober after a couple of glasses, swallowed between my landlady's kisses. Each drink I prefaced with a toast: "To. . . ." What I meant was that I was drinking to the piece I was writing.

After the fourth or fifth glass I remembered that I was really toasting the successful completion of their affairs. I began to feel sad and nauseous. But after a few more drinks, I was seized with a peculiar happiness. The whole gang I was drinking with that I hated so because they were contemptible criminals were really not so terrifying after all, our new government was stronger than they, it would root them out . . . I would help . . . the new order and I. . . .

This, it seemed to me, was a very important and profound point: Life is nasty, but the new order is cleaning it out. There's tremendous joy in helping our government!

I pushed my way to the table. I wanted to make a speech about it. But it was impossible to quiet the crowd; by the time I reached the table, I forgot my speech.

So I went back to drinking with the landlady. I dragged her off to a corner and, shaking my fist in her face, shouted the whole speech in her ear.

"You know something," I pulled her toward me, "you know something, you're a . . . you and your whole gang, you're a . . . stable . . . that's what you are. We'll clean the stable out, that's what we'll do . . . stink and all. You won't get by us with that stink of yours. . . . Look, I'm not being nasty—I've written up everything that's going on here, for the proper authorities. . . . Here, just touch it. . . . Here it is, in my breast pocket."

Only, the landlady was drunk by now, and tore herself away from me, back to the table where she had something much more important to say to her friends than anything I might have to say to her. And then she stared in my direction with terror in her eyes, her whole body trembling, because on the table, between the candlesticks . . . someone had turned over a couple of bottles, breaking some more glasses.

The people at the table went round and round; the room turned, too. The mandolins and guitar strummed harder, and somebody, pushing people and chairs aside, pulled off his jacket and started dancing.

Everybody began clapping, whistling, stamping. They got to their feet to stamp harder, urging the dancer on.

They were leaning over his feet in a circle, waving hands, pounding fists, rapping forks against glasses, pumping for him to leap higher, kick harder—when suddenly, very suddenly, the sound of knocking at the front door was heard. It had been going on for some time, and it was not just fists pounding, but something heavier and harder.

All at once it turned very quiet and everyone listened.

"I'm not giving him any more money," shouted the landlady hysterically. "It's my neighbor!"

She ran into the hall and there bumped into Maskileyson, looking sleepy and pale in his underclothes. He was struggling with idiotic uncertain movements to open the door.

To the general astonishment, instead of the drunken neighbor, when the door opened a medium-sized man, oddly quiet and dry, appeared standing in the doorway. At first glance, he impressed one as dumb.

He seemed so pitifully helpless that he had to be followed about by four or five heavily armed Red Army men. Taking a small wallet out of his pocket, he identified himself.

It turned out he could talk, after all. "Everybody into the room!" he said, very smooth and dry. "Your papers!"

In my confusion, instead of my papers I take my write-up of the gang out of my breast pocket and hand it to him.

"I'm a writer," I said to him, proudly.

Coldly, he takes the papers from my hand. "Writer?" He looks at me and at the gang with indifference.

"Scum," he says.

VI

It's gray outside, early morning. They take us through cobblestoned streets to a jail at the other end of town. About a dozen of us, including three women. At the line-up, it turns out they've been after this gang for some time.

Depressed, the prisoners barely drag their feet. All but me. I'm terribly excited, and deeply interested, and very preoccupied. I'm amazed at the remarkable ending I've found for my story tonight. This is how it will go:

"Damp shadows cool with evening. Sleepy janitors, dragging their brooms over the sidewalks, stop sweeping to look at the prisoners being marched past them. The sun comes up late over the great city. Up on high, over tall, many-storied walls, triangular patches of sky gaze down at the city. They seem far higher and far bluer than usual. . . ."

But I am disturbed at the name the man who arrested us called the gang—me included.

I can't fathom it: really to be able to describe the gang, I had to spend at least one night with them. And yet we deserved that name.

Was I right, or not?

* * *

Several days have passed since my arrest.

I think I'll have to cut some parts out of my story. Like the part where the landlady has a change of heart and becomes a woman of suffering.

The pale, fat Maskileyson boy shares my cell. He keeps hanging around me. He's very depressed, and constantly asks about his diploma and the old student's cap that were taken away from him at the line-up.

"What do you think? Will they give them back to me? They won't take them away from me, will they?"

But I barely listen. I'm delighted with the remarkable end of my story.

That word, though, keeps running through my head.

"Scum!"

Translated from the Yiddish by Jacob Sloan

May 1960

Lionel Abel

ART WHILE BEING RULED

"Abram Tertz," Brecht, and Calderón

Really surprising about the Pasternak affair was not so much that *Doctor Zhivago* was denied publication in the Soviet Union or that Boris Pasternak was prevented from accepting his Nobel Prize award: fundamentally, our astonishment sprang from the fact that his novel had been written at all. So it is possible, Western intellectuals were forced to admit, for creative work to be pursued in the Soviet Union, at least by some individuals; creative work, moreover, treating those very facts of life in Russia which the Soviet authorities want left undescribed. Pasternak, to be sure, was something of an oddity, being neither a product of the October Revolution nor of its Stalinist aftermath. The poet's sensibility had already been formed when the Bolsheviks came to power, and if it was not strange, after all, that a man of such culture and quality should have retained his critical sense, perspective, and feeling for individual judgment throughout the long period when literary and cultural thought in Russia were being bureaucratized, yet it *was* extraordinary that his unsparing and utter dislike for bureaucratization had been not only felt, but expressed, and clearly, and in a novel presented for publication in the Soviet state.

It is clear now that the writing of *Doctor Zhivago* was not an isolated event: Russian literature apparently has, and, in the future, is very likely to have, more surprises, both for the Communist leadership, and for us of the West. Not so long ago the French leftist review *Esprit,* the Italian periodical *Tempo Presente,* the British *Universities and Left Review,* and also the American quarterly *Dissent* published an article on "Socialist Realism" which is in many respects even more remarkable than Pasternak's *Zhivago.* The essay, moreover, is the work of a new and fairly young writer, a man who, I have been told on good authority, is in his middle thirties, and hence must have been formed culturally and psychologically under Communism; he is not someone from the old culture who managed to survive the revolution and Stalin. The author of the article on "Socialist Realism" is also the author of the long story—or short novel—"The Trial Begins," published in *Encounter* in January of this year, and bearing this signature: Abram Tertz.* "The Trial Begins," too, is an extraordinary work, though not, in my opinion, quite up to the article on "Socialist Realism" which so startled American readers when it appeared in *Dissent*. In any case, both works, of very high quality, are openly critical of at least certain aspects of Soviet life and culture. Evidently these pieces can tell us something about what is happening to the human spirit as it articulates itself in the new post-Stalin Russian literature.

I should add that neither the article nor the story by the new Russian writer who calls himself Abram Tertz—I shall from now on refer to him by that name—has been published in Russia. The manuscripts of these works, like that of *Doctor Zhivago,* were sent out of the country, no doubt surreptitiously, for publication in the West. The great difference, though, between these works and *Doctor Zhivago* is that the latter was fundamentally *addressed* to the West, not just published there. But the writings of Abram Tertz which have also been published in the West, and only there, are not, I think, fundamentally addressed to us. Nevertheless they have much to tell us, expressing as they do a new way of reacting to Communism, and to life from within a Communist culture and country.

Unfortunately, the two pieces of writing are by no means clear. Powerful, authentic, original—yes—but clear, no. I read Abram Tertz's article on "Socialist Realism" again and again without being able to be sure of what the author was saying; yet in the essay there is no sign of willful mystification; the man writes clearly and purposefully; but what he says is not clear, nor is his purpose in saying it evident. At first I thought he was trying to hide his real meaning behind irony, with a view to expressing his ideas in Soviet journals; but such an interpretation was, on reflection, impossible to hold to. There *are* occasions when Abram Tertz writes so clearly and so powerfully in denunciation of the Soviet regime that it is hard to conceive of why he would want to attenuate with irony criticisms less serious, or less bitter. Take this passage from his essay:

> So that prisons should vanish forever, we built new prisons. So that all frontiers should fall, we surrounded ourselves with a Chinese Wall. So that work should become a rest and a pleasure, we introduced forced labor. So that not one drop of blood be shed any more, we killed and killed and killed.

* The identity of "Abram Tertz" was eventually uncovered by the Soviet authorities—his real name is Andrei D. Sinyavsky. In February 1966 he was convicted of having maligned the Soviet people in his pseudonymous writings and was sentenced to seven years in a forced-labor camp.—Ed.

I submit: this is not the language of an author who is trying to hide his meaning.

What then is the meaning of Abram Tertz's article on "Socialist Realism"? At the outset, his main point seemed clear enough; the formula, socialist realism, is self-contradictory, and hence cannot be the guiding concept for an authentic Soviet literature. I think this *is* his meaning, and that in the rejection of socialist realism, at least, his thought is as unambiguous as one could wish. But when I tried to determine what kind of literature he wants to substitute for the kind that justified itself as socialist realism, his meaning suddenly became unclear. I could not tell, even after several readings of his article, whether the author wants Soviet literature in the future to be socialist *or* realist in character, and I am not sure that he himself knows which of these two terms, with all of the meanings each implies, he is ready to sacrifice for the other.

In any case, he has seen the self-contradictoriness of the concept of socialist realism, and nobody before him saw this or said it. His article is certainly the first serious criticism of Soviet literary policy to be made by a Soviet writer. So this is the moment to consider what Abram Tertz says that is understandable. Why, according to him, is the term "socialist" in contradiction to the term "realism" when applied to literature? Realism, of course, has traditionally meant direct inspection of what is going on in society or in the human mind, pursued with a critical alterness not to be inhibited by official pronouncements or received ideas. Such was the realism of Balzac and Flaubert, of Goncharov, Tolstoy, Chekhov, and Gorky. On the other hand, in Russia, the term "socialist" has come to stand for official pronouncements and received ideas. To put the matter in another way: realism was an instrument for attacking ideas that had been received from churchmen, aristocrats, and spokesmen for the bourgeoisie, but not received from Socialists or Communists; the "real" facts all non-socialist realists dealt with in the past were arguments against pronouncements by churchmen, aristocrats, or spokesmen for the bourgeoisie, but not arguments against pronouncements by Socialists or Communists. Realism, in other words, in its traditional character, was polemically motivated against an official view of things. Socialist realism, on the other hand, assumes that it is possible to synthesize the official Soviet view of things with such "real" facts as may have been "seen" by the writer. But an official view, Soviet or what have you, cannot but be just as polemically motivated against "real" facts as realism has been against official denials of fact. The incompatibility between the terms "socialist" and "realist" is both logical and psychological. The writer's impetus, if he is a realist, is to show that some official view is false, and without that impetus he has no motive for being especially realistic. Then there is the matter of logical incompatibility. The denial of real facts may be called "socialist" or "communist," whatever one pleases, but it can hardly be pursued in the name of "realism."

So far, so good. Abram Tertz's analysis of the impossibility of socialist realism as a literary concept is simply impeccable, and I have not in my brief summary done justice to all the richness of insight he brings to bear in his discussion. It is at this point, though, that the ambiguities of the author commence. For the question arises: which of the two terms, shown to be incompatible with the other, does he wish to retain as a guide for future Soviet writing, or even as a principle for his own work? Does he want a literature which will be socialist but not realist, or does he want a literature which will be realist but not socialist? Does he want writers, himself included, to point up all those facts which the official pronouncements of the Soviet government gloss over and even hide, or, committed to his government's basic policies, does he want a literature which will not gloss over real facts since it will not pretend to be describing them, a literature that will be fantastic rather than realist, and religious rather than critical? It does seem at times that this is the kind of literature Abram Tertz favors, but one cannot be sure. In what sense could such a literature be called socialist? Socialist? And yet leave unexplored what is actually taking place in the lives of people supposedly living under socialism? Now I cannot say that I have been able to determine what the author's judgment is on this matter. He can be interpreted as being for a realist literature or a socialist literature; he can be quoted on both sides of the question, and with about equal force. Yet the man is clear-headed. He writes:

> Our misfortune is that we are convinced social realists but not convinced enough. Submitting to its cruel rules, we are yet afraid to follow to the end the road that we ourselves have chosen. No doubt, if we were less educated, it would be easier for us to attain the integrity that is indispensable to a writer. But we went to school, read all kinds of books, and learned only too well that there were great writers before us—Balzac, Maupassant, Tolstoy, and, yes, what's his name?—Chekhov. This is what has undone us. We wanted to become famous and to write like Chekhov. This unnatural liaison produced monsters.

Here is Abram Tertz talking darkly. But why darkly? And what is one to think of his summation in the penultimate paragraph of the same essay?

> Right now I put my hope in a phantasmagoric art, with hypotheses instead of a Purpose, an art in which the grotesque will replace realistic descriptions of ordinary life. Such an art corre-

sponds best to the spirit of our time. May the fantastic imagery of Hoffmann and Dostoevsky, of Goya, Chagall, and Mayakovski (the most socialist-realist of all) and of many other realists and non-realists teach us how to be truthful with the aid of the absurd and the fantastic.

Why, one wonders, does one need the aid of "the absurd and the fantastic" in order to be "truthful"? And how could Mayakovski help with "fantastic imagery" if he is "the most socialist realist of all"? But even if we disregard the more obvious contradictions in the above, still another question remains which one is hard put to answer: is the actual predicament of Soviet writers under the present regime the *excuse* for creating a literature of fantasy, or *must* such a literature be created by Soviet writers who want to be in touch with the realities (the fantasies?) of their time?

Throughout his essay the author implies—he does more than that, he asserts—that there is no other purpose men could give themselves to besides Communism. No other ideal is worthy of man's devotion; and the highest ideal conceivable for any human effort merits being called divine, indeed (he does not scruple to use the word) God. So Communism is God. Does Abram Tertz mean to say—he implies it, and in many a passage—that since Communism is God, it transcends, or stands outside of any particular action undertaken to realize it? Then Communism is good in itself, no matter what Communists do in its name. A crime committed for the sake of Communism is not criminal or even wrong; quite the contrary; the Communist goal is too beautiful to be judged by human or moral standards. From this it follows—although one cannot be sure it does for the author—that a realistic literature describing the actual activities of present-day Communists would amount to a travesty of Communism itself. One cannot judge God by his priests. Thus we get some perception of why Abram Tertz seems to favor a non-realistic literature even though he does not state this in so many words. For a God is best represented by symbols and signs. But if we take this to be the author's final notion, we are prompted to ask how he would deal with the following difficulty: according to that notion, nothing happening in Russia, no matter how horrible, could be used as an argument against the Soviet regime. Obviously any criticism of the state would have to have a foundation in real fact; to attack a Soviet official or a Soviet policy one would have to confront the ideal by which the Soviet leader justified himself, or the norm by which the particular Soviet policy was justified, with the real content of the official's action, the real consequences of the particular policy. I repeat, to really criticize Soviet life one would have to be a realist. If Abram Tertz often seems hostile to realism, on the other hand, neither in his essay, nor in his story "The Trial Begins," does he refrain from criticizing Soviet life, and even by implication, the Soviet state. But from what point of view is the criticism made? One does not know. Here is another puzzling passage:

> The events of the last few years are dragging our art on a road of half-measures and half-truths. The death of Stalin inflicted an irreparable loss upon our religiously aesthetic system; it cannot be resuscitated through the now revived cult of Lenin. Lenin is too much like an ordinary man and his image is too realistic: small, bald, dressed in civilian clothes. Stalin seemed to be specially made for the hyperbole that awaited him: mysterious, omniscient, all-powerful, he was the living monument of our era and needed only one quality to become God—immortality.
>
> Ah, if only we had been intelligent enough to surround his death with miracles! We could have announced on the radio that he did not die but had risen to heaven, from where he continued to watch us, in silence, no words emerging from beneath the mystic mustache. His relics would have cured men struck by paralysis or possessed by demons. And children would have kneeled by the window and addressed their prayers to the cold and shining stars of the Celestial Kremlin.

Can this be irony? Once again, on reflection, one cannot be sure. Lenin's merits as a Communist leader were real, Stalin's were imaginary. From this fact, if we take Abram Tertz literally—which he may want us to do—it would follow that Stalin is the better symbolic representative of the divine purpose of Communism than was his predecessor in the Kremlin. If Lenin's authority came from the real force of his character, Stalin's could come only from the impersonal force of Communism itself; but Communism, if divine, would not need the devotion of gifted or even great men. Thus, Stalin, however criminal, however bureaucratic, would represent the idea of Communism better than could Lenin, for all the latter's real qualities of force, intelligence, selflessness. Clearly there is something in this peculiar judgment of the two Soviet political leaders similar to the peculiar evaluations of realism and fantasy in Abram Tertz's essay. One point the author has made clear at least: if Communism is a religion, a realistic literature would not serve it. But is this finally Abram Tertz's view?

I have concluded that I cannot determine what his view really is. Passing from the essay to the long story "The Trial Begins" did not prove helpful to an elucidation of the author's meaning. On the whole, his story seemed to me a less successful effort than his essay. There are in it the same puzzles, similar contradictions. Soviet life is described in bizarre, peculiar, fantastic terms. Typical positions taken by Soviet intellectuals and apologists for the regime are subjected to ridicule; yet the story does not add up to an indictment of the existing Soviet society or of its political leadership; in fact, it contains no indictment of anyone, or even of any institution, including the Soviet police. The inconsistencies by which the people of Russia manage to square their personal aims with the state's purposes are represented as the basic data of experience; if there are real problems, these lie elsewhere. Thus it is that of the two works I preferred the essay, which affected me more as a work of art should than did the story, and this leads me to the following explanation of the essay's theoretical inconclusiveness: in works of art, contradictions, without being obliterated, may be made to abate the bitterness of their antagonism. In a painter's landscape, the lion, without losing his characteristics, may lie down alongside the lamb. The reason, then, that we cannot penetrate to the message of the author on socialist realism is that in trying to state it he has created, out of his puzzles and confusions, a work of art. Nor is it so strange that the Russian writer's intellectual essay on the topic of socialist realism should succeed in a way not intended by him, while his story fails artistically. To begin with, the motives in Abram Tertz's story are too intellectual to be quite real. It is hard to believe that the young boy in "The Trial Begins" could be so concerned about the theoretical difference between just and unjust wars. It is not hard to believe that Abram Tertz himself is intellectually involved with such questions. The direct statement of his intellectual dilemmas is thus more moving than is his effort in "The Trial Begins" to distribute these dilemmas among his characters. For the author to say in his own person that Stalin should have been granted immortality is far more interesting than for him to describe, as he does in his story, the mighty-handed dictator blotting out the city of Moscow. But if the essay on socialist realism is a work of art, let us not forget that it contains the most annihilating criticism ever made of socialist realism as a literary concept; in fact, it is probable that this is the only real work of art which has even been instigated to any degree by the promotion of that inept and self-contradictory term.

A work of art, but art of what kind? Now there is only one way to understand any art work which is at first strange to us, and that is to compare it with other works to which it bears some significant resemblance. When we find two or more works which are strange in a similar way and were produced in different periods under conditions that somehow correspond or tally, we are in a better position to understand these works, and to evaluate them. Are two strange things that yet resemble each other less strange than one? Can this be? It is.

II

Reading Abram Tertz's essay, I was continually reminded of *The Measures Taken,* the play of Bertolt Brecht. Performed in 1930, it was attacked savagely by both Communists and anti-Communists. I do not think it has ever been performed since. It is inconceivable that it could be staged in the Soviet Union; yet indubitably this is a great play, maybe Brecht's masterpiece. While it would be wrong to think of *The Measures Taken* as an anti-Communist play, clearly it could not but be an unpleasant experience for party members to see it done. In reply to attacks on his work from the Communist press, Brecht was reported to have said that the play was not liked because it had been misunderstood. And the reason for the misunderstanding of his work was this: the playwright was more of a Marxist than the Marxists. But was he?

The Measures Taken is not a realistic play. Its construction is extremely formal, the story it tells is most fantastic; maybe it was this very play which suggested to Abram Tertz the genre of socialist-irrealism or socialist-superrealism toward which, from his essay, he seems inclined. Brecht's play, highly unified, simple in structure, presents four Communist agitators who report to the Control Commission of the party on their treatment of a young comrade whom they have liquidated. The reason they liquidated him, as they state openly, is this: the young comrade was too honest, too sincere, too bent on alleviating the sufferings of the masses. They had begged him to change his character and to become more like themselves: less honest, less sincere, less bent on alleviating the sufferings of the masses. Had he changed in accordance with their injunctions, he might have become a worthy agitator. He did not change. There was no alternative but to act:

> *We decided:*
> *Then he must disappear, and totally.*
> *For we must return to our work*
> *And cannot take him with us and cannot leave him behind*
> *We must therefore shoot him and throw him in the lime pit*
> *For the lime will burn him.*

The Control Commission approves their action as follows:

> *We agree to what you have done.*
> *Your report shows us how much it takes*
> *To change the world:*
> *Anger and tenacity, knowledge and indignation*

Swift participation, profound reflection
Cold acquiescence, endless persistence
Comprehension of the single man and of the whole:
*Change reality.**

Evidently, in his play, Brecht approves the action of the agitators in liquidating their young comrade. And in fact, at the crucial moments of the play, one is convinced that the action of the agitators was correct. Yet one sees at once why no Communist group would try to have Brecht's play performed. For why should Communists want to proclaim that individual virtues like honesty, sincerity, and sympathy for the masses are inconsistent with serious participation in party activity? On the other hand, the play is undoubtedly an exaltation of the Communist party.

Here we have a literary work which, intended as praise, can also be understood as an attack upon the object it is engaged in praising. A contradictory work, but not in the sense that its contradictions are fatal either to its aesthetic unity or to its dramatic force. A remarkable play, too; unhappily, one for which there is no audience.

Abram Tertz's essay reminded me of *The Measures Taken*. Brecht's plays in general have often made me think of Calderón's. In fact, I am somewhat puzzled that no literary critic (to my knowledge) has compared the German playwright with the 17th-century Spanish master.† In structure, the *autos* of Calderón are very like such of Brecht's morality plays as, for instance, *The Exception and the Rule* and *The Measures Taken*. Note that Calderón was the official poet of what was, for his time, an almost completely totalitarian society. Now Brecht conceived himself to be, and was finally recognized as, the representative writer of the Communist movement in its most totalitarian period. The play of Calderón which I want to compare with Brecht's *The Measures Taken,* and also with Abram Tertz's essay on socialist realism, is not a play dealing with political issues; however, it does express an attempt by the great Spanish dramatist to accept what must have been unpleasant and even horrible to him in his society.

Surgeon to His Own Honor—I prefer to translate Calderón's title less literally as "Physician for His Own Dishonor"—is a play of revenge, but of thwarted revenge, only half-consummated revenge. Don Gutierre, a Spanish nobleman, suspects that his wife may have feelings for another man that go beyond mere friendship; he decides to murder her. Gutierre

* Text is from Eric Bentley's English version, in *Modern Theater VI* (Anchor Books).

† The one European country, aside from Spain of course, where Calderón's plays had a real impact was Germany. Goethe greatly esteemed the playwright; Schlegel even overestimated him, having a keen eye for his virtues, no eye for his faults.

cannot attack the man she may be interested in; the latter belongs to the royal family. So Gutierre decides to have his wife bled to death by a surgeon—it will be thought that she died accidentally, or of illness, and thus there will be no reflection on Gutierre's honor. The nobleman carries out his purpose, his wife is dead, his honor intact. The King, who has had knowledge of the affair, and obviously approves the nobleman's action, suggests that he remarry. Don Gutierre demurs. What if a new wife prove unfaithful? In that case, says the King, you will know what to do. It would appear that the frightening cruelty of the husband has the poet Calderón's full endorsement.

But this is by no means sure. For Calderón has gone out of his way to lay bare a certain cruelty in the King himself, and thus is in a way indicting the whole society of which the King is the highest representative. In one scene the King threatens his clown thus: for each joke told which does not make His Highness laugh, the clown will have a tooth extracted. It is true that the ensuing dialogue cannot but be dramatically interesting, for we want to see the King, made to laugh, expose his teeth, while the clown, unsmiling, saves his. Nevertheless, there is something in the scene which goes beyond sheer dramatic interest. Unquestionably Calderón would not have written it had he not wanted to underscore the King's, and Gutierre's, cruelty. Yet the play breathes an almost pious devotion to the society for whose values the King and Gutierre stand.

III

The three works I have discussed, the contemporary Russian writer's essay on socialist realism, Brecht's play, and the drama of Calderón, are, it seems to me, aesthetically consistent works that simply lose meaning when we try to restate what they say in purely analytical terms. That which makes them consistent is never a clear idea, but a tone, a feeling, a formal quality, and perhaps something personal which cannot be made intelligible by any other means than the very ones these writers have employed. Self-contradiction, to be sure, far from being fatal to art, may actually engender it. That emotional instability which the clear-headed thinker tries to transcend in the sphere of ideas, can even be vindicated as order in an aesthetic work. Not, however, without a price. There is something peculiar, unnatural, and baffling about the two plays and the essay discussed above: art they are, but not art of the highest quality. In the three works, something humanly felt by the three writers is denied: Abram Tertz denies the value of Lenin's real character; Brecht denies the values of honesty, sincerity, and sympathy; Calderón denies the humanity of his hero and of his hero's King; but in all these works, too, the repressed values somehow assert themselves, even if obliquely. Each work can be described as a repression of part of the writer's personality; the repression is carried through successfully in a formal sense, but the repressed part speaks out too. Abram Tertz writes: "Art is elastic enough to fit into any bed of Procrustes that history presents to it." Here, I cannot but agree. The limbs of the human spirit, lopped or lengthened to fit the Procrustean bed of totalitarian ideology, may yet move in harmony, but only to the tune of some bizarre or fantastic music, suggestive both of triumph and of bafflement. One thinks of those dances of beggars during the Middle Ages, in which cripples, according to the pictures we have, often figured prominently. These dances may have had a weird beauty. Emaciated limbs, twisted spines, stumps and crutches were woven by music into patterns, but that weaving music must have been strange and wild. Does Abram Tertz think that some such music can order and save from dullness future Soviet writing? Here we get an inkling as to why the author, throughout his many contradictions, shows a constant resentment against realism (he does not finally reject it) and a definite predilection for images (he does not finally accept them) of the fantastic and the absurd.

My final reaction, after analyzing the young Russian writer's essay and comparing it with the two plays it may be said to resemble, was a feeling of wonder at the permanence and unmanipulability of literary form. The propagandist may say what he is told to say, but he can say it only in a certain manner, only with a certain gracelessness. With whatever he does not genuinely adhere to, he will not be able to touch our hearts. But when a writer strives against his own sensibility to accept values against which he continues to rebel, he may finally be able to touch us with his very effort to flog himself into conviction, and with his pain at being thus flogged. The Russian writer's essay is proof that art can be created today in the Soviet Union and that such art cannot but express, if only obliquely, some rejection of the society which it yet accepts. If not the very greatest kind of art, works of this sort can reach a high level, and it is comforting to realize that they are not altogether different from works produced in the past. We cannot finally understand what the author of the essay on socialist realism has said, but we can understand him as an artist, and his essay, if we think of it as art.

October 1961

Sidney Hook
H. Stuart Hughes
Hans J. Morgenthau
C. P. Snow

WESTERN VALUES AND TOTAL WAR

In May 1961, in observance of its fifteenth anniversary year, Commentary *invited* Sidney Hook, H. Stuart Hughes, Hans J. Morgenthau, *and* C. P. Snow* *to participate in a three-hour round-table discussion of the moral and political questions surrounding the possibility of a nuclear war. The discussion, held before a selected audience of writers, editors, clergymen, and educators at the Institute of Human Relations and moderated by* Norman Podhoretz, *was wholly spontaneous. What follows is a slightly abridged transcript of the entire proceedings.*

Norman Podhoretz: The problem we've selected for discussion this afternoon is a very, very broad one, "Western Values and Total War," but we're going to try to focus on several slightly narrower themes, the main one being the question of whether or not, in a situation that threatens thermonuclear war, there is an inherent contradiction between the job of preserving and extending the liberal-democratic heritage and the job of protecting the national interests of the various countries in the Western bloc who presumably represent that tradition.

There have been, crudely speaking, two schools of thought on the question of the nature of thermonuclear war, and most political positions follow ultimately from one or the other of these two sets of assumptions. The first school of thought—which is represented perhaps most prominently by Herman Kahn and certain members of the RAND Corporation

* C. P. Snow arrived late and did not take part in the opening stages of the discussion.

—believes that the possibility of thermonuclear war has changed nothing in kind but merely in degree. In other words, this school of thought is willing to contemplate the use of nuclear weapons and to calculate the point at which a civilization might rebuild itself after a thermonuclear war.

The other school of thought—which has been represented recently by Karl Jaspers—begins with the assumption that thermonuclear war is different in kind, not merely in degree, from all other forms of violence and armed conflict between nations. This school of thought believes that one cannot speak of preserving civilization, freedom, or values by resort to nuclear warfare, and therefore would consider that nuclear warfare must be ruled out as an instrument of national policy. I think spokesmen for this school might argue that we can conceive of preserving a nation *physically* even after a thermonuclear war, but that it is absurd to speak of preserving values—moral values, political values—and certainly impossible to speak of preserving a civilization like our own. I wonder, Professor Hook, whether you would begin to by commenting on this opposition that I've rather crudely described.

Sidney Hook: The situation that Mr. Podhoretz has laid out for us is even more complex and difficult. I do not know how great the destruction will be in the event of war. I don't think anybody knows because so many contingencies are involved. We can grant that in any case the upshot will be horrible. The main question to me in this context is the moral one—what price are we prepared to pay for the preservation of freedom in a world in which such things may happen? However, when we discuss this question, we must bear in mind the following: On the eve of the Second World War it was widely predicted that a world war would lead to the end of all civilization because of the use of poison gas. And for all I know, there existed at the time well-grounded possibilities that the use of gas would make human life impossible on this planet with as much or even more plausibility, in a technical sense, than the use of thermonuclear weapons. Despite these predictions, two things happened. Those who felt that the values of the West were worth preserving against the onslaught of fascism took the risk of war, despite the fact that they weren't sure that gas warfare wouldn't bring an end to mankind. And secondly, to the surprise of many, gas warfare was not used. Hitler was a madman; yet this madman realized that if he used gas he would provoke reprisals which would mean the end of the national existence of Germany. From this, I draw the following conclusion: If we surrender the deterrent—which is widely recommended by many—we invite the conquest of the world by Communist totalitarianism. And no matter how we define Western values, they are certainly incompatible with that system of organized terror. If we hold on to the deterrent, then, since Khrushchev is not a madman and does not want a war which would mean the end of Soviet existence, and since the Communists make a fetish of history—survival is the be-all and end-all for them—it might be possible, by preserving peace through the retention of the deterrent weapon, to work out a multilateral form of controlled disarmament, thus permitting the nations of this world to make their own decisions concerning the kind of life they wish to live.

I conclude this introductory statement with a reminder about our theme. I had hoped that we would begin with a discussion of the nature of Western values. As I read the history of Western culture it seems to me that survival at all costs is not among the values of the West. It was Aristotle who said that it is not life as such, or under any conditions, that is of value, but the good life. The free man is one who in certain situations refuses to accept life if it means spiritual degradation. The man who declares that survival at all costs is the end of existence is morally dead, because he's prepared to sacrifice all other values which give life its meaning. But our alternatives today are not limited to surrender to Communism or universal destruction by war. We can count upon the sanity of the men in the Kremlin—they're very sane and realistic. If we do not abandon our deterrent weapons, I believe that in time we can work out an alternative which will avoid the extremes described by our chairman.

Podhoretz: Mr. Hughes, you are one of the many people Mr. Hook was referring to who have advocated the abandonment of the deterrent as an instrument of national policy, and I know that you have a rather different view of the alternatives before us. So perhaps you'd care to comment on the statement just made.

H. Stuart Hughes: Yes, one thing I'd like to say at the start is that I'm not a pacifist, but as a historian I find very few wars worth fighting. I would almost limit those worth fighting to the Second World War. I would definitely not include the American Revolution, the American Civil War, or the First World War. You may say that I include the one war I fought in, but that's just how it happened. My position would be a non-pacifist one, but one extremely skeptical of wars in any case, and totally skeptical of wars of mass destruction. Where I differ from some of my friends is in feeling that the great change came not with the dropping of the atomic bomb on Hiroshima, but in 1943, when we began the terror bombardment of Germany. There's where I think the character of war changed and the use of weapons of mass destruction began.

Now, I think here one should apply a type of reasoning such as the theologians have always used. Presumably any war worth fighting—e.g., the Second World War—is in theological and moral terms a just war. I would argue to this day that the Second World War was a just war. But if I understand the theologians correctly, a war can only be considered just if the means are proportionate to the evil to be eradicated. Now it seems to me the means used against Hitler were proportionate until the terror bombing; and you did not need the terror bombing to win that war. It was both morally and technically stupid and wrong. I cannot see any way of fighting Communism by general war in which the means would be proportionate to the evil. I happen to think that Communism has a great deal of evil in it, but less than Nazism had. On this basis, then, I throw out all comparisons with the 1930's and Munich. I know this is the classic argument and I think people who hold my position should be prepared for it. We sound like appeasers. Well, we accept that charge and say that the situation is different. Remember, appeasement was not originally an ugly word. It became such after 1938.

If I may go on a moment more—I hope disarmament will come up eventually, but I want to leave that out for the present—it seems, then, we have to face the old "Red or Dead?" question, as Bertrand Russell and others express it in England. Which do you want, to be red or dead? To speak very crudely, I'm on the red side of this, and I gather Mr. Hook is on the dead side. But let me just suggest in this connection that people who hold my views do not think that they are inviting Soviet conquest and do not believe in surrender. We believe that the enemy should be met with real force, but real force on a human scale which would give men the old alternative of making a personal choice as to whether they wanted to die. If the Communists were to invade, I would like to take up a gun and fight. But that would be my personal choice. It wouldn't involve all sorts of neutrals, the animal world, unborn generations, etc. So, my point of view is: yes, we should be prepared to fight and to fight hard—but with conventional weapons, by guerrilla warfare, militia-type organizations, passive resistance, underground activity. And the most important task for this country is to begin to study these methods. I went just a month ago to the international congress in Milan on the history of resistance organizations during the Second World War, and I regard this as a most important type of study—to find out how you resist as human beings without weapons of mass destruction. I say these things to distinguish my position from a doctrinaire pacifist position or from a position of simply saying, "Let us let the red hordes wash over us."

PODHORETZ: Mr. Morgenthau, would you rather be red or dead, or neither? Is there a way of escaping this gruesome alternative?

HANS J. MORGENTHAU: I certainly would rather be neither, if I have a choice. I don't want to address myself at the moment to the grim question as to whether or not to surrender the nuclear deterrent. But I want rather to discuss the fundamental philosophic question—whether it is possible to defend the values of Western civilization by nuclear war. I'm indeed inclined to answer this question in the negative, while admitting the possibility, or even perhaps the likelihood, that we will have to fight a nuclear war. This likelihood is the measure of the dilemma we are facing and of the political and moral bankruptcy we are suffering because of our inability to devise a third alternative to those which have been mentioned—both of which are to me equally unacceptable.

I think a revolution has occurred, perhaps the first true revolution in foreign policy since the beginning of history, through the introduction of nuclear weapons into the arsenal of warfare. For from the beginning of history to the end of the Second World War, there existed a rational relationship between violence as a means of foreign policy, and the ends of foreign policy. That is to say, a statesman could ask himself—and always did ask himself—whether he could achieve what he sought for his nation by peaceful diplomatic means or whether he had to resort to war. A statesman, up to the beginning of the nuclear age, was very much in the position of a labor leader who asks himself, "Can I get what I want by the peaceful means of collective bargaining or do I have to resort to industrial warfare in the form of a strike?" To use another metaphor, the statesman in the pre-nuclear age was very much in the position of a gambler—a reasonable gambler, that is—who is willing to risk a certain fraction of his material and human resources. If he wins, his risk is justified by victory; if he loses, he has not lost everything. His losses, in other words, are bearable. This rational relationship between violence as a means of foreign policy and the ends of foreign policy has been destroyed by the possibility of all-out nuclear war.

I cannot accept the analogy with gas warfare. Before the outbreak of the Second World War, the possibility of gas warfare was infinitely more marginal than is the possibility of nuclear war today. Certainly, the United States today must rely primarily on the nuclear deterrent in defense of its national interest; and when the chips are down, it will be faced with either retreat or resort to nuclear war. No such simple, stark alternative existed before the Second World War with regard to either retreat or gas warfare. Gas warfare was one weapon among many from which nations could choose. Furthermore, it was not a rational deduction but practical considerations which made gas warfare appear inadvisable to Hitler. In the period of the *Blitzkrieg,* gas warfare was unnecessary because the German armies overran their neighbors on all sides, and afterward the initiation of gas warfare would have been suicidal for Germany. The question hardly arose for the Allies because they were engaged in a war of movement and therefore resort to gas warfare was also senseless for them. Furthermore, because they were so engaged, they would have had to kill not only the German armies but the populations of the occupied nations as well. So there is, I think, quite a difference between the fact that all belligerents refrained from gas warfare in the Second World War and the possibility, if not the likelihood, of nuclear war in the future.

However, the fundamental question is, in view of this disproportion between the means of violence and the ends of foreign policy, whether it is still possible today to defend the values of any civilization by resort to nuclear warfare. For if you assume—as even the most optimistic analysts such as Herman Kahn have assumed—that in a third world war fought with nuclear weapons, fifty, eighty, or a hundred million Americans would die, and nine-tenths, let me say, of the economic capacity of the United States would be destroyed, you must be possessed not only by an extreme optimism but by an almost unthinking faith to believe that civilization, any civilization, Western or otherwise, could survive such an unprecedented catastrophe. For the fundamental error in the reasoning to which I'm referring, it seems to me, lies in the assumption that the moral fiber of a civilization has an unlimited capacity to recover from shock. I would rather assume from individual personal experience as well as from the experience of history that there is a breaking point for a civilization, as there is a breaking point for an individual man. For, after all, when we speak of civilization we are speaking of an abstraction; we are really speaking of man in the mass, of Americans in the mass. Would Americans in the mass be able to hold to the values of Western civilization in the face of such an unimaginable, unprecedented catastrophe?

We are of course all guessing here, but I would dare to make the guess that Western civilization would not survive such a catastrophe. If this estimate is correct, then obviously an all-out nuclear war in defense of Western civilization is a contradiction in terms, an absurdity. I must say that this absurdity may occur, but if it should occur, I would still say that it was an absurdity.

HOOK: I think that both of my colleagues have been inconsistent.

PODHORETZ: With each other, or each with himself?

Hook: Not with each other, but with themselves. Mr. Hughes maintains that he'd rather be red than dead, and then tells us that of course he's prepared to die fighting against Communism. And he talks about means of underground warfare against totalitarianism without any regard for the great qualitative difference which totalitarianism makes where opposition is concerned. There is no underground in the Soviet Union, Mr. Hughes—you probably learned that at the congress you attended. One of the reasons there is no underground in the Soviet Union is that the Kremlin organizes its own opposition in order to destroy it. And this introduces a qualitative change of enormous magnitude.

But I want to go back for a moment to a very interesting thing Mr. Hughes said about mass bombing, which for him represented the great turning-point in history. He asserted that the use of weapons must be proportionate to the end. He deplored the mass bombings of Germany which, of course, the English did not initiate—Coventry preceded the mass bombings of Germany—and condemned them on the ground that they were strategically and militarily unnecessary. Some people with excellent hindsight have criticized the use of the atomic bomb at Hiroshima on similar grounds. I frankly don't know whether these criticisms are justified by military and strategic considerations or not, but my question to Mr. Hughes is this: suppose the only way in which the West could have prevented the world victory of Hitler was by this mass bombing of Germany? Would you have been in favor of it or not? Mankind paid the price of forty million dead to get rid of Hitler. It sounds macabre to make comparisons and weigh lives against values, but it seems clear that Mr. Hughes, who justifies the Second World War, thinks that forty million dead was not too high a price to pay for a free civilization. My contention is that both of my colleagues have overlooked the disproportion between the two alternatives of surrender and willingness to resist. Professor Morgenthau said that we might soon be confronted by a choice between the preservation of the United States—that is, the preservation of our freedoms—and the use of a nuclear deterrent. He didn't clearly indicate what his position would be if that were our choice. There was some intimation that he believed, if that were really our choice, we should have to surrender. . . .

Morgenthau: That is not what I meant to say.

Hook: I'm glad I misunderstood you on that point. But if we decide against surrender, then the question is: how can we best preserve ourselves? You face the same problem as Mr. Hughes. If conventional weapons won't prevent Khrushchev from taking the world, and if the only thing that can prevent him is the nuclear deterrent, should we use it or surrender? I don't see how we can avoid that point.

The main thing I want to stress, however, is that it is a mistake to make an easy equation of the alternatives between surrender on the one hand and resistance and the cost of resistance on the other. For if we are prepared to take the risk of fighting for freedom, then we must prepare ourselves in such a way that the costs are diminished. Here we're dealing with speculative notions. The one thing we can be sure about is that if we surrender, Communism, with all its evils, will take over the world. But if we are prepared to fight, then we may not have to fight, for the reasons which I have indicated; and if the enemy is foolish enough to attack us—which I don't believe for a minute he will do if we keep the deterrent—then, if we are prepared, the losses may not be as great as some anticipate. There are questions involved here whose answers are indeterminate. I challenge the accepted notion that all life necessarily must be impossible by virtue of any kind of nuclear combat independently of what we do. After all, Germany seemed finished at the end of the Second World War.

I would like my colleagues to address themselves to the question: whether when the chips are down they are prepared to sacrifice the integrity and existence of the free world to Communism? And further, whether they have done justice to two considerations: first, that our willingness to fight for our freedom may be the best way of preserving it, just as sometimes in personal life one's willingness to lose one's life may be the best way of defending his life; second, that for the Communist world nothing exists but history. Survival, I repeat, is the *summum bonum* for Communism, whereas the West, buttressed in part by belief in immortality, whether as a myth or fact, has always maintained that there are certain values which are more important than life itself. To the Communist world there is nothing worse than defeat. That is why Lenin always emphasized the importance of what he called the policy of strategic retreat, and its correlative maxim: avoid provocations! That is why the Communists will never start a war which they have reason to fear they will not survive. Consequently, in the light of all this, I say to Mr. Hughes that his position invites the Communists to take over the world. And when they do so, he has no guarantee even then of survival. He does not know whether or not the Chinese will use atomic weapons against the Russians. He may end up both red and dead.

PODHORETZ: Mr. Hughes, would you agree that the renunciation of the deterrent would automatically, or even probably, result in a Communist take-over?

HUGHES: I'd like to answer one thing before I answer that. For I do want to clear up this casualties-and-Second-World-War question. The question is: if the bombing had been necessary to winning the war, would it still have been right? I find this hard to argue because I think the mass bombing was such a cruel mistake even in the most hard-boiled military terms. As a staff officer during the war I spent a good deal of time arguing against it. But let us say if you balanced it against the destruction of six million in the extermination camps, I suppose if you had to do the arithmetic, you'd come out and say—all right, it would still fall within the just-war category. So I think I could give a qualified agreement on that.

As far as comparing the forty million dead during the Second World War with forty million dead in a thermonuclear war, this seems to me an unrealistic comparison. The holocaust of a day or two, and the particularly awful method of death, should not be balanced against the death of an equal number in regular warfare. And the figure of forty million —which, incidentally, is the lowest estimate that has been made—should not be balanced against deaths that happened over a six-year period in a very widely extended territory, most of them in the countryside rather than in the cities, at least as many by starvation and hardship as by violent death, at least half of them in the Soviet Union itself. Nothing, then, in our Western or even German experience would be remotely comparable to the contemplated forty million dead in a short thermonuclear war. Now, to get to the main question that the chairman wanted me to answer. I would say we would only be honest in answering that Soviet take-over in certain areas might be invited. . . .

PODHORETZ: *Might* be invited by unilateral disarmament?

HUGHES: By some sort of unilateral renunciation of thermonuclear deterrence. I dislike the term unilateral disarmament without qualification because it sounds as though one is going to strip down to one's underwear shorts tomorrow, and that is not it. It would be a question of starting a movement in this direction. Renouncing deterrence as an instrument of foreign policy might, I think, invite or at least facilitate Soviet penetration of certain areas, particularly in the underdeveloped world, but these areas are largely indefensible anyway.

PODHORETZ: What about Western Europe, Berlin?

HUGHES: No, I do not think so. I think in Europe deterrence has not deterred anything. Let's leave out Khrushchev as more rational, perhaps more humane, than Stalin, and get back to Stalin before 1953. What deterred Stalin from taking over Western and Central Europe? I would argue it was not our monopoly of atomic weapons, but the conviction that these would be very hard countries to rule. He was having enough trouble already.

HOOK: Excuse me, Mr. Hughes. We have some evidence on this, *viz.,* the exchange of letters between Tito and Stalin. Tito was willing and eager to take Trieste, but Stalin warned him not to because he said he was not prepared to go to war against the West, for this would spell disaster. One doesn't have to agree with Churchill that the atomic bomb prevented the Russian troops from marching to the Atlantic, but it's quite clear that wherever the West stood firm the Russians retreated. When it stood firm in Berlin they retreated. When it stood firm in Greece they retreated. And this wasn't because it was difficult to rule these countries. After all, Stalin was able to rule Poland, he was able to rule other satellite regions of the Soviet empire. He had enough terror at his disposal. I think you must give us more evidence that it wasn't fear of war that prevented Stalin from moving West, because a *prima facie* case can be made out that it was.

HUGHES: I think you have to make a distinction between areas occupied in the wake of Nazi conquest with the flow-back of the Nazi tide after the Second World War and areas occupied *de novo.* My own reading of history is that the Russians were frankly surprised at their lack of popularity in East-Central Europe. They may have been a little naive about this, but there is the fact of their permitting virtually free elections in Hungary, for example, in 1945—and then being enormously disappointed at the result. There is the famous incident of the Soviet Occupation Commander literally kicking the local Communist chief out of his office after the elections went bad, saying, "What happened? What's the matter with you people?" I think there is massive evidence that with the revulsion against Nazism, the Russians thought that occupation would be an easier job than in fact it turned out to be. So I wouldn't draw any analogies from experience in East-Central Europe as to Soviet computations of the risks and difficulties in governing a newly-conquered territory belonging squarely within Western civilization.

PODHORETZ: Well, I think there's probably too much evidence and not enough time to spell it out. The point of disagreement is clear. I wish, Mr. Hughes, you would just go on for another minute and sketch out for us your notion of what would happen in the event of a renunciation of deterrence by the West. You've already said that in certain underdeveloped countries the Communists would move in, but you implied or said that these countries would go Communist anyway. You are saying, then, that you don't think one ought to assume that the Russians would move into Berlin, for example, if we renounced thermonuclear deterrence? Do I understand you correctly?

HUGHES: Exactly.

PODHORETZ: Mr. Morgenthau, what is your reaction to all this? Do you believe, as a leading exponent of the school of *Realpolitik*—you have been called that, anyway. . . .

MORGENTHAU: I have been called lots of things.

PODHORETZ: Well, that probably more often than other things. Anyhow, do you think it's plausible to assume that the Russians have been deterred by American strength in the past ten years?

MORGENTHAU: I have absolutely no doubt. I am convinced that the Russians were deterred from advancing. I don't believe for a moment that the Russians today are imposing upon themselves a certain self-restraint because they are afraid that Western countries may be difficult to digest. After all, if you consider that since the end of the Second World War, in election after election, one out of every four Italians has voted the Communist ticket, it shouldn't have been very difficult for the Communists to digest Italy. In 1946 or 1947 it would have been relatively easy for the Russians, short of American deterrence through the threat of atomic war, to take over Italy and other such countries, not necessarily by sending the Red Army in but by letting the best organized and largest political group within those countries do the job.

PODHORETZ: Mr. Morgenthau, what then is your own position? I think that Mr. Hook was asking a few minutes ago what choice you would make.

MORGENTHAU: I would fully agree with Mr. Hook that I would not surrender. I would rather fight if I'm forced to fight a nuclear war. But I would be fully convinced of the utter absurdity, of the utterly suicidal character of such a war. It would be an absolutely senseless war, but it would be imposed upon us because it would be one of the two alternatives which not only Western statesmanship but the statesmanship of the world would have left to us.

HOOK: If I understand you, then, Mr. Morgenthau, you're prepared to be heroic even if foolish. I maintain (though I don't like to use these phrases) that if we're prepared to be heroic, we will not have to be foolish.

MORGENTHAU: Let me say a word about heroism. I believe the advent of nuclear power has also changed the character of heroism. I don't believe that it is appropriate to quote Aristotle in this context, because when Aristotle speaks of the value of life as over against the value of the good life, he does not contemplate—nor could he have contemplated—the mass extermination of large segments of a civilized population. He had in mind individual acts of heroism—Leonidas being slain at Thermopylae and Socrates drinking the hemlock. Those are deaths which carry a meaning. They are deaths which were worth dying, as it were, but the extermination of eight million New Yorkers within a fraction of a second is an entirely different type of thing. I see no meaning in the reduction of tens of millions of people to atomic dust, of the monuments of a civilization to radioactive rubble. I see no meaning at all, I see no heroism at all in this.

HOOK: Then why do you want to resist it?

HUGHES: I think Mr. Hook is logical and I think I'm logical, although we disagree; but I do not see your point about fighting a senseless war. If it is senseless, then why fight it?

MORGENTHAU: The other alternative is also senseless, but perhaps somewhat more. I'm not trying to be facetious.

PODHORETZ: Mr. Morgenthau, I think we'd all like to know what the sensible alternative might be. You spoke earlier of diplomatic means of conducting conflict between nations. Now the only diplomatic means we've heard about this afternoon so far are in the nature of military policy. Are there other diplomatic means that might get us out of this awful dilemma?

MORGENTHAU: The way out of the dilemma is to transcend the two equally unacceptable alternatives of surrender or fighting a suicidal atomic war, and that means taking nuclear power out of the arsenal of individual nations altogether.

HUGHES: By multilateral disarmament.

MORGENTHAU: Not necessarily by multilateral disarmament, but some kind of supra-national agency which we may call world government, because this is what it would be.

HOOK: We do not disagree about that. My main point was that it is a mistake to conceive of our situation as if it were limited to the two alternatives of surrender and world destruction. All I maintained, Mr. Chairman, was that if one were prepared when the chips were down to fight for freedom, one would thereby broaden the spectrum of possibilities. It would give us maneuverability. We could offer Khrushchev various peaceful modes of arbitrating our differences. We could continue to work through the UN and through renewed attempts at test controls. But once we abandon our deterrent, then I predict all of these other methods will surely fail. And if I may say so, I do not know any reasonable way by which one can choose between absurdities if one regards them as equally absurd. When Mr. Morgenthau says that surrender is more absurd than the readiness to fight, I interpret him to mean that it is *more sensible* to be prepared to fight than to surrender. I would also like to point out that in terms of the Western tradition, the view that it is not life but the good life which is the highest ideal—the essence of the liberal outlook—was not restricted merely to cases of individual heroism. Total war was also waged in the past. Let us stretch our imaginations a little. Imagine that we are living in Carthage, and the Romans are at the gates. Carthage fought a total war. So did Judea. Many illustrations can be cited of cities and entire settlements which went down to destruction fighting for what they thought was the good life, even when they had no assurance that their action would serve as a beacon to inspire the rest of mankind. The history of the Jewish people especially illustrates this. I am sometimes inclined to admire Josephus because he seemed so sensible. But I admire more those who fought against Roman despotism, who fought for the integrity of their belief, refused to bow down to the Roman Emperor, and suffered the destruction of their community in consequence.

If we surrender our values, we open the floodgates for totalitarianism to sweep through the world. That we can make certain distinctions between Communism and Nazism is irrelevant where the main issue is concerned. The Nazis incinerated six million Jews; the Communists destroyed even more millions—and I'm not thinking now of Jews or non-Jews or of the differences in the method of slaughter. We must never lose sight of the ethical issue. In the end, each one makes his own decisions on these matters.

But I would like to bring back our discussion from the abstract, ethical question to the question of political strategy. I ask Mr. Morgenthau, who is an expert—and deservedly so—on foreign policy, whether he does not think that we increase our maneuverability in trying to work out a genuine type of peaceful coexistence by remaining armed with the deterrent.

MORGENTHAU: I would certainly agree that the prospects of this kind of policy in the long run are likely to be self-destructive. It is exactly because we have not developed any other means of settling our disputes peacefully, which is the great issue of our times, that we are forced to alternate between those two equally unacceptable alternatives.

PODHORETZ: Mr. Morgenthau, it's recently been suggested—I think by Professor Seymour Melman of Columbia—that Western reluctance to contemplate the abandonment of deterrence as a strategy is based on the fear, the conviction, that in *political* warfare, even under the best conditions, the Communists would win. Mr. Melman was saying that we have not imagined how to compete politically and economically with the Communists and therefore we are forced continually to waver between these two grim alternatives. I'd like to hear some comments on that rather provocative statement.

MORGENTHAU: This is not, I think, so terribly provocative. It states an obvious fact.

HOOK: I would disagree that it states an obvious fact. I think it's a very problematic assertion. In fact, in certain areas of the world it's false. I do not think that the free world need fear political warfare with the Soviet Union if it's restricted to political warfare. If the peoples of Europe were given the choice, or even if the peoples of the Soviet Empire were given the choice, I have no doubt as to what their choice would be. If the Iron Curtains of this world were lifted, in what direction would the movement of peoples flow? In the Soviet Union it's a crime, punishable by death, to try to leave the country. We haven't reached that yet.

PODHORETZ: Excuse me, Mr. Hook—I think you've slightly diverted the point, which is perhaps why you were provoked. What Mr. Melman was getting at, I believe, is what is sometimes called the competition for the uncommitted nations. He probably was thinking of places like Latin America, in particular Cuba and other such countries, which seem to be attracted to the Communist bloc in one way or another in trying to carry out a social revolution. And he was further suggesting—and this I'd like to hear Mr. Hughes talk about for a moment—that American foreign policy has not in general backed such social revolutions on the ground that they would produce situations that they were not reliably anti-Communist.

HOOK: Mr. Podhoretz, before Mr. Hughes answers the question, perhaps you would make a little clearer what the question is. You are not saying, I assume, that countries, even in the uncommitted portions of the world, when given freedom of choice, have shown a natural inclination to join the Communist bloc. I'm aware of no underdeveloped country which when given freedom of choice through elections has ever decided to install a national Communist regime.

As a socialist, I certainly agree that our American policy has been bad in many of these countries. . . .

PODHORETZ: Well, that's one answer to the question I raised. Mr. Hughes, would you agree with that?

HUGHES: I'm delighted to find myself in agreement with Mr. Hook on one thing. I also regard myself as a socialist, and I think our view of the good society is almost identical.

HOOK: No, I'm afraid not.

HUGHES: We both believe in a democratic socialist society.

HOOK: No, you are prepared to surrender the world to the Communists.

HUGHES: But that is not a definition of a good society, and I would say that I was not prepared to surrender the world.

HOOK: That is the implication of your position today.

HUGHES: I feel slightly deflated. I was trying to agree.

MORGENTHAU: You can't get away with it.

HOOK: Excuse me.

HUGHES: I still think we agree. But I am surprised that Mr. Hook says, "Why discuss an abstract ethical question?" I thought that was the whole point, and I regard the central matter here as an abstract ethical question.

But let me go on to the question of our fearing political warfare. I think we do need to fear political warfare as long as we seem to represent in the world a status-quo power. We need to be not only tolerant of social revolution but behind social revolution. And I believe—and here perhaps Mr. Hook agrees with me also—that it is not just because we fear social revolutions will go Communist that we are against them, but because we fear that they will be anti-capitalist. It seems to me that American foreign policy will make no sense to the uncommitted world until we say that we do not have a capitalist foreign policy, that we have no quarrel with collectivism or Communism as an economic system, that all we are interested in is human freedom. It seems to me this could have enormously simplified our attitude toward Cuba and a number of other places. So until American foreign policy and American society change profoundly, in having a far greater socialist tinge than they do today, I think we are going to be handicapped in peaceful political competition.

HOOK: Mr. Hughes, let's be fair. As fellow socialists let us recognize the facts about American policy. I think it is demonstrably wrong to say that American policy has been motivated by a desire merely to preserve capitalism in countries which have been threatened by Communist and socialist movements.

PODHORETZ: If I may interrupt you, Mr. Hook, I'd like to find out what the director of the Center for the Study of American Foreign Policy [Morgenthau] thinks about that.

HOOK: Just let me have a few more sentences. I call attention not merely to the position taken by the American government in Mexico, I call attention especially to the attitude of the United States at the end of World War II. I should like Mr. Hughes to explain, on his view—and also have this clarified by Mr. Morgenthau—how it came about that when Britain was under a Labour socialist government, the United States canceled its debt and gave substantial aid even against the opposition of conservatives in this country. When Europe was in danger of breakdown at the end of World War II, the United States offered the Marshall Plan, Mr. Hughes, to all the countries of Western Europe—including Communist countries like Poland and Yugoslavia. The reason it did that, it seems to me, is that it wanted to preserve the structure of freedom in Western Europe. And it wasn't motivated by simple capitalist considerations. Our attitude toward Yugoslavia, a socialist country, our attitude toward Poland—though it could be better—certainly invalidates the extreme statement that you made. That's why I cannot accept what you said as a fact, but as a rather problematic assertion.

HUGHES: I know Mr. Morgenthau is waiting, but Mr. Hook misinterpreted me. I did not say American foreign policy was motivated by capitalist considerations. I simply said it was *limited* by them in its range of choice. Now it was one thing to accept a quasi-socialist *fait accompli* and say we would give it support—and that, furthermore, in a highly developed country where little threat seemed to be implied. (One must say, incidentally, that even in the British case, American sympathy for the Conservative party was well known.) But in places where we could throw our weight around, like certain German states before the formation of the Bonn government, the military government stepped right in. . . .

[C. P. Snow arrives]

PODHORETZ: Sir Charles, at the moment we are trying to decide whether American foreign policy can be called capitalist in the sense of being limited by capitalist considerations.

MORGENTHAU: Not being a socialist, I look at this intra-socialist quarrel with complete impartiality and detachment. I don't believe it can really be denied that in the competition for the minds of men, especially in the emergent nations, the United States is at a considerable disadvantage. The issue is not that American foreign policy is capitalistic. It is rather that it is in a doctrinaire way anti-Communist and that it will support any movement and any government and elite which is vociferously anti-Communist, and the more vociferously it is anti-Communist the more certain is it going to be of American support. By the logic of this position, we have been supporting throughout the world the most reactionary, the most sterile, the most unviable elites, governments, and social systems.

The handicaps which the United States suffers in competing with the Soviet Union for the allegiance of the emergent nations is existential and cannot be removed by some kind of political device. After all, the Soviet Union can say, and says every day—and with a great deal of at least surface plausibility—that it was an underdeveloped nation forty years ago; that it was a backward, weak nation, and that it has developed into the other great industrial and military power of the world by virtue of the political, social, and economic system of Communism. So the Soviet Union says to the emergent nations, "If you want to develop as we have developed, accept our system, imitate us." And there can be no doubt of the enormous impact the actual economic and technological achievements of the Soviet Union have made upon the emergent nations. I think it was on the occasion of the Fourth of July celebration of 1956 that a Russian journalist wrote in a Russian newspaper that from the 18th century to this moment, the United States had been the model for other nations to emulate: that the United States had always assumed that its social and political experiment was created not for the sake of Americans alone, but for sake of the world, and that the nations of the world had accepted this assumption. And now, this journalist said, the Soviet Union has taken the place of the U.S. Now it is the Soviet Union which gives an example to the rest of the world, which serves as a model to be emulated by other nations. I think this is a real challenge and this is a real problem, and whatever the voting might be in the Soviet Union if it were free, I think the facts of the situation point toward a real handicap which the U.S. suffers in the competition with the Soviet Union.

PODHORETZ: Sir Charles, do you think that the Soviet Union has stolen American thunder as a model for emulation throughout the world?

C. P. SNOW: I think there's no doubt of the fact at all. What Mr. Morgenthau said is undoubtedly true. It's part of the world situation at this moment, and quite clearly this country's got first to analyze that fact, and second to see in what respects it can be altered or softened. But of the fact there seems to me absolutely no doubt.

HOOK: If I may draw on my own experience in Asia, I should say the picture is a little more complicated. As far as the opinion-makers in countries like Japan and India and Burma are concerned, it is true that they have been very much impressed, especially on the mainland of Asia, by Soviet economic progress. Interestingly enough, in Japan this isn't the case. The Japanese intellectuals told me, "We industrialized our country in forty-five or fifty years, from the time of the Mehji restoration in the 1860's to the turn of the century." In Japan, the Soviet Union is not the star of first magnitude in the firmament of the discontented. Oddly enough it's China. And not in terms of Chinese achievement but rather in terms, I think, of racial pride and sympathy. The Japanese don't really regard themselves as part of Asia. In the Asian countries—I can't speak about Africa, Sir Charles—I think that the dominant opinion is still (though tinctured with admiration of Soviet achievements) sympathetic toward the West. I have found the Indian intellectuals profoundly influenced by the values which the British bequeathed to India. I think England is the most popular country in India today. The Indians want both to improve their standard of living and retain the values of the West. The United States has helped India, although the Congress party is overwhelmingly socialistic. If India fails, Mr. Morgenthau's analysis would hold true. If in ten years from now the per capita income of India is no greater than it is today—which, despite all our aid, might be the case unless the growth of population is restricted—then I think there would be a tendency to turn toward the Soviet Union and Communist China. But the whole situation of course has been aggravated by recent Chinese incursions into India. There is still a passion for freedom among the Indians, though its chief expression is for national freedom and national independence. I make these remarks not to take issue with Sir Charles, but to offer a more complete picture.

SNOW: I would accept that qualification. Of course India is a very odd and special case for all sorts of reasons.

HOOK: And Burma too.

SNOW: Yes.

PODHORETZ: I wonder if we might draw Sir Charles into one of the earlier themes of the afternoon's discussion. The major question that was raised earlier was whether it is possible for the West to preserve and extend the liberal-democratic heritage and still conceive of a thermonuclear war as a resort of policy. We've got the views of the other three gentlemen fairly clear. I wonder what yours would be on this, Sir Charles.

SNOW: It's a very difficult one. Remember I speak here—though I know you and love you—with some special coloration. After all, I am English, and behind the thinking of all English people, irrespective of politics, there's bound to be the feeling that for us, if there is a thermonuclear war, the country is absolutely finished, not just mutilated grossly, as would be the case here and in the Soviet Union, but absolutely finished. You see, we're a supply base. We're not in the position of France and Germany, which probably would not be exposed to an extreme thermonuclear war because they would be conquerable by arms. But we should have to be, in the grizzly military pharse, masked, and masked under these circumstances means the complete elimination of the country. So that is at the back of all our attitudes. I don't think it need determine them completely, but there it is, and I think you Americans must take account of that when you find from all kinds of Englishmen much more reserve on this topic than you'd normally adopt.

Having said that, I find myself in something of a dilemma. I would have thought that any thermonuclear war, if it actually happened, would probably not leave much of the Western values behind. It's very difficult to see how it can. If there's going to be a catastrophe so great that it makes previous catastrophes insignificant, then it's hard to think that there would be anything much left in the way of democratic institutions. And I've never been able to see that there is a coherent military strategy for such a war. It seems to me that all the tough, sophisticated, complex thinking has very little relation to what is actually happening in fact. It seems to me to be the intellectual play of people who have not been concerned with military decisions, but are concerned with a kind of academic theory. And yet it's not easy to see how this country or the Soviet Union can get rid of nuclear weapons at once. I think we might hope that there will be a scaling down. That seems to be possible. It seems to me extremely important that this country should build up conventional weapons in a way that it has—very erroneously in my view—neglected to do since 1945. Both qualitatively and quantitatively this country is hopelessly behind the Soviet Union in that particular field. As to the constant use of this particular nuclear thinking not only as a threat but as a kind of support to society, my general inclination is that we probably have to damp that down or we're simply going to die on our feet.

HOOK: I gather then, Sir Charles, that you are not urging a policy of unilateral disarmament on the part of the West.

SNOW: No, I have never.

HOOK: This mood of thinking in England which you describe, and with which I can sympathize, is shared very widely, by Macmillan as well as Gaitskell. On the basis of it, it's still possible to elaborate alternative policies.

SNOW: Yes, oh yes. I don't think it's an all-or-nothing situation in that kind of way. There are really two different sets of conditions. One is, I think—coming down again to the sort of things military theorists talk about—that between this country and the Soviet Union at the moment there is a relatively stable balance which would not be affected either by the increase or the diminution of nuclear weapons on either side by quite a large factor. I would think that either country during the next decade is going to have enough material to do the other devastating harm.

PODHORETZ: The so-called technological breakthrough that would put somebody far ahead is highly unlikely?

SNOW: That's highly unlikely. In fact, if you've got the stuff and you've got any means of delivering it, then technological breakthroughs don't count. No, I don't believe in that. What I'm more worried about immediately is the rapid coming into possession of these weapons by large numbers of people. Because that seems to me to alter the dangers of accident, error, and so on quite out of proportion to the number of bombs. The number won't be very much greater, because the gross number of these weapons is so large in American and Russian hands that the six or eight powers that are going to possess them, or already possess them, won't alter them appreciably. But they do enormously alter the possibilities of some of these things going off, and I bet—in fact I've stated that I'm sure that they will go off, unless we can contain this dispersion. Whether their going off in a particular circumstance is going to start the whole holocaust, of course, is a matter partly of luck. It depends where the chance happened, in what circumstances it happened, in what hands these things were. The optimistic theory is that just as there is a fairly stable locking between this country and the Soviet Union, there will equally be lockings between, say Israel and Egypt, and what not. That, I confess, I am far less confident about. Secondly, I would have thought that if this country and the Soviet Union go on regardless, increasing their armaments in this particular way, the position which may be stable now is bound to become unstable. I can't imagine an arms race of that type going on for very long without becoming unstable.

HOOK: Unless there were countervailing considerations, I would agree with you. If one speaks in terms of a long-run building up of weapons, at some critical point it would lead to a denouement; but as Keynes said, in the long run we shall all be dead. But suppose we take into account the possibilities of modifying the trend. There are so many contingencies, as you pointed out, that enter the situation. They depend upon what we do to control tests, and limit the extension of the bomb with respect to the N+1 countries. But I've always been puzzled, to be perfectly frank with you, Sir Charles, about the theory of probability you were using in your speech before the AAAS [American Association of Atomic Scientists] when you predicted that there was almost a mathematical certainty that in ten years these things would go off.

PODHORETZ: I think the term used was "statistical certainty," wasn't it, Sir Charles?

SNOW: What I was actually prophesying—and I prophesy it here and now again—was that some of these things will go off. I didn't say that a thermonuclear war need break out, and that is why I was qualifying it here. It depends enormously on the particular way in which this accident happens. For instance, if by some unfortunate chance, a nuclear bomb went off in or over New York this afternoon, I wouldn't think that would give us much hope of avoiding the worst. We would have to show great prudence and wisdom for that sort of contingency not to bring about the thermonuclear war. And similarly, if by any chance one went off over Moscow, my expectations wouldn't be very cheerful. But I can imagine that somewhere in the remoter parts of Asia Minor, so to speak, one could go off, by accident or by some mad action, which wouldn't have decisive results. That, I think, needn't lead to a nuclear war.

MORGENTHAU: It's not only a matter of accidental nuclear war. Once nuclear weapons have been dispersed to an indefinite number of nations, the very mechanics of mutual deterrence as they exist today, stabilizing within certain limits the international situation, would disappear.

SNOW: I agree.

MORGENTHAU: For if tomorrow an atomic bomb exploded in New York, everybody would know whose atomic bomb it was, and the retaliation would be swift and devastating. For this reason we don't need to worry about an atomic bomb going off tomorrow in New York.

SNOW: Except by chance.

MORGENTHAU: Well, that possibility is extremely slim. We don't need to worry about that. But if you imagine for a moment, as we must, that within five or ten years ten nations have atomic weapons and tension exists between the United States and, let me say, two or three different nations, and an atomic bomb goes off in New York—against whom are you going to retaliate? Are you going to blow up the whole world in order to make sure that the culprit doesn't escape? Furthermore, you will then have a new refinement of diplomacy, trying to make it appear that the atomic bomb originated from some country other than the one which actually dropped it. You will then have a very interesting new Machiavellian situation, which I suppose you will not survive for long. Before you came in, Sir Charles, I painted a rather glum picture of two different types of absurdity with which we are confronted. I think that the situation will not only be more difficult to handle in diplomatic and military terms but will also be intellectually and morally infinitely more grave than it is now, once the atomic club is wide open and an indefinite number of nations have joined.

HOOK: How can we prevent the extension of nuclear weapons to the N+1 countries? Have you any ideas, Mr. Morgenthau, about procedures? In the next ten years if scientific knowledge is dispersed throughout the world, even if the Soviet Union and the United States were to renounce the use of thermonuclear weapons, what's to prevent some small nation from. . . .

MORGENTHAU: You are absolutely right. You see, this is really my main argument against unilateral nuclear disarmament. It may work in a bi-polar nuclear situation. But it is bound not to work when you have a multi-polar situation, when you have five or ten nations, because it doesn't do the United States any good to renounce for itself the use of atomic weapons, when the nine other nuclear powers don't renounce such use.

HUGHES: It may be true that it is going to be too late even for a unilateral solution. This is the really nightmarish possibility. But it seems to me, Mr. Morgenthau, that you and Sir Charles, who seem to be occupying the center of this discussion. . . .

SNOW: But not by my wish.

MORGENTHAU: We two are marginal men here.

HUGHES: I think you are in positions that are very close to each other, and you lead yourselves almost up to unilateralism and then stop short of it by describing the present situation as impossible. Actually I think you differ with Sir Charles, Mr. Morgenthau, in believing the present situation is less stable than he does. I would say that your arguments finally reduce to the absolute necessity of breaking the circle, the vicious circle, of mutual distrust between us and the Soviet Union, and doing it fast, and arriving at what amounts to an American-Soviet alliance for the preservation of the peace and the denial of nuclear weapons to other nations. And I would maintain that the only way that circle can be broken, and broken fast, is by a dramatic act of renunciation on one side or the other. Since we are not sitting in the Soviet Union, it has to be done here. Q.E.D.

PODHORETZ: Well, that's a dramatic point at which to end the discussion at the table and throw the floor open to questions from the audience. Rabbi Isidore Hoffman.

HOFFMAN: Don't you gentlemen think that our dependence on deterrence, our willingness to use the bomb, has been a major factor in our not pursuing other ways of solving the present crisis? Since we have depended so much on the deterrent, if we were to give up that dependence, wouldn't we be doing a much more serious job of finding other solutions?

PODHORETZ: Rabbi Hoffman is on the national board of SANE; Mr. Hughes, who is one of the leading members and founding spirits of the Committees of Correspondence, will reply.

HUGHES: I just say aye, amen, and everything else. I'm glad to find an ally in the audience. I agree totally with you.

Hook: I didn't understand, Rabbi Hoffman, that that was the upshot of the views of the other members of the panel. What I understood Mr. Morgenthau to say was that the deterrent had contributed to keeping both the peace and freedom of the world at least in Western Europe. I also understood him to say—and I'm in agreement with him—that the use or the retention of the deterrent is not incompatible with other means of keeping the peace: military—as Sir Charles pointed out, by building up our conventional weapons—as well as social and political. Where I differ from you is that you would surrender the deterrent, despite the evidence that it has had some limited good, in order to pursue other means, whereas I'm willing to do all the other reasonable things that you want done, without surrendering the deterrent.

Hoffman: If we weren't spending enormous sums building up the deterrent, wouldn't we be doing a better job with the underdeveloped nations?

Morgenthau: If we didn't have the deterrent, we wouldn't have a chance to pursue any other foreign policy to begin with. For the only alternative to deterrence is unilateral disarmament and letting the Soviet Union do as it pleases. However, I agree with what is implicit in your question, Rabbi Hoffman, and that is the unsoundness of our past policy in looking at the deterrent—an ever bigger and, if possible, cheaper deterrent—as the be-all and end-all of our foreign and military policy, as if the foreign and military policies of the United States could be defined in terms of the number of H-bombs and of the delivery systems we possess. This is certainly a self-defeating and ultimately, I am convinced, a suicidal policy. But the issue is not to give up the deterrent and to do something else instead. The issue is rather to maintain the deterrent and to do something else in addition.

Snow: May I just make a comment? I think that Rabbi Hoffman has a point which is of great historical substance, though I think that as history has gone on, the position has become more complex. In fact, there was no necessity for the West, say in 1945, to throw its entire faith into the "deterrent," which is what we did. Remember the population of the West in 1945 was very much larger than that of the Soviet Union. China had not become a Communist country. The only reason—it's a very deep reason—why the West relied on the deterrent was the implied disbelief in the willingness of Western men to bear arms. There is no other reason, and it is exactly the same military heresy which dictated a lot of our policy in World War II itself. It is a thing we must constantly remember. It was not because we were hopelessly outmanned by the Soviet Union. It was not that. In fact, the population of the West was about 50 per cent or more larger, but nevertheless, as a choice which seems to be inherent in the fiber of our society, we thought we could only maintain military and diplomatic superiority by the use of a particular weapon and not through armed forces in the ordinary sense. I think we really ought to examine our hearts about this. Though now the position is somewhat different, some of the thinking remains.

MORGENTHAU: But even today what you have said, I think, is correct. The attempt to base NATO military strategy on so-called tactical atomic weapons in order to save manpower goes back to the same failure of nerve.

PODHORETZ: Mr. Ernest van den Haag.

VAN DEN HAAG: I am not quite clear about Mr. Hughes's position. Do you prefer the certainty of surrender to the risk of atomic war? What I want to emphasize is that we are not choosing between two certainties, but between, on the one hand, a risk, and on the other hand, a certainty. Do you then prefer the certainty of surrender to the risk of a possible atomic war?

HUGHES: I'm glad you asked that question, and I will answer it in the crude and over-simplified fashion in which you asked it. I think, slightly extending Sir Charles's statement, that under present conditions (which I regard as much less stable than he does—I think I am closer to Mr. Morgenthau on this), thermonuclear war is a virtual certainty. Surrender is merely a risk. I would just take your statement and turn it around.

PODHORETZ: Mr. Joseph Kraft.

KRAFT: I have a question for Mr. Hughes. One of the few things on which there was general agreement was that it would be useful to have some kind of international control over thermonuclear weapons. The question is this: If the United States renounced the use of thermonuclear weapons in any believable way, wouldn't it be removing one of the few incentives for the Russians to enter into a control agreement?

HUGHES: I don't know. This is a really "iffy" question, but I maintain that one of the fallacies we commit in the ordinary conventional-wisdom discussion of the Soviet Union is to believe that the only argument they understand is force. I think it's been implicit around this table that the Russians, at least under Khrushchev, understand other arguments.

My guess is that to renounce thermonuclear weapons would be worth more in terms of breaking the vicious circle of mutual distrust—and I apologize for using the phrase again—I think this would be more effective in bringing about an agreement than continuing with deterrence. It may be that I am very wrong, and I think this is where a really crucial choice-point comes. I've made my choice, but I can see there's an extremely logical argument for the other one.

PODHORETZ: I suspect that Mr. Hook would like to provide that logical argument.

HOOK: Logic, of course, isn't sufficient, but it's necessary. In these questions we are dealing with historical evidence. Mr. Hughes has spoken about faith in the Soviet Union and implied that distrust is unreasonable or vicious. But I submit, Mr. Hughes, and as a historian you will agree, that—I take the risk of repeating Santayana's *bon mot*—"Those who have forgotten the past are doomed to repeat it." We can base ourselves only on probabilities. Whether we have faith or distrust in the Soviet Union depends upon the record of its performance. When Henri Spaak at one UN meeting turned to Molotov, who had charged the West with mistrust, and said, "What else can we have in the light of your behavior since the Second World War?" it seemed to me he was phrasing what was in everybody's mind. In 1948 Bertrand Russell urged the West to use atomic bombs against the Soviet Union if it wouldn't accept reasonable conditions of international atomic control. The U.S. at that time had a monopoly of atomic power. If it had been guilty of the imperialism the Soviet Union charged it with, it would have dropped the bombs. But in an act which was unprecedented in the history of hostile nations, the U.S. offered to surrender its monopoly of these weapons to an international authority with the sole provision that measures be taken to prevent bombs from being dropped on the U.S. Every nation of the world accepted this proposal save the USSR. Do you really think it's unjustified to be mistrustful of the USSR? The experience of all Western nations with the Soviet Union justifies a profound mistrust.

HUGHES: May I say that this is really off the subject. Let me just say once and for all, because I'm so often misunderstood, that I agree with everything you say about Communist tyranny. We don't have to argue that old one again.

HOOK: But we were talking about *trust*.

HUGHES: No, but I was talking about trust only on the narrow question of attitude toward thermonuclear weapons. What seems to me has to happen is that the U.S. and the Soviet Union must come to a realization of their mutual interest in having a world totally free of thermonuclear weapons. Now, I think that even in terms of absolute power-political, totally unscrupulous, unprincipled Soviet behavior, this makes sense. They would do better in the world competition without nuclear weapons than by having this nightmare hang over them. I don't really think we'd be giving up much.

HOOK: That's all very well, but let us examine your notion of trust, not on the broad historical level but on the narrow level of weapons control. I ask you, Mr. Hughes, what is your evidence—you must have some evidence—that we can reasonably have trust great enough to justify a policy of unilateral disarmament, that the Soviet Union will accept our opening gambit? If it were England we were dealing with, there'd be no question about it. If it were any other non-Communist country in the world, we could have reasonable trust. Look what happened in Geneva at the conference to prohibit further bomb tests. All the concessions since last year have been made by the Americans. The Russians repudiated the agreement made previously that the enforcement group would be headed by a neutral. They have insisted upon a built-in veto by specifying a three-man control which parallels Khrushchev's proposal for the UN. In the light of this action in the narrow sphere of weapons control, I ask you, Mr. Hughes, what are the grounds of your faith?

HUGHES: I think they think we don't mean it, and we think they don't mean it. On the test-ban issue, I believe that they've become bored. They want the big discussion. But again, this seems to me rather irrelevant. The main point, it seems to me, is that there need be no ethical ground for faith or belief in benevolent intentions. The main point is, looking at it from the angle of Moscow, that the subversion of non-Communist peoples could progress far more readily and far more predictably if there were no thermonuclear weapons around. This throws off all the Marxist calculations of the future.

MORGENTHAU: I must disagree with this prediction, for if there were no thermonuclear weapons, the U.S. would not be compelled to pursue the same kind of abstentionist and cautious policy which it has pursued consistently vis-à-vis Communist expansion. It is exactly because it fears thermonuclear war evidently more than does the Soviet Union that it finds itself in this situation. Remove that threat and limit the use of violence to conventional weapons, and any number of wars would have broken out in the world, in some of which the U.S. would have been fully involved.

Hughes: I am afraid I disagree totally. I do not think we have deterred the Soviet Union and I don't think they've deterred us. The reason we do not spring to the defense of Laos at this point has nothing to do with thermonuclear weapons. It is simply that Laos is indefensible, and that the American population is not that interested.

Hook: What about Hungary? One of the specific reasons given for our not coming to the aid of the Hungarian people who rose partly because of our promise to aid in liberating them, was that this would mean a thermonuclear war. We stayed out of Hungary. We stayed out of East Germany, too, when the people rose in 1953.

Hughes: That was a most specious bit of reasoning to cover up for a failure of foreign policy. We made the ghastly error of giving the Hungarians the impression that we would come to their aid when we didn't have the slightest intention of doing so. Then when this was exposed to the world, we dragged in the thermonuclear weapons. It seems to me if one thing is true of America and American public opinion, it is that there is a general conviction that there should be no more Koreas. Truman tried it once and got very much burned on it. And I don't think we'll reach any clarity in foreign policy vis-à-vis our own people until we realize that there is very little enthusiasm for local wars, even with conventional weapons, in this country.

Podhoretz: Sir Charles, do you want to get in on this one?

Snow: Only to make the mild comment that since 1945 there have been several acts of aggression on both sides. That is, there have been about two genuine acts of aggression by the East—Hungary and Korea—and two genuine acts of aggression by the West—Suez and Cuba.

Hughes: And Guatemala.

Snow: And I would have thought that you mustn't have all this discussion on a high moral plane. As though we don't do any of these things ourselves, and as though we were entirely governed by the highest motives. I would have thought—and here I am with Mr. Hughes—that in local wars the deterrent has deterred nothing.

Podhoretz: Mr. Lionel Abel.

Abel: I have a question for Mr. Hughes. Since you say you are not a pacifist, would you also be in favor of militarizing the entire American people—bearing in mind Sir Charles's remark about the unwillingness of Americans to bear arms?

HUGHES: I think, and I've drawn from George Kennan on this, that there should be a military system not unlike the Swiss. I think that universal military service on a militia basis with serious summer training and a serious plan of how you retreat to your mountains and of how you organize guerrilla activities—I think this might make a great deal of sense. I think the Swiss have the best army in the Western world and the one best adapted to contemporary conditions. But the Swiss are not a military people. I would object to your term "militarization" because it implies the acceptance of military values and the prestige of generals in the national life and a big war-production effort that influences foreign policy. I may have a very romantic 19th-century view, but the Swiss make it work in the 20th century. I have much more the "nation-in-arms" point of view, which has never been a militarist point of view.

SNOW: I'd like to chime in on this because I think it is important. It would be a very cheap price to pay for a real lessening of the thermonuclear tension if everyone had to do a certain amount of military training. I'd pay that price with the utmost grace, and I should have thought that most people of good will would agree.

PODHORETZ: Are you talking about conventional armies, or are you talking about the kind of militia Mr. Hughes was describing?

SNOW: There are various alternatives, and some countries have gone in for more orthodox military establishments. Very highly civilized and democratic countries have taken this line with no loss that I can see. Sweden, for instance, which is a highly civilized country, has done this.

HOOK: In conversations with people in Switzerland and people in Norway, I got the impression they hoped that the United States would not surrender its deterrent. They would hate to be dependent exclusively upon their militia system. As I see the Communist system in operation, I think it is highly romantic to imagine that a militia alone could prevent a country from being occupied and its population deported to other regions of the world. Sir Charles was right when he said that at the end of the Second World War there was a great reluctance on the part of the Western powers to continue military training. I don't know whether you are aware of it, Sir Charles, but in this country at the end of the last war there was a mass movement, which some of us tried to stop, mobilized under the slogan, "Bring the boys back home." I think one of the great disasters of

American policy was the withdrawal of the U. S. Army from Europe—an act which, despite all our trust in the Soviet Union, was not met with a corresponding withdrawal. Russian armies remained astride of Europe while the Americans turned back to normal business. In fact, the reason so many people believed the boys should come home was the same touching faith in the Soviet Union that Mr. Hughes has.

HUGHES: May I say once again that I do *not* have a touching faith in the Soviet Union. I've said it twice already. How many more times do I have to say it?

PODHORETZ: Mr. Hughes, what kind of faith *do* you have in the Soviet Union?

HUGHES: I don't have much more than Mr. Hook. We draw different conclusions from the same data.

MORGENTHAU: Whatever kind of faith it is, it isn't touching.

HOOK: Well, it's not touching, but very profound. Let us return to a very important point. I believe there is no doubt that at the end of the war the peoples of Great Britain and the U.S. thought that they could work out a *modus vivendi* with the Soviet Union. NATO came into existence not as a result of Western aggression but as a defense against Soviet incursions in Western Europe, particularly after Czechoslovakia. It was with great reluctance that both Great Britain and the U.S. adopted this posture of defense. I agree with you, Sir Charles, that "he is all fault who owns none," and that none of us is free of guilt. But, perhaps not behind your position so much as behind Mr. Hughes's position, I find a kind of unconscious, and sometimes I think conscious, equation between the Soviet Union and its record of aggressions in the world, and that of the U.S. and the West. I think that the record. . . .

HUGHES: Let me interrupt you. Let me put on the record again, since it seems to be necessary to spell out the obvious, that Western aggressions have been far less serious than Soviet aggressions, since 1945, or whatever date you wish.

HOOK: Then I can only conclude that whatever the basis of Mr. Hughes's faith and trust in the Soviet Union is, it has no grounds either in logic, psychology, or historical fact.

PODHORETZ: That's a lot of ground.

Mr. Robert Bierstadt.

BIERSTADT: I'd like to ask a question about Sir Charles's statement that in the event of a thermonuclear war England would be finished. It seems to me that the United Kingdom has one alternative that is denied to us, and that is the neutralist position that is recommended now by the anti-Gaitskell wing of the Labour party, and of course by Bertrand Russell, and even implied by the Conservative government's decision not to proceed with the Blue Streak missile program. Isn't it possible that by making a commitment to neutralism the United Kingdom might have an alternative that is denied to us?

SNOW: I don't think it's a very real alternative. I don't think that the strategic position in the world would be affected. I think in any conceivable war between the United States and the Soviet Union England would be a very important aircraft carrier, so to speak. I never have thought that neutralism is anything more than an extraordinarily remote and chancy last resort. I doubt that there's very much in it. I think, on quite different grounds, it might be entirely reasonable and would help some of this Nth-power problem if England said: "We're not going to have our own nuclear arms." That would make, I think, very good military sense. In fact, we really can't deliver the damn things; even if we've got them, we're bound to depend on yours. I think I should be in favor of that, and it probably would be the one way of getting the French to renounce theirs.

PODHORETZ: Mr. Robert Silvers.

SILVERS: Mr. Morgenthau was asked whether he knew of some way of escaping the "red or dead" alternative, and he never had a chance to answer. Could he answer that now?

MORGENTHAU: I was rather happy that this chance passed by me. Now I have to face the inevitable. Of course, I am very frequently asked similar questions and can never answer them to the satisfaction of the questioner, because there is no honest possibility of pulling out a blueprint and saying that's it. But I can try to lay before you the general principles which I think must guide any concrete policy, if we want to escape those equally absurd alternatives which I discussed before.

It is a fundamental fact of contemporary history that the so-called sovereign nation-state has been made as obsolete by the recent technological revolutions of transportation, communications, and weaponry as the feudal principle of political organization was made obsolete by the first industrial revolution of the steam engine. We saw this very clearly during the Suez crisis when the great nation-states of Europe were no longer able to pursue independent political and military policies. In a sense we see it right now in this country when so powerful a nation as the United States is no longer able to pursue an independent policy with regard to Cuba or Laos, and is no longer able to protect its interests vis-à-vis nations which by any standard of comparison are infinitely weaker in the material sense than the United States. So we are living in a political world which has been left behind by technological developments. Nothing short of a political revolution commensurate with the technological revolutions through which we have passed, through which we are in the process of passing, and which are still ahead of us, will solve the problem to which you have referred.

To be more specific: the crucial importance of the Geneva negotiations concerning the cessation of atomic tests lies exactly in that if they should be successful, the world would have taken a first step beyond the nation-state toward at least one supra-national agency controlling one very limited technical aspect of atomic power. I think in this direction lies the only salvation I can see.

PODHORETZ: Mr. Philip Green.

GREEN: Mr. Hook, I'd like to ask you one question. I understand the ethical system by which you personally choose what we might call death rather than dishonor. But I do not understand, and I wish you'd clarify, the ethical system that gives you the right to make that choice for other people who have never been consulted—for example, the Okinawans who live as American chattels and who would be among the first to go in the event of a thermonuclear war.

HOOK: First of all, I should like to point out that I am not asking for the power to make that decision. I am making a proposal which, if accepted, would obviate the necessity of making a decision of that sort. On the other hand, I maintain that your position and the position of Mr. Hughes makes it more likely that this fateful decision will be taken by somebody. I am a democrat and therefore prepared to accept the consensus of opinion in this country on the policy we should follow. Of course, I make a distinction between a personal decision and a social decision. Morally, I don't have to be bound by what the majority decides; but so long as I am a democrat, then I have to accept, *as* a democrat, the freely-given judgment of the majority. However, if our democracy were to act in the way in which, say, Hitler's or Khrushchev's regimes act, I would surrender my belief in democracy and try to overthrow it. But I wouldn't pretend that I was a democrat and at the same time try to overthrow a properly arrived-at democratic consensus.

Behind your question, Mr. Green, and in your charge against me, I find a great deal of moral hypocrisy. You ask whether I am prepared to support a decision which will affect the lives of those who did not have a choice in making it. Did you ask a question of that sort when we decided to go to war against Hitler? Against Japan? When we bombed occupied France? When our weapons destroyed people who did not themselves have an opportunity to make that decision? Every war that has been conducted in the West in the history of mankind has involved this morally tragic situation. Would it be different if we surrendered to Communism? Wouldn't we be deciding the fate of others too?

You are worried about the Okinawans; were you worried about them when we fought against Japan? Yes, we bombed the Japanese islands, but what was the alternative? The alternative was defeat, and acceptance of a system of infamy. It is a question of our basic values and whether we are prepared to accept life in a community under any circumstances. Bertrand Russell, who has soft-pedaled this note recently, once said that he could conceive of a world that morally had eaten of some poisoned root, and in which therefore the cessation of life might be the lesser evil. As a theoretical possibility, no matter what kind of moral economy one adopts, one can conceive of a situation in which the conditions of life for a people, like the conditions of life for an individual, would be unendurable. This, as I have said, was the decision made historically by the Jewish people in fighting against Rome. It was made by many communities in fighting against Hitler. As far as these people were concerned, that constituted their whole world.

I do not want to be taxed with the monstrous cruelty of snuffing out somebody else's life because of a decision *I* make. If one generalized the principle behind your position, it would be impossible to adopt any kind of social legislation whatsoever. Every law limits the freedom of some individual. If we pass a law which forbids night work for women, some women will lose jobs which they badly need. In the end we make a decision on the basis of the over-all ethical values we're committed to. I am prepared to defend these values in a concrete historical situation.

I conclude with this point: we are confronted with a political choice. My view is really an appeal to our political common sense. The only faith that I have in the Russians is the faith that they want to survive. I believe that if they know *they* cannot survive a nuclear attack against the West, there will be none. Once that has been made clear to them, I would present them with alternatives again and again and again for multilateral disarmament under adequate controls. I would try by using our tremendous wealth to build up a freedom-loving welfare economy—an open society—everywhere in the world. And I would fight for the minds of people everywhere, including the Soviet Union, in the hope of preserving a stalemate—that tired phrase of Churchill's, "the balance of terror," is still useful—until changes take place in the Communist empire, and they move in their own way toward a community which would make it possible to establish a world state. I am not a fanatic who thinks *all* the problems of the day are those posed by Communism. But I do think it is sober truth to say that if there weren't a Communist totalitarian empire in the world today, it would be possible to develop a world community, in which the chances of these nuclear nightmares would be increasingly small. But we must take the facts as we find them, using whatever intelligence and courage we have in hopes of finding a solution.

GREEN: I did not say that I would not fight or that I would surrender. I merely was trying to make the point that when I fight it will be for myself and for whoever wants me to fight for them. I would like to associate myself with Mr. Hughes's remark that every war with the exception of World War II was unnecessary and that many facets of World War II were immoral.

HOOK: What I said seems to me still valid. If you were prepared to support the Second World War, then you were responsible for a decision which destroyed the lives of people who had no choice in making that decision and who did not want you to fight for them. There were a great many people in Western Europe who were prepared to live under Hitler. Why did you approve destroying them? And so I add to my charge of moral hypocrisy, one of logical inconsistency.

PODHORETZ: A much more serious charge.
Mr. Irving Kristol.

KRISTOL: I have a question to the panel in general on this matter of faith in the Soviet Union. I think I see what Mr. Hughes is getting at and I don't think this question has been adequately discussed. What Mr. Hughes is saying, if I understand him correctly, is that it does not make sense from the Russian-Communist point of view to have a world in which there is a threat of thermonuclear destruction; that from the Communist point of view it makes sense to enter into a nuclear disarmament agreement. The question therefore is, why don't they do it? I personally think they don't do it because they are Communists, because they are not rational, because there are elements of mythology in Communism which dictate their policies. But I should like to hear what the members of this panel think.

HUGHES: I think they don't do it because they think we don't mean it. And so we have to do something dramatic to show that we mean it.

MORGENTHAU: It is of course obvious that the Russians as rational beings have the same interest as everybody else in not being destroyed in a nuclear war. But there is a very long step from this simple recognition of a rational interest to political action putting this rational interest into practice. The statesmen of Russia are no more motivated by one simple rational consideration than anybody else. We all have contradictory motives; we all are torn by different tendencies, and so are the Russians. On the one hand, Mr. Khrushchev knows that a nuclear war would make an end to the Bolshevik regime in Russia, if not to the very national existence of Russia. But on the other hand, he says to Walter Lippmann that there are neutral nations, but no neutral men. I shall never surrender the security of the Soviet Union to a non-Communist, he says, any more than you would surrender the care for your security to a Communist.

So you have here two incompatible positions within the mind of the same man. And the question arises, how do you transcend these two incompatible positions? Mr. Hughes says we ought to make a dramatic gesture, which would really be an unprecedented act of renunciation, in order to show the Russians the right way. This assumes that Mr. Khrushchev is motivated by nothing but his rational interest in surviving in the present world. But he is certainly also very much motivated by the specter of a Communist world which he firmly believes the process of history is bound to bring about. Presented with such an opportunity, I must say my faith in Mr. Khrushchev's rationality in terms of survival would certainly yield to my distrust of Mr. Khrushchev as the apostle of Communism.

HOOK: Mr. Kristol's question as to why the Russians don't accept a disarmament treaty brought from Mr. Hughes the rejoinder, "Because they don't believe we mean it." Now that's a little ambiguous. First of all, we did make a dramatic gesture at the time of the Acheson-Lilienthal proposals. We made it, and the Communists rejected it. Will Mr. Hughes say that we didn't mean it? If he does, again I would like to ask for evidence.

HUGHES: Incidentally, I didn't say we didn't mean it. I said they *thought* we didn't. That's a different thing.

HOOK: Oh, well, that just puts the question further back. Why did they believe we didn't mean it? What could we do to make them believe that we mean it, short of surrendering to them? We made them this offer and they turned it down. I doubt that they thought we didn't mean it. There is another plausible explanation. It's this: the Russians do not fear that we will use the nuclear weapon. On several occasions, I believe, they have actually implied that it's morally impossible for the West to use the nuclear weapon without being provoked. Mr. Morgenthau indicated another line of thought that moves them. If they know their flank is covered, so to speak, that they needn't worry about an atomic Pearl Harbor on our side, why should they forgo the position of strength that they get from a war of nerves? I think Khrushchev is counting upon the growing hysteria in the West. And by hysteria I don't mean fear—intelligent fear is a good thing—I mean blind fear. He's counting upon the growth of hysterical fear in the West to force it to retreat again and again. Obviously that's the logic—or psychology—of the situation. If you say to the Russians, "Short of war we will use all means to stop you," what's to prevent them from closing their iron fingers around Berlin? Step by step they will march on, or to use an analogy of Kissinger's, we can lose a football game by a series of five-yard dashes as much as by one end-run. If the Communists can count upon our hysterical fear of world destruction, then they can sit pretty. And they *are* sitting pretty. They *are* winning the world. They're winning the world because we haven't worked out other alternatives. However, they can't be finally sure of winning the world until we surrender the deterrent.

SNOW: I'm getting rather left out of this party and I'm going to say something which I don't particularly like to say. The Russians have at least as much suspicion of you as you have of them. This is very real. They lost twenty million people in the last war—twenty million, one out of ten—and I've never been in a Russian family where someone hadn't had an immediate casualty. They've seen American bases around the Soviet perimeter, and this seems to them extremely immediate. They just do not trust you any more than you trust them. And I must say—and I've got to say this—that traveling a lot in this country, it's been extremely hard to get people to discuss the Soviet Union or any Russian attitude on the plane of rationality. Remember there is a naive skepticism, naive suspicion, that is quite as real as naive credulity, which Mr. Hook has been accusing Mr. Hughes of. A superb example of naive skepticism was of course the folly of thinking that Gagarin's flight wasn't absolutely authentic.

PODHORETZ: Mr. Moshe Decter.

DECTER: I'd like to ask Sir Charles to whom he's referring when he talks about "they" being suspicious of us in the Soviet Union? If you mean ordinary people, that can hardly amount to very much, because ordinary people don't constitute public opinion in the Soviet Union. If you mean the authorities, then surely they can't be naive enough to believe that the bases with which we have ringed their territory were created by us unprovokedly. There seems to me to be a false equation behind what Sir Charles is saying.

SNOW: This is an example, I think, of the difference in moral balance with which we view our own actions and the actions of others. When I say "they," by the way, I mean the people I know in Russia; they're very roughly scientists, writers, and a certain number of politicos, very much the same kind of people professionally as are gathered here this afternoon. You may think, and I dare say you're right to think, that having bases in Turkey is a fine pacific action and a very valuable action from every point of view. But the idea that the Russians think that is really stretching the point. If they had bases in Mexico, would you think that was such an admirable gesture?

DECTER: But why did we get bases in Turkey in the first place?

SNOW: I'm simply trying to answer the question that was asked: what do they really think? Why aren't they falling immediately for a nuclear pact? If they thought they could get a nuclear pact, a real nuclear pact, my bet is that they would take it with their arms open.

PODHORETZ: Sir Charles, could you elaborate a little on what you mean by a real nuclear pact?

SNOW: Well, I'm afraid that here the depth of suspicion on both sides, and for very good historical reasons, is absolute. Until that is broken —and I think that here I agree with Mr. Morgenthau—any small thing will help (and this is why I attach great importance to the nuclear test ban). A test ban would be the first sign that we can discuss more important and bigger things on the plane of reason. But I don't believe that the plane of reason is the plane on which these discussions have been taking place in either country.

PODHORETZ: Sir Charles, on the test-ban question, you disagree then with Mr. Hook who sees Russian actions at Geneva recently as an indication that they are not serious about negotiating a test ban. Is that so?

HOOK: I didn't go that far; I said that the upshot of the negotiations in Geneva is discouraging. . . .

SNOW: Oh, yes.

HOOK: And I could not take seriously Mr. Hughes's statement that the Russians are bored by it and that they're interested in the disarmament conference. If they're interested in the disarmament conference, why should they blow up a step leading to it? I said it was discouraging. I am in favor of a test ban with decent facilities for inspection. I agree with all the concessions which the West has made. After all, the British have been a moderating influence, Sir Charles, in these negotiations. I don't know what sentiment you've run up against in the United States, but I think our negotiators at Geneva have been very patient. The conference is on the verge of being suspended now only because, as I understand it—subject to correction by those who have studied the matter more carefully—the Russians themselves have reneged on their agreement that the controlling directorate would be in the hands of some neutral person. My discouragement is the basis for doubt of progress. If tomorrow the Russians reversed themselves, I would welcome it. I am not committed to a policy independently of the consequences and of fresh evidence.

SNOW: Let me say at once, I am worried too. We all know President Kennedy's chief scientific adviser, Jerome Wiesner, who has expressed his views. He's a man for whom scientists everywhere have the utmost respect—both for his intellect and for his good will. I've no question of that whatsoever, and I'm sure I can say that many Soviet scientists would feel the same. So I'm worried and puzzled.

PODHORETZ: You have no explanation, then, to offer for the behavior of the Russians? Mr. Morgenthau, can you perhaps offer an explanation?

MORGENTHAU: I think one can explain the Russian behavior at Geneva quite rationally on the basis of their utter distrust of our intentions. For the Russian negotiators made the point—and I think Mr. Khrushchev himself made the point—that the negotiations would not affect testing by France, and that if under present conditions we and the Russians were to sign a test-ban treaty, we would simply continue testing under the guise of French operations. And in that case we would take advantage of what the French learned while the Russians would stick to the agreement. So again you have the same kind of distrust which is at the basis of the whole situation.

HOOK: Mr. Morgenthau, I don't understand your analysis at this point. If this is the consideration which moves the Russians, how would the acceptance of their counter-proposal for a three-man secretariat meet it? Even under those conditions you couldn't stop the French, could you?

MORGENTHAU: That is correct; but of course, the three-man proposition is a mere subterfuge. Mr. Khrushchev is not serious about this—he can't be.

PODHORETZ: Mr. Spencer Brown.

BROWN: I'd like to ask the panel their views on why the Communists are so enthusiastic about the campaign for nuclear disarmament.

HUGHES: I think it's true that the Soviet Union is enthusiastic over Western agitation for unilateral disarmament. But I would say this is no reason for our not doing it. I've always said we should do what's right whether the Soviet Union applauds or hisses us. We cannot constantly gear our action to the Soviet reaction. But it's obvious why they're enthusiastic—because the threat to their existence would be removed. It's so obvious that I can't understand why you asked the question.

HOOK: The question was naive, but Mr. Hughes's answer was also naive. The Russians would like us to adopt unilateral disarmament because this would make it possible for them to dominate the world without any opposition. In other words, this is their political goal and therefore one reason for us to be suspicious. And now for my own position on unilateral disarmament—the only kind I favor is unilateral disarmament by the Soviet Union, on the ground that objectively they have nothing to fear from us.

MORGENTHAU: I have nothing to add to what has already been said, but I will make one general comment. If I were in favor of unilateral disarmament it wouldn't bother me one way or the other if the Soviet Union were in favor of it or against it. It so happens, for instance, that I am in favor of racial equality and I am against discrimination. So is the Soviet Union. That doesn't make any difference to me.

PODHORETZ: I think everybody in this room is in favor of unilateral disarmament by the Russians. On that we can all probably agree.
Mr. William Phillips.

PHILLIPS: I'm a little puzzled by the question of what the political consequences of multilateral disarmament might be. As I understand it, the consensus of the panel has been that at the moment the non-nuclear forces of the Soviet Union are stronger than those of the United States.

And, as Sir Charles said, the Communists seem to have a greater willingness to keep men under arms than we do. If that is so, and if nuclear weapons have constituted *the* deterrent to a Soviet take-over, what would deter a Soviet take-over if we arrived at multilateral disarmament? Perhaps the answer to this question might explain why bilateral nuclear disarmament has not been agreed upon.

HOOK: When I say I believe in multilateral disarmament I have two points in mind. First, assuming that we have adequate inspection, it has to be a phased disarmament—that is to say, not sudden, overnight. And in the nature of the case we should be grateful for even a little progress. We should feel our way; we can't be certain of our positions no matter how strongly we hold them. We live in a contingent universe. Maybe we shall discover some enemies of Earth on Mars, and then we can all agree. My program of multilateral disarmament envisages the extension to conventional weapons too, because if it didn't, then what we would be saying is that we want to reduce the West to the position of a nation that wields clubs against other powers using conventional weapons. Ultimately, I would like to abolish all weapons. But I want to begin with the most dangerous ones first.

PHILLIPS: In discussing many of the military and political problems that came up this afternoon, Mr. Hook, you applied the criterion of whether it might not permit a Russian take-over. In other words, your anti-Communism—and I don't disagree with much of your anti-Communism—is a part of your total position on disarmament. In answering my question you don't tell me how Khrushchev will be prevented from taking over West Berlin if the kind of disarmament that you say you are for were to be achieved.

HOOK: I still don't understand the drift of your question. After all, we did offer to give up our atom-bomb monopoly in 1948. I am in favor of multilateral disarmament starting with atomic weapons. There would be a certain risk involved, but the risk of a Soviet take-over would not be as great if the Russians only had conventional weapons. If the West really relies on conventional weapons, and is prepared to make the effort and pay the price, it has the manpower to equal Soviet strength. I don't think the Soviet Union will go to war with any weapons unless it's sure to win. And so I would gradually scale down weapons on both sides, and leave to the peoples of the world the free decision as to whether they want to live under Communism or not.

PODHORETZ: Having come in late, Sir Charles has had less opportunity to speak than the others, and perhaps it's fitting that he should have the last word on this point.

SNOW: Mr. Phillips' question is a very simple one, but of course a deep one. That is, what is the position in the world if in fact you get an effective disarmament agreement? This is a real and very interesting question. I would have thought that certainly some opposition to nuclear disarmament from the West has come because they are very troubled about the answer. . . .

PODHORETZ: I'm afraid I must interrupt you, Sir Charles. Our time is up, and we only have enough left for me to thank all of you for an extremely stimulating discussion.

November 1962

Oscar Gass

CHINA AND THE UNITED STATES

When you shall these unlucky deeds
relate, . . . Nothing extenuate,
Nor set down aught in malice.
—OTHELLO

I. War and Revolution, 1941-49

Chiang Kai-shek and his Kuomintang regime were swept from the mainland of Asia in 1949 because of their failure in all that relates to the building of an army. In the China of 1941-49, the customary foundations of consent and obedience were in dissolution. Clubs were trumps. But the Kuomintang was not capable of creating a steady, efficient organization of wielders of clubs.

At no time, from Pearl Harbor to the Japanese surrender, was there serious warfare against the Japanese in mainland China.* Chiang simply waited for his allies to defeat Japan. While waiting, he supported General Chennault's aerial strategy—and, in this, was abetted, for some years, by Roosevelt and Hopkins. If only Chennault were given a comparative handful of planes, his brave airmen would defeat Japan without further burdening a sorely tired China!

While Chiang rested, the Chinese Communists did assiduously train troops. They were determined never again to be dependent on non-Communist war lords, as they had been in their smashing defeat of 1925-27. They fought Chiang bitterly, whenever necessary. But, against the Japanese, the Communists did not fight. Instead, they untiringly urged Chiang on. What a traitor *he* not to devote himself single-mindedly to the liberation of the national territory! For themselves, publicity first. And

* The most valuable study establishing this fact is the distinguished official U.S. history of *The China-Burma-India Theater,* by C. F. Romanus and Riley Sunderland, 3 vols. (1953-59).

indeed the Communists so succeeded in magnifying the image of their pinprick guerrilla raids against the Japanese that they provided strong competition, in world propaganda, for the Chiang-Chennault journalists.

In fact, in October 1938 the Japanese advance in China came to a halt. No strategic offensive was ever resumed. Already from mid-1938 Japan was fighting a more powerful opponent. In August 1939, the Russians gave them a beating, inflicting at least 16,000 casualties. The Japanese repeatedly explored moving their maximum strength against Russia. Then, in the middle of 1941, the attack on Russia was set aside, for the present, There was no oil or rubber in far eastern Siberia, and Japan had no disposition to do Germany's work, at day laborers' wages. It was a time for rich prizes, and the ones selected by the Imperial Conference of Japan were the Dutch and British possessions in southeast Asia. If success in seizing these prizes necessarily involved war with the United States, that trial would have to be borne—though with a heavy heart and in a mood of desperation. But there would be no margin for side shows. The Japanese accordingly put their China forces on a garrison basis. In the supply plan for 1942, munitions for the garrison in China were set at a level enough only for one battle; the resupply factor for rifle ammunition was set at 0.3. The war in China was called off.

This Japanese choice of priorities has eased the way for the growth, in febrile minds, of a legend—invincible China. The legend mingles with half-remembered pictures of the *Grande Armée* bleeding its heart out on the retreat from Moscow. And that image merges, in confusion and misunderstanding, with memories of Stalingrad. So are born two myths—an invincible China and an invincible Russia. These notions may evanescently serve peace, but they close the eyes of understanding. The Japanese choice does not bear witness to an unconquerable China. No territory is unconquerable. No natural obstacle but can be surmounted unless passage is denied by fire. If there be an invincible people, it is made so by politico-military strength, not by geography and numbers. Nature is—and always has been—powerless to create safe havens. "Whatever flames upon the night/Man's own resinous heart has fed."

When Japan surrendered, the Kuomintang armies had about 4 million men. Perhaps 2 per cent had been trained to U.S. standards. Another 4 or 5 per cent had been through one thirteen-week cycle of training, and a similar number had received *some* training. There were more modern weapons on hand than soldiers who knew how to use them. But, most important, the great mass of common soldiers were weakened by hunger and disease, and demoralized by neglect and brutality. American officers described Kuomintang military hospitals as extermination camps. In August 1945, only a few days before the surrender, General Wedemeyer found it necessary to remind Chiang Kai-shek that Kuomintang China had no soldiers. Wedemeyer then gave Chiang a memorandum, entitled *Conscription,* from which I quote:

> A Chinese conscript's pay can be pocketed [by his officer] and his ration sold. That makes him a valuable member of the Chinese Army. . . . As they march along they turn into skeletons; they develop signs of beriberi, their legs swell and their bellies protrude, their arms and thighs get thin. Scabies and ulcers turn their skin into a shabby cover of an emaciated body which has no other value than to turn rice into dung and to register the sharp pains of an existence as a conscript in the Chinese Army. . . . Many of those who run away run off during the first few days. Later they are too weak to run away. Those who are caught are cruelly beaten. They will be carried along with broken limbs and with wounds in maimed flesh in which infection turns quickly into blood poisoning and blood poisoning into death.

Millions of such conscripts went over to the Communists without fighting.

A month before Wedemeyer gave Chiang this *Conscription* memorandum, the Military Intelligence Division of the War Department submitted a special study entitled *Report on the Chinese Communist Movement.* This stated:

> . . . the Chinese Communist Regular Army is a young, well fed, well clothed, battle-hardened volunteer force in excellent physical condition, with a high level of general intelligence, and very high morale. Training . . . may be rated as fair . . . even though it is woefully inadequate by American standards. Military intelligence, for their purposes, is good. The most serious lack . . . is in equipment.
>
> The outstanding weaknesses . . . include lack of sufficient small arms ammunition, lack of artillery, lack of engineers and other technical personnel, lack of signal equipment . . . and heavy casualties among officers with consequent weakness in junior leadership.

The Kuomintang army was not weakened by "heavy casualties among officers."

Stalin seems not to have believed that the Chinese Communists could prevail over the Kuomintang. (He is even reported, by Dedijer, to have told the Chinese comrades to join the Chiang Kai-shek government *and* dissolve their army!) He therefore apparently gave them little assistance, and that he gave covertly and while maintaining formally correct relations with Chiang. The United States, for its part, was not neutral and did not pretend to be neutral.* The U.S. air force and the U.S. navy transported whole Kuomintang armies, so that they could occupy the country and assert their authority. Chiang's forces were given military supplies of every kind—much of which they promptly surrendered to the enemy. In sum, in 1945-49 the United States did everything for the Kuomintang short of the deed of engaging the soldiers, sailors, and airmen of the American forces in combat with the Communists. But being short of this, the Kuomintang regime lacked the politico-military basis to sustain itself in mainland China.

II. Chinese Governments, Fascist and Communist

In the most decisive period of recent Chinese history, Franklin D. Roosevelt chose General Patrick J. Hurley to be Personal Representative of the President to Chiang Kai-shek. After a few months, Hurley was also made Ambassador. By March 1945 he had spent seven months negotiating to bring the Communists and Kuomintang together, and then Hurley reported:

> . . . two fundamental facts are emerging: (1) the Communists are not in fact Communists; they are striving for democratic principles; and (2) the one party, one man personal Government of Kuomintang is not in fact fascist; it is striving for democratic principles.

Was ever more error compressed into so few words?

Fascist *is* a reasonably apt name for the Kuomintang regime of 1927-49. True, the Kuomintang, in greater degree than the European fascisms, was a government for landlords. In China, the urban economy was secondary. Land was so scarce that farm rents were commonly 50 per cent (and even 70 per cent) of the whole produce. The livelihood of the peasant could be improved quickly only by reducing or eliminating his payments to the landowner. Hunger drove on one side; on the other side stood the desperate desire for a mode of life above the human subhuman. The Kuomintang protected the landowner and repressed the peasant. This landlord-peasant conflict was not equally the fulcrum of European fascisms.

In the urban social conflict, the similarity with Europe was greater. Both the Italian and German fascisms rose to power, in part, as shielders of property and society against Bolshevism. Chiang's rise had a similar history. (Many, even in the West, will know well the story of Chiang's decisive shift, in April 1927, to the role of repression of the urban working

* Of this aspect, a very fair account is given by Herbert Feis in *The China Tangle* (1953).

class, from the brilliant fictionalized account of this turning point given by André Malraux in *Man's Fate,* first published in 1933. Some will know these events even better from Harold R. Isaacs' impassioned essay, *The Tragedy of the Chinese Revolution,* first published in 1938.) From 1927, Chiang's regime was, at all times, the terror of the urban working class. It is a terror that will not be forgotten by Chinese who lived through those years. And they are receiving assistance in teaching the memory of it to their children.

In terrorism, Chiang had nothing to learn from Europe. The U.S. State Department counts Chiang's purges after April 1927 responsible for "several hundred thousand deaths." Then it was settled policy to kill all active and determined opponents. Strike leaders, recalcitrant peasants, or even student demonstrators were beheaded or shot on the spot. In prison, execution was preceded by torture and mutilation. In the countryside, peasants were buried alive, burned to death with kerosene, or cut to pieces. Imprisonment, torture, and execution were used not only in social warfare: they were employed also to extort ransoms and to satisfy personal grudges. The secret police and the thought-control police were not limited by legal process. And they were not pedantic about evidence: at times, bobbed hair was evidence enough to execute a girl.

The Kuomintang leadership, shut out from the richer areas of China by enemy occupation, returned in 1945 hungry. Soon all classes of the Chinese population were comparing their restored national government unfavorably with the departed Japanese. Then, in Formosa, the government prepared its ultimate retreat. Under fifty years of Japanese rule, Formosa had achieved a far higher standard of literacy and prosperity than China. Now came the Kuomintang. In the spring of 1947, it launched a campaign to kill off the Formosan leadership class. Teachers, students, editors, lawyers, doctors, and businessmen were rounded up and shot. School enrolment lists were used to find and kill educated young people. Soldiers went everywhere, in city and village, killing and looting as they pleased—evidently to show the Formosans that the Chinese had better be obeyed. On April 18, 1947, Ambassador Leighton Stuart wrote to Chiang Kai-shek:

> The continuing presence of fresh bodies in Keelung Harbor and other evidence indicate that the elimination of the informed opposition is continuing. . . . It is reported at Taipei that although shots and screams in the night have become less frequent, they continue, and that there is no palpable difference in the tense atmosphere of the city.

Chinese Communism never concealed its ultimate objectives. In this, Mao has as great a claim to candor* as Lenin or Hitler. The Communists

* The English translation of *Selected Works of Mao Tse-tung,* 5 vols., is un-

could join the Kuomintang in 1924: this reflected a public arrangement between the Kuomintang and the Comintern. They could also make a "united front" with Chiang in 1936 and talk coalition with him endlessly a decade later: in these things, they had the public approval of Stalin. Similarly, the Chinese Communists were under no pressure to pronounce for early agricultural collectivization. In Kiangsi (from 1930) and Yenan (from 1935) and even after taking power in Peking (1949), the Communists could advocate first rent reduction and lower interest rates and then more equal redistribution of land in private ownership. Had not Lenin, for a time, adopted the tactical policy of "The land to the peasants"? Again, in relation to urban capitalism, Mao was able to proclaim even *after* the occupation of Peking, that there was a constructive role in the new China for "the petty bourgeoisie and the national bourgeoisie." Why not? This policy was not incompatible with Communism. Had not Lenin utilized capitalists temporarily under the New Economic Policy? But the longer-run objectives were never obscured: China would be made a modern industrial country, free of imperialist influences; all ownership of capital would reside in the state; all power would be held by the Communist party; all opposition would be reformed or obliterated; China would help less fortunate countries to join the world society of Communism. The approach to these goals might involve zigzags; the goals themselves were never denied or attenuated.

They are, I think, in error who speak of a Maoist, peasant Communism in contrast with a fancied Russian, proletarian Communism. The single-party dictatorship, whether personalist or collegial, is surely neither peasant nor proletarian. When Chiang drove them from the cities, the Communists had to look to peasants for rank-and-file supporters and soldiers. But peasants have never touched the reins of power in Chinese Communism, and the peasantry has had no more influence over the Communist leaders than a flock has over a capable shepherd. These leaders never acquired a peasant outlook. On the contrary, it was their boast that the party had learned to swim in the sea constituted by the peasantry. It never occurred to the Communists to tolerate a society in which parties and peasants would swim alike in the same sea, where political activity permits alternative organizations and choices—also to peasants.

Of still more limited significance—except for purveying to the ignorant—is Mao's hundred-times-repeated claim that the new China is "under the leadership of the working class and the Communist party." Where two are named, one suffices. The working class, as distinguished from the Communist party, has no political weight in the new China. The govern-

---

trustworthy in detail because of Orwellian revision, but it suffices for the gross general line.

ment-appointed chief of the Chinese trade unions, Lai Jo-yu, could say explicitly, in 1953, "It is not permissible to express dissatisfaction with the party either openly among the members or at trade-union meetings." But the symbol, the working class, does apparently still play a self-justifying psychological role among Chinese Communists. Mao writes:

> The people's democratic dictatorship needs the leadership of the working class, because only the working class is most farsighted, just, unselfish, and richly endowed with revolutionary thoroughness. The history of the entire revolution proves that without the leadership of the working class, the revolution is bound to fail, and with the leadership of the working class, the revolution is victorious. In the era of imperialism, no other class in any country can lead any genuine revolution to victory.

How lavishly incense is here burned before the shrine of the abandoned Marxist idea of the historic role of a self-determining working class! Where fair is foul and foul is fair, the Chinese may yet, on a memorial to Mao, one day inscribe the epigram of Marx, "The emancipation of the working class is the work of the working class itself."

Nevertheless, it would be quite wrong to make for ourselves an image of the Chinese Communist leaders as people intellectually capable only of self-deception. They are much more considerable personalities than that. Five months after the occupation of Peking, Mao reviewed the long road behind, and then he was, in part, both perceptive and balanced:

> We had plenty of invaluable experiences, and the following were our three main experiences: (1) A party with discipline, armed with the theories of Marx, Engels, Lenin, and Stalin, employing the methods of self-criticism, and linked up closely with the masses; (2) an army led by such a party; (3) a united front of revolutionary strata and groups led by such a party.

Properly translated, Mao's summation will stand.

The disciplined party is the primary instrument. In 1937, there were only 40,000 members. But on its 40th anniversary, in 1961, the number was announced as 17 million—about one in forty of the population. Under the hierarchical control of his superior, the party cadre has the last word in all matters, to every person. In spite of civil war and party purges, the top leadership has survived from the first years of the party's existence. The four with greatest authority (Mao Tse-tung, Liu Shao-ch'i, Chou En-lai, and Chu Teh) are intellectuals and soldiers who have been close associates from the beginning. The decisions of these party leaders are law.

But theirs may not be a law more willingly accepted than the rule of other dictatorships which have prevailed in Asia and Europe in our time. Outward discipline is greater than has been achieved in any other modern society, but inward conformity is not complete. If consent were more uncoerced, repression would not need to be so total. In May and June 1957, during the Hundred Flowers episode, silence was briefly pierced, and the world could hear something of the pent-up distaste with which the Chinese Communist party is regarded by many among the Chinese people.* I quote one voice, Ke P'ei-ch'i, a faculty member of the Communists' prized Chinese People's University:

> . . . the party members and cadres . . . used to wear wornout shoes but now ride in luxury cars and wear woolen uniforms. . . . When the party wants to use a person, he is highly prized even if he has murdered friends, comrades and people within the party . . . the common people, with good reason, have come to distrust the Communist party . . . the masses want to overthrow the Communist party and kill the Communists. . . .

Such voices cannot be enumerated. They were quickly silenced. In September 1957 the Communists were executing student demonstrators, just as the Kuomintang had.

The Chinese Communists resemble the grosser European communisms and fascisms in bragging about being free of any reluctance to engage in terrorism. No sentimentalists they! These non-sentimentalists apparently did not find enough Historical Reality in the victory which came in 1949 through the disintegration of the enemy and with little occasion for killing. Instructions were accordingly given in 1950 that land reform must not be carried out by peaceful means. There must be violence. Many landlords must be killed. And great numbers of people must put their hands to the killing. Otherwise blood would not run between past and future. The revolution would not be Real. Where the local people were too placid, as in Manchuria, the party transported bands of hooligans from village to village, to get the killing started. Chou En-lai, who bears a great reputation in the world for gracious manners, was chosen to explain: "No exploiting class voluntarily makes its exit from the stage of history, and the Chinese landlord class, which has a history of several thousand years, is no exception." It must, under no circumstances, be permitted to be an exception!

Before the enemy is killed, he must be labeled. *Counter-revolutionary* is the best label, but *reactionary* is enough. And the best execution is in the public square, after a mass trial, in which hundreds of accused are disposed of in lots, and a crowd shouts, "Kill! Kill! Kill!"

We do not know the numbers killed. Mao has been quoted as saying

* A good brief account is given in T.H.E. Chen, *Thought Reform of the Chinese Intellectuals* (Hong Kong, 1960).

that 800,000 were executed between 1949 and 1954. Others have estimated the executed, in those years, as between one and three million. We do not know. And equally little do we know the larger numbers taken for forced labor. Fragmentary reports provide glimpses into a secret police network and a labor-camp system possibly larger than the Russian under Stalin. But all precision is lacking.

What we do know, with all particularity, is that Chinese Communism makes more exacting demands on its subjects than has any other modern totalitarianism. All others preserve a place for the apolitical; they demand outward obedience but recognize some limits to the securing of inner assent. Not so Chinese Communism. It demands not only obedience but also enthusiasm. It demands proof that the leadership of the Communist party and the instruction of Comrade Mao are *gratefully* accepted. It will not tolerate a qualified pro-Communism. So we find the distinguished sociologist and pro-Communist Fei Hsiao-t'ung being compelled in 1957 to denounce his own critical frame of mind and to thank the party for ". . . clubbing me in order to awaken me in good time. . . . I hate my past. . . . I confess my sins. . . . I resolve to accept the education of the party. . . ." For the process by which this abject surrender is achieved, American professional psychologists have found the gracious name "coercive persuasion." But such persuasion cannot take its first step unless there lurks in the background the power to inflict imprisonment, torture, and death. Nikita Khrushchev has given us the ultimate explanation and it is simple:

> And how is it possible that a person confesses to crimes which he has not committed?
>
> Only in one way: because of the applying of physical pressure, torture, bringing him to a state of unconsciousness, deprivation of his judgment, taking away his human dignity.

No one has detected in the Chinese Communist leadership reluctance to take away human dignity.

III. China's Long-Range Economic Prospect

Now, after a mere thirteen years of Communist rule, China retains much of her traditional Asian poverty. Under any government, she will remain poor for a long time, not only by American standards, but also in comparison with Japan. Her population is now probably over 700 million, and it is increasing by 15 or 20 million a year. Gross national product is somewhere in the range of $100 per capita (on a purchasing-power basis).

Japanese population is now near 95 million and gross national product over $500 per capita (on a minimizing, exchange-rate basis). In the past decade, the percentage growth in per capita income has, I believe, been decidedly higher in Japan than in China. And Japan may very well continue to advance at the faster rate for a long time. (The so-called "dual economy" of Japan has a large labor reserve.) Japanese natural resources—land and minerals—are relatively more meager than Chinese. But the quality of Japanese economic organization and entrepreneurship is higher. And, especially since the failure of her imperial effort, Japan has increasingly chosen the path of an industrialization dependent on world trade.

China has chosen a quite different economic path—one might call it the way of Stalin. We have no basis for surmising when, if ever, Chinese economic development, proceeding along this special way, will match the economic development of Japan. At best, the time required will be decades.

Of the Chinese population of over 700 million, some 75 or 80 per cent today earn their living primarily from agriculture. In the United States, with a population of 187 million, the corresponding share is about 8 per cent. The Chinese farm population is therefore easily 35 times the American. Yet the farm output of China is possibly the smaller. Much of the work for American agriculture has been transferred to the factory—making fertilizers, pesticides, tools, machinery, power, etc. In China this transfer is far off, even where (as in fertilizers, pesticides, and tools) it would make economic sense now. The Chinese Communists have not put industry for agriculture among their first priorities. In this respect, China and Israel may be regarded as the two poles of economic-development policy.

Without constructive relation to China's need for higher production is the four-act drama of social conflict which has been fought in her countryside. These acts may be called: land reform through killing landlords (1950-52); coerced formation of collectives (1956); herding collectives into communes (1958); and the zigzag away from communes (since 1959). The retreat from the communes has apparently not yet succeeded in overcoming the stagnation in farm output that followed their establishment. For four years now, Chinese agricultural stagnation has been so pronounced that the government has found it necessary repeatedly to adduce the explanation of natural calamities—droughts, floods, typhoons, plagues —in a degree which independent observers have not confirmed. Much of this stagnation apparently has social causes, rather than natural ones.

For 1961, the government confessed agricultural inadequacy by purchasing abroad more than six million tons of grain, some milk powder, and some sugar. And in 1962 China is importing food again, though, up to now, on a lower level. Reports of food shortage have multiplied; the government has announced more natural calamities; and, for a time, refugees (mostly *with* exit permission) pressed more numerously at the border with Hong Kong.

This continuing food shortage has yielded a flood of crocodile tears. The refugees at Hong Kong were made the occasion for an orgy of commiseration. And indeed some were hungry, more fearful, all happy to get out. But they were not starving. In all past Chinese food crises, millions starved. Under the Kuomintang, at times of food shortage, the bodies of the starved lay on the streets of every city and by every roadside. The Communists have achieved greater equality in sharing scarce food supplies than has previously been known in Chinese society.

Most of China is mountain or desert. The area suitable for crops is smaller than in the United States, and China's endowment of good range and forest is minuscule compared with North America. The Chinese now cultivate around 275 million acres and, by double cropping, plant perhaps 385 million.* (In 1950 the U.S. total was 485 million, including cover and pasture.) Chinese yields are not uniformly high. She is the world's largest producer of rice and sweet potatoes, second in corn and cotton. But for none of these are her authenticated yields per acre more than two-thirds of the average achieved in the United States or Japan. And it will not uniformly be economical for China to incur the costs required for the highest yields. Even an agriculture as skilled and abundant in instruments as that of the United States would earn a miserable livelihood extracting from the soil of China an output adequate for a population approaching four times the population of the United States. Chou En-lai has said that it is the plan of the party that 80 per cent of the Chinese people shall work in agriculture. This is a plan for poverty.

In a more rational world economy, China might export manufactures requiring little capital and much labor, largely to North America and Western Europe, and she might import grains. This exchange would permit productive use both of China's labor and of the rich land surpluses of North America and Australia. Even for the late 1960's, this trade might reasonably involve China's importing annually perhaps 30 million tons of grain, with a value around $2 billion. But the world is not moving in this direction. In a silly hour, Mao stigmatized such trade as colonial dependency. And many American protectionists would, no doubt, reject the exchange, as exposing the United States to a double peril—Communist and yellow.

In industry, the way of Stalin means three priorities: industrial materials, machines for the making of machines, and munitions. The chosen time span is three Five Year Plans, ending in 1967. Then China is to have

* These figures should be understood to be very rough. Chinese rural statistics for the 1950's have been well described as 30 per cent deliberate fraud and 70 per cent disinterested guess-work.

laid the basis for a modern economy. But Mao is, for the present, less ambitious than Khrushchev. The USSR is to surpass the United States; China will pass only Great Britain!

Where none existed, pride is naturally taken in the first. The Chinese show visitors their steel mills and metal-working plants with something of the pride of the early Israeli *kibbutznik* in his cowshed. And there is something of the same defensiveness. Who will now deny that a Chinese can make steel—or a Jew tend a cow?

In coal, China has certainly achieved something. She has become one of the big three, with the U.S. and the USSR. But China has not become a modern country in energy supply. Coal is a poor third—after oil and natural gas—in U.S. energy consumption, and the USSR is moving the same way. Chinese petroleum production for a month may now be about equal to U.S. production in half a day. And China has no significant production of natural gas, where American output is larger than all of China's coal, in thermal content. China's latest reported electricity generation is for 1960; then it was given as 58 billion kilowatt-hours. That was half the electricity output of Japan and 7 per cent of U.S. generation.

Enthusiastic fellow-travelers have reported, like a well-rehearsed chorus, that New China smells everywhere of cement. Yet Chinese cement production (1960) of about 12½ million metric tons is not larger, per capita, than India's. It is only 55 per cent of Japan's cement production, and it is less than is produced by each of Great Britain, France, Italy, and West Germany. Any of these European countries could be hidden in a corner of China. Yet one does not recall travelers' reports from these smaller countries being loaded with the smell of cement.

Similarly in steel production. China's output is impressive by the standard of Asian poverty. Her 18½ million metric tons of ingot steel (1960) was nearly six times India's, but it was 4 million tons less than Japan's, 6 million less than Great Britain's, 16 million less than West Germany's. And *some* consideration must be given to the size of the population. Chinese use of steel per capita in 1960 was only 27 kilograms; Japan used 208 kg., the USSR 296 kg., and Sweden 545 kg. China's is not yet a steel-using economy.

In industry, the announced Great Leap Forward of 1958-59 was apparently followed by a great stumble and sharp retrenchment. Then, some time in 1959, it became settled Chinese policy to withhold systematic economic information. Perhaps it was felt too mortifying to claim again later, when it was indeed achieved, what had already been claimed, to the sound of trumpets, in 1958-59. Moreover, statistical facts had been misused by "rightists": they would get no more ammunition. Therefore in 1959 the statistical corps was sternly re-educated in "the partisanship principle." (For some, a tour of duty in the coal mines served as a useful propaedeutic.) Statisticians were to avoid ". . . an objectivist tendency devoid of political viewpoint or class platform." Above all, "In accordance with the partisanship principle, all statistical personnel must place their work under the absolute direction of the party. . . ."

The difficulties in industry were sharpened by the fact that the prolonged agricultural stagnation coincided, in time, with the withdrawal of Soviet aid. China had, of course, never received really sizable *financial* aid from abroad at any time. The little state of Israel, with its 2¼ million people, has received more "unrequited imports" since 1949 than have the 700 million people of China. But, until the summer of 1960, China did receive highly valuable technical assistance. Chou En-lai acknowledged in 1959 that China had received 12,300 technical experts from the Communist bloc. China also received mountains of technical data and blueprints. Some 7,000 Chinese technicians were trained in the USSR. Then, in the summer of 1960, all this came to an end. It is unlikely that the large Soviet aid agreements of August 1958 and February 1959 were ever executed. The Chinese were left to see what they could indeed do themselves alone.

By the end of 1960, Chinese industrial policy had accomplished a sharp about-face. (The "right deviation" having been disciplined, it became safe to adopt much of its policy.) The slogan of "leap forward" was indeed retained—like that of the communes—but it was a tattered banner. The new key words were "consolidation," "readjustment," and "quality improvement." On December 31, 1961, Po I-po, Director of the General Office of Industry and Communications, sang the new song: "The capital construction front and the production front of industry have been appropriately *shortened*" (italics mine). And he added, ". . . the enterprises, by rationally organizing labor, have released a large number of workers in support of the agricultural front. . . ."

For these workers, unemployment became the great problem. Millions were directed to return to agriculture, where nobody welcomed them: there were already too many mouths to feed. The government therefore urged discharged urban workers to become pioneers: "Go, reclaim the hills." The Communist leaders had been complaining for years of the "blind movement of peasants to the towns." Now they announced, in 1960, the Chinese cities held about 115 million people. That would mean perhaps 45 or 50 million employables. The government did not need so many. Let them go back to agriculture. True, the rural area had itself already perhaps 225 to 250 million employables. In the countryside, however, people were less immediately a government responsibility.

But, for the longer run, if the popular standard of living is among their concerns, the Chinese leadership will have their fill of economic problems.

IV. Foundations of United States Policy Regarding China

Chinese Communist slogans frequently run in numbers. They have "the three-anti," "the five-anti," "the four together," "the three red banners," and many more. Perhaps it is because of my exposure to such numbered slogans that I find it helpful to think of the foundations of United States policy regarding China in the light of four themes: The Open Door, The Collision Course, The Doctrine of Non-Recognition, and The House of Cards.

The Open Door. The words refract the light of the 18th century. If we would do justice to generous origins, it is to that age that our thought should first turn. And to its liberating catch-phrases, *laissez faire* of course, but more particularly *laissez passer*. Let man pass free! The robber-baron shall not bar, nor shall the tollgate stand across the way. No monopolies! Let every man follow the labor of his choice. Let him be free to produce, to trade, to invest—to create. All this from the 18th century, and called to service again by American Presidents and secretaries of state—and specifically in connection with China. Is not this Open Door a principle in which the United States can take pride, for its past, and make a ground of conduct for the future?

No. When, in August 1949, Secretary Acheson issued his China White Paper, he did indeed claim United States espousal of the Open Door as the first evidence of generosity in the long history of United States policy regarding China. But the Secretary's statements on the Open Door belong to that activity which endeavors to serve the present by rearranging the past. A generation of American historians had already put shade where the Secretary proclaimed light.* First, the Open Door is not a doctrine for which Americans can claim any originality; Secretary Hay bought discarded British clothing, from an unauthorized peddler. Second, responsible Americans always knew the Open Door doctrine had not accomplished much in China; Theodore Roosevelt conveyed their realistic conviction when he wrote: ". . . the 'Open Door' policy, as a matter of fact, completely disappears as soon as a powerful nation determines to disregard it." Third, President Taft developed the Open Door into a cover for pushing American investments into China, even when (as often) the bankers did not wish to go, and the Chinese did not want the money; however this pressure—and the work of subsequent administrations—accomplished, in economics, nothing: American trade and investment in

* Their best statement is still perhaps the fine book of A. Whitney Griswold, *The Far Eastern Policy of the United States,* first published in 1938 and reissued without change in 1962.

China remained negligible. Fourth, the libertarian aspects of the general Open Door philosophy were never applied to Chinese in the United States; Chinese accordingly resented—and continue today deeply to resent—the racial discrimination and persecution to which they were subjected by Americans. (President Theodore Roosevelt, the great figure of progressive Republicanism, regarded the Chinese as the very epitome of a degenerate yet dangerous race.) These four deficiencies were acknowledged by the Western critique.

But a more unqualified devaluation of the Open Door idea comes from Chinese sources. These quite simply reject, root and branch (and, as I think, in part irrationally), all the conventionally attributed benefits of foreign trade and, still more, of foreign investment. They argue that foreign enterprise was no good to China: it disrupted Chinese agriculture; ruined traditional handicrafts; prevented the growth of Chinese-owned industry; and drained China's wealth through remittance abroad of profits. This total rejection of the Open Door is not only a Communist position; the rejection is shared by a great variety of Chinese. As I can quote only one voice, I choose Fei Hsiao-tung, a scholar and so little a party man that he had to be brainwashed after the Hundred Flowers. Writing before the Communists took power (in his *China's Gentry*), Fei says:

> Straws of various sizes thrust into rural areas suck out the wealth of China into these ports. . . . The producers of goods for export do not get back an equal value in imports. . . . The force dislodging the rural industries is both powerful and deeply penetrating. Behind it are big battleships and guns, the "imperialism" of well-organized industrialized countries. . . . Under the present system . . . the countryside continues to support those who consume modern manufactured goods . . . without gaining any benefit from modern industrialism for itself. . . . China is being constantly drained of its wealth.

In this Chinese view, the Open Door is a charter not of liberation but of exploitation. The wisdom of the 18th century is named foolishness and hypocrisy.

The Collision Course. In the official view, after the Open Door, the second guiding star of long-term United States action, in the Far East, has been the policy of maintaining the territorial integrity of China and of defending its sovereignty from foreign encroachment. Much here turns on the distinction between policy and preference, indeed between policy and wish-fancy or daydream. I define policy as an intended course of conduct for which one is prepared to concert the related means. By this definition, the maintenance of the territorial integrity of China has only episodically been a United States policy.

I make nothing important, in this matter, of the one American aberration in the direction of seizing Chinese territory. In November 1900, the United States did make an effort to obtain from China a naval base and territorial concession at Samsah Bay, in the province of Fukien, across from Formosa. A Japanese protest ended the matter. The United States concealed what it had attempted till 1924. But this episode had no sequel, and it reflects no substantial continuing purpose. The United States has never wished to hold Chinese territory. (Even contemporary Formosa is not, I think, an exception—though few mainland Chinese would agree.)

More significant is the occasional cooperation of the United States with other powers in facilitating their violation of the territorial integrity of China and encroachments on Chinese sovereignty. In assisting Japan (in Korea and south Manchuria) before World War I, the United States was actively cooperative. Similar facilitating initiative, regarding Manchuria, was extended to Stalin by Franklin D. Roosevelt at Teheran and Yalta. Other trespassers on Chinese sovereignty—Britain in Tibet, Czarist Russia in Mongolia, or France in south China—were rarely regarded with more than tolerance. These abridgements of Chinese territorial integrity were, for the most part, accepted by the United States sorrowfully, as the way of the world. Almost all of the time, the United States did desire that the territorial integrity of China be preserved. Frequently the United States did speak for this object, did exhort in its favor, and did reprove other powers who endeavored to dominate China.

But, if we would understand what we are, we must not falsify the record of what we have done and not done. And we must not conceal from ourselves the long continuity of character, as displayed in action. On July 3, 1900, the United States government dispatched its first circular to the powers urging the preservation of "Chinese territorial and administrative entity." Japan inquired whether the United States was prepared to join in securing observance of this principle, and she received the classic reply: the United States was not of a mind ". . . to attempt singly, or in concert with other Powers, to enforce these views in the east by any demonstration which could present a character of hostility to any other Power." Copies of this classic should have been kept on hand in the State Department; they could have been used unchanged nearly forty years later. On July 19, 1937, as Japan moved to take over north China, the United States issued another circular acclaiming the principles of 1900. And, on July 20, the United States was invited to join Britain and France in mediation, to restrain further Japanese advances. Hull refused flatly. He would make no joint representation, and he would not say what the United States might do in the event of further Japanese advance.

The developments from the renewed Japanese invasion in 1937 to

Pearl Harbor also did not establish the territorial integrity of China as a United States policy. There is no evidence that the United States would have gone to war if Japan had merely taken Chinese territory. Indeed, just ten days before Pearl Harbor, General Marshall and Admiral Stark addressed a memorandum to President Roosevelt in which they viewed the enlargement of the Japanese position in China as the alternative, among probable Japanese actions, which should cause the United States least concern.

The deeper lessons of the years that led to Pearl Harbor are lost if that time is pictured as one of American policy, initiative, and activity. It is hard to believe that any sincere and intelligent person, who knew United States government in those years, could fall into such an error. The government of the United States did not act; it reacted. Routine held, and imagination failed. To the prevailing American mind, the larger aspirations and more violent means then proclaimed by the Japanese did not make sense. The bold and violent and adventurist were too uncomfortable to be acknowledged fully. The United States government did not take the measure of the mind and intent of the Japanese government, and it did not initiate commensurate policy. It did not carry out a policy to preserve the territorial integrity of China—or any contrary policy. The United States maintained a collison course that lay across the path of Japan.

Non-Recognition. The fitting complement of the collision course was —and is—the philosophy of non-recognition. Withhold recognition from the devil, and he may go away! The more sober and older American view had acknowledged the devil's presence in more places. Henry Clay said, in 1818: "As soon as stability and order are maintained, no matter by whom, we have always considered and ought to consider the actual as the true government." Woodrow Wilson set a new course, with a self-righteousness which continues to be non-recognition's unfailing companion: "We dare not turn from the principle that morality and not expediency is the thing that must guide us and that we will never condone iniquity because it is most convenient to do so. . . ." Refusing to condone iniquity, the United States would not recognize bad Mexican governments; Bryan warned the Japanese in May 1915 that the U.S. "cannot recognize" various agreements in China; and, for sixteen years, the United States withheld recognition of the super-bad government of the USSR. Henry L. Stimson, in 1932, again found the moral course in non-recognition. By enunciating this doctrine, Stimson convinced himself, and many others, that he had done something important—spoken for the good cause, given Satan his right name. But his principal accomplishment, like that of his predecessors, was to blur the true alternatives of international policy—resistance or accommodation.

Moral approval is of character or conduct. International recognition need be only of political facts. The facts that recognition must acknowledge are: the existence of a state; the identities of its officers; and the area where its rule runs. Recognition need signify no degree of moral or political approval, and indeed it communicates such approval at grave peril. Even the perfunctory diplomatic euphemisms that conventionally accompany the occasion of recognition are best thinned out, lest they be misunderstood. Surely the United States is not involved in approving the regimes of the USSR and Yugoslavia, or of Spain and South Africa, because we recognize their existence as states? Bitter as the act may be, we cannot usefully deny the formality of recognition even to victorious aggression or established tyranny—unless it is an aggression we intend currently to repel or a tyranny we are taking action now to overthrow. Recognition always adds some facility in communication, some chance in accommodation. Non-recognition is sterile.

The foreign policy of a mature people will acknowledge that there are evils beyond its remedy. But it will not deceive itself by withholding the formalities of recognition from evils with which it must live. And a foreign policy worthy of a mature people will acknowledge also that there are other evils that can be reached and remedied—it may be by acquaintance, understanding, and accommodation, and it may be by resistance, force, and violence. In these situations, too, there will be no gain from the powder-puff of non-recognition.

The House of Cards. The three previous themes, whether declared foreign policies or life-styles of operation, come to us from many decades. The House of Cards is a new motif. Like the others, it has in part generous origins. It bespeaks the era of the United Nations, a proclaimed general order of law, wide territorial perspectives, where small peoples once disregarded come also into consideration. And it speaks of tremors running through the whole earth, of a world public opinion, of the worldwide clash of social systems, and of a generous concern for the weak. Where all was previously isolated, all is now made one. If the Chinese prevail by genocide in Tibet, the veil of the temple is rent, and the world order is broken to bits. None will ever again put trust in law or limit or in the protection of any power or association! The House of Cards comes crashing down.

It is on the borders of China particularly that the theme of the House of Cards has riotous play. There we have not only a Tibet but also a Laos, a Cambodia, and many another somewhat larger but little more powerful. It is therefore particularly on the borders of China that sanity resides in the ability to draw distinctions of greater and less, bearable and not to be borne, even among evils. An all-or-none politics makes impossible that little of reason and value we may otherwise attain. Acceptance of the theme of the House of Cards, among the American people, is therefore profoundly disturbing; it suggests deep weaknesses of mind and character, manifesting themselves in an unwillingness to make controlled, limited political and moral distinctions. The wide reception of the theme of the House of Cards testifies to an inner disquiet, which can boil into mad outbursts of violence or dissolve into rigid, immobilized fear.

V. Communist China Enters World Affairs

Hate America is today one fundamental element in the politics of Communist China. I find it false to confront this element after dealing with the particular conflicts between the United States and China since the proclamation of the People's Republic of China on October 1, 1949. *Hate America* does not, I believe, derive primarily from these conflicts. Mao, I suspect, and perhaps Liu Shao-ch'i, already held this tenet, comparatively full-blown, when they arrived in Peking in 1949—just as Hitler held *Hate the Jew* before World War I and before he knew Bolshevism. In this matter, scholars have been quick with names, and they have come up with some big ones—ethnocentrism, xenophobia, wounded racial pride, Marxist Messianism, and even the secular impulse southward of the Han [Chinese] peoples. These names do not meet the test of sufficient reason: what they point toward has been present where *Hate America* (or its equivalent) was absent.

Marx also will not help us here, nor even Spinoza. We must set aside all historical determinisms. Idea and will—value and choice—come in irreducibly. The Communist leaders of China, out of a mixture of conviction and policy, chose to inculcate the idea *Hate America* among the Chinese people. Their totalitarianism is on a much higher level of painstaking thoroughness, in remolding thought, than was Hitler's. The Communists have also now been in power in China longer than the whole duration of the Nazi regime in Germany. Comparison of whole societies is hazardous. Yet I venture the opinion that the idea *Hate America* is now more deeply anchored in Chinese minds than *Hate the Jew* was in German minds at any time.

For a Chinese today, a personal relationship with any foreigner is dangerous. (Technical experts from Communist countries report themselves to have lived in China in total personal isolation.) Attachment to American persons or ideas is catastrophic. A Chinese suspected of such attachments will be designated a counter-revolutionary. He is guilty of "worship America," "pro-America," or "afraid-of-America." To avert the worst, the suspect had better make abject confession promptly and engage in vigorous self-criticism. Self-defense will be called resistance, and—if persistent—will lead to death. But even the suspect who yields immediately will not be let off until he demonstrates enthusiastic espousal of three official positions: "hate-America," "despise-America," and "belittle-America." Relapse into old errors will bring prison or a labor service perhaps worse than prison.

America is represented as vile but not strong. No need to fear. Fortunately, ". . . U.S. imperialists with all their viciousness and ferocity are only paper tigers. . . ." Chou En-lai is reported (by an eyewitness, Chou Ching-wen) to play particularly on these themes. The Americans are low, cheap types. "We must constantly attack them, scold them, and threaten them into confusion." Then give them one hard beating, and they will come begging to be let off. The American enemy is persistent and contemptible, but he is not formidable.

It would be wrong to conclude that *Hate America* is now lodged, for all time, in Chinese minds. What one Chinese leadership has chosen to implant, another may, one day, find the conviction or policy to uproot. But, for the next years, it is unlikely that any force from abroad will succeed—over the head of the Chinese government—in reaching large numbers of mainland Chinese with images and conceptions that will displace those of hate and contempt which the Chinese Communist leadership has chosen to instill.

Korea is a tribulation for those who believe in the consistent cleverness of the Communist leaderships. At the end of 1949 and early in 1950, Mao was in the Soviet Union. In January, many governments announced recognition of the People's Republic. Amid these recognitions, Secretary Acheson, on January 12, 1950, made a speech defining the defense perimeter of the U.S. in the Pacific. That perimeter, Acheson said: ". . . runs along the Aleutians to Japan and then goes to the Ryukyus [and] from the Ryukyus to the Philippine Islands. . . . So far as the military security of other areas in the Pacific is concerned, it must be clear that no person can guarantee these areas against military attack." Secretary Acheson thereby announced that the U.S. defense perimeter excluded Formosa. The United States would impose no barrier against a mainland Chinese effort to end the civil war by occupying Formosa. But Acheson also excluded Korea from the U.S. defense area. And there the Communist leadership's judgment of priority—or their coordination of action—slipped badly.

Had the Chinese moved first against Formosa, they would have encountered only the demoralized forces of Chiang Kai-shek. Victorious in Formosa, they would have had no surviving competitor for the name of China. Then they could proceed slowly, step by step, to mediatize their small mainland neighbors—leaving these neighbors the outward insignia of sovereignty, while depriving them of its reality. But the Communist leaders of China and the USSR failed to put first things first—or they did not act together. On June 25, 1950, before any invasion of Formosa, they opened military action against South Korea. Heavy offensive weapons were used, to assure a quick victory. But by June 27 President Truman had determined to defend Korea. Moreover, gravely disturbed by the apparent universality of Communist offensives, Truman reversed U.S. policy: he ordered the U.S. Seventh Fleet to block military movements across the Formosa strait. From the Communist point of view, the timing had gone all wrong.

When the Korean war was over, the United States had, in South Korea, total responsibility for survival but no means of development. United States net financial aid to the Republic of Korea (26 million people) is now about $5 billion. Nonmilitary aid continues at about $225 million annually. Economic improvement is visible only to very sharp eyes: statisticians put it under 2 per cent per capita annually. Dictatorship headed by civilians has been succeeded by dictatorship of military officers. The political program, as elsewhere, is anti-corruption and anti-Communism. Public morale is suggested by the attitude of a Korean student in Washington, who—like many another of the brighter foreign students in the United States, from poor countries—obviously did not intend to go home. When asked, "Why don't you go back to Korea?" he replied, "Because I do not believe in transmigration of souls. If I had many lives to live, I would give one of them for Korea—but not this only one."

The Chinese also have reason to regret the Korean war was ever started. They demonstrated military capability; November and December 1950, they outgeneraled MacArthur and outfought his troops. But, when the war was over, they had gained nothing they could not have had better without the war. Their offshore position was frozen. They continued to share influence in North Korea with the USSR. And they were privileged to sustain this balance of influence by providing the fewer than 9 million people of North Korea with several hundred million dollars of financial aid for economic development—an amount not incommensurable with the total financial aid provided the 700 million people of China by the Soviet Union!

The Kuomintang survives on Formosa (Taiwan) because of the Communist folly of starting the Korean war—that and American resistance. But let us not call this Free China. They hold freedom in little regard who so take her name in vain.

After the Kuomintang killed some 10,000 people from the Taiwanese leadership element, in the spring of 1947, the quiet of repression was established. Some two million mainland Chinese came to live among nine million Taiwanese. The natives spoke south Chinese dialects or Japanese; the mainlanders made Mandarin official. A military force of about 600,000 dominated the island. Its officers were mainlanders, but in 1954 conscription was established, and Taiwanese became privileged to fill out the aging ranks. Government remains, as it was on the mainland, the personal appanage of Chiang Kai-shek. In March 1960, a constitutional prohibition was "suspended" to permit Chiang to continue as President. Legally he rules by wide decree authority, factually by total power. The press is controlled. Strikes are prohibited. Genuine opposition brings arrest for treason.

The Kuomintang official slogan in Taiwan is: "Overthrow the Communists, Resist Russia, and Return to the Mainland." From across the water, the Communists have been declaiming, for thirteen years, "We shall certainly liberate Taiwan." Between two large military demonstrations, in 1954-55 and 1958, the Communists tried even sweetness. In 1957, Chou En-lai appealed alike to the Taiwanese and to Taiwan's military guests: "All decent Chinese should unite as patriotic members of one big family and together fight against and crush the schemes of United States imperialism."

The native Taiwanese has seen the Japanese go. Chiang would take him to a mainland in which he has no interest. Mao offers a liberation worse than the present servitude. Perhaps never in his lifetime will he be free of alien occupation.

But his economic condition has improved. The Americans induced Chiang to carry out land reform. First, rent was reduced—to 37½ per cent of the yield of the main crop. Then land was purchased by the government and resold on credit, so that now about 85 per cent of all farm land is operated by its owners. Agricultural productivity was always higher than on the mainland, and it has continued to rise faster than population growth. Moreover, U.S. aid has dribbled down. Since July 1945, the U.S. Treasury has provided Chiang over $5 billion. Military aid now still runs around $150 million and non-military $120 million per year. Also, some Chinese with business ability came to Taiwan. (More preferred Hong Kong.) Industrial production is three times pre-war. On a per capita basis, Taiwan produces (1960) about one-and-one-half times the cotton yarn of mainland China, four times the electricity, and six times the cement! By the standards of the Far East, Taiwan is not poor.

When the Chinese People's Republic was proclaimed, there were two prominent views of the probable character of China's relations with the Soviet Union. We may call them the known thesis of Acheson and the suspected thesis of Mao. Acheson, we know, announced that the Chinese Communists were front-men for the Russians. They had yielded to Russia the substance of Chinese sovereignty, and they were about to cede Chinese territory—in Manchuria, Mongolia, and Sinkiang. Mao, we may suspect, thought the shoe was on the other foot. He would lead the Russians a merry dance! As he said in 1949, ". . . in an era when imperialism still exists, it is impossible for a genuine people's revolution to win its own victory without different kinds of help from the international revolutionary forces." Moscow was the first center of the revolution; let it be forthcoming in supplying "the different kinds of help"!

Liu Shao-ch'i made it quite clear, in November 1949, that the Chinese comrades were prepared to supply the brains. Others might know something about Europe, but Mao's great mind had found the road for Asia and Africa. First, in each country, there should be created a united front of all ". . . who are willing to oppose the oppression of imperialism and its lackeys. . ."; this front must be under the leadership of the Communist party. Then, wherever possible, "It is necessary to set up . . . a national army which is led by the Communist party. . . . This way is the way of Mao Tse-tung . . . for winning emancipation by the people of the colonial and semi-colonial countries. . . ." With Chinese vision ("a new contribution to the treasury of Marxism-Leninism") and Russian resources, Communism would rapidly make a clean sweep.

Acheson was proven wrong first. What the Chinese paid Stalin was principally adulation. A song reported to be among Mao's favorites goes as follows:

The eastern sky reddens,
The sun rises,
And in China Mao Tse-tung has come!
He strives for the welfare of the people.
He is the Great Savior of the people!

When Mao went to Moscow in 1949-50, there appeared everywhere in China a picture of the "Great Meeting" of Stalin and Mao, and the song was reportedly amended: *"Mao Tse-tung! Stalin/They are shining as bright as the sun in the sky!"* However, sharing equality with the sun was a small price. An agreement was concluded, in February 1950, diminishing Russian rights in Manchuria; Stalin would not require of his party comrades as much as President Roosevelt had arranged for him to get from Chiang. At the end of 1952, these rights were in fact relinquished, apart from Dairen; that went at the end of 1955. Meanwhile, after the death of Stalin, the joint Sino-Soviet companies which operated in the Chinese borderlands—and were suspected to be instruments of Russian penetration—were terminated. The Russians sold their stock to the Chinese. The Chinese had turned out, very quickly, to be anything but complaisant Russian front-men.

But if Acheson was mistaken, Mao was more profoundly so. The Russians did not prove themselves effective instruments for the finer Chinese brains. The Russians failed to get China into the United Nations; they failed to assist in the liberation of Taiwan; and they failed to provide the Chinese any substantial financial assistance. When the Russians could not get the Chinese into the UN, they did show good faith by stamping out of the Security Council. But that boycott only enabled the United States to annex the symbol of UN sponsorship in the Korean war. After seven months' boycott, appreciating that they had made a tactical error, the Russians stamped back in—but they could still do nothing for the Chinese. Similarly, when in 1958 the Chinese—for the second time—beat the drums for an attack to liberate Taiwan, the Russians announced, with great solemnity, that the Soviet Union would certainly be found a faithful ally of China—if the United States were to attack the mainland! That was surely sealing non-cooperation with insult. (A less humorless Washington might have offered, in the spirit of the famous tender of Bismarck to Gorchakov, to issue a stamp bearing, in Chinese characters, the inscription "Khrushchev protects China.")

But perhaps most disappointing, the Russians never provided China any development finance worth mentioning—no grants and paltry loans: $300 million in 1950, another $130 million in 1954, and about $320 million in 1961 (as the funding of trade debts). Perhaps—though this is not clear—there was an early loan of a billion dollars or more in military supplies. But all together, chicken feed. The Chinese themselves provided *grants* to North Korea, North Vietnam, Mongolia, Hungary, Cambodia, Nepal, Ceylon, and Egypt. These added up to far more than all the economic development loans China got from Russia. What parsimony; what uncomradely behavior; what a disappointment! And it was climaxed in the summer of 1960, when the Russians withdrew all (or practically all) their technical experts and reportedly ordered their men not to leave in China even the blueprints of uncompleted projects.

This failure to secure Russian support for large ambitions had one curious consequence. It convinced some that the Chinese Communist leaders are distinctivey *cautious* people. (How this awakens memories of that State Department scholarship which, in the 1930's, spoke of the extreme caution—indeed the long, hesitant sequence of advance and retreat—which characterized the history of Japan from 1895!) But, in their differences with the Russians regarding world affairs, so far as we know, it has always been the Chinese who were the adventurers. In one or two other matters, it is true, the Chinese were the more conservative. They objected to the severe downgrading of Stalin. Had not Mao matched with him and the sun? And they objected to extreme derogation of established leadership status. During the Great Leap Forward (1958-59), and even subsequently, Mao was the object of a personal adulation quite out of fashion in the Soviet Union.

That was a time when (April 1958) Mao found it most fortunate that China was "poor and blank," adding, "A clean sheet of paper has nothing on it, so that the newest and most beautiful words can be written and the newest and most beautiful pictures painted on it." Mao prided himself on calligraphy. But also on economics. Marxism, he announced triumphantly, can grow grain. And he predicted (November 1958) that the 1958 grain harvest would be 100 per cent higher than 1957, while 1959 would again be 100 per cent higher than 1958. Khrushchev can perhaps be forgiven for conveying some suggestion, during this period, that he thought Mao deranged.

VI. Power and Abstention in East Asia

China's frontiers on the east Asian mainland do not harbor a Sweden or a Turkey, nor even a Finland or a Poland. Take the measure of what is absent. *Sweden:* a mature democracy; an advanced economy; capable in self-defense; neutral of any alliance, but not neutral in preference for democratic societies. *Finland:* less fortunately situated and less independent than Sweden; bent to give the USSR every reassurance regarding foreign relations; but retaining democratic institutions, and not an associate for any Soviet military initiative. *Turkey:* only episodically a democracy, but a popular national state; united in fear of Russian aggression; a slow-developing economy, unable to bear the cost of modern defense; joined in NATO, and contributing massively what it has—reliable manpower. *Poland:* a Communist government, but preserving national distinctiveness; permitting criticism that does not challenge the foundations of Communist society; paying its debt of neighborhood and comradeship by speaking frequently for Russian positions in world affairs indifferent to Poland's interest, but not an associate for any aggressive military adventure.

The four include neutral, dependent, allied, and Communist. If only the east Asian mainland were peopled with societies and governments equal to the least of these!

Among east Asian countries, only the island nation of Japan can usefully be drawn into close comparison with the four above. Japan moved easily into modern nationhood, repelling foreign political and economic penetration, but avid in acquiring Western knowledge. Elsewhere, in east Asian societies, compelling allegiances were attached to family and local groups, not to the larger states imposed by the Western imperialisms. Absent larger unities, resistance to the West could not succeed. Emancipation from traditional Asian values and ties commonly yielded a materialistic and amoral (elsewhere Levantine) individualism. Mainland east Asian societies remained, therefore, dominantly traditional and morally fragmented. But their urban centers contained elements thinly modern and morally pulverized. During and after World War II, the Western imperialisms were expelled from these mainland societies also—first by imperial

Japan. In this process, Asians learned again how much is decided with guns. And then Communism solidified its appeal. Where other modernisms bred individualism, it taught organization. Where others relied on argument, it taught the use of guns. ("What good are your better arguments," the Vietnamese boy asked, "when they shoot you anyway?")

From moral fragments and sand, were formed the new states of the east Asian mainland. Other cements failing, force was used: governments everywhere (except in Malay) became more or less military dictatorships. Up to now, these dictatorships have uniformly failed (even to the extent that Turkey, for example, has succeeded) in creating popular national societies. None has found the spirit that can breathe life into dust. And they are far from having learned the skills of modern economies.

Japan is the great contrast. Always a strong national society, she now possesses far greater sources of power than were in the hands of the imperial Japan which overturned east Asia two decades ago. In economic development, Japan is accomplishing what China is only advertising. In 1951, Japan (aided by a generous occupation) threw off the consequences of defeat and attained an output surpassing the pre-war. Eleven years later, in 1962, Japan's output is about 2¾ times the pre-war. Since 1951, population has increased by only one-eighth, but agricultural product has risen by two-fifths, and industrial production has quintupled! The representative Japanese urban wage-earner's household now has an annual income over $1,500. And the transformation is continuing. In the years 1956-61 alone, one farm person in every five left agriculture, and one person for every previous four was added to non-agricultural employments. One third of the total national product was invested, and without inflation: both wholesale and export prices remained stable. Doubling the national income again in a decade is now taken to be a conservative objective.

All this undeniably meant great social turbulence. But it has been accomplished—and is being carried further—without massacres or concentration camps, without thought control or political dictatorship, without even the acquisition by any foreign interest of a single control point in the Japanese economy. Here, and not in Communist China, is the great Asian model of Permanent Revolution.

But, while Japan has added greatly to the basis for power, power itself she has relinquished—one might say rejected, especially power's military form. The defeat of 1945 was a shattering experience for a people which had not previously known defeat, as a national community, though privation and defeat were well-known to it, as personal experience. Having once been a symbol for militarism, the Japanese have put away military things. In 1941, Japan had larger—and, the Japanese say, better trained—armed forces than Communist China has today. She had an army of 2½ million men, a navy of 320,000, and an air force with about 4,800 first-line planes. Today the total military force numbers under 240,000 men. And, on balance, as now, the Japanese do not wish to have larger armed forces.*

Shock of defeat and occupation; the sight of Americans everywhere on the frontiers of China; and continuance of American military bases in metropolitan Japan: these three have combined to foster a distinctive Japanese outlook on east Asian conflicts. And this outlook extends to military preparations and world politics generally. Abstention. "Count me out!" Israel and Japan are the starkest contrasts. To go from Israel to Japan is to leave a community which considers itself beleaguered and does not dream of questioning that military preparations are *for us,* for our defense, our survival, our living as we wish. It is to enter a community which has no fear of attack, but does have a strong suspicion that all the expense and discomfort and danger of military preparations is *for them*—for the Americans, who are selfish, who view Japanese with condescension, and who endanger the country with their military bases. An able student reports Japanese members of Parliament (left-wingers, it is true) to have asked him, rhetorically, "What threatens Japan?" and to have answered their own question, "Only American insistence on our rearmament, which antagonizes Russia, China, and even South Korea."

For the affairs of east Asia, the Japanese once claimed preeminent responsibility. Now they are conditioned to play the role of very small boys indeed. In Japan, as frequently elsewhere, American military bases, in metropolitan territories, undermine the moral and political foundations of the alliance with the United States. But, particularly under Japanese conditions, the shield afforded by American bases also indulges the conviction of automatic security, and it greatly strengthens tendencies toward abstention. The Americans, in their bases, are safe targets for Japanese criticism. And, so long as the Americans are here, why bother one's head about supposed dangers from China or Russia? The treaty under which the U.S. was given the right to maintain bases in Japan until 1970 threatens to become a Maginot Line, constituting the greatest barrier to the constructive rethinking of Japan's abstention from international responsibilities. The treaty thereby contributes weightily to solidifying the United States role of solitary policeman in east Asia.

Since 1949 the United States has been continually in conflict with Communist China in the Asian ruins of the French colonial empire. In Vietnam, the Chinese lent their strength boldly. The Vietnamese resistance forces, under Ho Chi Minh, may then have been—I think they were —drawing support from an anti-colonialism which was not, for most of its followers, primarily Communist. But the key Vietnamese leaders were Communist militants of old stamp. Ho Chi Minh had been in on the

* See the very informative little book by D. H. Mendel, *The Japanese People and Foreign Policy* (1961).

foundation of the French Communist party in 1920, and he had joined the Borodin mission to the Kuomintang in 1924. His chief lieutenants were Communist graduates of French prisons who had also been colleagues of Mao, Liu, and Chou in Canton and Yenan and Moscow. In December 1949, the Chinese Communists established themselves on the Vietnam frontier. Then they moved swiftly to accord recognition, in January 1950, to Ho Chi Minh's government. The USSR was second. That was extending a helping hand promptly to trusted party comrades!

Already in 1950, the Vietnamese comrades showed they were a good investment. After receiving training and equipment from the Chinese, they—for the first time—dropped guerrilla tactics. They went over to the offensive and defeated the French, in a series of engagemnts all along the northern frontier. In 1950-53, intelligent Vietnamese, in the resistance, certainly learned—if they had not known before—that Ho Chi Minh and his lieutenants were leading as distinctly a Communist movement as had Mao and *his* lieutenants a few years earlier. In 1953, the intellectuals of the Vietnamese resistance, in the north, had their brains washed, according to the Maoist prescription, and this Chinese-style thought reform was so productive as to yield materials for tens of thousands of published copies of confessions. The artillery for the Vietnamese victory at Dien Bien Phu (May 1954) came from China. A responsible eyewitness (Gérard Tongas) has testified that half of the soldiers who marched triumphantly in Hanoi, on October 10, 1954, were Chinese.

Since the summer of 1954, when Vietnam was partitioned at the 17th parallel, sincere Western democrats have increasingly suffered pangs of conscience regarding the government of South Vietnam. They discovered, to their dismay, that Ngo Dinh Diem's regime bore a distinct family resemblance to Chiang's government on Taiwan and to the successive dictatorships in South Korea. Diem's rule is neither popular nor efficient. There are no civil liberties. In family nepotism, Diem matches Chiang, but not in land reform. And the economic development of South Vietnam does not compare remotely with that of Taiwan; in that, Vietnam is more like South Korea. Some $2 billion has been transferred to Vietnam by the U.S. in seven years, but there is no economic development to show for it. Indeed Diem's regime cannot even maintain security on the roads at night—in this being like Sukarno's Indonesia. Diem also tolerates no serious political opposition; tens of thousands—some say 40,000—are held in concentration camps, for "political reeducation." The regime fights rural guerrillas with torture of suspects and destruction of whole villages.

Americans may well feel shame that Vice President Johnson goes to Saigon to pronounce such a regime "a bastion of freedom and progress" and to liken Diem to Churchill. And General Maxwell Taylor evokes sad memories of departed French generals when he says that political and economic reforms may indeed be needed in South Vietnam, but they can only follow pacification. Such words appear already on many tombstones.

After what we know of oppression and revolt in South Vietnam, it may come as a shock to learn, from our best witness,* that it is to the south that the miserable people of North Vietnam look for deliverance. In North Vietnam, the Communists (particularly from 1956) introduced a Chinese-style totalitarianism. Following specific Chinese guides, they carried out a Mao-style land reform, through mass hysteria and executions. Where there were no large landlords, they invented "cruel" landlords, so the mass trials would have enough people to kill. Less efficient than the Chinese, they have attempted the same total control of action and thought. And they have been rewarded with hunger, terror, and resentment. China and Russia continue to indicate appreciation of the importance of the Vietnamese front by a scale of financial aid very unusual in the Communist world. North Vietnam has received, since 1955, grants and credits in excess of $900 million, of which more than half from China. Professor Tongas summarizes his comprehensive eyewitness knowledge by saying that North Vietnam is a hell on earth. It is then one of the chambers of hell which the great Communist powers claim specially as their own.

On the east Asian frontiers of China, "the way of Mao Tse-tung," as proclaimed by Liu Shao-ch'i in November 1949, prevailed only in the ruins of the French colonial empire and in North Korea. Elsewhere (in Burma, Malaya, Indonesia, and the Philippines) Communist warfare was defeated. On his way home from Geneva, after concluding the 1954 partition of Vietnam, Chou En-lai visited both Nehru and U Nu. With each, he joined in putting forward principles of peace—*Five Principles* as they were called:

> Mutual respect for each other's territorial integrity and sovereignty; nonaggression; noninterference in each other's internal affairs; equality and mutual benefit; and peaceful coexistence.

These *Five Principles* were hailed as reflecting the mature policies of the thoughtful, statesman-like New China. They constituted the central ideas of the 1955 Asia-Africa conference at Bandung. There Chou En-lai vied with Nehru and won the popular award. How undogmatic this spokesman for the New China, how concerned for peace, how reasonable, good-humored, and altogether charming!

But in 1959, in perhaps the most interesting episode in the struggle against the "rightists" who had opposed the Great Leap Forward and the People's Communes, Marshal P'eng Teh-huai (then Minister of Defense

* Gérard Tongas, *l'Enfer Communiste au Nord Viêt-Nam* (1961).

and a member of the Politburo) was dismissed and imprisoned.* With him was removed, among a long list of others, a Vice Minister of Foreign Affairs, Chang Wen-t'ien. In March 1960, special party meetings were called to denounce Chang as ". . . a right opportunist who had propagated the erroneous view . . . that peaceful coexistence in accordance with Five Principles and Bandung should be the basis of China's foreign policy. . . ." Chou En-lai remained undisturbed, Prime Minister and number-three man (after Mao and Liu) in the hierarchy.

Poor Chang Wen-t'ien! Had his pacific views been erroneous also at the time of Bandung? Or had they become erroneous only somewhat later? My own guess is that to hold such nonmilitant views—except as a means to deceive innocents—embodied mortal party error, in mainland China, from the beginning. It may be long before we know the history. But the present position we *do* know.

VII. Palliatives and Doubtful Reconciliations

One China and one separate Taiwan: power sets the limit, and a choice among evils. For many decades, Americans imagined there would one day be a great, united China, and it would be *ours*. Then came the Communist take-over. And Americans—even the more clear-sighted—could not quite forbear the dream. Two Chinas then, and one of them ours! But the world did not accommodate itself to vagrant dreams. There is only one China, and it is *theirs*.

Two million mainland Chinese and their 9 million hosts on Taiwan: that does not make a China. Neither, however, does it make a luncheon morsel which we are permitted to offer the tiger, in reasoned expectation that, having eaten, he will first sleep and then wake as friendly as a house-bred pussycat. No, he will probably rise strengthened and contemptuous.

So far as can be known today, Taiwan has no considerable number of people who desire to be absorbed in Communist China. But, in time, they should be asked. A fair plebiscite would help clear the international atmosphere. And, after the plebiscite, there should be a reasonable interval—surely not less than a year—in which any that choose could leave.

Military considerations, so far as a layman understands them, need not be decisive. Communist China will, no doubt, in the next years, acquire nuclear weapons and some means, however primitive, of their delivery. China could then devastate Taiwan. But, similarly, mainland China could be devastated, by nuclear weapons, *from* Taiwan. As this is a game at which two can play, both would better desist. For occupation of Taiwan,

* See on this very informative essay by David A. Charles in *The China Quarterly* of October-December 1961.

Communist China lacks the requisite naval and air forces. And she is, I believe, quite unlikely to acquire such forces in the next ten or fifteen years.

For the United States also, Taiwan is not an indispensable military position, even from the most conventional point of view. In World War II, the United States and its allies reconquered the whole western Pacific without occupying Taiwan. In the years up to 1950, the highest United States military authorities found repeatedly that Taiwan was not indispensable to American defense. Military action is increasingly at a distance. What was dispensable in 1950 is doubly dispensable now. If the Taiwanese wish, and China agrees, Taiwan can be independent, and it need not serve as a base for United States forces.

Pinpricks, but dangerous ones, are the tiny islands of Quemoy and Matsu. To Chiang's forces, holding these islands sustains the illusion of steppingstones for the reconquest of the mainland. To the Communists, the islands are a cosy target whenever they wish to kick up a fuss. On this issue, Senator John F. Kennedy once wrote perceptively: ". . . Quemoy and Matsu . . . are in effect, by laws of geography, hostages held by Mao Tse-tung . . . our commitment there gives Peking an ever-ready occasion to put on the pressure, to take it off, to bring us to the brink of war. . . . It is a dangerous mistake to leave such a temptation standing." President Kennedy has not yet found the decisiveness to act on the Senator's understanding. At worst, failing agreement, Chiang could be put on notice that, after a reasonable interval, the President would simply announce that the government of the United States will no longer assist defense of these islands.

When the islands of Quemoy and Matsu are abandoned, the mainland Communists will, no doubt, exult and rant and brandish their weapons. "By the strength of my hand I have done it, and by my wisdom, for I have understanding; and I have removed the boundaries of peoples. . . ." But we must not be deterred from doing a reasonable thing because it will elicit a fool's boast.

Experience provides no ground for confidence that the government of the United States will have any considerable success in fostering democratic governments in the east Asian countries now dependent on the United States for survival. I mean Taiwan, South Korea, and South Viet-nam. The governments of the little states of the Caribbean and Central America have lived in the shadow of the United States much longer, and under far better conditions for the penetration of American example and influence. Yet those American governments have not become stable democracies. How then should United States influence and example accomplish more in east Asia, under conditions of latent or overt civil war? We may rather expect the doctrine of non-intervention to continue its service as our liberal fig-leaf, justifying intervention, with American government money and influence, to sustain these morally fragmented and dictatorial regimes. These are our associates against Communist China. In mainland east Asia (Malaya apart), there is no other kind.

American democracy is an inheritance, not a philosophy. Perhaps because the American democratic inheritance lacks concepts, it has little power of adaptation to other cultures. And many Americans have always doubted that democracy is something that can be learned by inferior peoples. Inferiority is not limited to Africans or Asians. In the late 1930's, I was in a position to observe some dealings of the government of the United States with Italy, and I could only conclude that most of the higher officers of the United States government who were concerned with those matters, at that time, thought that Mussolini's Fascism (as distinguished from German National Socialism) was not too bad—a good enough system of government for Italians. Vice President Johnson's recent plaudits to Diem's government, for freedom and Churchillian leadership, are not freak events, nor are they personal aberrations. In democracy, as in other matters, the first thorough examination must be of the therapist, before attention is directed to the patient. Doctor, heal thyself!

If we had conviction and determination, we would still lack much in capacity and welcome. To my observation, U.S. government representatives, in the poorer countries, are almost never sufficiently saturated in the local cultural and social situation to be qualified to contribute importantly to the understanding and resolution of fundamental social, economic, or political problems. And, alas, in those rare cases where Americans do have this qualification, they are still almost never, in the poorer countries, admitted to the local trust and confidence needed for effectiveness. The American is not a countryman, nor a comrade; fortunate that rare one who is, for a time and in some limited context, regarded as a colleague.

We come to the painful question of food for China. I make a confession: it is a question I would prefer to evade. I am not satisfied, in my own mind, concerning the answer I give it. But the question cannot be evaded. President Kennedy confused the issue by saying that the Chinese had not asked for food from the United States. In so speaking, the President utilized the privilege of high office to make a statement that was formally correct but substantially misleading. The Chinese *had* availed themselves of intermediaries to explore whether the United States government would be inclined to supply them some food. The Chinese made no direct, official request, and—after some American hesitations—they were given no indirect encouragement.

Maimonides has told us that charity does not await the request and is best given where donor and recipient remain unknown to each other. So community and self-respect are preserved. And to what purpose would we supply food to the Chinese under conditions which denied a common humanity? Mao already thirteen years ago made a hero of Chu Tse-ching, a university professor, bitter against U.S. support for Chiang Kai-shek, who preferred to starve (in August 1948) rather than accept U.S. relief food. Something in this is history, something legend. But how far both history and legend are from the mentality of the United States Congress, which insists that every relief package be profusely labeled as the gift of the generous American people!

And yet I cannot separate myself as far as I might like from these Congressmen. The Chinese Communists are perfectly capable of using an indirect, unofficial supply of food as a further occasion for attack against the United States. "What vile creatures, these American imperialists! They are so avid for money they will sell even to their bitterest enemies. We *never, never* asked them for food. But they found some dirty money grubber through whom to sell it, for a profit!"

For this reason, though troubled in mind, I see some merit in the policy that the Chinese government be required to ask for supply assistance before American government food is made available to China. Once an official request is made, there need be no niggling concern over labeling. The truth will out. And quantities of the order of 10 million tons of grain could be available immediately. Only the United States has such quantities. And yet these are trifles in the perspective of a contribution to the alleviation of hunger and the gain, however remote and problematical, of some increment of good will, some marginal enhancement of the probability of peace.

The government of the United States should now, I suggest, publicly tender formal diplomatic recognition—without euphemisms and without conditions—to the Communist government of mainland China. Recognition should be limited to the territory which Peking in fact governs. American and Chinese Communist representatives have been meeting occasionally for a decade, at Panmunjom, Warsaw, and Geneva. As recently as July 23, 1962, the United States again joined the no-government of China in signing a *Declaration on the Neutrality of Laos*. When we have swallowed so many camels, why strain at a gnat?

It would, however, be the utmost silliness to believe that American diplomatic recognition will provide an open road to accommodation, peace, and friendship. The Chinese will not first jump with joy and then promptly agree to exchange embassies and consulates, to provide visas for journalists, to welcome private travelers and merchants, etc., etc. The government of China has a great investment in *Hate America*. For thirteen years, this government has devoted its talents to building a wall of misinformation and hatred between the Chinese people and the United States. The Chinese government invests further in this wall, day by day. At best, therefore, the Chinese authorities, if they see a balance of other advantages, may allow a small crack in their precious wall. The crack would certainly consist of nothing more than agreement to exchange of embassies. Then it would be for the United States to devote patience and ingenuity to widening this crack, to the end that some Americans might gradually attain, with some elements of the Chinese people, what degree of understanding and fellowship is possible between societies in such different circumstances.

But, for Mao and his lieutenants, the Stalin who accepted Roosevelt's recognition in 1933 was a sissy (more classically, an opportunist). The greater likelihood is that the Chinese would reject the U.S. offer of diplomatic recognition. Wishing to hold whatever they have won with guns, the Communists demand also to be given what they have not won with guns—especially Taiwan.

In 1949 and 1950, fourteen non-Communist governments recognized Peking. The Chinese agreed promptly to establish diplomatic relations only with six. The other eight got a cold shoulder. The British government, having recognized Peking on January 5, 1950, found itself consigned to "doing ante-chamber," and, formally speaking, the British are doing ante-chamber in China to this day.* Their Foreign Office man in Peking is only a "Negotiating Representative": in Chinese eyes, he is still *negotiating* for the establishment of diplomatic relations!

In response to a United States public tender of diplomatic recognition, Mao might well accord the U.S. much less than he gave Great Britain—perhaps only a public curse. But even such an exchange would help set the international realities in a clearer light.

When making its public tender of diplomatic recognition, the United States should, I suggest, also indicate that we will no longer oppose the admission of China to the United Nations. An American spokesman has indeed said, with indignation, that China must not be permitted "to shoot its way into the United Nations." Pray, sir, why not? If a nation can shoot its way into existence, why not into the United Nations?

Responsible international political action requires that the United Nations be utilized for a number of highly important purposes: in all cases, communication, exchange of ideas, and exposure to the molding force of opinions; where the great powers can agree, contribution to the maintenance of peace; where great power rivalry does not preclude, assistance to the poorest countries. All these purposes would be aided by universality. The membership of the UN already includes every type of state; it would better include every state, without exception.

No illusions: admission of China to the UN will not revitalize that association. The instrument of collective security and collective action that was envisaged in the Charter of the United Nations is now largely para-

* On this, a good account is Evan Luard's *Britain and China* (1962).

lyzed. Paralysis grows out of the lack of unanimity of the great powers. And this absence of unanimity is not casual or coincidental. It does not reflect some secondary deficiency of skill or ingenuity. It is the consequence of the profound conflict of one great group of powers with another. The Communist group seeks, by varying means, to extend the Communist system, as opportunity affords, and it correspondingly clashes with the other great group of powers that seeks to support and strengthen non-Communist societies.

Presence in the United Nations of China, the second great Communist power, will add reality though not harmony. At the worst, two shoes, instead of one, will be banged on the same table.

VIII. American Initiatives and Chinese Responses

In our fashionable quasi-military language, present United States policy toward China is named Containment. If the aspect of coalition were given unwarranted prominence, this policy could also be named Balance of Power. Three other courses offer themselves as more fundamental. I give them names: the policy of Escalation; the policy of Camp David; the policy of Greater Asia.

Escalation is the bolder brother of Containment. (Both brothers have many admirers in Washington.) If we play for small stakes, all can play. If we fight with sticks, all can fight. But let us increase the wagers, raise the weapons toward the ultimate. Then the poor and weak must drop out. Perhaps they will even drop out without wagering if only we bluff hard—double the bet and threaten to redouble without limit. So, the Chinese may fight successfully by arming guerrillas to infiltrate South Vietnam. Very well, then *we* will arm insurgents to attack North Vietnam. But what if the Chinese prove more willing to lose infantrymen than we? Then we must escalate higher. Perhaps we will get our Kuomintang allies to shell the Chinese mainland from Quemoy. But what if the Chinese simply shell right back? Well, then we must escalate still higher. Let us get the Kuomintang air force from Taiwan to bomb Amoy—or Canton. When the mainland Chinese air force is engaged, it will encounter a superior air force from Taiwan. At last, escalation will have reached a level where *we* are superior. The Chinese will now have to back down. And we have won. (If, at this point, the mainland Chinese *do* get their big brother to use a nuclear weapon and destroy Taiwan, the game has been misplayed. The referees call a halt. A new Taiwan is produced, so that the game can be replayed without the over-escalation error.)

Camp David is an application of the Balance of Power: a cruder name would be The Russo-American Alliance. This need not be conceived as an alliance for all purposes. It might be limited to cooperation in restraining Chinese adventures. Both the U.S.A. and the USSR are much concerned to avoid nuclear warfare; the Chinese are relatively inclined to disparage the new dimension introduced into warfare by nuclear destructiveness. Both Americans and Russians are sharply aware of the danger that local wars may escalate into a general war; the Chinese first systematically minimize the likelihood of a general war and then add, "Well, if a general war must come, let it come. We are not afraid of it. Only capitalism will be destroyed." To celebrate the thirteenth anniversary of the foundation of the People's Republic of China, on October 1, 1962, Chou En-lai issued an advance statement of bitter recrimination against the USSR, for its coddling of Yugoslav revisionists and American imperialists. These are certainly grounds of Russo-American understanding and relative Chinese isolation.

But, alas, what Americans call adventures, the Russians do not necessarily regard as adventures—and vice versa. Camp David was followed by the U-2 incident. Who was then, in Russian eyes, the adventurer? And when the United States sent military supplies to the Royal Laotian government, the Russians—perhaps even ostentatiously—flew in military supplies to the Pathet Lao. The Russians continue to identify themselves vigorously with the world-wide extension of Communism, and this is not mere rhetoric, though the Russians do accept a slower pace and a lower level of risk than the Chinese.

Particularly in east Asia, there may be as many occasions when the Russians will side with the Chinese as with the Americans—and Russian hearts may even more frequently be with the Chinese. No responsible statesman will neglect the restraining influence of Russian power, where that influence is to be had. But, in a larger sense, I believe, Camp David is a mirage—at best, a temporary mutual indulgence of illusions. There is, I think, no basis in broad, continuing purpose for a Russo-American alliance.

A new model Greater East Asia Co-Prosperity Sphere is a serious idea. In the past, the Chinese Communists were difficult also in relations with Japan. But now, after Americans and Russians have failed, the Japanese feel they may be able to work better with the Chinese. Race and culture are on their side, and the Chinese may now appreciate the need to be more equable. No one should underestimate the seriousness, for China, of the breach with the USSR. The Soviet Union has ceased assisting China's economic development. From 1960 to 1961, Soviet exports to China fell from about $800,000,000 to $360,000,000. Soviet supplies of machinery and equipment fell from about $500,000,000 to $100,000,000; this reduction was, for China, a catastrophe.

Japan could supply China much of what was previously received from the USSR. More problematic is China's ability to export enough to pay. Exports may take time to develop. But all that is best left to the commercial judgment of the parties.

What is most disturbing is the attitude of official Washington. Japanese who have spoken, in Washington, of possible revival of trade with China have been warned and threatened, both in the Executive branch and by senior members of the Congress. But surely neither the United States nor the world at large profits by isolating China from Japan. Nothing is gained by the United States playing dog-in-the-manger. And why should Americans be so cowardly, so lacking in faith in their own values, as to believe that moral and political influences will run only in one direction?

If a new model Greater East Asia is to be created, the Japanese must take on far more than an enlargement of their merchandising territory. They must resume the care of their own security and bear their share of responsibility for the peace of Asia. Only after some years of experience can it begin to be clear whether they are prepared to carry these obligations. But the years will not begin until the termination of the present unequal treaty providing for United States bases in Japan. That treaty, now scheduled to run until 1970, is a misfortune for both parties. I suggest, therefore, that the government of the United States now promptly initiate discussions for the termination of the treaty.

In this, I am by no means suggesting termination of the United States alliance with Japan—provided Japan also wants it. Let Japan and the United States remain allies. But let the Japanese control and operate any military bases in their country, just as the United States does in ours. This does not mean that Japanese bases need be quarantined against American access—if the Japanese want us there. It might be desirable, in execution of the U.S.-Japanese alliance, for a handful of American liaison personnel to be stationed at Japanese bases. And there might be special readiness arrangements for shared use of bases by U.S. elements in case of hostilities. There is no reason, between allies, why the bases should not accommodate visits from U.S. ships or U.S. planes. These bases might also be used—if the Japanese agree—for mutual supply, repair, and temporary sojourn. But each base should be entirely manned and operated by Japanese and under undivided Japanese authority. The reality of national differences and national sensitivities should be recognized.

Clearly, however, the Greater East Asia of the future, if there is to be one, cannot be an *east* Asia. It must go south to Pakistan and particularly to India. For this more serious purpose, the West must restrain its present *Schadenfreude* over the clashes between India and China—a malicious pleasure at injury which the Indians have perhaps earned, but which helps nobody. If frontier differences could be composed, there might, after some years, be created the foundations of a Greater Asia, as a concert of its own nations. Japan and China and India might be its great powers. That would be something quite different from the Co-Prosperity Sphere of imperial Japan, which was an Animal Farm of one equal and many less equals.

For a realistic chance on a true Greater Asia, the United States would be well-advised to pay a great deal. Surely this Greater Asia would emerge in life as something other than the poet's imagining. It might well be cemented by deals of which the United States did not approve. But even a very rough and imperfect concert of Asian powers would be better than the present. The United States plays unamiably and uncomfortably its role as the last Western imperial power in mainland Asia. (The British positions in Hong Kong and Malaya are not positions of power. And Russian Siberia is not regarded, by contemporary Asians, as intrusive.) It is unwise to look forward to a long future as solitary policeman in alien communities. In my judgment, though these states are not pillars of a House of Cards, it would not be wise for the United States to withdraw military support *today* from South Korea, or Taiwan, or South Vietnam. But Americans should surely work for a Greater Asia of a kind that might, one day, permit the farthest military outpost of the United States, in the Pacific, to stand quietly in the American state of Hawaii.

We are required to endeavor, but we cannot be obligated to believe, lacking reason. I do not believe the Communist China of 1962 would respond cooperatively to American conciliatory initiatives. I do not think the government of China would meet the government of the United States half way or even a quarter of the way. Hate is too deeply anchored, as the only appropriate sentiment. War is too firmly clutched, as the only appropriate technique. "Political power," Mao has said, "grows out of the barrel of a gun." Mao makes no distinction of domestic and international political power, and he is not spoofing. For the present regime of Communist China, peace is a continuation of war by other means.

From direct American conciliatory approaches to China, which I favor, I see today little expectation of substantial political achievement. Perhaps hate would be somewhat tempered or confused if the United States were to offer to supply China food. But, even after such an offer, I doubt that there would be an affirmative response, from the government of China, to a U.S. tender of diplomatic recognition, without the surrender of Taiwan. The Chinese would probably accept admission to the United Nations—if it were accompanied by their acquisition of the position now held by the Kuomintang. But this admission would, no doubt, strengthen the conviction of the Chinese leadership that they had indeed shot their way into the organization: their strength and threats had eventually broken the way open—against the quaking hearts of paper tigers.

The indirect approach may possibly be more productive. "The stone the builders had rejected became the corner-stone." Perhaps the Japanese are qualified for this role. Were they permanently disabled by the experience that culminated in Hiroshima? Now we cannot know. But we do know that, in accommodation with China, America has failed, and Russia too has failed. The Japanese may fail also—or may be prevented from even trying. Then all major paths to conciliation are closed.

In December 1958, in the full enthusiasm of the Great Leap Forward (but when the second attack on Quemoy had already failed), Mao gave his manic summation of the international situation, which was then repeated over and over again by his lieutenants: "The enemy rots with each passing day, while for us things are daily getting better." What would happen on the happy day when things got still better had been made clear, in May, by General Liu Ya-lou, Commander of the Air Force and later a Vice Minister of Defense:

> American imperialism is nothing; its only advantage is to have more tons of steel. . . . [When] we can use atomic weapons and rockets made by the workers, engineers and scientists of our own country . . . another new turning point will probably be reached in the international situation. . . . The revolutionary movement in the world in general and Asia in particular will advance with more vigorous steps.

The correct time perspective must not escape us. In the summer of 1959, when the bubble of the Great Leap Forward had already burst, but the news of its bursting had not yet reached the West, C. P. Snow could write, "But for the task of totally industrializing a major country, as in China today, it only takes will to train enough scientists and engineers and technicians—will, and a few years time." With this statement, Snow earned a tall dunce's cap, in a corner beside Mao. China will not be "totally industrialized" even in many years more. Nor will China, in a few years, have great long-distance military striking power, across water. In warfare, it is improbable that China will be able to do in the 1960's what Japan could do in the 1940's. But China will, no doubt, soon be able to produce nuclear explosions. And, as the 20th century moves toward the 21st, long-range missiles will probably also come into the range of Chinese production. Then, if not by stupidity or mischance sooner, the United States will have with China a great nuclear war, unless far-reaching accommodations have been worked out sooner, with accompanying changes of spirit.

It is perhaps a noble illusion that an honorable peace will come if only we rectify *our* errors. But it is nevertheless an illusion, and one that can bring death. The continuance of peace between China and the United States, during the rest of the 20th century, depends on changes in China as well as in the United States. And we cannot be confident that those changes will occur.

January 1964

George Lichtheim

REFLECTIONS ON TROTSKY

Revolutions give rise to myths, and these myths then help to shape the course of later revolutions. In the 19th century, revolutionaries everywhere saw analogies to what had been happening in France between 1789 and 1799 (or, if they were Bonapartists, between 1789 and 1814). Every upheaval, however insignificant, was interpreted in terms of recent French history, usually misunderstood. Historians set the tone, and journalists caught the infection from them. When a rising took place, people referred knowingly to tumbrils and barricades. (Actually there had been no barricades in the revolutionary Paris of 1789-99, but it was assumed that there must have been because barricades figured in the insurrections of 1830 and 1848). Radicals came to be known as Jacobins, or if they were somewhat less radical, as Girondins. The nature of the real dispute between these factions was ignored. Robespierre, according to taste, was a bloodthirsty despot, an incorruptible republican, or the leader of the middle class, intent on keeping the proletariat in its place. The fact that there was no proletariat, merely a mob of unemployed and casual laborers of the sort that Marxists later came to call *lumpenproletarians,* was conveniently overlooked.

Above all, there was Thermidor. On the 27th of July 1794—the 9th of Thermidor, according to the short-lived republican calendar—Robespierre was overthrown by a hostile majority in the Convention, and the reign of terror came to an end. Thermidor pleased the liberals, but it distressed the more radical democrats, because the Thermidorians did away with Equality and instead put Liberty first. Liberty of course was bourgeois liberty—freedom to buy and sell. Thermidor was the triumph of the bourgeoisie, which on that day won control of the Revolution and held power for five years, until Bonaparte chased the lawyers out and established his personal dictatorship. But France remained bourgeois, and in 1830 the heirs of the Thermidorians once more returned to power, led by Louis Philippe and

Guizot; only now they were called Liberals and wore sober frock-coats instead of fanciful neoclassical dress. By 1840, the Socialists had begun to see through all this, and eventually Marx came along and explained that the French Revolution had really been a bourgeois revolution, though draped in Roman costume, and that the "heroic illusions" of its chief actors were an unconscious means of promoting the drab reality of modern industrial-capitalist civilization.

This interpretation—which was in tune with Hegel's sardonic view of world history as a procession of stages whose meaning is concealed from the participants (though plain to the philosopher)—had a sobering effect upon those who understood it. On others it acted as a tonic: if the secret of the bourgeois revolution had at last been pierced, it should now be possible to make a proletarian revolution, which would pass beyond the bourgeois stage and found Equality on the rule of the toilers. Hints that the toilers might be incapable of ruling, and that the proletarian revolution might turn out to be just another historical masquerade leading to a new form of inequality, were dismissed as unworthy skepticism. There were some warning voices, but in general the Russian revolutionary intellectuals, who from about 1840 onward began to ponder these matters, refused to be deterred. Their business, as they saw it, was to make sure that next time there was no Thermidor, and that the Revolution went on *in permanence.*

The relevance of this theme to the life and work of the man who, more than any other, made of the Permanent Revolution a working concept and a political model, requires no emphasis in these days, when Communists the world over debate among themselves what went wrong in the Soviet Union after 1917 (or, once more according to taste, after 1921, when Lenin and Trotsky suppressed the Kronstadt rising and banned all factions within the ruling party). Any lingering doubts as to the central importance of the French example for the Bolsheviks—all of them, including Stalin—are stilled by the perusal of Mr. Isaac Deutscher's massive three-part biography of Trotsky, the third and concluding volume of which has now appeared (*The Prophet Outcast: Trotsky 1929-1940*).

The literary merits of this work are considerable, but they alone do not account for the fascination of Mr. Deutscher's theme. Nor does the stature of his protagonist, though this final volume, which records Trotsky's eleven years in exile until his death in 1940, derives a tragic quality from the personality of the chief character. Prometheus on his rock, Lear wandering about his blasted heath—these comparisons spring readily to a mind nurtured on literature, and Mr. Deutscher misses few opportunities to ram the point home. He is entitled to his hero-worship, as others are entitled to their feeling that Trotsky—like other characters of tragedy ancient and modern—was largely instrumental in causing disasters to accumulate wherever he went: down to the personal tragedies which in his closing years struck within the inmost family circle. (His eldest son died mysteriously in Paris at the height of the Great Purge, a daughter from an earlier marriage committed suicide.) The harrowing tale unfolds to the last unbearable chapter in Mexico, where the assassin struck down an ailing, lonely, embittered man, whose creation lay in ruins, and who at the close of his life had begun to doubt his own inmost certainties. It is a story often told and destined one day to find its Buechner or its Brecht, for nothing is more inherently dramatic than this terrible finale to a life so crammed with triumphs and disasters; so paradigmatic too—as in a different key was Marx's stoical fortitude amid the grinding pressures of the Victorian era—of our turbulent and blood-stained epoch. Here one merely records that Trotsky has been fortunate in his biographer, for it would have been easy to sensationalize the subject, or to drown it in learned scholasticism. Mr. Deutscher has avoided these pitfalls, and his readers have cause to be grateful.

They will be wise, however, not to regard this impassioned account of Trotsky's last years as a key to the historical lock which Trotsky himself failed to turn. Mr. Deutscher shares most of the illusions of his hero, and where he has discarded them, he substitutes others. Thus he has at last worked himself free from the doctrinaire strait jacket imposed upon other writers by Trotsky's own interpretation of the "Soviet Thermidor" (in the first two volumes of the trilogy this emancipation was only half-complete). But while he now recognizes that most of these analogies were based on a misunderstanding, he himself goes on to promote new confusions. If Stalin is no longer the "grave-digger of the revolution," then he must be a combination of Robespierre and Napoleon incarnate, and his quasi-Bonapartist use of the Red Army to "export the revolution" from 1939 onward is obliquely defended by Mr. Deutscher as the only way out, and, all things considered, a "progressive" phenomenon. If Trotsky was wrong about the Soviet Union being on the road to a bourgeois restoration, and if his former adherents were also mistaken in calling its system "state capitalism," then it seems to follow for Mr. Deutscher that perhaps it is socialism after all, though to be sure the full socialist content still has to burst through the bureaucratic integument. These apologetics—an aspect of Mr. Deutscher's unwavering fidelity to Lenin and Leninism—occupy a not inconsiderable part of his third volume. He is generally fair-minded even in dealing with the *"literary Trotskisants"*—a number of names familiar to Americans are mentioned—who after 1940 broke away from Communism altogether; but his own essential orthodoxy is never left in doubt. Whatever the "literary intellectuals"—he is too polite to call them drawing-room Bolsheviks—may think about the matter, Mr. Deutscher's faith in the inherently progressive role of the USSR has not been shaken even by the Stalinist experience. That chapter anyhow is closed;

and does not history consist of a long list of just such episodes, which for all their incidental horrors have brought mankind a step nearer to the promised land?

Not that he is inclined to overlook the cost. There is in this third volume a blood-freezing account of the 1929-30 "liquidation of the kulaks" which conveys some sense of the havoc wreaked upon the countryside by Stalin's war against the peasantry. And there are some grim pages on the slaughter of the Old Guard in 1936-8, though otherwise the great purge—the *Yezhovchina*—which swept away so many countless people, appears only as the backdrop to what really interests him: the duel between his protagonist and the dictator in the Kremlin. Was it for this that so many thousands died and so many millions were packed off to Siberia? From Mr. Deutscher's account, one might almost suppose that Stalin staged the great massacre merely in order to affirm his personal hold over his own deeply riven faction. No doubt the purge had a logic of its own: once set in motion, the avalanche swept on, until millions of people not remotely connected with the power struggle found themselves in the camps. But surely at some stage a decision must have been taken to let the NKVD loose upon the whole terrorized country, until every vestige of opposition had been rooted out and every last individual in the whole of Russia battered into unthinking obedience. Mr. Deutscher half recognizes the probability of some such purpose. He points out that the purge prevented the bureaucracy—only the bureaucracy?—from settling down and developing a dangerous *esprit de corps*. But he is reluctant to investigate the full logic of totalitarianism, and thus tends to remain within the confines of Trotsky's own vocabulary: the purge was the major instrument of Stalinism, and Stalinism was the way in which backward Russia revenged itself upon the Revolution. Further than that he is not prepared to go.

This approach has its difficulties. Their nature is revealed in the densely packed chapter of Mr. Deutscher's third volume in which he comes to grips with Trotsky's own interpretation of Stalinism, as set out notably in one of his last writings, *The Revolution Betrayed* (1937). This, as Mr. Deutscher points out, contains Trotsky's "classical indictment of bureaucracy." It also embodies Trotsky's tentative revision of his own earlier (and quite misleading) discussion of what he had called the "Soviet Thermidor." Here it is necessary to bear in mind that this particular metaphor had already been employed in the savage factional in-fighting of the late 20's. In the second volume of his study (published in 1959) Mr. Deutscher gave some examples of how in 1926-7 Trotsky and Zinoviev fell back on this time-honored slogan when they had run out of other arguments. Talk of "Thermidor" was enough to make the strongest men blanch. In July 1927, five months before his expulsion from the party, Trotsky temporarily unnerved the Old Bolsheviks on the Central Control Commission with a speech on the fall of Robespierre and the destruction of the Jacobin regime. Earlier, Bukharin—the intellectual leader of the right wing—reacted with hysterical fury when charged with encouraging "Thermidorian" tendencies. All the factions were in the grip of genuine fear lest they unwittingly enact a repetition of that historic disaster. But it was a two-edged weapon: by 1929, when Stalin turned against Bukharin and began his war upon the peasantry, the exiled Trotskyists—then still living under a relatively liberal regime, and even allowed to circulate their manifestoes—began to wonder whether after all Stalin might not be in the "historic" succession to Robespierre, in which case *they* were the Thermidorians! The thought alarmed them to such a degree that by 1932 most of them had made their peace with Stalin (not that it saved them in the end). Unluckily for him, these were just the years when Trotsky, from his exile in Turkey, was least able to influence events. Left to brood in isolation, he readily convinced himself that his supporters had sold the pass, and that he alone saw matters in their true light. Stalin *could not* carry the Five Year Plan through! Or if he did, it was not the plan that Trotsky would have carried through: not a socialist plan, but a bureaucratic one! By 1937 this had become the new line imposed upon the Trotskyist movement: the Soviet bureaucracy had "confiscated" the Revolution for its own benefit, though it was still the ruling caste of a "workers' state." It was, to be sure, a tyrannical and parasitic caste, which must be swept away to make "Soviet democracy" possible; yet it was also the guardian of public property. As long as it defended the new "production relations" against the world bourgeoisie, and against bourgeois tendencies at home, its historic role was "progressive," and Trotsky would go on defending it, even though its leader slaughtered all the Trotskyists in the internment camps (Mr. Deutscher suggests that Trotsky was unaware of this) and in general did his best to imitate Ivan the Terrible. Caught in these insoluble contradictions, the Trotskyist movement—never more than a loose assemblage of small groups and individuals—destroyed itself in furious arguments, which in the end left Trotsky almost totally bereft of organized support.

In fact, the whole debate was unreal. A "workers' state" is no more conceivable than a "peasants' state," and the notion that the USSR was at any time after 1917 close to becoming the "Soviet democracy" of Lenin's or Trotsky's imagination, belongs to the category of what Marx called "heroic illusions," along with the Rousseauist dreams of Robespierre. Trotsky could have solved his problem by conceding frankly that "proletarian dictatorship" was an impossibility, and the proletariat not fit to rule. In the closing months of his life he actually came near to confronting this truth, at any rate to the extent of suggesting that, if the European working class did not seize power in the wake of the Second World War, the whole Marxist perspective might have to be written off. What really needed to be written off was not Marxism, but the myth of the October Revolution; but then Trotsky never drew any distinction between the two. In his eyes, the revolutionary message of Marxism had been validated by what Lenin had done in 1917. If in 1937 it looked as though the Revolution had been aborted, the disaster must be a temporary setback. Otherwise what would be left of the original message?

To these important problems Mr. Deutscher is not an altogether safe guide, since his own preconceptions incline him to believe that Trotsky's analysis "still offers the best clue to the subsequent social evolution": that is, to Khrushchev's eclectic aim of eliminating the worst features of Stalinism, while preserving the new class relationships. He argues that even in 1937 Trotsky did not really envisage anything so utopian as the total elimination of the bureaucracy, merely a drastic curtailment of its privileges; and he suggests that this is currently being undertaken. On which the only possible comment is that in this case the Soviet "toilers" will have to go on being content with very little. It is all very well for Mr. Deutscher to write: "The problem of a bureaucracy in a workers' state is indeed so new and complex that it allows little or no certitude." However uncertain other things may be, it is undeniable that in what he is pleased to call a "workers' state," the workers are not the rulers but the ruled. This doubtless is inevitable; and moreover, it is perfectly compatible with the usual definition of socialism (public ownership), though not with Communism (common ownership). But it is not what the Bolsheviks set out to accomplish in 1917, and what Communists the world over are today still being promised, and promising others. Mr. Deutscher, a disillusioned ex-Trotskyist himself, is at pains to correct the misconceptions of his protagonist, but only in the interest of assuring the reader that the imperfect realization of the original purpose, in the present-day USSR and the other Soviet bloc regimes, is about all that can be expected in this world. He is clearly right; what may strike his readers as odd is his evident conviction that the original plan is still worth pursuing.

II

The revolutionary in politics: this is not in actual fact the central theme of Mr. Deutscher's now completed biography, but he might easily have organized his three volumes around it, and it would have been difficult to blame him. Trotsky is the classic case of the revolutionary leader who is also an intellectual in the fullest sense of that much abused term: not one who makes use of other people's ideas, but one who *lives* his own thoughts, and whose commitment to an idea overrides all other loyalties. It is only when someone of Trotsky's stature appears that the full meaning of the phenomenon becomes evident. Here is the "union of theory and practice" incarnate in an orator who is also a statesman, a theorist who can move crowds, organize government departments, set armies on the march; a "professional revolutionary" with a matchless style and an educated taste for literature. No wonder he fascinated the youth of three continents. Is it possible, at our present distance from the scene, to find a niche for him, to bracket him with other major figures of recent history?

Not with Marx. Superficial resemblances to the contrary notwithstanding, the two men do not really inhabit the same universe—a circumstance Trotsky, not otherwise given to modesty, was always ready to acknowledge. The difference does not lie merely in their respective intellectual endowments, though Trotsky was aware that abstract theorizing of the kind that was child's play to Marx, was beyond his own capacity. There is also the difference in social circumstances and historical background. For all his radicalism and the revolutionary fling he enjoyed in his youth, Marx was profoundly integrated within the German and European culture of his age. At the deepest level, he was at one with the social order whose doom he prophesied. There is something very revealing in his public status as a famous, learned, and somewhat irascible scholar of the late 19th century: a true Great Victorian, the contemporary (and admirer) of Darwin. One need only read his correspondence with Engels to see how profoundly both men were rooted in the conditions of their time and how much, for all their contemptuous indifference to the creeds upheld by majority opinion, they enjoyed being alive at that particular moment. No, Trotsky does not—except for certain inherited sensibilities of temper—relate back to Marx. Curiously enough, he has more in common with Marx's arch-enemy, Michael Bakunin, and not only because Bakunin was a perpetual rebel who died in exile. He shares with the founder of Russian Anarchism a certain romantic conception of "the revolution" as a vast popular uprising against authority—*all* authority—which Marx (not to mention Engels) would have reproved. If the surviving Trotskyist sects in Europe, Asia, and Latin America have over the years become the successors of the vanished Anarchist and Anarcho-Syndicalist movements—one need only read their pamphlet literature to catch the essential similarity—they can find retrospective warrant for this curious "deviation" in Trotsky's personality and writings. With a vastly better intellectual equipment and far greater literary talent than Bakunin, Trotsky nonetheless had something of his romantic utopianism, his faith in "the people," his individualism, even his vanity: traits which Lenin sternly repressed in himself. Not surprisingly, a good many people found Trotsky intolerable.

This is an aspect of his hero's personality that troubles his biographer. Not that Mr. Deutscher is inclined to minimize Trotsky's literary and intellectual gifts: if anything he makes too much of them, notably in the first of his three volumes, where even Trotsky's pre-revolutionary journalism is extolled in somewhat excessive terms. The awkward fact is that it is not easy to be both a profound thinker and an effective pamphleteer. Marx managed it, but then he was unique. In Trotsky's case, it is possible to feel that the style of his pamphleteering was frequently superior to the thought-content that went into it. At times—e.g. in *The Revolution Betrayed*—form and content came together to make a real unity. More often the rhetorician took over from the theorist, and produced brilliant writing when what was required was hard thinking about unpalatable circumstances.

Mr. Deutscher, in his concluding volume, praises Trotsky's pamphlets on the German situation in the early 30's, just before Hitler's rise to power. Having been among those who were privileged to read them as they came off the press, I am in a position to assure the student of Mr. Deutscher's volume that he is quite wrong about their influence, which was close to nil, and about their grasp of the German situation, which was vague in the extreme. They were indeed very brilliant, and of course vastly superior to the lunatic Comintern literature, which treated Hitler as a minor nuisance compared to the real enemy, the Social-Democrats; but that is not saying a great deal. By any reasonable standard of political analysis, Marxist or otherwise, Trotsky's writings of the period must be judged a brilliant failure (though curiously he showed some grasp of the economic logic of fascism in an article he published in, of all places, the quarterly *Foreign Affairs* in April 1934: a year *after* Hitler had come to power). It is not enough to say that in his pamphlets of 1931-2 he made mincemeat of the Comintern line; of course he did. Anyone outside that madhouse in Moscow could see that Germany was heading straight for catastrophe. What he failed to do was to indicate an alternative to the official Communist line, which really amounted to letting Hitler seize power, in the expectation that he would shortly be overthrown by "the workers." Trotsky was almost as romantic about the capacity of "the workers" to resist a totalitarian dictatorship as were the German Communists, and as innocent as they were of any understanding of the real nature of "capitalist crisis," to employ the term then much in vogue. Moreover, he had not the faintest notion of what German National Socialism was really about, what were the emotional springs that fed it, and how far it could be expected to go. After the lapse of a generation one still recalls the amazement with which his own supporters greeted his confident announcement that the Storm Troopers—being of course "petty bourgeois"—were "human dust" which would evaporate at the first sight of a united working class. This was sad nonsense, though Mr. Deutscher treats it with dead seriousness, thereby giving at least one of his readers the impression that he has not learned much from the experience of the great catastrophe.

In reality the German debacle, and the simultaneous emergence of Stalinism in Russia as, so to speak, a going concern and a system of government, put the quietus upon the sort of revolutionary socialism that Trotsky believed in. His biographer has failed to grasp the connection between the Russian and the German catastrophes, because his gaze is too exclusively fixed on the bizarre dialectic of the Stalin-Trotsky duel for control of a totally disoriented world Communist movement. Moreover, his "realism" does not quite extend to a realization that Hitler, no less than Stalin, had something to teach the Communists. What he taught them (and what they subsequently applied in practice when their turn came in 1945) was the technique of the quasi-legal *coup d'état* and the subsequent reign of terror. The real answer to Hitler's seizure of power in Berlin in 1933 was the Communist seizure of power in Prague fifteen years later: using very similar methods, with the ailing Beneš substituted for Hindenburg. Since then there has scarcely been a Communist party in the world that has not tried its hand at the game. In 1933 all this still lay in the future, and Trotsky was the last to perceive the lesson of events, which was that the age of *genuine,* spontaneous, popular revolutions was over except in backward countries, from Cuba to Algeria. Even the October coup of 1917 had not been quite genuine, but it was still backed by a spontaneous mass movement. Since then all successful seizures of power in industrial countries have had to be elaborately organized, with the masses no less than their "leading cadres" drilled beforehand. Backward countries, of course, are another matter, which may account for the fact that Trotskyist groups have had some successes in Bolivia, Ceylon, and even Algeria, but cannot boast any conquests, however minor, in the industrial centers of the world.

It would not be quite true to say that in the 1930's no one had grasped this. Toward the end of the decade some people had, but they did not include Trotsky and his orthodox disciples. The point is connected with the wider subject of the intellectual's role in politics, which is why it is proper to note that Trotsky did not see what was obvious to some people who lacked both his mental powers and his background as leader of a victorious revolution. The explanation clearly is that he had been disoriented precisely by his and Lenin's triumph in 1917. Indeed he spent the remainder of his life in the blinding glare of this cataclysmic event. Whether Lenin—had he lived—would have done better, is questionable, though he had a marked streak of pragmatic adaptability lacking in both Trotsky and Stalin: "the two ablest men in the Central Committee," as he remarked on a famous occasion. Mr. Deutscher, who in general tends to see Stalin as the (frequently unconscious) executant of Trotsky's ideas, is silent on this particular point, though articulate enough on many others. He does have something to say, however, about a controversy which caused bitter dissension in Trotsky's entourage during his last years: the debate over what came to be known as the "managerial revolution," that is, the rise of a new ruling stratum. At the risk of boring some readers, this topic must be briefly considered.

It all began—as the reader of Mr. Deutscher's third volume can discover for himself in detail—with the Italian ex-Trotskyist Bruno Rizzi and his book, *La bureaucratisation du monde,* published in Paris not long after Trotsky had in 1937 given his own assessment of the "new class." Today, with the wisdom of hindsight and the accumulated experience of another quarter century, we are inured to the notion of "bureaucratic collectivism" as a new form of class rule; but in 1938-40 Rizzi—and James Burnham, who largely based himself on Rizzi—sounded very shocking. What they proposed was of course unacceptable to Trotsky, for it amounted to saying that the Russian Revolution (like the French before it) had merely replaced one form of exploitation by another. If they were right, the Soviet bureaucracy, which Trotsky saw as a pernicious growth to be removed or at least cut down to size at the first opportunity, was really the essence of the whole matter. "Bureaucratic collectivism" had come to stay. The Bolsheviks had been utopians, just like the Jacobins before them (save for those like Stalin who had adapted themselves to the new trend). The classless society was an illusion, and the working class, so far from being the harbinger of a new order, was condemned to remain the "mass basis" of a system of inequality.

It is a tribute to Trotsky's intellectual integrity that, while rejecting this thesis as unproved and improbable, he did not entirely exclude the likelihood that things might indeed go wrong. Writing in September 1939, shortly after the Second World War had broken out, he still maintained that the revolutionary potential of Europe was not exhausted; but for the first time he also envisaged the possibility that the working class might prove unable to throw up an adequate leadership and gain power for itself. In a pronouncement (already referred to above) that startled his supporters, he declared that if at the close of the Second World War there was still no socialist revolution in the West, the Marxist-Leninist perspective would have to be written off: "We would be compelled to acknowledge that . . . [Stalinism] was rooted not in the backwardness of the country and not in the imperialist environment, but in the congenital incapacity of the proletariat to become a ruling class. Then it would be necessary to establish in retrospect that . . . the present USSR was the precursor of a new and universal system of exploitation. . . . However onerous this . . . perspective may be, if the world proletariat should actually prove incapable of accomplishing its mission . . . nothing else would remain but to recognize that the socialist program . . . had petered out as a Utopia."

Thus at the close of his own life Trotsky stood on the threshold of a new epoch, and what he glimpsed was not the promised land, but an Egypt of perpetual bondage. With a stoicism that still evokes admiration he proceeded to outline the practical consequences to be drawn by those who, like himself, were determined to remain faithful to the cause—albeit hopeless—of the oppressed and the exploited: if Communism was an illusion "it is self-evident that . . . a new minimum program would be required—to defend the interests of the slaves of the totalitarian bureaucratic system." Coming from Trotsky, these are poignant words—among the most poignant ever uttered by a political leader in exile. They testify both to his intellectual candor and to his moral stature. Yet they also represent a devastating judgment upon his (and Lenin's) earlier certainties. If revolution and counter-revolution alike were about to issue in totalitarianism, the entire edifice of belief built upon the October Revolution lay in ruins.

That the dismantling of Utopia is by now in fact complete, would be the judgment of most present-day Marxian socialists, though not of Mr. Deutscher, who on this subject exudes a confident optimism of almost Khrushchevian proportions. The point would scarcely be worth pursuing further were it not that it is frequently confused with a quite extraneous topic, namely the role of the revolutionary intellectual in the labor movement. It would seem that the confusion is at least in part semantic and has to do with the different uses to which the term "intellectual" can be put. Because Marx, Engels, Luxemburg, Lenin, Trotsky, Gramsci, Kautsky, the Webbs, Bernard Shaw, Léon Blum, and other notable figures in the history of socialism, were all intellectuals (what else should they have been?); and because in our own age the so-called "technical intelligentsia" is indisputably at the core of the various bureaucratic-collectivist regimes which currently occupy so large a part in everyone's thinking—it has become fashionable to argue from the first circumstance to the second, as though every 19th-century theorist at his desk had been a precursor of present-day industrial society. Because socialism stands for planning, and because planners have to work with scientists and technologists, the conclusion is drawn that the intelligentsia as such is responsible for totalitarianism! Even the most democratic and libertarian writers are saddled—a century or more after their passing—with responsibility for regimes which do their best to make the work of the critical intellect impossible!

In reality the equation "intellectuals = authoritarianism" won't hold up, if only because intellectuals are plainly at the core of all the liberalizing and "revisionist" tendencies in the Soviet orbit and elsewhere. It is true to say, however, that the relationship of the intelligentsia to the labor movement was not clearly worked out by the Marxists, while other socialist schools (with the partial exception of the Fabians) never bothered their heads about it. What Lenin had to say was two-edged, and lent itself as easily to gross flattery of the supposedly faultless working class as to authoritarian whip-cracking over its head. Stalinism even managed to combine both features in a single system: the "toiler" was solemnly upheld as a model, while in everyday matters his basic rights (such as the right to strike) were filched away. Trotsky for his part never wearied of belaboring his own supporters for being too remote from the masses: quite oblivious to the fact that the masses preferred Stalin (even in countries like France), and that practically all his own adherents were intellectuals. This situation has persisted: the half-dozen Trotskyist sects which in recent years have somehow managed to acquire a following were all started by intellectuals and largely staffed by them, while the workers showed little interest. A sociology of the Trotskyist movement, if it is ever undertaken, will doubtless disclose that the few working-class adherents it has had were displaced Syndicalists who could find no other sect to attach themselves to. As an organization of the "revolutionary proletariat," Trotskyism has been as complete a failure as was Anarchism, and largely for the same reason: the industrial working class in advanced countries is not "revolutionary"—at any rate not in the sense that Trotsky (unconsciously following Bakunin rather than Marx in this matter) associated with the term. The final judgment on Trotsky as founder, leader, and almost sole existing theorist of the "Fourth International" must be that he launched it at the very moment when all the certainties it embodied had gone into the melting-pot.

III

It has been necessary to dwell at some length on Trotsky's role in Communist history, and on Trotskyism as a political phenomenon. But after all one is talking about the biography of a Russian revolutionary in the tradition of Herzen, Bakunin, and all those other "romantic exiles" to whom Mr. E. H. Carr years ago devoted an enthralling study (a lot more fascinating than some of his subsequent volumes). The essential "Russianness" of Trotsky and his circle is well conveyed by Mr. Deutscher; it introduces an element of human warmth, and even lends a note of charm to what is on the whole a very somber story. Trotsky possessed all the Russian gift for self-expression combined with a very Jewish talent for constant intellectual ratiocination; and though it is tiresome to go on laboring the obvious, it must be evident that as a person he could have walked out of the pages of any of the great Russian novels. Mr. Deutscher is aware of the advantage this gives a biographer, and he rarely falters in his endeavor to bring the flavor of Trotsky's personality home to the reader. Sentimentality is kept in check, but there is no lack of graphic detail, and one or two minor surprises await the reader who has the patience to work his way through these three volumes (of which, incidentally, the third and last is the most revealing, as well as the most stylish). Inevitably, as the tale unfolds, from the almost halcyon stay on Prinkipo island in 1929-33, via the wretched wanderings around Europe in the middle 30's, to the final agony in Mexico, the picture becomes progressively bleaker. But it is only near the close, with disaster crowding in from every side, and the assassin lurking on the doorstep, that the reader begins to share the author's sense of re-living a tragedy of almost Shakespearean dimensions. Then Trotsky himself began to reflect upon his sufferings and the fate of those nearest to him—the son whom Stalin had exiled to Siberia, the other son who had died in Paris, the daughter who had taken her life, the burden borne by his wife, his faithful companion of so many misfortunes—and for the first time something like self-pity creeps in. He had been reading the autobiography of a famed 17th-century heretic, the Archpriest Avakuum, banished as an "Old Believer" by the Orthodox Church to Siberia where his children died of disease and starvation, and later brought back to Moscow to be burnt at the stake. The thought crossed his mind that after all very little had changed in three centuries:

> Concerning the blows that have fallen to our lot, I reminded Natasha the other day of the life of the Archpriest Avakuum. They were stumbling on together to Siberia, the rebellious priest and his faithful spouse. Their feet sank in the snow, and the poor exhausted woman kept falling into snowdrifts. Avakuum relates: "And I came up, and she, poor soul, began to reproach me, saying: 'How long, archpriest, is the suffering to be?' And I said, 'Markovna, unto our very death.' And she, with a sigh, answered 'So be it, Petrovich, let us be getting on our way.' "

The quotation is from Trotsky's *Diary in Exile,* an account of his wanderings published in 1958 by Harvard, with a preface by Mr. Max Schachtman: one of the veterans of the Trotskyist movement, though today (to Mr. Deutscher's evident disapproval) a Social-Democrat. It is a very moving document, rather more moving than Mr. Deutscher's biography, though perhaps that is an unfair remark. It also has the advantage of being short (not much more than 150 pages), and should be read by everyone interested in Trotsky's personality. It is a great pity that it came much too late for Mr. Edmund Wilson to incorporate in his book *To the Finland Station,* whose account of Trotsky in exile is based on the 1930 *Autobiography.* In that year Trotsky was still hopeful, for real disaster had not yet struck. In 1935, the year of the *Diary,* he already had some cause to wonder about his resemblance to the Archpriest Avakuum, for in that year he was expelled from France, refused entry by most other countries, and finally allowed into Norway, only to be interned a year later under humiliating conditions, due to Soviet pressure on the rather philistinely fearful Norwegian Labor government. By 1940—when Mr. Deutscher perforce ends his tale—Trotsky still had some political illusions, but none about his own prospects. While waiting for the assassin to strike, he noted (in a brief Testament appended to the *Diary*): "My high (and still rising) blood pressure is deceiving those near me about my actual condition. I am active and able to work, but the end is evidently near." It came exactly six months later, on August 20, 1940, in an unexpected form, but under circumstances already pointing to the early extinction of his physical no less than his political life. The testament closes (after some remarks about suicide) with the words: "But whatever may be the circumstances of my death, I shall die with unshaken faith in the Communist future. This faith in man and his future gives me even now such power of resistance as cannot be given by any religion." He was wrong, of course: the faith he kept was very precisely of the religious kind.

Over the whole scene of the *Diary*—as indeed over Mr. Deutscher's final volume—there hangs the shadow of an approaching catastrophe. In December 1934, Sergei Kirov, the party boss of Leningrad, had been murdered—if one can believe Khrushchev, at the instigation of none other than Stalin—and the Kremlin reacted with a calculated ferocity that boded ill for the future (though it did not daunt the Webbs, who were just then about to compose their paean to the democratization of Russia under Stalin). The *Diary* reflects the atmosphere on the eve of the great bloodbath of 1936-8. Early in 1935 Trotsky's first wife, and his younger son from a second marriage, were deported to Siberia, though neither had been politically active. Soon, more arrests and deportations followed, mostly of old friends. The diarist recorded these calamities, and then mused idly over the fate of the Czar's family—apparently without noticing the connection. On April 9-10, 1935, a lengthy entry records that the decision in 1918 to execute not merely the Czar but his entire family was taken by the Politburo in Trotsky's absence, and that on hearing of it he voiced some mild surprise (his own preference had been for a public trial of Nicholas II alone). The note proceeds: "The Czar's family fell victim to that principle which constitutes the axis of monarchy: dynastic succession." On the following page there is a brief, troubled entry: "No news about Seryozha (his younger son), and perhaps there won't be any for a long time." There wasn't. Nor was there any further hint that the author of these reflections had a premonition of destiny recoiling upon his head.

Trotsky's self-examination—notably in the *Diary*—is an impossibly difficult subject, because the view he took of himself and his role was at once so penetrating and so wrong-headed. Gifted with a capacious intellect and with great imaginative powers, he saw quite clearly that he represented a lost cause. At the same time he was convinced that history would vindicate him in the not very distant future. Every now and then he could claim to have been proved right. Thus when the Norwegian government in 1936 first interned him, and then expelled him in distressing circumstances, he told the placid Labor Ministers (they included Mr. Trygve Lie, who comes out very badly) in thundering tones that before long it would be *their* turn to seek refuge in exile. When the blow fell in 1940 and the Norwegian government did have to flee before the invading Germans, Trotsky might have had cause to feel that his prophecy had come true, the more so since he had told Trygve Lie to his face, in the presence of all his assembled officials, that the day was near when the Nazis would drive them all out! (King Haakon, who led the sad procession in 1940, is reported to have reminded his bedraggled Ministers of "Trotsky's curse.")

On other occasions he was less successful as a prophet, and the *Diary* as a whole is shot through with the sort of exasperated nagging that comes naturally to political exiles: all his enemies must be cretins or criminals, and so, it turns out, were most of his friends. If they were not cowardly traitors, they failed through lack of imagination. All the Socialists without exception were useless, while the official Communists were slaves of the Kremlin—that "historically doomed clique" of "degenerate and moronic traitors," who unfortunately possessed power, while he had none. Meanwhile fascism was on the march, not merely in France (this was 1935), but in England too (!), and "bourgeois democracy" clearly was about to give up the ghost. Indeed, imbecility and corruption were spreading everywhere. "It is hard to imagine a more painful occupation than reading Léon Blum." "In Belgium, Spaak has become a Minister. A miserable character!" "Claude Farrère, whom I mentioned the other day, has been elected to the Academy. What a revolting pack of old clowns!" Western literature was mostly decadent; Soviet literature was unreadable; only the classics were still tolerable. Politically, there was no ray of hope anywhere: France was rapidly going to pieces, while England was merely "the last ward in the European lunatic asylum." The smaller countries were stupidly philistine, and their leaders a collection of buffoons. Much of this unfortunately was true, but he missed all the factors in the situation that did not fit his prepossessions: notably the underlying strength of simple things like patriotism and democracy, which later asserted themselves in the various Resistance movements. Indeed, on the assumptions made in the *Diary* and in his later writings, the Resistance was incomprehensible, the more so since it was predominantly non-Communist and actuated by sentiments that had no place in his thinking.

In fact the tide had begun to turn in the very month of his death, August 1940. It is a pity that he did not live long enough to take account of England's resistance under Churchill—a Tory romantic with whom temperamentally (though not intellectually) he had something in common. About this time, too, his erstwhile follower André Malraux changed sides and attached himself to de Gaulle: the fascist challenge was beginning to produce its own antidote, but the counter-movement was also a movement away from Leninism and the myth of the October Revolution. Since 1945 the elites of Western Europe have been in possession of their own home-made myth: that of the Resistance. This is one reason—perhaps the major reason—why the whole tradition associated with Trotsky has now faded out.

It will not be revived by Mr. Deutscher's biography, and not only because on its political side his book is very largely a discreetly veiled apology for Stalin (and even more for Stalin's heirs). The fact is that Bolshevism is now as dead as Jacobinism, though there are still some parts of the world where the original tragedy is being re-enacted (in tragi-comic form, to paraphrase Marx). Nothing can revive the illusions brought to birth and then destroyed by the October Revolution; not even the romantic halo which continues to surround the life and death of Leon Trotsky. Who, in this day and age, is going to believe in a proletarian revolution giving rise to a classless society, when the only revolutions actually under way are so clearly neither proletarian nor classless? For that matter, what Marxist is ever again going to entrust his faith to the proletariat: a dwindling minority in the West, and a passive object of manipulation in the East? Even Communists will have to do better if they want their cause to retain some relevance. (In practice they are increasingly coming to rely on the very "labor aristocracy" of technicians and skilled workers whom Lenin and Trotsky anathematized for so many years.) And behind the official façade of "Communism" in the Soviet orbit, there emerges with ever greater clarity the outline of a new society in which the planners hold control, while the technicians do their bidding, and the workers are left to applaud. If this is socialism, it is certainly not classless. The last word lies with those erstwhile followers of Trotsky who broke away from him when they glimpsed the truth. Still it remains that by 1940 Trotsky had wrung from himself the admission that a long, dark, totalitarian night seemed about to precede the dawn, and that "the slaves" would need someone to defend them. Whatever honor Communism still retains was saved by its arch-heresiarch.

III

THE LIGHT OF HISTORY

Isaac Babel

FIRST LOVE

A Story

When I was ten years old I fell in love with a woman—Galina. Her last name was Rubtsov. Her husband, an officer, went off to the Russo-Japanese War and returned in October 1905. He brought many trunks back with him. The trunks, weighing altogether twelve hundred pounds, contained Chinese souvenirs: screens, precious weapons. Kuzma, the porter, used to tell us that Rubtsov had bought all these things with money he had pilfered while serving in the engineer corps of the Manchurian Army. The Rubtsovs were happy, so it was hard for people not to gossip about them. Their house leaned against our property, the glass veranda jutting over our grounds, but my father did not make a fuss about it. The elder Rubstov, who was a tax collector, had a reputation in our town for being a fair-minded man; he was friendly with the Jews. When the officer, the old man's son, returned from the war, we could see how happily he and his wife lived together.

Galina would hold her husband's hand all day long. She stared at him incessantly, for she had not seen him in a year and a half. But her gaze frightened me—I turned away and shivered. In her ecstatic eyes I saw that obscure and shameful life of all people on earth. I longed to drop off to sleep in a rare dream, to forget this life that stretched beyond all my fantasy. Galina would glide through the rooms with a braid down her back, in elegant red boots and a Chinese robe. Under the lace of her deep-cut slip one could see the swelling of her white breasts, pressed together, and the gash between them, and on her robe were embroidered rosy silk dragons, birds and hollowed-out trees.

The whole day long she sauntered about with a meaningless smile on her moist lips, brushing against the trunks, not yet unpacked, and the gymnastic rope-ladders strewn over the floor. Galina would scratch herself, pull the robe above her knee, and say to her husband: "Kiss your baby." The officer bent his long legs in their narrow dragoon's trousers, the smooth, taut leather boots with spurs and, crawling across the dirty floor on his knees, he would smile and kiss the hurt flesh, just where a little bulge rose above the garter.

I saw these kisses from my window. They made me suffer. Unbounded fantasies tormented me—but what's the use of speaking about it? The love and jealousy of a ten-year-old boy is the same in all ways as the love and jealousy of a mature man, only such feelings are more ardent, mysterious, and feverish in children. I did not go near the window and avoided Galina for two weeks—until an event brought us together.

It was the pogrom against the Jews which broke out in 1905 in Nicolayev and other towns where Jews were permitted to live. A mob of hired murderers plundered my father's store and killed my grandfather Shoyl. All this happened while I was gone. That sad morning I had bought some doves from the hunter Ivan Nikodimytch. Five years of the ten I had lived, I had dreamed with my whole soul about doves. But when I finally bought them, the crippled Macarenko smashed them against my temples. Then Kuzma found me and brought me to Rubtsov's. On Rubtsov's gate a cross was chalked. Nobody molested them and they hid my parents in their house. Kuzma led me to the glass veranda. My mother and Galina were sitting there, in the green rotunda.

"Now we must wash," Galina said. "We must wash, my little rabbi. Our face is covered with feathers, and the feathers are bloody."

She embraced me, guiding me along a hallway pungent with odor. My head leaned against her hip—her hip that moved and breathed. We got to the kitchen and Galina put my head under the water-tap. A large goose was frying on the tile stove; glowing pots and pans hung on the wall, and next to them, in the cook's corner, was Tsar Nicolay, decorated with paper flowers. Galina washed off the last smear of the dove which stuck to my cheeks. "You'll look like a bridegroom now, my sweet boy," Galina said, after kissing my mouth with her full lips and turning away.

"My little rabbi," she said unexpectedly, "your dad has troubles, you see. He roams the streets all day long. Call your dad home."

I saw through the window the empty streets under the great sky, and my red-headed father walking on the pavement. He walked bare-headed, his soft red hair fluttering, his paper shirt-front askew and fastened to the wrong buttons. Vlasov, a drunken workman, dressed in a soldier's cotton rags, stubbornly pursued him.

"Babel," Vlasov was saying in an affectionate, hoarse voice, "we don't need freedom so that the Jews can get hold of business. . . . Give enlightenment to the worker for his toil, for this awful greatness. . . . You must give it to him, my friend, do you hear me, give it to him!"

The workman was begging my father for some unknown gift, grabbing his arm. Flashes of pure drunken inspiration and gloomy sleepiness appeared on his face interchangeably. "We should live like the Molokan sect," he mumbled, swaying on his weak legs. "We should live like the Molokans, but without that old orthodox God. Only the Jews get anything from him, nobody else does."

Vlasov yelled in wild desperation against that old orthodox God who took pity only on the Jews. Vlasov bellowed, stumbled, and tried to catch hold of his fabulous God, but at that moment a Cossack patrol rode by, barring his way. An officer, with stripes on his trousers and a parade belt of silver, rode in front of the patrol, a high peaked cap set stiffly on his head. The officer rode slowly and did not look to the side. He was riding as though through a mountain pass where one can look only ahead.

"Captain," my father mumbled when the Cossack came abreast of him. "Captain," my father said, grasping his head with his hands and kneeling in the mud.

"Do what I can," the officer answered, still looking straight ahead, and raising his hand in its lemon-colored chamois glove to the peak of his cap.

Right in front of them, at the corner of Fisk Street, the mob looted and demolished our store, threw out boxes filled with nails, machines, and my new portrait in the uniform of my school.

"Look," my father said, still on his knees, "they destroy everything I have. Captain, why is it?"

"At your service," the officer murmured, and again put the lemon glove to his cap. He tugged at the reins but his horse did not move. My father crawled in front of the horse on his knees, rubbed against its short, sturdy, tousled legs and its broad, patient, hairy nose.

"At your service," the officer repeated, pulled on his reins and rode off, the Cossacks following him. They sat unmoved in their high saddles riding through their imaginary mountain pass, and disappeared into Church Street.

Galina again gently motioned me to the window.

"Call father home," she said. "He hasn't had anything to eat since morning."

I leaned out of the window.

"Papa," I said.

My father turned around when he heard my voice.

"My little son," he stuttered in immeasurable tenderness, trembling with love for me.

Together we went to Rubtsov's veranda where my mother was lying on a couch in the green rotunda. Near her were scattered dumbbells and the gymnastic apparatus.

"That cursed money," my mother cried at us. "You gave up everything for it. Human life, the children, and even our wretched little happiness. . . . Cursed money!" she cried out in a deep, coarse, unnatural voice. She winced and fell silent.

Then, in the silence, my hiccoughs were heard. I was standing near the wall with my cap pulled down over my forehead and I could not stop the hiccoughs.

"What a shame, my sweet boy," Galina said with her mocking smile, flipping me with her stiff robe. She went to the window in her red boots and began to hang Chinese curtains on the ornate molding. Her bare arms were drowned in silk, her braid was alive, swinging down over her hips. Enchanted, I stared at her.

I was a studious, neurotic boy and I looked at her as at a distant scene, glaringly lighted. Then I imagined that I was Myron, the son of the coal man who had his shop at our corner. I imagined myself to be a member of the Jewish Defense Corps and, like Myron, I am wearing torn shoes and a rope holds up my pants. On my shoulder an antiquated rifle hangs from a green cord. I am kneeling near the old wooden fence and shooting at the murderers. Behind the fence an empty lot stretches, heaps of dusty coal lie there. The discarded rifle shoots badly. The murderers have beards and white teeth, they approach steadily. I sense the proud feeling of coming death, and in the skies, in the world's blueness, I see Galina. I see a garret window, cut out in the wall of a gigantic house built of myriads of bricks. This purple house weighs heavily over the alley on which the gray earth is loosely stamped. In the highest garret window Galina is standing, flushed with wintry, heartless joy, like a rich girl in a skating rink. From the garret window out of reach she smiles mockingly. Her husband, a half-dressed officer, is standing behind her, kissing her neck.

Trying to stop my hiccoughs, I imagined all this so that I might love Galina with a bitterer, warmer, more hopeless love—perhaps because a ten-year-old boy has no way to measure his suffering. Oh, foolish fantasies, help me to forget the death of the doves, and Shoyl's death!

Maybe I would have forgotten these murders, if Kuzma had not come to the veranda with the repulsive Aba, sexton of the synagogue. It was twilight when they arrived. On the veranda a poor lamp, somehow bent, was burning—a blinking flame, the flickering companion of unhappiness.

"I put the shroud on grandfather," Kuzma said as he entered. "He's beautiful now, lying there, and I brought the sexton along. Let him gab a bit over the dead."

Kuzma pointed to the bored sexton Aba.

"Let him squeak," Kuzma, the porter, said amiably. "If the sexton gets his belly full, he'll pester God all night long."

Kuzma was standing on the threshold, with his friendly, broken nose twisted in all directions, and he wanted to tell us with as much feeling as he could how he had bound the dead man's chin. But my father interrupted old Kuzma.

"Please, Reb Aba," my father said, "pray for the deceased. I will pay you."

"I commit a sin," she exclaimed, leaning forward from her rotunda, "I voice and placed his bearded, weary face on the table. "I'm afraid you'll take my rouble and go away with it to Argentina, to Buenos Aires. You'll open a wholesale business on my rouble . . . a wholesale business," said Aba, chewing with his disdainful lips and dragging the newspaper across the table to him. In the paper a story was printed about the Tsar's manifesto of October 17, about the proclamation of freedom.

". . . Citizens of free Russia," Aba read syllable by syllable, chewing a mouthful of his beard, "Citizens of free Russia, be greeted this day of the holy Resurrection. . . ."

The old sexton held the swaying newspaper sidewise. He read drowsily in his sing-song voice and strangely accentuated the unfamiliar Russian words. Aba's accent resembled the bewilderment of an African Negro who has just come to a Russian port from his native land. It even made my mother laugh.

"I commit a sin," she exclaimed, leaning forward from her rotunda, "I am laughing, Aba. . . . You'd better tell me how you feel and how your family is."

"Ask me something else," growled Aba without easing the grip of his teeth on his beard, and continued to read the newspaper.

"Ask him something else," said my father, echoing Aba's words, and then stepped to the center of the room. His eyes, smiling to us in tears, suddenly turned in their sockets, and focused on a point unseen by us.

"Oh, Shoyl," my father said in a false voice, all prepared to burst into a shout.

My father's face, contorted by convulsions, split open in victory, and he got ready to scream as Jewish women scream at funerals, or old women in Morocco, women struck by misfortune. We saw that he would yell appallingly, and my mother warned us.

"Manus," she shouted, her hair disheveled in an instant, tearing at his chest. "Look how sick our boy is. Why don't you hear his hiccoughs? Why not, Manus?"

My father grew still. His glazed eyes filled with tears.

"Rachel," he said fearfully, "I can't tell you how sad I am for Shoyl."

He went to the kitchen and came back with a glass of water.

"Have some water," Aba said, coming up to me. "Drink this water. It will help you as much as candles help the dead."

He was right. The water did not help me. My hiccoughs increased. A howl escaped from my throat. A swelling, pleasant to touch, rose on my neck. It was alive, it expanded, spread on my throat and bulged over my collar. Inside the swelling bubbled my torn and gasping breath. It bubbled like boiling water. And when, toward night, I was no longer just the frail boy I had always been, but a writhing mass, rolling in my green vomit, my mother covered herself with a shawl and, growing taller and straighter, she approached the death-frightened Galina.

"Dear Galina," my mother said in a sonorous, strong tone. "How we disturb you and your whole family. I am so ashamed, dear Galina."

Her cheeks burning, mother pushed Galina toward the door. Then she hurried to me and stuffed my mouth with her shawl to muffle my groans.

"Try to stand it," my mother whispered. "Try to stand it, my dear little Babel, for your mother's sake."

Even if it had been possible to endure, I would not have done it, for I no longer felt any shame. I tossed on the bed, fell to the floor, and did not take my eyes off Galina. I reveled in my detestable power over her big, wonderful body. Fear made her stagger, distorted her features. I roared in her face to prolong my power over her, and crying, triumphing, exhausted with the last strength of love, I vomited near her the green water that came from my heart.

Translated from the Russian by Esther and Joseph Riwkin

February 1952

Theodor H. Gaster

THE PASSING OF THE BATLAN

A Grasshopper Among the Ants of Learning

If the *batlan* is passing from our midst, as many allege, so much the worse for us all. Undoubtedly the Jews and Judaism will survive, but neither will be quite the same. For the *batlan* is the last relic of a noble tradition. You may translate *batlan* "idler" or "waster of time," but, if you do, you miss the point and malign rather than describe. The *batlan* is an idler in a special sense, and while he may waste other people's time, of his own he is merely oblivious. Amid the stir and bustle of modern life, your *batlan* is the mental saunterer, the intellectual *flâneur:* Jewish style. Though of humbler cast, he is yet of the same substance as Sam Johnson and Boswell themselves. He is the man who has learned to distinguish between idleness and indolence, who has made a business of leisure and is determined that it shall yield a profit. He knows that time is something to spend and not to save. His life is a continuous Sabbath afternoon; and on his spiritual escutcheon are emblazoned the words (which might also serve as his epitaph): Good Lord, is it already sunset?

In my father's house there were many *batlanim*. (This is not an aspersion upon a large family, though we all of us, to be sure, had our fair share of *batlanuth*.) They came from the four ends of the earth. Some of them were mere intellectual eavesdroppers—men who ambled in on a Sabbath afternoon to catch a little conversation, and maybe also a little gossip, and whose only contribution to the general talk was an introductory recitation of their pedigree and provenience and an occasional grunt of recognition at the mention of someone else's relative in Hamburg or Calcutta. But if they were inarticulate, they were nonetheless eager. When the talk turned to "words of Torah," to the things which, as the rabbis put it, stand at the very top of the universe, they would carefully deposit their teacups on the floor beside them, and shift to the edge of their chairs, and crane forward, with all the air of pigeons pecking at peanuts, anxious, as it were, to be at least on the periphery of learning. In time they might graduate into regular *talmidim*. In that case, they would come in on weekdays to help catalogue the library. How many cards they managed to write or file in a single afternoon was nobody's business, but when one got home from school one would find them darting around among the books on a constant voyage of discovery and reminiscence. Rusty bits of schoolboy Latin and *cheder* Hebrew would come back to them nostalgically as they copied title and imprint, and made out among the imprints the familiar names of Frankfurt and Ulm and Altona. Most of them were recent arrivals from abroad, grateful, albeit unconsciously, to find in an alien world some haven of ancestral and traditional values. Gradually, however, the winds of the world blew upon them and—in Bialik's wonderful phrase—they were drawn up and absorbed in the morning of their days. One came across them in later years—successful businessmen comfortably ensconced in their swivel chairs in New York or Chicago, a little self-conscious and deprecatory of their years of *batlanuth,* but also not a little nostalgic and not entirely innocent of a sense of treason and betrayal. And when one leafs today through the cards of the catalogue file, it seems, as one detects their various hands (*batlanim* do not type), that the wings of the *Shekhinah* rustle.

Yes, in my father's house I came to know the *batlan*—that happy cross between *luftmensh* and *nudnik*—between the peddler of dreams on the one hand and the importunate simpleton on the other. And it is just because he is so difficult to define, and because the lines are so thinly drawn, that he is so easily confused with either one or the other. If he is successful in the world, he is a *luftmensh*—an airy, expensive "man of ideas," an eccentric, a character, an artist; if he fails, he is a *nudnik*—a nuisance, a bore, an encumbrance.

The full-time *batlan* is as unmistakable as a red cardinal in a treeful of birds. He is as ubiquitous as the Holy Presence, though far more gregarious. He is to be found wherever men foregather. He has the next chair at the barber's, and the seat beside you in the subway. He is one row ahead at the public meeting and the theater, and he invariably shares the ride home from funerals. He is there like a specter in the lobby of the synagogue, and he sidles up to your table in the restaurant and sits down uninvited. If you slip out at night for a pack of cigarettes, you are almost sure to meet him in the street; and the chances are that he will be loitering at the Pearly Gates discussing with his fellows the manufacture of harps!

Not all of my father's *batlanim* were Jews. There was the venerable, bearded priest, who had been the trusted friend of Herzl and who was now nearly ninety years old, who came regularly on Monday afternoons and pulled out of the ample pockets of his cloak—a veritable Elijah's mantle—an ever lengthening roll on which, in a glory of varied inks, was set forth an elaborate chart of doom calculated from the prophecies of Daniel. He was far from being a gloomy man, but he knew full well that doom was nigh and ineluctable; for every limb of the heathen image which Daniel had described represented, in reality, an epoch of man's history, and now—as he once greeted our Welsh maid at the door—"we were near the toes." When I took him to his bus, he would stand upon the crowded platform and hold up its departure the while he solemnly pronounced upon me the threefold blessing of Aaron; and when the conductor kindly inquired his destination, he would reply that he was on his way from the Jerusalem on earth to the Jerusalem on high.

Then there was the Great Gnostic. In his youth, he had been one of the foremost authorities on the literature and religious philosophy of the Gnostics, and his works are to be found on the shelves of every scholarly library worthy of the name. But now, in his later years, he had turned to Spiritualism. He was a regular frequenter of seances, and his home was the scene of spectacular revelations from the Beyond. But he was no dotard, and he insisted on what he called objective, scientific data; and he could still discuss Plotinus and Hermes Trismegistus with a vigor of mind, a depth of sympathetic insight and intuition, and a Shavian sense of mischievous dialectic which could put more orthodox scholars to shame. He was one of the few men who could tell my father he was hopelessly wrong, and get away with it. The Great Gnostic sticks in my mind because of a terrifying incident in which he was the main figure. One day he came to the house in the usual way, and my father happened to be out. The Great Gnostic stayed awhile to await his return, and my brother and I did our best to entertain him. The talk turned to his favorite subject, evidence of the Beyond. After we had ribbed him for his credulity, he turned suddenly and declared in half-humorous, half-serious vein: "Well, boys, I promise you here and now that if there really is possibility of communication with the dead, I will come back after my death and tell you so." I thought nothing more about the matter. But several years later, when the old man had gone to his rest, I was dreaming one night about something entirely different and unrelated when, all of a sudden, right across my dream, came the voice of the Great Gnostic. "Well," he said, "I have kept my promise. And soon you will yourself have proof, for soon you are going to join me." I asked how long I had to go. Six years? "Less," he replied. "One year?" "Less." "Six months?" "Yes." For six months I lived in a cold sweat, and was extra careful about crossing the street and hopping on buses while they were moving. At the end of that time, I knew that the Great Gnostic was merely *batlanizing* beyond the grave.

One speaks of the *batlan* as "he" because the whole world of *batlanuth* is alien and even suspect to the more practical temperament of women;

there is necessarily no female of the species. The feminine equivalent of *batlanuth* is window-shopping and the white goods sale; and the *batlan* knows full well that the approach of a woman means death to his art. One can see this instinctive antagonism in action any warm Sabbath morning on Riverside Drive. There are the *batlanim* trekking home from their devotions, three and four abreast, walking, by time-honored tradition, a little ahead of the female contingent. But their independence is short-lived, for presently they come to a corner and the rearguard advances upon them. At once the little group stops in its tracks, there are hasty handshakes and farewells, and the exponents of the noble art disperse in their several directions like squirrels at the tread of a human foot.

The *batlan* is on nodding or buttonholing terms with everyone. There is no breath upon the communal waters but he observes it from the shore. He is full of inside and background stories, and though his information is rarely reliable, he insists on pouring it forth in a torrent of alternate reminiscence and fury. Yet—and this is what gives him distinction—he is not simply a gossip. The essence of *batlanuth* is a preoccupation with ideas, and personalities are but intriguing incidentals. The true *batlan* is the spiritual counterpart of the old-time peddler, and when he opens his *pekel,* what is revealed is a rich and varied assortment of "notions." He is a picker-up of unconsidered trifles, and the more expert and practiced he is, the more rarefied are his wares. (Not long ago I spent the better part of a night, with a real expert in the art, figuring out the Hebrew equivalent for "the cat's pajamas.")

No, the *batlan* is not altogether dead; his tribe is diminished in numbers, but one still runs into very lively specimens—or rather, they run into one, or let us better say, sidle.

The latter-day genus, in my experience on two sides of the ocean, has several species, and two claim special attention. The first is *batlanus bibliothecanus,* so called because his favorite haunts are the purlieus of a public library. There he sits, always in his overcoat, his chair turned sideways away from the desk, never reading but always turning pages. Every now and then he relieves the tedium by darting to the open shelves, scanning a few titles, and immediately resuming his seat. If the librarian is around and is not too busy, the librarian is invariably his first victim. (I have been on both sides of this fence, so I speak not only as the scribes but also as one having had authority.) He does not seek bibliographical information. As often as not, he passes in brief review all of the new books exhibited on the shelf, and proceeds thence by a process of free association to that cultured exploitation of his own leisure and his victim's time which is the essence of his calling. Alternatively, you may find him lurking furtively beside the card catalogue ready to pounce before his victim has a chance of getting settled. "Silence" notices are to him academic; the library is not a repository of books but an intellectual stock exchange and he is short-tempered and caustic with those officious functionaries who would endeavor to restrict its province to strictly utilitarian purposes.

Then there is *batlanus scholasticus*. This is at once the youngest and the deadliest of all. A mere fledgling, his eye has not yet been dimmed, nor his natural vigor abated. His usual age is between seventeen and twenty-three, and his haunt is the college classroom. What makes him so deadly is the fact that he is a hybrid, for through his veins courses the blood of that noxious termite, *nudnicus vulgaris*. His approach is forthright, not insidious. Its warning gesture is the upraised hand (though this is often omitted), and it is followed in short order by the Ideological Discussion. *Batlanus scholasticus* is usually full of wide but undisciplined reading—he is a kind of intellectual Levengro—and the principle upon which he works is that anything the lecturer may say *must* link up somewhere and somehow with the miscellany of his own erudition and must possess wider "implications" which demand revelation, discussion, and exposition, if the rest of the class is not to be left in that state of unenlightenment from which he himself has providentially escaped. He is usually a person of astute intelligence, even of brilliance, but to him *batlanuth* is the technique rather than the adjunct of learning. No complete antidote to him has yet been discovered. He often graduates into a Viennese feuilletonist; his sister follows Vedanta and collects swamis.

Thus the full-time, professional *batlanim*. But forget not the amateurs—men who follow the gleam without being burned by the fire, to whom *batlanuth* is a hobby rather than a vocation, a tingling in the blood rather than a ferment. Many of these "honorary" *batlanim* are humble men who find themselves unable to trek the wilderness without intermittent pauses at the oases. But others are—or have been—great scholars who have recognized in occasional or periodic *batlanuth* a necessary instrument in the process of intellectual creation.

Full-time or part-time, *batlanuth* was once held in due honor as a necessary ingredient in the process of civilization. The derivation of the word *school* from the Greek *schole,* "leisure," is trite but eloquent testimony to this fact; while when the Roman spoke of *otium cum dignitate* ("leisure with dignity") as an enviable ideal, what he meant, of course, was refined *batlanuth*. Nor, indeed, has the tradition entirely died out; for the Athenaeum Club on the one hand and the professorial common room on the other may be considered, to a large extent, as latter-day survivals of that wondrous Mecca of *batlanim,* the 18th-century coffeehouse.

Within the narrower confines of our Jewish life, *batlanuth* has certainly served us well, and few of those who have really enhanced our heritage have ever disdained it. Scripture itself is witness that the Law was revealed not only in a moment of thunder and lightning but also in forty days and forty nights of quiet conversation, when God spoke familiarly with Moses "even as a man speaketh with his friend." One may suppose also that several of the rabbinic discussions recorded in the Talmud owed their origin, in large measure, to the leisurely consort of mind with mind.

Nor, indeed, need our evidence be either so ancient or so exalted. It suffices to think only of the goodly dose of *batlanuth* (again in the better sense of the term) which went into the making of the Hasidic masters, or—in more modern times—of the intellectual ferment that must have ensued and the stimulus that must have resulted from every session of "The Wandering Jews," that wonderful coterie of Schechter, Zangwill, Joseph Jacobs, and Israel Abrahams (to name but a few), which met weekly in the house of Asher Myers in London for the express purpose of practicing the noble art and of thereby sharpening mind upon mind. (On a somewhat less illustrious level, Myers' son, Maurice, kept up the tradition in his own generation, and all of us who frequented the gatherings at his home hold his memory cherished and blessed.)

Much, too, of the prime foundation of Zionism was laid by men who were not ashamed to be *batlanim*—to devote their time and energy (and sometimes, like Herzl, their lives) to a project which then seemed both visionary and impractical; and no one who is at all acquainted with the history of Jewish cultural movements will gainsay the contention that the cocoon of the chrysalis is almost invariably *batlanuth*. Most of those movements have, in fact, been launched by a couple of *batlanim* sipping tea with lemon.

But deny the facts, resist them as you will, today undeniably the *batlan* has fallen upon evil times. The accelerated pace of modern life has caused him to be regarded, more or less, as a jalopy on an arterial highway. He has to apologize for his existence; the spark from the altar fire is too apt to be dismissed as useless and "afunctional" and no adequate substitute for central heating. One perceives the evidence of this change and decay the moment one walks into the office of any of the leading communal organizations. In the old days, what one would have found, as often as not, would have been either some lean and hungry Cassius or a big, florid, dyspeptic, and untidy man sitting in a dingy room before a stained and weather-worn table, taking time out to compose a Yiddish feuilleton (maybe even a poem or a play about the Maccabees), eager to talk about anything but the matter in hand, full of local and international intelligence, bursting with untempered indignations and fantastic schemes, and ready at any moment to switch the conversation to the appraisal of some current literary controversy or to the novel (and probably incorrect) exegesis of some difficult passage of Scripture or Talmud. In short, one could be reasonably sure of a good hour of *batlanuth,* secure in the knowledge that where two are met together in this way, the Holy One, blessed be He, invariably makes a third.

So today the glory is departed from Israel. Today it is a trim receptionist who greets one impersonally from behind a window and efficiently flicks a button so that presently one may be ushered into the plush-and-airy holy of holies of some brisk, clean-shaven functionary, with glasses a little too brightly polished and tie a little too tightly knotted, who dismisses as purely academic the question of where he is going and what he expects to get. Here are no battered volumes of Hamaggid strewn over table and chairs and floor, no tired copy of Graetz or Dubnow leaning for support, upon a dusty shelf, between the Annual Report on the one side and the Hebrew Bible on the other. Here, on the desk, are no scattered slips filled with cryptic citations of Biblical verses or mysterious mnemonic hieroglyphs. Here, instead, there is a gleaming steel cabinet, two little trays labeled demurely "In" and "Out," and a sectional glass bookcase in which are imprisoned, rather than ensconced, serried volumes of *The Statesman's Yearbook* and *Who's Who in the East.*

One can never visit these fanes of Efficiency—at least, I cannot—without a sense of melancholy and regret. (*O God, the heathen are come into Thine inheritance. . . . They have set up their own signs for signs.*) Unless one's thoughts are interrupted by some importunate *batlan,* one begins invariably to wonder how much has been lost to both Jewish and general life by this invasion of the ancient shrines, this substitution of strategy for philosophy, of technique for concept, of routine for passion . . . and of the latter-day streamlined "conference" for the old-fashioned *shmoos.*

There is a prayer in the Sabbath Grace after Meals which beseeches the All-Merciful to "cause us to inherit a world which shall be always Sabbath and tranquil leisure for ever." This is, indeed, the prayer of the *batlanim*. When that world is ushered in, they will surely return to their own as citizens of the Kingdom of God. Having been a little chastened, they shall have great reward.

December 1960

Midge Decter

THE LEGACY OF HENRIETTA SZOLD

The year 1961 has been set aside by the Zionist movement, Hadassah particularly, for celebrating the centennial of the birth of Miss Henrietta Szold. In addition to being the founder, first president, and ideal personification, as it were, of Hadassah—the American women's General Zionist organization—Henrietta Szold had the kind of extraordinary life and career that must surely give her a place among the modern Zionist saints. She was largely responsible for both conceiving and realizing the major public health and welfare programs in Jewish Palestine; she was the director of Youth Aliyah, an agency which after 1935 performed the feat of rescuing, settling in Palestine, and educating 30,000 children from Nazi Europe and elsewhere; and she must also be credited, although indirectly, with the passage of countless millions of dollars from America and other Western countries to the Palestinian community. Not the least extraordinary fact about this career is that it took its most practical turn when she was sixty years old.

Perhaps no people is so intransigently equalitarian in its legend-making as the Jews: with their heroes they must share a secret—a wink, a double meaning, a small vice—from the rest of the uncomprehending world. Chaim Bialik, Chaim Weizmann, Shemarya Levin, David Ben Gurion—to mention a few of the Zionist saints—carry the aura of a greatness made all the more real by a certain reducing intimacy. There is, however, no familiar legend of Henrietta Szold. Somehow the secret is not possible with her, who always appears—even in the descriptions of those who knew her best—wrapped in her record of achievement, splendid, abstract, a little forbidding. The tiny, exquisitely gnome-like, white-haired lady who worked for eighteen hours a day until she was in her eighties is called "our founder," "our leader," "our guiding spirit" in tones of hushed reverence, almost as if to talk with familiarity about Henrietta Szold might be to take some unwarranted liberty.

Henrietta Szold was born in Baltimore on December 21, 1860, and was therefore an infant during the American Civil War. Her father, a Hungarian-born, Vienna-educated Conservative rabbi, was a man of learning and advanced social and religious ideas, and she his eldest and favorite child. The culture of her home was that peculiar and short-lived species of German Jewish Romantic enlightenment overlaid with a post-bellum American passion for social betterment. In her father's study, where she very early became both confidante and amanuensis, "Miss Henrietta" learned Jewish history and classical languages—and doubtless in an earnest young way shared her father's dream of a universally enlightened and cultivated Jewry. (This dream had a material effect on her life; from 1893 until 1916 she was to serve as editor of the Jewish Publication Society, an enterprise originally founded for the purpose of making great Jewish books available to American Jews in English translation.) When she completed high school, Miss Henrietta joined the staff of an elegant girls' academy, where for several years she taught German, botany—all her life she remained an ardent amateur botanist—and mathematics.

People have tended to draw a parallel between Henrietta Szold's coming to Zionism and that of Theodor Herzl: she and Herzl were contemporaries, both "Western," both brought up on German culture. But the parallel is faulty. Herzl's Zionism was a shocked response to his discovery, through the Dreyfus Affair, that Emancipation was a cheat as far as the Jews were concerned. Hers was the inevitable result of what can only be called her Jewish feelings. She was a pious Jew, but historically and culturally, rather than theologically, pious—after the tradition of her father. And in fact, the Conservative movement, with its twin notions of the historical development, and the fulfillment within history, of Judaism, was from the very beginning a most logically fertile ground for the breeding of Zionism.

Her difference from Herzl seems worth dwelling on because it points to something significant both about Henrietta Szold's life and work and about the Zionist movement in general. Herzl, with his dashing Viennese manners and his aspirations to aristocracy, grand gestures, and historic moments, was sufficiently detached from the real concerns of the masses of his fellow Jews to become the kind of romantic figure who might serve as a symbol of their new movement. Furthermore, as he moved through the courts and salons of Europe, pleading for the rightful estate of the Jews and dreaming of their eventual glory, Herzl gave Zionists the sense that what they wanted for themselves could be allied with the respectable impulses of European nationalism—and so without really understanding these Jews, he was able to activate them. Henrietta Szold belonged in the far more complicated if more commonplace tradition that fed into the mainstream of modern Zionism. What she and the early "Lovers of Zion" wanted was not so much to save the Jews from the degradation of statelessness as such: she wanted a way of giving the individual Jew a new sense of his own dignity and the Jewish people as a whole a sense of security that were both lacking in the Diaspora. Henrietta Szold's education, like Herzl's, was grounded in Western culture (many years later she was to tell a group of children just arrived in Palestine from Nazi Germany, "Do not forget your Goethe and your Schiller. They are Germany, too"); but in her upbringing there was also an element of East European Haskalah, which pronounced: the mission of the Jews is to become again as whole and as live and as valuable as we once were. For Herzl the object was always the Jewish people. For Henrietta Szold and those at the spiritual center of the Zionist movement the object was Jews. And with them she shared that loving antipathy for what had become of Jewish life and institutions as a result of centuries in the Diaspora that made real-world Zionism, and ultimately the State of Israel, possible.

Actually, there was an event—of the kind biographers find so useful in determining the sources of their subjects' ideas—that undoubtedly pushed her into accepting the need for Jewish statehood. In 1881 refugees from the Russian pogroms began pouring into Baltimore and gravitating, the learned and eager among them, to the hospitable home of Rabbi Benjamin Szold. By 1889, Miss Henrietta was devoting every minute to be spared from an already formidable routine of teaching, botanizing, and activity in such groups as the Women's Literary Club, to "my Russians." With her help, they established night classes in English and American history for the new immigrants. She undertook to procure rooms and supplies for this "school"—the model for what later became the predominant pattern in immigrant Americanization—to plan the curriculum, supervise, provide teachers, and teach herself. She was clearly hit hard by "her" Russians, but not—as Herzl would have been—so much by their collective plight as by her recognition of kinship with this new and strangely impressive breed of Jews. Coming into contact with them helped her formulate the political Zionism which had been latent in her commitment to Jewish tradition. Under the proper conditions of freedom and cultural autonomy, what might not these marvelous people accomplish—these people whose aspirations she found were vibrating in the depths of her own nervous system?

By 1893 she was helping to organize a Zionist society in Baltimore. Then in New York, where she and her mother settled in 1902 after the death of Rabbi Szold, she joined a women's Zionist study circle which called itself Hadassah, after the Jewish queen of Persia. It is not entirely clear by what impulse these early Zionist groups in America were organized or for what specific purpose. There were several of them scattered across the country, all founded around the same time—that is, more or less at the turn of the century. All were, it may be imagined, study groups, much like the New York Hadassah: the members prepared papers on aspects of Jewish history or ritual, and they held discussions of the new Zionist literature.

On her first trip to Palestine, in 1909, Henrietta Szold (or, as the story goes, her mother) found something useful for herself and her fellow Hadassah members to do. Prophetically enough, they were to translate their Zionism into action by doing something about health conditions in Palestine. Henrietta Szold returned to America with the proposal that the Hadassah group send a couple of public health nurses to Palestine to help combat such diseases as the trachoma she and her mother had found raging among the schoolchildren there. Even this tiny venture would have been too expensive for the single group to undertake, but the eminent philanthropist Nathan D. Straus offered to pay the nurses' first year's salary and also to equip a settlement house—on the model of the Henry Street Settlement—for their base of operation. Then in 1912, eight women's Zionist groups from several different cities met in Buffalo and constituted themselves a national organization, which was to take over responsibility for the public nursing venture. After some discussion, the organization adopted the name of the original New York group—Hadassah.

In any single life it is easy to detect recurring patterns; in Henrietta Szold's they were sharply marked out. The founding of Hadassah and its first project appeared in the same rhythm of development that she imposed on things and events over and over in her life: first came the work, conceived in the most direct and unpretentious way, then the organization, and then the burst of imagination and ambition that committed everyone, including Henrietta Szold, far beyond her original intentions. Much is made of Henrietta Szold's modesty and public shyness—so much that one must credit the reports. But modesty by itself cannot explain her peculiar mode of operation; no truly shy woman could have pushed her will so far. She had become the editor of the Jewish Publication Society after first doing some difficult and painstaking work as a volunteer; then she assumed full editorial responsibility—for the Society and for the American Jewish Year Book as well—that involved her in the most minute questions of scholarship, translation, and bibliography. In Palestine later, she was to begin each job as a kind of office manager, sweeping her small and punctiliously collected details into ever more grandiose heaps: a nurse's school, a hospital, a medical school, a youth welfare program, finally a national social service network. She was a woman who backed into everything she did. Once in, however, it never occurred to her that she was out over her head; nor was she ever.

Two things about her, it seems to me—one ideological, one personal—accounted for this pattern. First, she was a pragmatic liberal who abhorred the visionary—and abhorred it all the more for being so beset, so tempted by visions herself. Anything there was to be done, no matter how great or difficult, she believed, must be done step by simple step. This belief was to plague her—and yet serve her magnificently well—in the Palestine of the 20's and 30's, where almost everything that had to be done was either bizarre or seemingly impossible. And secondly, she was someone who hated making final commitments, hated both their demands on the soul and their effects on the personality. She lived and worked most productively while dreaming of doing, of being, something else somewhere else.

Henrietta Szold's life in New York continued to be, as it had in Baltimore, a crowded one. She attended the Jewish Theological Seminary—the first and for a long time the only woman there. She was never without a heavy burden of galley proofs to read or indexes to complete. There were several articles to write for the Jewish Encyclopedia, then in preparation. She was involved in a voluminous correspondence with friends and with her four sisters, who were married and scattered. What was, from the standpoint of her future, to be her most significant activity, namely her association with a small group of friends in the Hadassah study circle, seemed then only a minor aspect of her general busyness.

Henrietta Szold was not, however, that phenomenon we recognize as a "career woman." At the very height of her activities in the world of men—who conceded to her enormous talent and power—she far more closely resembled one of those old-fashioned spinsters doing good works who have been associated in the American imagination with Abolitionism and Women's Suffrage.

She nowhere showed the marks of a great ambition, either to fame or power. Yet, though she had lived what might have been regarded as the best part of her life respected and valued and surrounded by loving friends —fulfilling, in fact, the highest demands of her time and culture—at the age of sixty (in 1920) Henrietta Szold took herself off to a distant and never quite acceptable country and remained there to become famous and powerful—and to die. The Palestine to which she went, moreover, was a wilderness, whose physical conditions were almost intolerable to people much younger and much less kindly treated by life than she, and in whose language she was not fluent.

The twenty-four years she spent in Palestine converted Henrietta Szold from an admirable woman of her day into a great woman. Yet for all those years she refused to regard herself as anything but an American on a particular mission about to return home. Anyone inclined to be mystical would have to feel that her whole life of backing into things had been a preparation for its final phase: it was greatness she was backing into.

The Palestine Henrietta Szold and her mother had seen in 1909 was a primitive place, undeveloped and disease-ridden. The Jews she found there were mostly Orientals, with a sprinkling of very early East European Zionist settlers, and of course the small Orthodox community of Jerusalem. Insofar as it could be regarded as subsisting, this early Yishuv subsisted largely on foreign philanthropy. The two Hadassah nurses who went to Palestine in 1913 must have made little enough impact on the country, medicating the fly-infested eyes of children, trying to improve the standards of pre-natal and infant care.

But during World War I, the Turks deported the nurses and most of the few doctors who had been in the country. When Henrietta Szold returned to Palestine in 1920, this time to help administer the American Zionist Medical Unit, the country was in a state of acute postwar emergency, medical, social, and economic. In 1916 Hadassah, at the behest of the American Provisional Committee for Zionist Affairs, whose chairman was Louis D. Brandeis, had undertaken to organize a relief medical group. Hadassah then had about 4,000 members. In 1916, too, a group of Henrietta Szold's friends settled a small income on her for life. This income not only freed her of the necessity to earn her living, thereby releasing all her time to the Zionist movement; it also officially placed her in the aristocratic relation to her work that was truly consonant with her character. The American Zionist Medical Unit sailed in the summer, 1918, with a first year's budget, including transportation, of $250,000. Hadassah and the Joint Distribution Committee were to share the costs.

The dependence of this first major project on so much non-Zionist money may have been responsible for one extraordinary organizational principle of Hadassah, laid down immediately by Henrietta Szold and adhered to with astonishing rigor through the years: exactly 100 per cent of the funds raised by Hadassah for projects in Palestine must go to Palestine; the money required for organization, propaganda, and fund-raising in America must come from membership dues. Forty-four years and hundreds of millions of dollars later, that percentage has been reduced to 96.

When Henrietta Szold sailed for Palestine in February 1920, it was ostensibly to represent the American Zionist Organization on the Executive Committee of the Medical Unit. She of course had no idea that the move was to be more or less permanent. She seemed not to have a very clear notion of her responsibilities (soon she was sharing responsibility with the Unit's director for administering the entire program). One thing was certain; she did not regard herself as involved in an emergency relief measure. For her the purpose of the Medical Unit (whose staff had grown in two years from forty-four to four hundred and whose budget "ought to" have been $1,000,000) was to create a standard of medical practice, public health, and medical education for the new Yishuv. What the unit succeeded in doing in the establishment of hospitals, clinics, sanitation, and the elimination of such diseases as malaria and trachoma, would provide the basis for all future handling of these problems. The outgrowth of her ideas about the Unit was the Hadassah Medical Organization and the Hadassah Hospital, a major medical center in the Middle East and cosponsor of the Hebrew University medical school. It is interesting to note in this connection that both Henrietta Szold and Dr. Isaac Rubinow, the Unit's director, fought unsuccessfully to socialize medicine. Both their staff and the labor union movement opposed it (though subsequently the Histadrut created its own system of socialized medicine for its membership). A nurses' training school was opened and graduated its first class in November 1921. Just about this time Henrietta Szold also organized a school hygiene campaign and school lunch program.

The rest of Henrietta Szold's career is by now a matter of quite familiar record. In 1923 she returned to America for a while and resumed the active presidency of Hadassah. From its limited and highly selective character as an expanded study group, the organization was growing steadily in membership and scope and assuming more and more its ultimate character as a peculiarly representative, mass organization of American Jewish women. In 1927 Henrietta Szold returned to Palestine as a member of the three-man Executive of the World Zionist Organization with the portfolio for Health and Education. The Yishuv was in the throes of an internal crisis. The Zionist Organization had overextended its budget in prematurely grandiose schemes for development and was bankrupt. Unemployment was critical. Relations with the British Mandatory government were strained to the breaking point. The Arabs threatened. Most of Henrietta Szold's time in those years was spent juggling non-existent budgets, sometimes, as in the case of the school system, to the fine point of two or three pounds. She was bitter about the school system—made up of three separate school systems operated by the labor, capitalist, and religious parties with their separate curricula reflecting their respective party ideologies—which she considered vicious in itself for the education of the young and insane at a time when classes had to be shut down for lack of funds. She was also at swords' points with many American Zionists over matters of policy.

In 1930 she returned once again to America, this time discouraged and despondent. But Hadassah had much for her to do in the way of stirring up the membership, as she by her very presence was able to do; and her seventieth birthday was celebrated with great fanfare. It is not far-fetched to imagine that she, who had spoken so much (and was to speak again) of her longing to return home, could no longer find being in America meaningful. As she wrote of her birthday round with Hadassah: ". . . I feel like a bubble filled, not even with gas, but with that 'inspirational' fluid I am expected to give out all the time. The worst of such a regime is that it unfits one for the real things." The "real things" she had now tasted for good—building institutions and making them work—in Palestine. Very likely it was a fear that her Palestine days were over that made her despondent. And so, when in 1931 she was called again—not by the Zionist Organization but by the Yishuv itself—she hurried gratefully back. This time another portfolio, in some ways her most cherished one, for Social Welfare, was given her by the Vaad Leumi, the General Council of the Asefat Hanivharim, the elected representative body of Jewish Palestine. Her new position meant two things: personally, it meant her full acceptance by the Yishuv, without the suspicions or reservations that had interfered with their early relations (an unprecedented crossing of political lines had made possible her being seated on the Vaad Leumi); administratively it meant the opportunity for doing something she had dreamed of since 1920, the establishment of an indigenous Palestinian social welfare program. Her insistence that such a program was necessary had previously fallen on deaf ears; the labor ideologists thought it smacked too much of capitalist-style palliation; others had been indifferent. Now, without funds, and backed by very little general interest in the program, she hopefully organized classes and discussion groups in the problems of Palestinian social welfare. She was yet to have her way: in 1937 the Vaad Leumi and the municipality of Tel Aviv jointly opened a work village called Kfar Avodah for delinquent boys.

Some years before Kfar Avodah, however, in 1933, she embarked on her most memorable project. Characteristically, she was just about to leave for home when the new job presented itself.

Hitler had come to power in Germany and the Yishuv began to mobilize its money and resources for a German immigration. In Berlin a woman named Recha Freier had conceived the idea of sending German adolescents to live on the *kvutzot* as part of their secondary education and for this purpose had begun organizing the children into the Juedische Jugendshilfe. In 1932 Henrietta Szold had opposed the plan and refused Mrs. Freier's request to take over the work. She had felt strongly that it was wrong to take children from their families and commit them to a life in the Palestine settlements before they were old enough to make such a decision for themselves. One year later, with Hitler firmly in power, she understood there was no choice and became the director of a new agency called Youth Aliyah. Her fears for the responsibility she and Youth Aliyah and the Yishuv were assuming reflected themselves in every aspect of the program, and she was adamant about the arrangements. The children in Germany were to be fully prepared, on training farms and by thorough orientation courses, for the life they were about to lead. Their secondary education (in the beginning all the children transferred to Palestine were fifteen to seventeen years of age) must be completed under the aegis of Youth Aliyah. Henrietta Szold selected the *kvutzot* on which the children were to be settled and made detailed agreements with their members; she herself carefully inspected the housing and other facilities. As each boatload of young people arrived in Palestine, she was at Haifa harbor waiting. She personally interviewed most of the children and in the central office of Youth Aliyah kept voluminous files on the personal adjustment, aptitudes, and special problems of each and every child. The children were supervised in their various settlements by *madrichim*—the *madrich* was a combination youth leader, teacher, and case worker—who were obligated to keep in constant close touch with Henrietta Szold. After two years of Youth Aliyah training, the children were to choose an occupation and place to live.

By 1938, of course, these very high standards had to break down. By then, children all over Europe had to be transferred as quickly as possible to Palestine; setting limits to their age or requiring that they be properly prepared was out of the question. The British were both difficult and unpredictable about issuing immigration certificates; sometimes the children languished in temporary camps and sometimes boatloads of them had to be dispersed and settled in a matter of hours. Still an amazing degree of personal contact and individual accommodation was maintained in the Youth Aliyah procedure. Henrietta Szold simply continued to regard these children as her own charges, and—until the war closed Europe off totally—as children belonging to families elsewhere. Twice after 1933 she went to Berlin on business, once in 1935 and once, with special permission of the Gestapo, in 1937. Twice she had to face meetings with hundreds of parents, tearing at her for word of their children already in Palestine or for promises that she would take out those still in Germany. It was in some way those parents, and all the ones unconfronted, who presided over her plans and methods; at least until the children who came under her care were the ragged bands who had wandered through Europe and the Middle East, or those for whom home had been the Nazi camps.

Once again Hadassah took responsibility for Henrietta Szold's most pressing work. Its convention of 1935 voted to take on the raising of funds for Youth Aliyah in the United States (which under the circumstances meant about 75 per cent of the total budget). The organization was pledged to raise $30,000 a year for two years, a sum representing the amount of money required to keep and educate one hundred children. However, during those first two years Hadassah was able to transmit to Youth Aliyah no less than $250,766. By 1948 a total of 30,000 children, including those rescued before the war and those taken after the war from the camps of Europe and the Arab countries, had come under the care of the program. During the first decade of the State of Israel an expanded Youth Aliyah (now including those Palestine-Israel adolescents who needed some sort of special disposition) provided for 60,000 more. From 1935 to 1959 Hadassah had contributed $38,000,000—this in addition to its responsibility for the Hadassah Medical Organization, the hospital and medical school, a child welfare program, and a vocational high school.

On her eightieth birthday, Henrietta Szold invited a group of friends to hear her read her will. She was not to die for another four years, but she had saved a sum of money—an accumulation of gifts given her by Hadassah and individual friends—and she wished to preside over the execution of her last project. This was to be a children's fund, patterned after the Pro Juventute of Switzerland, which would provide a center for research and publication, and the coordination of national youth activities. After her death, in February 1945, the children's bureau was named the Mosad Szold.

So much of the drama of Henrietta Szold's career is bound up with the apocalyptic Hitler period in Palestine and with the unbelievable matter-of-course heroism of the Yishuv in those days that it becomes practically impossible to separate the woman from her institutional dimensions. All political partisanship aside, who can doubt the systematic, instinctive, incredibly heroic self-sacrifice of the Yishuv during the 30's and 40's? Desperation was part of it, true—and what the Israelis call "no alternative"—but there was something else we cannot quite manage to understand and can speak of even at the most detached only with a touch of oratory. Everything in Henrietta Szold's own style militates against thinking of her against a background of apocalypse; but her final destiny—the mother of 90,000 Jewish orphans—makes it impossible not to.

Yet the real meaning of her service to the Yishuv lay elsewhere. In 1921, after one year in Jerusalem, she wrote to her family:

> The new people—a war-created generation—who are coming here are wonderful. But I cannot accept them. I want to—and I cannot. I love order. Disorder nauseates me. And they are systemless. . . . Yet *they* are heroic, not I. If indeed I am fine and aristocratic as you say I am, why do I not embrace them?

These "new people" were the East European pioneers—the *halutzim*—who were coming into the country armed with their socialism and their ideologies of labor and a Jewish return to the soil. The feeble economy of those times offered them nothing in the way of occupation but a little road-building. Economic problems, however—in fact, all that order of things the rational world calls by the name of hard realities—were beside the point: the *halutzim* established their communes and cooperatives, made themselves into farmers and laborers, not out of the existence of possibility but solely from their possession of a new truth.

Henrietta Szold could not embrace them, while passionately admiring their heroism, because they represented the overturning of her world and her apprehension of it as no evil she might ever encounter could. Ideology was as real an element in the social topography of Palestine as the hardship, poverty, disease, disorganization she *was* equipped to contend with—indeed, in the end it proved realer than any of them. The systemlessness she complained of was actually something other than that: it was a new system of its own, which enthroned a kind of order both uncongenial to and never fully comprehended by her. The *halutz* was peculiarly a creature of order; everything material, to come into being for him, had first to be adjusted and shaped to his abstractions. And without his abstractions, the Jewish National Home—itself the highest abstraction—could neither have existed nor have been prepared for the most concrete moment in its history—namely, the moment when it undertook to save the salvageable remnant of European Jewry.

If the early socialist pioneers in Palestine were a species of madmen—and it has become the better part of both reason and Zionist theology to think so—it is important to remember that Henrietta Szold was no less mad in her own way. In a contemporary world dominated by the grandeur of social forces and historic movements, she was afflicted with the wild-eyed conviction that people move forward by placing one foot in front of another. She said good public health depends on a good hospital, good education depends on good attitudes among the children, and she said: Do you want to rescue children? Very well then, let us establish proper training farms. Enraged as she was by a politically divided school system that was as inevitable to Palestine as the sun or the rain, it was she who found the means to keep the schools open and the teachers teaching when economics and social reality said no. Thus without the anachronism of Henrietta Szold's spirit, much would have had to remain unadjusted to the *halutz*'s order.

It is perhaps in relation to the Arab problem that her peculiar position in the Yishuv was worked through most completely. Practically on her arrival in Palestine she began to fret about Arab hostility—blaming now the Jews, now the British, now the Arabs—and she accurately saw the problem as the obstacle against which the entire Palestinian community might founder. "Here lies my attitude," she wrote in August 1937: "we must have another five years of sympathetic trial to solve the Arab-Jewish problem. I believe there is a solution; and if we cannot find it, then I consider that Zionism has failed utterly." Here again, and most significantly, she ignored historical inevitability, which might now be stated in the simple proposition that the Arabs did not want the Jews in Palestine and that if the Jews remained, there was going to be war. It was this view—that Zionism must stand justified by an amicable settlement with the Arabs—which brought her to join Ihud, a group dedicated to the principle of a binational state. The official Zionist movement has had bitter thoughts and feelings about Ihud, which it is not necessary to rehearse here; in any event, Henrietta Szold was exempted from them. To those to whom the proposal for a bi-national community seemed a breach of discipline at a time when discipline above all was called for, she at least needed to present no credentials of a thoroughgoing Zionist loyalty. Apart from the ultimate political fate of bi-nationalism, and apart from all the just arguments that can be mustered on either side of the question, Henrietta Szold's membership in Ihud is of a piece with her entire approach to the movement she served: the real problems of the Jewish state must have concrete, and concretely Jewish, solutions, or else the purpose will have been cut off from those whose purpose the Jewish state is.

Since the establishment of the State of Israel, the Zionist movement has faced still another crisis. No one really knows what Zionism means any more—or what it can be made to mean. In America, Zionist organizations are languishing for want of an ultimate goal—such as the creation of a Jewish state once was—to which to direct their longings and energies. Hadassah, too, insofar as it is an organization deeply committed to the *ideas* of Zionism, is now going through the troublesome business of redefining its larger purpose. But Hadassah, alone within the whole Zionist movement, carries the unique legacy of Henrietta Szold. Ideologies come and go but orphans and the sick and the socially or psychologically disabled will be with us forever; Zionism will come to mean this thing or that—or, in a happier world, maybe nothing—but the 318,000 members of Hadassah, regardless of what they may finally come to say about their relations with the State of Israel, will not be left looking for ways to concretize their attachment to it. Perhaps Henrietta Szold—the stranger to the Yishuv who was not a stranger, the holder of enormous power who remained staunchly non-political, the woman who did the work cut out for her and left behind a string of useful institutions—perhaps she has provided the clue for the future behavior of those who wish to call themselves Zionists while continuing to live outside the State of Israel.

June 1962

R. H. S. Crossman

GENTILE ZIONISM AND THE BALFOUR DECLARATION

The Balfour Declaration was issued on November 2, 1917, and took the curious form of a letter from the British Foreign Secretary, Arthur James Balfour, to Lord Rothschild. The text is as follows:

Dear Lord Rothschild,

I have much pleasure in conveying to you, on behalf of His Majesty's Government, the following declaration of sympathy with Jewish Zionist aspirations which has been submitted to, and approved by, the Cabinet.

"His Majesty's Government view with favour the establishment in Palestine of a national home for the Jewish people, and will use their best endeavours to facilitate the achievement of this object, it being clearly understood that nothing shall be done which may prejudice the civil and religious rights of existing non-Jewish communities in Palestine, or the rights and political status enjoyed by Jews in any other country."

I should be grateful if you would bring this declaration to the knowledge of the Zionist Federation.

Yours sincerely,
Arthur James Balfour

Thus the actual Declaration consists of one single flabby sentence—the ambiguous product of three months' drafting and counter-drafting. Yet, unlike most famous political declarations, which merely ratify a decision already taken, these sixty-seven words changed the course of history. Once they had been published, Britain, then at the height of her imperial power, became involved in a Middle Eastern policy which committed her inexorably to plotting for and obtaining mandatory control of Palestine under the League of Nations, and thereby making herself responsible to the Jews of the world for the establishment of the National Home and to the Arabs for strangling it before it threatened their existence. If the Balfour Declaration had not been issued in the first week of November 1917, there would have been no Mandate and no National Home. Israel would have remained unborn and Arab nationalism might not have been transformed into an anti-Western movement.

Here, then, is one of those seminal episodes in human history, the study of whose details enables us to comprehend better the whole succeeding epoch. Unfortunately, however, the historical truth about the Balfour Declaration is a rock overlaid by successive deposits of myth and countermyth. There is the human interest story, to which Lloyd George gave some authenticity in his memoirs, that the British War Premier presented Palestine as a gift to Chaim Weizmann in return for services rendered when he was Minister of Munitions. The unknown Russian chemist, according to this version, had, singlehanded, saved the British Navy by developing a new process for the production of acetone, an essential ingredient in the making of TNT. "I am Weizmann's proselyte," Lloyd George told a Jewish audience in 1925. "Acetone converted me to Zionism."

It is a nice story, but no one believes it. Moreover, Jew and Arab alike have felt the need for a profounder explanation of this extraordinary British decision. The Arab version, of course, starts from the agreements with which the British tempted their leaders to revolt and then shows that, at the self-same moment these agreements were being negotiated, the British government was making a compact with the Jewish financiers of America, whose dollars were desperately needed. The Jewish version, on the other hand, prefers to see the episode as the masterpiece of Weizmann's diplomatic skill, a rare example of a change in the course of history wrought by the efforts of a single man.

Until now, in the absence of an authoritative study, one could take one's choice according to one's prejudice, but now no longer. *The Balfour Declaration,* by Leonard Stein, is a 660-page study, at once monumental in scale, scholarly in its standard of research, and perceptive in its analysis of human weakness. Unfortunately it is composed with a style so dry and an exactitude so pedantic that it is likely to put off all but the academic reader. Because I am pretty sure that it is the kind of book which will be read in review and not in the original, I have decided to make what should have been a critique of Mr. Stein into the summary of the astonishing story he has to tell.

II

Mr. Stein starts by reminding us what an insignificant little thing Zionism was in 1914. At that time there were only 8,000 members of the Zionist

Federation in Great Britain, and the situation in the United States was even worse. Out of three million Jews, some 12,000 were Zionists. Nor did there seem any prospect of their ideals being realized. Palestine was a backward, insignificant province of the Ottoman Empire, and the Zionist Executive, with its headquarters in Berlin, was strictly neutral in Great Power politics and vociferously asserted that "the Turks possess in the whole world no more generous and self-sacrificing friends than the Zionists." The Zionist aim, in fact, was to add a few more hundreds to the 35,000 Jews who then formed a tiny minority among the two million Arabs in Palestine. But the rise of the Young Turks, and of the new, fiercer nationalism in which they believed, made such hopes remote indeed. As Stein drily comments, "These protestations fell upon deaf ears. The Turks were unimpressed, and did all they could to keep the Jews out of Palestine."

Suddenly the situation was transformed by the outbreak of World War I, and, on November 5, 1914, by the British declaration of war against Turkey. In his speech at the Lord Mayor's Banquet four nights later, Mr. Asquith, then Prime Minister, made it clear that, in the new situation, Britain had abandoned her traditional policy of "propping up the Sick Man of Europe" and now included among her war aims the dismemberment of the Ottoman Empire. In the Cabinet next day, Lloyd George referred to the ultimate destiny of Palestine, and that very evening the president of the Local Government Board—now the nonogenarian philosopher-king, Lord Samuel—had a talk with Lloyd George on the subject and urged on him the need to establish a Jewish State in Palestine. That afternoon he went to see the Foreign Secretary, Sir Edward Grey, to whom he suggested that "British influence ought to play a considerable part in the formation of a Jewish State, since the geographical situation of Palestine, and especially its proximity to Egypt, would render its good will a matter of importance to the British Empire."

The fact that members of the British Cabinet were talking in this way was completely unknown to the official Zionist organization. After all, the headquarters were still in Berlin, and the leaders can hardly be blamed for announcing a policy of neutrality and giving their full support to the Germans. In the eyes of every Jew, Czarist Russia was the chief enemy; and, since Russia was the enemy of the Germans and the ally of the British, it was natural for European Jewry, including the Zionists, to feel more sympathy with the former than with the latter.

One Zionist alone saw instantaneously and incisively the new opportunity created by Turkey's entry into the war. Even before that, Weizmann had written to Zangwill (in October 1914): "My plans are based naturally on one cardinal assumption, viz. that the Allies will win. . . . I have no doubt in my mind that Palestine will fall into the sphere of England. It will be the Asiatic Belgium, especially if it is developed by the

Jews. We could easily move a million Jews into Palestine within the next fifty to sixty years, and England would have an effective barrier [against Russia] and we would have a country." On December 10, 1914, Weizmann met Samuel for the first time, and was amazed to discover that this buttoned-up, assimilated, ambitious Anglo-Jew had discovered a Zionist policy of his own, though he continued to refuse any contact with the Zionists. With Weizmann's encouragement, he circulated a memorandum to the Cabinet, of which the revised and final text was that of January 1915. By now the crude notion of British annexation and of a Jewish State had both been dropped. Instead, the hope was now expressed that "under British rule Jewish immigration, carefully regulated, would be given preference, so that in the course of time the Jewish inhabitants, grown into a majority and settled in the land, may be conceded such degree of self-government as the conditions of that day might justify." All we know for sure about this memorandum is that it evoked the Premier's scorn. "I confess I am not attracted by the proposed addition to our responsibilities," remarked Asquith, "but it is a curious illustration of Disraeli's favourite maxim that 'race is everything' to find this almost lyrical outburst proceeding from the well-ordered and methodical brain of H.S."

Nevertheless the collaboration of Weizmann and Samuel had its effect inside the British Establishment. In no social oligarchy are ideas as much a matter of fashion as in the British. For years a policy remains the monopoly of some eccentric outsider. Then, quite suddenly, it becomes accepted in the Establishment as a whole, enthused over by the *Times* and the *Guardian* and approved over the luncheon table at the Athenaeum, the Reform, and the Travellers' Club. Something of this sort happened to Zionism in the first two years of World War I. Weizmann, never unsusceptible to female charm, was lionized by the hostesses, and his home in Addison Gardens was frequented by the great. On March 20, 1916, Mrs. Weizmann could write in her diary: "Mrs. James de Rothschild has been to dinner at Lady Crewe's, and overheard the conversation between Lord Robert Cecil and Lady Crewe. She asked Cecil what he thought of Zionism, declared that 'we all in this house are Weizmannites' and asked whether the time was ripe to start a campaign."

It must be understood that this *succès fou* had nothing to do with the official Zionist organization. The Cabinet were Weizmannites, not Zionists. Nevertheless, it upset the anti-Zionist forces that still securely controlled British Jewry. These forces were led by Lucien Wolf. Wolf was one of those assimilated Jews who regarded Weizmann's concept of Jewish homelessness as rank anti-Semitism. Nevertheless, he realized that, in the United States as well as in Britain, Zionism was gaining ground among the Eastern Jews, and he decided to out-trump the Zionists by submitting a moderate declaration in favor of Jewish colonization in Palestine to Sir

Edward Grey at the Foreign Office. Although Asquith still regarded Zionism as crazy nonsense, he encouraged Grey to accept Wolf's draft and telegraph it to the British ambassadors in Paris and Petrograd, with the following significant addition, which shows how far Weizmann's ideas had begun to influence the British Cabinet:

> This formula seems to us unobjectionable. But we consider that the scheme might be made far more attractive to the majority of Jews if it held out to them the prospect that when in course of time the Jewish colonists in Palestine have grown strong enough to cope with the Arab population, they may be allowed to take the management of the internal affairs of Palestine (with the exception of Jerusalem and the Holy Places) into their own hands. . . . Our sole object is to find an arrangement which would be so attractive to the majority of Jews as to enable us to strike a bargain for Jewish support.

This completely cynical proposal lapsed, because the French government was not interested and the Czarist government was, not unnaturally, strenuously opposed to any declaration of this kind.

Weizmann was probably unaware that this telegram had been dispatched. If he had known of it, he would have been appalled at the irresponsibility which inspired it. The truth is that, in March 1916, the moment for such an appeal had not come. On the one hand, world Jewry was still profoundly suspicious of Britain as the ally of Russia and unwilling to give its support to any proposal which might seem to be inspired by British plans for annexing Palestine. On the other hand, the penetration of the British ruling class that Weizmann had achieved was still superficial. Much more hard work would have to be done before he was prepared to urge a British initiative.

So, in the intervals of his chemical work at the Ministry of Munitions, Weizmann settled down to prepare the ground. In the first place, he made his credentials both as a British citizen and as a supporter of the Western cause impeccable by cutting off all contact with the official Zionist headquarters in Berlin. He had come to the conclusion that, whatever the professional Zionists might believe, the Jewish State could only be achieved under British patronage, and he had equally convinced himself that Britain could only consolidate her Middle Eastern position after the break-up of the Ottoman Empire by establishing the Jews north of the Suez Canal. He had, in fact, evolved the concept of the identity of interest between the British and the Jewish peoples which was to inspire his greatest successes —and in the end to break him, when it became clear that the identity of interest had been repudiated by Ernest Bevin.

In the second place, Weizmann had begun to concern himself actively with the position of American Jewry. Here, fortunately, Mr. Justice Brandeis was as convinced as he of the need for an Allied victory in order to achieve a Zionist return to Israel. Nevertheless, Brandeis was forced to warn Weizmann that the vast majority of American Jewry, though increasingly sympathetic to Zionist ideas, were still either suspicious of Britain or, in the case of the German Jews, actively hostile.

III

Here it may be well to pause in our narrative and ask what it was that made so many British politicians in World War I susceptible to Jewish pressure. One can, I think, trace three motives, represented by three of the most prominent Gentile Zionists of the period—Lloyd George, A. J. Balfour, and Winston Churchill. What inspired Lloyd George was, first and foremost, the belief of a Welsh Nonconformist, brought up on the Bible, that Britain was the right country to liberate Palestine from the Turks and that, under British protection, the Jews of the Bible were the right people to inhabit it. Lloyd George was not a philosophical Zionist but, thanks to his Bible reading, he knew more about Palestine than about any country save his own, and his sense that it was Britain's destiny to plant the Jews there grew with his premiership.

A rather different type of Gentile Zionism was represented by Winston Churchill. I doubt whether he was ever deeply influenced by the Bible or by any romantic desire to help small nations. For Churchill, the key question was imperial convenience, and he saw in the support of Jewish claims in Palestine an effective method of limiting French expansion in the Middle East and simultaneously safeguarding the Canal. For Churchill, the essential point was the security of Suez; and the support of Zionism was a convenient moral justification for this imperial requirement to obtain control of Palestine.

A third and very different kind of Gentile Zionism was represented by A. J. Balfour. Mr. Stein appears surprised that Balfour, like so many other staunch supporters of the National Home, revealed strong anti-Semitic tendencies. He seems to have forgotten Weizmann's doctrine that anti-Semitism is endemic in the Gentile world and that the justification of Zionism lies precisely in this fact. It is because the Jews of the Diaspora must always, by definition, remain in danger of homelessness that a Jewish State is a necessity of Jewish survival.

From this central doctrine Weizmann drew one important practical consequence. Instead of being shocked by the fact that many of the Gentiles he dealt with felt strong anti-Semitic prejudices, he assumed that the most reliable support for his cause would be drawn from those Gentiles who were ashamed of their hostility to the Jews and from those Jews who were ashamed of their fear of the *goy*. As far as we know, neither Lloyd George nor Churchill ever worried about anti-Semitism, but Balfour certainly did, and Mr. Stein, in one fascinating passage of his book, reminds us that the famous first meeting between Balfour and Weizmann, during the general election of 1906, originated from the fact that, whereas Churchill's conscience about the Jews was clear, Balfour's was not.

A few years before the election a Conservative government, under Balfour's premiership, had introduced an odious immigration bill, chiefly designed to make difficulties for Jews entering Britain from Eastern Europe. The bill had been opposed by the Liberal opposition, not least by Churchill himself. When the government went to the country, Churchill and Balfour were both fighting seats in Manchester, and Churchill, who had a large Jewish vote in his constituency, was advised to ask Dr. Weizmann to intervene on his behalf. Anxious not to involve himself in British politics, Weizmann refused. Then Balfour's political managers got cold feet and suggested that it might be useful for their candidate to see the Zionist leader in order to reduce Jewish hostility. Because Balfour was Prime Minister, Weizmann agreed, and the famous conversation took place in which, by playing on Balfour's uneasy conscience, Weizmann converted him to a Zionism more altruistic than that of Churchill or Lloyd George. Feeling within himself the emotions from which the pogrom rises, Balfour dedicated himself to removing the cause of anti-Semitism by creating a Jewish State. Whereas his colleagues had to be persuaded that the British Empire would gain from Zionism, Balfour treated the creation of the Jewish State as an end in itself and, indeed, by 1921 was pressing that America, not Britain, should have the mandate.

Weizmann showed himself a maestro in the art of playing on these three species of British Gentile Zionism. Precisely because he was not an assimilated British Jew but an East European who combined his foreignness with a deep sense of loyalty to the country whose passport he had obtained; precisely because he was proud and not subservient; precisely because he wanted to lead the Jews out of the ghetto of finance and back to the wholesome life of the farm, Weizmann appeared to the British ruling class not as the kind of "Yid" they disliked but as a representative of the Jew they had learned to admire in their reading of the Bible. There is not another Jewish leader with whom Weizmann can be compared. Only Thomas Masaryk, the founder of Czechoslovakia, revealed the same powers and exerted the same magical attraction upon hard-headed Anglo-Saxon politicians.

IV

In December 1916 the intrigues of Lord Beaverbrook were successful. Asquith was overthrown and a new war coalition was established, with Lloyd George as Premier and a small War Cabinet, soon to be dominated by four leading Gentile Zionists—the Prime Minister himself, Balfour, Milner, and Jan Smuts. Now Weizmann's patience was rewarded: events began to press toward a declaration of British policy in regard to Palestine. The famous top-secret Sykes-Picot agreement for partitioning the Ottoman Empire had now been negotiated, first with the French and then with the Russians, and as soon as the signatures had been set to it the British Foreign Office began to seek methods of invalidating it—in particular, by keeping the French out of Palestine. What more useful excuse for Britain to go back on her secret agreement with France than the insistence of world Jewry that Britain and Britain alone could look after their interests in the Holy Land? In the second place, as a result of the collapse of the Czarist regime, the War Cabinet was obsessed by the need for keeping Russia in the war. To this end it seemed essential to counteract the ascendancy that the Russian left—Social Democrats, Mensheviks, and Bolsheviks—had achieved over the masses and, in particular, over the Jews. Could not a promised return to Zion under British patronage turn Russian Jewry into opponents of Menshevism and Bolshevism? That, at least, was the belief of the *Times*'s Foreign Editor, Wickham Steed. Though Kerensky had to complain of the *Times*'s anti-Semitic outbursts, Wickham Steed was soon giving his full support to Zionism, on the ground that "Herzl's ideas might exert a regenerating influence upon the Jewish intellectuals and serve as a counterpoise to the revolutionary elements in Jewry."

The final factor that transformed the situation was the American declaration of war. In April 1917 Balfour, as Foreign Secretary, visited Washington and had long talks with Brandeis, whom he regarded as the most notable American and the most wholesome influence on the President. Now that America was an ally and Czarism had collapsed, suspicions of Britain had markedly declined. But, despite Brandeis's influence, it was still not possible to win American Jewry to the idea of a British protectorate in Palestine. And these hesitations were greatly strengthened by the fact that, though the United States was at war with Germany, Wilson had maintained its neutrality toward Turkey and therefore could not be concerned in any plans for dividing up the Ottoman Empire.

But it was in Britain that Weizmann found his toughest opposition. Despite the recent incursion of Eastern Jews, British Jewry was still a small community, dominated by a rich oligarchy of distinguished and implacable anti-Zionists. On May 24, 1917, the anti-Zionists decided to take the initiative and declared war on Zionism in the columns of the *Times*. Despite all Weizmann's work, the battle was closely contested and the Board of Deputies only disowned the anti-Zionists by 56 votes to 51. Moreover, this victory was rapidly followed by a reverse, when a leading assimilated Jew, Edwin Montagu, whose slogan it was that he had been striving all his life to escape from the ghetto, joined Lloyd George's Cabinet.

Nevertheless, the decision could no longer be delayed. By now Weizmann had won the support of three brilliant young men with key positions in the Cabinet offices—Sir Mark Sykes, negotiator of the Sykes-Picot agreement, Harold Nicolson, and L. S. Amery. After consultation with them, it was decided to submit a draft declaration to the Cabinet on September 3.

And now there occurred one of those curious contretemps that so often disturb democratic proceedings. Neither Lloyd George nor Balfour could attend the meeting and, as a result, Edwin Montagu was able to deliver a passionate indictment of Zionism as a surrender to anti-Semitism and a successful plea that nothing more should be heard of the proposal until President Wilson's advice had been asked.

It was a typical delaying tactic, and it succeeded. On September 11, Colonel House replied in a curt telegram, stating that "Wilson had been approached as requested and had expressed the opinion that the time was not opportune for any definite statement further perhaps than one of sympathy, provided it could be made without conveying any real commitment." Apparently the President had acted without consulting Brandeis. At once Weizmann set all the wheels in motion and by September 23 Brandeis could wire Weizmann: "From talks I have had with the President and from expressions of opinion given to closest advisers I feel that I can answer that he is in entire sympathy with declaration quoted in yours of 19th." Mr. Truman was not the first occupant of the White House to find himself confused by contradictory advice on the Jewish question! In 1917 the State Department was already resolutely anti-Zionist and it was only Brandeis's influence inside the White House that saved the day.

Even so, the draft declaration had fallen out of the Cabinet agenda and could not be put back except by the Premier's express decision. On September 28, C. P. Scott, Editor of the *Manchester Guardian*, and Weizmann had breakfast with Lloyd George and achieved their purpose. By this time Edwin Montagu was on his way to India, but he had succeeded in his main purpose. The straightforward acceptance of the principle of a National Home in Palestine, which was the essence of the first draft, was now hedged round by the limitations which caused all the trouble about the Mandate. The first draft had run: "His Majesty's Government accepts the principle that every opportunity should be afforded for the establishment of a home for the Jewish people in Palestine." The draft of October 4 merely states that H.M.G. "views with favour the establishment in Palestine of a national home," and then goes on to add, "it being clearly understood that nothing shall be done which may prejudice the civil and religious rights of existing non-Jewish communities in Palestine, or the rights and political status enjoyed by Jews in any other country who are fully contented with their existing nationality." This new draft, it was now agreed, should be submitted to eight leading British Jews, including the Chief Rabbi, and resubmitted to President Wilson. This was duly done and on October 30 came the final Cabinet meeting.

As so often happens, the great occasion was a sad anti-climax. No one bothered to discuss the larger aspects of the Zionist question or the long-term advantages of a British association with the National Home. Balfour, who introduced the topic, concentrated entirely on the propaganda advantages of issuing the Declaration at once, arguing that it would win support among the Jews in America, as well as rallying the Jews in Russia against the Bolsheviks. Apart from the discussion of some minor amendments, there was no debate, and it was decided, for no clear reason, to issue the Declaration in the form of a letter to Lord Rothschild, although he held no office in the Zionist Federation.

V

So, on November 9, the Declaration was finally given to the press. It received little notice because the main news of the day was the entry of the British Army into Gaza and the beginning of the Bolshevik coup d'état in Russia. Indeed, the ironic feature of the Balfour Declaration is that, from the very moment of its adoption by the British government, it ceased to be of any service to British imperial interests. The seizure of power by the Bolsheviks finally destroyed the fantastic illusion that the Russian Jews could be persuaded to keep their country at war in defiance of the Revolution. Moreover, the beginning of the British occupation of Palestine meant that it was unnecessary any longer to use Zionism in order to keep the French out of the Middle East. Even the argument that the Declaration was necessary to prevent the German government from issuing its own pro-Zionist policy was found to have little validity. Though there were a few people in the German Foreign Office who would have liked a policy of this kind, the need to prop up an unstable Turkish regime made it completely impracticable. For the time being the Declaration seemed to have been stillborn and its opponents in the United States were successful in preventing President Wilson from giving it any support.

Mr. Stein's investigations have conclusively shown that, if the Declaration had not been passed on October 30, the British Cabinet would never have adopted it, since the reasons of state and the propaganda advantages which the British expected to derive from it had all been invalidated within three weeks of its proclamation. Throughout, indeed, one is struck by the regularity with which the British Foreign Office gave the wrong advice, advocated the Declaration for the wrong reasons of imperial utility, and never once warned the government that the Arabs might prove an obstacle to its achievement. One is also impressed by the minor role that public opinion was allowed to play in Britain as well as in America. Britain was still an oligarchy and in World War I power was concentrated in very few hands. It was the supreme achievement of Weizmann to avoid wasting time on influencing a public opinion that was completely ineffective. He concentrated his attention on the few score personalities who really mattered, showed patience when the time was not ripe, and exerted extreme and ultimately successful pressure when he felt that the opportunity was slipping away. The Jewish tradition that the Balfour Declaration was the product of a single man's diplomatic skill is no exaggeration.

But, almost as soon as it had been made, the Declaration became an embarrassment to the British, who began the attempt to wriggle out of it. Within a matter of weeks Balfour was arguing that Britain should persuade the United States to take over the Mandate—a view in which he persisted to the end, while General Allenby in Palestine was suppressing the text, in the interests of placating the Arabs, and seeking to get the policy reversed. Only Lloyd George and, to a lesser extent, Winston Churchill persisted in the belief that British imperial interests would be sustained by the establishment of a Jewish nation to the north of the Suez Canal. And even they, in 1922, were compelled by the rising tide of Arab nationalism to whittle the commitment down. By the middle of the 1930's, when the victims of Hitler's persecution were pouring into Palestine, and the Arabs were in armed revolt, it had become clear that the Balfour Declaration could only be fulfilled at the cost of jeopardizing Britain's Middle Eastern empire and imperiling the huge new oil interests along the Persian Gulf that had only emerged after Britain's acceptance of the Palestine Mandate. Alas for Chaim Weizmann! The identity of interest between the British Empire and the Jewish State, on which he had pinned his faith, had broken down. The State of Israel would have to be created not under the protection of Britain but in a war of independence against her.

September 1962

Isaac Bashevis Singer

YENTL THE YESHIVA BOY

A Story

After her father's death, Yentl had no reason to remain in Yanev. She was all alone in the house. To be sure, lodgers were willing to move in and pay rent; and the marriage brokers flocked to her door with offers from Lublin, Tomashev, Zamosc. But Yentl didn't want to get married. Inside her, a voice repeated over and over: "No!" What becomes of a girl when the wedding's over? Right away she starts bearing and rearing. And her mother-in-law lords it over her. Yentl knew she wasn't cut out for a woman's life. She couldn't sew, she couldn't knit. She let the food burn and the milk boil over; her Sabbath pudding never turned out right, and her *challah* dough didn't rise. Yentl much preferred men's activities to women's. Her father Reb Todros, may he rest in peace, during many bed-ridden years had studied Torah with his daughter as if she were a son. He told Yentl to lock the doors and drape the windows, then together they pored over the Pentateuch, the Mishnah, the Gemara, and the Commentaries. She had proved so apt a pupil that her father used to say:

"Yentl—you have the soul of a man."

"So why was I born a woman?"

"Even Heaven makes mistakes."

There was no doubt about it, Yentl was unlike any of the girls in Yanev—tall, thin, bony, with small breasts and narrow hips. On Sabbath afternoons, when her father slept, she would dress up in his trousers, his fringed garment, his silk coat, his skull-cap, his velvet hat, and study her reflection in the mirror. She looked like a dark, handsome young man. There was even a slight down on her upper lip. Only her thick braids showed her womanhood—and if it came to that, hair could always be shorn. Yentl conceived a plan and day and night she could think of nothing else. No, she had not been created for the noodle board and the pudding dish, for chattering with silly women and pushing for a place at the butcher's block. Her father had told her so many tales of yeshivas, rabbis, men of letters! Her head was full of Talmudic disputations, questions and answers, learned phrases. Secretly, she had even smoked her father's long pipe.

Yentl told the dealers she wanted to sell the house and go to live in Kallish with an aunt. The neighborhood women tried to talk her out of it, and the marriage brokers said she was crazy, that she was more likely to make a good match right here in Yanev. But Yentl was obstinate. She was in such a rush that she sold the house to the first bidder, and let the furniture go for a song. All she realized from her inheritance was one hundred and forty rubles. Then late one night in the month of Av, while Yanev slept, Yentl cut off her braids, arranged sidelocks at her temples, and dressed herself in her father's clothes. Packing underclothes, phylacteries, and a few books into a straw suitcase, she started off on foot for Lublin.

On the main road, Yentl got a ride in a carriage that took her as far as Zamosc. From there, she again set out on foot. She stopped at an inn along the way, and gave her name there as Anshel, after an uncle who had died. The inn was crowded with young men journeying to study with famous rabbis. An argument was in progress over the merits of various yeshivas, some praising those of Lithuania, others claiming that study was more intensive in Poland and the board better. It was the first time Yentl had ever found herself alone in the company of young men. How different their talk was from the jabbering of women, she thought, but she was too shy to join in. One young man discussed a prospective match and the size of the dowry, while another, parodying the manner of a Purim rabbi, declaimed a passage from the Torah, adding all sorts of lewd interpretations. After a while, the company proceeded to contests of strength. One pried open another's fist; a second tried to bend a companion's arm. One student, dining on bread and tea, had no spoon and stirred his cup with his penknife. Presently, one of the group came over to Yentl and poked her in the shoulder:

"Why so quiet? Don't you have a tongue?"

"I have nothing to say."

"What's your name?"

"Anshel."

"You *are* bashful. A violet by the wayside."

And the young man tweaked Yentl's nose. She would have given him a smack in return, but her arm refused to budge. She turned white. Another student, slightly older than the rest, tall and pale, with burning eyes and a black beard, came to her rescue.

"Hey, you, why are you picking on him?"

"If you don't like it, you don't have to look."

"Want me to pull your sidelocks off?"

The bearded young man beckoned to Yentl, then asked where she came from and where she was going. Yentl told him she was looking for a yeshiva, but wanted a quiet one. The young man pulled at his beard.

"Then come with me to Bechev."

He explained that he was returning to Bechev for his fourth year. The yeshiva there was small, with only thirty students, and the people in the town provided board for them all. The food was plentiful and the housewives darned the students' socks and took care of their laundry. The Bechev rabbi, who headed the yeshiva, was a genius. He could pose ten questions and answer all ten with one proof. Most of the students eventually found wives in the town.

"Why did you leave in the middle of the term?" Yentl asked.

"My mother died. Now I'm on my way back."

"What's your name?"

"Avigdor."

"How is it you're not married?"

The young man scratched his beard.

"It's a long story."

"Tell me."

Avigdor covered his eyes and thought a moment.

"Are you coming to Bechev?"

"Yes."

"Then you'll find out soon enough anyway. I was engaged to the only daughter of Alter Vishkower, the richest man in town. Even the wedding date was set when suddenly they sent back the engagement contract."

"What happened?"

"I don't know. Gossips, I guess, were busy spreading tales. I had the right to ask for half the dowry, but it was against my nature. Now they're trying to talk me into another match, but the girl doesn't appeal to me."

"In Bechev, yeshiva boys look at women?"

"At Alter's house, where I ate once a week, Hadass, his daughter, always brought in the food. . . ."

"Is she good-looking?"

"She's blond."

"Brunettes can be good-looking too."

"No."

Yentl gazed at Avigdor. He was lean and bony with sunken cheeks. He had curly sidelocks so black they appeared blue, and his eyebrows met across the bridge of his nose. He looked at her sharply with the regretful shyness of one who has just divulged a secret. His lapel was rent, according to the custom for mourners, and the lining of his gaberdine showed through. He drummed restlessly on the table and hummed a tune. Behind the high furrowed brow his thoughts seemed to race. Suddenly he spoke:

"Well, what of it. I'll become a recluse, that's all."

It was strange, but as soon as Yentl—or Anshel—arrived in Bechev, she was allotted one day's board a week at the house of that same rich man, Alter Vishkower, whose daughter had broken off her betrothal to Avigdor.

The students at the yeshiva studied in pairs, and Avigdor chose Anshel for a partner. He helped her with the lessons. He was also an expert swimmer and offered to teach Anshel the breast stroke and how to tread water, but she always found excuses for not going down to the river. Avigdor suggested that they share lodgings, but Anshel found a place to sleep at the house of an elderly widow who was half blind. Tuesdays, Anshel ate at Alter Vishkower's and Hadass waited on her. Avigdor always asked many questions: "How does Hadass look? Is she sad? Is she gay? Are they trying to marry her off? Does she ever mention my name?" Anshel reported that Hadass upset dishes on the tablecloth, forgot to bring the salt, and dipped her fingers into the plate of grits while carrying it. She ordered the servant girl around, was forever engrossed in story-books, and changed her hairdo every week. Moreover, she must consider herself a beauty, for she was always in front of the mirror, but, in fact, she was not that good-looking.

"Two years after she's married," said Anshel, "she'll be an old bag."

"So she doesn't appeal to you?"

"Not particularly."

"Yet if she wanted you, you wouldn't turn her down."

"I can do without her."

"Don't you have evil impulses?"

The two friends, sharing a lectern in a corner of the study house, spent more time talking than learning. Occasionally Avigdor smoked, and Anshel, taking the cigarette from his lips, would have a puff. Avigdor liked baked flatcakes made with buckwheat, so Anshel stopped at the bakery every morning to buy one, and wouldn't let him pay his share. Often Anshel did things that greatly surprised Avigdor. If a button came off Avigdor's coat, for example, Anshel would arrive at the yeshiva the next day with needle and thread and sew it back on. Anshel bought Avigdor all kinds of presents: a silk handkerchief, a pair of socks, a muffler. Avigdor grew more and more attached to this boy, five years younger than himself, whose beard hadn't even begun to sprout. Once Avigdor said to Anshel:

"I want you to marry Hadass."

"What good would that do *you?*"

"Better you than a total stranger."

"You'd become my enemy."

"Never."

Avigdor liked to go for long walks through the town and Anshel frequently joined him. Engrossed in conversation, they would go off to the water mill, or to the pine forest, or to the crossroads where the Christian shrine stood. Sometimes they stretched out on the grass.

"Why can't a woman be like a man?" Avigdor asked once, looking up at the sky.

"How do you mean?"

"Why couldn't Hadass be just like you?"

"How like me?"

"Oh—a good fellow."

Anshel grew playful. She plucked a flower and tore off the petals one by one. She picked up a chestnut and threw it at Avigdor. Avigdor watched a ladybug crawl across the palm of his hand. After a while he spoke up:

"They're trying to marry me off."

Anshel sat up instantly.

"To whom?"

"To Feitl's daughter, Peshe."

"The widow?"

"That's the one."

"Why should you marry a widow?"

"No one else will have me."

"That's not true. Someone will turn up for you."

"Never."

Anshel told Avigdor such a match was bad. Peshe was neither good-looking nor clever, only a cow with a pair of eyes. Besides, she was bad luck, for her husband had died in the first year of their marriage. Such women were husband-killers. But Avigdor did not answer. He lit a cigarette, took a deep puff, and blew out smoke rings. His face had turned green.

"I need a woman. I can't sleep at night."

Anshel was startled.

"Why can't you wait until the right one comes along?"

"Hadass was my destined one."

And Avigdor's eyes grew moist. Abruptly he got to his feet.

"Enough lying around. Let's go."

After that, everything happened quickly. One day Avigdor was confiding his problem to Anshel, two days later he became engaged to Peshe, and brought honey cake and brandy to the yeshiva. An early wedding date was set. When the bride-to-be is a widow, there's no need to wait for a trousseau. Everything is ready. The groom, moreover, was an orphan and no one's advice had to be asked. The yeshiva students drank the brandy and offered their congratulations. Anshel also took a sip, but promptly choked on it.

"Oy, it burns."

"You're not much of a man," Avigdor teased.

After the celebration, Avigdor and Anshel sat down with a volume of the Gemara, but they made little progress, and their conversation was equally slow. Avigdor rocked back and forth, pulled at his beard, muttered under his breath.

"I'm lost," he said abruptly.

"If you don't like her, why are you getting married?"

"I'd marry a she-goat."

The following day Avigdor did not appear at the study house. Feitl the Leatherdealer belonged to the Hasidim and he wanted his prospective son-in-law to continue his studies at the Hasidic prayer house. The yeshiva students said privately that though there was no denying the widow was short and round as a barrel, her mother the daughter of a dairyman, her father half an ignoramus, still the whole family was filthy with money. Feitl was part-owner of a tannery; Peshe had invested her dowry in a shop that sold herring, tar, pots and pans, and was always crowded with peasants. Father and daughter were outfitting Avigdor and had placed orders for a fur coat, a cloth coat, a silk *kapote,* and two pair of boots. In addition, he had received many gifts immediately, things that had belonged to Peshe's first husband: the Vilna edition of the Talmud, a gold watch, a Chanukah candelabra, a spice box. Anshel sat alone at the lectern. On Tuesday when Anshel arrived for dinner at Alter Vishkower's house, Hadass remarked:

"What do you say about your partner—back in clover, isn't he?"

"What did you expect—that no one else would want him?"

Hadass reddened.

"It wasn't my fault. My father was against it."

"Why?"

"Because they found out a brother of his had hanged himself."

Anshel looked at her as she stood there—tall, blond, with a long neck, hollow cheeks, and blue eyes, wearing a cotton dress and a calico apron. Her hair, fixed in two braids, was flung back over her shoulders. A pity I'm not a man, Anshel thought.

"Do you regret it now?" Anshel asked.

"Oh, yes!"

Hadass fled from the room. The rest of the food, meat dumplings and tea, was brought in by the servant girl. Not until Anshel had finished eating and was washing her hands for the Final Blessings did Hadass reappear. She came up to the table and said in a smothered voice:

"Swear to me you won't tell him anything. Why should he know what goes on in my heart! . . ."

Then she fled once more, nearly falling over the threshold.

The head of the yeshiva asked Anshel to choose another study partner, but weeks went by and still Anshel studied alone. There was no one in the yeshiva who could take Avigdor's place. All the others were small, in body and in spirit. They talked nonsense, bragged about trifles, grinned oafishly, behaved like *shnorrers.* Without Avigdor the study house seemed empty. At night Anshel lay on her bench at the widow's, unable to sleep. Stripped of gaberdine and trousers she was once more Yentl, a girl of marriageable age, in love with a young man who was bethrothed to another. Perhaps I should have told him the truth, Anshel thought. But it was too late for that. Anshel could not go back to being a girl, could never again do without books and a study house. She lay there thinking outlandish thoughts that brought her close to madness. She fell asleep, then awoke with a start. In her dream she had been at the same time a man and a woman, wearing both a woman's bodice and a man's fringed garment. Yentl's period was late and she was suddenly afraid . . . who knew? In *Medrash Talpioth* she had read of a woman who had conceived merely through desiring a man. Only now did Yentl grasp the meaning of the Torah's prohibition against wearing the clothes of the other sex. By doing so one deceived not only others but also oneself. Even the soul was perplexed, finding itself incarnate in a strange body.

At night Anshel lay awake; by day she could scarcely keep her eyes open. At the houses where she had her meals, the women complained that the youth left everything on his plate. The rabbi noticed that Anshel no longer paid attention to the lectures but stared out the window lost in private thoughts. When Tuesday came, Anshel appeared at the Vishkower house for dinner. Hadass set a bowl of soup before her and waited, but Anshel was so disturbed she did not even say thank you. She reached for a spoon but let it fall. Hadass ventured a comment:

"I hear Avigdor has deserted you."

Anshel awoke from her trance.

"What do you mean?"

"He's no longer your partner."

"He's left the yeshiva."

"Do you see him at all?"

"He seems to be hiding."

"Are you at least going to the wedding?"

For a moment Anshel was silent as though missing the meaning of the words. Then she spoke:

"He's a big fool."

"Why do you say that?"

"You're beautiful, and the other one looks like a monkey."

Hadass blushed to the roots of her hair.

"It's all my father's fault."

"Don't worry. You'll find someone who's worthy of you."

"There's no one I want."

"But everyone wants you. . . ."

There was a long silence. Hadass' eyes grew larger, filling with the sadness of one who knows there is no consolation.

"Your soup is getting cold."

"I, too, want you."

Anshel was astonished at what she had said. Hadass stared at her over her shoulder.

"What are you saying!"

"It's the truth."

"Someone might be listening."

"I'm not afraid."

"Eat the soup. I'll bring the meat dumplings in a moment."

Hadass turned to go, her high heels clattering. Anshel began hunting for beans in the soup, fished one up, then let it fall. Her appetite was gone; her throat had closed up. She knew very well she was getting entangled in evil, but some force kept urging her on. Hadass reappeared, carrying a platter with two meat dumplings on it.

"Why aren't you eating?"

"I'm thinking about you."

"What are you thinking?"

"I want to marry you."

Hadass made a face as though she had swallowed something.

"On such matters, you must speak to my father."

"I know."

"The custom is to send a matchmaker."

She ran from the room, letting the door slam behind her. Laughing inwardly, Anshel thought: "With girls I can play as I please!" She sprinkled salt on the soup and then pepper. She sat there lightheaded. What have I done? I must be going mad. There's no other explanation. . . . She forced herself to eat, but could taste nothing. Only then did Anshel remember that it was Avigdor who had wanted her to marry Hadass. From her confusion, a plan emerged: she would exact vengeance for Avigdor, and at the same time, through Hadass, draw him closer to herself. Hadass was a virgin: what did she know about men? A girl like that could be deceived for a long time. To be sure, Anshel too was a virgin but she knew a lot about such matters from the Gemara and from hearing men talk. Anshel was seized by both fear and glee, as a person is who is planning to deceive the whole community. She remembered the saying: "The public are fools." She stood up and said aloud: "Now I'll really start something."

That night Anshel didn't sleep a wink. Every few minutes she got up for a drink of water. Her throat was parched, her forehead burned. Her brain worked away feverishly of its own volition. A quarrel seemed to be going on inside her. Her stomach throbbed and her knees ached. It was as if she had sealed a pact with Satan, the Evil One who plays tricks on human beings, who sets stumbling blocks and traps in their paths. By the time Anshel fell asleep, it was morning. She awoke more exhausted than before. But she could not go on sleeping on the bench at the widow's. With an effort she rose and, taking the bag that held her phylacteries, set out for the study house. On the way whom should she meet but Hadass' father. Anshel bade him a respectful good morning and received a friendly greeting in return. Reb Alter stroked his beard and engaged her in conversation:

"My daughter Hadass must be serving you leftovers. You look starved."

"Your daughter is a fine girl, and very generous."

"So why are you so pale?"

Anshel was silent for a minute.

"Reb Alter, there's something I must say to you."

"Well, go ahead, say it."

"Reb Alter, your daughter pleases me."

Alter Vishkower came to a halt.

"Oh, does she? I thought yeshiva students didn't talk about such things."

His eyes were full of laughter.

"But it's the truth."

"One doesn't discuss these matters with the young man himself."

"But I'm an orphan."

"Well . . . in that case the custom is to send a marriage broker."

"Yes. . . ."

"What do you see in her?"

"She's beautiful . . . fine . . . intelligent . . ."

"Well, well, well. . . . Come along, tell me something about your family."

Alter Vishkower put his arm around Anshel and in this fashion the two continued walking until they reached the courtyard of the synagogue.

Once you say "A," you must say "B." Thoughts lead to words, words lead to deeds. Reb Alter Vishkower gave his consent to the match. Hadass' mother Freyda Leah held back for a while. She said she wanted no more Bechev yeshiva students for her daughter and would rather have someone from Lublin or Zamosc; but Hadass gave warning that if she were shamed publicly once more (the way she had been with Avigdor) she would throw herself into the well. As often happens with such ill-advised matches, everyone was strongly in favor of it—the rabbi, the relatives, Hadass' girl friends. For some time the girls of Bechev had been eyeing Anshel longingly, watching from their windows when the youth passed by on the street. Anshel kept his boots well polished and did not drop his eyes in the presence of women. Stopping in at Beila the Baker's to buy a *pletzl,* he joked with them in such a worldly fashion that they marveled. The women agreed there was something special about Anshel: his sidelocks curled like nobody else's and he tied his neck scarf differently; his eyes, smiling yet distant, seemed always fixed on some faraway point. And the fact that Avigdor had become betrothed to Feitl's daughter Peshe, forsaking Anshel, had endeared him all the more to the people of the town. Alter Vishkower had a provisional contract drawn up for the betrothal, promising Anshel a bigger dowry, more presents, and an even longer period of maintenance than he had promised Avigdor. The girls of Bechev threw their arms around Hadass and congratulated her. Hadass immediately began crocheting a sack for Anshel's phylacteries, a *challah* cloth, a *matzoh* bag. When Avigdor heard the news of Anshel's betrothal, he came to the study house to offer his congratulations. The past few weeks had aged him. His beard was disheveled, his eyes were red. He said to Anshel:

"I knew it would happen this way. Right from the beginning. As soon as I met you at the inn."

"But it was you who suggested it."

"I know that."

"Why did you desert me? You went away without even saying goodbye."

"I wanted to burn my bridges behind me."

Avigdor asked Anshel to go for a walk. Though it was already past Succoth, the day was bright with sunshine. Avigdor, friendlier than ever, opened his heart to Anshel. Yes, it was true, a brother of his had succumbed to melancholy and hanged himself. Now he too felt himself near the edge of the abyss. Peshe had a lot of money and her father was a rich man, yet he couldn't sleep nights. He didn't want to be a storekeeper. He couldn't forget Hadass. She appeared in his dreams. Every Sabbath when her name occurred in the Havdala prayer, he turned dizzy. Still it was good that Anshel and no one else was to marry her. . . . At least she would fall into decent hands. Avigdor stooped and tore aimlessly at the shriveled grass. His speech was incoherent, like that of a man possessed. Suddenly he said:

"I have thought of doing what my brother did."

"Do you love her *that* much?"

"She's engraved in my heart."

The two pledged their friendship and promised never again to part. Anshel proposed that, after they were both married, they should live next door or even share the same house. They would study together every day, perhaps even become partners in a shop.

"Do you want to know the truth?" asked Avigdor. "It's like the story of Jacob and Benjamin: my life is bound up in your life."

"Then why did you leave me?"

"Perhaps for that very reason."

Though the day had turned cold and windy, they continued to walk until they reached the pine forest, not turning back until dusk when it was time for the Evening Prayer. The girls of Bechev, from their posts at the windows, watched them going by with their arms round each other's shoulders and so engrossed in conversation that they walked through puddles and piles of trash without noticing. Avigdor looked pale, disheveled, and the wind whipped one sidelock about; Anshel chewed his fingernails. Hadass, too, ran to the window, took one look, and her eyes filled with tears. . . .

Events followed quickly. Avigdor was the first to marry. Because the bride was a widow, the wedding was a quiet one, with no musicians, no wedding jester, no ceremonial veiling of the bride. One day Peshe stood beneath the marriage canopy, the next she was back at the shop, dispensing tar with greasy hands. Avigdor prayed at the Hasidic assembly house in his new prayer shawl. Afternoons, Anshel went to visit him and the two whispered and talked until evening. The date of Anshel's wedding to Hadass was set for the Sabbath in Chanukah week, though the prospective father-in-law wanted it sooner. Hadass had already been betrothed once. Besides, the groom was an orphan. Why should he toss about on a makeshift bed at the widow's when he could have a wife and home of his own?

Many times each day Anshel warned herself that what she was about to do was sinful, mad, an act of utter depravity. She was entangling both Hadass and herself in a chain of deception and committing so many transgressions that she would never be able to do penance. One lie followed another. Repeatedly Anshel made up her mind to flee Bechev in time, to put an end to this weird comedy that was more the work of an imp than a human being. But she was in the grip of a power she could not resist. She grew more and more attached to Avigdor, and could not bring herself to destroy Hadass' illusory happiness. Now that he was married, Avigdor's desire to study was greater than ever, and the friends met twice each day: in the mornings they studied the Gemara and the Commentaries, in the afternoons the Legal Codes with their glosses. Alter Vishkower and Feitl the Leatherdealer were pleased and compared Avigdor and Anshel to David and Jonathan. With all the complications, Anshel went about as though drunk. The tailors took her measurements for a new wardrobe and she was forced into all kinds of subterfuge to keep them from discovering she was not a man. Though the imposture had lasted many weeks, Anshel still could not believe it: How was it possible? Fooling the community had become a game, but how long could it go on? And in what way would the truth come to the surface? Inside, Anshel laughed and wept. She had turned into a sprite brought into the world to mock people and trick them. I'm wicked, a transgressor, a Jeroboam ben Nabat, she told herself. Her only justification was that she had taken all these burdens upon herself because her soul thirsted to study Torah. . . .

Avigdor soon began to complain that Peshe treated him badly. She called him an idler, a *shlemiel,* just another mouth to feed. She tried to tie him to the store, assigned him tasks for which he hadn't the slightest inclination, begrudged him pocket money. Instead of consoling Avigdor, Anshel goaded him on against Peshe. She called his wife an eyesore, a shrew, a miser, and said that Peshe had no doubt nagged her first husband to death and would Avigdor also. At the same time, Anshel enumerated Avigdor's virtues: his height and manliness, his wit, his erudition.

"If I were a woman and married to you," said Anshel, "I'd know how to appreciate you."

"Well, but you aren't. . . ."

Avigdor sighed.

Meanwhile Anshel's wedding date drew near.

On the Sabbath before Chanukah Anshel was called to the pulpit to read from the Torah. The women showered her with raisins and almonds. On the day of the wedding Alter Vishkower gave a feast for the young men. Avigdor sat at Anshel's right hand. The bridegroom delivered a Talmudic discourse, and the rest of the company argued the points, while smoking cigarettes and drinking wine, liqueurs, tea with lemon or raspberry jam. Then followed the ceremony of veiling the bride, after which the bridegroom was led to the wedding canopy that had been set up at the side of the synagogue. The night was frosty and clear, the sky full of stars. The musicians struck up a tune. Two rows of girls held lighted tapers and braided wax candles. After the wedding ceremony the bride and groom broke their fast with golden chicken broth. Then the dancing began and the announcement of the wedding gifts, all according to custom. The gifts were many and costly. The wedding jester depicted the joys and sorrows that were in store for the bride. Avigdor's wife Peshe was one of the guests but, though she was bedecked with jewels, she still looked ugly in a wig that sat low on her forehead, wearing an enormous fur cape, and with traces of tar on her hands that no amount of washing could ever remove. After the Virtue Dance the bride and groom were led separately to the marriage chamber. The wedding attendants instructed the couple in the proper conduct and enjoined them to "be fruitful and multiply."

At daybreak Anshel's mother-in-law and her band descended upon the marriage chamber and tore the bedsheets from beneath Hadass to make sure the marriage had been consummated. When traces of blood were discovered, the company grew merry and began kissing and congratulating the bride. Then, brandishing the sheet, they flocked outside and danced a Kosher Dance in the newly fallen snow. Anshel had found a way to deflower the bride. Hadass in her innocence was unaware that things weren't quite as they should have been. She was already deeply in love with Anshel. It is commanded that the bride and groom remain apart for seven days after the first intercourse. The next day Anshel and Avigdor took up the study of the Tractate on Menstruous Women. When the other men had departed and the two were left to themselves in the synagogue, Avigdor shyly questioned Anshel about his night with Hadass. Anshel gratified his curiosity and they whispered together until nightfall.

Anshel had fallen into good hands. Hadass was a devoted wife and her parents indulged their son-in-law's every wish and boasted of his accomplishments. To be sure, several months went by and Hadass was still not with child, but no one took it to heart. On the other hand, Avigdor's lot grew steadily worse. Peshe tormented him and finally would not give him enough to eat and even refused him a clean shirt. Since he was always penniless, Anshel again brought him a daily buckwheat cake. Because Peshe was too busy to cook and too stingy to hire a servant, Anshel asked Avigdor to dine at his house. Reb Alter Vishkower and his wife disapproved, arguing that it was wrong for the rejected suitor to visit the house of his former fiancée. The town had plenty to talk about. But Anshel cited precedents to show that it was not prohibited by the Law. Most of the townspeople sided with Avigdor and blamed Peshe for everything. Avigdor soon began pressing Peshe for a divorce, and, because he did not want to have a child by such a bitch, he acted like Onan, or, as the Gemara translates it: he threshed on the inside and cast his seed without. He confided in Anshel, told him how Peshe came to bed unwashed and snored like a buzz saw, of how she was so occupied with the cash taken in at the store that she babbled about it even in her sleep.

"Oh, Anshel, how I envy you," he said.

"There's no reason for envying me."

"You have everything. I wish your good fortune were mine—with no loss to you, of course."

"Everyone has troubles of his own."

"What sort of troubles do *you* have? Don't tempt Providence."

How could Avigdor have guessed that Anshel could not sleep at night and thought constantly of running away? Lying with Hadass and deceiving her had become more and more painful. Hadass' love and tenderness shamed her. The devotion of her mother- and father-in-law and their hopes for a grandchild were a burden. On Friday afternoons all of the townspeople went to the baths and every week Anshel had to find a new excuse. But this was beginning to awake suspicions. There was talk that Anshel must have an unsightly birthmark, or a rupture, or perhaps was not properly circumcised. Judging by the youth's years, his beard should certainly have begun to sprout, yet his cheeks remained smooth. It was already Purim and Passover was approaching. Soon it would be summer. Not far from Bechev there was a river where all the yeshiva students and young men went swimming as soon as it was warm enough. The lie was swelling like an abscess and one of these days it must surely burst. Anshel knew she had to find a way to free herself.

It was customary for the young men boarding with their in-laws to travel to nearby cities during the half-holidays in the middle of Passover week. They enjoyed the change, refreshed themselves, looked around for business opportunities, bought books or other things a young man might need. Bechev was not far from Lublin and Anshel persuaded Avigdor to make the journey with her at her expense. Avigdor was delighted at the prospect of being rid for a few days of the shrew he had at home. The trip by carriage was a merry one. The fields were turning green; storks, back from the warm countries, swooped across the sky in great arcs. Streams rushed toward the valleys. The birds chirped. The windmills turned. Spring flowers were beginning to bloom in the fields. Here and there a cow was already grazing. The companions, chatting, ate the fruit and little cakes that Hadass had packed, told each other jokes, and exchanged confidences until they reached Lublin. There they went to an inn and took a room for two. On the journey, Anshel had promised to reveal an astonishing secret to Avigdor in Lublin. Avigdor had joked: what sort of secret could it be? Had Anshel discovered a hidden treasure? Had he written an essay? By studying the Cabbala, had he created a dove? . . . Now they entered the room and while Anshel carefully locked the door, Avigdor said teasingly:

"Well, let's hear your great secret."

"Prepare yourself for the most incredible thing that ever was."

"I'm prepared for anything."

"I'm not a man but a woman," said Anshel. "My name isn't Anshel, it's Yentl."

Avigdor burst out laughing.

"I knew it was a hoax."

"But it's true."

"Even if I'm a fool, I won't swallow this."

"Do you want me to show you?"

"Yes."

"Then I'll get undressed."

Avigdor's eyes widened. It occurred to him that Anshel might want to practice pederasty. Anshel took off the gaberdine and the fringed garment, and threw off her underclothes. Avigdor took one look and turned first white, then fiery red. Anshel covered herself hastily.

"I've done this only so that you can testify at the courthouse. Otherwise Hadass will have to stay a grass widow."

Avigdor had lost his tongue. He was seized by a fit of trembling. He wanted to speak, but his lips moved and nothing came out. He sat down quickly, for his legs would not support him. Finally he murmured:

"How is it possible? I don't believe it!"

"Should I get undressed again?"

"No!"

Yentl proceeded to tell the whole story: how her father, bedridden, had studied Torah with her; how she had never had the patience for women and their silly chatter; how she had sold the house and all the furnishings, left the town, made her way disguised as a man to Lublin, and on the road met Avigdor. Avigdor sat speechless, gazing at the storyteller. Yentl was by now wearing men's clothes once more. Avigdor spoke:

"It must be a dream."

He pinched himself on the cheek.

"It isn't a dream."

"That such a thing should happen to me . . . !"

"It's all true."

"Why did you do it? *Nu,* I'd better keep still."

"I didn't want to waste my life on a baking shovel and a kneading trough."

"And what about Hadass—why did you do that?"

"I did it for your sake. I knew that Peshe would torment you and at our house you would have some peace. . . ."

Avigdor was silent for a long time. He bowed his head, pressed his hands to his temples, shook his head.

"What will you do now?"

"I'll go away to a different yeshiva."

"What? If you had only told me earlier, we could have . . ."

Avigdor broke off in the middle.

"No—it wouldn't have been good."

"Why not?"

"I'm neither one nor the other."

"What a dilemma I'm in!"

"Get a divorce from that horror. Marry Hadass."

"She'll never divorce me and Hadass won't have me."

"Hadass loves you. She won't listen to her father again."

Avigdor stood up suddenly but then sat down.

"I won't be able to forget you. Ever. . . ."

According to the Law, Avigdor was now forbidden to spend another moment alone with Yentl; yet dressed in the gaberdine and trousers, she was again the familiar Anshel. They resumed their conversation on the old footing:

"How could you bring yourself to violate the commandment every day: 'A woman shall not wear that which pertaineth to a man'?"

"I wasn't created for plucking feathers and chattering with females."

"Would you rather lose your share in the world to come?"

"Perhaps. . . ."

Avigdor raised his eyes. Only now did he realize that Anshel's cheeks were too smooth for a man's, the hair too abundant, the hands too small. Even so he could not believe that such a thing could have happened. At any moment he expected to wake up. He bit his lips, pinched his thigh. He was seized by shyness and could not speak without stammering. His friendship with Anshel, their intimate talk, their confidences, had been turned into a sham and delusion. The thought even occurred to him that Anshel might be a demon. He shook himself as if to cast off a nightmare; yet that power which knows the difference between dream and reality told him it was all true. He summoned up his courage. He and Anshel could never be strangers to one another, even though Anshel was in fact Yentl. . . . He ventured a comment:

"It seems to me that the witness who testifies for a deserted woman may not marry her, for the Law calls him 'a party to the affair.'"

"What? That didn't occur to me!"

"We must look it up in Ibn Ezer."

"I'm not even sure that the rules pertaining to a deserted woman apply in this case," said Anshel in the manner of a scholar.

"If you don't want Hadass to be a grass widow, you must reveal the secret to her directly."

"That I can't do."

"In any event, you must get another witness."

Gradually the two went back to their Talmudic conversation. It seemed strange at first to Avigdor to be disputing holy writ with a woman, yet before long the Torah had reunited them. Though their bodies were different, their souls were of one kind. Anshel spoke in a singsong, gesticulated with her thumb, clutched her sidelocks, plucked at her beardless chin, made all the customary gestures of a yeshiva student. In the heat of argument she even seized Avigdor by the lapel and called him stupid. A great love for Anshel took hold of Avigdor, mixed with shame, remorse, anxiety. If I had only known this before, he said to himself. In his thoughts he likened Anshel (or Yentl) to Bruria, the wife of Reb Meir, and to Yalte, the wife of Reb Nachman. For the first time he saw clearly that this was what he had always wanted: a wife whose mind was not taken up with material things. . . . His desire for Hadass was gone now, and he knew he would long for Yentl, but he dared not say so. He felt hot and knew that his face was burning. He could no longer meet Anshel's eyes. He began to enumerate Anshel's sins and saw that he too was implicated, for he had sat next to Yentl and had touched her during her unclean days. *Nu,* and what could be said about her marriage to Hadass? What a multitude of transgressions there! Willful deception, false vows, misrepresentation!—Heaven knows what else. He asked suddenly:

"Tell the truth, are you a heretic?"

"God forbid!"

"Then how could you bring yourself to do such a thing?"

The longer Anshel talked, the less Avigdor understood. All Anshel's explanations seemed to point to one thing: she had the soul of a man and the body of a woman. Anshel said she had married Hadass only in order to be near Avigdor.

"You could have married me," Avigdor said.

"I wanted to study the Gemara and Commentaries with you, not darn your socks!"

For a long time neither spoke. Then Avigdor broke the silence:

"I'm afraid Hadass will get sick from all this, God forbid!"

"I'm afraid of that too."

"What's going to happen now?"

Dusk fell and the two began to recite the Evening Prayer. In his confusion Avigdor mixed up the blessings, omitted some and repeated others. He glanced sideways at Anshel who was rocking back and forth, beating her breast, bowing her head. He saw her, eyes closed, lift her face to Heaven as though beseeching: You, Father in Heaven, know the truth. . . . When their prayers were finished, they sat down on opposite chairs, facing one another yet a good distance apart. The room filled with shadows. Reflections of the sunset, like purple embroidery, shook on the wall opposite the window. Avigdor again wanted to speak but at first the words, trembling on the tip of his tongue, would not come. Suddenly they burst forth:

"Maybe it's still not too late? I can't go on living with that accursed woman. . . . You. . . ."

"No, Avigdor, it's impossible."

"Why?"

"I'll live out my time as I am. . . ."

"I'll miss you. Terribly."

"And I'll miss you."

"What's the sense of all this?"

Anshel did not answer. Night fell and the light faded. In the darkness they seemed to be listening to each other's thoughts. The Law forbade Avigdor to stay in the room alone with Anshel, but he could not think of her just as a woman. What a strange power there is in clothing, he thought. But he spoke of something else:

"I would advise you simply to send Hadass a divorce."

"How can I do that?"

"Since the marriage sacraments weren't valid, what difference does it make?"

"I suppose you're right."

"There'll be time enough later for her to find out the truth."

The maidservant came in with a lamp but as soon as she had gone, Avigdor put it out. Their predicament and the words which they must speak to one another could not endure light. In the blackness Anshel related all the particulars. She answered all Avigdor's questions. The clock struck two, and still they talked. Anshel told Avigdor that Hadass had never forgotten him. She talked of him frequently, worried about his health, was sorry—though not without a certain satisfaction—about the way things had turned out with Peshe.

"She'll be a good wife," said Anshel. "I don't even know how to bake a pudding."

"Nevertheless, if you're willing. . . ."

"No, Avigdor. It wasn't destined to be. . . ."

It was all a great riddle to the town: the messenger who arrived bringing Hadass the divorce papers; Avigdor's remaining in Lublin until after the holidays; his return to Bechev with slumping shoulders and lifeless eyes as if he had been ill. Hadass took to her bed and was visited by the doctor three times a day. Avigdor went into seclusion. If someone ran across him by chance and addressed him, he did not answer. Peshe complained to her parents that Avigdor paced back and forth smoking all night long. When he finally collapsed from sheer fatigue, in his sleep he called out the name of an unknown female—Yentl. Peshe began talking of a divorce. The town thought Avigdor wouldn't grant her one or would demand money at the very least, but he agreed to everything.

In Bechev the people were not used to having mysteries stay mysteries for long. How can you keep secrets in a little town where everyone knows what's cooking in everyone else's pots? Yet, though there were plenty of persons who made a practice of looking through keyholes and laying an ear to shutters, what happened remained an enigma. Hadass lay in her bed and wept. Chanina the herb doctor reported that she was wasting away. Anshel had disappeared without a trace. Reb Alter Vishkower sent for Avigdor and he arrived, but those who stood straining beneath the window couldn't catch a word of what passed between them. Those individuals who habitually pry into other people's affairs came up with all sorts of theories, but not one of them was consistent.

One party came to the conclusion that Anshel had fallen into the hands of Catholic priests, and had been converted. That might have made sense. But where could Anshel have found time for the priests, since he was always studying in the yeshiva? And apart from that, since when does an apostate send his wife a divorce?

Another group whispered that Anshel had cast an eye on another woman. But who could it be? There were no love affairs conducted in Bechev. And none of the young women had recently left town—neither a Jewish woman nor a Gentile one.

Somebody else offered the suggestion that Anshel had been carried away by evil spirits, or was even one of them himself. As proof he cited the fact that Anshel had never come either to the bathhouse or to the river. It is well known that demons have the feet of geese. Well, but had Hadass never seen him barefoot? And who ever heard of a demon sending his wife a divorce? When a demon marries a daughter of mortals, he usually lets her remain a grass widow.

It occurred to someone else that Anshel had committed a major transgression and gone into exile in order to do penance. But what sort of transgression could it have been? And why had he not entrusted it to the rabbi? And why did Avigdor wander about like a ghost?

The hypothesis of Tevel the musician was closest to the truth. Tevel maintained that Avigdor had been unable to forget Hadass and that Anshel had divorced her so that his friend would be able to marry her. But was such friendship possible in this world? And in that case, why had Anshel divorced Hadass even before Avigdor divorced Peshe? Furthermore, such a thing can be accomplished only if the wife has been informed of the arrangement and is willing, yet all signs pointed to Hadass' great love for Anshel, and in fact she was ill from sorrow.

One thing was clear to all: Avigdor knew the truth. But it was impossible to get anything out of him. He remained in seclusion and kept silent with an obstinacy that was a reproof to the whole town.

Close friends urged Peshe not to divorce Avigdor, though they had severed all relations and no longer lived as man and wife. He did not even, on Friday night, perform the *kiddush* blessing for her. He spent his nights either at the study house or at the widow's where Anshel had found lodgings. When Peshe spoke to him he didn't answer, but stood with bowed head. The tradeswoman Peshe had no patience for such goings-on. She needed a young man to help her out in the store, not a yeshiva student who had fallen into melancholy. Someone of that sort might even take it into his head to depart and leave her deserted. Peshe agreed to a divorce.

In the meantime Hadass had recovered, and Reb Alter Vishkower let it be known that a marriage contract was being drawn up. Hadass was to marry Avigdor. The town was agog. A marriage between a man and a woman who had once been engaged and their betrothal broken off was unheard of. The wedding was held on the first Sabbath after Tisha B'Ov, and included all that is customary at the marriage of a virgin: the banquet for the poor, the canopy before the synagogue, the musicians, the wedding jester, the Virtue Dance. Only one thing was lacking: joy. The bridegroom stood beneath the marriage canopy, a figure of desolation. The bride had recovered from her sickness, but had remained pale and thin. Her tears fell into the golden chicken broth. From all eyes the same question looked out: why had Anshel done it?

After Avigdor's marriage to Hadass, Peshe spread the rumor that Anshel had sold his wife to Avigdor for a price, and that the money had been supplied by Alter Vishkower. One young man pondered the riddle at great length until he finally arrived at the conclusion that Anshel had lost his beloved wife to Avigdor at cards, or even on a spin of the Chanukah *dreidl*. It is a general rule that when the grain of truth cannot be found, men will swallow great helpings of falsehood. Truth itself is often concealed in such a way that the harder you look for it, the harder it is to find.

Not long after the wedding, Hadass became pregnant. The child was a boy and those assembled at the circumcision could scarcely believe their ears when they heard the father name his son Anshel.

Translated from the Yiddish by Marion Magid and Elizabeth Pollett

September 1965

David Daiches

PRESENTING THE BIBLE

Something under four thousand years ago a troubled citizen of the Central Mesopotamian city of Haran left the community in which he had been born and brought up to wander westward to the country that was later known as Palestine. The Hurrian society from which he became a voluntary refugee had long been subject to Babylonian influence and was part of a complex of Mesopotamian civilization whose nature is now reasonably well known to scholars from a variety of records and texts. Cosmopolitan, stable, sophisticated, law-abiding, with flourishing literary and scientific activities, an exciting architecture, enlightened agricultural methods and prospering commercial enterprises—this is the picture that modern scholarship has built up. Was this a civilization for a sensible and sensitive man to flee from? Perhaps its very stability and prosperity oppressed him; perhaps the complex but smooth-running machinery of political and ethical life left out too much. For it was a spiritual quest on which the wanderer set out. In embarking on it he began what the late Professor Ephraim A. Speiser, in his introduction to the Anchor Bible Genesis, calls "the biblical process." In Abraham's belief that he had been called from his native land to seek a new way of life elsewhere lies the beginning of that extraordinary historical and religious development that produced the story of the Patriarchs, of Joseph in Egypt, of the Exodus, of the giving of the Law to Moses on Mount Sinai, and the subsequent history of Israel and Judah, the progress of Judaism, and the emergence of Christianity. The Bible, and biblical history, and all the consequences of biblical history, begin in fact with Abraham's migration.

The great medieval Jewish biblical commentator Rabbi Solomon ben Isaac (generally know as Rashi), looking at the five Books of Moses in traditional Jewish fashion as the Torah, the Law, remarked at the beginning of his commentary on Genesis that the Torah should really have commenced not with the story of the Creation but with the second verse of the twelfth chapter of Exodus, where the first actual precept is found. He added, however, that the earlier parts were necessary to show to the world the divine claim of the Jewish people to their Palestinian homeland. But if one looks at the whole biblical process, one is inclined to disagree both with Rashi and with those ancient biblical writers and editors who apparently adapted Babylonian accounts of primeval history to provide as it were a cosmic introduction to the story of Abraham's quest and its consequences. "The biblical process" begins neither with chapter 1 of Genesis nor with chapter 12 of Exodus: it begins with the divine words recorded in Genesis 12:1-3 as having sounded in Abraham's ears while he still lived in his native Haran. *Lech lecha*—"Get thee out of thy country, and from thy kindred, and from thy father's house, unto the land that I will show thee." That is the familiar King James rendering, and certainly "get thee out" captures the pithy forcefulness of the Hebrew *lech lecha*. Speiser, rightly seeing this divine message as a little inset poem, translates thus:

Go forth from your native land
And from your father's home
To a land that I will show you.
I will make of you a great nation,
Bless you, and make great your name,
That it may be a blessing.
I will bless those who bless you,
And curse those who curse you;
And through you shall bless themselves
All the communities on earth.

So Abraham and his wife and his nephew, with all their possessions, "set out for the land of Canaan and arrived in the land of Canaan."

But is it true? Was there a real, historical Abraham who really did leave his native Haran for the land of Canaan in obedience to a sense of divine call to engage in a spiritual quest? The paradox is that the evidence provided by all those modern tools of research into the Bible that are so shunned by right-wing Jewish Orthodoxy—the evidence of history, anthropology, textual criticism, comparative religion, linguistic scholarship—is on Abraham's side. The Bible says that Abraham migrated from Haran to the land of Canaan, and there is abundant evidence in the text of Genesis that the narrator of the story of the patriarchs was dealing with an original Hurrian character in a non-Hurrian context so that he did not understand the meaning of the Hurrian customs that he was recording. Abraham twice, and Isaac once, claimed that his wife was his sister when visiting a foreign notable. The three accounts in the Bible remain puzzling, and cast little credit on either patriarch. But Speiser explains that "in Hurrian society a wife enjoyed special standing and protection when the law recognized her simultaneously as her husband's sister, regardless of actual blood ties. Such cases are attested by two separate legal documents, one dealing with the marriage and the other with the woman's adoption as sister. This dual role conferred on the wife a superior position in society." Now Abraham, who originally came from the old Hurrian center of Haran, was of course familiar with Hurrian social practices. "Hence when he and his son, in visits to foreign lands, spoke of their wives as sisters, they were apparently intent not so much on improving their own prospects as on extolling and protecting their wives." It is important to note that "these particular wife-sister customs were peculiar to the Hurrians." The author of the accounts in Genesis of Abraham and Isaac claiming that their wives were their sisters clearly hadn't a clue as to what it all meant and was forced to invent the only plausible (and unfortunately rather discreditable) reason for this odd behavior that he could think of. Only if we imagine a later writer producing in the land of Israel (Canaan) an account of genuine old traditions some of which, being Hurrian, he could not understand, can we find any convincing explanation of this and other oddities in Genesis.

The Hurrian origin of the patriarchs is further evidenced by the puzzling story of Jacob's tricking Esau out of the eldest son's blessing. "On this point we now have pertinent illustrations in the Hurrian sources from Nuzi, which in turn mirror social conditions and customs in the patriarchal center at Haran. Birthright in Hurrian society was often a matter of the father's discretion rather than chronological priority. Moreover, of all the paternal dispositions, the one that took the form of a death-bed declaration carried the greatest weight." The whole situation recorded in the 27th chapter of Genesis, continues Speiser, reflects "an old and authentic usage," and he refers to the relevant supporting documents in the Annual of the American Schools of Oriental Research and elsewhere. "On the socio-legal level . . . the account is a correct measure of early relations between Hurrians and Hebrews."

Again, in chapter 28 of Genesis Jacob leaves Beer-sheba and sets out for his grandfather's birthplace, Haran, to escape Esau's anger and find a wife (as his father had done) from among his relations there. He returns, that is, to Mesopotamia, though of course only temporarily. It is on his way there that he has his famous dream in which he sees a stairway set on the ground, with its top reaching the sky. On waking, he exclaims: "How awesome is this place! This is none other than the abode of God, and that is the gateway to heaven!" (Speiser's translation.) He calls the place where he had the dream Bethel, or House of God. Is it a coincidence that on this journey to Mesopotamia Jacob dreams of something remarkably like a Mesopotamian temple tower or ziggurat? "For a ziggurat rose hard by the main temple on the ground . . . to provide on its summit a place for the deity to visit . . . and communicate there with mortals: a spiritual symbol, in short, of man's efforts to reach out to heaven." So Speiser comments, and he adds: "The phraseology is much too typical of the temple tower to be merely coincidental, and the underlying imagery cannot be mistaken." The irresistible conclusion is that the author of this passage is reporting an authentic tradition.

In chapter 29, similarly, we are told how Laban, Jacob's maternal uncle, gives Jacob his daughter Leah in marriage, though Jacob was really in love with her younger sister Rachel; later in the same chapter Jacob gets Rachel too. In each case the narrator sticks in the parenthetical note that with the daughter Laban handed over a maid to wait on her. "Laban had assigned his maid-servant Zilpah as maid to his daughter Leah." "Laban had assigned his maid-servant Bilhah as maid to his daughter Rachel." These brief interpolated sentences have their exact parallel in the Nuzi tablets; in a document printed in the Harvard Semitic Series (V. no. 67), dealing in part "with a marriage involving a young woman of high standing in the local community," we find that, after all the relevant details have been set out, the text adds parenthetically: "Moreover, Yalampa [a slave girl] is herewith assigned to Gilimninu [the bride] as her maid." The authenticity of the custom is thus vouched for.

Lastly, in chapter 31 we find the puzzling story of Rachel stealing her father's household images when Jacob and his family finally return from Haran to Canaan. The significance of the incident can now be seen to derive "from underlying social practices as they bear on the nature of the patriarchal narratives in general. According to the Nuzi documents, which have been found to reflect time and again the social customs of Haran, possession of the house gods could signify legal title to a given estate, particularly in cases out of the ordinary, involving daughters, sons-in-law, or adopted sons."

This is only a selection of those passages in Genesis which remain puzzling or meaningless until seen as the recording of Hurrian customs by a Hebrew writer who had lost touch with their original meaning and purpose. If all this does not prove beyond any possible doubt that a man called Abraham (or Abram, as we are told his name originally was) left Haran for the land of Canaan about 1700 B.C.E., it certainly helps to authenticate the traditions recorded in Genesis and confirms the biblical view of Abraham's origins. Nothing, in fact, in Genesis is inconsistent with the historicity of Abraham, and there is considerable external supporting evidence for the basic truth of the biblical account of the patriarchs' migrations and questings.

It is this deft and scholarly use of supporting material out of the abundance of his own knowledge of the whole world of the ancient Middle East that makes Speiser's notes and comments in the first volume of the enormously ambitious Anchor Bible* so illuminating and indeed so exciting. To translate the text afresh in the light of the best modern knowledge and to reconstruct the background with every available tool of scholarship is the aim of this series, and it could not have got off to a better start. On the question of translation, the editor of each volume has had to make his own decision. On the whole the editors of the six Old Testament volumes here considered agree in preferring accuracy to liturgical grace, in jettisoning the antique if beautiful forms of the King James Bible and its later revisions in favor of starting from scratch with an appropriate modern English, and at the same time in giving some clear indication of the nature of the literary form to be found in the original.

Some surprises result. It may come as a shock to the layman to be told that the very first words of the Bible do not mean "In the beginning." The text as vocalized by the Masorites (the Jewish editors who preserved and normalized the text of the Hebrew Bible, which they fixed about the 2nd century C.E., though they did not develop the full vocalization for another four centuries or so) shows the opening word as clearly in the "construct" form, meaning "in the beginning of." Speiser renders the opening thus: "When God set about to create heaven and earth—the world being then a formless waste, with darkness over the seas and only an awesome wind sweeping over the water—God said, 'Let there be light.' And there was light." This should not disturb Jewish scholars who know (or should know) that both Rashi and Ibn Ezra suggested a similar rendering. "In the beginning of God's creating the heaven and earth . . ." is the meaning according to Rashi, which is also how Speiser understands it—though he does not give Rashi's further reason for repudiating the traditional translation, "In the beginning God created the heaven and the earth," which was that it is clear from verse 2 that God did *not* first create heaven and earth, but rather the waters. The modern scholar is less concerned to eliminate apparent inconsistencies than to use them as evidence of different hands engaged in the composition of the narrative.

No modern scholar can discuss Genesis without giving some account of the cogent evidence suggesting the different hands in the book. Speiser presents a scholarly and balanced summary of this evidence, and while some of his attributions must inevitably remain problematical, there can be little doubt in the mind of the unprejudiced reader that the different

* The Anchor Bible, under the general editorship of William Foxwell Albright and David Noel Freedman (there will be 38 volumes in all). Genesis, translated with an introduction and notes by E. A. Speiser; I Chronicles, translation, introduction, and notes by Jacob M. Myers; II Chronicles, translation, introduction, and notes by Jacob M. Myers; Jeremiah, translated with an introduction and notes by John Bright; Job, introduction, translation, and notes by Marvin H. Pope; Proverbs and Ecclesiastes, introduction, translation, and notes by R. B. Y. Scott.

versions of the same story, differences in style and vocabulary, differences in main preoccupations and attitude, and differences in point of view (such as the extraordinary chapter 14, where we suddenly, and for the only time, get an outside view of "Abram the Hebrew" as a prosperous chief who can mobilize his own army at short notice), all add up to proof of multiplicity of authorship. Genesis, like all of the first books of the Bible, is a carefully wrought compilation from a variety of sources. Once again we are faced with the paradox that a recognition of this increases our admiration for what has actually been achieved in that remarkable book, just as our awareness of the Babylonian origins of the Creation and the Flood stories enchances our wonder at the radically different tone and meaning imposed on the material by the biblical authors. Speiser links these differences with Abraham's protest against the Mesopotamian civilization from which he withdrew. "The migration . . . was in protest against the local religious solution [*sic;* "situation"?]. And reflections of that protest can still be detected throughout the account of Primeval History. *P's** statement about Creation differs from its Mesopotamian analogue by its overriding concept of an omnipotent Creator. *J's** version of the Flood receives a moral motivation. Most revealing of all is the same writer's narrative about the Tower of Babel. The scene of the episode is Babylon itself, and some passages in that story read as though the author had had the Babylonian prototype before him. Yet the purpose of the tale is not a direct though unacknowledged transcript, but a stern criticism of the builders' monumental presumption."

Of the three main authors of Genesis who can be identified, *P* is distinguished by his use of *Elohim* and *El Shaddai* for God, by his interest in genealogies, and by his concern for the purity of the line through which God implemented His purpose; *J* is the great storyteller, who handles the Joseph story so magnificently, and he uses the tetragrammaton YHWH for God; *E* is also a good storyteller, though not so lively and individual as *J*, interested in dreams as God's way of communicating with men, and inclined to elaborate explanation and justification of the actions of his characters. The mysterious name of God, YHWH, has traditionally been translated "the Lord" in English versions, following the age-old Jewish custom of reading it as *"Adonai,"* "my lord (s)." The name itself was in Jewish tradition ineffable and not to be spoken except once a year in a moment of great awe by the High Priest. Whether it was ever pronounced "Yahweh" by the earliest readers of any part of the Bible is surely doubtful. The old Hebrew tradition of putting the vowels of *"Adonai"* under the consonants YHWH to show that the word should be read *"Adonai"* suggests an ancient inhibition. (It was a misunderstanding of this shorthand device that led Renaissance Christian Hebraists to read the word as

* See below for an explanation of *P, J,* and *E.*

"Jehovah," a non-existent name and a philological monstrosity.) The translators of all these volumes regularly render YHWH as "Yahweh": I confess that this makes me feel slightly uncomfortable.

The general problem presented by translating from biblical Hebrew into modern English is difficult. The two languages are so very different in sound, structure, and behavior. By means of a system of prefixes and suffixes Hebrew can compress into a single word what it may take three or four to express in English. The whole concept of verbal tenses is radically different from English and indeed from Indo-European languages in general. Many idioms, if rendered literally, may sound picturesque but may well give quite a wrong impression of the true meaning. A word or even a phrase may change its meaning in virtue of a difference in context, and to render them identically on each occasion when they occur may result in mistranslation.

In addition to these and similar problems, there are the problems presented by the state of the text itself. For the fixing of the Hebrew text by the Masorites, while it provided a stable text, did not necessarily provide a consistently accurate one. A long process of transmission, some of it originally oral, had been going on for many centuries before the Masorites got to work; such an extended interval always implies some degree of corruption. The problems presented by the text of the Hebrew Bible are bound up with the history and the transmission of this diverse anthology of Hebrew religious literature (for the Hebrew Bible is nothing less than that). The Masoretic text (MT) represents a late stage in the development of the biblical text and it has come down to us in manuscripts of no great antiquity. The Septuagint, the Greek translation made from a pre-Masoretic Hebrew text centuries before MT was established, points to an underlying Hebrew which sometimes differs from and sometimes may be superior to MT. One of the problems of the modern translator is to get behind MT where it is obviously or even possibly corrupt. So long as MT is regarded as sacrosanct, as it is by Jewish Orthodoxy (even though there are cases where pre-Masoretic readings are preserved in the Talmud), textual scholarship is limited.

Among the numerous differences between the Anchor Bible and the attractively produced Soncino Books of the Bible put out by the Soncino Press in England in the 1940's is that the latter, edited by Jewish rabbis and ministers throughout, sticks to MT and never seeks to emend or get behind it. The Soncino Bible prints the Hebrew as well as the English (in the translation of the Jewish Publication Society of America) and its commentary is less academic, or at least less rigorously professional, aimed more at the religious layman. In this respect it resembles more the volumes of the Pentateuch put out under the general editorship of the late J. H. Hertz, British Chief Rabbi, which are conservative and edifying rather than genuinely scholarly and, while attractively produced for the worshipper, skate over and sometimes simply ignore the really difficult and disturbing problems. It must be admitted that, with some notable exceptions, of which the Anchor Genesis is one, Christian scholarship on the Hebrew Bible has been more enterprising and often more genuinely scholarly than Jewish scholarship on the same subject has been. The Anchor Bible, where Jewish scholars contribute some volumes and Protestant and Catholic scholars contribute others, provides a fine proving ground for the biblical scholarship of all three groups.

Genesis is the first book of the Bible for both Jews and Christians. The name "Genesis" is of course Greek, and was first given to it by the Greek translators of the Septuagint in the 3rd century B.C.E. In Hebrew it is known by its first word, *bereshit,* "In the beginning" (or, more accurately, as we have seen, "In the beginning of"—a good example of how Hebrew can get into one word what English has to do in four). It combines Primeval History with Patriarchal History and brings the story up to the settlement of the Children of Israel in the land of Goshen and the death of Joseph. The three following books of the Hebrew Bible deal with the Exodus from Egypt, the giving of the Law on Mt. Sinai, the wandering in the wilderness, and further details of legal and ritual enactments. But the fifth book—the last book of the Pentateuch, the last of the so-called Five Books of Moses, the final volume of the Torah in the Orthodox Jewish view—is rather different. While in many respects the first four constitute a unity and the same hands can be traced in each of them, the fifth, Deuteronomy, appears as we have it to be the work of a writer who was trying to recall Israel to the fundamental principles of the Mosaic Law and worship of the one God; it was a reformist manifesto gathering up, recapitulating, classifying, reaffirming the religion of Moses partly under the inspiration of the idealism of the prophets Hosea and Isaiah.

It is important to recall the historical background. The Children of Israel (to give them the traditional biblical name) finally conquered the original inhabitants of Canaan and settled there, in accordance with the primal promise made to Abraham. Their Golden Age was the era of David and Solomon (10th century B.C.E.) when those great kings successively ruled over an Israelite empire which fell apart on the death of Solomon (c. 922 B.C.E.) into the northern kingdom of Israel with its capital eventually at Samaria and the southern kingdom of Judah with its capital at Jerusalem. For two hundred years those tiny (by modern standards) kingdoms survived side by side, sometimes in enmity and sometimes in alliance, enabled to do so because, as Professor John Bright points out in his introduction to the Anchor Jeremiah, the world situation permitted it. "One must realize that Israel's entire history since her occupation of Palestine had until this time been spun out in a great power vacuum; it was one of those interludes in which no world empire existed—neither in the Nile Valley, nor in Mesopotamia, nor elsewhere."

But in the second half of the 8th century B.C.E. things began to change; the accession to the Assyrian throne of Tiglath-pileser III inaugurated Assyria's period of empire. Israel, reduced to a tributary kingdom by Tiglath-pileser in the course of that king's conquest of all western Asia, was finally destroyed by Tiglath-pileser's successor Shalmaneser V in c. 722 B.C.E. Samaria was totally destroyed, and the inhabitants of Israel carried off into exile whence they never returned: they were eventually absorbed into their new environment and disappeared from history—though some may have trickled into Judah later. Judah carried on, but as an Assyrian dependency after 734 B.C.E., its kings alternately vainly trying to throw off Assyrian domination by alliance with Egypt or (like King Manasseh, so detested by the author of the Book of Kings) submitting voluntarily to Assyria and imitating Assyrian ways.

This naturally threatened the traditional religion, for the Jews seem to have been only too ready to give way at almost any time to idolatrous practices and cults from other nations. It was Manasseh's grandson Josiah who tried to stop the rot and restore his people to the true religion of the God of Israel. In the eighteenth year of Josiah's reign (i.e., 622), according to Kings, a copy of "the book of the law" was discovered in the Temple while repairs were being made there. The book was read to the king, and it gave further impetus to his religious reforms. It was clearly some form of Deuteronomy, whose reformist author or reviser went on to produce the historical books of the Bible from Joshua through II Kings. The work of the Deuteronomist (as this author is now called) had as its aim, in the words of Professor Jacob M. Myers, editor of the Anchor Chronicles, "to exhibit the effectiveness of the word of the Lord in Israel's history, both as judgment and salvation, and to foster the hope of a revitalization of the promise to David, in the face of a weakening Assyria if king and people heeded the lessons of the past." For Assyria, at the very moment of her greatest expansion, was beginning her decline and fall. Religious reform and feeling for national independence went together, as so often in Israel's history. (It should be noted that although the northern kingdom of Israel had now disappeared, the term "Israel" still existed and was still in use—as it is today—to describe those of the ancient people who retained their identity. The "ten lost tribes" of the northern kingdom were not in fact ten distinct tribes at the time of the Assyrian conquest; the inhabitants of Judah took over the whole inheritance of Israel.)

The work of the Deuteronomist presented Israel with a problem that was to enage the attention of many of the Hebrew Prophets. Would adherence to the Mosaic Law, as recapitulated and reaffirmed in Deuteronomy, insure the preservation of national independence and identity? And if, in spite of Josiah's reforms, Assyria or some other pagan foreign power were to subdue the country and overthrow its institutions, would this mean that God's promises were false and the confidence that He would look after His people if they did His will had all along been misplaced?

Meanwhile, the political situation was worsening. Assyria joined with Egypt in an attempt to check the rising power of Babylon; Josiah, either alone or in alliance with Babylon, tried to stop the joint Assyrian-Egyptian army, and was defeated and killed. In 598-7 the Babylonians marched against Judah and conquered it, though Nebuchadnezzar allowed the state to exist under Babylonian suzerainty; in 587, after a final Jewish rebellion, the Babylonians destroyed Jerusalem and deported the population to Babylon. In 539 the conquering Cyrus the Great of Persia subdued Babylon and issued an edict allowing all the Jewish deportees and their descendants who so desired to return to Judah. The author of Chroncicles wrote that it was the Lord who aroused the spirit of Cyrus to do this, and records his decree in this way: "Thus has Cyrus the king of Persia said: Yahweh God of the heavens has given me all the kingdoms of the earth and he has appointed me to build for him a house in Jerusalem which is in Judah. Whoever among you belongs to all his people, may Yahweh his God be with him and let him go up." (Myers' translation.)

The Deuteronomist had tried to prove to the people that obedience to the Mosaic Law would preserve them in freedom and security. Professor Myers comments: "Deuteronomy may have contributed [to the religious and moral decline that followed the death of Josiah] by the creation of a misdirected sense of security on the part of officials who trusted in externals to the exclusion, or nearly so, of a deep inner commitment to the will of God." At any rate, Josiah's reforms had not preserved national independence. The author of Chronicles ("the Chronicler") set himself to rewrite the history of Israel from the death of Saul and the accession of David to the decree of Cyrus in order to serve the needs of the returned exiles. His object was threefold: "to demonstrate that the true Israel was the one perpetuated in Judah—the one which began in the Davidic kingdom, continued right through the history of Judah, and more to the point, was now represented in the exilic community"; to create the proper conditions for true religious worship and centralize it in Jerusalem; and to provide an institutional structure that could resist " the manifest political and social pressures exerted upon the new community." He drew on a variety of sources, including, of course, the historical books of the Deuteronomist, but selected, organized, and emphasized in his own way for his own purpose. "He did not," says Professor Myers, "deliberately distort history to fit his purpose; he employed those phases that were apropos and, at numerous points, he manifestly relied on sources sometimes more accurate than those used by the Deuteronomist. In view of that fact one cannot accuse him of writing imaginative history, as has been charged so often. That he had his own way of filling in the gaps, with some embellishments no doubt, was due to the interests of the cause. The political aspects of the Davidic line had come to an end and there was no hope of re-establishment, at least not so far as he could see. Hope for Israel lay in the fortification of the religious institutions that survived the tragic experiences of 587 B.C. and the long years of the Exile."

It is fascinating to go through Chronicles and, with the aid of Professor Myers' notes, see how the Chronicler has focused attention on David, Solomon, and the Temple cult in order to present to his people the kind of history that would best serve them in their crisis. The Chronicler was, says Professor Myers, "above all else a churchman of the highest order" whose aim was to help his people by strengthening "a living religious institution rather than through the royal messianism proclaimed by the prophets—a messianism which had signally failed in the early stages of the post-exilic community." The Hebrew Bible in its traditional Jewish ordering ends with Chronicles: this makes sense, for the Chronicler (who was probably also the author of Ezra and Nehemiah) recapitulated Jewish history in such a way as to provide the basis for the survival of the Jewish people as essentially a religious community, thus preparing them for the greater *Galut*. It is surely ironical that a work designed to help the exiles returned from Babylon to re-develop their national religious life in their own country should have in fact helped to prepare their descendants for permanent exile.

Professor Myers' edition of Chronicles lacks the fine verbal grace we find in Speiser's Genesis (both in introduction and translation): no one who persistently uses the word "returnees" can claim the highest linguistic sensitivity. But the translation of Chronicles does not call for any great stylistic subtlety, and Myers does a scholarly and workmanlike job. His introduction, if not a model of English prose, is consistently illuminating. He perhaps exaggerates, in the interests of clarity of presentation, the difference between the Chronicler's position and that of the prophets, whose message can certainly not be adequately summed up in the phrase "royal messianism." The prophets saw the little states of Judah and Israel caught up in the great power struggles of the time, and counseled a contracting out of the whole game of power politics in favor of concentration on practicing justice, mercy, and righteousness. Between the decline of the Davidic empire and the final fall of Jerusalem to Babylon, these extraordinary men, speaking with total conviction in the name of God, exhorted, warned, castigated, and comforted their people in the firm belief that goodness rather than political strength or cunning would save the nation. By the same token, if Israel was oppressed by an outside power, it was by the will of God, and the duty of the people was to return to God rather than to rebel. This was the anguished message of Jeremiah, who prophesied in Judah from the beginning of the period of Babylonian domination of the country until after the final Babylonian conquest and the carrying off of so many of the people into exile. In a sense he was a Quisling, a traitor, counseling submission to Babylon because he saw no way out through political or military resistance. Babylon was God's instrument: he was convinced of this. Yet the knowledge tortured him, and he spoke out only because he felt that God was urging him to do so. After the final victory of the Babylonians, the victors offered him specially favorable treatment if he would come to Babylon with them. They misunderstood him, as so many of his own people misunderstood him. He stayed with the remnant of his people in devastated Judah until forcibly taken to Egypt.

Professor John Bright, in his Anchor Jeremiah, paints in the historical background with a vigorous brush, covering some of the same material dealt with by Professor Myers in his introduction to Chronicles but with a different focus. The center of the picture remains Jeremiah, the reluctant prophet, castigating his people for their faithlessness to their God and for preferring mere ritual to ethical action, prophesying with horrified conviction the defeat and destruction that God had prepared for His faithless people, protesting against his own prophetic mission and cursing his fate that he should be born into such a world and entrusted with such a message, and in the end advising the exiles in Babylon to seek the welfare of the country to which they had been deported and comforting them with visions of future restoration.

The Book of Jeremiah, with its prophetic poems, its historical and biographical narrative, and its terrifying autobiographical outbursts, is far from orderly (either chronologically or logically) as we now have it, and Professor Bright does some useful explaining and rearranging, sorting out the different strands and relating them to their background. In his translation he seeks a mean between a wooden literalness and a paraphrase, endeavoring to put the sense of the original into clear modern English and at the same time, in the poetic passages, trying to give the reader some impression of the effect of Hebrew poetry by keeping the lines at about the same length as the original and keeping the same number of accented syllables. This last aim sometimes leads him to use contractions that sound a bit too colloquial, but more often there is an immense gain in immediacy. Compare the following:

King James: Be not dismayed at them.
Bright: Don't lose your nerve because of them.

* * *

King James: And they shall fight against
thee; but they shall not

prevail against thee.
Bright: Attack you they will; overcome you they can't.

* * *

King James: And send unto Kedar and consider
diligently; and see if there hath
been such a thing.
Bright: Send out to Kedar and closely observe!
And see—was there ever the like?

* * *

King James: And my people love to have it so;
and what will ye do in the end
thereof?
Bright: And my people—they love it that way.
But what will you do when it ends?

* * *

King James: Oh that I had in the wilderness
a lodging place of wayfaring men;
that I might leave my people, and go
from them! for they be all adulterers,
an assembly of treacherous men.
Bright: O that I had in the desert
A wayfarer's lodge,
And so could leave my people,
Get away from them!
For they're all adulterers,
A gang of crooks.

"A gang of crooks" is an admirable rendering of the Hebrew *atseret bog'dim* and brings the phrase immediately out of the realm of the antique-poetic into that of vigorous market-place talk, which, after all, is what Jeremiah was engaged in.

The question of whether the prophets were right in believing that the practice of virtue could have saved the people from foreign domination—what does a small nation *do* when ringed round by mighty military powers?—may bother the modern reader, but it is worth noting that, in Professor Bright's words, "precisely in that Jeremiah's was a message of judgment, it was a saving message. By ruthlessly destroying false hope, by ceaselessly asserting that the tragedy was Yahweh's doing, his righteous judgment on the nation for its sin, Jeremiah as it were drew the national disaster within the framework of faith, and thus prevented it from destroying faith." The disaster proved not the death of God but the very present existence of God. In making the people see this, Jeremiah helped to lay down a basic article of creed that the Jewish people clung to through subsequent centuries. "And because of our sins we were exiled from our land" is a phrase repeated by Orthodox Jews every New Year (in the *musaph* service). Two thousand years of exile and intermittent persecution, culminating in the murder of the six million by Hitler, because of the sins of some remote ancestors? If Jeremiah had seen further into the future he would surely have been appalled, and been even more reluctant to prophesy than he in fact was, and the eloquent messages of future comfort that we find in chapters 30 and 31 might never have been announced.

Jeremiah did not, however, accept the word of the Lord tamely; he not only protested against the burden laid on him but also questioned God directly about His treatment of him. But it was in a different kind of context that the intractable question of the prosperity of the wicked and the suffering of the innocent was most fully treated in biblical literature. Among the third division of the Hebrew Bible (the traditional division is into Law, Prophets, and "Writings") we find that curiously attractive yet oddly anomalous group of books which belong to the "Wisdom" literature —that somewhat sophisticated, international, sometimes apparently agnostic, often worldly-wise, sometimes hedonistic, sometimes sad and world-weary to the point occasionally of anguish, trilogy of works, Job, Proverbs, and Kohelet (Ecclesiastes). Job, essentially a dialogue on theodicy inserted into the framework of an old folk tale, raises in a way so straightforward as to amount almost to blasphemy the question of unmerited suffering and challenges squarely the older doctrine that sin brings physical punishment and that the virtuous prosper. "I have been young and now I am old; yet have I not seen the righteous forsaken, nor his seed begging for bread," wrote the Psalmist. Nonsense, replies the author of Job. Life isn't that at all. And of course it isn't. Suffering does not prove antecedent sin, nor does righteous living guarantee happiness. While Job's friends try to persuade him that since he has been afflicted with such misfortunes he must have sinned, Job flatly refuses to accept this and keeps asking God to show him the indictment against him, to give him a proper trial instead of punishing him without even letting him know what he stands accused of. God replies, oddly enough, by castigating Job's friends and praising Job, yet at the same time humiliating Job by reciting a chain of natural wonders which God had created and which Job cannot possibly understand or control. The solution lies in wonder. God's ways are mysterious; we cannot hope to understand them. His is the power and the mystery, and we must just trust that He knows what He is doing.

The text of Job is difficult and sometimes corrupt, and the matter is made worse by the attempts of the Masorites to smooth away some of Job's more daring outbursts. Thus the exclamation, ". . . he will slay me; I shall have nothing to hope for" was changed by reading the Hebrew *lo,* meaning "not," as the word *lo,* meaning "to him" (same sound, difference in spelling of one letter), with the result that it could be translated, as the King James version has it: "Though he slay me, yet will I wait for him." (Professor Marvin H. Pope, in the Anchor Job, renders it: "He may slay me, I'll not quaver.") Job is full of such passages which Professor Pope's edition lucidly explains and clarifies. Some of the most famous sentences attributed to Job, which have rung down the ages as professions of faith, are clearly misreadings of the Hebrew, though they have developed a life of their own in religious thought and literature.

Like Professor Bright with Jeremiah, Professor Pope makes a good attempt to capture the feeling of the original poetry, using a much shorter line than more traditional translations. Here are some examples:

King James: As God liveth, who has taken away my right;
And the Almighty, who hath vexed my soul;
(For my life is yet whole in me,
And the spirit of God is in my nostrils;)
Surely my lips shall not speak unrighteousness,
Neither shall my tongue utter deceit.

Pope: As God lives, who withholds my right,
Shaddai who has embittered my soul,
While I have life in me,
God's breath in my nostrils,
My lips will not speak falsehood,
Nor my tongue utter deceit.

* * *

King James: Let the day perish wherein I was born.
And the night which said, there is a man child conceived.

Pope: Damn the day I was born,
The night that said, 'A boy is begot.'

Pope's rhythms are much more like those of the Hebrew.

Job sounds fevered and desperate beside the mellow skepticism of Kohelet, that curiously unbiblical work which is the best and most characteristic representative of straight Wisdom literature to manage to get into the canon. It didn't get in without a struggle, and the addition of an editorial conclusion to turn the genial skepticism of the author into a reason for faith and obedience. (One is reminded of the fun David Hume had with the idea of skepticism as the basis of faith in his *Dialogues on Natural Religion*.) Professor R. B. Y. Scott, who edits the Anchor Proverbs and Ecclesiastes (in a single volume), gives us a scholarly and workmanlike translation preceded by a clear if far from concise account of the background of the Wisdom literature. Some of the information he provides duplicates the material provided in Professor Pope's Job, but this is inevitable if each volume is to be regarded as independent. He does tend to be verbose, though, not only in his introduction but also occasionally in his translation. I can see no conceivable reason why that fine verse in Proverbs traditionally (and absolutely literally) translated:

Her ways are ways of pleasantness,
And all her paths are peace

should be rendered by Professor Scott as:

Her ways are ways to delight
And all her paths lead to felicity.

"Ways to delight" might just be defended on the grounds that it gives the sense of the Hebrew more accurately (though "ways of pleasantness" is both literal and charming, if considerably longer than the Hebrew), but what can possibly be said for changing "all her paths are peace" to "all her paths lead to felicity"? Scott admits in his notes that the substitution "seems literary sacrilege" but defends it on the grounds that it makes the meaning a little clearer. I confess that I cannot see how it does that. He tells us in an earlier note that the Hebrew *shalom* really means "wholeness, harmonious well-being." I do not for a moment question Professor Scott's formidable scholarship; but I can't help wondering what would happen if, the next time I visited Israel, I greeted someone there with: "Harmonious well-being to you!"

But this is a minor point. To present Proverbs and Kohelet together in a single volume with a translation which, even if occasionally infelicitous, does genuinely clear up (particularly with respect to the latter book) some of the beautiful mystifications of the King James translators and sets both works in their time and place and in the whole context of Wisdom literature of the Near East is a fine and welcome achievement. It is interesting to put the present translation beside that of Robert Gordis, whose work on Kohelet is one of the noblest monuments of American Jewish biblical scholarship. Gordis emends MT less frequently than Pope, but his translation is sometimes even freer. Gordis renders "Cast thy bread upon the waters" as "Send your goods overseas," which is not what the Hebrew says, though it may well be its implication; Pope renders with absolute literalness: "Throw your bread on the surface of the water," and in doing so gives us nine English words for the five Hebrew.

The whole question of how to render the imagery of Kohelet is beset with difficulties; sometimes the idiom rendered literally is meaningless; sometimes it is suggestive but in the wrong way; sometimes again (as, surely, with the example just quoted) the literal translation can be left to achieve its own suggestion. Sometimes emendation is absolutely necessary to achieve any sense at all; at other times it may improve the sense or at least make it seem more logical. King James renders the opening of the last chapter, "Remember also thy Creator in the days of thy youth." Gordis has, "Remember your Creator in the days of your youth" (the Jewish Publication Society's version retains the dubious force of the Hebrew prefix *u-* by rendering "Remember *then* thy Creator in the days of thy youth"). But Scott decides to emend MT *bor'ĕcha* ("your creator") to read *bor'cha* ("your grave")—though the common meaning of *bor* is "pit"—and renders, "In the days of your youth, remember your grave," which *is* more logical, since the passage goes on to describe the coming of old age and death. But this whole chapter is full of problems. Let anyone compare the mysteriously eloquent King James version with those of Gordis and Scott, and he will realize that the poetry of King James often produces a pleasing fuzz of meaning which is nevertheless fuzz.

As for Proverbs, they are an interesting collection of secular and religious sayings and didactic poems reflecting many of the characteristics of Near Eastern Wisdom literature. Many of the sayings keep reminding me of that bogus oriental proverb we used to joke about as schoolboys: "The rich man is kind to his dog, but the poor man rises early in the morning." After rereading the whole book of Proverbs more carefully than I have ever done before, and pondering on one of the categories of proverbs listed by Professor Scott (the pattern of *"non-identity, contrast,* or *paradox"*), I realize that this fake oriental proverb of my childhood really makes sense: the rich can afford the luxury of indulging animals, while the poor are too busy scratching a living to be able to afford that kind of indulgence. But I prefer the snappier sayings, some of which Professor Scott renders most incisively. "Go to the ant, thou sluggard," the well known King James rendering, does not leap out of the page like:

Go watch an ant, you loafer!

Now that is something you can really say to people.

Sof davar hakol nishma (Kohelet, 12:13, rendered by Professor Scott as "The sum of the matter when all has been heard is this") is that the Anchor Bible is the most exciting development in biblical studies in the English-speaking world at the present time. The endeavor to give a new rendering of each book of the Bible in the light of the knowledge now possessed by the sum of biblical scholars and to set that translation in an account of the context and background drawn similarly from every relevant branch of knowledge from archaeology to textual criticism must be warmly welcomed by anybody who considers himself in any degree literate. The Bible is a quite extraordinary anthology of religious literature which, quite apart from the special part it has played in the history of Judaism and Christianity, is of the highest literary, historical, anthropological and general human interest. It is good that expert knowledge about its nature and meaning should be released from the pages of learned journals and made available to the layman. For myself, I would have preferred an edition with the original text facing the translation. (In reviewing these volumes I have had to have a semicircle of Hebrew texts around me.) But that is probably a special taste. Of more universal value would have been the provision of maps and full indexes to each volume. One must not complain, though. This is a remarkable and quite exceptionally valuable series, and I look forward to its future volumes.

IV
GROUPS

Saul Bellow

LOOKING FOR MR. GREEN

A Story

Whatsoever thy hand findeth to do,
do it with thy might. . . .

Hard work? No, it wasn't really so hard. He wasn't used to walking and stair-climbing, but the physical difficulty of his new job was not what George Grebe felt most. He was delivering Relief checks in the Negro district, and although he was a native Chicagoan this was not a part of the city he knew much about—it needed a depression to introduce him to it. No, it wasn't literally hard work, not as reckoned in foot-pounds, but yet he was beginning to feel the strain of it, to grow aware of its peculiar difficulty. He could find the streets and numbers, but the clients were not where they were supposed to be, and he felt like a hunter inexperienced in the camouflage of his game. It was an unfavorable day, too—fall, and cold, dark weather, windy. But, anyway, instead of shells in his deep trench coat pocket he had the cardboard of checks, punctured for the spindles of the file, the holes reminding him of the holes in player-piano paper. And he didn't look much like a hunter, either; his was a city figure entirely, belted up in this Irish conspirator's coat. He was slender without being tall, stiff in the back, his legs looking shabby in a pair of old tweed pants, gone through and fringy at the cuffs. With this stiffness, he kept his head forward, so that his face was red from the sharpness of the weather; and it was an indoors sort of face with gray eyes that persisted in some kind of thought and yet seemed to avoid definiteness of conclusion. He wore sideburns that surprised you somewhat by the tough curl of the blond hair and the effect of assertion in their length. He was not so mild as he looked, nor so youthful; and nevertheless there was no effort on his part to seem what he was not. He was an educated man; he was a bachelor; he was in some ways simple; without lushing, he liked a drink; his luck had not been good. Nothing was deliberately hidden.

He felt that his luck was better than usual today. When he had reported for work that morning, he had expected to be shut up in the Relief office at a clerk's job, for he had been hired downtown as a clerk, and he was glad to have, instead, the freedom of the streets and welcomed, at least at first, the vigor of the cold and even the blowing of the hard wind. But on the other hand he was not getting on with the distribution of the checks. It was true that it was a city job; nobody expected you to push too hard at a city job. His supervisor, that young Mr. Raynor, had practically told him that. Still, he wanted to do well at it. For one thing, when he knew how quickly he could deliver a batch of checks, he would know also how much time he could expect to clip for himself. And then, too, the clients would be waiting for their money. That was not the most important consideration, though it certainly mattered to him. No, but he wanted to do well, simply for doing-well's sake, to acquit himself decently of a job because he so rarely had a job to do that required just this sort of energy. Of this peculiar energy he now had a superabundance; once it had started to flow, it flowed all too heavily. And, for the time being anyway, he was balked. He could not find Mr. Green.

So he stood in his big-skirted trench coat with a large envelope in his hand and papers showing from his pocket, wondering why people should be so hard to locate who were too feeble or sick to come to the station to collect their own checks. But Raynor had told him that tracking them down was not easy at first and had offered him some advice on how to proceed. "If you can see the postman, he's your first man to ask, and your best bet. If you can't connect with him, try the stores and tradespeople around. Then the janitor and the neighbors. But you'll find the closer you come to your man the less people will tell you. They don't want to tell you anything."

"Because I'm a stranger."

"Because you're white. We ought to have a Negro doing this, but we don't at the moment, and of course you've got to eat, too, and this is public employment. Jobs have to be made. Oh, that holds for me too. Mind you, I'm not letting myself out. I've got three years of seniority on you, that's all. And a law degree. Otherwise, you might be back of the desk and I might be going out into the field this cold day. The same dough pays us both and for the same, exact, identical reason. What's my law degree got to do with it? But you have to pass out these checks, Mr. Grebe, and it'll help if you're stubborn, so I hope you are."

"Yes, I'm fairly stubborn."

Raynor sketched hard with an eraser in the old dirt of his desk, left-handed, and said, "Sure, what else can you answer to such a question. Anyhow, the trouble you're going to have is that they don't like to give information about anybody. They think you're a plain-clothes dick or an installment collector, or summons-server or something like that. Till you've been seen around the neighborhood for a few months and people know you're only from the Relief."

It was dark, ground-freezing, pre-Thanksgiving weather, the wind played hob with the smoke, rushing it down, and Grebe missed his gloves, which he had left in Raynor's office. And no one would admit knowing Green. It was past three o'clock and the postman had made his last delivery. The nearest grocer, himself a Negro, had never heard the name Tulliver Green or said he hadn't. Grebe was inclined to think that it was true, that he had in the end convinced the man that he only wanted to deliver a check. But he wasn't sure. He needed experience in interpreting looks and signs, and, even more, the will not to be put off or denied and even the force to bully, if need be. If the grocer did know, he had got rid of him easily. But since most of his trade was with reliefers, why should he prevent the delivery of a check? Maybe Green, or Mrs. Green, if there was a Mrs. Green, patronized another grocer. And was there a Mrs. Green? It was one of Grebe's great handicaps that he hadn't looked at any of the case records. Raynor should have let him read files for a few hours. But he apparently saw no need for that, probably considering the job unimportant. Why prepare systematically to deliver a few checks?

But now it was time to look for the janitor. Grebe took in the building in the wind and gloom of the late November day—trampled, frost-hardened lots on one side; on the other, an automobile junk yard and then the infinite work of Elevated frames, weak-looking, gaping with rubbish fires; two sets of leaning brick porches three stories high and a flight of cement stairs to the cellar. Descending, he entered the underground passage where he tried the doors until one opened and he found himself in the furnace room. There someone rose toward him and approached, scraping on the coal grit and bending under the canvas-jacketed pipes.

"Are you the janitor?"

"What do you want?"

"I'm looking for a man who's supposed to be living here. Green."

"What Green?"

"Oh, you maybe have more than one Green?" said Grebe with new, pleasant hope. "This is Tulliver Green."

"I don't think I c'n help you, mister. I don't know any."

"A crippled man."

The janitor stood bent before him. Could it be that he was crippled? Oh, God! what if he was. Grebe's gray eyes sought with excited difficulty to see. But no, he was only very short and stooped. A head awakened from meditation, a strong-haired beard, low, wide shoulders. A staleness of sweat and coal rose from his black shirt and the burlap sack he wore as an apron.

"Crippled how?"

Grebe thought and then answered with the light voice of unmixed candor, "I don't know. I've never seen him." This was damaging, but his only other choice was to make a lying guess, and he was not up to it. "I'm delivering checks for the Relief to shut-in cases. If he weren't crippled he'd come to collect himself. That's why I said crippled. Bedridden, chair-ridden . . . is there anybody like that?"

This sort of frankness was one of Grebe's oldest talents, going back to childhood. But it gained him nothing here.

"No suh. I've got four buildin's same as this that I take care of. I don' know all the tenants, leave alone the tenants' tenants. The rooms turn over so fast, people movin' in and out every day. I can't tell you."

"Then where should I ask?"

The janitor opened his grimy lips but Grebe did not hear him in the piping of the valves and the consuming pull of air to flame in the body of the furnace. He knew, however, what he had said.

"Well, all the same, thanks. Sorry I bothered you, I'll prowl around upstairs again and see if I can turn up someone who knows him."

Once more in the cold air and early darkness, he made the short circle from the cellarway to the entrance crowded between the brickwork pillars and began to climb to the third floor. Pieces of plaster ground under his feet; strips of brass tape from which the carpeting had been torn away marked old boundaries at the sides. In the passage, the cold reached him worse than in the street; it touched him to the bone. The hall toilets ran like springs. He thought grimly as he heard the wind burning around the building with a sound like that of the furnace, that this was a great piece of constructed shelter. Then he struck a match in the gloom and searched for names and numbers among the writings and scribbles on the walls. He saw "WHOODY-DOODY GO TO JESUS," and zigzags, caricatures, sexual scrawls, and curses. So the sealed rooms of pyramids were also decorated, and the caves of human dawn.

The information on his card was, TULLIVER GREEN—APT 3D. There were no names, however, and no numbers. His shoulders drawn up, tears of cold in his eyes, breathing vapor, he went the length of the corridor and told himself that if he had been lucky enough to have the temperament for it he would bang on one of the doors and bawl out "Tulliver Green!" until he got results. But it wasn't in him to make an uproar and he continued to burn matches, passing the light over the walls. At the rear, in a corner off the hall, he discovered a door he had not seen before and he thought it best to investigate. It sounded empty, when he knocked, but a young Negress answered, hardly more than a girl. She opened only a bit, to protect the warmth of the room.

"Yes suh?"

"I'm from the district Relief station on Prairie Avenue. I'm looking for a man named Tulliver Green to give him his check. Do you know him?"

No, she didn't; but he thought she had not understood anything of what he had said. She had a dream-bound, dream-blind face, very soft and black, shut off. She wore a man's jacket and pulled the ends together at her throat. Her hair was parted in three directions, at the sides and transversely, standing up at the front in a dull puff.

"Is there somebody around here who might know?"

"I jus' taken this room las' week."

He observed that she shivered, but even her shiver was somnambulistic and there was no sharp consciousness of cold in the big smooth eyes of her handsome face.

"All right, miss, thank you. Thanks," he said, and went to try another place.

Here he was admitted. He was grateful, for the room was warm. It was full of people, and they were silent as he entered—ten people, or a dozen, perhaps more, sitting on benches like a parliament. There was no light, properly speaking, but a tempered darkness that the window gave, and everyone seemed to him enormous, the men padded out in heavy work clothes and winter coats, and the women huge, too, in their sweaters, hats and old furs. And, besides, bed and bedding, a black cooking range, a piano piled towering to the ceiling with paper, a dining-room table of the old style of prosperous Chicago. Among these people Grebe, with his cold-heightened fresh color and his smaller stature, entered like a school lad. Even though he was met with smiles and good will, he felt that all the currents ran against him and that he would make no headway. Without having spoken a single word he knew that he was already outweighed and overborne. Nevertheless he began: "Does anybody here know how I can deliver a check to Mr. Tulliver Green?"

"Green?" It was the man that had let him in who answered. He was in shirt sleeves, in checkered shirt, and had a queer, high head, profusely overgrown, long as a shako; the veins entered it strongly from his forehead. "I never heard mention of him. Is this where he live?"

"This is the address they gave me at the station. He's a sick man, and he'll need his check. Can't anybody tell me where to find him?"

He stood his ground and waited for a reply, his crimson wool scarf wound about his neck and drooping outside his trench coat, pockets weighted with the block of checks and official forms. They must have realized that he was not a college boy employed afternoons by a bill collector, trying foxily to pass for a Relief clerk, recognized that he was an older man who knew himself what need was, who had had more than an average seasoning in hardship. It was evident enough if you looked at the marks under his eyes and at the sides of his mouth.

"Anybody know this sick man?"

"No suh." On all sides he saw heads shaken and smiles of denial. No one knew. And maybe it was true, he considered, standing silent in the earthen, musky human gloom of the place as the rumble continued. But he could never really be sure.

"What's the matter with this man?" said shako-head.

"I've never seen him. All I can tell you is that he can't come in person for his money. It's my first day in this district."

"Maybe they given you the wrong number?"

"I don't believe so. But where else can I ask about him?" He felt that his persistence amused them deeply, and in a way he shared their amusement that he should stand up so tenaciously to them. Though smaller, though slight, he was his own man, he retracted nothing about himself, and he looked back at them, gray-eyed, with amusement and also with a sort of effrontery. On the bench, some man spoke in his throat, the words impossible to catch, and a woman answered with a wild, shrieking laugh, quickly cut off.

"Well, so nobody will tell me?"

"Ain't nobody who knows."

"At least, if he lives here, he pays rent to someone. Who manages the building?"

"Greatham Company. That's on 39th Street."

Grebe wrote it in his pad. But, in the street again, a sheet of wind-driven paper clinging to his leg while he deliberated what direction to take next, it seemed a feeble lead to follow. Probably this Green didn't rent a flat, but a room. Sometimes there were as many as twenty people living in an apartment; the real estate agent would know only the lessee. And not even the latter could tell you who the renters were. In some places the beds were even used in shifts, watchmen, or jitney drivers or short-order cooks in night joints turning out after a day's sleep and surrendering their beds to a sister, a nephew, or perhaps a stranger, a transient who paid something for it. There were large numbers of these transients in this terrific, blight-bitten portion of the city between Cottage Grove and Ashland, wandering from house to house and room to room. When you saw them wander, how would you know? They didn't carry bundles on their backs or look picturesque. You simply saw a man, a Negro, walking in the street or riding in the car, like everyone else, with his thumb closed on a transfer. And therefore how were you supposed to tell? Grebe fancied the Greatham agent would only laugh at his question.

But how much it would simplify his task to be able to say that Green was old, or blind, or consumptive. An hour in the files, taking a few notes, and he need not have been at such a disadvantage. When Raynor gave him the block of checks, he had asked, "How much should I know about these people?" Then Raynor had looked as though he were preparing to accuse him of trying to make the job more important than it was. He smiled, because by then they were on fine terms, but nevertheless he had been getting ready to say something like that when the confusion began in the station over Staika and her children.

Grebe had waited a long time for this job. It came to him through the pull of an old schoolmate in the Corporation Counsel's Office, never a close friend, but suddenly sympathetic and interested—pleased to show, moreover, how well he had done, how strongly he was coming through these miserable times. Well, he was coming through strongly, as strongly as the Democratic administration itself. Grebe had gone to see him in City Hall, and they had had a counter lunch or beers at least once a month for a year, and finally it had been possible to swing the job. He didn't mind being assigned the lowest clerical grade, nor even being a messenger, though Raynor thought he did.

This Raynor was an original sort. Grebe had immediately taken to him. As was proper on the first day, Grebe had come early, but he waited long, for Raynor was late. At last he darted into his cubicle of an office as though he had just jumped from one of those hurtling huge red Indiana Avenue cars. His thin, rough face was windstung and he was grinning and saying something breathlessly to himself. In his hat, a small fedora, and his coat, the velvet collar a neat fit about his neck, and his silk muffler that set off the nervous twist of his chin—he swayed and turned himself in his swivel chair, feet leaving the ground; so that he pranced a little as he sat. Meanwhile he took Grebe's measure out of his eyes, eyes of an unusual vertical length, a trace sardonic. So the two men sat for a while, saying nothing, while the supervisor raised his hat from his miscombed hair and put it in his lap. His cold-darkened hands were not clean. A steel beam passed through the little makeshift room from which machine belts once had hung. The building was an old factory.

"I'm younger than you; I hope you won't find it hard taking orders from me," said Raynor. "But I don't make them up, either. You're how old, about?"

"Thirty-five."

"And you thought you'd be inside doing paper-work. But it so happens I have to send you out."

"I don't mind."

"And it's mostly a Negro load we have in this district."

"So I thought it would be."

"Fine. You'll get along. *C'est un bon boulot.* Do you know French?"

"Some."

"I thought you'd be a university man."

"Have you been in France?" said Grebe.

"No, that's the French of the Berlitz School. I've been at it for more than a year, just as I'm sure people have been, all over the world, office boys in China and braves in Tanganyika. In fact, I damn well know it. Such is the attractive power of civilization. It's overrated, but what do you want? *Que voulez vous?* I get *Le Rire* and all the spicy papers, just like in Tanganyika. It must be mystifying, out there. But my reason is that I'm aiming at the diplomatic service. I have a cousin who's a courier, and the way he describes it is awfully attractive. He rides in the *wagons-lits* and reads books. While we . . . What did you do before?"

"I sold."

"Where?"

"Canned meat at Stop and Shop. In the basement."

"And before that?"

"Window shades, at Goldblatt's."

"Steady work?"

"No, Thursdays and Saturdays. I also sold shoes."

"You've been a shoe-dog, too. Well. And prior to that? Here it is in your folder." He opened the record. "St. Olaf's College, instructor in classical languages. Fellow, University of Chicago, 1926-27. I've had Latin, too. Let's trade quotations—*Dun spiro spero.*"

"Da dextram misero."

"Alea jacta est."

"Excelsior."

Raynor shouted with laughter, and other workers came to look at him over the partition. Grebe also laughed, feeling pleased and easy. The luxury of fun on a nervous morning.

When they were done and no one was watching or listening, Raynor said rather seriously, "What made you study Latin in the first place. Was it for the priesthood?"

"No."

"Just for the hell of it? As a luxury? Oh, the things people think they can pull!" He made his cry hilarious and tragic. "I ran my pants off so I could study for the bar, and I've passed the bar, so I get twelve dollars a week more than you as a bonus for having seen life straight and whole. I'll tell you, as a man of culture, that even though nothing looks to be real, and everything stands for something else, and that thing for another thing, and that thing for a still further one—there ain't any comparison between twenty-five and thirty-seven dollars a week, regardless of the last reality. Don't you think that was clear to your Greeks? They were a thoughtful people, but they didn't part with their slaves."

This was a great deal more than Grebe had looked for in his first interview with his supervisor. He was too shy to show all the astonishment he felt. He laughed a little, aroused, and brushed at the sunbeam that covered his head with its dust. "Do you think my mistake was so terrible?"

"Damn right it was terrible, and you know it now that you've had the whip of hard times laid on your back. You should have been preparing yourself for trouble. Your people must have been well off to send you to the university. Stop me, if I'm stepping on your toes. Did your mother pamper you? Did your father give into you? Were you brought up tenderly, with permission to go out and find out what were the last things that everything else stands for while everybody else labored in the fallen world of appearances?"

"Well, no, it wasn't exactly like that." Grebe smiled. *The fallen world of appearances!* no less. But now it was his turn to deliver a surprise. "We weren't rich. My father was the last genuine English butler in Chicago. . . ."

"Are you kidding?"

"Why should I be?"

"In a livery."

"In livery. Up on the Gold Coast."

"And he wanted you to be educated like a gentleman?"

"He did not. He sent me to the Armour Institute to study chemical engineering. But when he died I changed schools."

He stopped himself, and considered how quickly Raynor had reached him. In no time he had your valise on the table and your things unpacked And afterwards, in the streets, he was still reviewing how far he might have gone, and how much he might have been led to tell if they had not been interrupted by Mrs. Staika's great noise.

But just then a young woman, one of Raynor's workers, ran into the cubicle exclaiming, "Haven't you heard all the fuss?"

"We haven't heard anything."

"It's Staika, giving out with all her might. Reporters are coming. She said she phoned the papers, and you know she did."

"But what is she up to?" said Raynor.

"She brought her wash and she's ironing it here, with our current, because the Relief won't pay her electric bill. She has her ironing board set up by the admitting desk, and her kids are with her, all six. They never are in school more than once a week. She's always dragging them around with her because of her reputation."

"I don't want to miss any of this," said Raynor jumping up. Grebe, as he followed with the secretary, said, "Who is this Staika?"

"They call her the 'Blood Mother of Federal Street.' She's a professional donor at the hospitals. I think they pay ten dollars a pint. Of course it's no joke, but she makes a very big thing out of it and she and the kids are in the papers all the time."

Scores of people, staff and clients divided by a plywood barrier, stood in the narrow space of the entrance, and Staika was shouting in a gruff, mannish voice, plunging the iron on the board and slamming it on the metal rest.

"My father and mother came in a steerage, and I was born in our own house, Robey by Huron. I'm no dirty immigrant. I'm a U.S. citizen. My husband is a gassed veteran from France with lungs weaker'n paper, that hardly can he go to the toilet by himself. These six children of mine, I have to buy the shoes for their feet with my own blood. Even a lousy little white communion necktie, that's a couple of drops of blood; a little piece of mosquito veil for my Vadja so she won't be ashamed in church for the other girls, they take my blood for it by Goldblatt. That's how I keep goin'. A fine thing if I had to depend on the Relief. And there's plenty of people on the rolls—fakes! There's nothin' *they* can't get, that can go and wrap bacon at Swift and Armour any time. They're lookin' for them by the Yards. They never have to be out of work. Only they rather lay in their lousy beds and eat the taxpayers' money." She was not afraid, in a predominantly Negro station, to shout this way about Negroes.

Grebe pressed himself forward to get a nearer view of the woman. She was flaming with anger and with pleasure at herself, broad and huge, a golden-headed woman who wore a cotton cap laced with pink ribbon. She was barelegged and had on black gym-shoes, her hoover apron was open and her great breasts, not much restrained by a man's undershirt, hampered her arms as she worked at the kid's dress on the ironing board. And the children, silent and white, with a kind of locked obstinacy, in sheepskins and lumberjackets, stood behind her. She had captured the station, and the pleasure it gave her was enormous. Yet her grievances were true grievances, if wrongly aimed, and she put the whole force of her spirit into them. But she attacked with her voice. Her small eyes she kept averted, and her look was hidden, so that she seemed to be spinning and planning as she raged.

"They send me out college case-workers in silk panties to talk me out of what I got comin'. Are they better 'n me? Who told them? Fire them. Let 'em go and get married, and then you won't have to cut electric from folks' budget."

The chief supervisor, Mr. Ewing, could not silence her and he stood with folded arms at the head of his staff, bald, trying to appear mocking, saying to his subordinates like the ex-school principal he was, "Pretty soon she'll be tired and go."

"Nothing doing," said Raynor to Grebe. "She'll get what she wants. She knows more about the Relief even than Ewing. She's been on the rolls for years, and she always gets what she wants because she puts on a noisy show. Ewing knows it. He'll give in soon. He's only saving face. If he gets bad publicity, the Commissioner'll have him on the carpet, downtown. She's got him submerged; she'll submerge everybody in time, and that includes nations and governments." Grebe replied with his characteristic smile, disagreeing completely. Who would ever take Staika's orders, and what changes could her yelling bring about?

No, what Grebe saw in her, the power that made her a real center of attention, and made obedient and attracted people listen, was that her cry expressed the war of flesh and blood, made a little crazy and intensely ugly, on place and condition. And at first, when he went out, she somehow presided over the whole district for him, and it took color from her; literally her color, in the spotty curb-fires, and the fires under the El, the straight alley of flamey gloom. Later too, when he went into a tavern for a shot of rye, the sweat of beer, by way of West Side Polish streets, led him to think of her again.

He wiped the corners of his mouth with his muffler, his handkerchief being too deep in his pocket to reach for, and went out again to get on with the delivery of his checks. The air bit cold and hard and a few flakes of snow formed near him. A train struck by and left a quiver in the frames and a bristling icy hiss over the rails.

Crossing the street, he descended a flight of board steps into a basement grocery, setting off a little bell. It was a dark, long store and it caught you with its stinks of smoked meat, soap, dried peaches, and fish. There was a fire wrinkling and flapping in the little stove, and the proprietor was waiting, an Italian with a long, hollow face and stubborn bristles. He kept his hands warm under his apron.

No, he didn't know Green. You knew people, but not names. The same man might not have the same name twice. The police didn't know, either, and mostly didn't care. When somebody was shot or knifed they took the body away and didn't look for the murderer. In the first place, nobody would tell them anything. So they made up a name for the coroner and called it quits. And in the second place, they didn't give a goddam anyhow. But they couldn't get to the bottom of a thing even if they wanted to. Nobody would get to know even a tenth of what went on among these people. They stabbed and stole, they did every corrupt thing you ever heard of, men and men, women and women, parents and children, worse than the animals. They carried on their own way, and the crimes passed off like a smoke. There was never anything like it in the history of the world.

It was a long speech, deepening with every word in its fantasy and passion and becoming increasingly senseless and terrible: a swarm amassed by suggestion and by steady invention, a huge, hugging, despairing knot, a human wheel rolling through his shop.

Grebe felt that he must interrupt him. He said, sharply, "What are you talking about! All I asked was whether you knew this man."

"That isn't even the half of it. I been here six years. You probably don't want to believe this. But suppose it's true?"

"All the same," said Grebe, "there must be a way to find a person."

The Italian's close-spaced eyes had been queerly concentrated, as were his muscles, while he leaned across the counter trying to convince Grebe. Now he gave up the effort and sat down on his stool. "Oh . . . I suppose. Once in a while. But I been telling you, even the cops don't get anywhere."

"They're always after somebody. It's not the same thing."

"Well, keep trying if you want. I can't help you."

But he didn't keep trying. He had no more time to spend on Green. He slipped Green's check to the back of the block. The next name on the list was FIELD, WINSTON.

He found the back-yard bungalow without the least trouble; it shared a lot with another house, a few feet of yard between. Grebe knew these two-shack arrangements. They had been built in vast numbers in the days before the swamps were filled and the streets raised, and they were all the same—a boardwalk along the fence, well under street level, three or four ball-headed posts for clotheslines, greening wood, dead shingles, and a long, long flight of stairs to the rear door.

A twelve-year-old boy let him into the kitchen, and there the old man was sitting by the table in a wheel chair.

"Oh, it's d' government man," he said to the boy when Grebe drew out his checks. "Go bring me my box of papers." He cleared a space on the table.

"Oh, you don't have to go to all that trouble," said Grebe. But Field laid out his papers: Social Security card, Relief certification, letters from the state hospital in Manteno and a naval discharge dated San Diego, 1920.

"That's plenty," Grebe said. "Just sign."

"You got to know who I am," the old man said. "You're from the government. It's not your check, it's a government check and you got no business to hand it over till everything is proved."

He loved the ceremony of it, and Grebe made no more objections. Field emptied his box and finished out the circle of cards and letters.

"There's everything I done and been. Just the death certificate and they can close book on me." He said this with a certain happy pride and magnificence. Still he did not sign; he merely held the little pen upright on the golden green corduroy of his thigh. Grebe did not hurry him. He felt the old man's hunger for conversation.

"I got to get better coal," he said. "I sent my little gran'son to the yard with my order and they fill his wagon with screening. The stove ain't made for it. It fall through the grate. The order says Franklin County egg-size coal."

"I'll report it and see what can be done."

"Nothing can be done, I expect. You know and I know. There ain't no little ways to make things better, and the only big thing is money. That's the only sunbeams, money. Nothing is black where it shines, and the only place you see black is where it ain't shining. What we colored have to have is our own rich. There ain't no other way."

Grebe sat, his reddened forehead bridged levelly by his close-cut hair and his cheeks lowered in the wings of his collar—the caked fire shone hard within the isinglass and iron frames but the room was not comfortable—sat and listened while the old man unfolded his scheme. This was to create one Negro millionaire a month by subscription. One clever, good-hearted young fellow elected every month would sign a contract to use the money to start a business employing Negroes. This would be advertised by chain-letters and word of mouth, and every Negro wage-earner would contribute a dollar a month. Within five years there would be sixty millionaires.

"That'll fetch respect," he said with a throat-stopped sound that came out like a foreign syllable. "You got to take and organize all the money that gets thrown away on the policy wheel and horse race. As long as they can take it away from you, they got no respect for you. Money, that's d' sun of human kind!" Field was a Negro of mixed blood, perhaps Cherokee, or Natchez; his skin was reddish. And he sounded, speaking about a golden sun in this dark room, and looked, shaggy and slab-headed, with the mingled blood of his face and broad lips, the little pen still upright in his hand, like one of the underground kings of mythology, the old judging Minos himself.

And now he accepted the check and signed. Not to soil the slip, he held it down with his knuckles. The table budged and creaked, the center of the gloomy, heathen midden of the kitchen covered with bread, meat, and cans, and the scramble of papers.

"Don't you think my scheme'd work?"

"It's worth thinking about. Something ought to be done, I agree."

"It'll work if people will do it. That's all. That's the only thing, anytime. When they understand it in the same way, all of them."

"That's true," said Grebe, rising. His glance met the old man's.

"I know you got to go," he said. "Well, God bless you, boy, you ain't been sly with me. I can tell it in a minute."

He went back through the buried yard. Someone nursed a candle in a shed, where a man unloaded kindling wood from a sprawl-wheeled baby buggy and two voices carried on a high conversation. As he came up the sheltered passage he heard the hard boost of the wind in the branches and against the house fronts, and then, reaching the sidewalk, he saw the needle-eye red of cable towers in the open icy height hundreds of feet above the river and the factories: those keen points. From here, his view was unobstructed all the way to the South Branch and its timber banks, and the cranes beside the water. Rebuilt after the Great Fire, this part of the city was, not fifty years later, in ruins again, factories boarded up, buildings deserted or fallen, gaps of prairie between. But it wasn't desolation that this made you feel, but rather a faltering of organization that set free a huge energy, an escaped, unattached, unregulated power from the giant raw place. Not only must people feel it but, it seemed to Grebe, they were compelled to match it. In their very bodies. He no less than others, he realized. Say that his parents had been servants in their time, whereas he was not supposed to be one. He thought that they had never owed any service like this, which no one visible asked and probably flesh and blood could not even perform. Nor could anyone show why it should be performed; or see what the performance would lead to. That did not mean that he wanted to be released from it, he realized with a grimly pensive face. On the contrary. He had something to do. To be compelled to feel this energy and yet have nothing to do—that was horrible; that was suffering; he knew what that was. It was now quitting time. Six o'clock. He could go home if he liked, to his room, that is, to wash in hot water, to pour a drink, lie down on his quilt, read the paper, eat some liver paste on crackers before going out to dinner. But to think of this actually made him feel a little sick, as though he had swallowed hard air. He had six checks left, and he was determined to deliver at least one of these: Mr. Green's check.

So he started. He had four or five dark blocks to go, past open lots, condemned houses, old foundations, closed schools, black churches, mounds, and he reflected that there must be many people alive who had once seen the neighborhood rebuilt and new. Now there was a second layer of ruins; centuries of history accomplished through human massing. Numbers had given the place forced growth; enormous numbers had also broken it down. Objects once so new, so concrete that it could never have occurred to anyone they stood for other things, had crumbled. Therefore, reflected Grebe, the secret of them was out. It was that they stood for themselves by agreement, and were natural and not unnatural by agreement, and when the things themselves collapsed the agreement became visible. What was it, otherwise, that kept cities from looking peculiar? Rome, that was almost permanent, did not give rise to thoughts like these. And was it abidingly real? But in Chicago, where the cycles were so fast and the familiar died, and rose changed, and died again in thirty years, you saw the common agreement or covenant, and you were forced to think about appearances and realities. —He remembered Raynor and he smiled; that was a clever boy—. Once you saw that a great many things became intelligible. For instance, why Mr. Field should conceive such a scheme. Of course, if people were to agree to create a millionaire, a real millionaire would come into existence. And if you wanted to know how Mr. Field was inspired to think of this, why, he had within sight of his kitchen window the chart, the very bones of a successful scheme—the El with its blue and green confetti of signals. People consenting to pay dimes and ride the crash box cars, it was a success. Yet how absurd it looked; how little real to start with. And yet Yerkes, the great financier who built it, had known that he could get people to agree to its reality. Viewed as itself, what a scheme of a scheme it seemed, how close to an appearance. Then why wonder at Mr. Field's idea? He had grasped a principle. And then Grebe remembered, too, that Mr. Yerkes had established the Yerkes Observatory and endowed it with millions. Now why did the notion reach him in his New York museum of a palace or his Aegean-bound yacht to give money to astronomers? Was he awed perhaps by the success of his bizarre enterprise and therefore ready to spend money to find out where in the universe being and seeming were identical? Yes, he wanted to know what abides; and is flesh Bible-grass; and offered money to be burned in the fire of suns. Okay, then, Grebe thought further, these things exist because people consent to exist with them—we have got so far—and also there is a reality which doesn't depend on consent but within which consent is a game. But what about need, the need that keeps so many vast thousands in position? You tell me that, you private little gentleman and *decent* soul—he used these words against himself scornfully. Why is the consent given to misery? And why so painfully ugly? Because there *is something* that is dismal and permanently ugly? Here he sighed and gave it up, and thought it was enough for the present moment that he had a real check in his pocket for a Mr. Green who could be real beyond question. If only his neighbors didn't think they had to conceal him.

This time he stopped at the second floor. He struck a match and found a door. Presently a man answered his knock and Grebe had the check ready and showed it even before he began. "Does Tulliver Green live here? I'm from the Relief."

The man narrowed the opening and spoke to someone at his back.

"Does he live here?"

"Uh-unh. No."

"Or anywhere in this building? He's a sick man and he can't come for his dough." He held the check up into the light, which was smoky and smelled of charred lard, and the man held off the brim of his cap to study it.

"Uh-unh. Never seen the name."

"There's nobody around here that uses crutches?"

He seemed to think, but it was Grebe's impression that he was simply waiting for a decent interval to pass.

"No, suh. Nobody I ever see."

"I've been looking for this man all afternoon," Grebe spoke out with sudden force, "and I'm going to have to carry this check back to the station. It seems strange not to be able to find a person to *give* him something when you're looking for him for a good reason. I suppose if I had bad news for him I'd find him quick enough."

There was a responsive motion in the other man's face. "That's right, I reckon."

"It almost doesn't do any good to have a name if you can't be found by it. It doesn't stand for anything. He might as well not have any," he went on, smiling. It was as much of a concession as he could make to his great desire to laugh.

"Well, now, there's a little old knot-back man I see once in a while. He might be the one you lookin' for. Downstairs."

"Where? Right side or left? Which door?"

"I don't know which. Thin face little knot-back with a stick."

But no one answered at any of the doors on the first floor. He went to the end of the corridor, searching by matchlight, and found only a stairless exit to the yard, a drop of about six feet. But there was a bungalow near the alley, an old house like Mr. Field's. To jump was unsafe. He ran from the front door, through the underground passage and into the yard. The place was occupied. There was a light through the curtains, upstairs. The name on the ticket under the broken, scoop-shaped mailbox was Green! He exultantly rang the bell and pressed against the locked door. Then the lock clicked faintly and a long staircase opened before him. Someone was slowly coming down—a woman. He had the impression in the weak light that she was shaping her hair as she came, making herself presentable, for he saw her arms raised. But it was for support that they were raised; she was feeling her way downward, down the walls, stumbling. Next he wondered about the pressure of her feet on the treads; she did not seem to be wearing shoes. And it was a freezing stairway. His ring had got her out of bed, perhaps, and she had forgotten to put them on. And then he saw that she was not only shoeless but naked; she was entirely naked, blundering down and talking to herself, a heavy woman, naked and drunk. The contact of her breasts on his coat made him go back against the door with a blind, rousing shock. See what he had tracked down, in his hunting game! He hadn't reckoned with such prey. The woman was saying to herself, furious with insult, "So I cain't——, huh? I'll show that—kin' I, cain't I."

What should he do now? Why, he should go. He should turn and go. He could not talk to this woman. He could not keep her standing naked in the cold. However, he could not go. He could not acknowledge that what he had found was too much for him.

He said, "Is this where Mr. Green lives?"

But she was still talking to herself and did not hear him.

"Is this Mr. Green's house?"

At last she turned her furious drunken glance on him. "What do you want?"

Again her eyes wandered from him, a dark wink of blood in their enraged brilliance. He wondered that she didn't feel the cold.

"I'm from the Relief."

"Awright, what?"

"I've got a check for Tulliver Green."

This time she heard him and put out her hand.

"No, no, for *Mister* Green. He's got to sign," he said ridiculously. How was he going to get Green's signature tonight!

"I'll take it."

He desperately shook his head, thinking of Mr. Field's precautions about identification. "I can't let you have it. It's for him. Is he upstairs?"

"Awright. Take it up yourself, you goddam fool."

Yes, he was a goddamned fool. Of course he could not go up. Green would be drunk and naked, too. And perhaps he would appear on the landing soon. He looked eagerly up to the narrow height of the green wall. Empty! It remained empty!

"Hell with you, then!" he heard her cry and suddenly saw, with burning self-ridicule, how far his desire had carried him. Then why didn't he leave? He made ready to go.

"I'll come tomorrow, tell him."

"Ah, hell with you. Don' never come. What you doin' here in the night-time. Don' come back." She yelled so that he saw the breadth of her tongue. She stood astride in the long cold box of the hall and held on to the bannister and the wall. The bungalow itself was shaped something like a box, an immense sentry box pointing into the freezing air and sharp, wintry lights.

"If you are Mrs. Green, I'll give you the check," he said, changing his mind.

"Give here, then." She took it, took the pen offered with it in her left hand, and tried to write on the wall. He looked around, almost as though to see whether his madness was being observed, and came near believing that someone was standing on a mountain of used tires in the auto-junking shop next door.

"But are you Mrs. Green?" he now thought to ask. But she was already climbing the stairs with the check, and it was too late, if he had made an error, if he was now in trouble, to undo the thing. However, a moment came, illuminated from the greatest height, when you could not refuse to yield a check, a municipal check, and therefore his worry stung him only superficially. Besides, though she might not be Mrs. Green, he was convinced that Mr. Green was upstairs. Whoever she was, the woman stood for Green whom this time he was not to see. "Well, you silly bastard," he said to himself, "so you found him. So what?" But it was important that there was a real Mr. Green whom they could not keep him from reaching because he seemed to come as an emissary from hostile appearances. And though the self-ridicule was slow to diminish, and his face, throat and chest, arms, his whole body blazed with it, he had, nevertheless, a reason for elation, too. "For after all," he said, "I *did* get to him."

Bernard Malamud

THE LOAN

A Story

The sweet, the heady smell of Lieb's white bread drew customers in droves long before the loaves were baked. Alert behind the counter, Bessie, Lieb's second wife, discerned a stranger among them, a frail, gnarled man with a hard hat who hung, disjoined, at the edge of the crowd. Though the stranger looked harmless enough among the aggressive purchasers of baked goods, she was at once concerned. Her glance questioned him but he signaled with a deprecatory nod of his hatted head that he would wait—glad to (forever)—though his face glittered with misery. If suffering had marked him, he no longer sought to conceal the sign; the shining was his own—him—now. So he frightened Bessie.

She made quick hash of the customers, and when they, in response to her annihilating service, were gone, she returned to him her stare.

He tipped his hat. "Pardon me—Kobotsky. Is Lieb the baker here?"

"Who Kobotsky?"

"An old friend"—frightening her further.

"From where?"

"From long ago."

"What do you want to see him?"

The question insulted, so Kobotsky was reluctant to say.

As if drawn into the shop by the magic of a voice, the baker, shirtless, appeared from the rear. His pink, fleshy arms had been deep in dough. For a hat he wore jauntily a flour-covered, brown paper sack. His peering glasses were dusty with flour, and the inquisitive face white with it so that he resembled a paunchy ghost; but the ghost, through the glasses, was Kobotsky, not he.

"Kobotsky," the baker cried almost with a sob, for it was so many years gone Kobotsky reminded him of, when they were both at least young, and circumstances were altered—ah, different. Unable, for sentimental reasons, to refrain from smarting tears, he jabbed them away with a thrust of the hand.

Kobotsky removed his hat—he had grown all but bald where Lieb was gray—and patted his flushed forehead with an immaculate handkerchief.

Lieb sprang forward with a stool. "Sit, Kobotsky."

"Not here," Bessie murmured.

"Customers," she explained to Kobotsky. "Soon comes the supper rush."

"Better in the back," nodded Kobotsky.

So that was where they went, happier for the privacy. But it happened that no customers came so Bessie went in to hear.

Kobotsky sat enthroned in a private corner of the room, stoop-shouldered, his black coat and hat on, the stiff, gray-veined hands drooping over thin thighs. Lieb, peering through full moons, eased his bones on a flour sack. Bessie lent an attentive ear but the visitor was dumb. Embarrassed, Lieb did the talking: ah, of old times. The world was new. We were, Kobotsky, young. Do you remember how both together, immigrants out of steerage, we registered in night school?

"Haben, hatte, gehabt." He cackled at the sound of it.

No word from the gaunt one on the tall stool. Bessie fluttered around an impatient duster. She shot a glance into the shop: empty.

Lieb, acting the life of the party, recited, to cheer his friend: "'Come, said the wind to the trees one day, Come over the meadows with me and play.' Remember, Kobotsky?"

Bessie sniffed aloud. "Lieb, the bread!"

The baker bounced up, strode over to the gas oven and pulled one of the tiered doors down. Just in time he yanked out the trays of brown breads in hot pans, and set them on the tin-top worktable.

Bessie clucked at the narrow escape.

Lieb peered into the shop. "Customers," he said triumphantly. Flushed, she went in. Kobotsky, with wetted lips, watched her go. Lieb set to work molding the risen dough into two trays of pans. Soon the bread was baking, but Bessie was back.

The honey odor of the new loaves distracted Kobotsky. He deeply breathed the sweet fragrance, as if this were the first air he was tasting, and even beat his fist against his chest at the delicious smell.

"Oh, my God," he all but wept. "Wonderful."

"With tears," Lieb said humbly, pointing to the large pot of dough.

Kobotsky nodded.

For thirty years, the baker explained, he had been never with a penny to his name. One day, out of misery, he had wept into the dough and thereafter his bread was so sweet it brought customers in from everywhere.

"My cakes they don't like so much, but my bread and rolls they run miles to buy."

Kobotsky blew his nose, then peeked into the shop: three customers. "Lieb"—a whisper.

Despite himself the baker stiffened.

The visitor's eyes swept back to Bessie out front, then, under raised brows, questioned the baker.

Lieb, however, remained mute.

Kobotsky coughed clear his throat. "Lieb, I need two hundred dollars." His voice broke.

Lieb slowly sank onto the sack. He knew—had known. From the minute of Kobotsky's appearance he had weighed in his thoughts this against the remembrance of the lost and bitter hundred, fifteen years ago. Kobotsky swore he had repaid it, Lieb said no. Afterwards a broken friendship. It took years to blot out of the system the memoried outrage.

Kobotsky bowed his head.

At least admit you were wrong, thought Lieb, waiting a cruelly long time.

Kobotsky stared at his crippled hands. Once a cutter of furs, driven by arthritis out of the business.

Lieb gazed too. He breathed with pain on the right side. The button of a truss bit into his belly. Both eyes were cloudy with cataracts. Though the doctor swore he would see after the operation, he feared otherwise. He sighed. The wrong was in the past. Forgiven: forgiven at the sight of him.

"For myself, positively, but she"—Lieb nodded shopwise—"is a second wife. Everything is in her name." He held up empty hands.

Kobotsky's eyes were shut.

"But I will ask her—" Lieb looked doubtful.

"My wife needs—"

The baker raised a palm. "Don't speak."

"Tell her—"

"Leave it to me."

He seized the broom and circled the room, raising clouds of white dust.

When Bessie, breathless, got back she threw one look at them, and with tightened lips, waited adamant.

Lieb hastily scoured the pots in the iron sink, stored the bread pans under the table and stacked the fragrant loaves. He put one eye to the slot of the oven: baking, all baking.

Facing Bessie, he broke into a sweat so hot it momentarily stunned him.

Kobotsky squirmed atop the stool.

"Bessie," said the baker at last, "this is my old friend."

She nodded gravely.

Kobotsky lifted his hat.

"His mother—God bless her—gave me many times a plate of hot soup. Also when I came to this country, for years I ate at his table. His wife is a very fine person—Dora—you will someday meet her—"

Kobotsky softly groaned.

"So why I didn't meet her yet?" Bessie said, still, after a dozen years, jealous of the first wife's prerogatives.

"You will."

"Why didn't I?"

"Lieb—" pleaded Kobotsky.

"Because I didn't see her myself fifteen years," Lieb admitted.

"Why not?" she pounced.

Lieb paused. "A mistake."

Kobotsky turned away.

"My fault," said Lieb.

"Because you never go anyplace," Bessie spat out. "Because you live always in the shop. Because it means nothing to you to have friends."

Lieb solemnly agreed.

"Now she is sick," he announced. "The doctor must operate. This will cost two hundred dollars. I promised Kobotsky—"

Bessie screamed.

Kobotsky got off the stool, hat in hand.

Pressing a palm to her bosom, Bessie lifted her arm to her eyes. She tottered. They both ran forward to catch her but she did not fall. Kobotsky retreated quickly to the stool and Lieb returned to the sink.

Bessie, her face like the inside of a loaf, quietly addressed the visitor. "I have pity for your wife but we can't help you. I am sorry, Mr. Kobotsky, we are poor people, we don't have the money."

"A mistake," Lieb cried, enraged.

Bessie strode over to the shelf and tore out a bill box. She dumped its contents on the table, the papers flying everywhere.

"Bills," she shouted.

Kobotsky hunched his shoulders.

"Bessie, we have in the bank—"

"No—"

"I saw the bankbook."

"So what if you saw a few dollars, so have you got life insurance?"

He made no answer.

"Can you get?" she taunted.

The front door banged. It banged often. The shop was crowded with customers clamoring for bread. Bessie stomped out to wait on them.

In the rear the wounded stirred. Kobotsky, with bony fingers, buttoned his overcoat.

"Sit," sighed the baker.

"Lieb, I am sorry—"

"Sit."

Kobotsky sat, his face lit with sadness.

When Bessie finally got rid of the rush, Lieb stirred, went into the shop. He spoke to her quietly, almost in a whisper, and she answered as quietly, but it took only a minute to set them quarreling.

Kobotsky slipped off the stool. He went to the sink, wet half his handkerchief and held it to his dry eyes. Folding the handkerchief he put it away in his overcoat pocket then took out a small penknife and quickly pared his fingernails.

As he entered the shop, Lieb was pleading with Bessie, reciting the embittered hours of his toil, the enduring drudgery. And now that he had a cent to his name, what was there to live for if he could not share it with a dear friend? But Bessie had her back to him.

"Please," Kobotsky said, "don't fight. I go away now."

Lieb gazed at him in exasperation, Bessie stayed with head averted.

"Yes," Kobotsky sighed, "the money I wanted for Dora, but she is not sick, Lieb, she is dead."

"Ai," Lieb cried, wringing his hands.

Bessie faced the visitor, pallid.

"Not now," he spoke kindly, "five years ago."

Lieb groaned.

"The money I need for a stone on her grave. She never had a stone. This Sunday is five years that she is dead and every year I promise her, Dora, this year I will give you a stone, and every year I give her nothing."

The grave, to his everlasting shame, lay uncovered before all eyes. He had long ago paid a fifty-dollar deposit for a headstone with her name on it in clearly chiseled letters but had never got the rest of the money. If there wasn't one thing to do with it there was always another: the first year an operation, the second he couldn't work, imprisoned again by arthritis, the third a widowed sister lost her only son and the little Kobotsky earned had to help support her, the fourth incapacitated by boils that made him ashamed to walk out into the street, this year he was at least working, but only for just enough to eat and sleep, so Dora still lay without a stone, and for aught he knew he would someday return to the cemetery and find her grave gone.

Tears sprang into the baker's eyes. One gaze at Bessie's face—at the odd looseness of neck and body—told him that she too was moved. Ah, he had won out. She would now say yes, give the money, and they would then all sit down at the table and eat supper together.

But Bessie, though weeping, shook her head, and before they could guess what, had blurted out the story of her afflictions: how the Bolsheviki came, when she was a little girl, and dragged her darling father into the snowy fields without his shoes on; the shots scattered the blackbirds in the trees and the snow oozed blood; how, when she was married a year, her husband, a sweet and gentle man, an educated accountant—rare in those days and that place—died of typhus in an epidemic in Warsaw; and how she, abandoned in her grief, years later found sanctuary in the home of an older brother in Germany, who sacrificed his own chances to send her, before the war, to America, and as a result, in all probability ended up with his wife and daughter and her two blessed children in Hitler's incinerators.

"So I came to America and met here a baker, a poor man—who was always in his life poor—without a penny and without enjoyment in his life, and I married him, God knows why, and with my both hands, working day and night, I fixed up for him his piece of business and we make now, after twelve years, a little living. But Lieb is a sick man, with weak lungs, and eyes that he needs an operation, and this is not yet everything. Suppose, God forbid, that he died, what will I do alone by myself? Where will I go, where, and who will take care of me if I have nobody?"

The baker, who had often heard this tale, munched, as he listened, chunks of soft white bread.

When she had finished he tossed the shell of the loaf away. Kobotsky, at the end, had held his hands over his ears.

With copious tears streaming from her eyes, Bessie raised her head and suspiciously sniffed the air. Screeching suddenly, she ran into the rear and with a cry wrenched open the oven door. A cloud of smoke billowed out at her. The loaves in the trays were blackened bricks—charred corpses.

Kobotsky and the baker embraced and sighed over their lost youth. They pressed mouths together and parted forever.

March 1958

Wallace Markfield

THE COUNTRY OF THE CRAZY HORSE

A Story

As the train began the long crawl under the tunnel to Brooklyn I thought again of the crazy horse. It was Saturday morning, and all the mothers sat before the stoop on bridge chairs, opening tangerines and helping themselves from a big bag of polly seeds, budging not one inch as the super shot his dirty looks about and warned of summonses for each and every one who blocked his path to the cellar. The movie-house was not yet open; my crew and I waited, waited for the moment to draw near, killing the time with marvelous deathfalls—the slow, coin-flipping sag of George Raft; the sharp flinch and spin of the settler as the arrow strikes; the stool pigeon's slow crumple as they cut him down in the phone booth, behind the billboard, atop the church steps.

When all of a sudden the horse came clopping down the street. Heavy and handsome he was, the kind Buck Jones and Hoot Gibson sat, looking smart enough to pull you out of quicksand or loosen your bonds with his teeth, and white as a centaur. He bucked and wove through the traffic, taking little hip-hops up and down the sidewalk, kicking at the hedges that lined the one- and two-family houses. The cluster of mothers broke and scattered, then joined together again to form a circle around us like a wagon train. One, wilder even than the rest, made a run for her boy's two-wheeler, crying, for no good reason, "What did he need it for? What, tell me, what?" From an open window someone sloshed a pail of water. We began throwing pebbles and bottle caps and flipping little cardboard squares with our rubber band guns, but they fell short. The laundryman turned the corner in his truck and let go on the horn. Seymour, my best friend, who could imitate anything, brought up from deep within his chest the spang of bullets on rocks and trumpeting of wild bull elephants spotting the white hunter. Somehow stung by this, the horse whinnied back. He lowered his head, took delicate little steps to the sidewalk and stopped before the house of Ringleman, the dentist. He reared up, he flared his nostrils and showed his terrible teeth. Then, in a movement that seemed as precise and formal as a dance step, he made a long, low leap. And impaled himself upon the iron fence.

They removed the carcass later, on an open truck, and washed down Ringleman's lawn with a hose. My mother dragged me upstairs, bore me into the bedroom and caught fiercely at the neckband of my shirt. Her face trembled, and she opened and closed her mouth as if there lay in her mind some fearful pronouncement no tongue could utter. I saw the horse heave and rear between us again, his eyes glittering like the future. I stand, awaiting my mother's explanation for all that has passed. But there is only her hand, heavy as brass upon my face, and the cry, "Look at him. Feel him. How perspired he is, how it drips from him!"

Two stops now from my station and I am drenched with sweat again. I move to another seat, fleeing the fan's powerful draft, conscious of how vulnerable I am, of my tendency to colds and swollen glands, of the way I load my stomach with rich and spicy foods. From across the aisle a woman jumps up and, marvelously balancing against the pitching and bucketing, looms over me. She is plump and moon-faced and there is a tenderness in her eyes, as though she would like to stroke me as I sit there. A swift half-turn, a languid shrug, and she allows herself to fall heavily upon the seat next to mine, with a smile that stretches from one end of the world to the other. Her hands begin to flutter nervously, and I move closer to the window, pretending to lose myself in the boring vista of playgrounds and cemeteries and television antennae that spear the last light like crucifixes. She is stooped over, working very hard and furtively at something; once, she lifts her head to smile again, as though there was a secret between us. I watch her like a grim eavesdropper, awaiting the fulfillment of events. She strains, she wriggles, she falls back, spent. Then, gathering all her forces for one compulsive effort, she reaches deep into the straw cushion and draws out a maimed magazine.

"I used to love to read," she says at last, blinking her mad, moist brown eyes.

I nod profoundly and slowly spread my arms, the gesture of one who sees no escape from his miserable existence.

"But now, who has the mind for it? And every day to the hospital, that can knock anybody out. Not that the traveling bothers me. It's the going up and down to change trains. But it's the very least I can do for him. My brother-in-law. Oh, I knew already, even before the operation, when he complained that he can't eat any more, that he lost his appetite. Because that was an eater! Yeah, yeah! I knew already when they finished, I looked at the doctor's face. I didn't have to ask. They opened him up, they took a look, and they sewed him up again. And you know what he got it from? From one thing only. Aggravation."

"Oh yes, oh yes," I chant liturgically. "I can imagine, I can believe it. Aggravation. . . ." Till the age of fourteen I had been certain it was a Yiddish word.

"Since he's sick I don't give a damn for anything. I walk out of the house without even—you should pardon the expression—a girdle on. Though before I complain I should first bite my tongue off. A person has his health, he has everything."

"That's it. To be healthy is the main thing," I echo. Then, thank God, I recognize my station, like the beginning of an old movie, and I hustle for the door.

"Goodbye, good luck," she howls after me. "In whatever you undertake. You're a very, very nice person."

I feel a tickle of nervous excitement as I enter the streets. There's a brand-new community center where my old lot was and a hive of garden apartments whose brick is colored the sickly pink of a rabbit's eye. I stare inside the picture windows, into each living room with its Van Gogh sunflowers, its kidney-shaped coffee tables, its gigantic mohair chairs with their cold unrumpled covers. For a moment the acres of cement under my feet seem to turn into wall-to-wall carpeting, and I have a sudden impulse to shout something wild and crazy—*"God is Love!"* or *"Sauve qui peut!"* But I content myself with the idea as Flatbush sprawls vast and arctic and baffling before me, holding only the etherized silence of a museum. Not a gurgle anywhere, not a cheep, not even the yap of a backyard dog. I fondle the reassuring bulk of the candy box under my arm, dreaming of myself as a good son, an accountant, a chiropodist, a professional certainly, one who phones his mother each day from the office, even before his wife. At that moment I hear a cry that sounds as though it rose from a throat clogged by blood and rage. I stand, dumbfounded, till I catch the one terrible word, the speaking of the unspeakable: "Ma!" A yowl, a lunatic roar and then, with rising fervor, "Ma, open the window, Ma!"

I move along, tense and poised as a tightrope walker. Every corner, every garage, every alleyway and clothesline is an announcement of old sins. Here I broke, here I tore, here I mocked, here I raged, here I stole. . . . I near the candy store where I'd once applied my criminal mind to loose cigarettes and comic books, fighting it out with old man Teller over the water-bag I'd hurled into his fountain. "Oh, you killed him," his wife announced when the stroke came to finish him, "you ate him up alive, you and yours." Yet business was business, and she went on selling me my cockemamies, my skate keys and pencil boxes, and when she had to, sent me out to pick up a few pennies calling people down to the phone.

A powerful longing for an egg-cream assails me; I assure myself that it will wash down the nauseous sense of homelessness. With the chilly, menacing air of a movie gunfighter I walk past the little group of shmoozers clumped around the magazine racks and plant my elbows on the fountain. I give my order to the runty owner, making foolish conversation as he works the syrup dispenser. "It's a very strange thing," I say, "but I notice that you just cannot get a decent egg-cream in Manhattan. Why is that? After all, chocolate is chocolate, milk is milk and seltzer is seltzer.

He puts the drink before me and whispers dramatically, "It's all the syrup. What I use, I have to pay forty cents more on the gallon."

I let out a cunning, portentous "Ah!" Then I drain the glass in two long swigs and finish up with a big fig newton. The mixture turns bitter in my mouth. I wonder if, somehow, I have not been taking in the body and blood of old man Teller.

He wipes his hands on a soiled apron. "A malted," he moans. "They don't know how to make it and they don't want to know. You got to freeze the milk. Otherwise, tastes like *pishachs.*"

"Yes, oh yes, now I see." I nod my head as though I'd just heard the seven proofs for the existence of God. "No wonder! You freeze the milk. Yes!"

I put down a quarter and he flicks the change at me. Swiveling around fiercely, he lets out a bellow at a young wise-guy who blocks the doorway and makes too free with the comic books. "Moron," he yells, in rage and despair, "the whole store should burn with you in it!" He coughs and coughs, choking on a cold lump of grief.

"Kids," I soothe, as I stalk to the door. "Kids."

"Sure," he says, wiping and wiping at the marble counter. "But he's old enough to die."

I quicken my steps for the last two dark blocks, palms perspiring, whistling tonelessly through clenched teeth, like a man getting ready for his bride. Even from the corner I can make out my mother's face; it seems to have the eerie luminosity of one of Chagall's angels. I keep to the shadow, but she spots me anyway, hanging out the window to make the neighborhood ring with her "Sonny!" The nitwit yell shakes me up, as it did in the old days, when it would sour my life on the streets, following me wherever I went to catch me *in flagrante delicto*—with a stolen deposit bottle in my hand or a snotty word on my lips. Methodically, I check myself for failings: Am I wearing a hat against the changing weather? Do I strain my eyes on too many movies? Paying fancy prices at the all-night delicatessens? Ignoring overdue notices from the library? And roughage? Does my system get enough roughage? All clear, and I enter the lobby, where the super has long since given up his mop-work against the track of dogs and baby buggies.

"Welcome, stranger," my mother says. "I'm glad you still remember how to get here."

She moves in for the kiss, lowering her head and placing both hands on my shoulders. I block her deftly with the candy box. She averts her eyes, as though it was a telegram announcing disaster.

"No?" I threaten, making a mock grab. "Then here and now it goes out and down, down, into the incinerator."

"Take it home," she pleads. "Do me a favor and take it home." Her enlarged and plaintive eyes fix on the walls behind me, where my honor cards and graduation pictures hang. "He has a few cents and he must spend them. That's him. Even when he was a child."

"Don't you worry." I laugh a big booming Edward Arnold laugh, indicating I can afford this and much more.

"Sidney!" she summons. "Come! He's here!"

And my father drifts in, bearing the magazine section from last Sunday's *Times*. All his life he's never been able to catch up with the papers. His face is overcast with bafflement and a vague horror; at any moment he seems to expect the raising of my hand against him. Ten weeks ago he got himself a coronary, and he keeps rubbing his left side and nodding at me, as if to say, "Now you're a wise-guy, but wait, only wait a while." He leans over, plucking at my sleeve. "That suit," he snorts in derision. "Where did you pick up the bargain?"

My mother winks and bites her lip. "What's the matter?" she asks, a little shrilly. "It's a nice suit. Honest to God, I think it's very, very nice on him."

"Fine," my father grunts. "You bought it. You like it. Wear it in good health."

"In the *best* of health," my mother murmurs, looking passionately into my eyes. "Now come. You'll go inside, you'll have a bite. I have pot cheese. I have sour cream. I can slice in some vegetables."

So it's been, as long as I remember. You can die before you'll get a piece of meat in my mother's house. Still, for all her Gandhi ways my mother keeps alive a marvelous image of herself as a hotsy-totsy cooker, a wonder-woman with stuffed derma and sweetbreads and Old Country soups.

I mumble something to the effect that I have eaten, that I put away a big meal uptown, a costly meal.

Bitterly, tenderly, she says, "You come visit your mother and you eat on the outside."

"Ah, come on, Ma. Ma, come on." I hang my head and scrape my feet like a movie adolescent.

"I shopped. I prepared. I made a special trip."

"Don't force it." My father turns both palms up in his man-of-peace gesture. "You did your duty. You did the right thing."

"You'll take some home with you."

"I'll take."

"I'll wrap a nice little bundle and you'll enjoy it later."

"I'll enjoy."

We move out of the foyer, my mother pulling ahead and steering a desperate course for the kitchen. "Wait, Ma, wait," I tell her. "Why don't we go and sit in the living room? Come, we'll sit in the living room."

"Hah!" my mother cries in terror and disbelief. She back-tracks fast to cut off the living room door. "It's an icebox in there. I had to shut off the steam, it was turning all the drapes yellow. So help me God."

"Oh no, you don't!" I link arms, imprisoning her frail and fearful flesh and lead her tenderly into the living room's cluttered bleakness. We have not sat together here since the druggist came to claim I'd laid hands on his crazy daughter.

I didn't remember so many flowers. Lilies mostly, though here and there a few fat roses. Wherever I look there is the image of a flower. On the draperies, on the seat covers, on the lamp shades. Imbedded in plaster wreaths on the wall. Spilling all over my mother's apron and housedress. I begin to get a headache and breathing comes harder, as though they're draining oxygen from the air.

Then we get down to business. My father opens with a "What's new?"

To which I make reply, "What should be new?"

This stumps them. They expect more from me, their prophet and augur, their Hamlet and Tamburlaine. From the end table my Bar Mitzvah picture smirks at me. Hey, hey, he calls, this back-talker, this crafty fatso, where's that family chronicle you began at twelve? The ball of tin foil you were saving? And the instruction book in Judo? Gone now, with the old NRA Blue Eagle, with Dickie Moore, with hard-faced Frankie Darro and Garfield in his blackened T-shirt.

My father unfolds his magazine section; he has decided to readmit the present. My mother, in desperation, talks of aunts and uncles and cousins long forgotten. She permits nothing to rest in peace, she treads upon every grave in the family plot. This one owes her money, that one brought no gift to my father as he lay in his hospital bed. They have used her, they have sucked her and drained her, they have turned her heart into a huge festering sore. It's almost beautiful to watch the way she boils and blazes, a regular Old Testament queen, fire-eyed and calling down curses. She plays the clown too, getting her satire across with deviling malice, fingers pulling and probing as though they were molding effigies. And I begin to see how much I've taken from her. I catch a gesture I used at a party, a gibe I delivered the week before, a whine that enters my voice in cafeteria debates. I feel like an anthology of old sorrows.

Spent, consumed, a clawed hand punishing her breast, my mother says, "Strangers. Sometimes they treat you better than your own."

My father warms to the theme. "She's telling me something new. Strangers. When I was in the hospital they couldn't do enough for me. I'm not exaggerating. The nurse once saw that I couldn't digest the milk they were giving out. She made a special trip to get me a little tea when the kitchen was closed. And they would all talk to me. Do you know that when I left, the social worker came over and shook my hand and gave me a kiss? She told me, 'We're all crazy about you, we love you, but we don't want to see you again, you hear. That's an order.'" He laughs, aroused and deeply pleased. "Which reminds me. Tomorrow, without fail I want to give Mostag a ring. He was the one in the next bed who let me use his electric shaver. That's a prince, a real prince. To look at him, would you believe he's worth close to a quarter of a million?"

"'To look at him'? What do you mean 'to look at him'?" my mother mimics. "When you would sleep I used to sit and talk to him for an hour at a time and he'd have a big, big steamer basket by the bed with fruits and nuts and candy and he wouldn't once say, 'Here, take a piece.' Did you ever notice, the more they have—"

"Come on, get away!" Violently, my father shakes his paper. "I assure you, if you had helped yourself he would not have begrudged it to you. Men don't think of those things, it's not in their make-up."

"You don't let a person sit like a dummy. I didn't need his piece of candy. Thank God, I can afford to go out and buy a box. But be a sport, at least make the gesture."

"You know a lot! As far as I'm concerned and from the way he acted to me, why he's as decent as they come. Money or no money, you'll find goddamn few people who'll run around when you can't wait for the nurse and empty your you-know-what for you; goddamn few!"

My father's eyes are shining, burning with all his energies, and a queer look comes over his face. It's the look of a small boy shaking hands with a cop or a cowboy star, the look he'd get when he spoke of Debs and Norman Thomas, then F.D.R. and the manager of his local. In an instant he can shed his self, ecstatic with mediocrity. He becomes the one who sits in the back, always in the back of group photographs, the one who holds the umbrella over the principal speaker at a street rally or springs from the heart of a crowd to joggle the assassin's gun. . . . Years ago he broke down and wept scalding tears at the dinner table. And when we begged and pleaded for the reason he ground his teeth and quivered and answered, "You didn't see. You didn't read. Westbrook Pegler. What he had the gall to say about the Roosevelt boys!"

My mother rises. She's spotted the imprint of a finger on a window pane and she chases after it, relentless as Old Dutch cleanser. Then, swaying gently from her heels to her toes, she utters a great wrenching groan. "Tell me," she says, "do you remember Mr. Wasserman?"

I indicate my uncertainty with a limp disparaging hand.

"Ah, you should certainly recall," my mother says, a shallow sweetness invading her tones. "He lived near the Parkway, he used to be here day and night. The one who made your suit for the graduation. Everybody talked about it, they couldn't get over his workmanship."

"A mechanic," my father announces. "A pair of golden hands."

"Last week he called me. I couldn't get off the phone. I had to pretend the bell rang, and excuse myself."

Any moment now I know the shaft will come.

"So—" She draws and holds a long breath and her face pales and swells. "Two days ago. A hemorrhage. Go imagine."

"Never, never," my father cries, taking over. "In a million years, never. He wasn't a man, he was a giant. In the old days, when everybody was stretched out from the heat he'd be working the presser. And then first, late, late at night, he'd run around to pick up, to deliver. Yes, yes, oh yes, he was going to be president of the Society, he had big plans, he was going to build and renovate."

My father hunches forward. His words become thick and hazy, his fingers spread and whiten by their grip on his paper. He works and works to bring his awful feelings forth, but it's no go. Then names come scuttling through his mind. One by one he reels them off, a whole Book of the Dead. Kornfeld and Baumgarten . . . Ellinger and Glick . . . Horwitz and Kaplan . . . Old Man Fine, who chased a daughter out of the house for wearing a sleeveless dress . . . Rosen, scarred long ago by gangster acid . . . they've gone out now, the men my father loved, each and every one of them, who had never been before and would never be again, like brilliant stars at the end of night. And what people they were, what snap, what class and quality they had! Who's to keep the Society's books now, send out post cards for unveilings, throw the first clods of earth, and trim the cluttering weeds from grave beds? Nah! Their children were no children, keeping nothing up, paying no dues, coming to meetings only to eat and make stupid jokes.

"You know," my father says thoughtfully, "they'll send a check for five hundred dollars when I die. Thank God, it won't cost you a penny."

"Poo-poo!" My mother spits with a dry mouth against evil eyes and menaces.

"You think he'll bother to say *Yizkor* once in a while?"

"He'll say, he'll say," my mother assures.

A cold wave of penance moves through the room. I feel suddenly like promising all kinds of things: long visits, phone calls to relations, a greater interest in the fortunes of the family, a donation to the Synagogue. My father leans back against the chair. How bad he looks, I realize, how narrow and gray his face, how thin his hair and flabby his jaws, how cruelly shaven his cheeks.

"It's time, it's time," I announce, like a nervous innkeeper.

They rise with me, my father laying aside his paper finally, my mother commenting on the shortness of my stay, promising fantastic dishes, a veritable love-feast for my return. At the door my father describes a new way of returning to the city, and forces me to wait while he writes down the trains and stations, pointing out that I can save myself an extra fare.

"It's the 'D' train," he bellows, as I flee into the hall. "Make sure!"

"I'll make sure," I promise, waving and clutching the directions like a passport.

I've barely made the corner when I seem to hear my name called and the rush of heavy feet. What, I wonder, is it my old crazy horse again, clopping out of the past? Again, the calling of my name, and my mother catches up, proffering a soiled shopping bag.

"The pot cheese and cream. And a few cans of sardines. I made a nice package."

"Ma, Ma," I say. "For God's sake, Ma."

"What does it hurt? You'll enjoy."

"I'll enjoy." I give her a furry kiss and walk away, faster and faster, the shopping bag bulging against my side like an obscene growth.

Dan Jacobson

THE EXAMPLE OF LIPI LIPPMANN

A Story

In Lyndhurst, if a Gentile spoke enviously to a Jew about how rich the Jews of Lyndhurst were, how clever they were, how well they did in business, the reply was often made, "Well, it's not really true about all the Jews. Just look at Lipi Lippmann!" No one, not even the biggest anti-Semite in the world, could say that Lipi Lippmann was rich or clever or did well in business.

Lipi Lippmann once said that the Jews of Lyndhurst should pay him to remain poor, his poverty was so useful in arguments. But the joke was received in silence; it was felt to be in bad taste. The Jews of Lyndhurst were ready to use Lipi Lippmann's poverty to propitiate an envious Gentile, but they were ashamed of him nevertheless; ashamed of his old Ford lorry, laden with fruit and vegetables, going from door to door; ashamed that Lipi was the only white man who bickered among the colored and Indian hawkers at dawn in the market place. Every other Jew in town was a licensed wholesaler or a licensed hotelkeeper, a licensed dentist or a licensed doctor; but Lipi Lippman had remained nothing but a licensed hawker. And his only son, Nathan, was nothing but a licensed radio operator in the South African Airways, who still did not earn enough to support his aging father. What a ridiculous job Nathan's seemed to be, anyway, for a son of Lipi Lippmann! "How's the airman?" people sometimes asked Lipi patronizingly, when they saw him; and Lipi looked up at the sky, wrinkling his brow, and said, "He's fine, still up in the air." In fact, Nathan had been in the ground staff for a long time, but Lipi did not know this, for he and Nathan wrote to each other so seldom. Lipi himself had never flown in an airplane; he never listened to the radio either.

Lipi was a small man, with the head of a large one: his cheekbones were strong and prominent, his nose was bony and arched, his eyes were set wide apart. He was a widower, and lived by himself in a tiny single-storied house in one of the oldest suburbs of Lyndhurst. Around Lipi's house were houses as small and as shabby as his own, with the same high *stoeps* in front, and the same iron roofs above. In the back yards behind the houses there lived troops of raucous African servants who, with their dirty bare feet and torn clothes, were as different from the trim, white-overalled servants in the wealthier suburbs as the employers in the one district were from those in the other. All Lipi's neighbors in the street were Afrikaner railwaymen or mine workers, and their children sometimes shouted *"Koelie-Jood"* after him—*Koelie* being an insulting term for an Indian, and thus being a disdainful way of referring to Lipi's trade. But the mothers of these children always waited for Lipi to return home at the end of the afternoon, when they bought from him at cut-prices the softened carrots and moulting cabbages he had been unable to sell elsewhere. Then the children also came round, and asked Lipi if he had any *ertjies* for them. And often enough Lipi would produce a handful of pea-pods which were no longer green, but gray and pale brown or white, and distribute them among the clamoring children. When they had dispersed, he would pack the empty crates neatly together in the back of the van, tie them down with rope, and go into his house.

Nobody followed him inside it. Once inside, he took off his hat, collar, and tie (he always wore rather stiff detachable collars, even in the fiercest heat), and washed himself in the small, smelly bathroom. His "girl"—a withered Basuto woman whose grandchildren played about in the back yard—served him his supper. Soup, meat and vegetables, and stewed fruit followed one another in unvarying succession, while Lipi slowly read the paper from front to back. After supper he sat on his *stoep,* with the light burning above him, listening to the street noises and the shunting of trains in the distance. He never sat up late. Saturday was his busiest day, so he went to synagogue only on the high festivals; but he always went to the evening meetings of the local Zionist society. At these meetings he sat in the front row, listening intently and nodding his large head, almost like a man at prayer, to every word that was said.

That nod was Lipi's characteristic gesture; it seemed to be a gesture of profound acquiescence, of acceptance; yet it never brought to an end the debate he appeared to be having with himself. He nodded at Zionist meetings, he nodded when he drove his lorry, when he bargained with the housewives, when he sat alone on his *stoep*. And he nodded in the same way when he came home from work one day and found that while he had been away and the girl had been paying her regular afternoon visit to a friend in the back yard of a nearby house, someone had broken into his house and robbed him of everything that could be put into a trunk and carried out of the house. Almost all his clothes were gone, including his best *shul*-going suit; so was the money-box in which he kept the few pounds he earned one day and laid out for stock the next day. The thief or thieves had also taken the single bottle of whiskey Lipi kept hidden in his wardrobe; an old gold fobwatch and chain he had bought on the occasion of his marriage, and which he had not worn for years; two silver napkin-rings, with his own and his wife's initials engraved upon them; a couple of tablecloths. Someone, it was clear, had been unable to believe that Lipi was as poor as he had appeared to be; someone must have had the fantasy that Lipi was a miser, and had been hoarding money and valuables over the years. Whoever it was—a black man or a white one—was no doubt disillusioned now; and he had left the marks of what looked like rage in the splintered drawers thrown upon the floor, the razor-rents in the armchair in the front room and the mattress in the bedroom, the wanton destruction of the basin in the bathroom.

Because the basin was smashed, Lipi went into the kitchen and washed himself carefully at the sink, and then, in his shirtsleeves, came into the front room of the house. All day it had been hot; now, with the sun hanging low in the west, the heat seemed to have a settled, brooding quality, quite different in its intensity from the morning's direct glare, or the throb of noon. The windows of the room were wide open, but no breeze came in through them; it was as warm indoors as it was outside. Lipi stood in the middle of the room, staring at the drawers of the sideboard upside down on the floor, and the hideous lumps of blue and white stuffing protruding from the ripped armchair. A strange, cracked sound came from his breast; this sharp noise was followed by a sigh, as if something broken inside him sought to knit itself together again. He hunched his shoulders higher and went to the window. His shoulders shook, and again he uttered that abrupt sound, which was again followed by the faint complaining wheeze.

Lipi was laughing. When his girl came back she found him standing at the window, looking across the *stoep* and garden into the bit of street beyond. Seeing the wreckage in the room and the blood on Lipi's knuckles, she thought he had been in a fight with the intruders; and Lipi could not explain to her how he had laughed and bitten at his own knuckles, laughed and bitten at himself, like a madman, with the smashed room behind him.

It was the girl who went running to the neighbors with the news, and the neighbors who telephoned the police. The police found Lipi standing alone in the room. While one man in the police squad went around looking for fingerprints, the other, perturbed by the fixity of Lipi's expression and the sudden jerky nods of his head, tried to get him to sit down. But Lipi would not move; he did not seem to know what the man wanted of him. Readily enough, however, when the policemen asked him to make a statement, he began to detail what had been taken from him. There was his best suit, and the other clothes; his gold watch and the bottle of whiskey; there was his money-box.

"Money-box?" the policeman interrupted. "What kind of money-box? How much was in it? Where did you keep it?"

"How much was in it?" Lipi repeated. He laughed loudly, and his eyes stared forward without expression, looking beyond the policeman. "A fortune, what do you think? The work of a lifetime was in the money-box. Isn't that enough? Enough—enough—for what? What do I want? I want to go to *Eretz Yisroel* before I die. That's how much money there was in the money-box."

"Mr. Lippmann—"

"Yes," Lipi cried out, "put it down in your book, why not, put it down that there was money to go to *Eretz Yisroel* in the money-box, put it down. What difference does it make now?" Lipi laughed and shouted, he gnawed at his fists, he cried out that before he died he wanted to go to the Holy Land, and now he knew he never would be able to. He was a poor man, he had always been poor, but he had had one ambition, one hope; now he saw what nonsense it had always been. "I look around and see my whole life is rubbish, here it is in this room." When the policeman told him that he should get in touch with his insurance company, Lipi laughed for the last time. "Where am I insured, who insures me? It is lost, everything is lost. Put it down." Lipi began kicking at the furniture, tearing at the few strands of black and gray hair that usually lay flat on his scalp. Eventually, a doctor was called and he administered a sedative; Lipi fell asleep in the bedroom, on the torn mattress, with the wardrobe doors still hanging open and various articles the thieves had not bothered to take scattered about the floor. By that time a small curious crowd of people had gathered on the pavement outside, and the news of Lipi's loss had spread all over the neighborhood. The amount of the loss was greatly exaggerated as the story went from one servant or housewife to the next, though no single exaggeration was greater than the one that the policeman, at Lipi's bidding, had written into his book.

The next morning the story was in the local paper. Lipi was described as "a well-known city fruiterer and green-grocer"; his loss was estimated at "several hundred pounds, which Mr. Lippmann had been saving to fulfill his lifelong ambition of visiting the Holy Land." The police, the report added, were continuing their inquiries.

A few days later another report appeared, in which it was stated that several leading members of the Lyndhurst Jewish community were offering a reward for information leading to the arrest of the thief or thieves; the report stated also that it had been decided that, should the money not be recovered, a fund would be established to make good Mr. Lippmann's loss, and thus enable him to fulfill his lifelong ambition of visiting the Holy Land.

For Lipi had become a hero, even something of a martyr in Lyndhurst, and especially so to the members of the Lyndhurst Jewish community. If they felt any embarrassment or shame in connection with him now, it was only because they had been ashamed of him and embarrassed by him in the past. His poverty now appeared to them noble; his ambition to visit Israel exemplary; his attempts to realize that ambition inspiring; his defeat pitiable. There was none among the well-to-do-Jews of Lyndhurst who did not feel himself humbled by Lipi's humility, shamed by his self-sacrifice. When Lipi went to *shul* he was now greeted with great friendliness, even with deference; in the streets Jews and Gentiles alike stopped his lorry to express their sympathy with him and to assure him that from now on they would buy all their fruit and vegetables from him. The police continued their investigations, without success. And three months after the burglary had taken place, the paper published a photograph showing Lipi being presented with a return air ticket to Israel and a check large enough to cover his expenses during the visit. The presentation was made by half a dozen leading members of the Jewish community, among them an ex-Mayor of Lyndhurst, the local rabbi, and the chairman of the Zionist society. Many Gentiles, including some of Lipi's neighbors, it was said, had contributed to the fund.

Lipi dreamed that he was in Palestine. It was a dream he very often had, and the landscape was familiar to him, though it was unlike any he had ever seen. In front of him, pale ploughed fields stretched away to a group of white houses with red-tiled roofs, in the distance; behind the houses were hills, vaguely outlined. Nothing grew from the fields, yet they were not barren; there was no sun in the sky, but the scene was evenly filled with light; no one stirred about the houses, yet Lipi knew that there were people living in them. As he had done a hundred times before, Lipi began walking toward the houses.

As always, Lipi awoke before he reached the houses. And immediately he was fully awake, in the darkness, confronting once again, with the poignance of the dream still upon him, the enormity of his lie, his crime, and its consequences. Lipi had not anticipated anything of what had happened since he had told the policeman, in a frenzy of rage and self-hatred, that the thieves had stolen from him savings he had never had. Lipi could not even remember telling the lie to the policeman; if it had not been for the report in the newspaper the next morning he would never have believed that he had in fact done so. All Lipi could remember of that afternoon when he had come back to find his house in disorder, was a stunned sense of humiliation and anger, which had not at all been directed against the strangers who had come into the house, fingered and thrown about his meager possessions, and taken those few they had thought it worth their effort to carry. Lipi's rage had been directed against himself; against his own poverty and powerlessness; against the lifetime he had spent toiling in the sun, for so little reward, for a house that ten minutes could despoil, for possessions that ten pounds could buy.

These emotions, as he lay in his bed at night, with his departure for Israel only a few days off, Lipi could remember. But what had taken place subsequently was all an absurdity, a confusion of noise, of darkness and light. His own frenzy, and the faces of the policemen, the reports in the newspaper and the friendliness of strangers, the rumors of the collection that was being made for him and the tense, jovial little ceremony when he had been handed his tickets and money—all these were less substantial than a dream, far less substantial than the dream he had just had of Israel. But the tickets and the money were real, and had been given to him: they were waiting for him now at the bank. (How many jokes had been made at the ceremony about the money being safe from burglars in the bank; how many about Lipi being able to teach his son to fly when he came back from the trip.) What a lifetime of work had failed to bring him a single lie had made possible; and Lipi lay in his bed and marveled at the world, and especially, of all the world, at the city of Lyndhurst. With a satisfaction that was sweeter than any he had felt since he had been a young man lying beside his wife, Lipi knew that at last, at last, he would be able to settle the problem that had for so long been a dear, familiar, secret riddle to him: he would be able to see if Israel really looked as it did to him in his dreams.

But later that same night, Lipi woke again. His own beating heart had shaken him out of sleep; his body was filled with a dread that his mind was still ignorant of. Baffled by the warm, thick darkness around him, hardly knowing who or where he was, Lipi again remembered, as when he had woken earlier, the journey he was about to make. But this time the recollection came slowly, painfully, and seemed to carry the dread with it. Was he afraid of the burglars? Did he fear that the police might find them, or that they might come forward themselves, and expose his fraud? But that was an anxiety that had visited him before, and that had never had the power to make him lose his own sense of himself. It was another fear that possessed him now, and it was as formless, impenetrable, and insistent as the darkness around him. And even when he had recognized it, the dread remained formless to Lipi, and as compelling as before. He could not believe that the landscape of his dreams would accept him, if he came to it as a liar and a fraud. It would reject him—he did not know how—it would thrust him from itself, it would disgorge him as unclean, a tainted thing.

In the morning Lipi rose and went to see the ex-Mayor, who had formally handed to him his travel tickets and money, on behalf of the Lyndhurst Jewish community. The ex-Mayor was a wholesale merchant who had inherited his business; he was twenty years younger than Lipi and twice Lipi's size; his manner was authoritative and his complexion rubicund; he wore spectacles with heavy black rims, though his eyesight was excellent without them. He had not only been Mayor of Lyndhurst for a time; he had also been the captain of the local golf club and the president of the local Red Cross Society; he was still chairman of the Chamber of Commerce and a member of the City Council; and at public meetings, and even when he was alone with his wife, he was in the habit of putting forward his own career as an illustration of the cordiality of "interfaith relations" in Lyndhurst. He received Lipi with the benevolence of a man who knows he has done well by his visitor; but his benevolence had altogether disappeared by the time Lipi had finished his confession. However, the ex-Mayor was a man of decision; and he said nothing to Lipi of his rage at the deception Lipi had practiced upon the people of Lyndhurst, or of his own personal indignation at having been shown up as a sentimental fool, or even of his anxieties about the possible effects of Lipi's confession on "interfaith relations" in Lyndhurst. Instead, he told Lipi, "Look, I want you to leave for Johannesburg at once, and wait for your plane there. You can go on the train tonight. And I don't want you to say a word of this to anyone else, do you hear? Not a word. As far as I'm concerned, this conversation never took place. I haven't heard you, and no one else ever will. Now go, go on, go on, I'll send my car around to pick you up tonight. Do you understand? Just go!" Only at the very end did the ex-Mayor add, with sudden ferocity, "And I wish you'd never come back!"

Bewildered, Lipi allowed himself to be hustled out of the office; he found himself on the placid sunlit pavement, his hat in his hand. Around him the people of Lyndhurst went about their business, and Lipi joined them, though he had no business to attend to. In his ears there was a voice that shrieked that everyone, everything in the world was tainted; that he had nothing to fear, for Israel was tainted too. All day he wandered about the town; he was seen standing outside the shops in the commercial district and walking down the middle of streets in residential areas far from his own; he was even seen in the African locations around the town, where people stared in amazement at the spectacle of a white man, alone and on foot, making his way between the mud and iron huts laid down in rows upon the veld. At nightfall Lipi found himself in the railway shunting yards; and there, too late, he was glimpsed by a horrified engine driver, in front of whose slowly moving locomotive Lipi threw down his body. What the engine driver most vividly remembered, what he always mentioned when he subsequently told his tale to others, was how Lipi had brought his hands to his ears, at the very moment he fell.

At the inquest it was declared that Lipi had committed suicide while the balance of his mind was disturbed. The coroner added that the death was all the more tragic in view of the efforts that had recently been made to restore to the deceased his own hopes for himself and his faith in the good will of the people around him. Lipi's funeral was enormous; and it was noted that the ex-Mayor of the town was among those who seemed most affected by grief at the graveside.

February 1963

Norman Podhoretz

MY NEGRO PROBLEM—AND OURS

> *If we—and . . . I mean the relatively conscious whites and the relatively conscious blacks, who must, like lovers, insist on, or create, the consciousness of the others—do not falter in our duty now, we may be able, handful that we are, to end the racial nightmare, and achieve our country, and change the history of the world.*
>
> JAMES BALDWIN

Two ideas puzzled me deeply as a child growing up in Brooklyn during the 1930's in what today would be called an integrated neighborhood. One of them was that all Jews were rich; the other was that all Negroes were persecuted. These ideas had appeared in print; therefore they must be true. My own experience and the evidence of my senses told me they were not true, but that only confirmed what a day-dreaming boy in the provinces—for the lower-class neighborhoods of New York belong as surely to the provinces as any rural town in North Dakota—discovers very early: *his* experience is unreal and the evidence of his senses is not to be trusted. Yet even a boy with a head full of fantasies incongruously synthesized out of Hollywood movies and English novels cannot altogether deny the reality of his own experience—especially when there is so much deprivation in that experience. Nor can he altogether gainsay the evidence of his own senses—especially such evidence of the senses as comes from being repeatedly beaten up, robbed, and in general hated, terrorized, and humiliated.

And so for a long time I was puzzled to think that Jews were supposed to be rich when the only Jews I knew were poor, and that Negroes were supposed to be persecuted when it was the Negroes who were doing the only persecuting I knew about—and doing it, moreover, to *me*. During the early years of the war, when my older sister joined a left-wing youth organization, I remember my astonishment at hearing her passionately denounce my father for thinking that Jews were worse off than Negroes. To me, at the age of twelve, it seemed very clear that Negroes were better off than Jews—indeed, than *all* whites. A city boy's world is contained within three or four square blocks, and in my world it was the whites, the Italians and Jews, who feared the Negroes, not the other way around. The Negroes were tougher than we were, more ruthless, and on the whole they were better athletes. What could it mean, then, to say that they were badly off and that we were more fortunate? Yet my sister's opinions, like print, were sacred, and when she told me about exploitation and economic forces I believed her. I believed her, but I was still afraid of Negroes. And I still hated them with all my heart.

It had not always been so—that much I can recall from early childhood. When did it start, this fear and this hatred? There was a kindergarten in the local public school, and given the character of the neighborhood, at least half of the children in my class must have been Negroes. Yet I have no memory of being aware of color differences at that age, and I know from observing my own children that they attribute no significance to such differences even when they begin noticing them. I think there was a day—first grade? second grade?—when my best friend Carl hit me on the way home from school and announced that he wouldn't play with me any more because I had killed Jesus. When I ran home to my mother crying for an explanation, she told me not to pay any attention to such foolishness, and then in Yiddish she cursed the *goyim* and the *schwartzes,* the *schwartzes* and the *goyim*. Carl, it turned out, was a *schwartze,* and so was added a third to the categories into which people were mysteriously divided.

Sometimes I wonder whether this is a true memory at all. It is blazingly vivid, but perhaps it never happened: can anyone really remember back to the age of six? There is no uncertainty in my mind, however, about the years that followed. Carl and I hardly ever spoke, though we met in school every day up through the eighth or ninth grade. There would be embarrassed moments of catching his eye or of his catching mine—for whatever it was that had attracted us to one another as very small children remained alive in spite of the fantastic barrier of hostility that had grown up between us, suddenly and out of nowhere. Nevertheless, friendship would have been impossible, and even if it had been possible, it would have been unthinkable. About that, there was nothing anyone could do by the time we were eight years old.

Item: The orphanage across the street is torn down, a city housing project begins to rise in its place, and on the marvelous vacant lot next to the old orphanage they are building a playground. Much excitement and anticipation as Opening Day draws near. Mayor LaGuardia himself comes to dedicate this great gesture of public benevolence. He speaks of neighborliness and borrowing cups of sugar, and of the playground he says that children of all races, colors, and creeds will learn to live together in harmony. A week later, some of us are swatting flies on the playground's inadequate little ball field. A gang of Negro kids, pretty much our own age, enter from the other side and order us out of the park. We refuse, proudly and indignantly, with superb masculine fervor. There is a fight, they win, and we retreat, half whimpering, half with bravado. My first nauseating experience of cowardice. And my first appalled realization that there are people in the world who do not seem to be afraid of anything, who act as though they have nothing to lose. Thereafter the playground becomes a battleground, sometimes quiet, sometimes the scene of athletic competition between Them and Us. But rocks are thrown as often as baseballs. Gradually we abandon the place and use the streets instead. The streets are safer, though we do not admit this to ourselves. We are not, after all, sissies—that most dreaded epithet of an American boyhood.

Item: I am standing alone in front of the building in which I live. It is late afternoon and getting dark. That day in school the teacher had asked a surly Negro boy named Quentin a question he was unable to answer. As usual I had waved my arm eagerly ("Be a good boy, get good marks, be smart, go to college, become a doctor") and, the right answer bursting from my lips, I was held up lovingly by the teacher as an example to the class. I had seen Quentin's face—a very dark, very cruel, very Oriental-looking face—harden, and there had been enough threat in his eyes to make me run all the way home for fear that he might catch me outside.

Now, standing idly in front of my own house, I see him approaching from the project accompanied by his little brother who is carrying a baseball bat and wearing a grin of malicious anticipation. As in a nightmare, I am trapped. The surroundings are secure and familiar, but terror is suddenly present and there is no one around to help. I am locked to the spot. I will not cry out or run away like a sissy, and I stand there, my heart wild, my throat clogged. He walks up, hurls the familiar epithet ("Hey, mo'f——r"), and to my surprise only pushes me. It is a violent push, but not a punch. A push is not as serious as a punch. Maybe I can still back out without entirely losing my dignity. Maybe I can still say, "Hey, c'mon Quentin, whaddya wanna do *that* for. I dint do nothin' to *you,*" and walk away, not too rapidly. Instead, before I can stop myself, I push him back—a token gesture—and I say, "Cut that out, I don't wanna fight, I ain't got nothin' to fight about." As I turn to walk back into the building, the corner of my eye catches the motion of the bat his little brother has handed him. I try to duck, but the bat crashes colored lights into my head.

The next thing I know, my mother and sister are standing over me, both of them hysterical. My sister—she who was later to join the "progressive" youth organization—is shouting for the police and screaming imprecations at those dirty little black bastards. They take me upstairs, the doctor comes, the police come. I tell them that the boy who did it was a stranger, that he had been trying to get money from me. They do not believe me, but I am too scared to give them Quentin's name. When I return to school a few days later, Quentin avoids my eyes. He knows that I have not squealed, and he is ashamed. I try to feel proud, but in my heart I know that it was fear of what his friends might do to me that had kept me silent, and not the code of the street.

Item: There is an athletic meet in which the whole of our junior high school is participating. I am in one of the seventh-grade rapid-advance classes, and "segregation" has now set in with a vengeance. In the last three or four years of the elementary school from which we have just graduated, each grade had been divided into three classes, according to "intelligence." (In the earlier grades the divisions had either been arbitrary or else unrecognized by us as having anything to do with brains.) These divisions by IQ, or however it was arranged, had resulted in a preponderance of Jews in the "1" classes and a corresponding preponderance of Negroes in the "3's," with the Italians split unevenly along the spectrum. At least a few Negroes had always made the "1's," just as there had always been a few Jewish kids among the "3's" and more among the "2's" (where Italians dominated). But the junior high's rapid-advance class of which I am now a member is overwhelmingly Jewish and entirely white—except for a shy lonely Negro girl with light skin and reddish hair.

The athletic meet takes place in a city-owned stadium far from the school. It is an important event to which a whole day is given over. The winners are to get those precious little medallions stamped with the New York City emblem that can be screwed into a belt and that prove the wearer to be a distinguished personage. I am a fast runner, and so I am assigned the position of anchor man on my class's team in the relay race. There are three other seventh-grade teams in the race, two of them all Negro, as ours is all white. One of the all-Negro teams is very tall—their anchor man waiting silently next to me on the line looks years older than I am, and I do not recognize him. He is the first to get the baton and crosses the finishing line in a walk. Our team comes in second, but a few minutes later we are declared the winners, for it has been discovered that the anchor man on the first-place team is not a member of the class. We are awarded the medallions, and the following day our home-room teacher makes a speech about how proud she is of us for being superior athletes as well as superior students. We want to believe we deserve the praise, but we know we could not have won even if the other class had not cheated.

That afternoon, walking home, I am waylaid and surrounded by five Negroes, among whom is the anchor man of the disqualified team. "Gimme my medal, mo'f——r," he grunts. I do not have it with me and I tell him so. "Anyway, it ain't yours," I say foolishly. He calls me a liar on both counts and pushes me up against the wall on which we sometimes play handball. "Gimme my mo'f——n' medal," he says again. I repeat that I have left it home. "Let's search the li'l mo'f——r," one of them suggests, "he prolly got it *hid* in his mo'f——n' *pants.*" My panic is now unmanageable. (How many times had I been surrounded like this and asked in soft tones, "Len' me a nickle, boy." How many times had I been called a liar for pleading poverty and pushed around, or searched, or beaten up, unless there happened to be someone in the marauding gang like Carl who liked me across that enormous divide of hatred and who would therefore say, "Aaah, c'mon, le's git someone else, *this* boy ain't got no money on 'im.") I scream at them through tears of rage and self-contempt, "Keep your f——n' filthy lousy black hands offa me! I swear I'll get the cops." This is all they need to hear, and the five of them set upon me. They bang me around, mostly in the stomach and on the arms and shoulders, and when several adults loitering near the candy store down the block notice what is going on and begin to shout, they run off and away.

I do not tell my parents about the incident. My team-mates, who have also been waylaid, each by a gang led by his opposite number from the disqualified team, have had their medallions taken from them, and they never squeal either. For days, I walk home in terror, expecting to be caught again, but nothing happens. The medallion is put away into a drawer, never to be worn by anyone.

Obviously experiences like these have always been a common feature of childhood life in working-class and immigrant neighborhoods, and Negroes do not necessarily figure in them. Wherever, and in whatever combination, they have lived together in the cities, kids of different groups have been at war, beating up and being beaten up: micks against kikes against wops against spicks against polacks. And even relatively homogeneous areas have not been spared the warring of the young: one block against another, one gang (called in my day, in a pathetic effort at gentility, an "S.A.C.," or social-athletic club) against another. But the Negro-white conflict had—and no doubt still has—a special intensity and was conducted with a ferocity unmatched by intramural white battling.

In my own neighborhood, a good deal of animosity existed between the Italian kids (most of whose parents were immigrants from Sicily) and the Jewish kids (who came largely from East European immigrant families). Yet everyone had friends, sometimes close friends, in the other "camp," and we often visited one another's strange-smelling houses, if not for meals, then for glasses of milk, and occasionally for some special event like a wedding or a wake. If it happened that we divided into warring factions and did battle, it would invariably be half-hearted and soon patched up. Our parents, to be sure, had nothing to do with one another and were mutually suspicious and hostile. But we, the kids, who all spoke Yiddish or Italian at home, were Americans, or New Yorkers, or Brooklyn boys: we shared a culture, the culture of the street, and at least for a while this culture proved to be more powerful than the opposing cultures of the home.

Why, *why* should it have been so different as between the Negroes and us? How was it borne in upon us so early, white and black alike, that we were enemies beyond any possibility of reconciliation? Why did we hate one another so?

I suppose if I tried, I could answer those questions more or less adequately from the perspective of what I have since learned. I could draw upon James Baldwin—what better witness is there?—to describe the sense of entrapment that poisons the soul of the Negro with hatred for the white man whom he knows to be his jailer. On the other side, if I wanted to understand how the white man comes to hate the Negro, I could call upon the psychologists who have spoken of the guilt that white Americans feel toward Negroes and that turns into hatred for lack of acknowledging itself as guilt. These are plausible answers and certainly there is truth in them. Yet when I think back upon my own experience of the Negro and his of me, I find myself troubled and puzzled, much as I was as a child when I heard that all Jews were rich and all Negroes persecuted. How could the Negroes in my neighborhood have regarded the whites across the street and around the corner as jailers? On the whole, the whites were not so poor as the Negroes, but they were quite poor enough, and the years were years of Depression. As for white hatred of the Negro, how could guilt have had anything to do with it? What share had these Italian and Jewish immigrants in the enslavement of the Negro? What share had they—down-trodden people themselves breaking their own necks to eke out a living—in the exploitation of the Negro?

No, I cannot believe that we hated each other back there in Brooklyn because they thought of us as jailers and we felt guilty toward them. But does it matter, given the fact that we all went through an unrepresentative confrontation? I think it matters profoundly, for if we managed the job of hating each other so well without benefit of the aids to hatred that are supposedly at the root of this madness everywhere else, it must mean that the madness is not yet properly understood. I am far from pretending that

I understand it, but I would insist that no view of the problem will begin to approach the truth unless it can account for a case like the one I have been trying to describe. Are the elements of any such view available to us?

At least two, I would say, are. One of them is a point we frequently come upon in the work of James Baldwin, and the other is a related point always stressed by psychologists who have studied the mechanisms of prejudice. Baldwin tells us that one of the reasons Negroes hate the white man is that the white man refuses to *look* at him: the Negro knows that in white eyes all Negroes are alike; they are faceless and therefore not altogether human. The psychologists, in their turn, tell us that the white man hates the Negro because he tends to project those wild impulses that he fears in himself onto an alien group which he then punishes with his contempt. What Baldwin does *not* tell us, however, is that the principle of facelessness is a two-way street and can operate in both directions with no difficulty at all. Thus, in my neighborhood in Brooklyn, *I* was as faceless to the Negroes as they were to me, and if they hated me because I never looked at them, I must also have hated them for never looking at *me*. To the Negroes, my white skin was enough to define me as the enemy, and in a war it is only the uniform that counts and not the person.

So with the mechanism of projection that the psychologists talk about: it too works in both directions at once. There is no question that the psychologists are right about what the Negro represents symbolically to the white man. For me as a child the life lived on the other side of the playground and down the block on Ralph Avenue seemed the very embodiment of the values of the street—free, independent, reckless, brave, masculine, erotic. I put the word "erotic" last, though it is usually stressed above all others, because in fact it came last, in consciousness as in importance. What mainly counted for me about Negro kids of my own age was that they were "bad boys." There were plenty of bad boys among the whites—this was, after all, a neighborhood with a long tradition of crime as a career open to aspiring talents—but the Negroes were *really* bad, bad in a way that beckoned to one, and made one feel inadequate. *We* all went home every day for a lunch of spinach-and-potatoes; *they* roamed around during lunch hour, munching on candy bars. In winter *we* had to wear itchy woolen hats and mittens and cumbersome galoshes; *they* were bare-headed and loose as they pleased. *We* rarely played hookey, or got into serious trouble in school, for all our street-corner bravado; *they* were defiant, forever staying out (to do what delicious things?), forever making disturbances in class and in the halls, forever being sent to the principal and returning uncowed. But most important of all, they were *tough;* beautifully, enviably tough, not giving a damn for anyone or anything. To hell with the teacher, the truant officer, the cop; to hell with the whole of the adult world that held *us* in its grip and that we never had the courage to rebel against except sporadically and in petty ways.

This is what I saw and envied and feared in the Negro: this is what finally made him faceless to me, though some of it, of course, was actually there. (The psychologists also tell us that the alien group which becomes the object of a projection will tend to respond by trying to live up to what is expected of them.) But what, on his side, did the Negro see in me that made me faceless to *him?* Did he envy me my lunches of spinach-and-potatoes and my itchy woolen caps and my prudent behavior in the face of authority, as I envied him his noon-time candy bars and his bare head in winter and his magnificent rebelliousness? Did those lunches and caps spell for him the prospect of power and riches in the future? Did they mean that there were possibilities open to me that were denied to him? Very likely they did. But if so, one also supposes that he feared the impulses within himself toward submission to authority no less powerfully than I feared the impulses in myself toward defiance. If I represented the jailer to him, it was not because I was oppressing him or keeping him down: it was because I symbolized for him the dangerous and probably pointless temptation toward greater repression, just as he symbolized for me the equally perilous tug toward greater freedom. I personally was to be rewarded for this repression with a new and better life in the future, but how many of my friends paid an even higher price and were given only gall in return.

We have it on the authority of James Baldwin that all Negroes hate whites. I am trying to suggest that on their side all whites—all American whites, that is—are sick in their feelings about Negroes. There are Negroes, no doubt, who would say that Baldwin is wrong, but I suspect them of being less honest than he is, just as I suspect whites of self-deception who tell me they have no special feeling toward Negroes. Special feelings about color are a contagion to which white Americans seem susceptible even when there is nothing in their background to account for the susceptibility. Thus everywhere we look today in the North, we find the curious phenomenon of white middle-class liberals with no previous personal experience of Negroes—people to whom Negroes have always been faceless in virtue rather than faceless in vice—discovering that their abstract commitment to the cause of Negro rights will not stand the test of a direct confrontation. We find such people fleeing in droves to the suburbs as the Negro population in the inner city grows; and when they stay in the city we find them sending their children to private school rather than to the "integrated" public school in the neighborhood. We find them resisting the demand that gerrymandered school districts be re-zoned for the purpose of overcoming *de facto* segregation; we find them judiciously considering whether the Negroes (for their own good, of course) are not perhaps pushing too hard; we find them clucking their tongues over

Negro militancy; we find them speculating on the question of whether there may not, after all, be something in the theory that the races are biologically different; we find them saying that it will take a very long time for Negroes to achieve full equality, no matter what anyone does; we find them deploring the rise of black nationalism and expressing the solemn hope that the leaders of the Negro community will discover ways of containing the impatience and incipient violence within the Negro ghettos.

But that is by no means the whole story; there is also the phenomenon of what Kenneth Rexroth once called "crow-jimism." There are the broken-down white boys like Vivaldo Moore in Baldwin's *Another Country* who go to Harlem in search of sex or simply to brush up against something that looks like primitive vitality, and who are so often punished by the Negroes they meet for crimes that they would have been the last ever to commit and of which they themselves have been as sorry victims as any of the Negroes who take it out on them. There are the writers and intellectuals and artists who romanticize Negroes and pander to them, assuming a guilt that is not properly theirs. And there are all the white liberals who permit Negroes to blackmail them into adopting a double standard of moral judgment, and who lend themselves—again assuming the responsibility for crimes they never committed—to cunning and contemptuous exploitation by Negroes they employ or try to befriend.

And what about me? What kind of feelings do I have about Negroes today? What happened to me, from Brooklyn, who grew up fearing and envying and hating Negroes? Now that Brooklyn is behind me, do I fear them and envy them and hate them still? The answer is yes, but not in the same proportions and certainly not in the same way. I now live on the upper west side of Manhattan, where there are many Negroes and many Puerto Ricans, and there are nights when I experience the old apprehensiveness again, and there are streets that I avoid when I am walking in the dark, as there were streets that I avoided when I was a child. I find that I am not afraid of Puerto Ricans, but I cannot restrain my nervousness whenever I pass a group of Negroes standing in front of a bar or sauntering down the street. I know now, as I did not know when I was a child, that power is on my side, that the police are working for me and not for them. And knowing this I feel ashamed and guilty, like the good liberal I have grown up to be. Yet the twinges of fear and the resentment they bring and the self-contempt they arouse are not to be gainsaid.

But envy? Why envy? And hatred? Why hatred? Here again the intensities have lessened and everything has been complicated and qualified by the guilts and the resulting over-compensations that are the heritage of the enlightened middle-class world of which I am now a member. Yet just as in childhood I envied Negroes for what seemed to me their superior masculinity, so I envy them today for what seems to me their superior physical grace and beauty. I have come to value physical grace very highly, and I am now capable of aching with all my being when I watch a Negro couple on the dance floor, or a Negro playing baseball or basketball. They are on the kind of terms with their own bodies that I should like to be on with mine, and for that precious quality they seem blessed to me.

The hatred I still feel for Negroes is the hardest of all the old feelings to face or admit, and it is the most hidden and the most overlarded by the conscious attitudes into which I have succeeded in willing myself. It no longer has, as for me it once did, any cause or justification (except, perhaps, that I am constantly being denied my right to an honest expression of the things I earned the right as a child to feel). How, then, do I know that this hatred has never entirely disappeared? I know it from the insane rage that can stir in me at the thought of Negro anti-Semitism; I know it from the disgusting prurience that can stir in me at the sight of a mixed couple; and I know it from the violence that can stir in me whenever I encounter that special brand of paranoid touchiness to which many Negroes are prone.

This, then, is where I am; it is not exactly where I think all other white liberals are, but it cannot be so very far away either. And it is because I am convinced that we white Americans are—for whatever reason, it no longer matters—so twisted and sick in our feelings about Negroes that I despair of the present push toward integration. If the pace of progress were not a factor here, there would perhaps be no cause for despair: time and the law and even the international political situation are on the side of the Negroes, and ultimately, therefore, victory—of a sort, anyway—must come. But from everything we have learned from observers who ought to know, pace has become as important to the Negroes as substance. They want equality and they want it *now,* and the white world is yielding to their demand only as much and as fast as it is absolutely being compelled to do. The Negroes know this in the most concrete terms imaginable, and it is thus becoming increasingly difficult to buy them off with rhetoric and promises and pious assurances of support. And so within the Negro community we find more and more people declaring—as Harold R. Isaacs recently put it in these pages*—that they want *out:* people who say that integration will never come, or that it will take a hundred or a thousand years to come, or that it will come at too high a price in suffering and struggle for the pallid and sodden life of the American middle class that at the very best it may bring.

The most numerous, influential, and dangerous movement that has grown out of Negro despair with the goal of integration is, of course, the Black Muslims. This movement, whatever else we may say about it, must

* "Integration and the Negro Mood," *Commentary,* December 1962.

be credited with one enduring achievement: it inspired James Baldwin to write an essay* which deserves to be placed among the classics of our language. Everything Baldwin has ever been trying to tell us is distilled here into a statement of overwhelming persuasiveness and prophetic magnificence. Baldwin's message is and always has been simple. It is this: "Color is not a human or personal reality; it is a political reality." And Baldwin's demand is correspondingly simple: color must be forgotten, lest we all be smited with a vengeance "that does not really depend on, and cannot really be executed by, any person or organization, and that cannot be prevented by any police force or army: historical vengeance, a cosmic vengeance based on the law that we recognize when we say, 'Whatever goes up must come down.'" The Black Muslims Baldwin portrays as a sign and a warning to the intransigent white world. They come to proclaim how deep is the Negro's disaffection with the white world and all its works, and Baldwin implies that no American Negro can fail to respond somewhere in his being to their message: that the white man is the devil, that Allah has doomed him to destruction, and that the black man is about to inherit the earth. Baldwin of course knows that this nightmare inversion of the racism from which the black man has suffered can neither win nor even point to the neighborhood in which victory might be located. For in his view the neighborhood of victory lies in exactly the opposite direction: the transcendence of color through love.

Yet the tragic fact is that love is not the answer to hate—not in the world of politics, at any rate. Color is indeed a political rather than a human or a personal reality and if politics (which is to say power) has made it into a human and a personal reality, then only politics (which is to say power) can unmake it once again. But the way of politics is slow and bitter, and as impatience on the one side is matched by a setting of the jaw on the other, we move closer and closer to an explosion and blood may yet run in the streets.

Will this madness in which we are all caught never find a resting-place? Is there never to be an end to it? In thinking about the Jews I have often wondered whether their survival as a distinct group was worth one hair on the head of a single infant. Did the Jews have to survive so that six million innocent people should one day be burned in the ovens of Auschwitz? It is a terrible question and no one, not God himself, could ever answer it to my satisfaction. And when I think about the Negroes in America and about the image of integration as a state in which the Negroes would take their rightful place as another of the protected minorities in a pluralistic society, I wonder whether they really believe in their hearts

* Originally published in *The New Yorker* under the title "Letter from a Region in My Mind," subsequently published in book form (along with a new introduction) under the title *The Fire Next Time.*

that such a state can actually be attained, and if so *why* they should wish to survive as a distinct group. I think I know why the Jews once wished to survive (though I am less certain as to why we still do): they not only believed that God had given them no choice, but they were tied to a memory of past glory and a dream of imminent redemption. What does the American Negro have that might correspond to this? His past is a stigma, his color is a stigma, and his vision of the future is the hope of erasing the stigma by making color irrelevant, by making it disappear as a fact of consciousness.

I share this hope, but I cannot see how it will ever be realized unless color does in *fact* disappear: and that means not integration, it means assimilation, it means—let the brutal word come out—miscegenation. The Black Muslims, like their racist counterparts in the white world, accuse the "so-called Negro leaders" of secretly pursuing miscegenation as a goal. The racists are wrong, but I wish they were right, for I believe that the wholesale merging of the two races is the most desirable alternative for everyone concerned. I am not claiming that this alternative can be pursued programmatically or that it is immediately feasible as a solution; obviously there are even greater barriers to its achievement than to the achievement of integration. What I am saying, however, is that in my opinion the Negro problem can be solved in this country in no other way.

I have told the story of my own twisted feelings about Negroes here, and of how they conflict with the moral convictions I have since developed, in order to assert that such feelings must be acknowledged as honestly as possible so that they can be controlled and ultimately disregarded in favor of the convictions. It is *wrong* for a man to suffer because of the color of his skin. Beside that clichéd proposition of liberal thought, what argument can stand and be respected? If the arguments are the arguments of feeling, they must be made to yield; and one's own soul is not the worst place to begin working a huge social transformation. Not so long ago, it used to be asked of white liberals, "Would you like your sister to marry one?" When I was a boy and my sister was still unmarried, I would certainly have said no to that question. But now I am a man, my sister is already married, and I have daughters. If I were to be asked today whether I would like a daughter of mine "to marry one," I would have to answer: "No, I wouldn't *like* it at all. I would rail and rave and rant and tear my hair. And then I hope I would have the courage to curse myself for raving and ranting, and to give her my blessing. How dare I withhold it at the behest of the child I once was and against the man I now have a duty to be?"

December 1964

Nathan Glazer

NEGROES AND JEWS: THE NEW CHALLENGE TO PLURALISM

If today one re-reads the article by Kenneth Clark on Negro-Jewish relations that was published in *Commentary* almost nineteen years ago,* one will discover that tension between Negroes and Jews is neither of recent origin nor a product of the civil rights revolution. In that article Dr. Clark described the bitter feelings of the masses of Northern Negroes toward Jews. Not that these feelings hampered cooperation between Negro and Jewish leaders—an effective cooperation which was to play an important role in the following years in bringing fair-employment, fair-housing, and fair-education legislation to many communities, and indeed to most of the large Northern and Western states. But whatever the relationships were at the top, the fact was that down below, the Negro's experience of the Jew was not as a co-worker or friend or ally, but, in a word, as an exploiter.

As Dr. Clark wrote: "Some Negro domestics assert that Jewish housewives who employ them are unreasonably and brazenly exploitative. A Negro actor states in bitter terms that he is being flagrantly underpaid by a Jewish producer. A Negro entertainer is antagonistic to his Jewish agent, who, he is convinced, is exploiting him. . . . Antagonism to the 'Jewish landlord' is so common as to become almost an integral part of the folk culture of the Northern urban Negro." And, of course, one would have to add to this catalogue the Jewish merchants in the Negro business districts, believed by their customers to be selling them inferior goods at high prices and on poor credit terms (a charge the merchants might answer by explaining that they were simply covering the greater financial costs—through payment delinquency and robbery—of doing business in a Negro area, plus compensation for the physical danger involved).

In any case, long before many of those Negro youths were born who took part last summer in the destruction and looting of Jewish businesses in Harlem and Bedford-Stuyvesant and Philadelphia, Dr. Clark explained

* "Candor on Negro-Jewish Relations," February 1946.

clearly enough the basis for the anti-Semitism prevalent in the Negro ghettos. It was, he said, a special variant of anti-white feeling, encouraged by the more direct and immediate contact that Negroes had with Jews than with other whites, and encouraged as well by the inferior position of Jews in American society, which permitted the Negro to find in the luxury of anti-Jewishness one of his few means of identifying with the American majority. Two years later, also in *Commentary,* the young James Baldwin told the same story in one of his first published articles,* underlining the point with his elegant acidity: "But just as a society must have a scapegoat, so hatred must have a symbol. Georgia has the Negro and Harlem has the Jew." One still feels the shock of that cold ending: is *that* what the Jew was to Harlem in 1948?

If, however, we knew decades ago that the ironic historic confrontation of Jew (as landlord, merchant, housewife, businessman) with Negro (as tenant, customer, servant, and worker) in the North had produced hatred on the part of many poor and uneducated Negroes, we now have to record two new developments in this confrontation. First, the well of ill-feeling has moved upward to include a substantial part of the Negro leadership, mainly some of the newer leaders thrown up in the North by the civil rights revolution; and second, Jewish feeling toward the Negro has undergone changes of its own.

There is little question that his feeling has never been hatred. It has ranged from passionate advocacy of Negro rights by Jewish liberals (and Communists and Socialists too), through friendly cooperation on the part of Jewish leaders who saw Negroes as allies in the fight for common goals, to a less effective but fairly widespread good will on the part of ordinary Jews. The hatred of poor Negroes for Jews was not reciprocated by Jews; in the way that Harlem "needed" the Jew, the Lower East Side, Brownsville, and Flatbush perhaps needed the *goy,* but they never needed the Negro. If there was prejudice against Negroes (and, of course, there was), it was part of the standard Jewish ethnocentrism which excluded all outsiders. The businesslike adoption of the norms of behavior of the white world (in refusing to rent to Negroes in New York, or serve them in department stores in the South) was just that—businesslike rather than the reflection of a deeply held prejudice. The Irish had had experiences which had taught many of them to dislike or hate Negroes: their competition with Negroes for the worst jobs in the early days of immigration, their antagonism to a Civil War draft that forced them to fight—as they thought—for Negroes. But the Jews had never come into direct competition with Negroes, in North or South. The tenant or customer might hate the landlord or storekeeper—the feeling was not mutual.

In the North, then, in the late 40's and 50's, well-staffed and well-

* "The Harlem Ghetto: Winter 1948," February 1948.

financed Jewish organizations usually had the support of much more poorly staffed and poorly financed Negro organizations in fighting for legislation that advanced the interests of both groups, even though they stood on very different steps in the economic and occupational ladder. For the same law permitted a Jew to challenge exclusion from a Fifth Avenue cooperative apartment and a Negro to challenge exclusion from a much more modest apartment building.

This situation is now changing. As the Negro masses have become more active and more militant in their own interests, their feelings have become more relevant, and have forced themselves to the surface; and Jewish leaders—of unions, of defense and civil rights organizations—as well as businessmen, housewives, and home-owners, have been confronted for the first time with demands from Negro organizations that, they find, cannot serve as the basis of a common effort. The new developments feed each other, and it would be impossible to say which came first. The resistance of Jewish organizations and individual Jews to such demands as preferential union membership and preferential hiring, and to the insistence on the primacy of integration over all other educational objectives, breeds antagonism among former Negro allies. The "white liberal," who is attacked as a false friend unwilling to support demands which affect him or his, and as probably prejudiced to boot, is generally (even if this is not spelled out) the white *Jewish* liberal—and it could hardly be otherwise, in view of the predominance of Jews among liberals, particularly in major cities like New York, Chicago, Philadelphia, and Los Angeles. This Jewish resistance, however, is often based not only on the demands themselves, but on a growing awareness of the depths of Negro antagonism to the world that Jewish liberalism considers desirable.

One importat new element in the situation, then, is that the feelings of the Negro masses have become politically relevant and meaningful in a way that they were not in 1935 or 1943. In those years, too, the Negroes of Harlem rioted, and broke the show windows of the Jewish-owned stores, and looted their contents. But these earlier outbreaks—which in terms of the feelings involved were very similar to the outbreaks of last summer—were not tied up with a great civil rights movement. While the Negro leaders of today could deny all responsibility for such outbreaks, and could point out that this kind of hoodlumism had been endemic in the Negro ghettos since the depression, the growing tendency toward militancy in the civil rights movement meant that the leadership would inevitably be charged with responsibility—as they were not in 1935 and 1943 (except for Communists and race radicals). Moreover, the feelings of the Negro masses were now in greater measure *shared* by middle-class and white-collar and leadership groups. And this is also strikingly new.

For the Negro no longer confronts the Jew only as tenant, servant, customer, worker. The rise of Negro teachers, social workers, and civil servants in considerable numbers means another kind of confrontation. Once again, the accidents of history have put the Jew just ahead of the Negro, and just above him. Now the Negro teacher works under a Jewish principal, the Negro social worker under a Jewish superivisor. When HARYOU issued its huge report, *Youth in the Ghetto,* last summer, only one of some 800 school principals in the New York system was a Negro, and only four of the 1,200 top-level administrative positions in the system were filled by Negroes! But as significant as these ridiculously tiny percentages is the fact that most of the *other* principalships and administrative positions are filled by Jews who poured into the educational system during the 30's and are now well advanced within it, while thousands of Negroes, comparative latecomers, have inferior jobs. And what makes the situation even worse is that part of the blame for the poor education of Negro children can be placed on this white (but concretely Jewish) dominance. As the HARYOU report states (though indicating that this is only one possible point of view):

> Public school teachers in New York City come largely from the city colleges, which have a dominant pupil population from a culture which prepares the child from birth for competition of a most strenuous type. These students are largely white, middle-class, growing up in segregated white communities where, by and large, their only contact with the Negro finds him in positions of servitude. . . . Responsible positions, even within the neighborhood schools, are in the main held by people who perceivably differ from [the Negro pupils]. The dearth of Negro principals, assistants and supervisors is a most glaring deficit and one which leaves a marked, unwholesome effect upon the child's self-image. . . . The competitive culture from which the bulk of the teachers come, with the attendant arrogance of intellectual superiority of its members, lends itself readily to the class system within the school . . . which in effect perpetuates the academic pre-eminence of the dominant group.

This new confrontation of middle-class Negroes, recently arrived at professional status, and middle-class Jews, who got there earlier and hold the superior positions, is most marked in New York, because of its huge Jewish population. It is there that the animus against the white liberal reaches its peak, and where the white liberal tends most often to be a Jew. But the confrontation is only somewhat less sharp in Philadelphia, Detroit, Chicago, Los Angeles, and other cities with substantial Jewish populations. Perhaps the only place where the term "white liberal" is not used to mean the "Jewish liberal" is in San Francisco. The reason is that radicalism in San Francisco has a peculiarly non-Jewish base in Harry Bridges's International Longshoreman's and Warehouseman's Union; moreover, the Jewish group there contains many early settlers who are closely identified with San Franciscans of the same class and origin. Indeed, in San Francisco, there was never even a Jewish ghetto available to become transformed into a Negro ghetto; yet the fragment of a Jewish ghetto that did exist is now part of a Negro ghetto.

And this brings us to yet another new twist in the historic confrontaiton of Jew and Negro. I do not know why in so many American cities Negro settlement has concentrated in the very areas that originally harbored Jewish immigrants. There are possibly three reasons. First, Jews have on the whole favored apartment-house living, and apartments provide cheap quarters for newcomers. Second, Jews have been economically and geographically more mobile than other immigrant groups who arrived around the same time (for example, Italians and Poles), and consequently their neighborhoods opened up to Negroes more rapidly. And finally, Jews have not resorted to violence in resisting the influx of new groups—in any case, most of them were already moving away.

But as Jews kept retreating to the edges of the city and beyond, the Negroes, their numbers and in some measure their income rising, followed —in recent years, as far as the suburbs. This is a problem, of course, for the same reasons that it is a problem for any white property-owner or home-owner: fear of the declining real-estate values that can be occasioned by a flight of panicky white residents; fear of changes in the neighborhood affecting the schools and the homogeneity of the environment. Obviously, Jews are not the only people caught up in such concerns; but since migrating urban groups generally follow radial paths outward (a pattern that is not so marked in New York, broken up as it is by rivers and bays, but that is very clear in inland cities like Detroit, Chicago, Cleveland, and Cincinnati), this new Negro middle class has moved into Jewish areas far more often than statistical probability alone would lead one to expect. Here again, therefore, a novel type of tension—specifically involving middle-class groups and home-owners—has been introduced.

In a number of suburbs Jewish home-owners of liberal outlook have banded together in an effort to slow down the outflow of whites and thus create an integrated community (which, of course, also helps to maintain the value of their homes). But to create an integrated community not only means slowing down the outflow of whites; it also means reducing the influx of Negroes. In some cases these good—from the Jewish point of view—intentions (and they usually *are* good) have looked, from the Negro point of view, like just another means of keeping Negroes *out,* but this time using the language of liberalism instead of race prejudice. We are all acquainted with the paranoia of persecuted minorities, and many jokes that used to be told of Jews (for example, the one about the stutterer who could not get a job as a radio announcer because of "anti-Semitism") could now be told of Negroes—and would be just as true.

All this forms part of the background of Negro-Jewish relations today. But in the immediate foreground are the new demands that have come to be made in the North and West by the civil rights movement. Negroes are acutely aware of how few of their young people even now get into the good colleges, and they see as a critical cause of this the small proportion of Negroes in good public elementary and high schools; they are acutely aware that their large-scale entry into the ranks of the clerks and typists of our huge public bureaucracies has not been accompanied by any equivalent entry into the higher positions of the civil service; they know that their new junior executive trainees in the large corporations are matched by hardly any Negroes higher up in these great private bureaucracies. And since political pressure and organized group pressure have been effective in breaching segregation in the South, and in bringing about some of these entries in the North, they see no reason why similar pressures should not be equally effective in making good the deficiences that continue to be apparent. If whites say, "But first you must earn your entry—through grades, or examinations," Negroes, with a good deal more knowledge of the realities of American society than foreign immigrants used to have, answer, "But we know how *you* got ahead—through political power, and connections, and the like; therefore, we won't accept your pious argument that merit is the only thing that counts."

There is some truth to this rejoinder; there is, I believe, much less truth when it is made to Jews. For the Jews have, indeed, put their faith in the abstract measures of individual merit—marks and examinations. Earlier, before school grades and civil-service test scores became so important, they depended on money: it, too, could be measured, and the man who had it could manage without any ties of blood or deep organic connection to the ruling elite of the land. In addition to this, the reason merit and money have been the major Jewish weapons in overcoming discrimination, rather than political power and pressure, is that only in exceptional cases (New York City is one of them) have they had the numbers to make these latter means of advancement effective. As a result, their political skills are poor (where are the master Jewish politicians in America?), but their ability to score the highest grades in examinations and to develop money-getting competence still shows no sign of declining.

The ideologies that have justified the principle of measurable individual merit and the logic of the market place, where one man's money is equal to any other man's, have always appeared to Jews, even more than to other Americans, almost self-evidently just and right. And the New York *Times,* which most of the newer Negro leaders dislike intensely, expresses this liberal ideology in its purest form. The *Times* has never been tolerant toward the accommodations that others have sometimes seen as necessary in our mixed and complex society—the balanced ticket, for example, which has nothing to do with the abstract principles of merit.

But the liberal principles—the earlier ones arguing the democracy of money, the newer ones arguing the democracy of merit—that have been so congenial to Jews and so much in their interest are being increasingly accepted by everyone else nowadays under the pressures of a technological world. We are moving into a diploma society, where individual merit rather than family and connections and group must be the basis for advancement, recognition, achievement. The reasons have nothing directly to do with the Jews, but no matter—the Jews certainly gain from such a grand historical shift. Thus Jewish interests coincide with the new rational approaches to the distribution of rewards.

It is clear that one cannot say the same about Negro interests. And so the Negroes have come to be opposed to these approaches. But when Negroes challenge—as they do in New York—the systems of testing by which school principals and higher officials in the educational bureaucracy are selected and promoted, they are also challenging the very system under which Jews have done so well. And when they challenge the use of grades as the sole criterion for entry into special high schools and free colleges, they challenge the system which has enabled Jews to dominate these institutions for decades.

But there is another and more subtle side to the shift of Negro demands from abstract equality to group consideration, from color-blind to color-conscious. The Negroes press these new demands because they see that the abstract color-blind policies do not lead rapidly enough to the entry of large numbers of Negroes into goods jobs, good neighborhoods, good schools. It is, in other words, a group interest they wish to further. Paradoxically, however, the ultimate basis of the resistance to their demands, I am convinced—certainly among Jews, but not Jews alone—is that they pose a serious threat to the ability of other groups to maintain *their* communities.

In America we have lived under a peculiar social compact. On the one hand, publicly and formally and legally, we recognize only individuals; we do not recognize groups—whether ethnic, racial, or religious. On the other hand, these groups exist in actual social fact. They strongly color the activities and lives of most of our citizens. They in large measure determine an individual's fate through their control of social networks which tend to run along ethnic, racial, and religious lines. Even more subtly, they determine a man's fate by the culture and values they transmit, which affect his chances in the general competition for the abstract signs of merit and money.

This is not an easy situation to grasp. On the one hand (except for the South) there is equality—political equality, equal justice before the law, equal opportunity to get grades, take examinations, qualify for professions, open businesses, make money. This equality penetrates deeper and deeper into the society. The great private colleges now attempt to have nationally representative student bodies, not only geographically, but socially and economically and racially. The great private corporations reluctantly begin to accept the principle that, like a government civil service, they should open their selection processes and their recruiting procedures so that all may be represented. On the other hand, these uniform processes of selection for advancement, and the pattern of freedom to start a business and make money, operate not on a homogeneous mass of individuals, but on individuals as molded by a range of communities of different degrees of organization and self-consciousness, with different histories and cultures, and with different capacities to take advantage of the opportunities that are truly in large measure open to all.

Here we come to the crux of the Negro anger and the Jewish discomfort. The Negro anger is based on the fact that the system of formal equality produces so little for them. The Jewish discomfort is based on the fact that Jews discover they can no longer support the newest Negro demands, which may be designed from the Negro point of view to produce equality for all, but which are also designed to break down this pattern of communities. We must emphasize again that Jewish money, organizational strength, and political energy have played a major role in most cities and states in getting effective law and effective administration covering the rights to equal opportunity in employment, housing, and education. But all this past cooperation loses its relevance as it dawns on Jews, and others as well, that many Negro leaders are now beginning to expect that the pattern of their advancement in American society will take quite a different form from that of the immigrant ethnic groups. This new form may well be justified by the greater sufferings that have been inflicted on the Negroes by slavery, by the loss of their traditional culture, by their deliberate exclusion from power and privilege for the past century, by the new circumstances in American society which make the old pattern of advancement (through formal equality plus the support of the group) less effective today. But that it *is* a new form, a radically new one, for the integration of a group into American society, we must recognize.

In the past, the established groups in American society came to understand, eventually, that the newer groups would not push their claims for equality to the point where the special institutions of the older groups would no longer be able to maintain their identity. There were certainly delicate moments when it looked as if the strongly pressed and effectively supported Jewish demand for formal equality, combined with Jewish wealth and grades, would challenge the rights of vacation resorts, social clubs, and private schools of the old established white Protestant community to serve as exclusive institutions of that community. But after a time the established Protestant community realized there were limits to the demands of the Jews, as there were limits to the demands of the Catholics. They realized that Jews and Catholics could not demand the complete abolition of lines between the communities because they too wanted to maintain communities of their own. Most Jews wanted to remain members of a distinctive group, and regardless of how consistent they were in battering against the walls of privilege, they always implicitly accepted the argument that various forms of division between people, aside from those based on the abstract criteria of money and achievement, were legitimate in America. Thus, when John Slawson of the American Jewish Committee argued against the discriminatory practices of various social clubs, he did not, I believe, attack the right of a group to maintain distinctive institutions. He argued rather that Jews in banking or high politics could not conduct their *business* if they were not accepted as members of these clubs. He did not attack social discrimination as such—he attacked it because of its political and economic consequences and suggested it was abetting economic and political discrimination. The grounds he chose for his attack are revealing, for they indicate what he felt were the legitimate claims that one group in American society could raise about the way the other groups conducted their social life.

Now it is my sense of the matter that with the Negro revolution there has been a radical challenge to this pattern of individual advancement within an accepted structure of group distinctiveness. The white community into which the Negro now demands full entrance is not actually a single community—it is a series of communities. And all of them feel threatened by the implications of the new Negro demand for full equality. They did not previously realize how much store they set by their power to control the character of the social setting in which they lived. They did not realize this because their own demands generally did not involve or imply the dissolution of the established groups: they never really wanted to mingle too closely with these established groups. They demanded political representation—which assumed that the group continued. They demanded the right to their own schools, or (like the Catholics today) support for their own schools—which again proceeded from the assumption of group maintenance. They demanded equal rights in employment, in education, in housing. But as a matter of fact many of their jobs were held in business enterprises or in trades controlled by members of their own group. Many of them set up their own educational institutions to create the kind of higher education they thought desirable for their young people. If freedom of housing became an issue on occasion, such freedom was nevertheless used as much to create voluntary new concentrations of the group as to disperse it among other people.

The new Negro demands challenge the right to maintain these sub-communities far more radically than the demands of any other group in American history. As Howard Brotz has pointed out, the exclusion of the Negro from his legitimate place in American society was so extreme, so thoroughgoing, so complete, that all the political energy of the Negro has been directed toward beating down the barriers. The corollary of this exclusive focus is that most Negroes see nothing of value in the Negro group whose preservation requires separate institutions, residential concentration, or a ban on intermarriage. Or rather, the only thing that might justify such group solidarity is the political struggle itself—the struggle against all barriers. What other groups see as a value, Negroes see as a strategy in the fight for equal rights.

We have become far more sophisticated in our understanding of the meaning of equality, far more subtle in our understanding of the causes of inequality. As a result, political equality alone—which the Negro now enjoys in most parts of the country—is considered of limited importance. The demand for economic equality is now not the demand for equal opportunities for the equally qualified: it is the demand for equality of economic *results*—and it therefore raises such questions as why some businesses succeed and others fail, and how people are selected for advancement in large organizations. When we move into areas like that, we are not asking for abstract tolerance, or a simple desisting from discrimination. We are involving ourselves in the complex relationships between people, and we are examining the kinds of ties and judgments that go to make up our American sub-communities. Or consider the demand for equality in education, which has also become a demand for equality of *results*, of *outcomes*. Suppose one's capacity to gain from education depends on going to school with less than a majority of one's own group? Or suppose it depends on one's home background? Then how do we achieve equality of results? The answers to this question and many similar ones suggest that the deprived group must be inserted into the community of the advantaged. For otherwise there is no equality of outcome.

The force of present-day Negro demands is that the sub-community, because it either protects privileges or creates inequality, *has no right to exist*. That is why these demands pose a quite new challenge to the Jewish community, or to any sub-community. Using the work of Oscar Handlin and Will Herberg, the Jewish community has come up with a convenient defense of Jewish exclusiveness—namely, that everyone else is doing it, too. The thrust of present-day Negro demands is that everyone should *stop* doing it. I do not interpret Jewish discomfort over this idea as false liberalism—for Jewish liberalism, even if it has never confronted the question directly, has always assumed that the advancement of disadvantaged groups, both Jews and others, would proceed in such a way as to respect the group pattern of American life. But the new Negro leaders believe Negroes cannot advance without a modification of this pattern. The churches, one of the major means by which group identities maintain themselves, are challenged by the insistent Negro demand for entry into every church. And if the Jews, because their church is so special, are for the moment protected against this demand, they are not protected against demands for entry on equal footing into other institutions which are the true seats of Jewish exclusiveness—the Jewish business, for example, the Jewish union, or the Jewish (or largely Jewish) neighborhood and school. Thus Jews find their interests and those of formally less liberal neighbors becoming similar: they both have an interest in maintaining an area restricted to their own kind; an interest in managing the friendship and educational experiences of their children; an interest in passing on advantages in money and skills to them.

The Negro now demands entry into a world, a society, that does not exist, except in ideology. In that world there is only one American community, and in that world, heritage, ethnicity, religion, race are only incidental and accidental personal characteristics. There may be many reasons for such a world to come into existence—among them the fact that it may be necessary in order to provide full equality for the Negroes. But if we do move in this direction, we will have to create communities very different from the kinds in which most of us who have already arrived—Protestants, Catholics, Jews—now live.

Milton Himmelfarb

HOW WE ARE

Like Everyone Else, Only More So?

The ancients knew it and we learn it anew every day: no opinion is so absurd as not to be professed by some learned man. A favorite and long-lived absurd opinion of many who are learned and many who are intellectual (they are not entirely identical), especially if they are Jews, is about the Jews. In a current formulation, by a Jewish professor-social scientist-intellectual-radical (M.M. Tumin, "Conservative Trends in Jewish Life," *Judaism*, Spring 1964), it is this:

> . . . it would indeed be radical in American politics if there were an identifiable Jewish vote . . . [which] stood for a morally radical position on the political spectrum. And it would be a beautiful challenge to America. . . . [But] what do Jews stand for in America? For a normal distribution of political opinions along the same spectrum and in the same proportions as non-Jews. . . .
>
> The American Jewish community seems to be living on the rapidly shrinking psychic income from the capital investment of Jews of the last two thousand years—or the last thirty years. What can it mean, in all honesty, for the average Jew in America to claim . . . a heritage and tradition of social justice, of respect for knowledge and learning, of concern for culture? He appears today to care for these things no more than anyone else around him.

Here is an important sociological generalization. It would be all true if it were not, transparently, all false.

First, as to the assertion that we "stand for . . . a normal distribution of political opinion . . . in the same proportions as non-Jews": if Tumin had tried he could not have said anything more unreal. In 1948 *Public Opinion Quarterly* published a graph of attitudes toward guaranteed economic security. It was an ascending line from predominant hostility in denominations with a low proportion of manual workers, like the Congregationalists, to predominant support in denominations with a high proportion of manual workers, like the Baptists and Catholics. Seven major American denominations were represented by points on that line. One was not: the Jews, as low in manual workers as the Congregationalists, were as high in support for guaranteed security as Catholics and Baptists. When seven successive points are on a graph line and an eighth is completely off the line, the thing represented by that point must differ materially from the things represented by all the other points.

If a similar graph were to be drawn today, for voting, the Jewish point would still be off the line. In November 1964 we voted about 90 per cent for Johnson, i.e., against Goldwater—more than any other white group, whether defined by income, region, religion, or ethnic character, and possibly as much as the Negroes. (Of those Jews who did not vote for Johnson, not all voted for Goldwater. There were some Jewish votes for minority parties and some abstentions from voting for any Presidential candidate.) In Memphis, Tennessee, a defeated Republican candidate for the House of Representatives annoyed the Jews by his bewilderment about them: "I had hoped against hope that the Jewish group would see things my way. I am a businessman. They are businessmen. Apparently I didn't succeed. I am amazed that I couldn't. If ever there was a group that should be conservative, they should."

Earlier in 1964, in a Democratic Presidential primary, the Jews of Baltimore and the rest of Maryland voted against Governor Wallace of Alabama more than any other group of whites, and almost as much as the Negroes. In 1960, at each level of income, proportionately many more Jews voted for Kennedy (or against Nixon) than anyone else—including the Catholics, with their special reason for wanting to see Kennedy elected. In 1952 and 1956, and again during the Democratic convention in 1960, Jews were more enthusiastically for Stevenson than any other body of Americans. Tumin's "last thirty years" must mean the era of Franklin D. Roosevelt. We have not changed, in any essential way, from what we were then. In 1965 whose political worship is oriented to Roosevelt's shrine but the Jews'?

Second, as to a living tradition of social justice: in Tumin's 30's, as we know, Jews made up half of the membership of the radical movements. (Let us not inquire too closely into the beauty of some aspects of *that* "beautiful challenge," which as late as 1948 drew so many Jewish dupes to the other Wallace—who later realized he himself had been a dupe—that Truman lost New York to Dewey.) In the *Commentary* symposium of 1961 a young man not long out of college reported scornfully that *only* half of the campus radicals in his time had been Jews. In 1964 half or more of the white young men and women who went down to Mississippi to work with the Negroes and risk their lives were Jews. Most of them feel as superior to the Jewish solid-citizen community as Tumin, but are they so totally different from the community as they would like to believe? Proportionately, more rabbis have gone South, and have been jailed or beaten, than any other white clergymen. The Jews of Baltimore are solid citizens, and we have seen how they voted about Governor Wallace. The Jews of Kansas City and Detroit, in referenda on open housing (to benefit Negroes), have voted for it in a huge disproportion to other whites. In California, in November 1964, two-thirds of all the votes were *for* Proposition 14, an anti-Negro constitutional amendment on housing; but two-thirds of the Jewish votes were *against* it.

In the 1961 symposium one writer said that he had always been for Negro equality, because members of one minority naturally sympathize with other minorities. Last year was a good one for testing his proposition that minorities naturally sympathize with each other. The commentators singled out, above all, Polish backlash and Italian backlash within the general category of white backlash. Governor Wallace and Senator Goldwater were not strikingly unpopular with the ethnic minorities—who, in the referenda across the country, were almost solidly against open housing. (Yet objectively the others have as much of a stake in a liberal society as the Jews. A country ruled by Goldwaters and Wallaces could not be a happy place for Slavs and Mediterraneans.) These differences between the Jewish and the other minorities just possibly could mean that when the Jewish minority behaves well, it does so less because it is a minority than because it is Jewish.

If we think of social justice to the poor, no others nearly so prosperous as the Jews, on the average, so ardently favor a welfare state. That is as much so now as in 1948, the year of the graph. If we think of social justice as including civil liberties, the polls consistently found a much higher proportion of Jews than others opposed to Senator McCarthy, and more strongly opposed. (Gallup, June 1954, "intense disapproval" of McCarthy: Jews 65 per cent, but Protestants 31, Democrats 38, college graduates 45; Roper, March 1957, gauge of attitudes toward McCarthy expressed as an index number: Jews -46, and executives and professionals—the next most disapproving group—only -18.) And does anyone imagine that the membership and financial support of, say, the American Civil Liberties Union are proportionately Jewish and no more?

Third, as to respect for knowledge and learning: let the colleges and universities testify. At a time when America has broken every precedent the world has ever known by sending almost 30 per cent of its young people to college, the American Jewish community is sending almost 80 per cent. Short of hiring truancy officers to round up abstainers, we could hardly send more. Or are we to understand that few young Jews are studying for advanced degrees? That would be news in the graduate schools. Or is the professor asserting that Jews have been turning their backs on teaching in the universities? The mind, as Mr. Wodehouse might say, boggles.

Finally, as to a deficient concern for culture: who, us? A few years ago someone in the publishing business, writing in the *New Leader,* estimated that something like a quarter of the buyers of books in the United States were Jews. (We are barely 3 per cent of the population.) In his recent *Culture Consumers,* Alvin Toffler is struck by the share of Jews among those who go to concerts, theaters, and museums, support orchestras, and buy works of art. What appears in print only confirms what everyone knows by direct observation. That is the way things are, and it is the way they used to be in Berlin and Vienna, Budapest and Prague. When the bourgeoisie stopped saying daily prayers, Hegel said, it started reading daily newspapers. When the Jews of those cities became modern, they put a piano in the parlor and the collected works of Goethe, Lessing, and Schiller in the bookcase; and many, especially the women, went so far as to play the pianos and read the books. Though the outer form may change, the inner substance remains. In America today, where you find culture vultures there you will not find Jews lacking.

As I was reading Tumin's jeremiad against the backsliding of the children of Israel, I had a feeling of *déjà lu:* Jeremiah, of course, and the other prophets; and of course the Jewish preachers in every generation, as Marshall Sklare suggested in the comments accompanying the paper, who were convinced that there had been a sad decline in piety and learning from the days of their grandparents. (A distinguished historian, Jacob Katz of Jerusalem, has discussed the difficulty of using sermons as data for social reality.) But then it came to me. Tumin was raising the standard of the Jewish 30's, and the Jews of the 30's had been judged in a 1944 symposium in *Commentary's* predecessor, the *Contemporary Jewish Record*. Alfred Kazin, Lionel Trilling, and Clement Greenberg, among others, took part. Tumin might have been quoting them.

Kazin: ". . . timidity . . . parochialism . . . dreary middle-class chauvinism. . . ."

Trilling: ". . . provincial and parochial . . . no sustenance to . . . the artist or intellectual. . . ."

Greenberg: ". . . suffocatingly middle-class . . . No people on earth are more correct, more staid, more provincial, more commonplace. . . ." (There was yet another symposium, in 1951, to discuss Morris Freedman's anticipation of Tumin—an accusation that the Jewish student was not what he had been in the former, great times. In the meanwhile, the woman who never let you forget her son the doctor was being overtaken and surpassed by the woman who was quick to remind you of her son the assistant professor.)

Tumin is no more alone now than the symposiasts of 1944 were then. In 1964 a Gentile sociologist issued a preposterous report alleging that the Jews studied by his graduate students were more prejudiced than others. The students had done the rating of prejudice. Probably most of them were Jews, and it would be no surprise if they were so eager to see the Jews as no better than the rest that they rated them as worse than the rest. Similarly, in a work that appeared a few years ago on the sociology of a Jewish community, the Jewish authors adduce the Jewish country club as proof that the Jews are as bad as the Gentiles. A few pages later they note that an applicant for membership had better have a record of substantial contributions to Jewish philanthropies. Is that bad? For the authors, it shows that the Jews vie with each other in splashy expenditure.

Anyone who looks at country clubs must note real differences between Jewish and Gentile clubs, which ought to be particularly notable to sociologists. Since the sociologists in question are Jews, it is left to *Sports Illustrated* (March 5, 1962) to instruct us:

> Discrimination aside, Jewish country clubs generally differ from their Christian counterparts in a couple of ways. For one, the Jewish clubs put greater emphasis on charity; a prospective member is expected to be philanthropic (one club in the New York area requires that an applicant must have given $10,000 to United Jewish Appeal). For another, members of Jewish clubs habitually eat more and drink less than do Christian club members. It is possible to pick out the Jewish clubs from the clubs surveyed in Horwath and Horwath's annual anonymous study simply by checking the food and beverage expenditures of the average member. In one Jewish club, for instance, the average member spent $455 on food and only $134 on drink. At a comparable Christian club the average member spent $275 for food and $240 for drinks.

I have never been, am not, and do not expect ever to be a member of any country club; and I am mindful of what Lionel Trilling said in 1944 about American Jews being "self-indulgent" (that would go with eating more than Gentiles) "and self-admiring" (for drinking less, I suppose, and exacting large sums for philanthropy). The point of all this is that on the evidence that has been amassed, even about country clubs, no objective sociologist could deny Jewish difference.

Radicals and intellectuals may not know it, but they have enthusiastic allies in pretending that the Jews are like everyone else, only more so. Most Jews, at one time or another, believe it and say it, but those who say it loudest and most often are the kind one would suppose to be at the furthest remove from the radical intelligentsia. Tumin says that we stand for "a normal distribution of political opinions . . . in the same proportions as non-Jews." For its part, the American Council for Judaism is reported in the New York *Times* as having said, after the 1964 election, that "although [Republican] Senator Keating [of New York] had 'made the strongest appeal in history [?] to Jewish voters, as Jews,' he had made only small gains among Jewish voters." Small gains? In Jewish districts Keating's Democratic opponent, Robert Kennedy, did more than 20 per cent worse than President Johnson—and more than 15 per cent worse than his brother, the President, had done in 1960. He did not do so poorly in other Johnson-President Kennedy districts. The radicals and intellectuals, on the one hand, and the American Council for Judaism types, on the other, are united in insisting that in those things where we are in fact significantly different the Jews are like-everyone-else-only-more-so.

Why should ACJ and the radicals agree with each other in rejecting the plain evidence of their senses? For ACJ the answer is simple. They do not want the Jews to be different, and particularly do they not want the Jews to look different. Only Jewish invisibility could make them comfortable, and they try by incantation to persuade themselves—even they must know they are not persuading others—that the Jews are an optical illusion.

For the radicals and intellectuals, suitably, the answer is less simple. As the independent repetition of the words must demonstrate, they detest provincialism and parochialism. Particularisms are obstacles in the way of the Messianic Age, secular style. The Jewish community, or Jewish society, is particular and also—so they say—provincial and parochial. But they are upset because something is clearly wrong in this chain of observation, reasoning, and profession of faith. If they were not upset, so many intelligent people would not be saying so many foolish things.

You have to deny the special propensity of Jews, because they are Jews, for the very values you cherish. Otherwise you would have to ask yourself, more insistently than you would like, how attached you yourself would be to those values if you had not been born to Jewish parents. That sort of thing could shake a faith blended of cosmopolitanism and individualism. (Individualism is my shy conviction that when all is said and done, I have achieved my present moral and intellectual grandeur unassisted because in the inmost core of my self, I am—no two ways about it—morally and intellectually pretty grand. In a bourgeois this appears as the myth of the self-made man. "For he says: 'By the strength of my hand I have done it, and by my wisdom, for I have understanding. . . .'")

Worse still, you might have to recognize that: if you truly want people who care for social justice, respect knowledge and learning, and are concerned about culture—why, the hard fact is that such people are more likely to be found among the Jews than anywhere else. Since that has also been the hard fact in so many other places for so long, a good breeding ground for those desirable propensities might be the Jewish community, that distressingly particular and parochial thing. The Jewish community, though obviously quite awful, must equally obviously be less awful than practically anything else. Instead of your values requiring a dissolution of the Jewish community, may they not rather need a Jewish community to assure that an important base of support for them will continue to exist?

But to go on with such thinking could lead to all kinds of reactionary conclusions, possibly even of a personal character. There is a way out. All you have to say is what your predecessors said—that while the Jewish community may have been all right somewhat earlier, the contemporary Jewish community has practically nothing in common with it; and to say that, all you have to do is to prefer fable to fact. The difficulty is that each succeeding generation has less excuse for the preference.

Postscript. Engineers know that Murphy's Law is inexorable: what can go wrong will go wrong. Soldiers have Moltke's Law: what can be misunderstood will be misunderstood. The more general law is in itself neither pessimistic nor optimistic: what can be will be. Its unceasing operation was again revealed to me after I had finished the part about the unexpected agreement of the radical intellectuals and their opposites, the American Council for Judaism. A colleague showed me some ACJ publications, and there it was, almost as explicitly as if it had been written to make my point. What can be will be.

ACJ's *Briefs* for November-December 1964 was shocked because Rabbi Joachim Prinz had declared from his pulpit before Election Day: "A Jewish vote for Goldwater is a vote for Jewish suicide." It impeached Rabbi Prinz for three sins: violating the political neutrality of the pulpit, unpatriotically suggesting—ACJ is nothing if not patriotic—that the United States was threatened by something fascist, and thus encouraging Jewish self-ghettoization.

On Goldwater and a fascist threat, Tumin must be closer to Rabbi Prinz than to ACJ. Yet ACJ's *Education in Judaism* for June-July 1964 is filled with admiration for "Tumin's article": "provocative"—O.K.—and "well worth reading." Why so? Because he said: "No one has a right to self-ghettoization." Blessed word! For its sake much is forgiven and an embrace is offered.

Politics, as someone said when a candidate went back to living with his wife, makes strange bedfellows.

When Good Clashes with Good

For most of us it is hard to concede that a passion for one good thing can conflict with a passion for another good thing: if Liberty, Equality, and

Fraternity are simultaneously desirable, why should they not be simultaneously attainable?

Professor Tumin takes it for granted that there can be no tension, let alone conflict, between a desire for social justice and respect for knowledge and learning. Yet when the Jews' zeal for justice is blunted, it is apt to be blunted precisely by their zeal for education. For instance, too many Jews in New York go along with Parents and Taxpayers in opposing Negro demands on the school system, afraid that meeting those demands will result in lowering the quality of their own children's education.

The particular issue about which PAT has been able to mobilize is the pairing of mostly white and mostly Negro elementary schools. That issue by itself does not come close to justifying the anxiety it has aroused, but if we look beyond we must recognize that as things stand now, there is in fact and in principle a tension, or outright conflict, between the requirements of justice for the Negroes and the requirements of first-rate education. What is more, Negroes seem to think so, too. In essence, they say this: "You whites have so contrived matters that we Negroes are unable to meet what you are pleased to call your objective, color-blind tests. We will no longer submit to rules that put us at a disadvantage. Admit us to your schools. If that means a lowering of standards for you, it will mean a raising of standards for us—and it is the only way for them to be raised. The lowering of standards will be temporary, until we have been qualified to compete with a fair chance of success. But whether it is more temporary or less, that is the price you must pay now for the profit you have reaped all these many years from keeping us down."

To which whites respond with the old self-evident truths—which apparently are not evident to Negroes—about impersonal tests and *les carrières ouvertes aux talents*. Jews, especially, hold those truths to be self-evident. They are our ideology and they are our self-interest, because we do well when they prevail. For us those rules, those truths, define justice itself. Most of us are not even aware of a tension between our desire for justice and our passion for education. In resisting Negro demands that give a secondary place to objective standards, we really think we are on the side of justice.

Negroes are more candid with themselves than Jews in recognizing privately, and often publicly, that their ideology is designed to serve their interest. A good illustration, in which a conflict over high educational standards figures centrally, is an alliance now in the making between New York City Negroes and conservative upstate Republicans favoring tuition fees in the City University of New York, against the liberal city Democrats fighting to maintain the century-old policy of no fees. Why should Negroes, mostly poor, ally themselves with conservatives, and why should they want to get rid of the City University's no-fee policy? Professor Lester

H. Granger, formerly the executive secretary of the Urban League, lets us see why in a report to a State Senate committee. According to the newspapers,

> The report . . . suggested that by charging tuition the university could take in 3,000 students now excluded by entrance requirements that are artificially inflated [i.e., traditionally high] because of lack of facilities.
>
> Scholarship assistance to low-income students [i.e., Negroes, mostly] would limit the tuition charges to those who could afford it [i.e., lower-middle-class Jews, mostly]. . . .
>
> Professor Granger proposed that admissions to the university "be allocated among the various high schools of the city—a uniform percentage of the ranking graduates of each school." [This would mean fewer students from the better high schools, with their heavy Jewish concentration, and more from the other schools, especially the mostly Negro ones.]

Is justice on Professor Granger's side? If so, it is at odds with high educational standards. To prefer it to those standards would mean the city colleges having to abandon their old norms even more than they are alleged to have done already. Or is justice on the conventionally liberal side, which would retain the no-fee, entrance-by-merit, color-blind policies? If so, it would favor the well-fed over the ill-fed. One is rightly suspicious of that kind of justice.

In New York today, the educational self-interest of Jews clashes with the educational self-interest of Negroes. It is a serious clash because education is a serious matter, determining how much your children will earn, what kind of life they will live, and what they will be able to do for *their* children. It is also a matter in which Jews have a big investment of tradition and emotion; and Negroes, of aspiration and resentment. Wherever justice lies in that clash of self-interests, there is going to be a fight.

Nevertheless, if there is no way of solving the dilemma, there may be a way of bypassing it. The fight is over the distribution of a scarce resource, cheap higher education. Make the resource more plentiful and there will be less need to fight. To do that, much more money will have to be raised in taxes for higher education. Fortunately for our moral credit and our consciences, Jews always vote enthusiastically for improving or expanding education, on any level—even when the direct beneficiaries are not our children.

The Case of Senator Keating

There must have been something about Kenneth Keating that caused the Jews of New York State to give him a far greater share of their votes (though not a majority) than they normally give a Republican. In looking for that cause, the first thing we can rule out is conservative trends. For the Jews who backed Keating, he was more, not less liberal than Robert Kennedy. Even if they were prepared to admit that the two were equally liberal, they thought a vote for Keating would serve liberalism better.

The most compelling urgency of all was to defeat Goldwater—crushingly, conspicuously, exemplarily. Keating had made an honorable, acceptably liberal record for himself. He won sympathies by firmly dissociating himself from Goldwater and so earning the hatred of the Goldwater enthusiasts that the rightist Conservative party ran a candidate and directed most of its propaganda against him. In voting for such a man, his Jewish supporters reasoned, they would be rewarding someone who deserved it and at the same time helping to discredit right-wing fanaticism. Especially if he won, but even if he did not lose badly—while Goldwater was losing very badly indeed, they hoped—the Republican party thenceforth might see the advantage of nominating people like him, and America might be blessed for a long time to come with the happy necessity of choosing between liberals called Democrats and liberals called Republicans.

Since his election to the Senate in 1958, Keating had been cultivating the Jews. He had made himself heard repeatedly in favor of Israel and against Soviet anti-Semitism, and he had seen to it that his person and his words came to the attention of people assembled as Jewish audiences and people whose names were on the mailing lists of Jewish organizations. During the campaign he could not be accused of neglecting this means of recalling to the Jews who he was and what he stood for. Neither could Kennedy. Both, of course, worked just as hard at doing the same sort of thing with the Italians, the Negroes, the Puerto Ricans, and all the rest.

To determine how much this helped Keating with the Jews, or how much it ever helps any other candidate who does it, is extraordinarily hard. The more sophisticated the politician, the better he knows that the Jews are fairly sophisticated, too, on the whole, and that you have to approach us with something else than simple pro-Jewish oratory. What we want is a broadly liberal program and tone, with a subtle, barely audible Jewish undertone of recognizable Jews on the speaker's platform and recognizably Jewish names on the letterhead or in the advertisements. The Jews I heard praising Keating did not mention his specifically pro-Jewish stands, but presented the "unparochial" argument I have been summarizing. If anything, they were probably a little embarrassed by the Jewish note that was sounded. (Of course, there are Jewish voters, generally less sophisticated, who respond to political appeals couched in explicitly Jewish language. It is a question of proportions. More than others, we have, or want to think we have, a broad view of political questions.)

But perhaps the subtleties are even subtler than that. Some who spoke the language of unparochial liberalism on behalf of Keating—and meant it—may have secretly wanted, too, to show their approval of his specifically pro-Jewish deeds and intentions. Either they were uneasy about it within themselves or they feared that even to mention it would get them lectured at by the other Jewish liberals they were talking with—who themselves may have had the same feelings, and therefore did not say anything aloud, either.

Possibly, also, some would have been more dissatisfied with the absence of an explicitly pro-Jewish appeal than they were embarrassed by its presence. If a groupy appeal is made to everyone else, if it is normal American practice, what could be the meaning of not making one to the Jews? Are we abnormal? Or so taken for granted that a candidate can believe that only for us need he not bestir himself? If a big part of politics is the competition of interests, and if in many things the general interest is defined as a kind of moment of the forces of particular interests, why exclude ours? Jewish abnegation would not abolish self-interest, it would only injure Jewish self-interest; and by remaining quiet while everyone else was shouting, we would be allowing the final consensus to be worse (from our point of view, at least) than if we, or our representatives, had spoken up, too.

This kind of thinking should not prevail at the expense of liberalism, but neither is it to be disdained. It has intrinsic worth. And let those who dislike it for extrinsic reasons, out of an anxiety about what the Gentiles will say, remember this: what is natural rarely puzzles or alarms, and nothing is more natural than the ties of like people with each other. One knows where one is with that. It is familiar, limited, of the same order as all the other ties of all the other families of mankind. More than a hundred years ago it was an American, a naval officer leading his squadron without authorization to the rescue of a British flotilla in China, who said that blood is thicker than water.

An apparent lack of such natural impulses, a devotion to what seems to others only abstract, general, ideological, altruistic—that is what puzzles and alarms. There is something almost uncanny about it, making for discomfort in the beholder. If that Republican candidate had had it explained to him that the Jewish businessmen of Memphis were voting as they did because they saw in the Goldwater movement a threat to themselves as Jews, as well as a threat to liberal values, even he might have understood.

What no one can understand is claptrap—like a denial of anything specifically Jewish about the way all those individual businessmen, who happened to be Jews, also happened to vote differently from the Gentile businessmen.

Bayard Rustin

FROM PROTEST TO POLITICS

The Future of the Civil Rights Movement

The decade spanned by the 1954 Supreme Court decision on school desegregation and the Civil Rights Act of 1964 will undoubtedly be recorded as the period in which the legal foundations of racism in America were destroyed. To be sure, pockets of resistance remain; but it would be hard to quarrel with the assertion that the elaborate legal structure of segregation and discrimination, particularly in relation to public accommodations, has virtually collapsed. On the other hand, without making light of the human sacrifices involved in the direct-action tactics (sit-ins, freedom rides, and the rest) that were so instrumental to this achievement, we must recognize that in desegregating public accommodations, we affected institutions which are relatively peripheral both to the American socio-economic order and to the fundamental conditions of life of the Negro people. In a highly industrialized, 20th-century civilization, we hit Jim Crow precisely where it was most anachronistic, dispensable, and vulnerable—in hotels, lunch counters, terminals, libraries, swimming pools, and the like. For in these forms, Jim Crow does impede the flow of commerce in the broadest sense: it is a nuisance in a society on the move (and on the make). Not surprisingly, therefore, it was the most mobility-conscious and relatively liberated groups in the Negro community—lower-middle-class college students—who launched the attack that brought down this imposing but hollow structure.

The term "classical" appears especially apt for this phase of the civil rights movement. But in the few years that have passed since the first flush of sit-ins, several developments have taken place that have complicated matters enormously. One is the shifting focus of the movement in the South, symbolized by Birmingham; another is the spread of the revolution to the North; and the third, common to the other two, is the expansion of the movement's base in the Negro community. To attempt to disentangle these three strands is to do violence to reality. David Danzig's perceptive article, "The Meaning of Negro Strategy" (*Commentary,* February 1964), correctly saw in the Birmingham events the victory of the concept of collective struggle over individual achievement as the road to Negro freedom. And Birmingham remains the unmatched symbol of grass-roots protest involving all strata of the black community. It was also in this most industrialized of Southern cities that the single-issue demands of the movement's classical stage gave way to the "package deal." No longer were Negroes satisfied with integrating lunch counters. They now sought advances in employment, housing, school integration, police protection, and so forth.

Thus, the movement in the South began to attack areas of discrimination which were not so remote from the Northern experience as were Jim Crow lunch counters. At the same time, the interrelationship of these apparently distinct areas became increasingly evident. What is the value of winning access to public accommodations for those who lack money to use them? The minute the movement faced this question, it was compelled to expand its vision beyond race relations to economic relations, including the role of education in modern society. And what also became clear is that all these interrelated problems, by their very nature, are not soluble by private, voluntary efforts but require government action—or politics. Already Southern demonstrators had recognized that the most effective way to strike at the police brutality they suffered from was by getting rid of the local sheriff—and that meant political action, which in turn meant, and still means, political action within the Democratic party where the only meaningful primary contests in the South are fought.

And so, in Mississippi, thanks largely to the leadership of Bob Moses, a turn toward political action has been taken. More than voter registration is involved here. A conscious bid for *political power* is being made, and in the course of that effort a tactical shift is being effected: direct-action techniques are being subordinated to a strategy calling for the building of community institutions or power bases. Clearly, the implications of this shift reach far beyond Mississippi. What began as a protest movement is being challenged to translate itself into a political movement. Is this the right course? And if it is, can the transformation be accomplished?

II

The very decade which has witnessed the decline of legal Jim Crow has also seen the rise of *de facto* segregation in our most fundamental socioeconomic institutions. More Negroes are unemployed today than in 1954, and the unemployment gap between the races is wider. The median income of Negroes has dropped from 57 per cent to 54 per cent of that of whites. A higher percentage of Negro workers is now concentrated in jobs vulnerable to automation than was the case ten years ago. More Negroes attend *de facto* segregated schools today than when the Supreme Court handed down its famous decision; while school integration proceeds at a snail's pace in the South, the number of Northern schools with an excessive proportion of minority youth proliferates. And behind this is the continuing growth of racial slums, spreading over our central cities and trapping Negro youth in a milieu which, whatever its legal definition, sows an unimaginable demoralization. Again, legal niceties aside, a resident of a racial ghetto lives in segregated housing, and more Negroes fall into this category than ever before.

These are the facts of life which generate frustration in the Negro community and challenge the civil rights movement. At issue, after all, is not *civil rights,* strictly speaking, but social and economic conditions. Last summer's riots were not race riots; they were outbursts of class aggression in a society where class and color definitions are converging disastrously. How can the (perhaps misnamed) civil rights movement deal with this problem?

Before trying to answer, let me first insist that the task of the movement is vastly complicated by the failure of many whites of good will to understand the nature of our problem. There is a widespread assumption that the removal of artificial racial barriers should result in the automatic integration of the Negro into all aspects of American life. This myth is fostered by facile analogies with the experience of various ethnic immigrant groups, particularly the Jews. But the analogies with the Jews do not hold for three simple but profound reasons. First, Jews have a long history as a literate people, a resource which has afforded them opportunities to advance in the academic and professional worlds, to achieve intellectual status even in the midst of economic hardship, and to evolve sustaining value systems in the context of ghetto life. Negroes, for the greater part of their presence in this country, were forbidden by law to read or write. Second, Jews have a long history of family stability, the importance of which in terms of aspiration and self-image is obvious. The Negro family structure was totally destroyed by slavery and with it the possibility of cultural transmission (the right of Negroes to marry and rear children is barely a century old). Third, Jews are white and have the *option* of relinquishing their cultural-religious identity, intermarrying, passing, etc. Negroes, or at least the overwhelming majority of them, do not have this option. There is also a fourth, vulgar reason. If the Jewish and Negro communities are not comparable in terms of education, family structure, and color, it is also true that their respective economic roles bear little resemblance.

This matter of economic role brings us to the greater problem—the fact that we are moving into an era in which the natural functioning of the market does not by itself ensure every man with will and ambition a place in the productive process. The immigrant who came to this country during the late 19th and early 20th centuries entered a society which was expanding territorially and/or economically. It was then possible to start at the bottom, as an unskilled or semi-skilled worker, and move up the ladder, acquiring new skills along the way. Especially was this true when industrial unionism was burgeoning, giving new dignity and higher wages to organized workers. Today the situation has changed. We are not expanding territorially, the western frontier is settled, labor organizing has leveled off, our rate of economic growth has been stagnant for a decade. And we are in the midst of a technological revolution which is altering the fundamental structure of the labor force, destroying unskilled and semi-skilled jobs—jobs in which Negroes are disproportionately concentrated.

Whatever the pace of this technological revolution may be, the *direction* is clear: the lower rungs of the economic ladder are being lopped off. This means that an individual will no longer be able to start at the bottom and work his way up; he will have to start in the middle or on top, and hold on tight. It will not even be enough to have certain specific skills, for many skilled jobs are also vulnerable to automation. A broad educational background, permitting vocational adaptability and flexibility, seems more imperative than ever. We live in a society where, as Secretary of Labor Willard Wirtz puts it, machines have the equivalent of a high school diploma. Yet the average educational attainment of American Negroes is 8.2 years.

Negroes, of course, are not the only people being affected by these developments. It is reported that there are now 50 per cent fewer unskilled and semi-skilled jobs than there are high school dropouts. Almost one-third of the 26 million young people entering the labor market in the 1960's will be dropouts. But the percentage of Negro dropouts nationally is 57 per cent, and in New York City, among Negroes 25 years of age or over, it is 68 per cent. They are without a future.

To what extent can the kind of self-help campaign recently prescribed by Eric Hoffer in the *New York Times Magazine* cope with such a situation? I would advise those who think that self-help is the answer to familiarize themselves with the long history of such efforts in the Negro community, and to consider why so many foundered on the shoals of ghetto life. It goes without saying that any effort to combat demoralization and apathy is desirable, but we must understand that demoralization in the Negro community is largely a common-sense response to an objective reality. Negro youths have no need of statistics to perceive, fairly accurately, what their odds are in American society. Indeed, from the point of view of motivation, some of the healthiest Negro youngsters I know are juvenile delinquents: vigorously pursuing the American Dream of material acquisition and status, yet finding the conventional means of attaining it blocked off, they do not yield to defeatism but resort to illegal (and often ingenious) methods. They are not alien to American culture. They are, in Gunnar Myrdal's phrase, "exaggerated Americans." To want a Cadillac is not un-American; to push a cart in the garment center is. If Negroes are to be persuaded that the conventional path (school, work, etc.) is superior, we had better provide evidence which is now sorely lacking. It is a double cruelty to harangue Negro youth about education and training when we do not know what jobs will be available for them. When a Negro youth can reasonably foresee a future free of slums, when the prospect of gainful employment is realistic, we will see motivation and self-help in abundant enough quantities.

Meanwhile, there is an ironic similarity between the self-help advocated by many liberals and the doctrines of the Black Muslims. Professional sociologists, psychiatrists, and social workers have expressed amazement at the Muslims' success in transforming prostitutes and dope addicts into respectable citizens. But every prostitute the Muslims convert to a model of Calvinist virtue is replaced by the ghetto with two more. Dedicated as they are to maintenance of the ghetto, the Muslims are powerless to effect substantial moral reform. So too with every other group or program which is not aimed at the destruction of slums, their causes and effects. Self-help efforts, directly or indirectly, must be geared to mobilizing people into power units capable of effecting social change. That is, their goal must be genuine self-help, not merely self-improvement. Obviously, where self-improvement activities succeed in imparting to their participants a feeling of some control over their environment, those involved may find their appetites for change whetted; they may move into the political arena.

III

Let me sum up what I have thus far been trying to say: the civil rights movement is evolving from a protest movement into a full-fledged *social movement*—an evolution calling its very name into question. It is now concerned not merely with removing the barriers to full *opportunity* but with achieving the fact of *equality*. From sit-ins and freedom rides we have gone into rent strikes, boycotts, community organization, and political action. As a consequence of this natural evolution, the Negro today finds himself stymied by obstacles of far greater magnitude than the legal barriers he was attacking before: automation, urban decay, *de facto* school segregation. These are problems which, while conditioned by Jim Crow, do not vanish upon its demise. They are more deeply rooted in our socio-economic order; they are the result of the total society's failure to meet not only the Negro's needs, but human needs generally.

These propositions have won increasing recognition and acceptance, but with a curious twist. They have formed the common premise of two apparently contradictory lines of thought which simultaneously nourish and antagonize each other. On the one hand, there is the reasoning of the New York *Times* moderate who says that the problems are so enormous and complicated that Negro militancy is a futile irritation, and that the need is for "intelligent moderation." Thus, during the first New York school boycott, the *Times* editorialized that Negro demands, while abstractly just, would necessitate massive reforms, the funds for which could not realistically be anticipated; therefore the just demands were also foolish demands and would only antagonize white people. Moderates of this stripe are often correct in perceiving the difficulty or impossibility of racial progress in the context of present social and economic policies. But they accept the context as fixed. They ignore (or perhaps see all too well) the potentialities inherent in linking Negro demands to broader pressures for radical revision of existing policies. They apparently see nothing strange in the fact that in the last twenty-five years we have spent nearly a trillion dollars fighting or preparing for wars, yet throw up our hands before the need for overhauling our schools, clearing the slums, and really abolishing poverty. My quarrel with these moderates is that they do not even envision radical changes; their admonitions of moderation are, for all practical purposes, admonitions to the Negro to adjust to the status quo, and are therefore immoral.

The more effectively the moderates argue their case, the more they convince Negroes that American society will not or cannot be reorganized for full racial equality. Michael Harrington has said that a successful war on poverty might well require the expenditure of a $100 billion. Where, the Negro wonders, are the forces now in motion to compel such a commitment? If the voices of the moderates were raised in an insistence upon a reallocation of national resources at levels that could not be confused with tokenism (that is, if the moderates stopped being moderates), Negroes would have greater grounds for hope. Meanwhile, the Negro movement cannot escape a sense of isolation.

It is precisely this sense of isolation that gives rise to the second line of thought I want to examine—the tendency within the civil rights movement which, despite its militancy, pursues what I call a "no-win" policy. Sharing with many moderates a recognition of the magnitude of the obstacles to freedom, spokesmen for this tendency survey the American scene and find no forces prepared to move toward radical solutions. From this they conclude that the only viable strategy is shock; above all, the hypocrisy of white liberals must be exposed. These spokesmen are often described as the radicals of the movement, but they are really its moralists. They seek to change white hearts—by traumatizing them. Frequently abetted by white self-flagellants, they may gleefully applaud (though not really agreeing with) Malcolm X because, while they admit he has no program, they think he can frighten white people into doing the right thing. To believe this, of course, you must be convinced, even if unconsciously, that at the core of the white man's heart lies a buried affection for Negroes—a proposition one may be permitted to doubt. But in any case, hearts are not relevant to the issue; neither racial affinities nor racial hostilities are rooted there. It is institutions—social, political, and economic institutions—which are the ultimate molders of collective sentiments. Let these institutions be reconstructed *today,* and let the ineluctable gradualism of history govern the formation of a new psychology.

My quarrel with the "no-win" tendency in the civil rights movement (and the reason I have so designated it) parallels my quarrel with the moderates outside the movement. As the latter lack the vision or will for fundamental change, the former lack a realistic strategy for achieving it. For such a strategy they substitute militancy. But militancy is a matter of posture and volume and not of effect.

I believe that the Negro's struggle for equality in America is essentially revolutionary. While most Negroes—in their hearts—unquestionably seek only to enjoy the fruits of American society as it now exists, their quest cannot *objectively* be satisfied within the framework of existing political and economic relations. The young Negro who would demonstrate his way into the labor market may be motivated by a thoroughly bourgeois ambition and thoroughly "capitalist" considerations, but he will end up having to favor a great expansion of the public sector of the economy. At any rate, that is the position the movement will be forced to take as it looks at the number of jobs being generated by the private economy, and if it is to remain true to the masses of Negroes.

The revolutionary character of the Negro's struggle is manifest in the fact that this struggle may have done more to democratize life for whites than for Negroes. Clearly, it was the sit-in movement of young Southern Negroes which, as it galvanized white students, banished the ugliest features of McCarthyism from the American campus and resurrected political debate. It was not until Negroes assaulted *de facto* school segregation in the urban centers that the issue of quality education for *all* children stirred into motion. Finally, it seems reasonably clear that the civil rights movement, directly and through the resurgence of social conscience it kindled, did more to initiate the war on poverty than any other single force.

It will be—it has been—argued that these by-products of the Negro struggle are not revolutionary. But the term revolutionary, as I am using it, does not connote violence; it refers to the qualitative transformation of fundamental institutions, more or less rapidly, to the point where the social and economic structure which they comprised can no longer be said to be the same. The Negro struggle has hardly run its course; and it will not stop moving until it has been utterly defeated or won substantial equality. But I fail to see how the movement can be victorious in the absence of radical programs for full employment, abolition of slums, the reconstruction of our educational system, new definitions of work and leisure. Adding up the cost of such programs, we can only conclude that we are talking about a refashioning of our political economy. It has been estimated, for example, that the price of replacing New York City's slums with public housing would be $17 billion. Again, a multi-billion dollar federal public works program, dwarfing the currently proposed $2 billion program, is required to reabsorb unskilled and semi-skilled workers into the labor market—and this must be done if Negro workers in these categories are to be employed. "Preferential treatment" cannot help them.

I am not trying here to delineate a total program, only to suggest the scope of economic reforms which are most immediately related to the plight of the Negro community. One could speculate on their political implications—whether, for example, they do not indicate the obsolescence of state government and the superiority of regional structures as viable units of planning. Such speculations aside, it is clear that Negro needs cannot be satisfied unless we go beyond what has so far been placed on the agenda. How are these radical objectives to be achieved? The answer is simple, deceptively so: *through political power*.

There is a strong moralistic strain in the civil rights movement which would remind us that power corrupts, forgetting that the absence of power also corrupts. But this is not the view I want to debate here, for it is waning. Our problem is posed by those who accept the need for political power but do not understand the nature of the object and therefore lack sound strategies for achieving it; they tend to confuse political institutions with lunch counters.

A handful of Negroes, acting alone, could integrate a lunch counter by strategically locating their bodies so as *directly* to interrupt the operation of the proprietor's will; their numbers were relatively unimportant. In politics, however, such a confrontation is difficult because the interests involved are merely *represented*. In the execution of a political decision a direct confrontation may ensue (as when federal marshals escorted James Meredith into the University of Mississippi—to turn from an example of non-violent coercion to one of force backed up with the threat of violence). But in arriving at a political decision, numbers and organizations are crucial, especially for the economically disenfranchised. (Needless to say, I am assuming that the forms of political democracy exist in America, however imperfectly, that they are valued, and that elitist or putschist conceptions of exercising power are beyond the pale of discussion for the civil rights movement.)

Neither that movement nor the country's twenty million black people can win political power alone. We need allies. The future of the Negro struggle depends on whether the contradictions of this society can be resolved by a coalition of progressive forces which becomes the *effective* political majority in the United States. I speak of the coalition which staged the March on Washington, passed the Civil Rights Act, and laid the basis for the Johnson landslide—Negroes, trade unionists, liberals, and religious groups.

There are those who argue that a coalition strategy would force the Negro to surrender his political independence to white liberals, that he would be neutralized, deprived of his cutting edge, absorbed into the Establishment. Some who take this position urged last year that votes be withheld from the Johnson-Humphrey ticket as a demonstration of the Negro's political power. Curiously enough, these people who sought to demonstrate power through the non-exercise of it, also point to the Negro "swing vote" in crucial urban areas as the source of the Negro's independent political power. But here they are closer to being right: the urban Negro vote will grow in importance in the coming years. If there is anything positive in the spread of the ghetto, it is the potential political power base thus created, and to realize this potential is one of the most challenging and urgent tasks before the civil rights movement. If the movement can wrest leadership of the ghetto vote from the machines, it will have acquired an organized constituency such as other major groups in our society now have.

But we must also remember that the effectiveness of a swing vote depends solely on "other" votes. It derives its power from them. In that sense, it can never be "independent," but must opt for one candidate or the other, even if by default. Thus coalitions are inescapable, however tentative they may be. And this is the case in all but those few situations in which Negroes running on an independent ticket might conceivably win. "Independence," in other words, is not a value in itself. The issue is which coalition to join and how to make it responsive to your program. Necessarily there will be compromise. But the difference between expediency and morality in politics is the difference between selling out a principle and making smaller concessions to win larger ones. The leader who shrinks from this task reveals not his purity but his lack of political sense.

The task of molding a political movement out of the March on Washington coalition is not simple, but no alternatives have been advanced. We need to choose our allies on the basis of common political objectives. It has become fashionable in some no-win Negro circles to decry the white liberal as the main enemy (his hypocrisy is what sustains racism); by virtue of this reverse recitation of the reactionary's litany (liberalism leads to socialism, which leads to Communism) the Negro is left in majestic isolation, except for a tiny band of fervent white initiates. But the objective fact is that *Eastland and Goldwater* are the main enemies—they and the opponents of civil rights, of the war on poverty, of medicare, of social security, of federal aid to education, of unions, and so forth. The labor movement, despite its obvious faults, has been the largest single organized force in this country pushing for progressive social legislation. And where the Negro-labor-liberal axis is weak, as in the farm belt, it was the religious groups that were most influential in rallying support for the Civil Rights Bill.

The durability of the coalition was interestingly tested during the election. I do not believe that the Johnson landslide proved the "white backlash" to be a myth. It proved, rather, that economic interests are more fundamental than prejudice: the backlashers decided that loss of social security was, after all, too high a price to pay for a slap at the Negro. This lesson was a valuable first step in re-educating such people, and it must be kept alive, for the civil rights movement will be advanced only to the degree that social and economic welfare gets to be inextricably entangled with civil rights.

The 1964 elections marked a turning point in American politics. The Democratic landslide was not merely the result of a negative reaction to Goldwaterism; it was also the expression of a majority liberal consensus. The near unanimity with which Negro voters joined in that expression was, I am convinced, a vindication of the July 25th statement by Negro leaders calling for a strategic turn toward political action and a temporary curtailment of mass demonstrations. Despite the controversy surrounding the statement, the instinctive response it met with in the community is suggested by the fact that demonstrations were down 75 per cent as compared with the same period in 1963. But should so high a percentage of Negro voters have gone to Johnson, or should they have held back to narrow his margin of victory and thus give greater visibility to our swing vote? How has our loyalty changed things? Certainly the Negro vote had higher visibility in 1960, when a switch of only 7 per cent from the Republican column of 1956 elected President Kennedy. But the slimness of Kennedy's victory—of his "mandate"—dictated a go-slow approach on civil rights, at least until the Birmingham upheaval.

Although Johnson's popular majority was so large that he could have won without such overwhelming Negro support, that support was important from several angles. Beyond adding to Johnson's total national margin, it was specifically responsible for his victories in Virginia, Florida,

Tennessee, and Arkansas. Goldwater took only those states where fewer than 45 per cent of eligible Negroes were registered. That Johnson would have won those states had Negro voting rights been enforced is a lesson not likely to be lost on a man who would have been happy with a unanimous electoral college. In any case, the 1.6 million Southern Negroes who voted have had a shattering impact on the Southern political party structure, as illustrated in the changed composition of the Southern congressional delegation. The "backlash" gave the Republicans five House seats in Alabama, one in Georgia, and one in Mississippi. But on the Democratic side, seven segregationists were defeated while all nine Southerners who voted for the Civil Rights Act were re-elected. It may be premature to predict a Southern Democratic party of Negroes and white moderates and a Republican Party of refugee racists and economic conservatives, but there certainly is a strong tendency toward such a realignment; and an additional 3.6 million Negroes of voting age in the eleven Southern states are still to be heard from. Even the *tendency* toward disintegration of the Democratic party's racist wing defines a new context for Presidential and liberal strategy in the congressional battles ahead. Thus the Negro vote (North as well as South), while not *decisive* in the Presidential race, was enormously effective. It was a dramatic element of a historic mandate which contains vast possibilities and dangers that will fundamentally affect the future course of the civil rights movement.

The liberal congressional sweep raises hope for an assault on the seniority system, Rule Twenty-two, and other citadels of Dixiecrat-Republican power. The overwhelming of this conservative coalition should also mean progress on much bottlenecked legislation of profound interest to the movement (e.g., bills by Senators Clark and Nelson on planning, manpower, and employment). Moreover, the irrelevance of the South to Johnson's victory gives the President more freedom to act than his predecessor had and more leverage to the movement to pressure for executive action in Mississippi and other racist strongholds.

None of this *guarantees* vigorous executive or legislative action, for the other side of the Johnson landslide is that it has a Gaullist quality. Goldwater's capture of the Republican party forced into the Democratic camp many disparate elements which do not belong there, Big Business being the major example. Johnson, who wants to be President "of all people," may try to keep his new coalition together by sticking close to the political center. But if he decides to do this, it is unlikely that even his political genius will be able to hold together a coalition so inherently unstable and rife with contradictions. It must come apart. Should it do so while Johnson is pursuing a centrist course, then the mandate will have been wastefully dissipated. However, if the mandate is seized upon to set fundamental changes in motion, then the basis can be laid for a new mandate, a new coalition including hitherto inert and dispossessed strata of the population.

Here is where the cutting edge of the civil rights movement can be applied. We must see to it that the reorganization of the "consensus party" proceeds along lines which will make it an effective vehicle for social reconstruction, a role it cannot play so long as it furnishes Southern racism with its national political power. (One of Barry Goldwater's few attractive ideas was that the Dixiecrats belong with him in the same party.) And nowhere has the civil rights movement's political cutting edge been more magnificently demonstrated than at Atlantic City, where the Mississippi Freedom Democratic Party not only secured recognition as a bona fide component of the national party, but in the process routed the representatives of the most rabid racists—the white Mississippi and Alabama delegations. While I still believe that the FDP made a tactical error in spurning the compromise, there is no question that they launched a political revolution whose logic is the displacement of Dixiecrat power. They launched that revolution within a major political institution and as part of a coalitional effort.

The role of the civil rights movement in the reorganization of American political life is programmatic as well as strategic. We are challenged now to broaden our social vision, to develop functional programs with concrete objectives. We need to propose alternatives to technological unemployment, urban decay, and the rest. We need to be calling for public works and training, for national economic planning, for federal aid to education, for attractive public housing—all this on a sufficiently massive scale to make a difference. We need to protest the notion that our integration into American life, so long delayed, must now proceed in an atmosphere of competitive scarcity instead of in the security of abundance which technology makes possible. We cannot claim to have answers to all the complex problems of modern society. That is too much to ask of a movement still battling barbarism in Mississippi. But we can agitate the right questions by probing at the contradictions which still stand in the way of the "Great Society." The questions having been asked, motion must begin in the larger society, for there is a limit to what Negroes can do alone.

V
THOUGHT IN CRISIS

June 1953

Clement Greenberg

THE PLIGHT OF OUR CULTURE

Industrialism and Class Mobility

T. S. Eliot's most recent book on a non-literary subject, *Notes Towards the Definition of Culture,* proceeds largely on the assumption, familiar by now, that our culture is in decline. The book, when it appeared in 1949, received an amount of attention proportionate to its author's fame, but the quality of that attention did not match the importance of the problems raised. The assumption as to cultural decline was neither questioned nor explicitly rejected. Most of the regular reviewers scolded *Notes Towards the Definition of Culture* for its reactionary tendencies and left it at that, whereas the literary magazines, with even greater obtuseness, treated it as one more item to be placed in the temple of Eliot's reputation. (William Barrett and Robert Gorham Davis, in *Kenyon Review* and *Partisan Review,* respectively, formed exceptions, as did also the contributors to a symposium in *Scrutiny* in England.)

True, the assertion that our culture was deteriorating was made without being argued, just as Eliot tended throughout to pontificate rather than consider evidence and draw conclusions from it, though professing in all earnestness to be writing as a responsible sociologist. And just as, too often in general, partial glimpses of partial truths were offered as complete answers, truisms as fresh contributions. Nevertheless, Eliot did pose a problem of enormous importance, state cogently some of the limits within which it would have to be solved, and remind us of our failure, so far, to have thought about it seriously enough.

In any case, his book would be important as an influence and a symptom. We cannot forget who Eliot is: one of the very greatest of all literary critics, a remarkable poet, and a writer whose prestige at the moment is probably larger than that enjoyed by any other English-speaking literary man during his own lifetime. Also, he has been a great reformer of sensibility, outside as well as inside literature, with consequences felt in areas of intellectual life seemingly remote from *belles-lettres* or art. Sensibility may not be identical with intelligence, but prepossessions of feeling can become premises of thought, and limitations of thought, limitations of emotion and experience.

Eliot has done as much as anyone in our time to expose the superficialities that have accompanied the popularization of the ideas of the Enlightenment, of Utilitarianism, and "scientism"—but by criticizing a kind of sensibility, not systems of ideas. Nor does his quarrel seem in the beginning to have been with the ideas of liberalism as such, or with any set of ideas, but with deadness of sensibility wherever he found it, on the right and left, in church and out; and if he found it more often on the left, it was not so much because he wanted, at first, to find it there. Only later, when he began to deal publicly with non-literary matters, did he fix on liberalism as the main enemy, and adopt a consciously "anti-modern" religious and political position. But it was then, too, that his own sensibility showed the first symptoms of the same ailment he had diagnosed. His cure turned out to be a variant of that malady, and he, too, became an ideologue, remaining fixed, with no further understanding, in his original disgust with "modernism." And as he has gone on flogging the same tired horse—omitting in his criticism of the Enlightenment to distinguish between the root ideas and their vulgarization—he has become less and less able to distinguish between insight and banality in the notions he himself advances.

Nowhere in Eliot's later writings do we find so much evidence of this inability as in *Notes Towards the Definition of Culture*. Its disconcerting mixture of sense and superficiality, penetration and obtuseness, makes it a treacherous springboard for further discussion, and I can understand why most reviewers should have drawn back from the plunge. For this very reason, however, and for others, it may be worth going a little further into the deficiencies of the *Notes* before considering independently some of the issues that it raises.

Eliot has obeyed that rule established in the 18th century according to which the eminent man of letters begins to feel in middle age that literature is not enough, and aspires to some larger power over public opinion. But like Thomas Mann, he has made the big mistake of offering himself as a head as well as conscience. Victor Hugo knew better; so, really, did Matthew Arnold, and even Carlyle: they lectured and admonished, confident of their instinct for moral issues, but, for all their *obiter dicta,* seldom tried to theorize consistently. Besides, literary men have a tendency to confuse aesthetic with social values (see, for example, Arnold on America). This, I think, has been particularly the case with Eliot. And he is also prone to adopt attitudes that, however honestly meant, are not honestly come by (whence sometimes a note of involuntary parody enters—as if seriousness, especially that with which he wishes to take himself, were a strain requiring comic relief).

Whether or not he got his first political notions from the late Charles Maurras, Eliot has been chronically susceptible (perhaps because early impressed by the high cultural level of French reaction) to the kind of thing Maurras expressed most consistently: that type of reaction, trimmed out with Catholicism, "tradition," "classicism," "hierarchism," "authority," ultra-nationalism, and anti-Semitism, which an eminent section of French literary, if not political, opinion has professed ever since de Maistre and de Bonald, in the first half of the 19th century, laid down a systematic basis for rejecting the French Revolution. The main trouble with this position is less that it is reactionary than that it is irrelevant, and their own half-suppressed realization of this has the effect of driving its adherents to but further extremes of irrelevance—as we saw when Maurras collaborated with the Germans under the Occupation (for which he sat in jail for six years). Eliot, repeating a number of the same ideas to an English-speaking public in books like *After Strange Gods* and *The Idea of a Christian Society,* has been, if anything, more irrelevant, and some of his published remarks on politics, made over the last two decades, belong together with many leftist expressions of the period in an anthology of political nonsense. That, as I have heard, he voted Labour in 1945 would only bear out the charge.

Like most inveterate aesthetes, Eliot appears to lack a sense of the urgent reality of politics as a matter of weal and woe, and to regard correct opinion as an end in itself. Nor does he seem to appreciate the multiplicity and variability of the factors that determine social reality. This is as much a deficiency of sensibility as of intelligence, and the fact that Eliot shows a real awareness of historical movement inside literature does not gainsay this, but only demonstrates, once again, how much better his mind functions—and how much more he respects his subject—where aesthetic ends are the decisive ones.

But in *Notes Towards the Definition of Culture* we will also find things chargeable to what has to be called mindlessness, not just want of sensibility. It is startling to come across sentences like ". . . it may be argued that complete equality means universal irresponsibility. . . ." Or: "A democracy in which everybody had an equal responsibility in everything would be oppressive for the conscientious and licentious for the rest." Such statements are neither correct nor incorrect, but simply useless. The writer settles a very large and complicated question at a stroke by repeating an old saw sententiously, thus sparing himself further thought—which is exactly the function of cant. And when he apologizes, with that elephantine humor which can astound us again and again in Eliot, for a paragraph, otherwise full of good sense, that ends with the words "destroying our ancient edifices to make ready the ground upon which barbarian nomads of the future will encamp in their mechanized caravans," by adding that this was but an "incidental flourish to relieve the feelings of the writer and perhaps a few of his more sympathetic readers," we are far from sure that he himself realizes what a threadbare piece of journalism he has just repeated. Eliot can begin another paragraph with the sentence: "The colonization problem arises from migration." And refer to "vast impersonal forces." And "the oriental cast of the Russian mind." American movies are called "that influential and inflammable article the celluloid film." Something even worse than mindlessness is involved in: "I do not approve of the extermination of the enemy; the policy of exterminating or, as is barbarously said, liquidating enemies, is one of the most alarming developments of modern war and peace, from the point of view of those who desire the survival of culture. One needs the enemy." (Who, in modern times, has needed what exterminated enemy?) Never was a humane sentiment expressed with such barbaric and fatuous humor. At this point one becomes alarmed for the author's soul, not his mind. And, after all, Eliot is, or was, a great writer.

One can see why this present book of his is so difficult to deal with. Yet this does not make the issues he deals with any the less momentous; nor does this tendency to clown of which I have given examples prevent him from saying much that is arresting and true—if not exactly original.*

I

Eliot writes in his introductory chapter: "The most important question that we can ask, is whether there is any permanent standard, by which we can compare one civilization with another, and by which we can make some guess at the improvement or decline of our own. We have to admit, in comparing one civilization with another and in comparing the different stages of our own, that no one society and no one age of it realizes all the values of civilization. Not all of these values may be compatible with each other; what is at least certain is that in realizing some we lose the appreciation of others. Nevertheless, we can distinguish between higher and lower cultures; we can distinguish between advance and retrogression. We can assert with some confidence that our own period is one of decline; that the standards of culture are lower than they were fifty years ago; and that the evidences of this decline are visible in every department of human activity." Nowhere does Eliot even hint at the "permanent standard" of com-

* To be wholly fair to Eliot, a "note" on culture that he published in *Partisan Review* in 1944 should be taken into account. No part of this "note" has been retained in original form in the present book, although it says more in fewer, apter, and carefuller words than does any chapter in the latter.

parison that enables him to make this assertion with "some confidence"; he appears to assume, simply, that the reader's own experience will confirm it, and leaves the question of the "permanent standard" itself—theoretically, a far more important one—wide open. If he had tried to close it, perhaps his book would have done more to stimulate a fruitful discussion.

At the same time his definition of culture is not (as the title of his book might indicate) worked "towards" but merely handed down. Culture, in Eliot's view, is, as Marxists would say, entirely "superstructural"; it excludes political, social, religious, and economic institutions, which come, presumably, under the broader term of *civilization*. Culture "includes all the characteristic activities and interests of a people: Derby Day, Henley Regatta . . . the pin table, the dart board, Wenslyedale cheese, boiled cabbage cut into sections . . . 19th century Gothic churches and the music of Elgar." There is the individual's culture, which depends on that of his class and group, which derives in turn from the culture of the "whole society." Obviously, much has to be investigated and weighed before one can assert with *any* confidence that every present aspect of culture, even under this definition—much less "every department of human activity"—bears evidence of a decline of cultural standards. Little in Eliot's book testifies to such an investigation.

A reasonable question is whether enough evidence of cultural improvement might not be discovered in each "department of human activity" to balance the evidence of decline. I would agree with Eliot that decline predominates in most of the arts, in standards of taste, in some departments of learning, and many aspects of manners, but would hesitate to say this of *all* the arts, *all* areas of taste, *all* departments of learning, or manners on *all* social levels. Do the *majority* of people in England and America eat more poorly prepared food than fifty years ago? Have dress and décor declined since then? Has—particularly—architecture? The majority of people in the industrial countries of the West are certainly gentler in their relations with one another than they used to be, whatever the upper classes have lost in formal grace. The poor remain the most numerous, and fifty years ago they were not only poorer, but, according to the mass of evidence, much more brutal and brutish. Culture has lost much on its higher levels, but may there not have been some compensation on those where the multitude find their "characteristic activities and interests"?

Such questions are not easy to answer, least of all with "confidence." The problem is far more complicated than Eliot actually does acknowledge, however much he seems to do so. And in its complication may lie reasons for hope as well as despair. The reasons for the latter—the war, the exterminations, the oppression, the present tawdriness of our machine-made environment with its commercial culture and its leveling, etc.—are obvious, all too obvious. By seizing upon the obvious so confidently, Eliot, and others like him, collaborate with journalists in diverting attention from causes to effects, though they may think they are doing the opposite. The general readiness to cry woe, the crisis-mongering, may itself be the symptom of a decline of culture.

Granted, nevertheless, that our culture is in decline on its highest levels: what can be done about it? The weight of Eliot's short book is placed on a description of three conditions he deems more or less indispensable to a recovery. He does not propose that we set about directly to establish or restore these, but hopes rather to clarify the problem by dissipating false hopes: we are to infer that certain social and political conditions now present will largely frustrate any *ad hoc* measures to remedy the plight of culture, and that these conditions must be changed first.

The first desirable condition is an "organic (not merely planned, but growing) structure, such as will foster the hereditary transmission of culture within a culture; and this requires the persistence of social classes. The second is the necessity that a culture should be analyzable, geographically, into local cultures: this raises the problem of 'regionalism.' The third is the balance of unity and diversity in religion—that is, universality of doctrine with particularity of cult and devotion." But: "The reader must keep in mind that I am not pretending to account for all the necessary conditions for a flourishing culture: I discuss three which have especially struck my attention . . . so far as my observation goes, you are unlikely to have a high civilization where these conditions are absent."*

Yet almost nothing is presented of the content of the "observation" that has led to this important conclusion; we can only surmise that Periclean Athens, the medieval West, Elizabethan England, Renaissance North Italy, 17th-century France, and so forth, are meant—the accepted golden ages of art and literature. It is implied that successful *novelty* in the social and political structures which support culture is by and large impossible: as culture developed in the past, so must it in the future.

We can quibble over the necessity or importance, even in the past, of the second and third conditions that Eliot lays down, but the indispensability, so far in history, of class differences to a high urban culture cannot be denied, since there is no record of any such culture without them. The big question is whether class divisions—or, to be exact, the traditional alignment of small upper class over against large lower class—will continue to

* Eliot's discussion (pp. 27 to 32) of the relations between religion and culture, and more particularly, art, is, in my opinion, the most original part of his book. He is as cavalier here with the rules of discourse and evidence as elsewhere (of what use is it to say that culture is impossible without religion when we know of no society—not even the USSR—that has existed without religion?) but at least he seems to have experienced a good deal of what he talks about. And because he reveals more frankly, if unintentionally, the profound aestheticism that sways him in his religious convictions no less than in his political and social ones, he rings truer.

be as necessary to high culture as in the past. Eliot's answer in the affirmative provoked most of the hostile comment his book received (in their heat the reviewers overlooked his introductory statement that class divisions may not be essential to the achievement of other, perhaps higher, values than culture; though later on, it is true—on page 47—he does imply that a "graded" society is the best form of society in general).

Marx pointed out that productivity in even the most materially advanced societies of the past was always so low that the majority had to work full time to provide, in addition to their own necessities, the material surplus to support the leisure and ease of the relatively tiny minority that maintained high culture wherever it appeared. Marx's prognosis of a socialist future was founded on the assumption that science and industrial technology would eventually make it possible for society to produce material goods in such plenty as to render social differences unnecessary and put the dignified leisure required for the pursuit of high culture within reach of everyone. Whether this expectation is utopian or not, Marx did at least sense the big difference that industrialism would make as far as the *structure* of society was concerned. Eliot's failure to give more than a passing glance to industrialism, on the implied assumption that it contains little but harm for culture, prevents his discussion of modern culture from advancing, in effect, beyond the point at which Spengler left it.

Like Spengler, Eliot gives one to infer that industrialism is but another of the time-bound phenomena that, along with skeptical rationalism and hugeness of cities, accompany the decline of any high civilization. But to judge from the past again, humanity, barring some unprecedented catastrophe, will no more forget industrial technology than it has, amid the rise and fall of civilizations, forgotten the use of metal tools, the wheel, domestic plants, or domestic animals. Technological progress has been irreversible by and large; that is, there has been a cumulative gain in our control of the material environment. As a rule, once a people learned to use bronze it never went back to stone, and once it learned to handle iron it never went back to bronze. There have been temporary retreats, especially in quality of workmanship, but the evidence shows that these have almost always been made good. (Franz Borkenau, in "Will Technology Destroy Civilization?" in *Commentary* of January 1951, quotes Alfred Weber, the German historian, to this effect.) That industrialism will remain with us in one form or another would seem to be the largest single circumstance to be taken into account in any discussion of the future prospects of our culture.

Radical changes in technology have in the past always transformed the inner, or cultural, as well as the outer, or social, structure of society. We have reason to expect that industrialism—to which, really, we are still new—will, in the long run, effect more radical and comprehensive changes in the fundamental *scheme* of culture and civilization (as Franz Borkenau pointed out in his *Commentary* article of January 1951) than anything that has happened since the Neolithic revolution which some eight or nine thousand years ago replaced the hunting and gathering economy of the Paleolithic Age with an agricultural and herding one. Hence many premises based on observation of the relatively recent past must be discarded, and the prospects of culture, now as well as in the hypothetical future, viewed within a new perspective—not altogether new, of course, but new enough to demand a re-examination of the assumptions that ideologues of "tradition," like Eliot, proceed on.

At best one can reason from past experience only under the most general terms. The "Iron Age" civilizations of the past three millennia form in their aggregate only one part of the history of civilization as such, and at this point in time it is as hazardous to reason toward the future on their basis as it would have been, a thousand years before Jesus, to do so in terms of the material and cultural premises of the Bronze Age civilizations. Novelty has always to be allowed for, if not believed in. Spengler, Toynbee, *et al.,* may still be right in seeing the present as a period of decline that will end relatively soon in the collapse or paralysis of Western civilization, in accordance with the pattern followed by all other high civilizations so far; nevertheless science and industrialism do, and will, make a great difference, and the future is likely to present a scheme, and possibilities, radically different from those of the expired or moribund civilizations we already know. Many of the conditions under which a flourishing culture again becomes possible will therefore be different from those that made one possible in the past.

It would be wiser, accordingly, not to speculate so exclusively on the basis of past precedent. Rather we ought to examine more closely the situation of culture here and now, and try to ascertain its inherent tendencies and drift, to see what in the situation is so new that it cannot be understood in terms of anything we know from the past.

II

As has been observed, culture in the urban, industrial West is now stratified on three main levels. First, there is commercialized, "mass," "popular," "jukebox," or "lowbrow" culture; then there is "middlebrow" culture; and finally—and traditionally—high or "highbrow" culture.* All three be-

* "Highbrow," "middlebrow," and "lowbrow" are terms of brutal simplification. Nor were they coined to denote types of culture so much as types of social personality, and all three in an invidious sense—as if any kind of personal culture were a foible, and all the more a legitimate object of ridicule because revealed in one's

long to the city; rural, folk, or peasant culture is now, for the first time since it appeared thousands of years ago, practically extinct over much of the countryside in the Western world. This in itself amounts to a very radical piece of novelty. What, however, is almost equally novel is that the stratification of culture no longer coincides as uniformly as before with class lines. Whereas in the past the culture of the highest level usually received the greatest social as well as economic support, today the greatest economic support is given to the bottom level, and the greatest social support to the middle. Yet the uppermost level still carries the main history of culture, and exerts the most influence on the other levels.

The culture of the majority of the *rich* in a country like ours has by now become definitely middlebrow, with only a small minority directly supporting highbrow culture. The middle classes furnish more customers in absolute numbers for lowbrow than middlebrow culture, yet still make up the bulk of the audience for the latter. Everybody with a high school education gets at least a taste of middlebrow culture, and almost everybody in American society comes in daily contact with the lowbrow variety. Only among the poorest classes, who can be presumed to belong altogether to the lowbrow audience, does social level seem to determine cultural level as consistently as it used to do.

The middle, for a variety of reasons, has become the crucial level as far as social power is concerned, and deserves special attention. At the same time it is the most difficult level to define. "Middlebrow" is no longer a term with which to "relieve one's feelings," but means a very large if disorderly piece of reality. Eliot remarks in his book on the desirability of "a structure of society in which there will be, from 'top' to 'bottom,' a continuous gradation of cultural levels. . . ." This is not as lacking in an advanced industrial country like our own as he seems to imply. There is a vast distance between high culture and lowbrow—vaster, perhaps, than anything similar in the past—but it is covered without apparent break by the infinite shadings and gradings of middlebrow culture, which is defined roughly by the fact that, though its audience shrinks from the trials of highbrow culture, it nonetheless refuses to let its culture be simply a matter of entertainment and diversion on the lowbrow order. Middlebrow culture has to do in one way or another with self-improvement, and is born almost always out of the desire and effort of newly ascended social classes to rise culturally as well.

Something like middlebrow culture emerged in Western Europe in the 17th century—say, with Bunyan and Defoe in England—but did not

---

physiognomy. But I am afraid that no other terms available fit the realities I am trying to deal with as well as these three. And the reader, I feel sure, will understand immediately what they mean, and at the same time realize that the distinctions they make are not hard and fast ones.

quite establish a separate identity, and so remained for a time more or less tributary to aristocratic and patrician high culture. It was during the 19th century, as industrialism raised newer, rawer, and larger middle classes out of petty bourgeois or proletarian obscurity, and these tried to turn high culture to their own purposes, that middlebrow culture began really to differentiate itself. However, these new classes, for all their buying power, did not yet form a large enough proportion of society to upset the old balance between huge sweating majority and small leisured minority upon which traditional high culture had depended so far; they could still be assimilated, or at least controlled, by the old educated classes. Therefore middlebrow culture remained an ambiguous thing, largely subservient to high culture in social prestige if not economic power. Only within the last decades, and chiefly in this country, has this relation changed, and middlebrow culture acquired a positive identity and become an unmistakable force.

The revolutionary cultural phenomenon of the recent past has been not so much the spread of "mass" or lowbrow culture—which was already here a hundred years ago—as the rapid expansion of the middlebrow kind and the multiplication of its degrees and shades. This is owing to the appearance, for the first time, of a middle class large enough to amount to a *mass,* if not a majority—a mass that is now, thanks to industrial prosperity, in the material position at least to aspire to the kind of culture that used to be the exclusive prerogative of a small minority. This position does not automatically produce aspirations toward higher culture—in the 1920's the newest, and largest, American middle class did not feel them—yet material ease does in the long run tend to awaken them if only because culture, and cultivation, assert social status.

Behind the shrill and spectacular lowbrow culture that holds the foreground of American life, just such aspirations have begun lately to spread in ever-widening circles as standards of living are consolidated and continue to rise. The fact is being remarked upon in many places. Whatever its immediate causes, the "culture boom" that started shortly before the recent war was due, fundamentally, to the settling in of the enormous new middle class created by the more rapid development of industrialism after 1914, and to the coming of age of its second generation. And the largest increment by far of this boom has to be booked to the account of our middlebrow culture.*

* A similar boom started in England—and in Scandinavia, too—in the late 1930's, and the causes were somewhat the same. However, the spread of higher living standards may have been less of an immediate factor abroad than the popularization of socialist ideas—which meant increased self-awareness on the part of lower classes and, with that, a desire for adult education and an interest in self-education in general. The most typical phenomena of the British culture boom are the BBC's Third

High culture, however—authentic, disinterested culture—has so far suffered more than it has gained in the process. Being, among other things, the expression of unconscious taste and habit, of assumptions that never get stated, of a way of life and an ingrained sense of proportion, it has as a rule to begin being acquired during childhood, from the immediate and everyday just as much as from books and works of art. The antecedents of the new middle classes do not lie in such childhoods; higher culture comes to them from the outside, in adolescence at most, and has to be acquired by conscious effort, therefore tends to remain somewhat external and artificial. According to everything we know so far, Eliot is right when he repeats that the family is still "by far the most important channel of transmission of culture." Nor is this the whole story.

Other handicaps are imposed by the very scale and rapidity (both proportional and absolute) with which the new American middle classes have been expanding. Every generation since the Civil War, but especially since 1918, has brought a new mass of people to the social surface. And each new mass, being larger usually than the one before, yet quickly rising to the same social level, has acted as a drag, culturally, on its predecessors. The traditional structure of culture, which could assimilate these newcomers as long as they arrived in limited numbers and at sufficient intervals, cannot maintain itself when they come in such steady and huge throngs (the increase of the population in absolute figures alone is enough to unsettle the situation). By sheer demographic weight and buying power, the newcomers force all levels of the cultural market down to meet the lower standards they bring with them from their culturally inferior origins. The old upper classes become helpless in the matter. Nor, for that matter, do these classes enjoy the prestige in connection with culture that the old upper classes of, say, England do, and they are that much the less able to maintain the continuity of traditional standards—which are in their care if they are in anyone's—with enough authority to tame parvenus.

At the same time lowbrow, "machine," commercial culture is there everywhere to offer its relief to all those who find any sort of higher culture too much of an effort—lowbrow culture being powerful not only because it is "easy" and still suits the majority, but also because it has replaced folk culture as the culture of *all* childhood, and thereby become our "natural," "autochthonous" culture. (And, unlike folk culture, lowbrow culture neither contributes—at least not fundamentally—to high culture nor effaces itself in its social presence.)

Armed with their new wealth, their optimism, and their political

---

Program, with its magazine, *The Listener,* and the success of the Penguin books, whereas the emphasis in America is not so much on self-education as on gentility, correctness of taste, knowingness, "gracious living"—that is, emblems of status.

power, the new American middle classes have in this situation been able to ask with more confidence and success than any upstart class before them that high culture be delivered to them by a compromise, precisely, with their limitations. Hence, above all, middlebrow culture.

The liberal and fine arts of tradition, as well as its scholarship, have been "democratized"—simplified, streamlined, purged of whatever cannot be made easily accessible, and this in large measure by the same rationalizing, "processing," and "packaging" methods by which industrialism has already made lowbrow culture a distinctive product of itself. Almost all types of knowledge and almost all forms of art are stripped, digested, synopsized, "surveyed," or abridged. The result achieved in those who patronize this kind of capsulated culture is, perhaps, a respect for culture as such, and a kind of knowingness, but it has very little to do with higher culture as something lived.

The middlebrow in us wants the treasures of civilization for himself, but the desire is without appetite. He feels nostalgia for what he imagines the past to have been, and reads historical novels, but in the spirit of a tourist who enjoys the scenes he visits because of their lack of resemblance to those he has come from and will return to. A sense of continuity with the past, a continuity at least of truth, of enduring relevance, belongs to genuine culture almost by definition, but this is precisely what the middlebrow does not acquire (the fault is not entirely his own). He might be able to do so, eventually, by exerting humility and patience, but these he is somehow never able to muster in the face of culture. In his reading, no matter how much he wants to edify himself, he will balk at anything that sends him to the dictionary or a reference book more than once. (Curiosity without energy or tenacity is a middlebrow trait wherever and in whomever it appears.) Toward his entertainment, no matter how much he wants it to be "significant" and "worthwhile," he will become recalcitrant if the "significance" is not labeled immediately and obviously, and if too many conditioned reflexes are left without appropriate stimuli. What the middlebrow, even more conspicuously than the lowbrow, wants most is to have his expectations filled exactly as he expects to have them filled.

Middlebrow culture, because of the way in which it is produced, consumed, and transmitted, reinforces everything else in our present civilization that promotes standardization and inhibits idiosyncrasy, temperament, and strong-mindedness; it functions as order and organization but without ordering or organizing. In principle, it cannot master and preserve fresh experience or express and form that which has not already been expressed and formed. Thus it fails, like lowbrow culture, to accomplish what is, perhaps, the most important task of culture for people who live in a changing, *historical* society: it cannot maintain continuity in the face of novelty, but must always forget and replace its own products.

But I said "in principle." Like lowbrow, middlebrow culture is not all of a piece. The good and the bad are mixed, all the way from Class A movies and the *Reader's Digest* through *The Saturday Evening Post* and *South Pacific* to the *Times Book Review* and Rouault. Middlebrow art, if not middlebrow learning or thought, is not wholly adulteration and dilution. Novelists like Hemingway, Faulkner, Fitzgerald, and O'Hara can profit as well as lose by a certain middlebrow impatience with intellectual distinctions that enables them to make new distinctions in experience itself. And while the middlebrow's respect for culture may be too pious and undifferentiated, it has worked to save the traditional facilities of culture—the printed word, the concert, lecture, museum, etc.—from that complete debauching which the movies, radio, and television have suffered under lowbrow and advertising culture. And it would be hard to deny that some sort of enlightenement does seem to be spread on the broader levels of the industrial city by middlebrow culture, and certain avenues of taste opened. Just as, in general, an authoritative part of the public has begun to show a greater sense of responsibility toward disinterested culture, and to censor its own philistine impulses.

But doesn't the damage still outweigh the gains, and can any amount of improvement at the lower levels compensate for deterioration at the highest, where the most authentic manifestations still have their being, where the forms and values of every other level originate—no matter how perverted subsequently—and where our experience is still most significantly and enduringly preserved?

October 1960

Emil L. Fackenheim

THE DILEMMA OF LIBERAL JUDAISM

The liberal Jew of today is in a dilemma. His Jewish conscience urges him to look for an authority which might guide and direct his Jewish life. But his liberal conscience frowns on that desire, as a temptation to be resisted. As a Jew he fears that, unless individuals such as himself accept an authority, there will soon be an end to Judaism. But as a liberal he fears that, should they in fact accept it, there will soon be an end to liberalism. These fears and doubts confront him with the possibility that he might in the end have to choose between his Judaism and his liberalism; that, as critics on both right and left have charted all along, liberal Judaism is a contradiction in terms.

If this dilemma, latently present ever since the rise of liberal Judaism, is becoming open and manifest in our time, it is because of three main conclusions toward which the conscientious liberal Jew is more and more ineluctably driven. Gone are the days when one could arbitrarily pick and choose from the Jewish past and persuade oneself that one's selection was Judaism. The selections have been too many and too varied, and too apt to reflect less the spirit of Judaism than that of those who selected from it, or that of their age or their class. If the liberal's Jewish life is to have a claim to authenticity, then, there must be a sense in which the Jewish past has authority. This is the first conclusion.

The second is a corollary of the first. Arbitrary picking and choosing may be done by the learned and the unlearned alike. But genuine contact with the past is possible, if at all, only through learning and scholarship. Hence if there is a sense in which the Jewish past has authority for the liberal Jew, there is also a sense in which Jewish learning has such authority. The views of the learned and those of the unlearned cannot carry equal weight; they can approach equality only as the unlearned themselves take steps to become learned.

The third conclusion is the deepest and hardest of all. Indeed, it is so deep and hard that, although it is well-nigh inescapable, the desire to escape from it is stubborn and widespread. If the Jewish past is to have authority for the liberal Jew, then this past cannot be a merely human past, however great. A merely human past could obligate the liberal Jew, if at all, only as a man; and the Jewish part of it, perhaps to a greater degree than other parts, but not differently in kind.* If Judaism is to continue to exist, there must be a sense in which the Jewish past has an altogether unique authority for the liberal Jew. But this is possible only if what speaks to him through it is not merely the voice of man but the voice of God. The third conclusion, then, toward which the liberal Jew is more and more ineluctably driven is that Judaism is not a purely human product: that it is, after all, a covenant between Israel and God. Hence he stands under still another authority, and this is the highest, of which indeed the other two are but means and instruments: the authority of God.

These conclusions, we say, are becoming increasingly inescapable for the serious liberal Jew. But because he is a liberal, he also finds them all but unacceptable. For they seem radically incompatible with that intellectual and spiritual freedom the exercise of which he considers both his right and his duty. As he sees his duty, he must criticize the past, not accept its authority; and he must criticize it in the light of standards which are modern and contemporary. It is by virtue of criticism that he sees the present to have progressed beyond the past; and to desist from such criticism and accept past authority would be, in his view, to betray his liberal conscience and lapse into reaction.

Liberal conscience, then, seems to rule out the authority of the past. It also seems to rule out the authority of learning and scholarship. A free believer must think for himself. He cannot be free if another thinks on his behalf. In the sphere of spiritual life, inferior thoughts which are the individual's own are better than superior thoughts which are not—simply because they *are* his own. How then can the authority of learning be acceptable? Hillel maintained that the ignorant cannot be pious.† To the liberal, these are hard and indeed intolerable words.

But the hardest authority for the liberal is not that of the past or of learning but that of God. Whether the divine word comes through the

* Any contribution of past "Jewish genius" is a contribution no doubt different from but not incommensurable with that of Greek genius. Why should the contemporary Jew have a qualitatively unique obligation to past Jewish contributions? The duty to assimilate Greek philosophy, if a duty at all, is incumbent, not on modern Greeks but on modern civilized men. This whole point is developed at greater length in my article, "Can There Be Judaism Without Revelation?" in *Commentary,* December 1951.

† It may be noted in passing, however, that Rabbinic Judaism balances this insistence on the importance of learning with an insistence on the importance of religious motive.

mouth of a prophet or a sacred writing or even through his own heart, he cannot, he feels, simply subject his conscience to it. He cannot but weigh that word against his own conscience; and in the end it must be *his* conscience and *his* judgment which are his authority, not a God other than they who legislates to them. If indeed there should be such a thing as revelation, it cannot be a voice *other* than the voice within. It must be identical with it. The voice of conscience, or of free thought, or of religious experience, must be the voice of God.

In an attempt to cope with the dilemma of the liberal Jew, our first task must be to consider more closely the concept of freedom which gives rise to it. That concept first achieved prominence in the Age of Enlightenment, and it has pervaded Western consciousness ever since.

It is well defined by Immanuel Kant. "Enlightenment," Kant writes, "is man's release from his self-incurred tutelage. Tutelage is man's inability to make use of his understanding without direction from another. Self-incurred is this tutelage when its cause lies not in lack of reason but in lack of resolution and courage."

In Kant's account, freedom is not the mere ability to choose. This would be altogether compatible with authority, that is, the taking of direction from another, provided only such direction is taken voluntarily. True freedom, for Kant, consists of autonomy. And by autonomy he means the ability to choose in the light of standards approved by one's own thinking, conscience, and experience. Freedom as so defined is radically and completely incompatible with authority, that is, the taking of direction from another. Kant thinks that true enlightenment consists of autonomy, and hence of emancipation from authority; and that autonomy is man's noblest goal. A noble goal: but not a goal that is easy or popular. Kant continues: "It is so easy not to be of age. If I have a book which understands for me, a pastor who has conscience for me, a physician who decides my diet . . . I need not trouble myself. I need not think, if I can only pay."

The modern concept of autonomy has had revolutionary implications for religious thought. The first of these was stated by Kant himself. Holy Writ cannot legislate to moral conscience. Moral conscience must legislate to Holy Writ. We cannot accept a law as moral because it is Biblical. Rather, we can accept a Biblical law only if it is moral; and it *is* moral if approved by moral consciousness. Moses and Jesus are not moral legislators who provide us with moral standards. They merely illustrate moral standards which we already possess.*

* See chiefly Kant's *Religion Within the Limits of Reason Alone* (transl. Greene and Hudson). Kant, who undoubtedly would have had a profound regard for Judaism had he possessed an adequate knowledge of it, thought of it as a mere

The second implication of the concept of autonomy became manifest in the course of the 19th century. Pre-modern historians accept past facts on the authority of reliable documents. And pre-modern Biblical historians accept Biblical facts on the authority of the Bible. But modern historians wholly dispense with authorities. They *reconstruct* the facts of the past, instead of accepting them on authority, and the reconstructing is done in the light of their critical reason. Documents are no longer authoritative statements of what has happened; they are merely one means among others which enable the historian to reconstruct what has happened.

To the modern Biblical historian, the Bible can be no exception. It too is not an authoritative statement of historical facts, but merely one source among others which aid in their reconstruction. Hence the discipline known as Biblical criticism is not a mysterious discipline in its own right. It is but a branch of modern critical history.

But is the Bible merely another book of moral maxims, or another historical record? What of its claim to being the record of a divine revelation? The most momentous of all implications of the concept of autonomy is that revelation is in principle impossible. Revelation is the incursion of a God who is *other* than man into the life of man; and man is receptive to his incursion. But such receptivity is in principle incompatible with autonomy. If indeed man is capable of autonomy, then autonomy is his highest possibility; and if and when he actualizes it, he has transcended all passivity and receptivity in creative self-realization. Only two possibilities therefore remain concerning revelation if man is capable of autonomy. Either God does not contact man at all, being non-existent or necessarily absent. Or else the God who contacts man is not other than man and present *to* man, but rather present *in* man. Revelation occurs, in that case, in great moments of human self-realization and is identical with it. Religious experience, or moral conscience, are not stimulated or caused by God. They are themselves divine.

It is in this re-interpretation alone, then, that revelation is compatible with autonomy. But if thus re-interpreted, revelation cannot be accessible through acceptance of the Bible. No doubt the Bible is the product of creative religious genius. But if later generations accept it as an authority they do not gain access to revelation but on the contrary bar themselves from it. For revelation consists of spiritual creativity whereas they have lapsed into receptivity and passivity. Only if they themselves achieve spiritual creativity can they penetrate, beyond the product of ancient creative genius, to that genius itself, achieving spiritual sympathy with it. But if they do achieve such creativity, then recourse to either the Bible or the

---

external legalistic system—a notion which seems to have reached him, ironically enough, through Spinoza and Moses Mendelssohn.

genius which produced it is no longer needed. That bold, iconoclastic reformed clergyman, D. F. Schleiermacher, was able to write: "Not he has true religion who believes in a Holy Scripture, but he who does not require such a Scripture, and indeed could compose one in his own right."

Such, then, are the main implications of the modern concept of autonomy, so far as they are relevant to religion. Whether or not that concept is valid we must in due course inquire. For the present it must be shown that the concept of autonomy has, at any rate, enough validity for the liberal Jew to make pre-modern concepts of religious authority in principle unacceptable. Indeed, it was through recognition of this fact that liberal Judaism first came into being.

Pre-modern Judaism was by no means blindly authoritarian. Tradition stresses that R. Akiba interpreted the Torah so freely that Moses himself could not recognize it; and that what matters in the observance of the 613 commandments is not the letter but the spirit. At the same time, R. Akiba thought that he was merely drawing out what was in the Torah, and tradition insists that the commandments be observed, preferably to be sure in spirit as well as in letter, but in letter in any case. R. Akiba's conviction and the insistence of tradition in the end rest on one single fundamental belief, and this belief is the ultimate basis of pre-modern Jewish authority: the belief, not only in revelation, but in verbal revelation; the conviction that the Torah is not a human product, even one produced under the impact of divine revelation, but quite literally a divine product, dictated by God.

In breaking with the Orthodox view of authority, it is with this belief that, in the final analysis, the liberal Jew broke. Nor can he, even in his most romantic moods, return to that belief today. He broke with it under the impact of the concept of autonomy. But whatever the validity of that concept, it has enough validity to make the break inevitable.

Orthodox apologists often harp on specific blunders or excesses of Biblical criticism. But the true impact of Biblical criticism does not lie in particular radical assertions, such as that Israel never stood at Mt. Sinai. It would be as great even if all the critics agreed that Isreal *had* stood at Mt. Sinai. The impact lies, not in specific assertions, but in basic assumptions. A medieval thinker such as Judah Halevi could accept Biblical facts absolutely, on the authority of 600,000 witnesses and an unbroken tradition. A modern historian can accept them, if at all, only tentatively, as a hypothesis capable of being overthrown. In the modern age, to follow the lead of Judah Halevi would be to exempt the Torah, alone among all historical documents, from the methodological requirements of modern history. But this is for the liberal Jew intellectually impossible. He can indeed, as we shall forthwith argue, believe in revelation. But he cannot possibly believe in verbal revelation, that is, in a divinely handed-down text.

To do so is not only an intellectual impossibility. It is a moral and spiritual impossibility as well. When confronted with Biblical laws and concepts which seemed offensive to his conscience, the pre-modern Jew had two basic choices. Believing as he did in verbal revelation, he could see himself forced to swallow his scruples. Thus the Orthodox Jew prays for the return of animal sacrifices even today. Or he could interpret what seemed offensive so as to make it acceptable; and believing as he did in verbal revelation, he could believe that his interpretation was faithful to the literal meaning of the Biblical text. For the liberal Jew, both of these escapes are impossible. He is too deeply imbued with the modern historical spirit to be able to believe that modern values are implicit in ancient laws and concepts whose letter contradicts them. Nor can he pray for the return of animal sacrifices. To him, these are ancient but long outmoded ways of worshipping God.

The upshot, then, is clear. Whether or not he can accept revelation, the liberal Jew cannot, at any rate, accept *verbal* revelation. To accept it would be to accept an authority which would silence or fetter his critical reason and his spiritual conscience. But he would cease to be a liberal if he betrayed his duty to give free rein to both.

But some liberal Jews have always thought it necessary to go far beyond these negative conclusions. The concept of autonomy was accepted by them completely, with all its implications. Indeed, some have gone so far as to make the concept of autonomy the central positive concept of liberal Judaism. The "Pittsburgh Platform," adopted by a representative group of Reform rabbis in 1885, may be cited as a significant illustration. That platform frankly replaces revelation with "the consciousness of the indwelling of God in man." It openly rejects all traditional laws except moral laws, and what is moral it determines by the standards of modern consciousness. It regards Judaism as "a progressive religion, ever striving to be in accord with the postulates of reason." Not Judaism, not revelation, not the Torah, but reason is the one and only standard of truth and value!

Still, liberal Jews have frequently hedged as regards the concept of autonomy, and they have done so in increasing numbers as time went on. Thus while the Pittsburgh Platform of 1885 is forthright, the "Columbus Platform," adopted by the Central Conference of American Rabbis in 1937, equivocates: speaking of religious experience, but also of revelation; and asserting religious progress, but also that prophetic insight is unique, and hence presumably still unsurpassed. Liberal hedging is epitomized in a prayer, known to us all, which bids us "welcome all truth, whether shining from the annals of ancient revelations or reaching us through the seers of our own time." Whether both truths are revelation or neither is; whether the ancient legislates to the modern, or the modern to the ancient: these are questions which remain unanswered.

Superficially a sign of intellectual cowardice, such liberal hedging in fact reflects a profound Jewish awareness. It springs from the realization that the concept of autonomy, if carried to its logical conclusion, and made the central concept of liberal Judaism, must necessarily destroy Judaism.

To demonstrate this assertion is not difficult: to judge the past by the standards of the present is to presuppose the absolute superiority of the present. It is not merely to reject blind submission to the authority of the past. It is also to deny that we can learn anything whatsoever from the past. The past may approximate or on occasion even reach the level of the present. But it cannot by definition ever and at any point surpass it. Precisely because present standards decide what is true and of value, a Judaism based on the concept of autonomy would therefore have to be a wholly contemporary Judaism, cut loose from all essential ties with the past.

Further, such a Judaism would have to be a wholly man-made product. If based on the concept of autonomy, it could leave no room for revelation, understood as the incursion of a God other than man into the life of man. The voice of God could be present in such a Judaism only if identified with the "religious genius" which had produced it; and the genius would have to be, in essence, contemporary.

How could such a Judaism be related to the modern Jew? It could be understood as a body of universal truths and values. But then there would be no reason why to accept this body one need be a Jew, or why a Jew need accept it *because* he is a Jew. We should be left, not with Judaism but with a "religion of mankind." Or it could be regarded as a body of particular Jewish truths and values, true and valid for Jews alone. But in that case we would save Jewishness and Judaism only at the cost of lapsing into chauvinism and idolatry. In the past, the Jew persisted in his Jewishness for the sake of the worship of God. But if God is not other than man but present in human vision, and if He is present for the Jew in his Jewish vision, then the Jew of the future would have to persist in his Jewishness, for the sake of the worship, not of God but of the Jewish vision of God.

This serves to show the most serious and indeed catastrophic implication of the belief in autonomy for Judaism. The God of traditional Judaism can be present *to* man. If man is autonomous then God can be present only *in* man, as "conscience" or "insight" or "creative genius." But to accept this is in the end to fall prey to idolatry. That the voice of the heart is the voice of God is a belief which could seem plausible in ages given to romantic enthusiasm. But this age cannot but see that the heart, while endowed with great spiritual power, is also, as Jeremiah said, deceitful above all things and exceeding weak. And we arrive at this crucial conclusion: God is accessible to man, either as He who is other than man and yet enters into human life; or He is not accessible at all. But this means that we must choose between Judaism and the belief in autonomy. We cannot have both.

The central problem of the liberal Jew has now become clear. Judaism requires a twofold receptivity: a receptivity toward the past, and a receptivity toward a God who speaks through both present and past. The problem is whether this twofold receptivity is compatible with freedom. And this *is* a problem because the concept of autonomy implies that it is not compatible.

But one may wonder whether true freedom is always autonomy. Let us first ask: must every free relation to the past assume the absolute superiority of the present over the past? No doubt one's first reaction is to answer in the affirmative. Present science is superior to past science, and present history, to the history of the past. To think otherwise would be to lapse into reaction.

But reflection gives rise to second thoughts. Present science builds on past science, and present history on past history. Is the same necessarily true of religion and morality? Science and history deal with concepts only. Religion and morality are concerned not only with concepts but also with human lives. Concepts can be built on other concepts. But lives cannot be built on other lives. Hence while in science and history there can be steady progress, progress in religion and morality is at best only haphazard and equivocal. Religious and moral truths, even if long discovered, must always be re-discovered; and they are re-discovered, not just by being rethought but by being re-lived. In short, in religion and morality, the present is not necessarily superior to the past.

This is why one cannot simply subject past religious and moral beliefs to present standards, any more than one can simply submit to their authority. To do the latter would be to avoid the responsibilities of freedom. To do the former would be to remain with a very limited freedom which, by idolizing the present, would become enclosed in its parochial bounds. A truly free spiritual relation to the past is not either of these one-way relations; it is the two-way relation of a genuine *encounter:* a relation in which the past, to be sure, is exposed to the judgment of the present, but in which the present also exposes itself to the judgment of the past. In such a relation there is acceptance from the past. But there is no blind acceptance. For what is unacceptable is not accepted, and what is accepted is appropriated by the recipient and made his own. But this is the crucial point: what the present recipient has accepted from the past is something he has truly learned. It is something new, something which he did not possess before the encounter. This is why, when he accepts it and makes it his own, his very being is transformed.

Such a receptivity, then, far from being incompatible with freedom, on the contrary enlarges and enhances it. It raises the recipient above the narrow dogmas of his time. No doubt a merely passive receptivity is incompatible with freedom. But not every receptivity is simply passive. We must therefore conclude that the problem of freedom and authority, as stated in terms of the concept of autonomy, is a falsely stated problem. And it is falsely stated because the concept of autonomy is itself invalid. Or rather, it is valid for the activities of abstract scientific and historical thought. But it is not valid as a concept of freedom which applies in human life.

This is our first important, positive conclusion, and it frees the liberal Jew from a time-honored but false dilemma. Critics on the right charge that to accept the past must be to accept it entire, and that all selective acceptance is arbitrary. Critics on the left charge that to select from the past is to be committed to present standards of selection, and that to be thus committed is to have no need of the past. Jointly these critics have always charged the liberal Jew with mere compromise.

But such charges have no force for the truly liberal Jew, who meets the Jewish past in a genuine encounter. For in this encounter he learns that not all selecting from the past is arbitrary; and not all acceptance from it a form of blind submission. No doubt his encounter with the past is fraught with danger. He will often project into the past what he believes himself to be discovering in it. And he will often fall prey to blind worship of the past when he believes himself to be freely accepting it. But he must resist the temptation of escaping from the encounter, by a flight either into or from the past. Rather he must cope with the dangers of the encounter in the encounter itself.

We conclude, then, that human freedom is compatible with receptivity to the past. But is it compatible also with receptivity to a God who speaks to man through present and past? With this question, we have come upon the crux of our whole inquiry. This question is the crucial question. The difficulties it poses are the crucial difficulties. Indeed, on our ability to answer this question the success of our whole inquiry depends. And in the final analysis, everything thus far said has been said to prepare just for this question: is human freedom compatible with human receptivity to a God other than man—a God under whose authority he therefore stands?*

* This is the crux of the present, but not of every, inquiry into revelation. The question "Is revelation compatible with human freedom?" is logically secondary to the question "Can a modern man believe in revelation at all?" After all, while in the case of receptivity to a human other, one can *know* the existence of this other, in the case of receptivity to a divine Other, one can accept the existence of this Other, if at all, only *on faith*. But an inquiry into faith and revelation is not part of our present purpose, which is confined to inquiring into the compatibility between the liberal and the Jewish faith. See, however, the article previously referred to and also "Jewish

Reception from a human other can appropriate what it receives; the recipient can make what he receives his own. But can he appropriate the gift of a divine Other, and make it his own? Appropriating reception is possible in the first case because giver and recipient are both human. But is it possible if only the recipient is human while the Giver is divine? It may seem that only two possibilities exist in this case. Either the human recipient can indeed appropriate what he receives. But then the divine Giver cannot, after all, be other than the human recipient, and we are led back to the view that the divine voice is in man, rather than being other than the voice of man. Or else the divine Giver is indeed wholly other than the human recipient. But then the latter must receive His gift in radical passivity, and we are led back to pre-modern authoritarianism. For if the prophet is the mere vessel of the divine revelation, then the words he speaks cannot be a human reflection of an event of divine incursion, but must be quite literally the words of God. In short, we should have landed in Orthodoxy. Thus it seems that the crucial dilemma of liberal Judaism is still unresolved.

As we at long last try to cope with this dilemma we must first turn for guidance to traditional Judaism. For while authoritarian, traditional Judaism is by no means blindly so. And we must never forget that what unites liberal with traditional Judaism is far more than what separates them.

Traditional Judaism is often pictured as a barren legalism, in which the observance of external laws takes the place of a relation with the living God. If this account were correct, then revelation, as understood by traditional Judaism, could reveal laws only, not God along with these laws. And the Jew bound by them would be related only to these laws, giving recognition to their divine origin merely by submitting to them in blind passivity. In fact, however, this legalistic picture is nothing but a gross caricature. Except for rare periods of spiritual decay, traditional Judaism was always a religion, not of *law,* but of *commandment.*

A law discloses only itself. A commandment discloses its giver along with itself. Obedience to a law does not necessarily create a relation to its giver. Obedience to a commandment necessarily creates such a relation. In Judaism, revelation is commandment rather than law. And this means that revelation does not disclose the will of God to the exclusion of God, just as it does not disclose God to the exclusion of His will. It discloses both in indissoluble union. And this disclosure calls for an appropriate response on the part of those to whom it is made: that is, that they should both accept the commandment, and accept it as God's commandment. In

---

Existence and the Living God" (*A People and Its Faith,* ed. A. Rose, pre-published in *Commentary,* August 1959).

prophetic utterances, the words "Thus saith the Lord" are not a mere preamble; they are an essential part of the message. To state the whole point very briefly we may say: traditional Judaism is not the mechanical observance of a system of laws. It is the living covenant between God and Israel.*

Where revelation is thus experienced and understood its reception cannot possibly occur in total passivity. Were this the case, the Divine presence would shatter the will of the human recipient, and indeed his very selfhood. The recipient would, as the mystic claims he does, dissolve into ineffable union with the Divine. But revelation which *commands* leaves the human *self* intact, for the commandment is addressed to him. It leaves his free *will* intact, for it is to his will that the commandment appeals. Indeed, the commandment accentuates this will, for it confronts it with a challenge from which there is no escape. Finally and most importantly, in Judaism revelation-as-commandment does not challenge the recipient merely to receive and fulfill the commandment, but to fulfill it with joy—that is, to appropriate it and make it his own.

To the mystic, revelation-as-commandment has always seemed an impossibility. How can finite man, touched by the Infinite, retain his finite identity? How can this touch even accentuate his will? Finally, how can he appropriate the gift of the Infinite, while himself remaining finite? This may seem an impossibility. Yet it is the innermost secret of Jewish faith and Jewish life that this "impossibility" is actual.

How can it be actual? It is actual by virtue of divine love. In the very moment of touch which threatens to devour finite selfhood, revelation turns into commandment which re-establishes and reassures that selfhood. In the instant in which the commandment confronts man with a radical otherness which threatens to destroy him, it divests itself of enough of its otherness to become capable of enhancing human life instead of destroying it. In Judaism, then, love is not a revelation separate from commandment, let alone an "idea which was evolved only later in religious development." The very disclosure of commandment is also and already a disclosure of love, and would be impossible without it. And the traditional concepts of God as commanding King who inspires fear, and as forgiving Father who inspires love, are not separate, let alone incompatible concepts. The King is Father, and the Father, King. Hence it has well been said: "Love and fear God; tremble and rejoice when you perform the commandments."

Where revelation discloses itself as commandment, later generations which are subject to it cannot be related to it as to a dead past. Were this the case, the commandment would be living commandment only to those

* The distinction here made between law and commandment is indebted to a celebrated exchange of letters between Martin Buber and Franz Rosenzweig. See Rosenzweig, *On Jewish Learning* (ed. N. N. Glatzer, New York 1955), pp. 109 ff.

who first received it. To all others it would be mere dead law. The past for traditional Judaism is not a dead past. Through it still speaks the God who gave it. He still speaks because He still lives, and because His covenant with Israel is still alive. And the Jew today, as the Jew of old, is enjoined to practice, not arid law, but living commandment. Hence the Midrash well says: "All souls, even those which had still to be created, were present at the revelation of Mt. Sinai."

Our crucial question has thus in part been answered, in terms of Jewish tradition. Is human receptivity to a God other than man compatible with human freedom? If revelation is neither arid law nor mystic union but *commandment,* it is not only compatible with freedom but impossible without it. The human self remains intact even in the moment of touch by the Divine. He is free to choose for or against His commandment. Finally and most importantly, he is free to appropriate His commandment: to observe it, not in blind, slavish fear, but in the kind of love which exists because the recipient has made God's commandment his own, and God's will his. There can be no greater freedom than this. We saw above that free appropriation of the human past raises man above the parochialism of the present. We see now that free appropriation of God's commandment raises him above a human parochialism which is the lot of man when he is divorced from God. The Midrash thus rightly says: "When the Torah came into the world, freedom came into the world."

Jewish tradition, then, solves most of the liberal's problems. But it leaves one serious problem unsolved, and to solve it, the liberal Jew must crucially depart from tradition. As for tradition, a recipient of the commandment is free to accept or reject it; and if accepting it, to observe it in fear, or in love as well as in fear. But it would appear that human spontaneity does not enter into the act of hearing itself, for the traditionalist holds that what he hears is quite *literally* the word of God. But this belief, as we have seen long ago, is to the liberal unacceptable.

Hence we are compelled to put forward a different doctrine. Human spontaneity enters not merely into the response to the commandment, but already into the *hearing* of it. Hearing does not precede the human response to the divine address. The hearing already contains elements of response. Hence every single word any prophet ever spoke is shot through with human interpretation. Yet had there been no event of divine revelation there would have been no human interpretation. Franz Rosenzweig rightly said: " 'He came down' [on Sinai]—this already concludes the revelation; 'He spoke' is the beginning of interpretation, and certainly 'I am.' "

This doctrine, if acceptable, removes all the remaining liberal difficulties. Regarding the Torah as the human reflection of a divine revelation, rather than as itself literal revelation, the liberal can regard it as a human book which is the legitimate object of historical criticism, and whose commandments do not have, in letter, authority over him. But he may at the same time regard it as the prime means of access to a divine revelation which addresses him, as much as his ancestors. In his quest for the commandment as it applies to him, he does well indeed to take the ancient human reflection of the revelation with the utmost seriousness. But were he to subject himself blindly to its authority, as if it were itself the liberal word of God, he would not fulfill God's commandment, but rather bar himself from it. He must hear with his own ears. He cannot hear with ears of yore.

But is the above doctrine acceptable? If all revealed content is shot through with human interpretation, must we not conclude that revelation, apart from this interpretation, is wholly without content and therefore irrelevant? Do we not, after all, return at this late point—in practice if not in theory—to the unacceptable doctrine of autonomy, the doctrine which identifies the word of God with that of man?

The answer is that revelation and interpretation can be distinguished in abstract thought, but not in the concrete existential situation in which both occur. To make the distinction between revelation and interpretation is important, lest we subject ourselves blindly to the authority of the ancient interpretation. But once we have made it we must ourselves return to the existential situation, and to its responsibilities. And to do so is to ask: what does the divine commandment demand of *us?* What can we hear? What can we do?

In search of an answer, the liberal Jew of today must encounter the ancient reflection of the divine incursion which constituted the covenant under which he still stands. He must also encounter the tradition of those of his ancestors who sought—and received—answers before him. But if and when he himself receives an answer as a result of this encounter, it will be—if the encounter itself is genuine—the answer heard by him with modern ears, and addressed to him in a modern situation. Heard by him, it will no doubt bear the stamp of his human interpretation, just as did the answers heard by earlier generations. But if it is a genuine answer, genuinely heard, his human interpretation will nevertheless be the result of God's address. For He, the God of Israel, still lives; and the liberal Jew, son of the covenant, still stands at Mt. Sinai, as did his fathers.

Gershom Scholem

MARTIN BUBER'S HASIDISM

A Critique

There can be no doubt that the contribution of Martin Buber to the Western world's knowledge of the Hasidic movement has been a most distinguished one. Before Buber took it upon himself to introduce and interpret Hasidism to Western readers, the movement was practically unknown to students of religion—despite the fact that it had been a major force in the life and thought of East European Jewry since it crystallized in western Ukraina in the middle of the 18th century. Throughout the period known in Jewish history as the Enlightenment, Hasidism was seen mainly as an outbreak of extreme obscurantism allied to those forces in the Jewish past to which the protagonists of a modern enlightened Judaism found themselves in fiercest opposition. So, too, with the great Jewish scholars of the last century who initiated the "scientific" study of the universe of Judaism—men like Heinrich Graetz, Abraham Geiger, and Leopold Zunz: mysticism and emotionalism held no attraction for them and they repudiated the values for which movements based on such tendencies stood. It was only toward the turn of the century that certain Jewish writers and scholars living in Russia tried to take a more sober view. This new view was linked to a general revaluation of Jewish history which treated it as the history of a living people rather than as the paradigm of an enlightened theology to be judged by the extent to which it lived up to abstract standards set by philosophers and religious thinkers. We can take it for granted that the new wave of Jewish nationalism which erupted in the late 19th century, and a romantic urge for discovering the deeper forces active in the life of the Jewish masses, played a great part in bringing about this change. Scholars like Simon Dubnow, enthusiasts like Samuel Horodezky, and great writers like Judah Leib Peretz, heralded the new era, and though Dubnow's pioneering researches into Hasidism were marked by a rather cool and reserved tone, this was more than outweighed by the glamor which the discovery of the world of Hasidic legend lent to the movement. Since Peretz, the poetic and emotional appeal of Hasidic legend has deeply influenced Jewish literature, especially in Hebrew, Yiddish, and German.

It is within this context that Buber's lifelong fascination with Hasidism and his contribution to the understanding of it has to be approached. Overwhelmed by what he took to be the message of Hasidism when it first presented itself to him in his youthful quest for a living Judaism, Buber has devoted nearly fifty years of an outstanding literary career to formulating and reformulating the meaning of this message. The Zionist credo that brought him to Hasidism in the first place became interwoven with the conviction that "no renewal of Judaism is possible that does not bear in itself the elements of Hasidism." Being a writer of great charm and vigor, he made an immediate impact with his first books, *The Tales of Rabbi Nachman* and *The Legend of the Baal-Shem,* and from that time on, an almost unending stream of Hasidic material and interpretative discussion has flowed from Buber's pen, reaching its climax in *Tales of the Hasidim* and other books of a more theoretical character which have been extremely influential over the last fifteen years.

Buber's influence is not hard to account for. Whereas the ardor of some other apologists for the teachings of Hasidism, like Horodezky, was essentially naive, and their writing sometimes lovely in its unaffected simplicity and sometimes boring, Buber has a deep and penetrating mind which not only admires intuition in others but has it at its own command. The earnest manner in which a writer of such literary refinement and intellectual subtlety propounded what to him seemed the very soul of Hasidism could not fail to produce a deep impression on our generation. He possesses that rare combination of a searching mind and literary refinement that makes for a great writer. As a matter of fact, many of us have come to think of Hasidism primarily in terms of Buber's philosophical re-interpretation, which has been accompanied by such a wealth of seemingly irresistible evidence in the shape of Hasidic legends and sayings as to baffle the would-be critic. Fifty years of neo-Hasidic teaching have evoked a strong response from the Jewish world; and, so far as I am aware, have found competent scholars somewhat unwilling to raise any fundamental questions about whether everything in this inspired and beautifully worded interpretation might stand the test of a sober and critical analysis. Dubnow, in a very general way, expressed certain doubts about the "modern" turn of Buber's Hasidism, but he did not substantiate them, and the emotional (to say nothing of the artistic) appeal of Buber's writings is, of course, so infinitely greater than that of Dubnow's rather arid discussion of Hasidic thought that there could be little question as to which side of the argument would prevail. Yet, while historical research has progressed far beyond Dubnow's achievement and has opened up many new vistas and insights into the origin and development of Hasidism, Buber's writings—especially those of his later years—have only recently begun to evoke critical discussion. Such a discussion seems to me very much called for, and I should therefore like to take up one here, necessarily limiting myself to a few points which I consider fundamental.

A critical analysis of Buber's interpretation of Hasidism has to confront certain special difficulties at the very outset. The biggest is that Buber, although a keen student of Hasidic literature, does not write as a scholar citing chapter and verse for his contentions. He combines facts and quotations as suits his purpose, which is to present Hasidism as a spiritual phenomenon and not as a historical one. He has frequently said that he is not interested in history, and in the context of our discussion this means two things, both of equal importance. First, he ignores much material which does not interest him, although for an understanding of Hasidism as a historical phenomenon it may be of the greatest value. And secondly, the material that he does select is frequently bound up with his own interpretation of its meaning. (I shall have to say more of this later.)

The other big difficulty facing the critical analyst of Buber is to be found in the fact of his own development. Buber started as an enthusiastic admirer or even follower of mystical religion, and it was his discovery of the mystical core of living Judaism in the Hasidic movement that struck him most forcefully when he first came into contact with its literature and tradition. He saw Hasidism as the flower of Jewish mysticism, as "Cabbala transformed into Ethos," and accordingly his earlier interpretation—as found in the famous chapter "The Life of the Hasidim" which introduces his *Legend of the Baal-Shem*—was colored by this view. Some years later, however, his thinking underwent a further development bringing about a deep change in his outlook, a change characterized in his own philosophical writings by the dialogue *Daniel* of 1913 on the one hand and *I and Thou* (1923) on the other. Here he foresook the world of mysticism and took a new stand which brought him into the forefront of what would today be called religious existentialism, however much he used to shun the term. But even in this new phase, Hasidism continued to serve as his paradigm. A little pamphlet like his *The Way of Man in Hasidic Teaching* is not only a gem of literature but at the same time an extraordinary piece of religious anthropology couched in the language of Hasidism and inspired by a great quantity of authentic Hasidic sayings. It is precisely this problem of determining the kind of inspiration Buber found in the old sayings, and how, interpreting them in his own way, he transformed them, to which I shall devote the main part of my discussion.

In this last phase of his selective presentation of Hasidism, Buber no longer stressed the essential identity of Cabbala and Hasidism, as he had done in his earlier work. Even while acknowledging strong links between the two phenomena, he strove to establish an essential distinction between Hasidism and Cabbala (which he now chose to call gnosticism). He saw two conflicting kinds of minds at work in Hasidism—although the creators of the movement may not have been conscious of the split. One kind was formed by the Cabbalistic tradition, which aimed at a knowledge of, or at least an insight into, the mysteries of divinity, and which led Hasidism into speculations of a theosophical character. Buber was fully aware that Hasidism developed within the framework of the Lurianic Cabbala; indeed he accepted and elaborated upon my own characterization of the Lurianic Cabbala as an outstanding example of a gnostic system of thought within the confines of Orthodox Judaism.* But this Cabbalistic gnosis was not, according to Buber, a creative element in Hasidism. Its conceptual apparatus was used by the great leaders of Hasidism, but they transferred its meaning from the sphere of divine mysteries to the world of man and his encounter with God. This, said Buber, was the truly creative aspect of Hasidism. And since only the creative impulse counts, he felt entitled to disregard the Cabbalistic (or "gnostic") element in Hasidism almost completely—conceiving of it as no more than a kind of umbilical cord that, once the new spiritual creation exists in its own right, must be severed if we are to see the new creation in its own genuine mode of being.

There are many formulations of this attitude in Buber's writings. Let me quote but one:

> The Hasidic movement takes over from the Cabbala only what it needs for the theological foundation of an enthusiastic but not over-exalted life in responsibility—responsibility of a single individual for the piece of world entrusted to him. Gnostic theologumena that are thus taken over are transformed; their ground and their atmosphere are transformed with them. From spiritualities enthroned in the unbinding [I think the translator meant The Absolute—G.S.], they became the core of authentications. . . . Therefore everything has become different. In the place of esoterically regulated meditations has stepped the unprescribable endowing of each action with strength of intention arising ever again from the moment. Not in the seclusion of the Ascetics and schools of Ascetics does the holy now appear, but in the joy in one another of the masters and their communities. And—what was unthinkable in the circles of the old Cabbala—the "simple man" is held in honor, that is, the man of the original *devotio,* the man by nature at one with himself who lacks the secret knowing as well as rabbinical knowledge, but can do without both because

* See Scholem, *Major Trends in Jewish Mysticism,* Chapter 7.

united he lives the united service. Where the mystic vortex circled, now stretches the way of man.*

This statement, although pronounced in a voice of authority, must nevertheless fail to carry conviction for anyone familiar with both Cabbalistic and Hasidic literature. In order, however, to understand the strange mixture of oversimplification, error, and truth it contains, we must turn our attention to a basic feature of Buber's approach to the phenomenon of Hasidism: namely his conviction that the chief source of our knowledge of Hasidism is its legends. This conviction, together with Buber's method of selection, is the only thing that can explain statements like the one quoted above.

At this point we must remember that the voluminous literature of Hasidism ultimately falls into two categories. There is a very large body of theoretical writings mostly comprising homilies, commentaries on Biblical texts, and tracts on prayer and other aspects of devotion. The most important of these works—which embodied the teachings of the great saints of Hasidism, the *Tsaddikim,* and which, by way of illustration, frequently quoted epigrammatic sayings by them or short tales about them—were written between 1770 and 1815, when Hasidism became a major force in Poland and Russia, propagating its views and mode of life both by word of mouth and by the pen. An even more voluminous literature of the same type was produced after 1815, but to a great extent it only contained variations on the motifs developed in the earlier books. The second category of Hasidic literature consists of a large body of legendary writings, biographies, and tales of the miraculous deeds and wonderful sayings of the *Tsaddikim*. This legendary literature developed during the closing years of the 18th century and enjoyed an ever-growing popularity among the Hasidic masses because, it was held, to relate stories about the saints was on the same spiritual level as studying the divine mysteries. The main features of Hasidic legend crystallized in the first half of the 19th century, incorporating in many cases legends of much older vintage and coming from circles outside and preceding Hasidism. Since about 1860, several hundred volumes of this type have been published, drawing into their orbit each and every figure among the Hasidic leadership, including those of later times.

Now Buber's presentation and interpretation of Hasidism is based almost entirely on this second category of Hasidic literature—on the legends, apothegmata, and epigrams of the Hasidic saints. He says: "Because Hasidism in the first instance is not a category of teaching but one of life, our chief source of knowledge of Hasidism is its legends, and only after them comes its theoretical literature. The latter is a commentary, the former the text, even though a text that has been handed down in a state of extreme

* *The Origin and Meaning of Hasidism, p.* 253.

corruption. . . . It is foolish to protest that the legend does not convey to us the reality of Hasidic life. Naturally, the legend is no chronicle, but it is truer than the chronicle for those who know how to read it." *

This continuous emphasis on the preeminence of legendary tradition over the theoretical literature reveals a methodological principle of approach which I consider more than questionable. Of course, the terms used by Buber are somewhat confusing. What is a "category of teaching" as opposed to one of "life" when it comes to analyzing a historical phenomenon whose teaching is inextricably tied to the life it preached? Buber's metaphors about text and commentary are misleading and conceal the fact that the so-called commentary was the first and most authoritative statement of the meaning of this life long before its legends developed. Furthermore, strictly speaking, these legends are themselves obviously no more than a commentary on what Buber would call life. Life is reflected both in teaching and legend, but we can say with assurance that the very coming into being of this Hasidic life was deeply influenced by ideas embodied in the theoretical literature, whereas at its origin it certainly was not influenced by legend.

I see this as one of the main pitfalls into which Buber's ambiguous use of the term "life" has precipitated him. No doubt, for the purposes of aesthetic presentation the legends have a greater advantage and appeal, and lend themselves to a subjectivist interpretation more easily than the theoretical writings which contain a sustained line of argument and on which, in my humble opinion, a discussion of the meaning of Hasidism—even if we call it "Hasidic life"—must be based. It is very interesting to note that in the course of the years, as Buber's existentialist and subjectivist "philosophy of the dialogue" became more developed and elaborate, his references to the theoretical literature of Hasidism became ever weaker and more scanty. I dare say that many readers of Buber would never so much as suspect that such a literature even exists.

Buber apparently regarded these sources as too dependent upon earlier Cabbalistic literature to be considered indigenously Hasidic. Dependent they indeed are. Many of them, and some of the most famous, are written entirely in the language of Cabbalism, and it is a task for subtle scholarship—by no means an easy one—to define exactly where their ideas depart from those of their Cabbalistic predecessors. The Hasidic authors obviously were not aware of having broken in any way with the gnostic tradition of Cabbalism, and they wrote plainly as gnostics—Buber's protest to the contrary notwithstanding. When Buber declared in favor of the legends of Hasidism as its truly creative contribution, he put himself into the rather paradoxical position of contending that the originality of the movement was revealed more genuinely in a genre of literature which mostly came

* *Ibid,* p. 27.

into being almost fifty years after the period when Hasidism was actually created—a period embodied in the theoretical books he has chosen to sidestep. This is a contention that cannot stand.

Buber, in short, by making his choice and omitting whatever clashes with its demands, assumes an authority which we cannot grant him. To describe the universe of Hasidism, the way of life it propagated, and the teachings of its masters exclusively on the basis of its legends is equivalent to describing Islamic mysticism by taking into account only the sayings of the great Sufis and disregarding their voluminous theoretical (equally "gnostic") literature; or to describing Roman Catholicism by selecting and interpreting the choicest epigrams of the saints of the Church without regard to its dogmatic theology. No doubt this could be done, and an analysis or even a mere compilation of the *obiter dicta* of their great spirits would certainly open up a wonderful vista into the worlds of Sufism and Catholicism. Sayings of this kind, which reflect an individual's response to and conception of the system of thought in which he lives, obviously have a strong tinge of what today is called existential meaning. But the pleasure and illumination we would derive from a compilation of such sayings or legends should not mislead us into thinking that they represent the actual teaching of Sufism or Catholicism, whose more dogmatic features would be apt to get blurred in a presentation of this character. And that is precisely the case with Buber's selection of Hasidic material. These legends and sayings are certainly impressive and they certainly possess a general human appeal, but to understand what they actually meant in their original context, one still has to go back to the primary sources which Buber has declared to be merely secondary. We shall presently see how important this original context is in discussing the most fundamental point in Buber's interpretation of Hasidism. As a man of letters—even as the preacher of a message—we willingly grant Buber the right to choose as he pleases, whatever ambiguity his choice may entail. However, such a choice will not serve him in making out a scholarly case for a true understanding of what most appeals to him in the phenomenon of Hasidism.

To be sure, there is some truth in Buber's idea of the relation between Hasidism and Cabbala. While the Hasidim never lost or foresook their enthusiasm for the teachings of the Zohar and the Lurianic Cabbala, and while no page of a Hasidic book can be understood without constant reference to these traditions, at the same time the Hasidic writers were not particularly creative in elaborating the theosophical points of Cabbalism, and all students of Hasidism are agreed that it is not here that their most valuable contribution lies. They use the old formulas, terms, and ideas, adding only a new twist. Thus Buber is right in saying that gnostic theologumena when taken over by Hasidism are transformed. Into what are they transformed? Into statements about man and his way to God. Cabbalistic terminology which originally referred to divine mysteries is interpreted by the Hasidic writers as referring also to values of the personal life of man and his relation to God, and great emphasis is placed on this "moral" reading of the old vocabulary. In the writings of Rabbi Baer of Mezritch—the 18th-century pupil of the Baal-Shem who actually organized the movement—we find a whole string of pages where Cabbalistic terms are almost systematically taken up with a view to explaining what they mean if understood as guiding principles in the personal life of the devotee. They are not robbed of their original meaning, which indeed continues to play its part; rather they acquire an additional one.

This far we can agree with Buber, but again he overstates his point in opposing the ideal of the Cabbalist initiated into the mysteries of God to that of the simple man who lacks gnostic and rabbinic knowledge but has achieved a "unity" in his life. This seems to be a false alternative. The Cabbalists never excluded the possibility of a simple unlearned person achieving the highest spiritual perfection, nor did Hasidism set up this kind of simple man as its highest ideal. He may appear here and there in Hasidic legend (which in this respect has absorbed a much older Jewish folk-tradition), but Hasidic teaching says nothing about his representing the highest ideal to be achieved by following the call. On the contrary, it never tires of expounding its doctrine of the necessary interrelation between the truly spiritual man—who is always seen as a gnostic initiate—and the simple people: only by binding themselves to their common roots can these two kinds of men arrive at the true Hasidic community, which needs them both. The Hasidic legends honoring the faith of the unlettered believer are essentially the same as are found in all religions, and only rarely do they throw light on the specific scale of values which Hasidic literature held up to be followed, and on the ways it prescribed for achieving communion with God. This latter concern—the achieving of communion with God—is the core of Hasidism.

But let us proceed to the main point. I agree with Buber when he says: "What Hasidism strives for as regards the Cabbala is the de-schematization of the mystery. The old-new principle that it represented is, restored in purified form, that of the cosmic-metacosmic power and responsibility of man. 'All worlds depend on his works, all gaze at and long for the teaching and the good deeds of man.' This principle, by virtue of the pure intensity of Hasidism, became a religious *meeting* . . . a center of a life force and of a community." * The notion that man's action constitutes a meeting with God is certainly, and quite rightly, central to Buber's point of view. It takes on enormous dimensions in his Hasidic writings, but is the meaning he gives to it a true representation, as he claims, of the very heart of Hasidism?

* *The Origin and Meaning of Hasidism*, p. 124.

Hasidism does indeed teach that man meets God in the concreteness of his activity within the world. What do the Hasidim understand by this? According to the great myth of exile and redemption which is Lurianic Cabbalism, "sparks" of divine life are exiled all over the world and long to be "lifted up" by the actions of man and restored to their proper place in the divine harmony of being. This Cabbalistic myth—whose details are too complicated to be spelled out here*—is probably the most important heritage Hasidism took over from Cabbalism. The upshot of the many variations on the myth was that since these holy sparks were supposed to be everywhere without exception, Hasidism denied in principle the existence of a purely secular sphere in life of no significance to the religious task of man. What appears to be profane and without relevance to religion, in fact contains a specific religious demand on man. Everywhere there is an opportunity, nay a necessity, for "uplifting," and everywhere there lurks the danger of failure. Thus religion is not a beaten track in a circumscribed sphere. New paths open up wherever one looks, and God is at the end of every path. The contemplative mind discovers the "spark" in every sphere of life and thereby turns the profane into something of immediate religious significance.

The formula for this mood was provided by Proverbs 3:6, "In all thy ways acknowledge Him," which the Hasidim interpreted to mean: by every action in which you are engaged you may come to know God, you may be meeting Him. As a matter of fact, the Talmud itself (Berakhoth 63a) calls this verse "a small thing on which all the fundamentals of the Torah depend." Some medieval commentators tried to sidetrack this principle by applying it rather narrowly, but Hasidism, in its own mystical way, restored it to its full significance. Rabbi Pinchas of Koretz is credited with the following remark: "How then is it possible to know God in *all* ways? It is, because when God gave the Torah, the whole universe was filled with Torah. There is thus nothing which does not contain Torah, and this is the meaning of the verse. And whoever says that the Torah is one thing and the secular sphere of life [*millei di-alma*] is another, is a heretic." Since the beginnings of Hasidism this doctrine has always been considered one of its basic principles.

Special emphasis was laid by the Hasidic writers on precisely those "forgotten" fields of "simple" activity, the transformation of which into media of holy worship was one of the most refreshing aspects of the movement. True to their innate radicalism—and it is as radicals that the Hasidim have come down in the history of Judaism—they were not afraid of paradoxical statements of their position. "Small talk with one's fellow can

* For a fuller exposition, see Professor Scholem's article, "Jewish Messianism and the Idea of Progress," in the April 1958 *Commentary*—Ed.

be the vehicle of deep meditation," says the Baal-Shem. "The cardinal principle in religious worship," says another Hasidic leader, "is to serve Him through profane, or material, things." "Even by political conversation and talk about the wars of the gentile nations [the *ne-plus-ultra* of insignificance and wasted time in the eyes of non-Hasidic moralists of the period!] may a man be able to attain communion with God," said a third. And this last is not a simple overstatement—the author of it gives detailed advice on how to perform the feat. The Rabbi of Polnoye, the pupil of the Baal-Shem, sums it all up: "There is no great or small thing isolated from God, for He is immanent in all being. Therefore, the perfect man can perform the deepest meditations and acts of unification even through his most earthly actions, such as eating, drinking, sexual intercourse, and business transactions." The contemplative acts of mystical concentration, called *Yihudim* in Cabbalistic parlance, are no longer performed in solitude and retreat from the world, but rather in the market-place and in supposedly non-spiritual areas. It is here that the true Hasid finds the perfect stage for a perfectly paradoxical achievement.

But is the achievement really paradoxical? At this point we come face to face with the main principle of Buber's interpretation of Hasidism. The doctrine which I have just expounded is a fact. But how is it to be understood? What kind of contact with the concrete reality of things does man achieve through the lifting up of the holy sparks, according to this radically mystical theory? Does he achieve communion with the concrete in its actual concreteness—with, that is to say, "life as it is"? In using this phrase, I am quoting Buber who says with much clarity and conviction that Hasidism "kindled its followers to joy in the world as it is, *in life as it is,* in every hour of life in this world as that hour is," and that it taught a "constant, undaunted, and exalted joy in the Here and Now."

This far-reaching thesis constitutes the basis of Buber's existentialist interpretation of Hasidism as a perfect realization of the Here and Now, and I think we can gain a better understanding of the truly dialectical nature of Hasidic teaching by considering what makes the thesis so questionable. In some sense, Hasidism does of course know of joy and of the affirmation of reality—a fact which has never escaped the attention of the many writers on Hasidism. But Hasidic doctrine, which seems to me very far from what Buber takes it to be, is ambiguous on this point. The ambiguity is clearly visible in the turn which Hasidic writers gave to the Cabbalistic doctrine of the uplifting of the sparks, and I wish to formulate it as precisely as possible.

The doctrine of the uplifting of the sparks by human activity means that there is indeed an element in reality with which man can, and should, establish a positive communion, but the liberation or realization of this element simultaneously *annihilates* reality insofar as "reality" signifies (as it does for Buber) the Here and Now. For the "undaunted and exalted joy" which Hasidism certainly did demand of its followers is *not* a joy in the Here and Now. In joy—or let me say in doing whatever he does in full concentration—man communes not with the Here and Now itself (as Buber would have it) but with what is *hidden* in the negligible garment of the Here and Now. Buber's joy in life as it is and in the world as it is—this strikes me as a rather modern idea, and I am bound to say that I find the Hasidic *dicta* expressive of quite a different mood. They do not teach us to enjoy life as it is; rather do they advise—nay enjoin—man to extract, I may even say distill, the perpetual life of God out of life as it is. This extracting must be an act of abstraction. It is not the fleeting Here and Now that is to be enjoyed but the everlasting unity and presence of Transcendence. Of course, it is precisely this notion of abstraction in joy and in the uplifting of the sparks to which Buber's interpretation of Hasidism takes exception. For it would go against the essence of his interest in Hasidism as an anti-Platonic, existentialist teaching. Buber says: "Here where we stand, the hidden divine life should be made to shine." This formula conveys true Hasidic teaching, but with an ambiguity of which Buber's reader would not be aware. For in the very act of making the hidden life shine through, we destroy the Here and Now, instead of—as Buber wishes—realizing it in its full concreteness.

Buber's statement, interestingly enough, is to be found almost word for word in Cabbalistic writers such as Moses Cordovero, and is a gnostic thesis whose meaning Hasidic teaching did not alter in the least. "If you see a beautiful woman"—says Rabbi Baer of Mezritch—"do not think of her beauty in its concrete, palpable shape [that is to say, as it exists in the Here and Now] but abstract from its concrete reality and concentrate your mind on the divine beauty that shines through the concrete phenomenon. Then you will no longer behold the beautiful and tempting Here and Now which is this woman, but the ideal and everlasting quality of beauty which is one of God's attributes, and from this you will proceed to contemplate the source of all beauty, namely God." *Dicta* of this kind are legion in Hasidic literature. They use the concrete meeting of man and reality in order to transcend reality, not to fufill it. And their truly Platonic ring sounds rather different from Buber's glorification of the Here and Now. The Here and Now is transcended and vanishes when the divine element makes its appearance in contemplation, and the Hasidim were tireless in pointing this moral.

Moreover, the Hasidic conception of the ultimate realization of the concrete contains an essential element of *destruction* which I fail to notice in Buber's analysis. The Baal-Shem and his followers, however, were perfectly well aware of it. I should like to quote only one characteristic saying of the Baal-Shem to make my point clear.

> Once [reports Rabbi Wolf of Zhitomir] the Baal-Shem asked one of the outstanding sages of his generation in regard to prayer: "How do you behave and where do your thoughts turn when praying?" He replied: "I unite with all the individual vitality that there is within created things. For in every thing that comes to be created, there must be a vital force which derives from the divine emanation. I unite with them when speaking my words before God to make my prayer penetrate up into the highest regions." Said the Baal-Shem to him: "If that is what you do, you are destroying the world because in draining off the vitality of things you leave their concrete individuality without their vital force." Said the man: "But how is it possible that I could drain off their vital force by uniting with them?" Answered the Baal-Shem: "Your question shows that your prayer is of little account, since you do not believe that by your prayer you have the power to lift up from them what is their vital capacity."

Here, then, we have the clear-cut and radical thesis which frequently recurs in Hasidic teaching: the complete and final realization of communion has a destructive quality. And the solution which the Baal-Shem offers shows the dialectical character of communion and lifting up. He says that this realization is only a momentary one which must not last. One draws out the vital force, but at the same moment one draws it in again. Or, as many Hasidic writers like to say, one reduces it to nothingness and thereby restores it. This is plainly an esoteric action, and it is called so in so many words by the Baal-Shem—for all that Buber believes that esotericism was renounced by Hasidism. Nor does this action amount, as Buber claims, to the realization of the concrete in all its concreteness. For, as is clearly indicated by the Baal-Shem's words, it is not of the essence of the act itself that it should be discontinued. The need to discontinue is only accidental, caused by man's decision to desist, or by his weakness and incapacity for sustaining his destructive concentration. Consequently, such concentration is calculated to empty concrete things of their concreteness rather than filling them to capacity with concrete being, as Buber would have it. We might say that the dialogue reported by the Hasidic writer could well-nigh have been a dialogue between the Baal-Shem and Buber.

Additional evidence against Buber's existentialist interpretation can be found throughout the classics of Hasidism, the writings of the great pupils of the Baal-Shem, where the individual and concrete being or phenomenon, the *pratiyut* or *lebush,* is always treated rather superciliously. The Here and Now indeed presents a supreme opportunity for a meeting between God and man, but such a meeting can only take place when man uncovers another dimension of the Here and Now—an act which makes the "concrete" disappear. The Here and Now of created being is not identical with what shines through it once it has become transparent. To assume such an identity is to contradict genuine Hasidic teaching which makes the awareness of the divine core of being dependent precisely on emptying the concrete phenomenon of its own weight and significance.

In Buber's careful wording this essential difference is always blurred. On the other hand he establishes a distinction between the Platonic raising-up of the concrete into the realm of Ideas and the existential seizing of the holy sparks hidden in all things. But this distinction is by no means as clear-cut in the Hasidic texts as it is with Buber. For the Hasidim, the realization of reality (if I may use the phrase) is a precarious enterprise: reality may break under the strain of such realization as the lifting-up of the sparks implies. It is not the *concrete* reality of things that appears as the result of the mystic's action, but the *messianic* reality in which all things have been restored to their proper place in the scheme of creation and have thus been transfigured. As a matter of fact, the terms reality and concreteness mean something quite different to Buber from what the Hasidim understood by them. He sometimes uses these terms to signify both the realm of the Here and Now and the realm of transfigured being—a circumstance which has tended to confuse the issue raised by his interpretation. Since the Hasidim laid great stress on the point that human activity cannot bring about or reveal the messianic reality (a point which is also blurred in Buber's writings), they were left with prescribing ways for the individual to use the concrete as a vehicle to the abstract and thereby to the ultimate source of being. This may be conventional theology, even if couched in the language of personal religion, and may be much less exciting than the novel interpretation read into it by Buber, but it is still what Hasidism stood for.

For all this, however, one should not underrate the possibility that the doctrine of the lifting up of the sparks was interpreted in practice by many Hasidim in a less dialectical sense than was originally intended. Hasidic theory—as presented by the Baal-Shem himself, the Rabbi of Polnoye, the Maggid of Mezritch, and their most important pupils—never lost its awareness of the destructive implications of the doctrine and tried to devise ways and means to escape its consequences. But the practice, attested to by the complaints on the part of friend and foe alike, was frequently less sophisticated than the theory. To many Hasidim, lifting up the sparks indeed meant living a fuller life: not emptying reality by taking the sparks *away,* but fulfilling it by bringing them *in.* Thus the holy sparks were interpreted not as metaphysical elements of divine being, but as subjective feelings of joy and affirmation projected into man's relation with his environment. This, however, is a view dictated not by the theology of the founders of Hasidism but by the mood of some of its followers. And it is of course precisely this kind of popularization or vulgarization which is sometimes reflected in the world of legend, where Buber's simplified view has its relative legitimation. But to call it the message of Hasidism would be wide of the mark.

In the preceding remarks I have been dealing in detail with one central point in Buber's interpretation of Hasidism. In analyzing other important concepts we would be faced with the same task of probing into Buber's assertions by referring back to the theoretical literature of Hasidism. We would then find that the curiously vague terms Buber uses are invariably almost Hasidic, but never quite. There could be no better illustration of this than the following quotation: "In the Hasidic message the separation between 'life in God' and 'life in the world,' the primal evil of all 'religion,' is overcome in genuine, concrete unity." This seems to mean that man's responsibility is infinitely more important than the dogmatic formulation of institutional religion. But the fact is that what Buber calls the "primal evil of all religion" is very much at the center of Hasidic teaching. Buber's so-called "concrete unity" is a fictitious one where Hasidism is concerned, for "life in the world" is no longer life in the world when its divine origins appear in contemplation, thereby transforming it into "life in God." I have still to discover a passage in Hasidic writings that does not maintain the basic separation that Buber so resents. The fact, of course, is—to put it bluntly—that Buber is a religious anarchist (a term that is not meant to disparage him; I am an anarchist myself, though not one of Buber's persuasion). True, Buber's philosophy asks man to *take* a direction and to *make* a decision, but he never says *which* direction and *which* decision. Moreover, he says that such direction and decision cannot be formulated except in the world of the *It,* so much disparaged in his own thinking. Whatever the merits of this view—which is intrinsically anarchic—Hasidism never could share it because Hasidism remained "committed" to Jewish tradition as a *teaching in which directions could be formulated,* that is to say, as a teaching about *what* should be done. In Buber's philosophy this belongs to the world of the It, in which the anarchic life of the dialogue is killed. Buber has always been very honorable and indeed admirable and courageous in standing by this principle. Commit yourself, he tells us, but he refuses to say what we should commit ourselves to (although he himself has made his own choice).

Therefore, references to the Torah and the Commandments, which to the Hasidim still meant everything, become extremely nebulous in Buber's presentation. It is true that Jewish mysticism, by a certain theory of the meaning of Revelation, expands the domain to which the Torah as a set of values refers, but it is still Torah, and that separation of which Buber speaks so disparagingly is still maintained. Where the separation is overcome it is overcome at the cost of the "life in the world," as is clearly shown by the saying of Rabbi Pinchas of Koretz quoted above.

Buber's interpretation stresses the uniqueness of the task confronting every single individual. "All men have access to God, but each in a way that is all his own" (*Der Weg des Menschen*). This is indeed true, but it is not a novelty introduced by Hasidism. On the contrary, the idea comes originally from the Lurianic Cabbala—that is to say, from that very gnosis at which Buber looks askance. It holds that each individual is enjoined to lift up the holy sparks specifically belonging to his own spiritual root in the great soul of Adam (which is the common soul of mankind), each according to the particular place he once had in Adam's soul. All Hasidism did was to formulate this theory in a popular way, thereby giving it a more personal turn.

Another instance of the peculiar vagueness in Buber's use of Hasidic terms is the way he employs the word *Yihud*. In both Cabbalistic and Hasidic parlance *Yihud* means a contemplative act through which man binds himself to the spiritual element by concentrating his mind on the holy letters of the Torah, which is also the holy book of nature. Buber's contention is that in Hasidism *Yihud* is no longer a magical formula or procedure as it was in Cabbalism. "It is nothing else than the ordinary life of man, but concentrated and aimed at unity as its goal." There may be other *Yihudim,* after the old fashion, but (says Buber) they never so much as touch the center of Hasidic doctrine. Yet I am bound to say that I am unable to find any new shade of meaning in the Hasidic usage of the term. There are always two meanings to *Yihud* in the older literature, and they have undergone no change in the Hasidic texts. The first derives from the Cabbalists and always signifies some special meditation attached to a particular action, a meditation by which one unites oneself to some spiritual reality—to the soul of a holy man or its sparks, to a name of God or a divine attribute. (In this usage, the term also signifies the result achieved by such meditation.) The second meaning of *Yihud,* however, derives above all from Bachya ibn Pakuda's ethical work, *The Duties of the Heart,* where it refers to the directing of one's mind or one's action toward God. In this sense, the term is used only in the singular. Used in the plural, it can only have the Cabbalistic meaning, which has to do with contemplation exclusively and not with the concrete unity of human life achieved by the intensity of concentration, as Buber would have it. The *Yihudim* (plural) are achieved by contemplative communion (*d'veḳut*) with the inwardness of the "letters" which are imprinted into being itself. In all the sayings of the Baal-Shem of which I know, the term is used in this precise and technical sense. Therefore I find Buber's translations of many passages on *Yihud* very modern and suggestive, but scientifically unacceptable.

To sum up, the merits of Buber's presentation of Hasidic sayings and legends are very great indeed and will to a large extent stand the test of time. But the spiritual message he has read into them in his more mature works is too deeply bound up with assumptions that have no root in the texts—assumptions drawn from his own very modern philosophy of religious anarchism. Too much is left out in his presentation of Hasidism, while what has been included is overloaded with highly personal speculations. These may be of a sublime character and they may appeal deeply to the modern mind, but if we are searching for an understanding of the actual phenomenon of Hasidism, both in its grandeur and its decay (which in many ways are bound together), we shall, I am afraid, have to start all over again.

June 1962

Lionel Trilling

SCIENCE, LITERATURE, AND CULTURE

The Leavis-Snow Controversy

It is now nearly eighty years since Matthew Arnold came to America on his famous lecture tour. Of his repertory of three lectures, none was calculated to give unqualified pleasure to his audience. The lecture on Emerson praised the then most eminent of American writers only after it had denied that he was a literary figure of the first order. The lecture called "Numbers" raised disturbing questions about the relation of democracy to excellence and distinction. "Literature and Science" was the least likely to give offense, yet even this most memorable of the three *Discourses in America* was not without its touch of uncomfortableness. In 1883 America was by no means committed—and, indeed, never was to be committed—to the belief that the right education for the modern age must be predominantly scientific and technical, and Arnold, when he cited the proponents of this idea, which of course he opposed, mentioned only those who were English. Yet his audience surely knew that Arnold was warning them against what would seem to be the natural tendency of an industrial democracy to devalue the old "aristocratic" education in favor of studies that are merely practical.

Arnold wrote "Emerson" and "Numbers" especially for his American tour, but he had first composed "Literature and Science" as the Rede Lecture at Cambridge in 1882. Its original occasion cannot fail to have a peculiar interest at this moment, for C. P. Snow's *The Two Cultures and the Scientific Revolution,* around which so curious a storm rages in England, was the Rede Lecture of 1959.

Sir Charles did not mention his great predecessor in the lectureship, although his own discourse was exactly on Arnold's subject and took a line exactly the opposite of Arnold's. And F. R. Leavis, whose admiration of Arnold is well known and whose position in respect to the relative importance of literature and of science in education is much the same as Arnold's, did not mention Arnold either, when, in his Richmond Lecture at Downing College, he launched an attack of unexampled ferocity upon the doctrine and the author of *The Two Cultures*.

In its essential terms, the issue in debate has not changed since Arnold spoke. Arnold's chief antagonist was T. H. Huxley—it was he who, in his lecture on "Culture and Education," had said that literature should, and inevitably would, step down from its pre-eminent place in education, that science and not "culture" must supply the knowledge which is necessary for an age committed to rational truth and material practicality. What is more, Huxley said, science will supply the very basis of the assumptions of modern ethics. In effect Snow says nothing different.

The word "culture" had been Arnold's personal insigne ever since the publication of *Culture and Anarchy* in 1867, and Huxley made particular reference to the views on the value of humanistic study which Arnold had expressed in that book.* Arnold's reply in "Literature and Science" could not have been simpler, just as it could not have been more temperate, although it surely did not surpass in temperateness Huxley's statement of his disagreement with Arnold's ideas; the two men held each other in high admiration and were warm friends. Arnold said that he had not the least disposition to propose that science be slighted in education. Quite apart from its practical value, scientific knowledge is naturally a delight to the mind, no doubt engaging certain mental temperaments more than others but holding out the promise of intellectual pleasure to all. Yet of itself science does not, as Arnold put it, "serve" the instinct for conduct and the instinct for beauty, or at least it does not serve these instincts as they exist in most men. This service, which includes the relating of scientific knowledge to the whole life of man, is rendered by culture, which is not to be thought of as confined to literature—to *belles lettres*—but as comprising all the humane intellectual disciplines. When Dr. Leavis asserts the primacy of the humanities in education, he refers more exclusively to literature than Arnold did, but in general effect his position is the same.

It may seem strange, and a little tiresome, that the debate of eighty years ago should be instituted again today. Yet it is perhaps understandable in view of the "scientific revolution" about which Sir Charles tells us. This revolution would seem to be one of the instances in which a change of quantity becomes a change in kind—science can now do so much more and do it so much more quickly than it could a generation ago, let alone in

* Arnold, I need scarcely say, did not use the word in the modern sense in which it is used by anthropologists, sociologists, and historians of thought and art; this is, more or less, the sense in which it is used by Snow. For Arnold, "culture" was "the best that has been thought and said in the world" and also an individual person's relation to this body of thought and expression. My own use of the word in this essay is not Arnold's.

the last century, that it has been transmuted from what the world has hitherto known. One of the consequences of this change—to Sir Charles it is the most salient of all possible consequences—is the new social hope that is now held out to us, of life made better in material respects, not merely in certain highly developed countries but all over the world and among peoples that at the moment are, by Western standards, scarcely developed at all.

The new power of science perhaps justifies a contemporary revival of the Victorian question. But if we consent to involve ourselves in the new dialectic of the old controversy, we must be aware that we are not addressing ourselves to a question of educational theory, or to an abstract contention as to what kind of knowledge has the truest affinity with the human soul. We approach these matters only to pass through them. What we address ourselves to is politics, and politics of a quite ultimate kind, and to the disposition of the modern mind.

II

The Two Cultures has had a very considerable currency in England and America ever since its publication in 1959, and in England it was for a time the subject of lively discussion. Indeed, the general agreement in England that it was a statement of great importance, to the point of its being used as an assigned text in secondary schools, was what aroused Dr. Leavis to make his assault on the lecture this long after the first interest in it had subsided. The early discussions of *The Two Cultures* were of a substantive kind, but the concerns which now agitate the English in response to Dr. Leavis' attack have scarcely anything to do with literature and science, or with education, or with social hope. These matters have now been made a mere subordinate element in what amounts to a scandal over a breach of manners. The published comments on Dr. Leavis' attack on *The Two Cultures* were, with few exceptions, directed to such considerations as the exact degree of monstrousness which Dr. Leavis achieved in speaking of Sir Charles as he did; whether or not he spoke out of envy of Sir Charles's reputation; whether or not he has, or deserves to have, any real standing as a critic; or writes acceptable English; or represents, as he claims he does, "the essential Cambridge."

Dr. Leavis' Richmond Lecture, "The Significance of C. P. Snow," was delivered in the Hall of Downing College, Cambridge, on February 28, 1962, and published in *The Spectator* of March 9.* In the next week's

* In an editorial note, Dr. Leavis is quoted as saying, "The lecture was private and representatives of the press who inquired were informed that there was no admission

issue of *The Spectator,* seventeen letters appeared, all defending Snow and most of them expressing anger at, or contempt for, Leavis. The following week brought fifteen more communications, of which eight expressed partisanship with Leavis; several of these deplored the tone of the previous week's correspondence. Many of the correspondents who defended Snow were of distinguished reputation; of the defenders of Leavis, the only one known to me was Mr. Geoffrey Wagner, who wrote from America to communicate his belief that the attack on Snow was much needed, for, despite a parody in *New Left Review* in which Snow appears as C. P. Sleet, despite, too, his own adverse criticism of Snow in *The Critic,* "the hosannas obediently continued on this side of the Atlantic, both from the Barzun-Trilling syndrome and the Book-of-the-Month Club, the worst of both worlds, as it were." Three of the writers of the Snow party touched upon the question of literature and science, the scientist J. D. Bernal, the historian of science Stephen Toulmin, and the literary critic G. S. Fraser. In a miasma of personality-mongering, their letters afforded a degree of relief, but they said little that was of consequence. Of the Leavis party two dons of the University of Birmingham in a joint letter touched rapidly but with some cogency on the relation between literature and science, deploring any attempt to prefer one above the other, concluding that if one must be preferred, it should be, for reasons not stated, literature.

From the *Spectator* letters, so many of them expressing small and rather untidy passions, there are no doubt conclusions to be drawn, of a sufficiently depressing sort, about the condition of intellectual life at the moment. But no awareness that we may have of the generally bad state of intellectual affairs ought to blind us to the particular fault of Dr. Leavis in his treatment of Sir Charles Snow. Intelligent and serious himself, Dr. Leavis has in this instance been the cause of stupidity and triviality in other men.

There can be no two opinions about the tone in which Dr. Leavis deals with Sir Charles. It is a bad tone, an impermissible tone. It is bad in a personal sense because it is cruel—it manifestly intends to wound. It is bad intellectually because by its use Dr. Leavis has diverted attention, his own included, from the matter he sought to illuminate. The doctrine of *The Two Cultures* is a momentous one, and Dr. Leavis obscures its large significance by bringing into consideration such matters as Sir Charles's abilities as a novelist, his club membership, his opinion of his own talents, his worldly success, and his relation to worldly power. Anger, scorn, and an excessive consciousness of persons have always been elements of Dr. Leavis' thought—of the very process of his thought, not merely of his

---

and that no reporting was to be permitted. The appearance in newspapers of garbled reports has made it desirable that the lecture should appear in full."

manner of expressing it. They were never exactly reassuring elements, but they could be set aside and made to seem of relatively small account in comparison with the remarkable cogency in criticism which Dr. Leavis so often achieved. But as they now appear in his valedictory address—for, in effect, that is what the Richmond Lecture was, since Dr. Leavis retired that year from his university post—they cannot be easily set aside, they stand in the way of what Dr. Leavis means to say.

And, indeed, our understanding of what he means to say is to be derived less from the passionate utterance of the lecture itself than from our knowledge of the whole direction of his career in criticism. That direction was from the first determined by Dr. Leavis' belief that the human faculty above all others to which literature addresses itself is the moral consciousness, which is also the source of all successful creation, the very root of poetic genius. The extent of his commitment to this idea results in what I believe to be a fault in his critical thought—he does not give anything like adequate recognition to those aspects of art which are gratuitous, which arise from high spirits and the impulse to play. One would suppose that the moral consciousness should, for its own purposes, take account of those aspects of art and life that do not fall within its dominion. But if the intensity of Dr. Leavis' commitment to the moral consciousness contrives to produce this deficiency of understanding, it is no less responsible for the accuracy and force which we recognize as the positive characteristics of his work. For Dr. Leavis, literature is what Matthew Arnold said it is, *the criticism of life*—he can understand it in no other way. Both in all its simplicity and in all its hidden complexity, he has made Arnold's saying his own, and from it he has drawn his strength.

If, then, Dr. Leavis now speaks with a very special intensity in response to *The Two Cultures,* we must do him the justice of seeing that the Rede Lecture denies, and in an extreme way, all that he has ever believed about literature—it is, in fact, nothing less than an indictment of literature on social and moral grounds. It represents literature as constituting a danger to the national well-being, and most especially when it is overtly a criticism of life.

Not only because Charles Snow is himself a practitioner of literature but also because he is the man he is, the statement that his lecture has this purport will be shocking and perhaps it will be thought scarcely credible. And I have no doubt that, in another mood and on some other occasion, Sir Charles would be happy to assert the beneficent powers of literature. But there can be no other interpretation of his lecture than that it takes toward literature a position of extreme antagonism.

The Two Cultures begins as an objective statement of the lack of communication between scientists and literary men. This is a circumstance which must have been often observed and often deplored. Perhaps nothing in our culture is so characteristic as the separateness of the various artistic and intellectual professions. As between, say, poets and painters, or musicians and architects, there is very little discourse, and perhaps the same thing could be remarked of scientists of different interests, say biologists and physicists. But the isolation of literary men from scientists may well seem to be the most extreme of these separations, if only because it is the most significant, for a reason which Sir Charles entirely understands: the especially close though never fully defined relation of these two professions with our social and political life.

The even-handedness with which Sir Charles at first describes the split between the two "cultures" does not continue for long. He begins by telling us that scientists and literary men are equally to blame for the separation—they are kept apart by "a gulf of mutual incomprehension," by distorted images of each other which give rise to dislike and hostility. But as Sir Charles's lecture proceeds, it becomes plain that, although the scientists do have certain crudities and limitations, they are in general in the right of things and the literary men in the wrong of them. The matter which causes the scales to shift thus suddenly is the human condition. This, Sir Charles tells us, is of its nature tragic: man dies, and he dies alone. But the awareness of the ineluctably tragic nature of human life makes a moral trap, "for it tempts one to sit back, complacent in one's unique tragedy," paying no heed to the circumstances of everyday life, which, for the larger number of human beings, are painful. It is the literary men, we are told, who are the most likely, the scientists who are the least likely, to fall into this moral trap; the scientists "are inclined to be impatient to see if something can be done: and inclined to think that it can be done, until it's proved otherwise." It is their spirit, "tough and good and determined to fight it out at the side of their brother men," which has "made scientists regard the other [i.e. the literary] culture's social attitudes as contemptible."

"This is too facile," Sir Charles says in mild rebuke of the scientists, by which he of course means that essentially they are right. There follows a brief consideration of a question raised not by Sir Charles in his own person but by "a scientist of distinction" whom he quotes. "Yeats, Pound, Wyndham Lewis, nine out of ten of those who have dominated literary sensibility in our time, weren't they not only politically silly, but politically wicked? Didn't the influence of all they represent bring Auschwitz that much nearer?" And Sir Charles in answer grants that Yeats was a magnanimous man and a great poet, but he will not, he says, defend the indefensible—"the facts . . . are broadly true." Sir Charles in general agrees, that is, that the literary sensibility of our time brought Auschwitz nearer. He goes on to say that things have changed considerably in the literary life in recent years, even if slowly, for "literature changes more slowly than science."

From the mention of Auschwitz onward, the way is open to the full assertion by Sir Charles of the virtues of the scientist. Although they are admitted to be sometimes gauche or stupidly self-assertive, although Sir Charles concedes of some of them that "the whole literature of the traditional culture doesn't seem relevant to [their] interests" and that, as a result, their "imaginative understanding" is diminished, he yet finds scientists to be men of a natural decency; they are free from racial feelings, they are lovers of equality, they are cooperative. And chief among their virtues, as Sir Charles describes them, is the fact that they "have the future in their bones."

Indeed, it turns out that it is the future, and not mere ignorance of each other's professional concerns, that makes the separation between the culture of science and the culture of literature. Scientists have the future in their bones. Literary men do not. Quite the contrary—"If the scientists have the future in their bones, then the traditional culture responds by wishing that the future did not exist." The future that the scientists have in their bones is understood to be nothing but a good future; it is very much like the history of the Marxists, which is always the triumph of the right, never possibly the record of defeat. In fact, to entertain the idea that the future might be bad is represented as being tantamount to moral ill-will—in a note appended to the sentence I have just quoted, Sir Charles speaks of George Orwell's *1984* as "the strongest possible wish that the future shall not exist."

It is difficult to credit the implications of this astonishing remark and to ascribe them to Sir Charles. As everyone recalls, Orwell's novel is an imagination of the condition of the world if the authoritarian tendencies which are to be observed in the present develop themselves—logically, as it were—in the future, the point being that it is quite within the range of possibility that this ultimate development should take place. In Orwell's representation of an absolute tyranny, science has a part, and a polemical partisan of science might understand this as the evidence of a literary man's malice toward science. But it is much more likely that, when Orwell imagined science as one of the instruments of repression, he meant to say that science, like everything else that is potentially good, like literature itself, can be perverted and debased to the ends of tyranny. Orwell was a man who, on the basis of actual and painful experience, tried to tell the truth about politics, even his own politics. I believe that he never gave up his commitment to socialism, but he refused to be illusioned in any way he could prevent; it lay within the reach of his mind to conceive that even an idealistic politics, perhaps especially an idealistic politics, can pervert itself.

We must be puzzled to know what can be meant when such a man is said to entertain the strongest possible wish that the future shall not exist.

Having characterized the culture of literature, or, as he sometimes calls it, "the traditional culture," by its hostility to the future, Sir Charles goes on to say that "it is the traditional culture, to an extent remarkably little diminished by the emergence of the scientific one, which manages the Western world." This being so, it follows that the traditional culture must be strictly dealt with if the future is to be brought into being: what is called "the existing pattern" must be not merely changed but "broken." Only if this is done shall we be able to educate ourselves as we should. As for the need to educate ourselves: "To say, we have to educate ourselves or perish is perhaps a little more melodramatic than the facts warrant. To say, we have to educate ourselves or watch a steep decline in our lifetime is about right." And Sir Charles indicates our possible fate by the instance—he calls it a "historical myth" —of the Venetian Republic in its last half-century:

> Its citizens had become rich, as we did, by accident. They had acquired immense political skill, just as we have. A good many of them were tough-minded, realistic, patriotic men. They knew, just as clearly as we know, that the current of history had begun to flow against them. Many of them gave their minds to working out ways to keep going. It would have meant breaking the pattern into which they had been crystallized. They were fond of the pattern, just as we are fond of ours. They never found the will to break it.

I quoted without comment Sir Charles's statement of the idea on which, we may say, the whole argument of *The Two Cultures* is based: "It is the traditional culture, to an extent remarkably little diminished by the emergence of the scientific one, which manages the Western world." It is a bewildering statement. In what way can we possibly understand it? That the Western world is managed by some agency which is traditional is of course comprehensible. And we can take in the idea that this agency may be described, for particular purposes of explanation, in terms of a certain set of mind, a general tendency of thought and feeling which, being pervasive, is hard to formulate, and that this is to be called a "culture." But for Sir Charles the words "traditional" and "literary" are interchangeable, and that this culture, as we agree to call it, is *literary,* that it bears the same relation to actual literary men and their books that what is called the "scientific culture" bears to scientists and their work in laboratories, is truly a staggering thought. The actions of parliaments and congresses and cabinets in directing the massive affairs of state, the negotiations of embassies, the movement of armies and fleets, the establishment of huge scientific projects for the contrivance of armaments and of factories for the production of them, the promises made to citizens, and the choices made by voters at the polls—these, we are asked to believe, are in the charge of the culture of literature. Can we possibly take this to be so?

It can of course be said that literature has some part in the management of the Western world, a part which is limited but perhaps not wholly unimportant. If, for example, we compare the present condition of industrial England with the condition of industrial England in the early nineteenth century, we can say that the present condition is not, in human respects, anything like what men of good will might wish it to be, but that it is very much better than it was in the early years of the Industrial Revolution. And if we then ask what agencies brought about the improvement, we can say that one of them was literature. Certain literary men raised the "Condition of England Question" in a passionate and effective way and their names are still memorable to us—Coleridge, Carlyle, Mill (I take him to be a man of letters; he was certainly a good literary critic), Dickens, Ruskin, Arnold, William Morris. They made their effect only upon individuals, but the individuals they touched were numerous, and by what they said they made it ever harder for people to be indifferent to the misery around them or to the degradation of the national life in which they came to think themselves implicated. These literary men helped materially, some would say decisively, to bring about a change in the state of affairs. This is not exactly management, but it is a directing influence such as literature in the modern time often undertakes to have and sometimes does have.

Yet in Sir Charles's opinion this directing influence of the literary men of the nineteenth century deserves no praise. On the contrary, his description of their work is but another count in the indictment of the culture of literature. Speaking of the response which literary men made to the Industrial Revolution, he says:

> Almost everywhere . . . intellectual persons did not comprehend what was happening. Certainly the writers didn't. Plenty of them shuddered away, as though the right course for a man of feeling was to contract out; some, like Ruskin and William Morris and Thoreau and Emerson and Lawrence, tried various kinds of fancies, which were not much in effect more than screams of horror. It is hard to think of a writer of high class who really stretched his imaginative sympathy, who could see at once the hideous back-streets, the smoking chimneys, the internal price—and also the prospects of life that were opening out for the poor. . . .

Nothing could be further from the truth. No great English writer of the nineteenth century, once he had become aware of the Industrial Revolution, ever contracted out. This is not the place to rehearse the miseries that were acquiesced in by those who comforted the world and their own consciences with the thought of "the prospects of life that were opening out for the poor." It is enough to say that there were miseries in plenty of a brutal and horrifying kind, by no means adequately suggested by phrases like "the hideous back-streets, the smoking chimneys, the internal price." (Auschwitz, since it has been mentioned, may be thought of as the development of the conditions of the factories and mines of the earlier Industrial Revolution.) If the writers "shuddered away," it was not in maidenly disgust with machines and soot; if they uttered "screams of horror," it was out of moral outrage at what man had made of man—and of women and little children. Their emotions were no different from those expressed by Karl Marx in his chapter on the working day, nor from those expressed in Blue Books by the factory inspectors, those remarkable men of the middle class whom Marx, in a moving passage of *Capital,* praises and wonders at for their transcendence of their class feelings.

I have mentioned Matthew Arnold among those writers who made the old conditions of the Industrial Revolution ever less possible. Like many of his colleagues in this undertaking, he did entertain "fancies"—they all found modern life ugly and fatiguing and in some way false, and they set store by certain qualities which are no doubt traditional to the point of being archaic. But Arnold's peculiar distinction as a literary critic is founded on the strong sensitivity of his response to the modern situation. He uniquely understood what Hegel had told the world, that the French Revolution marked an absolute change in the condition of man. For the first time in history, Hegel said, Reason—or Idea, or Theory, or Creative Imagination—had become decisive in human destiny. Arnold's argument in "Literature and Science" was the affirmation of the French Revolution; he was speaking on behalf of the illumination and refinement of that Reason by which man might shape the conditions of his own existence. This is the whole purport of his famous statement, "Literature is the criticism of life."

That saying used to have a rough time of it, perhaps because people found the word *criticism* narrow and dour and wished to believe that life was worthier of being celebrated than criticized. But less and less, I think, will anyone find the ground on which to quarrel with it. Whatever else we also take literature to be, it must always, for us now, be the criticism of life.

But it would seem to be precisely the critical function of literature that troubles Sir Charles. And perhaps that is why, despite all that he says about the need to educate ourselves, he does not make a single substantive proposal about education.

If we undertake to say what the purpose of modern education is, our answer will surely be suggested by Arnold's phrase, together with the one by which he defined the particular function of criticism: "to see the object as in itself it really is." Whenever we undertake to pass judgment on an educational enterprise, the import of these two phrases serves as our criterion: we ask that education supply the means for a criticism of life and teach the student to try to see the object as in itself it really is. Yet when Sir Charles speaks of the need to break the "existing pattern" and to go on to the right education which will help us to establish the necessary new pattern, he does not touch upon any such standard of judgment. Although he would seem to be the likeliest person in the world to speak intelligently about the instruction in science of students who do not intend to be scientists, actually he says nothing more on the subject than that ignorance of the Second Law of Thermodynamics is equivalent to ignorance of Shakespeare, or that the Yang-Lee experiment at Columbia should have been a topic of general conversation at college High Tables.

Nor does he propose anything for the education of the scientist, except, of course, science. He does say that scientists need to be "trained not only in scientific but in human terms," but he does not say how. Scientists —but eventually one begins to wonder if they are really scientists and not advanced technologists and engineers—are to play a decisive part in the affairs of mankind, but nowhere does Sir Charles suggest that, if this is so, they will face difficulties and perplexities and that their education should include the study of books—they need not be "literary," they need not be "traditional": they might be contemporary works of history, sociology, anthropology, psychology, philosophy—which would raise the difficult questions and propose the tragic complexity of the human condition, which would suggest that it is not always easy to see the object as in itself it really is.

Well, it isn't beyond belief that a professional corps of high intellectual quality, especially if it is charged with great responsibility, should learn to ask its own questions and go on to make its own ethos, perhaps a very good one. But Sir Charles would seem to be asking for more than the right of scientists to go their own way. What he seems to require for scientists is the right to go their own way *with no questions asked*. The culture of literature, having done its worst, must now be supplanted; it is not even to play the part of a loyal opposition. How else are we to understand Sir Charles's belief in the endemic irresponsibility of the literary mind, his curious representation of the literary culture as having the management of the Western world, that is to say, as being answerable for all the anomalies, stupidities, and crimes of the Western world, for having made the "existing pattern" which must now be broken if the West is to survive or at least not suffer steep decline? It is manifest that the literary culture has lost the right to ask questions.

No one could possibly suppose of Charles Snow that he is a man who wants to curtail the rights of free criticism. The line which he takes in *The Two Cultures* is so far from the actuality of his temperament in this respect that we can only suppose that he doesn't mean it, not in all the extravagance of its literalness. Or we suppose that he means it at the behest of some large preoccupation of whose goodness he is so entirely convinced that he will seek to affirm it even in ways that would take him aback if the preoccupation were not in control of his thought. And this, I think, is the case. I believe that the position of *The Two Cultures* is to be explained by Sir Charles's well-known preoccupation with a good and necessary aim, with the assuring of peace, which is to say, with the compounding of the differences between the West and the Soviet Union. It is an aim which, in itself, can of course only do Sir Charles credit, yet it would seem to have implicit in it a strange, desperate method of implementing itself.

For the real message of *The Two Cultures* is that an understanding between the West and the Soviet Union could be achieved by the culture of scientists, which reaches over factitious national and ideological differences. The field of agreement would be the scientists' common perception of the need for coming together to put the possibilities of the scientific revolution at the disposal of the disadvantaged of all nations. The bond between scientists, Sir Charles has told us, is virtually biological: they all have the future in their bones. Science brings men together in despite of all barriers—speaking of the way in which the very wide differences in the social origins of English scientists were overcome to make the scientific culture of England (and seeming to imply that this is a unique grace of scientists, that English men of letters never had differences of social class to overcome), Sir Charles says, "Without thinking about it, they respond alike. That is what a culture means." And in the same way, "without thinking about it," the scientists of the West and the scientists of the Soviet Union may be expected to "respond alike." And, since "that is what a culture means," they will have joined together in an entity which will do what governments have not done, the work of relieving the misery of the world. But in the degree to which science naturally unites men, literature separates them, and the scientists of the world cannot form this beneficent entity until we of the West break the existing pattern of our traditional culture, the literary culture, which is self-regarding in its complacent acceptance of tragedy, which is not only indifferent to human suffering but willing to inflict it, which asks rude and impertinent questions about the present and even about the future.

It is a point of view which must, I suppose, in desperate days, have a show of reason. In desperate days, it always seems wise to throw something or someone overboard, preferably Jonah or Arion, the prophet or the poet. Mr. G. S. Fraser, for example, seems to understand what Sir Charles wants, and he is rather willing to go along with him, rather open to the idea that the achievement of peace may require some adverse judgment on literature. "It does not matter," he says, "whether we save the real Cambridge within the actual Cambridge. . . ; what we want to save is our actual human world with all the spots on it. This will not be done by teaching English at universities; men like Snow, at home both in Russia and America, and in a simple blunt way trying to teach these two blunt simple giants to understand each other, may in the end prove greater benefactors than Dr. Leavis."

No, the world will not be saved by teaching English at universities, nor, indeed, by any other literary activity. It is very hard to say what will save the world. But we can be perfectly certain that denying the actualities of the world will not work its salvation. Among these actualities politics is one. And it can be said of *The Two Cultures* that it communicates the strongest possible wish that we should forget about politics. It mentions national politics once, speaking of it as the clog upon the activity of scientists, as the impeding circumstance in which they must work. But the point is not developed and the lecture has the effect of suggesting that the issue is not between the abilities and good intentions of scientists and the inertia or bad will of governments; the issue is represented as being between the good culture of science and the bad culture of literature.

In this denial of the actuality of politics, Sir Charles is at one with the temper of intellectuals today—we all want politics not to exist, we all want that statement of Hegel's to be absolutely and immediately true, we dream of reason taking over the whole management of the world, and soon. No doubt a beneficent eventuality, but our impatience for it is dangerous if it leads us to deny the actuality of politics in the present. While we discuss, at Sir Charles's instance, the relative merits of scientific philosopher-kings as against literary philosopher-kings, politics goes on living its own autonomous life, of which one aspect is its massive resistance to reason. What is gained by describing the resistance to reason as other than it is, by thinking in the specious terms of two opposing "cultures"?

But of course the fact is that politics is not finally autonomous. It may be so massively resistant to reason that we are led to think of its resistance as absolute—in bad times we conceive politics to be nothing but power. Yet it cannot be said—at least not so long as politics relies in any degree upon ideology—that politics is never susceptible to such reason as is expressed in opinion, only that it is less susceptible in some nations and at some times than in other nations and at other times. And nowhere and at no time is politics exempt from moral judgment, whether or not that judgment is effectual. But if we make believe, as *The Two Cultures* does, that politics does not exist at all, then it cannot be the object of moral judgment. And if we deny all authority to literature, as *The Two Cultures* does, going so far as to say that this great traditional agency of moral awareness is itself immoral, then the very activity of moral judgment is impugned, except for that single instance of it which asserts the rightness of bringing the benefits of science to the disadvantaged of the world. In short, Sir Charles, seeking to advance the cause of understanding between the West and the Soviet Union, would seem to be saying that this understanding will come if we conceive both that politics cannot be judged (because it does not really exist) and that it should not be judged (because the traditional agency of judgment is irresponsible).

III

I take *The Two Cultures* to be a book which is mistaken in a very large way indeed. And I find the failure of Dr. Leavis' criticism of it to consist in his addressing himself not to the full extent of its error but to extraneous matters. From reading the Richmond Lecture one gains the impression that the substance of the Rede Lecture is extremely offensive to Dr. Leavis, that all his sensibilities are outraged by it: we conclude that Sir Charles wants something which is very different from what Dr. Leavis wants, and that Dr. Leavis thinks that what Sir Charles wants is crude and vulgar. But we can scarcely suppose from Dr. Leavis' response that what Sir Charles says has a very wide reference—for all we can tell, he might have been proposing a change in the University curriculum which Dr. Leavis is repelling with the violence and disgust that are no doubt often felt though not expressed at meetings of curriculum committees. For Dr. Leavis, who has always attached great importance to educational matters, the proposed change is certainly important beyond the University. He understands it both as likely to have a bad effect on the national culture and as being the expression of something already bad in the national culture. But this, we suppose, he would feel about any change in the curriculum.

In short, Dr. Leavis, in dealing with the Rede Lecture, has not seen the object as in itself it really is, just as Sir Charles, in dealing with the culture of literature in its relation to politics, has not seen the object as in itself it really is.

An example of the inadequacy of Dr. Leavis' criticism of *The Two Cultures* is his response to what Sir Charles says, in concert with that "scientist of distinction," about the political posture of the great writers of the modern period. That statement, if we stop short of its mention of Auschwitz—which makes a most important modification—certainly does have a color of truth. It is one of the cultural curiosities of the first three decades of the twentieth century that, while the educated people, the readers of books, tended to become ever more liberal and radical in their thought, there is no literary figure of the very first rank (although many of the next rank) who, in his work, makes use of or gives credence to liberal or radical ideas. I remarked on this circumstance in an essay of 1946. "Our educated class," I said, "has a ready if mild suspiciousness of the profit motive, a belief in progress, science, social legislation, planning, and international cooperation, perhaps especially where Russia is in question. These beliefs do great credit to those who hold them. Yet it is a comment, if not on our beliefs then on our way of holding them, that not a single first-rate writer has emerged to deal with these ideas, and the emotions that are consonant with them, in a great literary way. . . . If we name those writers who, by the general consent of the most serious criticism, by consent too of the very class of educated people of which we speak, are thought of as the monumental figures of our time, we see that to these writers the liberal ideology has been at best a matter of indifference. Proust, Joyce, Lawrence, Yeats, Mann [as novelist], Kafka, Rilke, Gide [also as novelist] —all of them have their own love of justice and the good life, but in not one of them does it take the form of a love of the ideas and emotions which liberal democracy, as known by our educated class, has declared respectable."

To which it can be added that some great writers have in their work given utterance or credence to conservative and even reactionary ideas, and that some in their personal lives have maintained a settled indifference to all political issues, or a disdain of them. No reader is likely to derive political light from either the works or the table talk of a modern literary genius, and some readers (of weak mind) might even be led into bad political ways.

If these writers are to be brought to the bar of judgment, anyone who speaks as their advocate is not, as Sir Charles says, defending the indefensible. The advocacy can be conducted in honest and simple ways. It is not one of these ways to say that literature is by its nature or by definition innocent. Literature is powerful enough for us to suppose that it has the capability of doing harm. But the ideational influence of literature is by no means always as direct as, for polemical purposes, people sometimes say it is. As against the dismay of Sir Charles and the distinguished scientist at the reactionary tendencies of modern literary geniuses, there is the fact that the English poets who learned their trade from Yeats and Eliot, or even from Pound, have notably had no sympathy with the social ideas and attitudes of their poetical masters.

Every university teacher of literature will have observed the circumstance that young people who are of radical social and political opinion are virtually never troubled by the opposed views or the settled indifference of the great modern writers. This is not because the young exempt the writer from dealing with the serious problems of living, or because they see him through a mere aesthetic haze. It is because they know—and quite without instruction—that, in D. H. Lawrence's words, they are to trust the tale and not the teller of the tale. They perceive that the tale is always on the side of their own generous impulses. They know that, if the future is in the bones of anyone, it is in the bones of the literary genius, and exactly because the present is in his bones, exactly because the past is in his bones. They know that if a work of literature has any true artistic existence, it has value as a criticism of life; in whatever complex way it has chosen to speak, it is making a declaration about the qualities that life should have, about the qualities life does not have but should have. They feel, I think, that it is simply not possible for a work of literature that comes within the borders of greatness *not* to ask for more energy and fineness of life, and, by its own communication of awareness, bring these qualities into being. And if, in their experience of such a work, they happen upon an expression of contempt for some idea which they have connected with political virtue, they are not slow to understand that it is not the idea in its ideal form that is being despised, but the idea as it passes current in specious form, among certain and particular persons. I have yet to meet the student committed to an altruistic politics who is alienated from Stephen Daedalus by that young man's disgust with political idealism, just as I have yet to meet the student from the most disadvantaged background who feels debarred from what Yeats can give him by the poet's slurs upon shopkeepers or by anything else in his inexhaustible fund of snobbery.

If ever a man was qualified to state the case for literature, and far more persuasively than I have done, it is Dr. Leavis. His career as a critic and a teacher has been devoted exactly to the exposition of the idea that literature presents to us "the possibilities of life," the qualities of energy and fineness that life might have. And it is, of course, the intention of the Richmond Lecture to say just this in answer to Sir Charles's indictment. Yet something checks Dr. Leavis. When it is a question of the defense, not of literature in general, but of modern literature, he puts into countervailing evidence nothing more than a passage in which Lawrence says something, in a wry and grudging way, on behalf of social equality. This does not meet the charge; against it Sir Charles might cite a dozen instances in which Lawrence utters what Sir Charles—and perhaps even Dr. Leavis himself—would consider "the most imbecile expressions of anti-social feeling."

There is only one feasible approach to the anti-social utterances of many modern writers, and that is to consider whether their expressions of anti-social feeling are nothing but imbecile. It is the fact, like it or not, that a characteristic cultural enterprise of our time has been the questioning of society itself, not its particular forms and aspects but its very essence. To this extreme point has the criticism of life extended itself. Of the ways of dealing with this phenomenon, that of horror and dismay, such as Sir Charles's, is perhaps the least useful. Far better, it seems to me, is the effort to understand what this passionate hostility to society implies, to ask whether it is a symptom, sufficiently gross, of the decline of the West, or whether it is not perhaps an act of critical energy on the part of the West, an act of critical energy on the part of society itself—the effort of society to identify in itself that which is but speciously good, the effort to understand afresh the nature of the life it is designed to foster. I would not anticipate the answer, but these questions make, I am sure, the right way to come at the phenomenon.

It is not the way that Dr. Leavis comes at the phenomenon, despite his saying that the university study of literature must take its stand on "the intellectual-cultural frontier." Actually, when it is a question of the frontier, he prefers—it is an honorable preference—to remain behind it or to take a position at certain check-points. For example, of the two D. H. Lawrences, the one who descended from the social-minded nineteenth century and who did, in some sort, affirm the social idea, and the other, at least equally important, for whom the condition of salvation was the total negation of society, Dr. Leavis can be comfortable only with the former. His commitment to the intellectual-cultural frontier is sincere but chiefly theoretical; he has, as is well known, sympathy with very few modern writers, and he therefore cannot in good grace come to their defense against Sir Charles's characterization of them.

Mr. Walter Allen, writing in the *New York Times Book Review* shortly after the publication of the Richmond Lecture and the *Spectator* letters attacking and defending it, accurately remarked on "the common areas of agreement" between Dr. Leavis and Sir Charles. "One would expect . . . that Snow would be sympathetic to Leavis's emphasis on the all-importance of the moral center of literature," Mr. Allen said. "Both have attacked experiment in literature. Neither of them, to put it into crude shorthand, are Flaubert-and-Joyce men." The similarities go further. In point of social background the two men are not much apart, at least to the untutored American eye. Both spring from the provincial middle class in one or another of its strata, and whatever differences there may have been in the material advantages that were available or lacking to one or the other, neither was reared in the assumption of easy privilege. From these origins they derived, we may imagine, their strong sense of quotidian actuality and a respect for those who discharge the duties it imposes, and a high regard for the domestic affections, a quick dislike of the frivolous and merely elegant. Neither, as I have suggested, has any least responsiveness to the tendencies of modern thought or literature which are existential or subversive. A lively young person of advanced tastes would surely say that if ever two men were committed to England, Home, and Duty, they are Leavis and Snow—he would say that in this they are as alike as two squares.

There is one other regard, an especially significant one, in which they are similar. This is their feeling about social class. One of the chief interests of Sir Charles's novels is their explicitness about class as a determinative of the personal life, and in this respect *The Two Cultures* is quite as overt as the novels—its scientists make a new class by virtue of their alienation from the old class attitudes, and Sir Charles's identification of literary men with the traditional culture which supposedly manages the Western world implies that they are in effect the representatives of an aristocratic ruling class, decadent but still powerful. The work of Dr. Leavis is no less suffused by the idea of social class, even though its preoccupation with the subject is far less explicit. To my recollection, Dr. Leavis does not make use of any of the words which denote the distinctions of English society—he does not refer to an aristocracy, a gentry, an upper middle or lower middle or working class. For him a class defines itself by its idea of itself—that is, by its tastes and style. Class is for him a cultural entity. And when he conceives of class power, as he often does, it is not economic or political power but, rather, cultural power that he thinks of. It is true that cultural power presents itself to his mind as being in some way suggestive of class power, but the actualities of power or influence are for him always secondary to the culture from which they arose or to which they give rise.

And indeed, no less than Sir Charles, Dr. Leavis is committed to the creation of a new class. This, we might even say, is the whole motive of his work. The social situation he would seem to assume is one in which there is a fair amount of mobility which is yet controlled and limited by the tendency of the mobile people to allow themselves to be absorbed into one of the traditional classes. As against the attraction exerted by a quasi-aristocratic, metropolitan upper middle class, Dr. Leavis has taken it to be his function to organize the mobile people, those of them who are gifted and conscious, into a new social class formed on the basis of its serious understanding of and response to literature, chiefly English literature. In this undertaking he has by no means been wholly unsuccessful. One has the impression that many of the students he has trained think of themselves, as they take up their posts in secondary schools and universities, as constituting at least a social cadre.

The only other time I wrote about Dr. Leavis I remarked that the Cromwellian Revolution had never really come to an end in England and that Dr. Leavis was one of the chief colonels of the Roundhead party. His ideal readers are people who "are seriously interested in literature," and it is on their behalf that he wages war against a cultural-social class which, when it concerns itself with literature, avows its preference for the qualities of grace, lightness, and irony, and deprecates an overt sincerity and seriousness. "To a polished nation," said Gibbon, "poetry is an amusement of the fancy, not a passion of the soul," and all through his career it is against everything that Gibbon means by a polished nation and might mean by a polished class that Dr. Leavis has set his face. Bloomsbury has been his characteristic antagonist. But now, in Charles Snow, he confronts an opponent who is as Roundhead as himself, and as earnest and *intentional.*

To this confrontation Dr. Leavis is not adequate. It is not an adequate response to the massive intention of *The Two Cultures* for Dr. Leavis to meet Sir Charles's cultural preferences with his own preferences; or to seek to discredit Sir Charles's ideas chiefly by making them out to be vulgar ideas or outmoded ("Wellsian") ideas; or to offer, as against Sir Charles's vision of a future made happier by science, the charms of primitive peoples "with their marvellous arts and skills and vital intelligence." I do not mean to say that Dr. Leavis does not know where Sir Charles goes wrong in the details of his argument—he is as clear as we expect him to be in rebuking that large unhappy blunder about the Victorian writers. Nor, certainly, do I mean that Dr. Leavis does not know what the great fundamental mistake of Sir Charles's position is—he does, and he can be eloquent in asserting against a simplistic confidence in a scientific "future" the need of mankind, in the face of a rapid advance of science and technology, "to be in full intelligent possession of its full humanity (and 'possession' here means, not confident ownership of that which belongs to *us*—our property, but a basic living deference towards that to which, opening as it does into the unknown and itself immeasurable, we know we belong)." But such moments of largeness do not save the Richmond Lecture from its general parochialism. For example, of the almost limitless political implications of Sir Charles's position it gives no evidence of awareness. And if we undertake to find a reason for the inadequacy of Dr. Leavis' response, we will find, I think, that it is the same as the reason which accounts for Sir Charles having been in the first place so wholly mistaken in what he says—both men set too much store by the idea of *culture* as a category of thought.

The concept of culture is an idea of great attractiveness and undoubted usefulness. We may say that it begins in the assumption that all human expressions or artifacts are indicative of some considerable tendencies in the life of social groups or sub-groups, and that what is indicative is also causative—all cultural facts have their consequences. To think in cultural terms is to consider human expressions not only in their overt existence and avowed intention, but in, as it were, their secret life, taking cognizance of the desires and impulses which lie behind the open formulation. In the judgments which we make when we think in the category of culture we rely to a very large extent upon the style in which an expression is made, believing that style will indicate, or betray, what is not intended to be expressed. The aesthetic mode is integral to the idea of culture, and our judgments of social groups are likely to be made chiefly on an aesthetic basis—we like or do not like what we call their life-styles, and even when we judge moralities, the criterion by which we choose between two moralities of, say, equal strictness or equal laxness is likely to be an aesthetic one.

The concept of culture affords to those who use it a sense of the liberation of their thought, for they deal less with abstractions and mere objects, more with the momentous actualities of human feelings as these shape and condition the human community, as they make and as they indicate the quality of man's existence. Not the least of the attractions of the cultural mode of thought are the passions which attend it—because it assumes that all things are causative or indicative of the whole of the cultural life, it proposes to us those intensities of moralized feeling which seem appropriate to our sense that all that is good in life is at stake in every cultural action. An instance of mediocrity or failure in art or thought is not only what it is but also a sin, deserving to be treated as such. These passions are no doubt vivifying: they have the semblance of heroism.

And if we undertake to say what were the circumstances that made the cultural mode of thought as available and as authoritative as it now is, we must refer to Marx, and to Freud, and to the general movement of existentialism, to all that the tendencies of modernity imply of the sense of contingency in life, from which we learn that the one thing that can be disputed, and that is worth disputing, is preference or taste. The Rede Lecture and the Richmond Lecture exemplify the use to which the idea of culture can be put in shaking the old certainties of class, in contriving new social groups on the basis of taste.

All this does indeed give the cultural mode of thought a very considerable authority. Yet sometimes we may wonder if it is wholly an accident that so strong an impulse to base our sense of life, and conduct of the intellectual life, chiefly upon the confrontations of taste should have developed in an age dominated by advertising, the wonderful and terrible art which teaches us that we define ourselves and realize our true being by choosing the right style. In our more depressed moments we might be led to ask whether there is a real difference between being the Person Who defines himself by his commitment to one or another idea of morality, politics, literature, or city-planning, and being the Person Who defines himself by wearing trousers without pleats.

We can, I suppose, no more escape from the cultural mode of thought than we can escape from culture itself. Yet perhaps we must learn to cast a somewhat colder eye upon it for the sake of whatever regard we have for the intellectual life, for the possibility of rational discourse. Sir Charles envisages a new and very powerful social class on the basis of a life-style which he imputes to a certain profession in contrast with the life-style he imputes to another profession, and he goes on from there to deny both the reality of politics and the possibility of its being judged by moral standards. Dr. Leavis answers him with a passion of personal scorn which obscures the greater part of the issue and offers in contradiction truth indeed but truth so hampered and hidden by the defenses of Dr. Leavis' own choice in life-styles that it looks not much different from a prejudice. And the *Spectator* correspondents exercise their taste in life-styles and take appropriate sides. It is at such a moment that our dispirited minds yearn to find comfort and courage in the idea of mind, that faculty whose ancient potency our commitment to the idea of culture denies. To us today, mind must inevitably seem but a poor gray thing, for it always sought to detach itself from the passions (but not from the emotions, Spinoza said, and explained the difference) and from the conditions of time and place. Yet it is salutary for us to contemplate it, whatever its grayness, because of the bright belief that was once attached to it, that it was the faculty which belonged not to professions, or to social classes, or to cultural groups, but to man, and that it was possible for men, and becoming to them, to learn its proper use, for it was the means by which they could communicate with each other.

It was on this belief that science based its early existence, and it gave to the men who held it a character which is worth remarking. Sir Charles mentions Faraday among those scientists who overrode the limitations of social class to form the "scientific culture" of England. This is true only so far as it can be made consonant with the fact that Faraday could not have imagined the idea of a "scientific culture" and would have been wholly repelled by it. It is told of Faraday that he refused to be called a *physicist;* he very much disliked the new name, as being too special and particular, and insisted on the old one, *philosopher,* in all its spacious generality: we may suppose that this was his way of saying that he had not overridden the limiting conditions of class only to submit to the limitations of profession. The idea of mind which had taught the bookbinder's apprentice to embark on his heroic enterprise of self-instruction also taught the great scientist to place himself beyond the specialness of interest which groups prescribe for their members. Every personal episode in Tyndall's classic account of his master, *Faraday as a Researcher,* makes it plain that Faraday undertook to be, in the beautiful lost sense of the word, a *disinterested* man. From his belief in mind, he derived the certitude that he had his true being not as a member of this or that profession or class, but as—in the words of a poet of his time—"a man speaking to men."

No one now needs to be reminded of what may befall the idea of mind in the way of excess and distortion. The literature of the nineteenth century never wearied of telling us just this, of decrying the fatigue and desiccation of spirit which result from an allegiance to mind that excludes impulse and will, and desire and preference. It was, surely, a liberation to be made aware of this, and then to go on to take serious account of those particularities of impulse and will, of desire and preference, which differentiate individuals and groups—to employ what I have called the cultural mode of thought. We take it for granted that this, like any other mode of thought, has its peculiar dangers, but there is cause for surprise and regret that it should be Sir Charles Snow and Dr. Leavis who have jointly demonstrated how far the cultural mode of thought can go in excess and distortion.

September 1962

David T. Bazelon

THE PAPER ECONOMY

> *In time, immutable rules of conduct enforced under progressively changing conditions should logically result in a muddle.*
>
> THORSTEIN VEBLEN

There are immense changes under way in our social economy, as everybody senses; but through this whole earthquake alteration of circumstance, our ideas about the structure of our society have hardly mellowed, much less developed in a rough tandem with events. *The muddle is upon us,* and the days grow shorter.

The approaching crisis has been occasioned by the awful advance of technology; for the technology which has not been prepared for (or is not soon accommodated socially) is no blessing at all, but the deepest ironic disaster of the human race. The human being today stands poised to be destroyed by his primary biological blessing—his propensity to develop and his capacity to use *technique:* there is a direct line from the prehensile thumb to the nuclear bomb.

The political essence of the approaching crisis is that we have not been able to make our great power felt by *non-military* means, either at home or abroad. The domestic source of this impotence derives, for example, from such ritualistic activities as budget-balancing, devotion to the supposed stability of the dollar, fear of inflation (or federal action to forestall it), and accompanying under-use of productive facility and talent. Under-use and mis-allocation of our great industrial and technological power, except under and by virtue of military purpose, flow directly from the predominant bookkeeping considerations which go by the names of money, profit, price, return on investment, etc.—that is, *existing property rights, all of which and the system comprising which, I will here call "paper."* Taken as seriously and devoutly as it has been and still is today, the paper system is inadequate to insure full production at home and to fight the cold war on non-military terms. So this is the nature of the domestic crisis: we must achieve a political posture whereby we can take the Paper Economy less seriously in order to be able to modify it according to non-paper considerations. If we fail to do this, we will surely forsake the promise of the future and also fail in the cold war. Or worse, we will trap ourselves into fighting it out on military grounds, which could well be the end of all of us.

The traditional way out of an American crisis is no longer available to us. For one thing, you don't win the cold war (unless you are Senator Goldwater), you just keep the nuclear holocaust from occurring. For another thing, it is increasingly obvious that the war in which we are engaged is not to be fought with military hardware: the military part of it is simply a stand-off operation which allows the true conflict to go forward elsewhere and by other means. We could mobilize the economy for a World War II-type effort of several years duration: *but to mobilize the social economy for the kind of conflict in which we actually are engaged requires structural changes in our society, and these changes will be permanent.* Indeed, they will be continuing and cumulative. There's the rub—to accept or resist this new experimental form of mobilization.

It is a hard irony of history that calls upon the conservative leadership of the most conservative great nation in the world to choose freely the pursuit of a permanent social revolution. However, analysis and reflection reveal over and over again, and finally compel the conclusion, that this *is* the contour of the crisis—and that just such an unreasonable demand is now being made by *our* history.

Money and Scarcity

Money is not real. What made it *seem* real for so long was its scarcity. Since money is supposed to be spent on things, its scarcity can truly reflect reality only when that reality is made up of a general scarcity of things. It no longer is, except mostly by intention. Since the scarcity of money no longer mirrors the scarcity of things, and since money that is not scarce is not exactly money, the whole meaning of the symbol has changed profoundly.

We are the most productive society in history, and consequently are daily threatened by cumulative non-scarcity. In 1961, the Secretary of the Treasury said:

> We are no longer in a time of shortages. . . . There is unusual—and under-utilized—capacity everywhere in our land today; in

steel, in autos, in housing, in textiles, in chemicals—indeed, everywhere we look. We also—and unfortunately—are under-utilizing our labor force, which stands ready and willing to operate the unused capacity of our industrial plant.

Because capitalism and its paper world were based on actual scarcity, the drama of the system was to contend heroically with this condition. But the whole point about the new freedom, the new technology, is that it has made scarcity absurd. So our society can no longer dare to be based on it, heroically or otherwise.

The paper system is still conceived in terms of scarcity—still founded upon that concept. Since scarcity no longer occurs naturally in this country (unless the Paper Economy just as we have it today is considered "natural"), we are quickly approaching the point where the nation will have to make a fundamental decision about whether it can do without the whole baggage of historical ideas which were outgrowths of previously existing scarcities—the psychological basis of the Paper Economy. I think there is no question that man's sense of himself, and the traditional psychology accompanying it, have been substantially conditioned by these earlier scarcities. Consequently, the final result of the technological revolution will be a new conception of man.

This need disturb no one, since economics has always been based upon a psychological image of man—on some model of motivation. In this sense, what we are faced with is a revolution in motivation, and the conservatives don't want it—because they see it as an attack on their personalities. Indeed, it *is* frightening, as well as exhilarating. What on earth will we do with ourselves if making a dollar loses its allure? If "hewing to the line" no longer really matters? If the traditional idea of sacrificing the present for the sake of the future becomes fatuous? (The reason President Kennedy keeps asking for "sacrifice" from the nation is not that any real ones are needed, but because he shrewdly understands that the nation yearns for the mood.) How, then, will we face up to the prospect of a decent life?

American business prefers to call itself The Free Enterprise System—or even more expansively, The American Way of Life. The latter designation is so accurate that it leaves nothing to be discussed; but the former is a Big Symbol that can and has been discussed endlessly. This talkathon has been greatly facilitated by the fact that "free enterprise" cannot possibly be defined for reasonable people as something actually happening between New York and Los Angeles. Apart from everything else, the idea assumes a minuscule role for the federal government—and everybody knows better than that. No, the only existential meaning of *enterprise* is what businessmen generally happen to be doing at the moment, and *free* is merely the accompanying demand that they be left alone to do it.

Industrialism, the network of technology and productive industry, is not to be identified with free enterprise or capitalism or any other control-system which at a particular historical moment stands astride and determines how and why men shall operate the industrial complex. Capitalism is not the same thing as industrialism, any more than capital means the plants, machines, and other subjects and objects of technology which shape the physical world under industrialism. Capital is not Things—and neither are enterprises, free or otherwise. Capital is *assets;* and enterprises are more or less organized and more or less purposeful collections of assets. *An asset is a money-value:* another symbol-on-paper, in this instance that Torah of the Paper Economy, The Balance Sheet. But you could spend a whole day walking through the mammoth Fairless Works of the United States Steel Corporation without seeing the slightest piece of balance-sheet profit perched expectantly in the vicinity of a furnace. All the pieces are hidden in the heads of the personnel—in some heads more than other heads, but all of them in one head or another. In the early commercial days, before machine technology got moving, capital referred to a stock of goods. But now goods can be produced so quickly by machines that capital refers for the most part to the machines themselves, while goods are called "inventory." Goods are now felt by producers to be a liability as often as they are an asset. You *control* the machines, but you just *move* inventory. Indeed, you *have* to move inventory.

Competition?

The central idea of business ideology is Competition, because that makes all sorts of difficult, questionable, and downright unpleasant matters come out all right in the end. As J. K. Galbraith has engagingly put it: "Like marital fidelity, decent plumbing, or clean underclothing, competition is a prerequisite of respectability in our society."

The Idea of Competition asserts that competitive markets are the exclusive regulators of all practical and moral relations in society. The result has been that all conscious human intervention in the economic process, or planning, is accepted only as disaster threatens; and once its agonizing birth has been effected, the high priests of paper propriety revoke its birthright by denying or ignoring its existence. The Idea of Competition (*not* the occasional fact) is one of the most mindless notions ever to dominate the supposed thinking of a society of grown men.

The issue is not whether at some times and places competition functions as an effective allocative factor. It does, but look at it this way: in any fresh, unorganized situation you are going to have unorganized activity—

"competition"—until someone is able at last to organize the thing on some rational basis. Most of our great business heroes—Rockefeller, Carnegie, Morgan—were men of capacity who dramatically carried forward this process of organization. They recognized that competition was a dangerous form of internal warfare, of benefit to no one, and exactly the kind of senseless feuding which it has been the role and the justification of the state since time immemorial to suppress. So they suppressed it, and did a very good job of it for that time and place. Of course they were not the state *de jure,* but that was not an important matter.

American business relies on the Idea of Competition, along with a deep animus toward federal power, because it is bitterly embattled today. The business system is fighting a rear-guard action against the continuing transfer of power from private to governmental hands. That it is a cynical, hopeless, rear-guard action has been revealed by the recently-lived-through eight years of "Modern Republicanism." It turns out that American business interests are not counter-revolutionaries, but only determined saboteurs of a reasonable adjustment to the change. David Riesman has said: "We have been trained for a world of scarcity and we have developed an image of man under the psychology of scarcity." Our ruling business groups are extremely reluctant to modify the training or abandon the image.

Business has not and will never recover from its 1929 failure to run the society with a minimum of decency and competence. It had all the power it needed, and all the freedom in the world to use it—but the hand was overplayed, and the business system revealed itself once and for all to be incapable of resisting the easy exploitation of the money-credit-price mechanism. The Great Depression was the melodramatic end of effective private government in the United States.

Since then the federal government has underwritten the entire functioning of the economy. That is what the New Deal meant; that's all it meant; and that meaning stands under Modern Republicanism. The traditional underwriters—investment and commercial bankers, utilizing the central banking authority of the Federal Reserve System, and allied with corporate power in key industries—were unequal to the task. They were not able to fulfill their obligations. So, in 1933 a new underwriter was called in. The terms of the new underwriting contract were stated generally, the details being left to future needs and contingencies, and "arrangements" to be made with the former underwriters—as in any major bankruptcy. It is these details of the contract, of our new unwritten constitution, that make up the issues of our political life. But the remnants of private government are not negotiating in good faith with us, their creditors, nor are they acting reasonably with regard to the common enterprise. Rockefeller, Carnegie, and Morgan would never have behaved so badly.

What Is Property?

The ordinary idea of property is that it is is made up of Things. A man's property is what he owns—and he looks about him and sees a house, some furniture, clothes in the closet, a car in the garage, and his mother's amber beads. *His* property. But wait a minute: there's an insurance policy, some cash in his pocket, a bank account, and maybe even ten shares of AT & T. That's property, too. But of a very different kind. He doesn't own AT & T but only ten out of many millions of shares—which *share* only after some billions of dollars of debt. In fact, his ten shares have to be carefully punched out on an IBM card not to be lost sight of entirely. The stock certificate, the deposit, the policy, the cash are all paper. He just owns the paper—he doesn't own AT & T, the insurance company, the bank, or the Federal Reserve System. So his property consists of some things and some paper. But wait a minute again: he lives in the house, everybody on the block will tell you it's his house, but as a matter of fact the Nickel Savings Bank of Lower Sandusky has a greater right to the house than he has—it's worth $15,000 and his equity comes to only five as against the bank's mortgage of ten. Likewise the car, and mechanical trinkets in the house. (Maybe even the clothes on his back.)

Where does all that leave us with the idea of property? Well, the truth is that if you are talking about things, you hardly need the idea of property at all—until somebody tries to take some of it away from you. *Property is not the thing, it is rights in and to the thing.* Consequently, the ordinary notion of property, as being made up of things, is almost exactly wrong. Most frequently, property ends up being a right to force someone to act or refrain from acting in a certain way toward a certain thing, or to pay for the privilege of refusal—pay in that biggest of all forms of property, *money,* the great common denominator.

The generic form of property is a contract, an agreement, a promise. (I won't bother going into the textbook definition of a contract—let it suffice that contracts are made up of mutual promises, with the added proviso that in law a man may "promise" by his course of conduct, without opening his mouth and uttering that ringing law-school phrase, which still raises the hair on my neck, *"I accept!"*) The right to enter into contracts "freely" is the substance of the free market competition notion—a market being the place, or the habitual pattern by which, contracts of purchase and sale are supposed to be entered into freely. Economists have always been blinded by the glamor of the equilibrium of the free market. But when you look at the same phenomenon from the point of view of freedom of contract—the lawyers' point of view—you are much more apt to see this freedom for the lopsided license to steal that in large part it was.

And it was freedom of contract rather than the free market that served as the first grand bastion of defense to be raised by business, and then to fall in the course of the popular onslaught against unbridled capitalist plunder in the 19th century. Freedom of contract justified almost any predatory practice; the free market serves mostly to justify unfettered pricing power. The main reason that freedom of contract has never been as free as it is advertised—and it is a painfully obvious reason—is that sellers and buyers are not equal in bargaining power. This means that the terms of sale will simply reflect the power, or lack of it, that each party brings to the market place. So a market is also a financial slaughterhouse, where the strong chop up the weak.

The right of the dominant seller or buyer to his dominance in the market place is enforced by the state. Indeed, that is one of the chief functions of the state under capitalism. This big fact has been obscured in a big way by the historical circumstance that the bourgeois state supplanted autocratic monarchies, and in the course of the struggle, the bourgeoisie developed a non-state or anti-state, almost anarchistic, ideology. But when control of the state had been achieved, the new ruling class did not pursue its own anarchistic principles. To say the least.

Uses of the Property Idea

Many economists who are not lawyers, and most lawyers who are not especially conscious of what they are doing, see the world of production and things as controlled by the encompassing universe of money and credit; the independent concept of property may be lost somewhere in between. This is unfortunate, because the truth is that money-and-credit are simply the most generalized and therefore the most obvious form of property. It is the *whole* property system, not the money-and-credit system alone, that decisively represents our society's attempt to control and rationalize the real world of things and the people, *pari passu* thingified, who live in it.

In the massive corporate economy, the old market equilibrium theory is thoroughly bankrupt, whether or not supplemented by Keynes's money-manipulation notions. (Keynes's theories, as applied, are not adequate for a full production economy: he was an exceptionally clever and completely English dialectician who modified received theory no more than necessary for his purpose at the time. He did *not* revise economics in the light of corporate market power; he accepted existing theoretical baggage and then merely outlined a role for the government to save the whole works—in special circumstances—by monetary and fiscal maneuvering. And he buried the gold standard, that shining relic of pre-1914 confidence in the rightness of all things.) This market theory—which at best offers a passable description of certain aspects of the 18th and 19th centuries—is, along with Keynes's techniques for keeping a depression from downright destroying us, the basis of fateful governmental policy. It gives one pause.

In the new social economy, all rights-property is paper—and all the paper in the Paper Economy must be considered if a Keynesian effort to influence or control the real world of things is attempted. All the paper—not just federal debt and the money in central banks. But because of the stale distinction between "property" and money/credit, we don't usually take all the paper into account. As a consequence, we are trying quite unsuccessfully to deal with a runaway technology within the framework of an archaic business-profit system. The result is under-used and mis-used plant capacity, a circumstance covered over—just barely—by a puerile public-relations culture which is almost impossible to bear, even by its beneficiaries.

We have sown a 19th-century dream, and are reaping a whirlwind of 20th-century paper.

The Paper Dream

Money is a dream. It is a piece of paper on which is imprinted in invisible ink the dream of all the things it will buy, all the trinkets and all the power over others; a kind of institutionalized dream which, along with its companion dream institution of Success, constitutes the main fantasy on which our way of life has been built.

But the old, pure money-dream is dying in America; we are passing through a purgatory (or, if you prefer, a child's garden) of fantastically shaped automobiles and ineluctable electric can-openers, and what our new dream will be no one knows. But at least, before we begin again, we will have touched down for a time and even have lived a little in our current consumers' paradise.

The main point is this: the money that figures so prominently in the dream of money is not money for spending. You don't ever buy anything with it. It's for earning more money. And after you really get moving, you don't even buy anything with the money you earned on the money you used to earn it, and so on.

But what *is* money? Well, it is not just a dream. It is also not wealth, which exists in reality and is not merely a symbol. The paper in the world of paper we live in is supposed to order the creation and use of our wealth; but it is not itself wealth. This is an essential point, and is probably the most difficult idea to come to terms with in the whole discussion of property, money/credit, and the Paper Economy.

For one thing (closer to the facts), money is a contract—the freest, most gorgeous contract of them all. Money is somebody else's promise to pay, to give me what I want, when I want it: the fully alienable contract for anything, anytime, anywhere. Whatever else history may say of the Western bourgeoisie, this honor must be accorded them: *They perfected modern money, which is a contract with parties unknown for the future delivery of pleasures undecided upon.*

Gold as cash is irrelevant (except internationally, because we are so primitive in that arena); cash is paper immediately and universally exchangeable, also called currency; currency is a contract right currently accepted; and all such contract rights are based on credit of one kind or another (you only enter into a contract with someone you "credit" with the capacity to fulfill the contract). Therefore money is credit. And credit is based on reputation. So money is a function of reputation. And everybody knows what reputation is. Reputation, as a matter of fact, is what everybody knows about somebody. There you have, quickly, the story of money.

How It All Began

The whole paper show began historically with two great events, both growing out of the emergence of trading in Europe, the medieval fairs, etc., etc. The first event occurred when the first seller transferred his goods to a buyer, who at the time had no goods to trade and no gold to substitute for goods. This pioneer seller said to his buyer, probably in disgust, "OK, give me two pigs or one gold ducat next year—and if you don't show, I'll come and get you. And write it down on this piece of paper here, so there won't be any argument." The second great event begins like the first but adds a new twist—which turns out to be a creative act on about the same level as the invention of the wheel. Same scene, same characters, but when the seller goes home he's still boiling because he's stuck with a "worthless" piece of paper; his buyer may be dead next year, or impressed into military service, or go into another line of business somewhere else, or any number of things. He feels maybe he's been taken, and as so many people before and subsequently have done in that uncomfortable circumstance, he looks around for somebody to take in turn and so cut his loss, resolving firmly in his heart never to be taken again. Wonder of wonders, he finds a real patsy (he thinks) who is willing to take the buyer's paper in exchange for a half-ducat of gold payable immediately. This "patsy" happens to know that the buyer is a big man in a far country, vigorous and powerful, and well-respected: *a man of good reputation*. The gold is exchanged for the paper, and the Paper Economy is born.

Once we get past barter—the direct exchange of things—we are stuck with gold or something like it until men begin to write down their promises and accept these instead of gold. But gold is a very limiting factor—there never was enough of it—so it was absolutely necessary to create something "as good as gold." *The closest thing to gold-today is gold-tomorrow, and that's how the system was born.* All of our paper today is ultimately gold due in a tomorrow that never comes. And just as well—there isn't enough to go around.

Now most people, I should imagine, accept checks as money because they are under the impression that banks are loaded with *real* money. It is true that you can take a check to a bank and get some engraved paper for it, if you want to be fancy, but it would be a very long day indeed for the fellows operating the government printing presses if any large number of people had this idea at the same time. No, banks are mostly just like us—all they have is bank deposits. From where do they get them, you ask? They create them—that's their business. Nice business, you say? Yes, it's not bad. It used to be rather nerve-racking, but the New Deal took all the worry out of it. (I suppose that's why bankers loved FDR so much.)

So how does a bank begin? One line of banking started out in Europe with the goldsmiths, who knew all about gold, had a lot of it in their possession one way or another, and just naturally became bankers as the popular belief in gold and the need for banks joined to provide *one* basis for the money/credit system without which capitalist-exchange would have remained a gleam in our forefathers' eyes.

But if you are rich, or people think you are, they will assume you own gold or something "as good as gold," and such individuals became bankers, too. If they had a sufficient air of affluence, the banking customers-to-be did not bother to demand to see the color of their coin, but assumed it was a full, rich yellow. This Mr. Big did not have much gold around the house—if he had any at all it was certainly out working for him—so his stock in trade became gold-tomorrow. *All you have to do to become a banker is to go into debt.* Mr. Big's promises to pay gold-tomorrow circulated as money, especially when endorsed by other leading citizens.

If enough people leave their money with a banker, his notes can circulate at par without being endorsed by other wealthy men—*their deposits are endorsement enough.* At this stage of the game, bankers can engrave their notes on special paper and we are well on the way toward the fantastic shambles of 19th-century American banking. And not a moment too soon, either, because all the gold, faith, deposits, hope, paper engraved and otherwise, and pure charity that the new banker-merchants have sopped up and agglomerated will hardly be enough gold-tomorrow on which to build the railroads, the steel mills, and the rest of our great industrial establishment. The people engaged in that enterprise will, besides, find it incumbent upon them to print their own money. And even that won't suffice: they will unfortunately find it necessary to steal from the government and even, on very black days, from each other.

So they played out the hand, and everybody in on it got very rich. But they wanted central banking in some more viable form than that offered by the House of Morgan. After enough of the wrong people had been hurt in enough financial panics, and after Congressman Pujo's investigation of the banking system in 1905 had smelled up the atmosphere, the quaint Federal Reserve System was allowed to enter the union in 1913, half-slave and half-free, a compromise use of government power on behalf of private banking. Thus the paper created in the course of raping a continent was canonized. You might say the policeman waited in the hall until he was needed.

Credit Is Wonderful

The phenomenon of credit is one of the most profoundly engaging in the whole rainbow range of social life. Its significance, once grasped, is truly startling.

There is a lot of talk these days about status in our society. Well, compared to credit, status is about as exciting as Calvin Coolidge in deep thought. Because the point about status is rather obvious—the details can be fascinating and funny in revealing our nonsense to ourselves—but the thing itself is just there. Status is static, but credit is dynamic. As a matter of fact, *credit is the active arm of status,* it is status on the go, status in current use to effect some purpose in the world besides mere display: *credit is status capitalized.* (It is worth while to stop and realize that Veblen's most famous book was *The Theory of the Leisure Class,* a very perceptive and amusing cartoon on the subject of status, but that his most important and brilliant work all revolved around his insights into the function of credit in America—what he called the price system. The fact that the cartoon has impressed the American intellectuals so much more than his epochal thinking on credit does no due respect either to them or to Veblen.)

Under capitalism, the reputation of individuals has been commercialized—*literally turned into money.* Indeed, that is mostly what money is. Under prior aristocratic societies, all power felt to be necessary was achieved or maintained by the display of status, by a grand here-I-am gesture, and it was not the usual thing actively to "trade on one's reputation." To trade on one's reputation is to secure credit on it—that is, issue debt—which means to commercialize or capitalize it.

It is the reputation of individuals and institutions that holds society together, and makes the wheels run. Reputation is what-a-thing-is-known-for. That is, what it is believed to be. There has never been a society based on what-a-thing-is, and the closest approach to it is the society of modern physical scientists, the creators of our technology; or the tiny society of you and me when we are in agreement, and so can dispense with the troublesome distinction between what a thing is and what it is known for, and go forward on the basis of what we agree it *shall* be known for. (Physical scientists don't agree on anything—they allow only experience to confer the blessed quality of agreement.)

One sometimes wonders, however, what the leading people in our society think they have achieved by so completely commercializing their reputations. Most of the money they get in exchange for the respect due them is not for buying anything, and a great deal of it does not even lead to the creation of real national wealth. The process therefore becomes circular—reputation creates money and money creates reputation, and not enough happens in the meanwhile. In past societies, great reputations fulfilled a much more creative social function.

Behind the Debt

The question of collateral is fundamental to the whole marvelous business of reputation and borrowing, and, consequently, to the story of the Paper Economy. We all love money (or currency, metaphysically conceived), and money is debt—but *who* gets a leg up on going into debt? That is the question. The answer begins by reference to this idea of collateral—the what-with behind the debt. Now recollect that you *earn* on collateral, and *pay* on a debt. But you are allowed to get into debt because you have some kind of collateral. That is hypothecation or capitalization (as a matter of fact, that is life-as-hypothesis—or capitalism). In the typical case, first you make a profit (earn) or appear to be doing so, then you capitalize that apparent profit-making. The most substantial collateral for further credit is a recent success: the pre-belief that you will win again.

The standing (read, *status*) of successful buck-chasers substitutes for any more substantial collateral—just as in England the gentleman's overdraft is a loan secured by collateral no firmer than his proper gentlehood. Whether or not, in this process, engraved paper called stocks or bonds is used, is a matter of indifference. What is being collateralized or hypothecated or capitalized is a reputation for making money. The engraved paper simply makes it easier for the lender in turn to sell the debt or borrow against it—because that debt is now money, if anybody will accept it as such. And if your name is General Motors, they certainly will. (That's how consumer financing was born.)

Now in order to make all this collateralizing come out happily, it is repeatedly necessary to raise prices on goods in order to increase profits in order to make borrowing worthwhile. But everybody understands this necessity, and the important people involved are even quite knowledgeable in noting exactly the proper moment when the existing game has been played out at a particular level and another boost is in order. If necessary, production can be induced to drag its feet for a few months, everybody gets nervous about a possible deflation, and the Federal Reserve Board finally loosens up the process of creating money, thus making a rise in prices absolutely irresistible, and, with a national sigh of relief, they are once again upped. The ante having been raised, a new hand is dealt. The better technique is to blame the unions when raising prices for profit-and-credit reasons, because in that case it is not necessary to frighten everyone to death by sabotaging production; but it appears that this bit of public relations business has about had it.

The beauty of a bank is that in pooling reputations it creates a new and more glorious reputation for itself, without absolutely tying up the reputations collected in the pool. These are still more or less free to be used elsewhere. Notice how wonderfully circular this can become: individuals lend their reputations to a bank, which can even use the reputation thereby created to guarantee the paper of these individuals, its depositors—*vide,* cashier's check, banker's acceptances, etc. Consequently, I would suggest that central banking, which exists in one way or another in all advanced capitalist credit economies, is a form of underwriting. The central bank and its depositors underwrite each other's promises.

Underwriting is the greatest credit invention of them all, after alienable paper itself (gold-tomorrow). Really all it amounts to is endorsement or guaranty—*one man's credit standing behind, "written under," another's.* Here, reputation becomes superbly generalized—nothing at all is promised, that is, put on the line, except the promise to pay if the first fellow doesn't. This tones up the quality of the paper to a wonderful degree (and it can be quite lucrative for the underwriter, too). The more people who put their names on paper, the better it is; and the bigger their reputations (for paying when due, or earning all along, or just plain having it), the better than better it is. That's underwriting, and it doesn't cost very much unless everything goes to pot. And, of course, that doesn't happen anymore.

The Age of the Big Underwriter

The biggest underwriters in the world used to be the moneymen in the City of London. Then their American correspondents, like Morgan, took over—at first in America, but later being called upon to shore up the mother-lode during the First World War. Finally, Morgan and other similarly situated underwriters defaulted in 1929—the situation had gotten out of hand—and then the central government of the United States became the primary underwriter. It still is today. Now when you underwrite one-half of the civilized world, you do not accomplish this by endorsing a check. In principle, yes; but the actual process is much more complicated.

Today, the federal government stands behind all our paper—and like any competent underwriter, it intervenes in the actual processes of reality on occasion (when it can) in order to insure the validity of the various make-believe promises concerning that reality. It particularly intervenes, by specific guaranty or even *de facto* receivership, in all unprofitable activities which are nevertheless necessary for the functioning of the economy.

Big corporations, being in control of the actual production of goods and administering the prices of same according to their own convenience, are in effect their own best underwriters. They are the ones who underwrite paper by actual reference to their dominant position in existing social reality. So they are the great source of new paper, or the cause of increase in the value of old paper.

Probably what happened during the 20's which made the situation unmanageable and led to the default of the financiers was that the basic creative power in the business system had, without anyone clearly recognizing the significance of the fact, shifted decisively from the old-paper centers to the producing corporations themselves. As financial institutions, the corporations ended up making the big banks look like corner grocery stores.

"In the business world the price of things is a more substantial fact than the things themselves," said Veblen. The great power of our great corporations is not their magnificent capacity to produce goods, but the taxing authority inherent in the power to raise prices. If the basic purpose of these corporations were to produce goods—to create real wealth—then they would just produce and produce and produce, as they did during the Second World War for a few years, and there would be so much wealth lying around and the bother of dumping it in the ocean would be so great that the alternative of distributing it "unprofitably" to the people who could use it would become downright attractive. In order to avoid such an unpleasant alternative, the big corporations act more reasonably and view their essential power as the princely prerogative to create more paper-value. This is done periodically by raising prices, and continuously by not lowering them as costs are reduced—which they continuously are under modern technology.

Price Is the Thing

The bridge between the make-believe world of money/credit and other paper, and the real world of the production and exchange of things for other things, is *price*. The paper system rests absolutely on the price level, and the only way out of our paper-chasing madness is through rational control of the price level.

If prices are held steady, demand can be fed into the economy until the limits of supply (short-term) or technological capacity (long-term) are reached. The result is full production—full use of our productive capacity. The "demand" referred to is easily created by printing presses: it is just paper. Prices are not supposed to go up until demand, of whatever source, outdistances supply-capacity—and it just doesn't anymore, except rarely and in special circumstances. The reason prices go up anyway, thus insuring under-use of our plant, is that the people controlling them want them to go up. They prefer profit-paper to demand-paper—and it is they who control the printing presses of the Paper Economy, so to speak.

The whole awesome structure of conventional theory, including the sterilized Keynesianism of the Federal Reserve Board, is based on the assumed ubiquity of *price* competition. But in the most important sectors of the economy—especially where the big manufacturer stands astride the raw material supplier and the ultimate consumer—there just isn't enough price competition. Which raises a very serious problem.

The Paper Economy is like a balloon, which is why the key terms are inflation and deflation. The hole where the air goes in is labeled "Price—Blow Here." And they sure do. During the 50's it has been figured that the dollar lost value at the rate of 2¼ per cent a year—while the rest of the smart paper gained.

Now there is a great deal to be said on the subject of inflation, and most of it has already been said more than once. The Official Morning Line on inflation is simple and clear-cut: governments spend too much and workers get too many raises. Since governments and workers are the best spenders-on-things and the slowest creators-of-paper, the Official Morning Line is exactly wrong—and one can only hope, as usual, for better post-time comprehension.

There is no inflation in the real world of things, only allocation. Real values do not get inflated, they get allocated; only paper and balloons get inflated.

Inflation is the very essence of the paper system which capitalism has never even dreamed of living without, or even significantly altering, except *in* moments and *for* moments of extreme crisis, like World War II. Inflation is raising prices (it is *not* any particular theory as to why they are raised). Prices go up, they don't go down: since the 30's they haven't even dipped very much. This used to be called progress and now it is called inflation. The difference is that now it has become frightening, even to those who benefit most from it. Inflation, we were told endlessly in business advertisements, is the "cruelest tax of all." So was the previous progress, also known as the accumulation of capital.

Inventory is important in understanding modern inflation because it constitutes a sensitive contact-point between the two worlds of paper and things. If the price of an inventory-thing goes up, it is better to have a lot of it; if it goes down, money is better. Now most of the postwar recessions have featured inventory-panics among businessmen (these substitute for the financial panics of our early capitalist history, the last of which we shall ever see having occurred—along with much else—in 1929). Why should this be? The more inventory we have, the more "backing" there is to all the paper that's around. If inflation is blamed on too much spending-money and not enough things to spend it on, then why, as soon as there are enough things, do we have a recession? Because in such a situation more paper to buy goods must either be handed to those who will use it, or the price must be lowered so that the goods can be moved with the given quantity of purchasing-paper. But the price cannot be lowered without disturbing the value of all the non-purchasing paper which is sustained by it—and for the same reason there is a reluctance to raise either wages or taxes, which would also increase the quantity of purchasing-paper. The new inflation-recession cycle results from the continuing chase after paper-profit in a circumstance where too much product is too easily produced. The paper system is simply not adequate any longer to the job of clearing the shelves.

On the Downside

The other face of inflation is deflation, and that's like scarcity—it's in short supply.

There are no losers anymore. Prices don't go down, they only go up. Important quantities of paper-value are not wiped out any longer. The federal government has underwritten the Paper Economy—and the underwriter will not permit a really effective deflation.

Ah, but the old days were wonderful. Somebody yelled "Cheezit, the cops!" and everybody started to scamper around frantically trying to collect all debts at the same time. Quite a sight. The show amounted to a heretical worship of the ritual of payment—sort of a financial Holyrollerism—in which everything is going smoothly on Beneficent Wednesday but on Black Thursday it is arbitrarily decided that the "tomorrow" in gold-tomorrow is knocking at the door like Banquo's ghost. All the paper that can be called is called for clearing, and balances have to be settled in gold-today—right away. And nobody has the what-with to lend anymore. Well, there never was enough gold for *that* kind of religion (if there were, then gold would not be gold—it wouldn't even be as good as gold) and the fact became clear even to the High Priests themselves in 1907, when everybody was frightened by the mass passion to be paid in yellow metal. Thus the Federal Reserve System. There have to be limits to religious frenzy in any well-ordered church—you have to keep the True Believers in line. (Financial panics were also encouraged by the fact that markets—i.e., the domination of the consumer—were imperfectly organized: some real competition here and there, and as a consequence prices could on occasion be forced down faster than costs, which brings the whole related paper structure tumbling down.)

We have not yet figured out a workable substitute for the ritual of bankruptcy and other forms of price reduction and deflation—for letting the air out of the balloon. Meanwhile the air is getting fairly stale inside, even though we keep blowing fresh air in through the price-hole.

How can we deflate without interfering too much with the non-paper area of employment and production? The answer is simply to try, as we have been trying, to manipulate the mass of paper (but not just bank deposits) with a comprehension of its basic unreality, and to keep our attention focused on important matters, like real wealth and its rational allocation. A real Old Religion type of credit liquidation is really out of the question. That couldn't happen without production slowing down disastrously. We have had a steady government-underwritten (and business-benefited) inflation since 1933 (with a special and unnecessary spurt for 1946-48), with all the old and new paper protected, and we're stuck with that system.

But the fact that we live in the Age of the Big Underwriter, that prices don't go down, and that paper is never seriously deflated, is brand new, decisive, and changes the entire nature of our system.

The money-unit is not stable and it does not measure all things—it merely measures all paper. The value of the dollar has to shift in order for it to do its job. The fact that it no longer shifts upward is unfortunate, and of course makes the system of paper-value increasingly intramural. But the true historical purpose of the paper system was never to measure the value of things (that would have been an impossible task); its purpose was to value a future-with-more-things-in-it more highly, much more highly, than a present-deficient-in-things. It certainly achieved that purpose effectively, although not equitably. What has compromised the paper system is merely the superfluity of things in the present. The future has arrived—but the paper-chasers refuse to join the welcoming committee. The urgent point I want to make is that somebody ought to get out there and welcome it anyway.

What is the difference between one hundred dollars "saved"—even out of salary, or go further and say hoarded in Federal Reserve Notes—and one hundred dollars "made" by a one-point rise in a hundred-share smidgeon of Snappy Garter Inc., which rise, lasting only one day, resulted from an unfounded rumor that the Company's third-quarter earnings would snap back to 1961 levels? Freeze it in time, and you will notice upon dissection that all paper is created equal.

Nobody has to "save"—that is, wait and work a year to get an automobile—so that General Motors can build another factory. That would be true only under full production—and we haven't experienced that phenomenon except in limited sectors and for limited periods since the war. Moreover, under full production—this is a very revealing fact—the paper system with its price-airhole is utterly incapable by itself of rationally allocating materials and effort: to accomplish this, under full technological steam, reality as well as its conventional symbols must be consulted.

Paper is a useful and historically valid technique of accumulating capital, by means of a kind of privately distributed authoritarianism (relying on big banks and small governments), in those circumstances where the demand for goods is so great that all goods possible are actually produced, and new factories besides. That was some time ago. Probably the reason the Great Depression was so great (as W. W. Rostow suggests) is that we had by that time left those circumstances rather decisively behind.

The validity of paper in the absence of scarcity is unthinkable without conscious control of its quantity and/or value. When scarcity is in inadequate supply, so to speak, paper leads to a literal form of madness—a distortion or denial of reality in order to preserve the illusion of the absent condition. And when the power of great corporations is a part of the situation, reality itself gives way to the illusion—and a weird, glistening, new kind of scarcity appears, as an emanation from beyond the historical grave. It is Scarcity Regained—one of the ugliest of all human creations.

April 1964

Henry David Aiken

THE REVOLT AGAINST IDEOLOGY

Can it any longer be doubted that, on all sides of the Iron Curtain, the age of Leviathan is upon us? And for serious men does there remain any significant form of activity that is politically indifferent? We still profess loyalty to the ideal of "free inquiry," but the fact is that, directly or indirectly, governments supply the major resources, and politics most of the incentives, for our scientific research. And if some fortunate scientists of eminence are still encouraged to do "pure" or "basic" research, according to their interest, the primary reason is not that such studies exemplify one of man's essential intrinsic goods, but that the state cannot survive without them. Indeed, our universities and governments, along with our great industrial complexes, look increasingly like the interlocking arms of a great, if also headless, political establishment. Free enterprise (who doubts it?) is everywhere a dead issue save in the mythology of fundamentalist Republicanism, and whether our political leaders favor state capitalism or corporate socialism, the welfare state is accepted by all as an irremovable reality. Politics provide the primary themes of our literature, and when the critics charge a novelist or poet with "retreating from life," what they mean by "life" does not need to be construed. "Aesthetics" signifies merely enfeeblement and irrelevance; the "pure" artist, like the pure scientist, is a dying species, and none will mourn him save perhaps a few old "new critics" who, be it added, well understood the political meaning of their own dandified aestheticism. Our most exigent moral perplexities are overwhelmingly political, and our gods, such as they are, seem wholly preoccupied with affairs of state.

I must admit, however, that there still exists one quiet place where a man may go if he is nauseated by problems of politics and hence of power, and one course of study which he may still pursue without fear of political encroachment: he may go, that is, to the graduate school of any great university and take up the subject known there as "philosophy." Among the intellectuals, to my knowledge, we philosophers alone are politically inert. The meaning of the concept of political obligation fascinates some few of my colleagues, but I have rarely heard them, in congress assembled, discuss their political obligations. And if any were asked to offer their opinions concerning the ends, or limits, of government they would probably either decline to answer or regard the question as philosophically improper.

In order to prove the rule, there remain a few notorious exceptions such as Bertrand Russell, Jean-Paul Sartre, and Professor Sidney Hook. But we have Russell's own word for it that his politics, like his ethics, and his philosophy have nothing in common except that both were hatched under the same head of hair, and both Sartre and Hook are frequently dismissed by their more academic colleagues as publicists who have deserted philosophy for careers as ideologists and politicians. Recalling the greatest names in the history of philosophy from Socrates to Aquinas and from Hobbes to Mill, one may wonder momentarily how such a state of affairs could have come to pass. But when one remembers what men have done, and in many parts of the world are still prepared to do, in the name of a political philosophy, the answer seems evident: from a "pragmatic" point of view, political philosophy is a monster, and wherever it has been taken seriously, the consequence, almost invariably, has been revolution, war, and eventually, the police state. Russell himself once wrote an essay entitled, "The Harm That Good Men Do." Many would regard this as an appropriate subtitle for any honest and realistic history of political philosophy. With Socrates, political philosophy became a gadfly; in Plato, a monstrous dream; in Rousseau, Fichte, Hegel, Marx, and the rest, it has become a scourge and an obscenity.

Such is the prevailing view. And if Peter Laslett, the editor of a recent volume of essays *on* political philosophy, is correct in saying that "for the moment, anyway, political philosophy is dead," then none mourn its passing less than the philosophers themselves. Those few who, as philosophers, still suppose that they have a useful political role to play, discover it to be only that of unmasking the pretensions of other political philosophers.

Just what is wrong with political philosophy as a genre nonetheless remains obscure. Of course many political philosophies from Plato to Aquinas, and from Hobbes and Rousseau to Hegel and Marx, have been tied to the kites of theological or metaphysical systems. And for some, no doubt, this fact suffices to put them beyond the pale. But roundhouse objections to "metaphysics" are less fashionable than they were some years ago. In fact, under pressure from the philosophers of ordinary language, philosophical analysts are increasingly reluctant to proscribe as meaningless any established form of discourse on principle, as the positivists used to do with the propositions, not only of metaphysics and theology, but also of ethics. In this respect, recent analytical philosophy has steadily moved in the direction of pragmatism or, I had better say, the direction in which pragmatism has tended to move since the days of William James. Any form of utterance, so it is now argued, is to be interpreted and judged only in the light of its own characteristic "practical bearings." Thus, for example, if political philosophers in their own terms are given to general moral evaluations of political activities and institutions, the question is only whether such appraisals, all things considered, are acceptable as value judgments: that is to say, do they express commitments to which, on sober second thought and in view of the historical record, we should be ready to give our own conscientious assent? Do the lines of social action which they commend appear on the whole to be worth the trouble it would take to realize them? Above all, would we in conscience be able to give our blessings to the sort of "representative man" who might emerge if such lines of action were resolutely pursued?

Questions of this sort, which I take more seriously, have produced another round of objections which, although they do not rule out political philosophy on supposedly semantical or logical grounds, do nonetheless seem to condemn it virtually as a genre. These objections are all the more telling and all the more significant since they come from a quarter in which there has been no general animus against metaphysics and no self-denying ordinance which would exclude from the purview of philosophy any problem that is not purely a conceptual problem about the "logic" of expressions.

To my knowledge the most powerful attack upon political philosophy from this quarter (which for convenience may be called "existentialist") is to be found in Albert Camus' arresting work, *The Rebel*. Camus' indictment is easily misunderstood. To be sure, it is profoundly antirationalistic, but it is by no means based upon a romantic or nihilistic disillusionment with human reason or with the value of its exercise. Quite the contrary, reasonableness, in the more classical sense of the term, is Camus' forte. What he condemns, rather, are the crimes incited by the political philosophers in the name of Reason or of Reason's God. All men, say the philosophers, are created equal; *ergo,* let them be restored at once to their pristine estate, whatever the cost. All men are by nature free, yet everywhere they are in chains; *ergo,* Reason demands that they immediately be released, though ten thousand jailers perish in the process. Man is, above all, the rational animal, but because of the blinders which the ancient regime places before his mind, he cannot freely exercise his reason; then destroy the regime, let reason, or its self-appointed representatives, reign, and the devil take those who stand in the way. No doubt the political philosophers never meant to be quite so simple or so brutal as these caricatures suggest. But what of their followers, those who take them, or try to take them, at their word? Can the political philosophers altogether disclaim responsibility for their crimes? Is there not an ingrained metaphysical or moral pride, a fatal lack of continence in the very attempt of political philsophers to set forth, whether in the name of reason or of nature or of humanity, the absolute ends of government and the supposedly invariant forms of the just society?

But Camus' criticisms are by no means directed exclusively to the 18th-century *philosophes* and their descendants. They are extended also to the Hegelians and the Marxists who attempt to formulate a universal law, or dialectic, of historical development which is then made to double in brass as an immanent principle of justification for their own incitive prophecies about man's social destiny. Whether such prophecies proclaim a future of unlimited freedom, of absolute justice and equality, or of perpetual peace, in each case they too represent that criminal pride of reason which destroys the sense of limitation which for Camus is the beginning of political, as of every other form of, wisdom.

From these remarks it would be easy enough to conclude that Camus' indictment of traditional political philosophy is actually an indictment of philosophy itself. And so in a way it is, at least as philosophy has been conceived and executed in the dominant Western tradition. Yet Camus is not just another literary counter-philosopher. Nor is his indictment of rationalistic political philosophy a condemnation of political philosophy *per se*. For it is plain that, as Sir Herbert Read points out in his discerning preface to the English translation of *The Rebel,* Camus himself has a philosophy of politics. But it is, at any rate, a philosophy of politics radically different from those of his predecessors. For Camus makes no attempt to define *the* function or the end of government or to state *the* rightful basis of political authority. Nor does he propose any universal principle of political action save one of self-limitation or restraint. It is also characteristic of Camus that although he repudiates any and all forms of unlimited revolution, he accepts the necessity, on occasion, of rebellion or civil disobedience.

Despite many differences both in philosophical background and in literary style, there are striking parallels between Camus' existentialist critique of modern political philosophy and those to be found in the writings of the pragmatist, John Dewey. In Dewey one finds the same hatred of essentialism and apriorism, the same antipathy to utopianism, and the same distrust both of radical individualism and of radical collectivism. There is a similar emphasis upon the concrete "problematic situations" (as Dewey calls them) which alone he takes it to be the business of "creative intelligence" to resolve. And there is the same underlying humanism which opposes the sacrifice of living men to principles and to ideals realizable, if at all, only in an abstract and indefinite future. For obvious reasons, Dewey was more confident than Camus of the efficacy of democratic procedures, at least in "developed" societies. Yet he was by no means prepared to demand the immediate institution of such procedures in all countries and circumstances; nor did he, like more romantic majoritarians, regard the will of the many as an absolute source of rightful political authority. Democracy for Dewey is a method rather than an end. Or if, in certain writings, democracy also tends to become an end, then it is in a looser sense of the term which now begins to take on meanings more strictly associated with the concepts of community, fraternity, and social equality.

Dewey's pragmatic criticisms of earlier political philosophy are usually regarded as methodological rather than moral—although in his case, as in that of all pragmatists, it is always a question where problems of method leave off and problems of ethics (and politics) begin. Thus, whereas Camus ascribes the primordial fault of the political philosophers to their incontinent passion for absolute transcendence of the finite conditions of man's historical social existence, Dewey ascribes it to the illusory "quest for certainty" which, according to his reading, dominated virtually the whole history of philosophy before the 20th century. Yet in Dewey's case also, one senses that the more radical evil lies not in the illusion itself but in its attendant waste and destructiveness. The quest for certainty begins in hope and ends in skepticism and despair. In promising us an unlimited intellectual and moral security, it brings us by stages to the war of all against all. Dewey's more unfriendly critics have often charged him with advocacy of the gospel of human perfectibility. No criticism could be more perverse. Man, as Dewey conceives him, is, once for all, a mortal creature who lives and has his being within the orders of nature and of history. Indeed, this is the governing metaphysical principle underlying his logic, his theory of knowledge, and his moral philosophy. Uncertainty, and hence imperfection, are ingrained in the very texture of human existence. And no method, including the methods of science, can extricate us from them.

In other spheres, philosophical forgetfulness of this fact has been unfortunate; in politics, as in ethics, it has proved a calamity. This is not to deny that Dewey has a philosophy of politics, but like Camus' it is of a sort quite different from the major political philosophies of the tradition. He is sometimes criticized for offering us no explicit general theory of governmental authority, no principled statement of the grounds or proper limits of political obligation—above all, no settled position toward the most vexatious of modern political problems, namely, revolution. But Dewey's vagueness on these scores is quite intentional. In politics as in ethics, Dewey repudiates any and all fixed principles for the institution of the good society or for the establishment and maintenance of good government. His preoccupation as a political philosopher is solely with the controlling attitudes which men bring to their political deliberations.

II. Marxism and Ideology: The First Revolt

Impressive as they are, the foregoing criticisms of political philosophy are largely matters of individual judgment. And if the professional philosophers now decline to do political philosophy, it may be argued that this is owing to their own disillusionment with the achievements of their predecessors rather than to any inherent fault in political philosophy as a genre. It remains to ask whether there may be, after all, some deep-lying confusion of mind, some pervasive logical fault or category mistake, which really does afflict political philosophy as a form of discourse.

As a way of confronting this question, it may prove useful to examine certain aspects of the widespread attack against the modern offspring of and successors to political philosophy, namely, ideology. Most of the "anti-ideologists," as I shall call them, share certain attitudes in common with the existentialists; indeed, it is my impression that some of them owe more to the latter, and particularly to Camus, than they have as yet acknowledged. They owe something also to the pragmatists; in fact, most American anti-ideologists fancy their own point of view as essentially "pragmatic." But (generally speaking) they go beyond the existentialists and the pragmatists in contending that ideological thinking is the function of certain features of the social situation in which intellectuals as a group find themselves in an era of exact science, advanced technology, and the welfare state. In predicting the end of ideology, they thus imply that the social and intellectual conditions which have been conducive to ideological thinking are now disappearing. Their own role, in effect, is to make certain that the prediction will come true.

Now the primary target of our contemporary Western anti-ideologists is, of course, Marxism. And in prophesying the end of ideology, it is the end of Marxism of which they mainly dream. It is worth remembering, therefore, that: (a) Marx was the first great critic of political philosophy; and (b) he was also the first great prophet of the end of the ideological age.

According to Marx, ideology always involves a conception of reality which systematically "inverts" the whole relation of thought to being.* As

* In this section I have been aided by Stanley W. Moore's *The Critique of Capitalist Democracy: An Introduction to the Theory of the State of Marx, Engels, and Lenin.* Moore's fourth chapter, "Ideology and Alienation," is highly compressed and schematic, but I know of no other discussion of the subject which, within its limits, is so clear and so accurate. I have also benefited from Norman Birnbaum's "The Sociological Study of Ideology (1940-60)," *Current Sociology,* Vol. IX, No. 2, 1960. Birnbaum's essay, which he subtitles "A Trend Report," is a masterly survey of cur-

a form of thought, therefore, ideology is inherently confused; it stands to science, in Marx's words, as an inverted image in a "camera obscura" stands to a veridical perception. This inversion, of which Hegel's "objective" idealism is a prime philosophical example, results directly or indirectly from that process of "alienation" whereby human artifacts, including "ideas," are invested with a power and a reality that are supposedly independent both of their producers and of the material conditions and operations involved in their production. Such an investment, which philosophers call "reification," is also necessarily accompanied by "mystification," i.e., by an obscuring of the interests and relationships that actually determine social behavior. For example, in imputing an independent reality and power to their reified ideas and principles, their rights and duties, their ends and "reasons," men thereby conceal from themselves the fact that it is they, the creators of such entities, whose underlying actions and whose work alone give them whatever significance they may have.

Except for genuinely empirical science, the whole cultural "superstructure" of hitherto existing societies is permeated by the same process of alienation and ideological inversion. For this reason it would be a radical mistake to conceive of ideology as limited to political philosophy; on the contrary, ideology also includes, among other things, religion, ethics, art, metaphysics, and the "dismal science" of economics. Properly understood, political philosophies are merely special applications of far-flung ideological patterns that invest them with their own magical "authority" and "justification." Furthermore, since alienation is a social process, ideologies, whether as wholes or as parts, are to be understood as expressions, not of the interests of isolated individuals, but of the conflicting concerns—or better, tendencies—of social classes. It is thus only by relating political ideologies to their objective social conditions and causes that we can begin to interpret their true objective meaning (i.e., what they signify or portend within the order of nature), and hence, by stages, to correct the inverted images of reality which they present to the ideologists themselves. One of the primary functions of Marxism, in fact, is precisely to provide the intellectual, including the social-theoretical, tools for such interpretations and corrections, and thus for the first time to enable us, in principle, to demythologize ideology.

But it is one thing to explain ideology and another to overcome it. Mankind as a whole can permanently overcome ideological thought (and action) not by any process of purely conceptual analysis on the part of individual philosophers, but only by removing the material causes of alienation which, according to Marx, are rooted in the institution of private

rent literature on the subject of ideology, including Marxist ideological theory. It also contains an invaluable critical bibliography.

property. And it is for this reason, and this reason alone, that Marx's historical prophecy of the coming of world socialism amounts at the same time to a prophecy of the end of the ideological ages.

III. Disillusionment in the West: The Second Revolt Against Ideology

Marx's view of ideology underlies the thinking of most of our own anti-ideologists. However, they go beyond Marx in extending the pejorative associations of the term to the role of ideology in ordering human attitudes. Thus, they not only regard ideological doctrines as wrong-headed; they also object to their employment as vehicles for the formation, guidance, and control of social behavior. But they go Marx one better in another way, for they also regard Marxism itself as a prime example of ideology.

The first non-Marxist writer, so far as I know, explicitly to inquire whether we might be approaching the end of the ideological age was Raymond Aron in his book, *The Opium of the Intellectuals.* The prevailing temper of Aron's book is not unlike that of Camus' *The Rebel.* There are also a number of striking parallels between Aron's point of view and that of Karl Popper, as developed in the latter's *The Open Society and Its Enemies.* For example, there is the same constitutional distrust of large-scale social planning, the same insistence upon the impossibility of large-scale historical predictions of social behavior, and the same celebration of the virtues of "the open society." Above all, there is the same castigation of any attempt to determine the drift and meaning of human history as a whole and hence of the attempt to formulate universal and necessary laws of historical development.

"The last great ideology," says Aron, "was born of the combination of three elements: the vision of a future consistent with human aspiration, the link between this future and a particular social class, and trust in human values above and beyond the victory of the working class, thanks to planning and collective ownership." Aron believes that at the present time the hope aroused by that ideology is gone beyond peradventure. One main reason for this disillusionment, so he argues, is that "confidence in the virtues of a socio-technique has begun to wane." Furthermore, on this side of the Iron Curtain, no one believes any longer in the reality of a social class that will carry us, under the leadership of the socio-economic engineers, to the frontiers of the classless society. Like Camus and Popper, Aron cannot bring himself flatly to renounce the values of the Enlightenment; but in practice he is no more able than they to take them with absolute seriousness as governing ideals for the reconstruction of society in the 20th century. In his own terms, he no longer fully believes in the vision of a future consistent with "human aspirations." And it is this fact perhaps that accounts for the vein of pessimism and the self-division which run through his writing.

In any case, it is plain that for Aron the approaching end of the age of ideology represents also a crisis of faith and of hope for mankind. On the penultimate page of his book, Aron asks, "Does the rejection of fanaticism encourage a reasonable faith, or merely skepticism?" His analogical answer is that "one does not cease to love God when one gives up converting pagans or the Jews and no longer reiterates 'No salvation outside the Church.' " Coming as late as it does in Aron's book, this has something like the effect of an unprepared major cadence at the end of a funeral march. What is its basis? No matter how personal one's religion may be, it is hard to see how it could fail to be attenuated by a radical renunciation of one's belief that it should prevail. If one really gives up trying to convert the "pagans," does this not entail reservations about the value as well as the possibility of converting them? If so, does this not also suggest that one has ceased completely to love God or else that only a gesture toward the love of Him remains? Making due allowance for the analogy, I cannot, as a pragmatist, see how one can be said actively to seek a less cruel lot for humanity if one can trust no technique and no plan for its amelioration. To will the end is to will the means, and to reject the means is, in practice, to renounce the end. Like Peirce in another connection, one is minded to say to the political as well as to the epistemological moralists: "Dismiss make-believe!" This means also, so far as I can see, "Dismiss professions of 'reasonable faith' if you do not believe in the *power* of reason; and do not talk about abolishing 'fanaticism,' unless you believe that there is a way (or 'technique') of abolishing it." Like all anti-ideologists, Aron is opposed to the expectation of "miraculous changes" either from a revolution or an economic plan. Very well. The question is whether he gives us any reason to expect unmiraculous changes from any sort of concerted human action. "If tolerance is born of doubt, let us teach everyone to doubt all the models and utopias, to challenge all the prophets of redemption and the heralds of catastrophe." And, "If they alone can abolish fanaticism, let us pray for the advent of the skeptics." The rhetoric is appealing. But it smacks of ideology, in Aron's own sense. For toleration is also a principle and a method. And it too has its dangers.

These comments are not made in a spirit of mockery. My purpose is rather to make clear what may be implied in the prophecy that we are living at the end of the ideological age, the age, in Mr. Aron's own apt words, in which men still actively search "for a purpose, for communion with the people, for something controlled by *an idea and a will*" (my italics). As he points out, we Westerners have suffered an increasing fragmentation of our universe; our poetry becomes more and more obscure and diffuse, and our poets are isolated from one another as well as from "the big public" which "in their heart of hearts, they long to serve"; our scientists have ideas aplenty but no control over their use or indeed any consistent belief in the possibility of their control; our scholars control limited areas of specialized knowledge, but present-day science "seems to leave . . . [them] as ignorant of the answers to the ultimate questions as a child awakening to consciousness"; and our economists and sociologists, for all their facts and statistics, their jargon and their lore, have not the vaguest notion whether "humanity is progressing toward an atomic holocaust or Utopian peace." This process of fragmentation and dissociation, moreover, is not new; it has been going on at an ever more rapid pace, at least since the Renaissance. But here precisely, as Aron admits, "is where ideology comes in. . . ." For ideology represents the insistent demand for a coherent *way* of individual and social life, an orientation toward the world and toward the human predicament, controlled as he says both by an idea and by a will, or, rather, by a will infused with an idea and an idea animated by will. Ideology, as Aron tacitly acknowledges, is a creature of alienation; but it represents also a passion to reduce alienation, to bring it down to bearable human proportions. It also represents the belief that alienation may be reduced through collective human endeavors. Thus, by his own account, an end to the age of ideology would amount to this extent to a virtual skepticism about the possibility of reducing alienation through corporate planning and action (ideas infused with will). And this means that man has no choice but to live with alienation. Here, however, one faces precisely one of those metaphysical and historical "necessities" against which the anti-ideologists themselves rail when they find them in the writings of other ideologists. Here, too, it seems, we are faced with a "simplified" idea of man's fate which, as in the case of the Stoicism it is plainly a variant of, forms the basis of still another ideology, an idea that in this instance is, if I may say so, fused with inaction.

IV. The Sociological Critique of Ideology

Aron's analysis of ideology, although suggestive, does not take us very far. Let us therefore cross the ocean to the heartland of contemporary anti-ideology. In the United States perhaps the leading anti-ideologist is the sociologist and social critic, Profesor Daniel Bell. Bell, who knows his Marx, is also a good strategist. Already in the introduction to his book, *The End of Ideology,* he moves beyond Aron, for, unlike the latter, he proposes to make a positive virtue of alienation. "Alienation," he tells us flatly, "is not nihilism but a positive role, a detachment, which guards one against being submerged in any cause, or accepting any particular embodiment of community as final. Nor is alienation deracination, a denial of one's roots or country." This persuasive definition has its points. It is also an interesting instance of the notion of an idea fused with will which Bell, like Aron, tends to identify with ideology.

As befits a sociologist, Bell is concerned not just with the content of ideas but with their social origins, causes, and roles. Thus, in an attempt to locate the sources of ideological thinking, he begins his analysis with a characterological division of the intelligentsia into two main types: (a) the "scholars"; and (b) the "intellectuals." The scholar, as Bell conceives him, "has a bounded field of knowledge, a tradition, and seeks to find his place in it, adding to the accumulated, tested knowledge of the past as to a mosaic." He is, so to say, a "pro" for whom "the show must go on," however and whatever he himself may feel about it. Accepting the scholarly tradition within which he has found a place, he is able to judge himself, or at least his scholarly performance, by impersonal and objective standards. And if he performs with a modicum of efficiency and does not stray beyond the limits of his scholarly "competence," he is entitled to a modicum of self-respect. Indeed, his self-respect, like his role-governed conception of himself, is a function of his assurance of the respect of his peers and, more indirectly, of the society of which his discipline is an established part.

The intellectual, on the other hand, has no such responsibility or security. Lacking a scholarly discipline, perhaps lacking the talent for achievement within such a discipline, which can hold him continuously responsible to "objective" methods and to "facts" wholly independent of himself, his only recourse is an endless dialectic and critique of general ideas. And because he is without a legitimate social role to play within society, he perforce finds himself alienated from its institutions and is left to manipulate his "ideas" in a mood of unrequited and unfocused resentment. He doesn't so much think with his ideas as feel through them. In the discourses of an intellectual, therefore, the thing to look to is not his argument, which, where it exists, is merely a vehicle for his resentments, but rather to the effect which it is meant to induce. He presents his readers not with information but with a goad and with an outlet for their own repressed emotions of estrangement or violence. He may, in the process, tell them something, but it is doing something to them that is his real, if unavowed, aim. For him, the beginning and end of a process of reflection is not a specific problem about objective processes and events; as Professor Bell charges, he begins always with "*his* experience, *his* perceptions of the world, his privileges and deprivations, and judges the world by these sensibilities." For him, the "world" is not a thing in itself, but rather his will and his idea, and if there is something *there,* in itself, then he acknowledges it only as something which he is up against and which exists only in so far as he is up against it. His business, in Marx's words, is not to understand the world, but to change, or better, to overcome it. And if he can't change it in any other way, he may at least reject it, and thus, by an obvious inversion, still show his superiority to it.

In this way, every statement and every discussion becomes for the intellectual an implicitly political move in an endless game of power. Of course he fancies his own moves really to be in the interest (*n.b.*) of "justice" or "freedom," while those of his "opponents," whether they invoke the names of "legitimacy" or of "law and order," are actually made in the interest of business as usual which it is the function of the established order to protect and to promote. The sad fact remains, however, that the intellectual's power *is* severely limited by the existing system. Hence, in order to maintain the illusion of his freedom or of his power to realize it, he is obliged, as Bell puts it, to embark "upon what William James called 'the faith ladder,' which in its vision of the future cannot distinguish possibilities from probabilities, and converts the latter into certainties."

What is the nature of the conceptual tools with which the "free-floating" and unscholarly intellectual does his work? In order to answer this question, Bell is obliged to move from sociology to logic and semantics. Thus he speaks repeatedly, in terms which I find merely more explicit than Aron's, of ideology as being somehow a "fusion" of thought with emotion or passion which at one and the same time does the trick of "simplify[ing] ideas, establish[ing] a claim to truth, and, in the union of the two, demand[ing] a commitment to action." The result—and it is this which Bell most seriously objects to—is not just a "transformation" of ideas, but also a transformation of people. The typical effect of any ideological argument is, then, a kind of conversion. The road by which the ideologist comes to Damascus doesn't matter; what matters is that he is made to see the light. Says Bell: "Ideology is the conversion of ideas into social levers. Without irony, Max Lerner once entitled a book 'Ideas Are Weapons.' This is the language of ideology. It is the commitment to the consequences of ideas."

Bell is rarely more analytical than this, but toward the end of his study he does say one further thing which is at least symptomatic of the point of view which he represents: "If the end of ideology has any meaning, it [sic] is to ask for the end of rhetoric, and rhetoricians, of 'revolution,' of the day when the young French anarchist Vaillant tossed a bomb into the Chamber of Deputies, and the literary critic Laurent Tailhade declared in his defense: 'What do a few human lives matter; it was a *beau geste*.'" The general idea that concerns us here is not the tacit identification of ideology with revolutionary activity, especially of the more bizarre and feckless sort, but rather its identification with rhetoric.

If by "rhetoric" Bell means the use of language in order to persuade or influence others—and many things he says suggest that this is his meaning—then his vision of the end of ideology as an end to rhetoric is a utopian fantasy. Worse, it is an evil fantasy, for it implies a conception of human relations which would deprive us of the right to address one another except for the purpose of comparing notes about matters of fact. Consider what would happen were such a fantasy to come true. In any ordinary sense, it would mean a virtual end to discourse, to communication, and to argument. For it would mean an end to any speech-act addressed to others with a view to their guidance, their instruction, their edification, or their pleasure, with a view, in short, to changing their minds. Indeed, the image of man implicit in Bell's dream of the end of ideology is precisely one of an academic grind or functionary to which he himself, as a counter-ideologist and counter-rhetorician, is fortunately unable to conform.*

The American anti-ideologists, Bell included, regard themselves as pragmatists. However, we should remind ourselves that it is the great pragmatists who have insisted, time out of mind, that ideas have consequences and that, indeed, their operative meaning can only be construed in consequential terms. Rhetoric, from this point of view, is not necessarily a bad or degenerate form of expression; rather it is a dimension of any form of speech which is addressed to others. Furthermore, pragmatism is also a normative theory which asks us to evaluate any form of speech, and hence

* What Bell does not sufficiently emphasize is that the intellectuals' "faith ladders" have indeed converted possibilities into certainties. Otherwise it is hard to see why he and his fellow anti-ideologists make such a hullabaloo about ideology and why they are enthralled with the thought that we have reached the end of the age of ideology. The simple fact is that ever since the French Revolution the intellectuals, with the help of their ideologies, have been moving mountains. And if *their* ideologies are exhausted, as Bell contends, this does not necessarily entail the end of ideology as such. No doubt the old ideologies of the right and the left have lost much of their power to persuade, and no doubt, all over the world, radicalism and intellectualism in our time must inevitably take new forms. But they will persist, by Bell's own analysis, until every intellectual has become a scholar (or worker) and until every scholar becomes a scholar (or worker) merely; that is, until there are no full- or part-time "out-groups" (to employ a fashionable term of sociological analysis) and no general ideas for them to think with. At this point one begins to have visions of an academic utopia within which there are no "free-floating" intellectuals, no alienated, critical minds, such as Professor Bell's, that are not wholly committed to their vocations and that possess an over-plus of energy and passions that is not expended in the conduct of their own "researches." In such a utopia (if I may speak metaphorically) there would be no New York and no Concord, but only a series of semi-urban centers for semi-advanced study for semi-advanced scholars who would sternly deny themselves the use of any concept or the affirmation of any statement whose "practical bearings" cannot be shown to lie wholly within the range of their legitimate scholarly activity or work. Such a utopia, I fancy, would have no place even for counter-ideologists like Professor Bell whose own "restless vanity" (the phrase is his) is evidently not sated by the rewards that accrue from the performance of his scholarly labors.

of rhetoric, in terms of its consequences. The question, therefore, is not whether a discourse persuades or influences other minds and other hearts, but how it does so and with what effect. Not every rhetorician is a demagogue. Plato's Socrates professed to despise the Sophists because they were rhetoricians, and this Socrates, I surmise, is the grandfather of all the countless anti-rhetoricians and anti-ideologists from his day to Bell's. But it should not be forgotten that Socrates himself was a master rhetorician and that his admirers ignore the fact because they believe his cause was just. Moreover, Socrates was not only a lover of truth; he was also, politically, a reactionary whose hatred of the Sophists was directed not only to their rhetoric but also to their liberal, democratic, and plebeian political and social attitudes. In saying this, I do not mean to attack our latter-day anti-ideologists by innuendo. I do mean to say that the plain effect of *their* rhetoric is to reinforce acceptance of our own institutional status quo and to declass those "intellectuals" who seek to modify in any radical way the fundamental structures of "Western" political life.

There remains a secondary sense of the term "rhetoric" which Bell may also have in mind. In this sense, rhetoric means eloquence. So conceived, the demand for an end to rhetoric is tantamount to a request for plain talk and, so to say, for an age of prose. So far so good. But there may be more to it than this. Elsewhere Bell harps upon the theme that "Throughout their history, Americans have had an extraordinary talent for compromise in politics and extremism in morality." It is plain that Bell is repelled by "this moralism," though, I gather, not so much because it is hypocritical but rather because, as moral, it is uncompromising. "The saving grace, so to speak, of American politics, was that all sorts of groups were tolerated, and the system of the 'deal' became the pragmatic counterpart of the philosophic principle of toleration. But in matters of manners, morals, and conduct—particularly in the small towns—there has been a ferocity of blue-nosed attitudes unmatched by other countries." And again, "It has been one of the glories of the United States that politics has always been a pragmatic give-and-take rather than a series of wars-to-the-death." Of course this last is *not* true. Among our national "glories" have been a war for independence and a civil war, both of them (among other things) wars of principle. Our periods of "give-and-take" have usually also been periods of drift and complacency which have ended in orgies of political corruption and degradation. In one domain, however, Bell believes that our underlying political "postures" have not been "pragmatic." "One of the unique aspects of American politics is that . . . foreign policy has always been phrased in moralistic terms. Perhaps the very nature of our emergence as an independent country forced us to constantly adopt a moral posture in regard to the rest of the world; perhaps being distant from the real centers of interest conflict allowed us to employ pieties, rather than face realities. But since foreign policy has usually been within the frame of moral rather than pragmatic discourse, the debate in the fifties became centered in moral terms."

These passages are typical. In asking for an end to rhetoric, what Bell appears to be calling for is, among other things, an end to *moral* discourse and a beginning of consistent "pragmatic discourse" in every sphere of political life. What does this mean? So far as I can make out, it means an end to judgment and to principle, to praise and to blame, in the political domain and a beginning of plain, unvarnished "politicking" in the name of our "realistic" national, social, or individual "interests." It means, in effect, that in political discourse two and only *two* forms of expression are to be regarded as legitimate: (a) realistic, verifiable statements of fact; and (b) bald, undisguised expressions of first-personal (singular or plural) interest. On such a view, one would be permitted to say, "I don't like segregation and I will try—without, however, upsetting the apple cart—to do what I can to limit segregationalist practices," but not "Segregation is an affront to the humanity of the Negro people," or, "Those who practice segregation are unfair and unjust." What is wrong with moral, as distinct from "pragmatic," discourse? It is not to be doubted that moral discourse is more eloquent and more incitive, and in this sense more rhetorical, than the "pragmatic" forms of speech which Bell prefers. But what is wrong with eloquence *per se?* No doubt it should not be used to cloud an issue, to obscure relevant facts, or to promote unreason. But this is no more a necessary consequence of moral discourse than of any other form of eloquence. Without eloquence, especially in times of crisis, few great political movements would succeed. In fact, eloquence, including the eloquence of moral judgment, is native to the language of politics, and particularly so, as Bell himself admits, in democratic societies where persuasion of the great masses is a condition of success. Thus to put an end to eloquence would be to put an end, not only to "moralism" (which is usually nothing more than the morality of those with whom we disagree) and to "ideology," but also to any form of politics in which great issues are stated or argued in terms of human rights and responsibilities and in which it is essential to gain the approval of the people, or their representatives, before any fundamental change in governmental policy is made. Perhaps a tightly knit, self-interested, and all-powerful elite might get along (among its members) with "pragmatic discourse" alone. But despite Bell, democratic politics does not just mean "bargaining between legitimate groups and the search for consensus." It means also a form of politics in which men are governed by, and hence with reference to, principles and ideals—in a word, to morals and to ideology.

But now a word of caution: It is no part of my intention to suggest, much less admit, that ideology and morality *are* rhetoric; the equation is

Bell's, not mine. I contend only that if, as is true, ideological discourses are full of rhetoric (in the above senses), there is no reason to deplore the fact. Quite the contrary.

Webster also mentions a third sense (or senses) of "rhetoric" which for our purposes is perhaps the most interesting of all. In this sense, "rhetoric" means "ostentatious or artificial speech." That some ideologists and moralists are ostentatious need not be denied. My own impression, however, is that academic scholars, particularly in some of the more immature sciences of man, are at least as prone to ostentatious speech (and thought) as other intellectuals. Sociology, indeed, might almost be defined as the ostentatious science. But except in beautiful women, ostentation is surely a minor vice, and only a fool would write off a whole field of study or an entire form of expression because some of its practitioners, like Molière's learned ladies, tend to give themselves airs.

Artificiality is another matter, which will repay closer scrutiny. Now "artificiality" often connotes a way of doing things which, although not necessarily ostentatious, is mannered, contrived, studied, and "unnatural." On occasion, a rhetoric which is artificial in this sense can be very powerful, as for example, in the poetry of Milton or in the prose of Burke and Macaulay. Among moralists and men of letters one associates it with the conservative wits of the 18th century and with the elaborate courtesy and the elegant banter of Matthew Arnold and his disciples. For obvious reasons, it is not a rhetoric characteristic of revolutionary ideologists. In our own time one runs into it only occasionally among writers of the right or the right-center. In England, Michael Oakeshott employs it with some effect, as (in another way) do T. S. Eliot and his followers. In this country, some of the so-called southern agrarians, such as Allen Tate, are minor masters of this rhetoric. But I fancy that Tate, at least, is well aware that he is fighting in a lost cause, and his style, like a ruffled cuff, is intended to give us a heightened sense of the fact. To my unaccustomed ears, the Encyclicals of Leo XIII, which are among the modern masterpieces of Catholic ideology, are also effective examples of a rhetoric of this sort. Indeed, it is precisely the impervious, anachronistic artificiality of Leo's prose which makes one realize how remote, for better or worse, is the concessive modernity of his social thought from the radical liberalism of a Bentham or a Mill.

But "artificiality" has another connotation in this context that is more central to our theme. In this sense, I take it, rhetoric is to be contrasted with literal statement. Here I must limit my remarks mainly to political ideology, but what will be said holds also of all ideologies, including those we normally think of as religious or metaphysical. Now political ideology is nothing but political discourse (as distinct from political science) on its most general formative level. It is, that is to say, political discourse insofar as the latter addresses itself, not just to specific, piecemeal reforms, but to the guiding principles, practices, and aspirations by which politically organized societies, absolutely or else in certain typical situations, ought to be governed. This being so, political ideologies inevitably include, among their leading articles, statements of general principle or method and expressions of basic attitude, orientation, and concern which, as they stand, are so highly abstract as to appear to many minds preoccupied with day-to-day problems of "practical politics" virtually meaningless. Such statements are of course habitually formulated in terms like "general welfare," "common good," "justice," "equality," "democracy," "security," and the rest.

But these very terms, so natural or even essential, when one is defining and appraising political practices or systems, also tend through overuse to become mere counters which elicit from us the tired, stock response that leaves us, and hence the practices themselves, unchanged. Or worse, because our responses are dull and routine, and hence *practically* of no political importance, we may conclude that all general philosophical discussions of politics are pointless and that one political ideology is just as good—or bad—as any other. What does matter, so we feel, is not what we say or think about "the system," but only what we do within it. And so, by stages, we are led to the conservative conclusion that political manifestoes, declarations of independence, and constitutions (with their embarrassing ideological preambles) make no difference to society as a going concern. In short, so far as we are concerned, ideology is useless verbiage. On the other side, unfortunately, we discover to our dismay that other peoples, politically and intellectually less "advanced" than ourselves, are enflamed, sometimes to the point of revolution, by ideological discourses, fresher and more affecting, in part because less literal and less abstract, than those to which we are accustomed. And to our contempt for our own ineffectual ideological abstractions we now add a positive hatred (or fear) of an ideological rhetoric which suddenly endows those same abstractions with a new life that disturbs our own.

It should be observed, however, that our very hatred is itself a backhanded tribute to the power of ideology. And if, out of a misplaced loyalty to "reason," we merely limit ourselves to "exposing" it, we stand in danger of losing our world. Most of us, realizing that the world is *never* well lost, find ourselves drawn back inescapably into the ideological struggle which, if we are to win it for ends that are right and just, requires that we produce a counter-rhetoric more imaginative, more distinguished, and more durable than that of our opponents. But if, as literalists of the imagination, we still decline to go the whole hog, resorting now only to formal reaffirmation of the old abstract "principles" which no later than yesterday we professed to find meaningless, who will believe us? Why should they? They have heard the same golden words mouthed a thousand times on the party platforms by hacks who have no notion of their meaning. And, if it comes to that, what *do* they mean?

In science it normally suffices to state a fact, and one man may do this as well and as accurately as another. But in the sphere of conduct much more is involved. For here we have to do with matters of attitude and intention and with problems of authenticity, legitimacy, and authority. Here words must not only predict what will be but determine what shall be; they must not only inform but also prepare and initiate lines of action. And what *is* it that is being determined, prepared, and initiated? This, so I contend, can be fully revealed only through the "poetry" which the ideologist may afford us.

Since Plato, rationalists have ever been afraid of poetry. And even those who profess not to be so, worry lest "the people" confuse the true poet with the counterfeit. But just as true poetry, known and loved, is the only real protection against the malefactions of pseudo-poets, so also its ideological analogue is the only guarantee against the factitious "myths" of a Rosenberg, a Hitler, or a Mussolini. Our worry, in America, should be not that the false rhetoric of "foreign" ideologies may divert our people from their loyalties to our establishment, but that we do so little to replenish the fund of ideological poetry with which the founding fathers, along with Lincoln and a few others have provided us. Our contemporary ideology is, or seems to be, all ghost-written. The voice sounds as reedy and hollow as are the men who contrive it. But if we should lose the power both to create and passionately to respond to a great ideological rhetoric, we would also lose the power to tell the difference between the phony and the real thing.

Further, figurative and hence rhetorical language enables, or compels, men to perform in advance of experience those crucial symbolic actions and imaginative experiments upon which, as Dewey has persuasively argued, genuinely rational judgments of practice and of value entirely depend. Know the truth, and the truth will set you free: how dangerous and how misleading is this half-truth. How, in a moral and practical sense, *are* we to know it? I can assent to the proposition that on the first day of an atomic war every major city in the United States would be destroyed, without in the least *realizing,* in human terms, what the statement really means. In order that I may even remotely grasp such an idea, in absence of the event, I must somehow try symbolically to live through the horror and the agony of such a calamity. But this is precisely what the cold, literal, objective statement of fact does not require me to do. To this end, therefore, it is essential that I find a way of thinking and talking about the fact which will make me realize from a practical, and even, if you please, from a metaphysical point of view, what it comes to. For most of us, this can be done only through the artificial linguistic devices, known to every reader of fiction and of poetry, which enable us to perform "in imagination," as we say, those symbolic actions in which alone the "reality" of *literary* art exists. To disdain "rhetoric," therefore, is to disdain the very condition through which full practical understanding and judgment is possible. And to deny oneself its use is not to guarantee the preservation of scientific "objectivity" but to preclude the possibility of really being objective in trying to decide, in political terms, what one's way of life is to be.

It remains to say a word about "simplism," that final bogey of the anti-ideological mentality. Through rhetoric, according to Bell, ideology infuses ideas with passion, thus, as might be expected, winning friends and influencing people. But the principal underhanded intellectual (or is it, too, rhetorical?) trick of the ideologists is to "simplify ideas." It therefore seems necessary to remind the anti-ideologist that simplification, so far from being a fault peculiar to ideology, is, as William James well knew, a large part of the saving virtue of rationality itself. To oppose simplism on principle, in politics as in every other sphere of activity, is not to make a legitimate demand for recognition of the complexities and diversities of political life, but, in effect, to ask for an abandonment of policy and a fatal acquiescence in the drift of events. For simplification is an essential feature of any rational initiation of action. To refuse to simplify when one confronts a problem is in effect to reject the obligation to reach a solution; it is to make a game of possibilities and hence to move automatically outside the context of agency and choice. Every procedure that helps us to make decisions does so precisely by reducing the range of possibilities which we may reasonably be expected to consider. And every method, in setting a limit to the considerations that ought to be taken into account, thereby secures our deliberations against an endless spread of doubts.

On this score particularly, Professor Bell seems merely disingenuous when he tells us—incidentally letting a fair-sized ideological cat out of his own elastic bag—that although "There is now more than ever some need for utopia, in the sense that men need—as they have always needed—some vision of their potential, some manner of fusing passion with intelligence. . . . The ladder to the City of Heaven can no longer be a 'faith ladder,' but an empirical one; a utopia has to specify *where* one wants to go, *how* to get there, the costs of the enterprise, and some realization of, and justification for the determination of *who* is to pay." There is a rather terrible irony in the fact that Bell, who in other contexts is so prone to rail against those who think in terms of all or none, should find it so hard at this point to think in terms of degree. Were one seriously to try, in detail and at the outset, to meet all his requirements for a "good" utopia, the magnitude and complexity of the task would paralyze thought. The "good" utopian, like the unholy ideologist, must settle for considerably less if he is ever to bring his deliberations to a conclusion. And if he eventually does reach a conclusion, then no matter how long he reflects and however precise his calculations, it will have been conceived in sin. For it will always reflect a radical simplification of the possibilities and the alternatives which a more scrupulous utopian would think it obligatory to consider.

But Bell's advocacy of even his "good" utopias is, at best, half-hearted. For he really has no faith in any long-range scheme aimed at the amelioration of society as a whole. "Ideology," he tells us, "makes it unnecessary for people to confront individual issues on their individual merits." But in one sense this is true of any rule, any procedure, and any plan, including the plans of piecemeal social engineers like Bell and Popper. What would be the point of any such scheme, however limited in its scope, unless it relieved us of the necessity of confronting every blessed individual issue on its (otherwise) individual merits? And if it comes to that, what is an "individual issue," and what is it to confront one on its "individual merits"? Is the issue of desegregation, for example, one such issue or is it many? Indeed, is the issue of desegregating one individual classroom in one individual school in one God-forsaken county of the state of Mississippi an individual issue? And if it is, what, pray, are *its* individual merits? How far to these extend?

One of the overwhelming advantages of a bill of human rights (which is nothing but a schedule of enforced ideological commitments) is that it drastically reduces the number of "issues" over which men in societies must continue to quarrel. In this way it reduces the terrible wear and tear of political life which, even in the best-run societies, is nearly unendurable. Bell and his allies, following Popper (and at a distance Bergson), are admirers of the "open society." But of course a completely open society, if such ever existed, would not be a society, but a chaos. If an "open society" is one in which each individual issue is decided, *ad hoc,* on its own peculiar merits, then who wants an "open society"? And if a "closed society" is one in which, owing to the presence of a prevailing ideology (or constitution), many issues are, in any practical sense, dead issues, why then let us by all means continue to have a closed society. Were we Americans seriously to invoke the principle that individual cases should be settled exclusively on their (otherwise) individual merits, we would have to repudiate our Declaration of Independence and to dismantle our whole constitutional system and the characteristic rule of law which it provides.

Is this what the anti-ideologists want? The question is by no means merely "rhetorical." Consider, for example, what that most determined and most consistent of anti-ideologists, Professor Michael Oakeshott, has to say about the Declaration of Independence. It is, he tells us, "A characteristic product of the *saeculum rationalisticum*. It represents the politics of the felt need interpreted with the aid of an ideology. And it is not surprising that it should have become one of the sacred documents of the politics of Rationalism, and, together with the similar documents of the

French Revolution, the inspiration and pattern of many later adventures in the rationalistic reconstruction of Society." Whatever else may be true of Professor Oakeshott, he at least knows an ideology when he sees one and is candid enough to say so. It would clear the air if his fellow anti-ideologists on this side of the Atlantic would speak as clearly and unequivocally.

Let us no longer mince words. Our own anti-ideological foxes are no more "empirical" and no less rhetorical than their leonine opponents; they are, on broad issues, merely more indecisive and more eclectic. As it stands, their point of view is so lacking both in consistency and in clarity that, as I have discovered at some cost, it is virtually impossible to argue with them without fear of doing them some frightful injustice. Still, out of a sophisticated but paralyzing fear of over-simplification, they have managed to fashion a kind of counter-ideology, or fetish, of complexity, difficulty, and uniqueness. They tell us that "the present belongs to the living" and that we should lift from our shoulders "the heavy hand of the future" as well as "the dead hand of the past." Yet they evidently have not the courage to say that the preamble to the American Constitution, which speaks among other things of securing the "Blessings of Liberty to ourselves *and our Posterity,"* is so much wicked ideological flourish and moonshine. Their "pluralism" has become a kind of mania which, when pressed to its own counter-ideological extremes, leads inescapably (as William James long ago perceived) to anarchism and, at last, to nihilism. Were their political and social attitudes generally to prevail in the West—and it is primarily of the West that they speak in talking of the end of ideology—the result would be a pessimistic *carpe diem* philosophy which would render us helpless in the world struggle against the ideology of Communism. At home, in the political parties, in the Congress, and in the courts, it continually weakens what remains of our national commitment to the ideological principles that animate our constitutional system; in the Presidency, it provides merely the covering excuses for a spate of uncorrelated, "piecemeal" moves which, however admirable from a tactical point of view and however skillful as "pragmatic" politics, result in an ever increasing loss of basic political control and social direction. Curiously, the over-all picture is one of Hegelian "gray on gray." The only difference is that unlike our anti-ideologists Hegel knew that gray on gray is the color of barrenness, of late autumn and approaching winter.

November 1964

Leslie H. Farber

"I'M SORRY, DEAR"

And the eyes of them both were opened, and they knew that they were naked; and they sewed fig leaves together, and made themselves aprons.

GENESIS

Lust is more abstract than logic; it seeks (hope triumphing over experience) for some purely sexual, hence purely imaginary, conjunction of an impossible maleness with an impossible femaleness.

C. S. LEWIS

The modern dialogue which furnishes me my title is practiced throughout the Western world. As a theme with only a limited number of variations, it cannot sustain much repetition: familiarity breeds silence; although never really abandoned, the script quickly becomes implicit. When reduced to a dumb show—or perhaps no more than a monosyllabic token—it still remains faithful to its pathetic premise. However, for the purposes of introduction I shall try to represent its essence in a wholly explicit manner. The man speaks first.

"Did you?"

"Did *you?* You *did,* didn't you?"

"Yes, I'm afraid I—Oh, I'm sorry! I *am* sorry. I know how it makes you feel."

"Oh, don't worry about it. I'm sure I'll quiet down after a while."

"I'm *so* sorry, dearest. Let me help you."

"I'd rather you didn't."

"But, I . . ."

"What good is it when you're just—when you don't really want to? You know perfectly well, if you don't *really* want to, it doesn't work."

"But I *do really* want to! I *want* to! Believe me. It *will* work, you'll see. Only let me!"

"Please, couldn't we just forget it? For now the thing is done, finished. Besides, it's not really that important. My tension always wears off eventually. And anyhow—maybe next time it'll be different."

"Oh, it *will,* I *know* it will. Next time I won't be so tired or so eager. I'll make sure of that. Next time it's going to be *fine!* . . . But about tonight—I'm sorry, dear."

Unhappily, no end to talking and trying for our pathetic lovers. To deaden self-consciousness they may turn to alcohol or sedatives, seeking the animal indifference that is unencumbered with hesitations, reservations, grievances—in short, all those human tangles that create the sexual abyss they will themselves to bridge. To delay his moment, to quicken hers, they may try to assist the chemicals by thinking of other matters—football games and cocktail parties—in order finally to arrive at that mutual consummation which, hopefully, will prove their sufficiency unto each other, if not their love. All the strategies and prescriptions of sexology that have often failed them in the past are not cast aside but stubbornly returned to, if only because in such an impasse there is nothing else. Instead of alcohol or drugs or irrelevant reveries they may—in solitude or mutuality—resort to sex itself as their sedative, intending the first try to spend their energies just enough to dull self-consciousness and thicken their passion to the "spontaneity" necessary for their second and final attempt. Although normally truthful people, our lovers are continually tempted by deception and simulation: he may try to conceal his moment, she to simulate hers—as they stalk their equalitarian ideal. It can happen that they will achieve simultaneity by means of one or several or none of these devices. But their success—in the midst of their congratulations—will be as dispiriting as their failures. For one thing the joy the lovers sought in this manner will be either absent or too fictitious to be believed. Furthermore, once the moment has subsided they must reckon with the extraordinary efforts that brought it about—efforts that appear too extraordinary for ordinary day-to-day existence. Thus does it happen that success may bring as much as or more pathos than failure. And always lying between them will be the premise borrowed from romanticism: if they *really* loved each other it would work. Small wonder, then, as self-pity and bitterness accumulate, that their musings—if not their actions—turn to adultery: a heightened situation which promises freedom from the impingements of ordinary sexual life. Or, pushed gradually past heightening, past hope, they may even come to abstinence, which can seem—with some irony—the least dishonorable course.

My conviction is that over the last fifty years sex has for the most part lost its viability as a human experience. I do not mean there is any danger it will cease to be practiced—that it will be put aside like other Victorian bric-a-brac. The hunger will remain, perhaps even increase, and human beings will continue to couple with as much fervor as they can provoke, all the while that the human possibilities of sex will grow ever more elusive. Such couplings will be poultices after the fact: they will further extend the degradation of sex that has resulted from its ever-increasing bondage to the modern will. To those first pioneers at the turn of the century—sexologists, psychoanalysts, political champions of woman's suffrage—"sexual emancipation" seemed a stirring and optimistic cause. Who could have imagined then, as the battle was just beginning, how ironic victory would be: sex was emancipated, true, but emancipated from all of life—except the will—and subsequently exalted as the measure of existence.

At this point I think it only fair that I commit myself, even if briefly, on how sex was, is, or could be a viable human experience. My view is not that of St. Augustine—that man, by reason of the Fall, is necessarily subject to the lust of concupiscence. Nor can I subscribe, at the other extreme, to the position of the Church of England, as reported at the Lambeth Conference in 1958: "The new freedom of sexuality in our time is . . . a gate to a new depth and joy in personal relationship between husband and wife." Of the erotic life Martin Buber has remarked that in no other realm are dialogue and monologue so mingled and opposed. I would agree that any attempt to offer a normative description would have to include precisely such mingling and opposition. Even if we place it optimally within an ongoing domestic world of affection, in which sex bears some relation, however slight, to procreation, our task is still the difficult one of maintaining that sex is both utterly important and utterly trivial. Sex may be a hallowing and renewing experience, but more often it will be distracting, coercive, playful, frivolous, discouraging, dutiful, even boring. On the one hand it tempts man to omnipotence, while on the other it roughly reminds him of his mortality. Over and over again it mocks rationality, only to be mocked in turn at the very instant it insists its domain is solely within the senses. Though it promises the suspension of time, no other event so sharply advises us of the oppressiveness of time. Sex offers itself as an alternative world, but when the act is over and the immodesty of this offering is exposed, it is the sheer worldliness of the world we briefly relinquished and must now re-enter that has to be confronted anew. Residing no longer in the same room which first enclosed us, we now lie in another room with another topography—a room whose surfaces, textures, corners, knobs have an otherness as absolute and formidable as the duties and promises which nag us with their temporal claims. What began as relief from worldly concern ends by returning us to the world with a metaphysical, if unsettling, clarity.

Though sex often seems to be morality's adversary, it more often brings sharply in its wake moral discriminations that previously had not been possible. Because the pleasure of sex is always vulnerable to splitting into *pleasuring* and *being pleasured,* the nature of pleasure itself, as well as the relation between pleasure and power, are called into question. If pleasuring is the overpowering concern, intimations of the actual and immediate experience of slavery or peonage will appear. On the other hand, if being pleasured is most compelling, tyranny and oppression will invade experience with some urgency. And finally, should the lovers will equality between these two concerns, in their effort to heal the split, they will personally suffer the problematic character of democratic forms. To some extent our political past influences our sexual negotiations, but in equal measure sexual pleasure itself is a source of political practice and theory.

The list of oppositions and minglings could easily be extended, but such an extension would not change the fact that human sex inevitably partakes of human experience, for better or for worse, and through its claim on the body simultaneously asserts its particular difference, for better or for worse.

Its particular difference from everything else in this life lies in the possibility which sex offers man for regaining *his own* body through knowing the body of his loved one. And should he fail that *knowing* and *being known,* should he lapse into all those ways of *knowing about* which he has proudly learned to confuse with knowing—both bodies will again escape him. Increasingly, as D. H. Lawrence understood, man has become separated from his body, which he yearns to inhabit, such yearning understandably bringing sentimental and scientific prescriptions for the reunion eluding him. Yet it is through the brief reconciliation with his own and his loved one's body that he can now grasp—and endure—the bodily estrangement which has always been his lot, without succumbing to the blandishments that would betray the realities of both sides of this duality.

In order to develop more concretely my conviction that sex for the most part has lost its viability as a human experience, I wish to consider the Sex Research Project, directed by Dr. William H. Masters at the Washington University School of Medicine. Through the use of women volunteers Dr. Masters is endeavoring "to separate a few basic anatomic and physiologic truths" about "the human female's response" to what he calls "effective sexual stimulation." The subject, he believes, has been hopelessly beclouded by "literary fiction and fantasy," "pseudoscientific essays and pronouncements," and "an unbelievable hodgepodge of conjecture and falsehood." His debt to Kinsey is clear, though qualified. He acknowledges his "complete awe" for Kinsey's "time-consuming efforts" which have made his own research not only "plausible, but possible." On the other hand, he finds that the work of his predecessors, including Kinsey, has unfortunately been "the result of individual introspection, expressed personal opinion, or of limited clinical observation"—rather than "a basic science approach to the sexual response cycle." * Therefore, he has done what was indeed inevitable: he has moved the whole investigation into the laboratory.

I should make clear that Dr. Masters' project itself interests me far more than his exact findings. This project strikes me as one of those occasional yet remarkable enterprises which, despite its creator's intentions, quite transcends its original and modest scientific boundaries, so that it becomes a vivid allegory of our present dilemma, containing its own image of man—at the same time that it charts a New Jerusalem for our future. Such an enterprise, when constitutive, is apt to be more relevant and revealing than deliberate art. Because no actual artist is involved, it is not particularly rewarding to ask how this matter acquires its revelatory, even poetic, power. Often its director merely pursues the prevailing inclination in his field. Yet the pursuit is so single-minded, so fanatical and literal, that part of the power of the enterprise as constitutive symbol must be credited to the director's unflagging lack of imagination and his passionate naïveté, which stay undeterred by all the proprieties, traditions, and accumulated wisdom that would only complicate his course.

I shall not linger over the anatomical and physiological detail in Dr. Masters' reports, except to say it concerns the changes observed on the various parts of the bodies of his volunteers as they approach, accomplish, and depart from sexual climax. Of all the mechanical, electrical, and electronic devices at his command in this research, it is movie-making which seems to give Dr. Masters the clearest edge over the subjective distortions of his predecessors:

> Since the integrity of human observation of specific detail varies significantly, regardless of the observer's training or good intent, colored motion-picture photography has been used to record in absolute detail all phases of the human sexual response cycle.

This movie is often referred to in Dr. Masters' writing and, I am told, has been exhibited at a number of scientific institutes throughout the country. So fond is he of this medium that there seem to be occasions when his scientific prose seeks, however incompletely, to emulate not only the objectivity but the aesthetic brilliance of his movie sequences:

* These and all subsequent quotations are from Dr. Masters' article, "The Sexual Response Cycle of the Human Female" (*Western Journal of Surgery, Obstetrics, and Gynecology,* January-February 1960).

> If the bright pink of the excitement phase changes to a brilliant primiparous scarlet-red, or the multiparous burgundy color, a satisfactory plateau phase has been achieved.

There is even a point at which the movie medium itself becomes the inventor: like the accidental solution or the contaminated culture, which have heroic roles in older scientific romances, movie-making allows Dr. Masters to uncover "the vascular flush reaction to effective sexual stimulation" which had not been previously described in the scientific literature.

> With the aid of artificially-increased skin surface temperature, such as that necessary for successful motion-picture photography, the wide distribution of this flush becomes quite apparent. . . . With orgasm imminent, this measle-like rash has been observed to spread over the anterior-lateral borders of the thighs, the buttocks and the whole body.

Probably it was this discovery of the "measle-like rash" which inspired a more Pavlovian venture which, if read slowly, will be seen to have quite eerie dimensions:

> One observed subject, undergoing electroencephalographic evaluation, has been trained for 4 months to attain orgasm without producing concomitant muscle tension in order to provide significance for her tracing pattern. Yet, this patient repeatedly showed a marked flush phenomenon over the entire body during plateau and orgasm, and during resolution was completely covered with a filmy, fine perspiration.

If movie-making is Dr. Masters' main laboratory device, "automanipulative technics" constitute his "fundamental investigative approach" to "the sexual response cycle of the human female." His frankness here is to be commended—particularly since some scientists might feel that such automanipulation was inadequate to the verisimilitude necessary for laboratory demonstration. Dr. Masters himself does not discuss the issue, but his obvious preference for this approach over "heterosexual activity" does not appear to be ascribable to decorum. To some degree, I imagine, it was the laboratory procedures and devices—particularly motion picture photography—which determined the approach, automanipulation being clearly more accessible to scientific inspection than coition. But more important, there is evidence that Dr. Masters regards automanipulation to be a more reliable—that is, more predictable—technique than "heterosexual activity" in the pursuit of "the more intense, well-developed, orgasmic response" cycle.

> This type of total pelvic reaction is particularly true for an orgasmic phase elicited by manual manipulation, but it also occurs, although less frequently, with coition.

Little is told us about the volunteers in this research. Apparently the project began with prostitutes. But when objections were made that such a profession might not yield the best "normal" sample, subjects were chosen among medical students and medical students' wives who volunteered and were paid a modest fee for their activities. Naturally no studies could be made on those who, for whatever reason, would not volunteer. And presumably quickly eliminated were those young women who offered themselves out of their enthusiastic wish to contribute to science, only to discover they could not sustain their sexual excitement in the setting of the laboratory, the paraphernalia, the cameras, the technicians, the bright lights. And even more quickly eliminated were those women who on initial interview were not sure whether or not they had climax: "Our rule of thumb is if they're not sure about it they probably haven't had it."

Other circumstances surrounding the study can only be guessed at. Like much scientific research, this particular project must have been an orderly affair. It can be assumed that the investigators did not wait on the whim of their volunteers; that is, they were not subject to call day or night whenever the volunteer felt in the mood. No, the women were given regular appointments during the working day when the entire research crew was available. Doubtless, too, the directors of the project considered it scientifically unseemly to encourage sexual titillation in their volunteers—certainly out of the question would have been anything resembling a physical overture. Should suggestive reading matter be required by the research—as it indeed occasionally was—it would have to be offered the volunteers in a spirit of detachment; not even the hint of a smirk could be allowed to disrupt the sobriety of the occasion. On the whole, the erotic basis would have to be provided by the scientific situation itself, in addition to the actual manipulation: that is, the prospect of arriving at the laboratory at 10:00 A.M., disrobing, stretching out on the table, and going to work in a somewhat businesslike manner while being measured and photographed, would have to provide its own peculiar excitement. (Thank you, Miss Brown, see you same time next week. Stop at the cashier's for your fee.) So, back to one's ordinary existence.

If these speculations have any truth, what can be said about the qualities that the ideal subject for such experiments would have? In a general way, her sexuality would have to be autonomous, separate from and unaffected by her ordinary world. "World" here would have to include not only affection but all those exigencies of human existence which tend to shape our erotic possibilities. Objectively, her sexuality would be mechanically accessible or "on call"—under circumstances which would be, if not intimidating, at least distracting to most bodies. Hers would have to be indifferent to the entire range of experiences, pleasant and unpleasant, whose claim is not only not salacious but makes us forget there is such a thing as sexuality. Her lust would lie to hand, ready to be invoked and consummated, in sickness or in health, in coitus or "automanipulation," in homosexuality or heterosexuality, in exasperation or calm, hesitancy or certainty, playfulness or despair. (This would be the other side of that older, though not unrelated romanticism which just as willfully insisted on soft lights, Brahms, incense, and poetical talk.) In other words, her sexuality would be wholly subject to her will: whenever she determined—or the project determined—that she should have reached a climax, she would willingly begin those gestures that would lead to one. To use the modern idiom, all that would be unavailable to her sexological dexterity would be frigidity. Or, to speak more clearly, all that would be unavailable to her would be a real response to the laboratory situation. Insofar as her sexuality was under her will's dominion, she would resemble those odd creatures on the old television quiz programs—also ideal subjects in their own way —who were led from boarding houses to stand in a hot soundproof isolation booth, and when the fateful question was delivered from the vault, answered correctly and without a tremor how many words there were in *Moby Dick*—answered correctly in a loud clear voice under circumstances in which most of us could not even mumble our name. The popularity of these programs (at least until skull-duggery was revealed) suggests the audience looked with envy and/or admiration at this caricature of knowledge—a knowledge equally responsive to its owner's will, regardless of contingency or trapping.

A truly constitutive symbol should embody both an accurate rendering of contemporary life and a clear indication of what that life should be. Taking, for the moment, only the ideal contained in my description of the volunteer in these experiments, I would say that she is a latterday Queen of Courtly Love, a veritable Queen Guinevere. For most modern men and women, who grow ever more discouraged by their bodies' stubborn refusal to obey their owners' will, this Lady of the Laboratory has long been the woman of their dreams: men long to channel or claim this creature's prompt and unspecific response for their own specific overtures, while women dream of rivaling her capacity to serve her body's need whenever she so wills.

And what of those self-effacing scientists behind the camera who conceived and guided this research? Do they too reflect who we are and who we would become? We know as little about this research team as we know about the volunteers. How the scientific boundaries were staked out and protected against trespass is not described in the reports. Once again we can only surmise, but that there was difficulty is suggested by a remark Dr. Masters made in one of his lectures—namely, that he preferred to have a woman scientist alongside him in these investigations because she helped to make him or keep him more "objective." I assume he meant that having an actual woman present, fully clad in the white coat of science, reminded him not only of the point of the matter at hand but of the more hazardous life to be lived with women outside the laboratory—of the difference between the ideal and the actual. It would be a ticklish problem how to maintain the proper detachment to protect the scientists without at the same time inhibiting the volunteers. Here the equipment and rituals of research would help. And very possibly there would be a deliberate effort to eliminate even the ordinary frivolity that sometimes overcomes a surgical team in the midst of the most delicate operation, because frivolity in this sort of research might be only a way-station en route to the lubricious. Any falling-away into the most ordinary locker-room talk, in or out of the laboratory, would have to be regarded as a danger signal. I imagine each scientist, with all the resolution at his command, would remind himself continually it was just an ordinary day's work in the laboratory, no different from the work next door with the diabetic rats. At the end of the day, when his wife asked, "How were things at the lab today?" he would reply, "Oh nothing, just the same old grind." And if she pressed him in a jealous fashion, his justifications might resemble those of a young artist explaining his necessity to sketch nude models. Of course, there would be strict rules forbidding dalliance between scientist and volunteer after hours. But should they happen to run into one another in the cafeteria, each would keep his conversation casual, trying not to allude to those more cataclysmic events of a few hours before. Mindful of his professional integrity, the scientist would have to guard against prideful thoughts that he knew her, if not better, at least more microscopically than those nearest her. Most troublesome of his self-appointed tasks, it seems to me, would be his effort to prevent his research from invading his own ordinary erotic life, particularly if it were worried by the usual frustrations. In this regard he would be indeed heroic to withstand the temptation of comparing his mate's response to those unspecific, yet perfectly formed, consummations of the laboratory.

Again, if these imaginings have any truth, how may we characterize the ideal scientist in research of this immediate order? First of all, he would have to *believe,* far more than the volunteers, in a "basic science" approach to sex. This is not to say that he would consider the practice of sex a possible science, even though his practice might eventually be informed by his scientific theories. But it would have to be an article of faith for him that the visible palpable reactions of the organs themselves, regardless of whatever human or inhuman context they might occur in, would speak a clear unambiguous truth to all who cared to heed. In his hierarchy of beliefs, these reactions would take precedence in every sense. The questions we are apt to ask about human affairs, not excluding lust, ordinarily have to do with appropriateness, affection, etc.—in other words, right or wrong, good or bad, judged in human terms. On the other hand, the ideal Sexologist, as he presses his eye to his research, finds another variety of drama—inordinately complicated in its comings and goings, crises and resolutions—with its own requirements of right and wrong, good and bad, all writ very small in terms of "droplets" and "engorgements" and "contractions."

The will of the ideal Sexologist seems different from the will of the Lady of the Laboratory, but it may be the opposition is more illusory than actual. The latter wills orgasm through physical manipulation. Certainly the sexologist supports and approves her willing, such sexual promptness being ideal for laboratory study. However, while his approval may be invented by his will, it is by no means the most important expression of his will. As a scientist his will must be given to the systematic inspection of the sexual response of the "human female," literally portrayed. To this end he persists in his gadgetry, always at the expense of any imaginative grasp of the occasion. His will to be a scientist requires his further commitment to any number of willful enterprises; in the present circumstance he finds it necessary to will his own body to be unresponsive—not merely to the events on the laboratory table but to any fictional construction of these events his imagination might contrive, because imagination, at least in this arena, is his opponent in his pursuit of science. On the surface his dilemma may seem a familiar one, being comparable to older ascetic ventures, particularly of the Eastern yoga variety. But the sexologist's task is actually more difficult: asceticism is not his goal—the very nature of his enterprise points in an opposite direction. He wishes indifference which he can invoke at will: it may be the project which demands his not responding, but—as we shall see later—it may be other moments, unofficial and unscientific, which seem to call forth his willed lack of response. The will not to respond and the will to respond are related possibilities of the will. In this sense, the Lady of the Laboratory and the ideal Sexologist are collaborators rather than opponents. Of course, I speak in ideal terms—whether these ideals can be achieved is another matter. But if the Lady of the Laboratory is a latter day Queen of Courtly Love, then our ideal Sexologist is the modern Sir Galahad, and together—separately or commingled—they rule our dreams of what should be.

Let us remind ourselves that most of us could not hope to qualify for this research—either as volunteers or as scientists. But this does not mean the differences are great between us and them. True, compared to ours, their lives have an oversized quality, and true, they are in the vanguard.

But in a real sense our fleshly home is that laboratory. Whatever room we choose for our lovemaking we shall make into our own poor laboratory, and nothing that is observed or undergone in the real laboratory of science is likely to escape us. At this stage, is there any bit of sexology that is not in the public domain, or at least potentially so for those who can read? Whatever detail the scientific will appropriates about sex rapidly becomes an injunction to be imposed on our bodies. But it is not long before these impositions lose their arbitrary and alien character and begin to change our actual experience of our bodies. Unfortunately our vision of the ideal experience tends to be crudely derived from the failure of our bodies to meet these imperatives.

Our residence in the laboratory is recent: really only since the turn of the century has the act of sex been interviewed, witnessed, probed, measured, timed, taped, photographed, judged. Before the age of sexology, objectifications of the sexual act were to be found in pornography and the brothel, both illicit, both pleasurable in purpose, both suggesting the relatively limited manner in which will—given absolute dominion—could be joined to sexual pleasure. However else the Marquis de Sade may be read, he at least offered the most exhaustive inventory yet seen of techniques for exploiting the pleasure of the body's several parts, if one wholeheartedly put one's will to it. As a moralist he seemed to say, Why our particular rules? What if there were no limits? More recently, yet still before sexology, it was possible for shy erotomaniacs, disguised as greengrocers, to visit brothels, there to peek at the antics of the inmates. The bolder ones could join the sport. When the performance reached its final gasp our tradesmen, now satiated, would slink back to the propriety and privacy of their own quarters, convinced their ordinary domestic world was discreetly separate from the world of the peephole which they paid to enter. In fact, or so it seemed, the separateness of these two worlds heightened the erotic possibilities of each. The emancipation which sexology enforced gradually blurred this distinction, making it unclear whether each home had become its own brothel or whether every brothel had become more like home. The truth is that sexology eventually not only blurred the distinction, but by housing us all in laboratories, made both the brothel and pornography less exciting dwellings for our erotic investigations.

When last we left our pathetic lovers I suggested that as their self-pity and bitterness mounted, they might—in desperation—turn to adultery. Yet even for the person who believes himself to be without scruples, adultery—in fact or fantasy—is difficult to arrange, exhausting to maintain. Requiring, as it does, at least two persons and two wills, this illicit encounter risks the danger of further pathos. But if we heed our laboratory drama carefully, we can see there is another possibility preferable to adultery. According to the lesson of the laboratory there is only one perfect orgasm, if by "perfect" we mean one wholly subject to its owner's will, wholly indifferent to human contingency or context. Clearly, the perfect orgasm is the orgasm achieved on one's own. No other consummation offers such certainty and moreover avoids the messiness that attends most human affairs. The onanist may choose the partner of his dreams who very probably will be the Lady of the Laboratory, or he may have his orgasm without any imagined partner. In either case, he is both scientist and experimental subject, science and sex now being nicely joined. In his laboratory room he may now abstract his sexual parts from his whole person, inspect their anatomic particularities, and observe and enjoy the small physiologic events he knows best how to control. True, this solitary experience may leave him empty and ashamed. But as a citizen of his times he will try to counter this discomfort by reminding himself that sexology and psychoanalysis have assured him masturbation is a morally indifferent matter. As a true modern he tells himself that it is not as good as what two people have, but that does not make it bad. Superstitious people of other ages thought it drove one crazy, but he knows better; he knows that the real threat to *his* sanity is unrelieved sexual tension. In fact—he may decide—were it not for certain neurotic Victorian traces he has not managed to expunge from his psyche, he could treat the matter as any other bodily event and get on with his business. So we must not be too harsh with our pathetic lovers if they take refuge in solitary pleasures—even if they come to prefer them to the frustrations of sexual life together. Nor should we be too surprised if such solitary pleasure becomes the ideal by which all mutual sex is measured—and found wanting.

Let us now turn to the phenomenon being inspected and celebrated in our laboratory—the phenomenon which contributes most of all to our lovers' impasse. Of all the discoveries sexology has made, the female orgasm remains the most imposing in its consequences. De Tocqueville's prediction of life between the sexes in America* might not have been so sanguine, could he have anticipated first, the discovery of sexology and psychoanalysis, and second, their discovery of the female orgasm.

In the second half of the 19th century Western man began to see nature in a new and utilitarian way as a variety of energies, hitherto unharnessed, which could now be tamed and transformed into industrial servants which in turn would fashion never-ending progress and prosperity.

* ". . . I never observed that the women of America consider conjugal authority as an unfortunate usurpation of their rights, or that they thought themselves degraded by submitting to it. It appeared to me, on the contrary, that they attach a sort of pride to the voluntary surrender of their will. . . . Though their lot is different, they consider both of them as beings of equal value. . . . If I were asked . . . to what the singular prosperity and growing strength of that people ought mainly to be attributed, I should reply: To the superiority of their women." Alexis de Tocqueville, *Democracy in America.*

The health of the machine, powered by steam and electricity, and the sickness of the machine if those energies were misdirected or obstructed, were obsessive considerations of the period. It was entirely appropriate to regard the human body as still another natural object with many of the vicissitudes of the machine: this had always been medicine's privilege. But for the first time the scientists, in their intoxication, could forget the duality previous centuries knew: namely, that the body is both a natural object and not a natural object. And once it was decided the dominant energy of the human machine was sex, the new science of sexology was born. With the suppression of the second half of the dialectic, sexology and psychoanalysis could—with the assistance of the Romantics—claim the erotic life as their exclusive province, removing it from all the traditional disciplines, such as religion, philosophy, literature, which had always concerned themselves with sex as human experience. Qualities such as modesty, privacy, reticence, abstinence, chastity, fidelity, shame—could now be questioned as rather arbitrary matters which interfered with the health of the sexual parts. And in their place came an increasing assortment of objective terms like *ejaculatio praecox,* foreplay, forepleasure, frigidity—all intended to describe, not human experience, but the behavior of the sexual parts. The quite preposterous situation arose in which the patient sought treatment for *ejaculatio praecox* or impotence and the healer sought to find out whether he liked his partner.

If the Victorians found sex unspeakable for the wrong reasons, the Victorian sexologists found it wrongly speakable. (To what extent Victorian prudery was actually modesty or reticence, I cannot say. It has become habitual for us to regard Victorian lovemaking as an obscenity.) Science is usually democratic, and since sex now belonged to science, whatever facts or assumptions were assembled had immediately to be transmitted to the people, there to invade their daily life. Writing of the Kinsey Report, Lionel Trilling finds—correctly, I believe—a democratic motive for the study:

> In speaking of its motives, I have in mind chiefly its impulse toward acceptance and liberation, its broad and generous desire for others that they be not harshly judged. . . . The Report has the intention of habituating its readers to sexuality in all its manifestations; it wants to establish, as it were, a democratic pluralism of sexuality. . . . This generosity of mind . . . goes with a nearly conscious aversion from making intellectual distinctions, almost as if out of the belief that an intellectual distinction must inevitably lead to a social discrimination or exclusion.

If we disregard Kinsey's scientific pretensions, we still must recognize his eminence as arbiter of sexual etiquette. Like the lexicographer who finds his sanction in usage, Kinsey discovers his authority in practice: his democratic message is that we all do—or should do—more or less the same things in bed. And any notion lovers retain from an older tradition that what they have together is private and unique is effectively disproved by his cataloguing of sexual manners, providing they join him in equating behavior with experience. As a fitting disciple of Kinsey, Masters actualizes the "pluralism of sexuality" within the democratic unit of the laboratory and enlarges behavior to include the more minute physiological developments which, too, should belong to every citizen.

The political clamor for equal rights for women at the turn of the century could not fail to join with sexology to endow her with an orgasm, equal in every sense to the male orgasm. It was agreed that she was entitled to it just as she was entitled to the vote. Moreover, if she were deprived of such release her perturbation would be as unsettling to her nervous system as similar frustration was thought to be for the man. Equal rights were to be erotically consummated in simultaneous orgasm. On the one hand it was unhealthful for her to be deprived of release and, on the other hand, psychoanalysis decreed that an important sign of her maturity as woman was her ability to achieve it. In other words, without orgasm she was neurotic to begin with or neurotic to end with.

Though simultaneous orgasm seemed to be a necessary consequence of equal rights, the problem remained that in matters of lust more than a decree or amendment was required for such an achievement. True, the sexologists were most generous with instruction, but each citizen has had to discover over and over again the degree to which he is caught in the futile struggle to will what could not be willed—at the same time that he senses the real absurdity of the whole willful enterprise. The lover learns, as his indoctrination progresses, to observe uneasily and even resist his rush of pleasure if it seems he is to be premature. When no amount of resolution can force his pleasure to recede, he learns to suffer his release and then quickly prod himself to an activity his body's exhaustion opposes. In other words, he learns to take his moment in stride, so to speak, omitting the deference these moments usually call forth and then without breaking stride get to his self-appointed and often fatiguing task of tinkering with his mate—always hopeful that his ministrations will have the appearance of affection. While she is not likely to be deceived by such dutiful exercises, she neverthelesses wishes for both their sakes that her body at least will be deluded into fulfilling its franchise.

As far as I know, little attention was paid to the female orgasm before the era of sexology. Where did the sexologists find it? Did they discover it or invent it? Or both? I realize it may seem absurd to raise such questions about events as unmistakable as those witnessed in our laboratory. But I cannot believe that previous centuries were not up to our modern delights;

nor can I believe it was the censorship imposed by religion which suppressed the supreme importance of the female orgasm. My guess, which is not subject to laboratory proof, is that the female orgasm was always an occasional, though not essential, part of woman's whole sexual experience. I also suspect that it appeared with regularity or predictability only during masturbation when the more human qualities of her life with her mate were absent. Further, her perturbation was unremarkable and certainly bearable when orgasm did not arrive, for our lovers had not yet been enlightened as to the disturbances resulting from the obstruction or distortion of sexual energies. At this stage her orgasm had not yet been abstracted and isolated from the totality of her pleasures, and enshrined as the meaning and measure of her erotic life. She was content with the mystery and variety of her difference from man, and in fact would not have had it otherwise. Much that I have said, if we leave aside the erotomanias which have always been with us, applies to the male of previous centuries. For him, too, the moment of orgasm was not abstracted in its objective form from the whole of his erotic life and then idealized. And he too preferred the mystery of difference, the impact of human contingency, becoming obsessed with the sheer anatomy and mechanics of orgasm only when all else was missing, as in masturbation.

Theological parallelism is a treacherous hobby, especially when we deal with movements flagrantly secular. Nevertheless, the manner in which lovers now pursue their careers as copulating mammals—adopting whatever new refinements sexology devises, covering their faces yet exposing their genitals—may remind us of older heresies which, through chastity or libertinism, have pressed toward similar goals; one heretical cult went so far as to worship the serpent in the Garden of Eden. But the difference between these older heresies and modern science—and there is a large one—must be attributed to the nature of science itself, which—if we accept such evidence as the Lambeth Conference—by means of its claims to objectivity can invade religion and ultimately all of life to a degree denied the older heresies. So, with the abstraction, objectification, and idealization of the female orgasm we have come to the last and perhaps most important clause of the contract which binds our lovers to their laboratory home, there to will the perfection on earth which cannot be willed, there to suffer the pathos which follows all such strivings toward heaven on earth.

VI
WRITING

February 1948

Edmund Wilson

PAUL ROSENFELD: THREE PHASES

The death of Paul Rosenfeld has left me not only shocked at the unexpected loss of a friend, but with a feeling of dismay and disgust at the waste of talent in the United States. Paul, when I first knew him—in 1922, I think—was one of the most exciting critics of the "American Renaissance." I had read, while in the army in France, an essay on Sibelius in the *New Republic,* which had had upon me the exhilarating effect that wartime reading sometimes does; and later, when I was back in New York, a longer study on Richard Strauss, a great musical hero of the time, which brought into the writing itself something of the Straussian brilliance but probed with a very sure hand what was specious and vulgar in Strauss. It was the first really searching criticism that I had ever seen of this composer, and both these essays amazed me. They had a kind of fullness of tone, a richness of vocabulary and imagery, and a freedom of the cultural world that were quite different from the schoolmasterish criticism which had become the norm in the United States. *Musical Portraits,* in 1920, the first book that collected these pieces, seemed at the time absolutely dazzling. Paul told me, when I knew him later, that the point when he had felt his maturity was the moment when he had realized with pride that he could turn out as good an article as Huneker; but actually he much surpassed Huneker, who, useful though he was in his role, always remained a rather harried journalist, trying to produce a maximum of copy in order to get money to go abroad. Paul was a serious writer who was working from New York as a base. One had always had the impression that Huneker came in through the back door at Scribner's in a day when the arts were compelled to give precedence to money and gentility, and that there had been something in Bernard Shaw's prophecy that, if he stayed in the United States, he would never be anything but a "clever slummocker"; and one now heard depressing reports that he was old, poor and ill in Brooklyn. But Paul Rosenfeld seemed the spirit of a new and more fortunate age, whose cosmopolitanism was not self-conscious and which did not have to be on the defensive for its catholic interest in art and life. The portraits of Paul's first book dramatized modern music as no criticism had done before; they brought into range a whole fascinating world, united though international, of personality, poetics, texture, mood. Paul Rosenfeld at that time enjoyed a prestige of the same kind as Mencken's and Brooks's, though it was not so widely felt as the former's.

He had inherited a comfortable income, and he built himself at Westport, Connecticut, a small and attractive house, where he lived alone with his work and entertained his friends. The first time I ever saw him, I had not yet met him. It was in Paris sometime in the summer of 1921, and I was dining alone one night in a favorite Italian restaurant, very clean and rather austere—I remember it as always quiet and filled with a clear twilight—to which I had been taken first by somebody during the war and to which I liked to return, ordering almost always the same meal that I had had when I went there first: ravioli and Asti Spumante. A party of three sat down at the table just across from mine, and though I had never seen any of them before, I recognized them soon as Paul Rosenfeld, Sherwood Anderson and Anderson's wife, the sculptress, Tennessee Mitchell. I had heard in New York that Paul was taking the Andersons to Europe, where Anderson had never been, and I observed the party with interest and heard snatches of their conversation. Tennessee Mitchell had the aspect and the manner of a raw-boned prairie woman, and I was touched by Paul's obvious effort to approximate for her benefit to a modestly folksy manner. I was reminded of the incident later when I read in Sherwood Anderson's memoirs that he had sat in the Tuileries one day—he is here apostrophizing himself—with "the tears running from your eyes, because you thought everything around you so beautiful." It was all very typical of the period, and so are my first memories of Paul after I got to know him in New York. I spent a weekend with him once at Westport—sometime in 1922—and read him an article I had just written about T. S. Eliot's *Waste Land* on the occasion of its getting the *Dial* prize. In the city I had been leading at that time rather a frenetic life, and I remember what a relief it was to talk about art with Paul in an atmosphere completely free from the messy dissipation and emotion that were characteristic of the twenties, and for once to get a good night's sleep in a house where everything was quiet and simple. I had that night a delightful dream, which still comes back to me quite distinctly, of little figures that were really alive though much less than life-size, dancing with slow grace to an exquisite Mozartian music which filled me with peace and joy. It was an antidote to the stridencies of the jazz age, which Paul's spirit had managed to exorcise. He loathed jazz in all its raw forms and could only accept it transmuted by the style of a Stravinsky or a Copland.

With his fair reddish hair and mustache, his pink cheeks and his limpid brown eyes, his clothes which always followed with dignity the Brooks-cut college model, his presence, short though he was, had a certain authority and distinction. It was something that made Anderson call him the well-dressed man of American prose. He had a knack of turning pretty little speeches and he was also genuinely considerate in a way that was rare in that era, but he could be forthright when the occasion demanded, and, though naturally candid and warm, he would retire—which always amused me—at a suspicion of imposture or imposition, into a skeptical and ironic reserve. He was, I think, the only man I have known of whom it could truly be said that he possessed a Heinesque wit, and I always thought it a pity that his humor, which contributed so much to the pleasure of being with him, should have figured so little in his essays. (Since writing this, however, I have been looking into one of his later books, *An Hour with American Music,* and I see that it is full of *wit.* It was the humor of exaggeration, to which he sometimes gave rein in his talk, that rarely appeared in his work.)

When I got to know Paul better, we sometimes compared notes about our childhood and education. He had gone to school on the Hudson and had afterwards graduated from Yale, and the latter institution, though he seemed to feel a certain respect for it, had rather oppressed him at the time he had been there; but he had been fortunate in being able to escape to spend his summer vacations in Europe. When he had once found out, he told me, that there existed somewhere else an artistic and social and intellectual world larger and more exciting than anything he had known in America, and that he could always go back to it later, he found that he could endure New Haven, to which he was so ill-adapted, without fears of suffocation. He had grown up in uptown New York in a German-Jewish household, and he had never belonged to any church or been trained in any religion; but he had got from his parents a grounding in the classical German culture, musical and literary. When he went to Europe in summer, he loved to visit a German uncle, who was something of a *bon vivant.* His parents had both died when he was young, and his only close relative was a sister. He never married and, so far as I could see, had no real desire to marry, enjoying the bachelor's life which his moderate means made possible.

His strongest tie was undoubtedly with Stieglitz, toward whom he stood in something like a filial relation; and the group around Stieglitz became for him both family and church. The only traditionally and specifically Jewish trait that ever came, in my intercourse with Paul, as something alien that blocked understanding between us was the quality of his piety toward Stieglitz, whom he accepted and revered as a prophet, unquestioningly obedient to his guidance in the spirit that has been sometimes exemplified by the disciples of Freud and Schoenberg; and his range as a writer on the plastic arts was limited by the exclusiveness of his interest in the work of the Stieglitz group. It was difficult, if not impossible, to persuade him to pay attention to any contemporary American painter who was not a protégé of Stieglitz's, and if Stieglitz had excommunicated a refractory or competitive disciple, Paul Rosenfeld, following the official directive, would condemn him, not merely as an artist but as a reprobate who had somehow committed an unpardonable moral treason. He had the tone of the old-fashioned brother whose sister has fallen to shame, or the member of a Communist sect reacting to the name of a heretic.

For the rest, his affectionate and generous nature had to spend itself mainly in the sympathy that he brought to the troubles of his friends and in the tireless encouragement of talent. His judgment here was usually shrewd, his insight often profound; he was tactful and unobtrusive in helping people who needed help, and he did not want thanks in return. His taking the Andersons to Europe is an example that happens to be known of the kind of thing he liked to do, and one has heard of his providing, at a critical time, resources for a now famous composer; but he undoubtedly did more for more people than anyone will ever know. It has remained in my mind that he was present at the deathbed of Randolph Bourne, desperately feeding him with oxygen in the effort to keep him alive. Bourne had been one of the most remarkable of the group that founded the *Seven Arts*. As a hunchback, he was unfit for the services and thus free to repudiate the war as an able-bodied writer could hardly have done so roundly; and the intellectual light and the moral passion, the mastery of self-expression, that led people to forget his deformity as soon as he began to talk, made his friends of that era feel that he was keeping alive spiritual values that might otherwise have gone by the board. "When he died," Paul wrote, "we knew that perhaps the strongest mind of the entire younger generation in America had gone. . . . We see the size of him plainly in the bitter moments in which we realize how vacant the scene has become in the many fields to which he brought the light of his own clear nature!"

II

Paul later sold his house at Westport and took a little corner apartment in an old and elevatorless house on the west side of Irving Place. There, however, he continued to flourish. He liked to give evening parties which were none the less agreeable for their rather old-fashioned character. What was unusual in the dry twenties was that there was very little liquor served: a highball or two or a little punch; and poets read their poetry and composers played their music. One met Ornstein, Milhaud, Varèse; Cummings, Hart Crane, and Marianne Moore; the Stieglitzes and all their group; the Stettheimers, Mumford, Kreymborg. One of the images that remains with me most vividly is the bespectacled figure of Copland, at that period gray-faced and lean, long-nosed and rather unearthly, bending above the keyboard as he chanted in a high, cold and passionate voice a poem of Ezra Pound's—*An Immorality*—for which he had written a setting.

In those days I saw a good deal of Paul in a business as well as in a friendly way, for I was working first on *Vanity Fair,* then on the *New Republic,* and Paul wrote a good deal for both. He grew rather stout at this time, and his style betrayed a tendency toward floridity. He felt afterward, he told me, that his writing, like so many other things during the Boom, had, to its detriment, become somewhat overinflated. My impression is that when people say they do not like Paul Rosenfeld's style, they are thinking of characteristics that only became really rampant in some of his work of this period, and that they have no real acquaintance with his criticism either before or after. As an editor, I had sometimes to struggle with him over the locutions and vocabulary of his essays, and I am fully aware of his faults. He had spent so much time in Europe and he read so much French and German that he could never quite keep his English distinct from his other languages, and habitually wrote *ignore* as if it meant the same thing as *ignorer* and *genial* as if it meant possessing genius. He had also a way of placing adverbs that used to set my teeth on edge, as did some of these adverbs themselves, such as *doubtlessly* and *oftentimes*. There were moments when he *did* overwrite, working himself up into a state of exaltation with romantic Germanic abstractions that sounded a little ridiculous in English. But, going back to his essays today, one is not much bothered by this or even necessarily conscious of it. One finds a body of musical criticism that covers the modern field more completely than one had remembered and that stands up, both as writing and as interpretation, so solidly as to make quite unimportant these minor idiosyncrasies and slips.

There is of course an objection to Paul's writing which is based on disapproval on principle of the romantic and impressionistic school that he enthusiastically represented. In the serious literary journals, a new tone had just been set in the twenties by T. S. Eliot's *The Sacred Wood,* which was spare and terse in style, analytical and logical in treatment. Paul Rosenfeld, who lacked the intellectual instruments for dealing with literary ideas (though he was expert at dealing with musical ones), was somewhat less satisfactory—except when writing of certain kinds of poetry that had something in common with music—on the subject of literature than he was on music and painting; but it was very unjust that this fashion should have prejudiced against him the editors of the kind of magazine on which he most depended for a market. The same tendency appeared in the musical world; and the critics—though less, I think, the composers—complained of his lack of scholarship on the technical side of music. To this a writer who is not a musician can only reply that it seems to him that the moment the critic departs from the technical analysis of a score, he is writing impressionistic criticism; and that Berlioz in his essays on Beethoven's symphonies and Debussy when he is putting on record such an opinion as that Edvard Grieg was a bonbon stuffed with snow are just as much impressionistic critics as Paul Rosenfeld ever was. Berlioz and Debussy, of course, were a great deal more literary and programmatic than the generation of Schoenberg and Stravinsky have liked to be thought to be; but I believe that Paul was right in insisting that every valid work of art owes its power to giving expression to some specific human experience and connecting it with some human ideal. For musicians it must of course be profitable to read the kind of score-by-score study that has been made by Albert Berger, for example, of the development of Aaron Copland; but, as a layman who merely listens to music, I do not see that it is easy to dismiss the interpretations given by Paul of the emotional and social content of the more "abstract" modern composers: Schoenberg and Stravinsky, Bartók and Hindemith. It is just here, where the composer invites it least, that Paul's insight most proves his genius.

All those years we talked much of such matters. The kind of writing I did myself aimed at something rather different from his, and he horrified me once by saying that his idea of good prose was something that was laid on like a thick coat of paint; but we had in common a fundamental attitude and invoked a common cultural tradition, which it is easiest to call humanistic. Among the few things that I really look back upon with anything like nostalgia in the confusion and waste of the twenties are such conversations as those with Paul when we would sit in his corner room, beneath his little collection of Hartleys and O'Keeffes and Marins, surrounded by his shelves full of Nietzsche and Wagner, Strindberg, Shaw and Ibsen, Tolstoy and Dostoevsky, Flaubert, Claudel and Proust, Henry James and Poe, and the English poets that he had read at Yale, or walk back and forth at night between my place and his. He liked New York, was a thorough New Yorker, and—except for a few weeks in the summer, when he would visit the Stieglitzes at Lake George and, as Georgia O'Keeffe once told me, take the same walk every afternoon, or for an occasional out-of-town lecture or concert—he rarely ventured to leave the city. He did visit the Andersons in Virginia, and once got as far as New Mexico—when Georgia O'Keeffe was there—and even saw an Indian corn dance; but it was difficult to make him take an interest in any but the most self-consciously aesthetic aspects of American cultural life. I tried again and again to get him to read such writers as Ring Lardner and Mark Twain, but I never had the least success. When I finally resorted to the device of giving him *Huckleberry Finn* as a Christmas present, he obstinately refused to open it, having learned that Henry James had characterized Mark Twain as a writer for immature minds. I told Paul once later on, when the first liveliness of the twenties was spent, that he would not have lived very differently if he had been the leading music critic of Frankfurt, Dresden or Munich; but he protested at once against this. He could never be so free, he said, in Germany—or anywhere else except New York.

III

The depression was disastrous for Paul. His income dwindled almost to nothing; and he was forced to give up Irving Place, moving first to a small apartment on Eleventh Street just off Fifth Avenue, then later to a much less accessible one in the far reaches of West Eleventh Street. The *Dial* suspended publication in 1929; the *New Republic* was in the hands of an editor of whom it might almost be said, as the Nazis said of themselves, that when he heard the word *culture* he reached for his gun. Paul, for the first time in his life, was obliged to resort to real hackwork: little odd jobs and reviews, for which he was not well paid. He developed diabetes and grew thin; and something, I got the impression, went wrong with his personal affairs—though of this I never heard him speak. The staffs and the principal contributors of the *Dial* and the *New Republic,* both noncommercial affairs financed by rich patrons, had been groups of serious writers who had had lunches and dinners together, where plans and current events were discussed, and who had been part of Paul's social life as well as a stimulus to his work. But now, when endowments were drying up, there was a movement toward the political Left, and such groupings and common undertakings as the New York "intellectuals" (so called now rather than "writers" or "artists") continued to go in for in the thirties, were mostly oriented in the direction of Communism. Paul intensely disliked all this, and though one of the great merits of his criticism had been its sure sense of musical personalities as the reflections of their national and social backgrounds, he would indignantly deny at this time that art had anything to do with history. When I argued such questions with him, I found that "the Artist" meant for him a being unique and god-like, and that Paul would not admit for a minute that a philosopher or a scientist or a statesman could achieve an equal creative importance. On one occasion he was somehow persuaded to attend an election rally held by the Communists in Cooper Union, at which there were to be speeches by writers who had announced that they would vote for the Communists and who paid their homage to Communism as a literary restorative and bracer in the vein of the new convert to evangelism or the patent medicine testimonial; but, seated in a conspicuous place in one of the front rows, he attracted unfavorable attention by pointedly refusing to rise when the *International* was sung.

I was deep in Left activities myself, but I always continued to see him and occasionally went to concerts with him. If you dined with him in his apartment, he cooked and served the dinner; and the difficulty was, if you ate out with him in one of the Greenwich Village restaurants, ever to pay back his hospitality, as he invariably snatched the check and insisted on settling it himself. Even now that he had no regular platform, he continued to go to concerts and make notes on his impressions of the music and put them away in his files; and he continued to look for new talent and to acquire new protégés—though he sometimes had fits of gloom in which he would declare that American music was an abomination of desolation. He was sharply unsympathetic with the new tendency of American composers to abandon the abstruse researches into which they had been led by Schoenberg, the high seasoning and classicizing and virtuosity of abbreviation characteristic of Stravinsky and others, and to try to produce a music that could be heard and enjoyed by bigger audiences than those of the Composers' League. He was shocked, almost personally hurt, when Americans whose work he had thought promising did anything for the radio or Hollywood or published popular books. He expressed his views on this general subject in his essay on Kurt Weill and *Gebrauchsmusik*, in which he asserted that all music was useful, since "all works of musical art express essences and ideas and thus, with their symbols of the inner truth of life, provide the best of bases of social relationships," and that there was of course no reason why composers who "deeply felt the spirit and symbols of social rituals" should not provide these rituals with music—so long as the music provided "conveyed an individual interpretation of the meanings of the ritual" and not merely "general and conventional symbols and a sort of collective expression." He concluded: "Let us by all means have *Gebrauchsmusik*. But let it be the work of artists, not of 'revolutionary' academicians." It will be seen that these considered and formulated views were less severe than his instinctive attitude toward the practice of American composers; and I guessed that this attitude was due to his lately having felt himself a little out of things as well as to disappointment at any evidence that other artists cared anything for popular success.

But it worried me to feel, as time went on, that he was beginning to lose his self-confidence. He had put a good deal of work into the writing of what I gathered from his descriptions was a kind of symphonic novel based on a visit he had made to Rome, but he had decided that his whole conception was vitiated by some moral falsity and he withheld it from publication—which seemed to me a morbid symptom. A healthy writer either knows what he is doing or doesn't discover his error till after he has published the book. The persecution of the Jews by Hitler came later to weigh upon Paul and to become overpoweringly identified with the difficulties he was facing at fifty. The times had not brought to fulfillment that creative and enlightened era of which the sun had seemed to be rising in the days when the *Seven Arts* was founded: totalitarian states and class pressures were closing down on the artistic élite. The independent American journalism that had flared up for a while in the twenties had given way to the streamlined commercial kind, and the non-commercial magazines were composed for the most part by this time of second-rate academic papers and the commentaries of Talmudic Marxists. Even the *New Yorker,* more liberal and literate than most of the new magazines, and in its own way quite independent, was unable to find a place for Paul: it, too, had a conventional style, which sometimes ran to insipidity through the solicitous care of the editors to eliminate anything unexpected in the way that their writers expressed themselves. It was primarily a humorous weekly and had a department that exploited the absurdities that appeared in other papers, so that they had to be on their guard against writing that might be thought ridiculous. It was one of the most cruel blows of Paul Rosenfeld's later years that the *New Yorker* would not print his articles after asking him, as he assumed, to act as their regular art critic. Paul's prose, as I knew, had its blemishes, but at its best it would have been hopelessly refractory to the *New Yorker* processing mill. There was at that time not a single periodical which would print the work of a writer simply because he knew his subject and wrote about it well. Paul sometimes showed signs of a fear that he had been made the victim of a boycott; and at others was too ready to blame himself. He said to me once that his inheritance from his grandmother had unfitted him to struggle with the world; that he had thrown up his first and only job—as a reporter on a New York paper—when, finding that the work embarrassed him, he had reflected that he did not need a job to live. Certainly he was unfitted for putting himself over or making terms with editors and publishers; no one ever had less sense of business. He never could understand that writing was a commodity like any other, which, from the moment one lacked a patron, had to be sold in a hard-boiled way; and the world came more and more to divide itself for him into two classes, black and white: the negative forces of darkness that were closing down to crush him and the few pure children of light who survived and could heal and save.

I was distressed by him in these latter days and used to wonder how the circumstances had been combined to undermine so able a man, with the shift in economic conditions, by way of his very virtues even more than by way of his weaknesses. Certainly it was unwise of Paul to have depended as much as he did on the writing of musical criticism. Since he was himself not a musician but a writer, he should not have tied up his talent with the reporting of contemporary concerts. It is impossible for a master of words completely to express himself by merely rendering the effects of some other art; and I have never really understood why Paul did not tackle some bigger subject—a history of American music or a biography of some composer—which would have got him an advance from a publisher and supplied him with a sustaining interest. One might have said the same thing about Huneker; but it is no great comfort to realize that Paul Rosenfeld, in an age which prided itself on its emergence from the Philistinism of Huneker's, should have burned out in much the same way and been left in the same neglect. The burning-out and the public indifference seem somehow to work together. They are an old and depressing story in the American intellectual world.

When I got back to New York from Europe in the autumn of 1945, I spent with Paul a wonderful evening, which, though I may have seen him once or twice afterward, has left me with a last lively impression that I am extremely glad to have. He was in very much better spirits than he had been during the years of the war. He had received from a foundation a substantial grant to do a book of literary studies; and it seemed to cheer him up to hear talk about Europe again, now that the war was over and the arts might be expected to revive. I told him about my enthusiasm for Benjamin Britten's opera, *Peter Grimes,* which I had heard that summer in London. And both of us were glad to find someone to whom one could express oneself freely about the current state of letters and art. He was angry over his treatment at the hands of one of the highbrow quarterlies, the editor of which had first asked him to be a member of the advisory board and had then refused to print his articles, keeping them, however, for months without letting him know about them. I had had with this same magazine an almost equally annoying experience; and I managed to make Paul laugh by describing to him an essay in which this pedantic editor, in the course of a rigorous analysis of Macbeth's "Out, out, brief candle" speech, conducted in the rigorous spirit of the new "methodological" criticism, had said something like, "We cannot know why Shakespeare has chosen for death the curious adjective *dusty,* but the epithet has a quaint appropriateness that can be felt but hardly explained." We rapidly became so exhilarated, abounding so, as Henry James would say, in our own old sense, affirming our convictions so heartily and making such hilarious fun of the more tiresome of our contemporaries, that we went on till what was for Paul a late hour, walking the autumn streets and stopping off for coffee and beer at Childs' and the Lafayette, almost as if we had been back in the twenties, with the new era of American art just beginning to burst into life between Macdougal Street and Irving Place. Less than a year later, Paul died of a heart attack as he was coming out of a movie, to which he had gone alone.

And now, despite the miseries of his later years, he remains for me, looking back, one of the only sound features of a landscape that is strewn with distortions and wrecks: a being organically moral on whom one could always rely, with a passion for creative art extinguishable only with life. It has worried me to reflect that the rise in morale I thought I had noted in him when I talked to him last was not, after all, to lead to anything, and to remember how unhappy and insecure, how unrewarded, he was at the end. There are tragedies of untimely death which—coming at the end of a man's work or breaking off his career at a crisis—represent a kind of fulfillment. But one can find no justice in Paul's. His death had no dramatic appropriateness; nor was it preceded, I fear, by any very steady serenity. It had been obvious, in view of the interest that had been stimulated in American music, partly through Paul's own efforts, and of the quantity of books about music that were now getting into type, that it was time for a reprinting of Paul's criticism; and the suggestion had been made to two publishers that an omnibus be brought out. But he had not had even this gratification. One can only reassure oneself by remembering that the work he had done was of the kind that pays for itself, because it is done for love, in the desire to give life away, and because it brings, in the doing, elevation and liberation of spirit. To have had thirty years of such work is not the least enviable of destinies; and Paul's best writing bears on every page his triumph and his justification.

December 1957

Philip Rahv

SELF-DEFINITION IN AMERICAN LITERATURE

Experience and Fulfillment

"Characteristically American" is the phrase that occurs and recurs with virtually compulsive regularity in all the intensive discussions of the prospects and condition of the national letters conducted since the earliest years of the Republic. Quite often the phrase carries with it the suggestion that the user of it is far from certain in his own mind as to what the "characteristically American" actually comes to, and that he is in fact looking to the literary expression of his countrymen to provide him with the key to the enigma. Thus it would seem that one of the principal functions of literature in America has been to serve as a *vademecum* of Americanness, if not of Americanism. The latter term has by now acquired an unction compelling its surrender to the politicians; it is with Americanness, a category more existential than political, that our writers and critics have been concerned.

There is little to be wondered at in the uncertainty that has prevailed from the start as to the actual constituents of the "characterisically American." Henry James saw complexity in the very fate of being an American, and among the recognitions that this complexity entails is the fact that as a national entity we are uniquely composed of diverse and sometimes clashing ethnic and regional strains. Even more important is the fact that as a nation we are afloat in history without moorings in pre-history. Americans have no organic past, only ambiguous memories of European derivations. The decisive factor in the forming of American civilization, as the cultural historian F. G. Friedmann put it, is that "the American community had a beginning at a particular moment in history in contrast with the traditional communities that, far from having a precise historical origin, rose out of the bottomless darkness of time in that epoch of pre-history which is history, if at all, only in its latent and undeveloped stage."

Hence American society has the startling look about it of a human artifact, constructed for specific socio-political and economic purposes in a given period, a period well known and thoroughly documented. It is a society established on contractual rather than traditional foundations, the very existence of which makes for the impression that in the New World the legend of the "social contract" has finally been brought to visible life. And this very perceptibility, so to speak, of the national origins is not the least of the elements making for a profound sense of the problematical in the American awareness of cultural identity.

This sense of the problematical, this sense of always verging on a definition yet somehow missing it, enters significantly into many of the critical approaches that Americans have made to their own literature—approaches tending to turn into a search for America that takes on the aura of a spiritual adventure or mythic quest. Now the problematical is surely not so far apart from the fascinating; and the more committed minds among those who embarked on this search form a vital band of native spokesmen to whom the American character presents itself as a fascinating problem. The effects of this fascination, of this tall measure of devotion, are writ large in our criticism. Most of the famous testaments of our cultural history owe to it their verve in undertaking successively fresh appraisals of the national experience. Its operation is everywhere manifest in such works as Emerson's "American Scholar," Whitman's various prefaces and *Democratic Vistas,* Henry James's biography of Hawthorne, Henry Adams's *Education,* the letters and essays of Randolph Bourne, and the books full of passionate indictment that Van Wyck Brooks issued year after year before the change of front made evident in his *Makers and Finders* series.

Yet even this voluminous record of filiopietistic indulgence is quickened and given its rationale by the lasting fascination with the American character, a fascination which continues to serve at once as the goad and the charm of even such relatively late and sober-minded studies as F. O. Matthiessen's *American Renaissance* and Alfred Kazin's *On Native Grounds.* In the latter work Mr. Kazin alludes with insight to some of the consequences of this absorbing commitment on the part of American critics when he observes that "from Emerson and Thoreau to Mencken and Brooks, criticism has been the great American lay philosophy, the intellectual carryall. It had been a study of literature inherently concerned with ideals of citizenship, and often less a study of literary texts than a search for some imperative moral order within which American writing could live and grow. . . . It has even been the secret intermediary . . . between literature and society in America."

Among the earliest tasks that American critics set for themselves was that of locating and defining the differences between American and European writing. All through the past century and, in fact, until the renaissance that transformed the American literary consciousness in the earlier part of this century, this effort at definition met with resistance from the more genteel and agreeable writers and critics. These worthies, from Washington Irving and James Russell Lowell to William Crary Brownell and George Edward Woodberry, entertained expurgated notions of the creative life, and they were unable to countenance "the snapping asunder," in Poe's phrase, "of the leading strings of our British Grandmamma."

This prolonged resistance is to be explained by the fear of learning that the differences between the literature of the Old and the New World were indeed acute and real. "It is hard to hear a new voice," wrote D. H. Lawrence, "as hard as it is to listen to a new language; and there is a new voice in the old American classics." This new feeling originated in the psychic shift that occurred in the movement to the Western hemisphere. Lawrence called it a displacement, adding that "displacements hurt. This hurts. So we try to tie it up, like a cut finger, to put a rag round it." Whitman and Emerson exulted in the displacement; Hawthorne brooded about it and made what he could of it by searching for its beginnings in the annals of New England; Melville was heroic in his striving to do it justice but soon suffered a breakdown because he could not sustain the pitch of intensity at which he expended himself. A more easeful or complacent reaction was evolved by Longfellow, Lowell, Holmes, and the other distinguished authors of a tame reflective literature. They recoiled in paleface fashion from the tensions and hazards of the fresh experience thrown up by the dynamism of American life; and insofar as this experience came within their purview at all, they saw it in its crude, exposed state, judging it to be unfit for imaginative treatment.

Barrett Wendell, the Harvard professor who published *A Literary History of America* in 1900, was among the foremost exponents of the Genteel Tradition and one of those luminaries of the academy in America who could not bring themselves to treat American writers as anything but poor relations of the towering British figures to whom they looked up with reverence.* Yet even so, Wendell somehow hit upon the formula that accounts for the feebleness that affects us so discouragingly in studying the pre-modern period in American letters. (It has become habitual among us to regard Melville and Whitman as the representative creative

* In his *Days of the Phoenix* (1957), Van Wyck Brooks recalls that even as late as 1920, when American writing had come to seem important, it was "still ignored in academic circles where Thackeray and Tennyson were treated as twin kings of our literature and all the American writers as poor relations. It was regarded as 'a pale and obedient provincial cousin about which the less said the better,' in the phrase of Ernest Boyd; and Christian Gauss at Princeton, as Edmund Wilson pointed out, chimed in with Woodberry at Columbia and Wendell at Harvard."

types of that period. But this view indicates a loss of perspective on the past, for both were signally unsuccessful in gaining the esteem of the public of their time and in influencing the creative practice of their contemporaries. Whitman survived by making a fight of it, while Melville went under, his best work scarcely known.)

Wendell's formula is that this literature is in essence "a record of the national inexperience," and its "refinement of temper, conscientious sense of form, and instinctive disregard of actual fact" are its most characteristic traits. Thus he accurately noted, though with no objection on his part, the overriding fault—that of innocuousness—against which Melville warned in declaring that "the visible world of experience . . . is that procreative thing which impregnates the Muses." And if a novelist like William Dean Howells is virtually unread today, then surely it is because of the lack in him of "that procreative thing." Hence the failure of the recent efforts to stage his "revival." Evidently the absence of the "procreative thing" cannot be made up for by the clarity of design of his fiction and by the considerable intelligence and attractiveness of the personality that informs it. It is plain that whatever interest we may have in Howells today is not actual but falls somewhere on the borderline between the historical and the antiquarian; that is equally true of Longfellow, William Gilmore Simms, and others whose names are still honored in the textbooks.

Now modern American literature has attempted to overcome the fault so fatal to Howells and his predecessors by at long last seizing upon what the native genius had long been deprived of, by finding, in other words, its major stimulus in the urge toward and immersion in experience.* American writers were able to accomplish this transformation, however, not merely by accepting experience in all its indigenousness but also by overturning the tradition of the palefaces and by frequently making the most, in true redskin fashion, of experience precisely in its crude, exposed state, thus turning what had long been taken as a defect into a virtue. The law of over-compensation is as operative in art as in life.

It seems to me that it is only by facing up to the fact of the enfeeblement of the greater part of the older American literature, by its negative relation to experience, that we can properly evaluate the complaint against the native environment typically voiced by so many of the worst as well as the best of our 19th-century writers. Let us attend only to the best of them, noting the virtual identity of the terms in which they state the case against

* The true initiators of the line of modernity in American writing are Whitman and James, because both adopted a positive approach to experience even while defining its value and content in diametrically opposite ways. Hence the specifically modern in the national letters cannot be said to have had its start, as is usually assumed, in this century with the onset of the "new" poetry and the movement toward realism in fiction.

their country's capacity to provide them with imaginative substance. There is James Fenimore Cooper, for instance, asserting back in 1828 that among the main obstacles against which the native writer has to contend is sheer "poverty of materials." "There is scarcely an ore which contributes to the wealth of the author, that is found, here, in veins as rich as in Europe. There are no annals for the historian; no follies (beyond the most vulgar and commonplace) for the satirist; no manners for the dramatist; no obscure fictions for the writer of romance . . . nor any of the rich auxiliaries of poetry . . . no costume for the peasant . . . no wig for the judge, no baton for the general, no diadem for the magistrate."

This complaint is substantially repeated by Hawthorne some three decades later in his preface to *The Marble Faun,* where he remarks upon the difficulty of "writing a romance about a country where there is no shadow, no antiquity, no mystery, no picturesque and gloomy wrong, nor anything but a commonplace prosperity, in broad and simple daylight, as is happily the case with our dear native land." James, quoting these words in his biography of Hawthorne, is powerfully moved to enlarge upon them, and it is at this point in his book that the famous passage comes in ("No sovereign, no court, no personal loyalty, no aristocracy, no church, no clergy, no army," etc., etc.) enumerating the items of high civilization absent from American life. It is important to observe that James's version, by stretching Hawthorne's statement to the limit, no longer refers to "romance" alone but to artistic creation in general. Essentially he is duplicating Cooper's complaint in a more elaborate and conscious manner; and where Cooper speaks of "the poverty of materials" available to the American writer, James speaks of "the paucity of ingredients."

The justice and pathos of this standing complaint have been more or less recognized by our critics and historians of letters. No doubt it is justified insofar as we cannot but accept in some sense the Jamesian dictum that it takes "an accumulation of history and custom . . . to form a fund of suggestion for the novelist." But there is nonetheless a fallacy in the argument so strikingly concurred in by Cooper, Hawthorne, and James. For what they are saying, intrinsically, is that it is impossible to write European literature in America; the necessary ingredients are missing. And so they were if we are thinking in terms of a Walter Scott romance or a Jane Austen novel or the poems of Byron; no part of the United States was then a center of high civilization. Still, what is wrong is the tacit assumption that the ingredients are of a fixed kind, given once and for all.

But is it really true that the relationship between literature and high civilization is so completely binding? If that were strictly the case, we would be utterly at a loss to explain the appearance in backward Russia, and so early in the 19th century at that, of so great a poet as Pushkin and a master of narrative prose like Gogol. Whitman's "Song of Myself" is in no sense a poem of high civilization, but it is a magnificent poem nevertheless. Is it not more to the point to acknowledge that the genuinely new and venturesome in literary art emerges from a fresh selection of the materials at hand, from an assimilation, that is, to imaginative forms of that which life newly offers but which the conventions of past literature are too rigid to let through? And in the earlier as well as the latter part of the 19th century, life in America certainly offered sufficient experience for imaginative treatment, though not the sort of experience marked by richness and complexity of historical reference and safely certified for literary use by the past conventions of authorship. Actually, in creating the character of Leatherstocking, Cooper did break through those conventions; as Lowell wrote in his *Fable for Critics:* "He has drawn you one character, though this is new/ One wildflower he's plucked that is wet with the dew/ Of this fresh western world"; where Cooper failed in his Leatherstocking tales, however, is in being far too obedient to the established conventions in point of style and technique.

As for Hawthorne, he appears to have attached a disproportionate importance to the question of "romance," plainly because of his incapacity to come to terms with the kind of subject matter which is novelistic in essence. The fact is that in his time "romance" was a genre already far gone in obsolescence; it was the novel that was then full of promise and vitality. Let us recall, too, that some of "the follies" disdained by Cooper as much too "vulgar and commonplace" for literary exploitation served the French novel very well in the work of Balzac, Flaubert, and Zola. In his *Comédie humaine* Balzac intended to treat all strata of society, but in practice he assigned the major role to the trading and professional classes. There was no lack of such classes in the United States, and yet no indigenous version of a novel comparable to Balzac's *César Birotteau* was ever produced by a writer who knew his New York, Boston, or Philadelphia. A subject so lowly as Balzac tackled in his commercial saga of a Parisian linen draper was entirely at variance with the "abnormal dignity" which then prevailed in American letters.

Another example would be *Madame Bovary*. Can it really be claimed that the material fashioned by Flaubert into a work of art was unavailable a hundred years ago in America? After all, a pretty woman's boredom, adultery, and suicide are scarcely a monopoly of French life. Yet the sort of imaginative transaction represented by the story of Emma Bovary is unthinkable in mid-19th century America. It was not the absence of materials but the absence of writers prepared to cope with the materials actually at hand that decided the issue, and it is in this sense that the standing complaint cited above was misdirected. Allowing for Whitman and in part for Melville as formidable exceptions, what stood in the way was the fixed stance of the writers, their lack of inner freedom to break with tradition so as to be able to say the seemingly unsayable. "The immense and vague cloud-canopy of idealism," in Brooks's phrase, which then hung over the national culture made any such attempts prohibitive.

The truth is that there were no real novelists in America until the 80's and 90's, only pre-novelists and romancers. A conspicuous instance attesting to this fact is Melville's *Pierre,* the one work in which he undertook to possess himself of the forms of realism developed by his European contemporaries and in which he failed dismally. I am stressing this point in order to reinforce the contention in my essay "The Cult of Experience in American Writing," that in that period American literature was not yet in position to adapt for itself "the vitally new principle of realism by which the art of fiction in Europe was . . . evolving toward a hitherto inconceivable condition of objectivity and familiarity with existence."

This principle of realism—which the late Erich Auerbach defines in his *Mimesis* as "a serious representation of contemporary social reality against the background of a constant historical movement"—requires above all a give-and-take relation between the ego and experience. It is only with the appearance of narratives like Henry James's *Washington Square* (1881) and *The Bostonians* (1886) that we sense that this relation is perceptibly beginning to come into being. And if the former narrative, in its recreation of old New York focusing on the house in Washington Square with its chintz-covered parlor where Catherine Sloper is courted by Morris Townsend, still puts us under a spell, it is hardly because those young people are especially memorable or their case compelling, but because earlier American fiction is so poor in evocations of the actual in its time and place. It is a matter of the Americanness of a past age coming through as an aesthetic impression by virtue of the precision with which it is conveyed.

But James was soon to settle in London, taking his American characters with him. It was to be a question for him of becoming either a novelist of high civilization, even if mainly of its impact on his countrymen, or nothing at all. He removed himself from the scene, exerting an uncertain influence from afar. Not till after the turn of the century, when the qualities of national existence changed radically and a native intelligentsia rose to the surface of social life, did American literature liberate itself from its past inhibitions.

Of course, all through the 19th century the ideologues of nativity bent every effort to nullify the complaint against America's "poverty of materials." Whitman's prose is one long counter-argument. And at an earlier date, apart from the Young America group in New York led by the Duyckincks and Cornelius Mathews, of whom a thorough and entertaining account has recently been given by Professor Perry Miller in his study

The Raven and the Whale, powerful voices were raised in defense of America's creative possibilities.

There is Emerson, for example, writing in 1842 that

> we have as yet no genius in America, with tyrannous eye, which knew the value of our incomparable materials, and saw, in the barbarism and materialism of the times, another carnival of the same gods he so much admires in Homer. . . . Banks and tariffs, the newspaper and caucus, Methodism and Unitarianism, are flat and dull to dull people, but rest on the same foundations of wonder as the town of Troy and temple of Delphi. . . . Our log-rolling, our stumps and their politics, our fisheries, our Negroes and Indians . . . the northern trades, the southern planting, the western clearing, Oregon and Texas, are yet unsung. Yet America is a poem in our eyes; its ample geography dazzles the imagination, and it will not wait long for metres.

As usual, Emerson is being beautifully eloquent. His catalogue of materials is impressive, a splendid retort to disparagers and complainers. But a catalogue is one thing; the personal appropriation of materials is something else again. Only writers of a truly Balzacian grossness of appetite could conceivably have digested them. What was needed was not a "tyrannous eye" but a strong stomach above all; but unfortunately the men of letters of that period were typically inclined either toward a morbid type of spirituality or toward a propitiatory and at bottom escapist jocosity.

Whitman alone responded in programmatic fashion to Emerson's challenge, though his master was sometimes depressed by his want of meters. Moreover the master, along with the lesser partisans of nativity, was not content to submit his inventory of materials without at the same time prescribing an attitude of patriotic glow as the condition of their assimilation. Note that Emerson says of America that it is "a poem in our eyes," just as Whitman was to say in the 1855 preface to *Leaves of Grass* that "the United States are themselves the greatest poem." Thus dogmatic patriotism is turned into a prerequisite of artistic creation.

Historically speaking, this is indeed the vulnerable side of nativism in literature, that it cannot advocate the use of the American subject matter without at once demanding of the writer that he declare himself in advance to stand in an affirmative relation to it. Nativists can never understand that any attempt to enlist literature "in the cause of America" is bound to impose an intolerable strain on the imaginative faculty. The real issue in the times of Emerson and Whitman was not between love of America and disdain of it; neither Cooper nor Hawthorne nor James disdained it. The issue was rather the availability at home of creatively usable materials; their availability was the point, and the writer's readiness to benefit from it according to his lights, not the political or moral or philosophical valuation to be put upon them. It is through his achievement in his own medium that the important writer contributes to the spiritual development of his people. To ask that he commit himself to flattering the national ego is a proceeding as simple-minded as it is vicious. And it is a false idea of what affirmation comes to in the long run to believe that the literary artist who brings to his people not peace but a sword has failed in his spiritual task. As isolable qualities, neither pessimism nor optimism is definable as a value in art.

At the present time, when the issue of "poverty of materials" can no longer arise in America, the habit of demanding affirmation still persists. We are living in a period of renewed national belligerency, when pessimism is again regarded as "un-American." In many circles so recent a lesson as that taught us in the 20's, when American writing showed far more creative force than it does now even while engaging in a bitter assault on the national pieties, has been conveniently forgotten. As in the old days, so now the appeal to "the sanely and wholesomely American" is taken up as a weapon against the moral freedom of literature.

It is true, as Mr. Henry Bamford Parkes points out in his essay "The Metamorphoses of Leatherstocking," that a good deal of American writing, in the classic as in the modern period, is dominated by forms of flight from the organized pressures of society. Mr. Parkes brilliantly marshals the evidence to show that the Leatherstocking type of hero, who may be seen as a fugitive from society, reappears again and again in our fiction, which carries with it a specific emotion of disappointment in the consequences of civilization. In *Huckleberry Finn,* as in some of the novels of Sherwood Anderson, Dos Passos, Hemingway, and Fitzgerald, an antagonism is demonstrated between individual integrity and institutional disciplines and mores. To the texts cited by Mr. Parkes one might add so signal an expression of the same tendency as Faulkner's long story "The Bear," in which the principal character, Isaac McCaslin, relinquishes the land he has inherited, in the belief that rapacity was the prime motive power of subduing the wilderness and that civilization represents a fall from goodness and innocence requiring strict expiation.

One wonders, however, whether Mr. Parkes is right in the interpretation he puts upon the evidence at his disposal. Is not the pessimism which he perceives to be so strikingly characteristic of modern American literature to be found in even stronger ideological doses, though not expressed with the same heedless violence, in modern European writing? Are we justified in absolving civilization of sin and guilt while convicting writers of an impossible idealism derived from a Rousseauistic faith in natural virtue and natural religion? Is not discontent with civilization one of the major sources of the virulence of modernity? Literature, here as in Europe, has so long made a specialty of the depiction of evil in man that it can scarcely be said to tell us that he is good; but neither does it tell us that social institutions are admirable, endowed with "prescriptive" rights which the individual does wrong to challenge. Institutions are made and unmade by particular men under particular circumstances, and to confer a sacrosanct character upon their own handiwork is to turn them into idolaters and slaves.

A close observer of the creative process once finely remarked that the honor of a literature lies in its capacity to develop "a great quarrel within the national consciousness." One has only to think of the outstanding Victorian figures who decried the state of England, or of the French and particularly the Russian novel in the past century, to realize the truth of that statement. In a somewhat different way the modern American novel is likewise implicated in a "great quarrel within the national consciousness." To my mind, the principal theme of this novel, from Dreiser and Anderson to Fitzgerald and Faulkner, has been the discrepancy between the high promise of the American dream and what history has made of it. The inner feeling of this novel is one of nostalgic love and nativity combined with baffled (and sometimes angry) disenchantment. That is what comes so tellingly through to us, with plangent lyrical force, in the wonderful closing paragraphs of Fitzgerald's *The Great Gatsby,* when the narrator, Nick Carraway, wanders down to the beach at night:

> Most of the big shore places were closed now and there were hardly any lights except the shadowy, moving glow of a ferryboat across the Sound. And as the moon rose higher the inessential houses began to melt away until gradually I became aware of the old island that flowered once for Dutch sailors' eyes—a fresh, green breast of the new world. Its vanished trees, the trees that had made way for Gatsby's house, had once pandered in whispers to the last and greatest of all human dreams; for a transitory enchanted moment man must have held his breath in the presence of this continent, compelled into an aesthetic contemplation he neither understood nor desired, face to face for the last time in history with something commensurate to his capacity for wonder.
>
> And as I sat there brooding on the old, unknown world, I thought of Gatsby's wonder when he first picked out the green light as the end of Daisy's dock. He had come a long way to this blue dawn, and his dream must have seemed so close that he could hardly fail to grasp it. He did not know that it was already behind him, somewhere back in that vast obscurity beyond the city, where the dark fields of the republic rolled on under night.
>
> Gatsby believed in the green light, the orgastic future that

year by year recedes before us. It eluded us then, but that's no matter—tomorrow we will run faster, stretch our arms further. . . . And one fine morning—

So we beat on, boats against the current, borne back ceaselessly into the past.

Art has always fed on the contradiction between the reality of the world and the image of glory and orgastic happiness and harmony and goodness and fulfillment which the self cherishes as it aspires to live even while daily dying. If reality ever measures up to that image, art will witness its own dissolution in a beautiful world. But the world is what it is, in the New as in the Old. And in transposing this reflection into a national key, one feels compelled to say that America, whatever it looked like in its fresh flowering to Dutch sailors' eyes, is far more what its best artists have made it out to be than it is the achieved utopia invoked in our mass media and by officialdom in politics as in culture. In their relation to their native land those artists have never lost their capacity for wonder, and they are in no danger of losing it so long as they do not degrade wonder into submission, acquiescence, or an allegiance simple, uniform, and thoughtless.

January 1958

Dwight Macdonald

BY COZZENS POSSESSED

A Review of Reviews

The most alarming literary news in years is the enormous success of James Gould Cozzens' *By Love Possessed*. It sold 170,000 copies in the first six weeks of publication—more than all eleven of the author's previous novels put together. At this writing, it has been at the top of the best-seller lists for two months. Hollywood and the *Reader's Digest* have paid $100,000 apiece for the privilege of wreaking their wills upon it. And the *New Yorker* published a cartoon—one matron to another: "I was looking forward to a few weeks of just doing nothing after Labor Day when along came James Gould Cozzens."

There's nothing new in all this—after all, *something* has to be the No. 1 Best-Seller at any given moment. What is new appears if one considers Grace Metalious' *Peyton Place,* which was at the top for a full year, before *By Love Possessed* displaced it. *Peyton Place* is a familiar kind of best-seller, a pedestrian job, an artifact rather than a work of art (putting it mildly) that owes its popularity to nothing more subtle than a remarkably heavy charge of Sex; perhaps its best-known predecessor is *Forever Amber,* fabricated a decade ago by another notably untalented lady. But Cozzens is not of the company of Kathleen Winsor, Edna Ferber, Daphne du Maurier, Lloyd C. Douglas, and other such humble, though well-paid, artisans. Nor can he be "placed" at the middle level of best-sellerdom, that of writers like Herman Wouk, John Hersey, and Irwin Shaw, nor even (perhaps) on the empyrean heights occupied by Marquand and Steinbeck. He is a "serious" writer, and never more serious than in this book. That so uncompromising a work, written in prose of an artificiality and complexity that approaches the impenetrable—indeed often achieves it—that this should have become what the publishers gloatingly call "a runaway best-seller" is something new. How do those matrons cope with it, I wonder. Perhaps their very innocence in literary matters is a help—an Australian aboriginal would probably find *Riders of the Purple Sage* as hard to read as *The Golden Bowl*.

The requirements of the mass market explain a good deal of bad writing today. But Cozzens here isn't writing down, he is obviously giving it the works: *By Love Possessed* is his bid for immortality. It is Literature or it is nothing. Unfortunately none of the reviewers has seriously considered the second alternative. The book is not only a best-seller, it is a *succès d'estime*. Such reviews, such enthusiasm, such unanimity, such nonsense! The only really hostile review I have been able to find was by William Buckley, Jr., of all people, in his *National Review*. Granted that he was somewhat motivated by a non-literary consideration—the book is lengthily anti-Catholic—still I thought his deflation skillful and just.

Looking through Alice Payne Hackett's *Sixty Years of Best Sellers,* I find among the top ten novels between 1935 and 1955 just seven that I would call in any way "serious," namely: Wolfe's *Of Time and the River* (1935), Huxley's *Eyeless in Gaza* (1936), Virginia Woolf's *The Years* (1937), Steinbeck's *The Grapes of Wrath* (1939), Hemingway's *For Whom the Bell Tolls* (1941), Norman Mailer's *The Naked and the Dead* (1948), and James Jones's *From Here to Eternity* (1951). About one every three years, with a significant falling off in the last decade. It is a slim harvest, in both quantity and quality, but the difference between the least of these and *By Love Possessed* is the difference betwen a work of art on some level and to some extent achieved, and one that falls below any reasonable literary criterion. Yet the reviewers almost to a man behaved as if they were possessed. This sincere enthusiasm for a mediocre work is more damaging to literary standards than any amount of cynical ballyhoo. One can guard against the Philistines outside the gates. It is when they get into the Ivory Tower that they are dangerous.*

There seems little doubt that *By Love Possessed* has been selling on the strength of the reviews. (Word-of-mouth comment has probably worked the other way; I've found only two people who liked it, and the most common reply is: "I couldn't read it.") All the commercially important journals reviewed it prominently and enthusiastically. The Sunday *Times* and *Herald Tribune* book sections gave it front-page reviews, by Malcolm Cowley ("one of the country's truly distinguished novelists") and Jessamyn West ("Rich, Wise, Major Novel of Love"). *Time* put Cozzens on the cover—Herman Wouk was there a year or two ago—and pronounced *By Love Possessed* "the best American novel in years." Orville Prescott in the *Times* thought it "magnificent," Edward Weeks in the *Atlantic* found it "wise and compassionate," and Whitney Balliett in the *Saturday Review* divined in it "the delicate and subtle tension between action and thought that is the essence of balanced fiction."

* A similar case of demoniacal possession took place in London in 1956 apropos of Colin Wilson's *The Outsider*.

The most extraordinary performances were those of Brendan Gill in the *New Yorker* and John Fischer in *Harper's*. The former praised it in terms that might have been thought a trifle excessive if he had been writing about *War and Peace:* "a masterpiece . . . the author's masterpiece . . . almost anybody's masterpiece . . . supremely satisfying . . . an immense achievement . . . spellbinding . . . masterpiece." The mood is lyrical, stammering with heartfelt emotion: "No American novelist of the twentieth century has attempted more than Mr. Cozzens attempts in the course of this long and bold and delicate book, which, despite its length, one reads through at headlong speed and is then angry with oneself for having reached the end so precipitately."

Mr. Fischer was more coherent but equally emphatic. Speaking from "The Editor's Easy Chair," as *Harper's* quaintly styles it, he headed his piece: "NOMINATION FOR A NOBEL PRIZE," and he meant it. For one slip or another—sentimentality, neuroticism, subjectivism, sloppy plot construction, or habitual use of "characters who are in one way or another in revolt against society"—he faults all the other competitors (the habitual-use-of-deleterious-characters rap alone disposes of Faulkner, Hemingway, Steinbeck, Algren, Mailer, Capote, Bellow, Jones, Paul Bowles, and Tennessee Williams) until finally James Gould Cozzens stands out in superb isolation, a monument of normality, decency, and craftsmanship.*

The provincial reviewers followed their leaders: "COZZENS PENS ENDURING TALE" (Cleveland *News*), "ONE OF THE GREAT NOVELS OF THE PRESENT CENTURY" (San Francisco *Call-Bulletin*), "finest American novel I have read in many a year" (Bernardine Kielty in the *Ladies' Home Journal*), "COZZENS WRITES ABSORBING STORY IN EXCELLENT AND PROFOUND NOVEL" (Alice Dixon Bond in the Boston *Herald;* her column is called "The Case for Books"—is there an adjacent feature, "The Case Against Books"?). Leslie Hanscom in the New York *World-Telegram*—there are provincials in big cities, too—was impressed by Cozzens' "awesome scrupulosity as an artist." Mr. Hanscom's scrupulosity as a critic inspires little awe; "Hemingway and Faulkner, move over!" he summed up. The frankest of the provincials was Carl Victor Little in the Houston *Press:* "The *N.Y. Times,*

* Actually, even according to Mr. Fischer's absurd standards, Cozzens doesn't deserve this eminence. He is not "a classic mind operating in a romantic period" nor does his novel run counter to "the Gothic extravagance of current fiction"; as I shall show, his mind lacks clarity, control, and form—the typical classic virtues—and his prose is as Gothic as Harkness Memorial Quadrangle (also as unaesthetic). As for the alleged normality of his characters—"ordinary people, living ordinary lives, in ordinary circumstances" with whom the reader "can identify himself as he never can with the characters of an Algren or a Mailer"—they are normal only on the surface; once this is broken through, they are as neurotic and fantastic in their behavior as other current fictional people. The chief difference is that their creator often doesn't realize it.

Saturday Review and other publications have taken out of the ivory tower the most accomplished critics available to join in the hallelujahs. So about all I can do is ditto the dithyrambs."

The literary quarterlies have not yet been heard from, but the liberal weeklies have. They didn't exactly ditto the dithyrambs, except for Granville Hicks in the *New Leader:* ". . . a novel to which talk of greatness is not irrelevant." But they didn't exactly veto them, either. Howard Nemerov in the *Nation,* Sarel Eimerl in the *New Republic,* and Richard Ellmann in the *Reporter* were all critical but respectful.

Mr. Nemerov's review I thought especially interesting. He was much alive to the use of the novel by the middlebrow reviewers as a stick to beat the highbrows, but, like Ellmann and Eimerl, not at all alive to what seems to me the chief defect of a very defective novel: the atrocious style. My first thought was that this is odd because Nemerov is a poet. My second was that perhaps that's the trouble. Our taste may have been corrupted not only by mass culture but also by its opposite—as we learned in old Doctor Engels' dialectical kindergarten, opposites are first cousins—the anything-goes subjective style which some of our painters and poets have evolved as a protest against, and an escape from, mass culture. After all, *By Love Possessed* is not much harder to read than most contemporary poetry.

Perhaps we should now take a look at what Cozzens has to say in *By Love Possessed,* and how he says it. The normative hero is Arthur Winner, a reputable, middle-aged lawyer and family man who is exposed, during the two days and nights covered by the action, to a variety of unsettling experiences, which stimulate in him some even more unnerving memories. Winner is presented as a good man—kind, reasonable, sensitive, decent—and so he is taken by the reviewers: "The grandest moral vision in all Cozzens' work—a passionately good, passionately religious, yet wholly secular man, whose very failures are only bad dreams" (Balliett), "intelligent, successful, tolerant . . . the quintessence of our best qualities" (Gill). I'm unwilling to go farther than the Kansas City *Star:* "thoroughly honest, genteel, devoted to his work, and conscientious." Passion seems to me just what is most obviously missing in Arthur Winner; he's about as passionate as a bowl of oatmeal.

He is, in fact, a prig. His responses to the many appeals made to him in the course of the story—he's always on top, handing down advice and help, a great temptation to priggishness—while decent enough in form ("genteel") are in reality ungenerous and self-protective. To a Catholic lady who tries to justify her faith: "Where there are differences in religion, I think it generally wiser not to discuss them." To a seduced girl's father, who has flourished a gun: "Be very careful! Return the gun; and meanwhile, show it to no one else. Don't take it out of your pocket; and don't consider pointing it. Pointing a weapon is a separate indictable offense, and would get you an additional fine, and an additional jail term." To his teen-age daughter, who wants to go dancing: "A real gone band? I believe I grasp your meaning. Clearly a good place to know. Where is it?" "Oh, it's called the Old Timbers Tavern. It's down toward Mechanicsville, not far." "Yes; I've heard of it. And I'm afraid, whatever the reputed quality of the band, I must ask you not to go there." "Oh, Father!" That he is right in each case, that the Catholic lady is addlewitted, that the father is a fool and a braggart, that the Old Timbers Tavern is in fact no place for a young girl to go—all this is beside the point. A prig is one who delights in demonstrating his superiority on small occasions, and it is precisely when he has a good case that he rises to the depths of prigocity.

Although Winner behaves like a prig, he is not meant to be one, if only because the main theme of the novel, the moral testing and education of a good man, would then collapse, and the philosophical tragedy that Cozzens has tried to write would have to be recast in a satiric if not a downright farcical mode. Here as elsewhere, the author is guilty of the unforgivable novelistic sin: he is unaware of the real nature of his characters, that is, the words and actions he gives them lead the reader to other conclusions than those intended by the author.

His characters often speak brutally, for example, not because they are supposed to be brutes, but because their creator apparently thinks this is the way men talk. An elderly lawyer, civilly asked by a client to make some changes in the investing of her trust fund, replies: "You're getting senile, Maud. Try not to be more of a fool than you can help." A doctor, presented as a gentleman, meets the wife of a friend at a party, and, no dialogue or motivation given before, opens up: "What's your trouble, baby? Or can I guess? . . . Tell Pappy how many periods you've missed . . . . You know as well as I do you're one of those girls who only has to look at him to get herself knocked up." She leaves the room "indignantly" (the adverb implies she's a mite touchy) and he turns to Clarissa, Winner's wife:

> "I knew it as soon as I looked at her. Sure. One night she thinks: Too much trouble to get up; the hell with it! You two ought to trade apparatus. Then everybody'd be happy."
>
> Clarissa said: "Reg, you're not being very funny—"
>
> "That's right. I don't feel very funny. Sometimes you get your bellyful of women—their goddam notions; their goddam talk-talk-talk; their goddam sacks of tripes!"

No reason is given for any of these onslaughts, aside from the fact that all three recipients are women; this seems to be Cozzens' idea of manly straight-from-the-shoulder talk. Curious. Curious, too, Winner's pooh-

poohing attitude when he is appealed to by the feminine victims.

For Winner, too, is something of a brute, without his creator suspecting it. There is, for example, that odd business on page 428 when Mrs. Pratt, after her silly, hysterical religiosity has beaten vainly for some thirty pages against the rock of Winner's Episcopalian rectitude (Mrs. Pratt is a Roman Catholic), is finally checkmated. She has to go to the bathroom. For reasons obscure to me, this is presented as the decisive proof of hypocrisy: "At fact's surely unkindest prank of all, Arthur Winner must protest, generously indignant." ("Meanly delighted" would be more accurate.) For a page, Winner ruminates on his antagonist's discomfiture, concluding: "But how in the world of fancy did you put delightfully the human circumstance whose undressed substance was that Celia, Celia, Celia shits—or even that Mrs. Pratt most urgently requires to piss?" Methinks the gentleman doth protest too much, and methinks that Swift's allusion to Celia's necessity was positively healthy compared to Cozzens-Winner's resort to scatology to win an argument.

This leads us, in a way, to sex. The crucial episode, the one that more than any other shakes Winner's faith in himself and in the uprightness of his life, is something that happened years before the action begins and that keeps coming back into his mind: his affair with Marjorie, the wife of his close friend and law partner, Julius Penrose. On the day after his first wife's death, Marjorie—another silly, hysterical woman—comes to the house and in a rush of emotion offers herself to him. He is about to take her, on his wife's bed, when the phone rings. That time he is literally saved by the bell, but later, one summer when Penrose is away, they do have a frantic affair. At no time is love or even lust involved: "Far from coveting his neighbor's wife, he rather disliked her, found her more unattractive than not." The only reason given for Winner's reaction to Marjorie is that she was there. Like that mountain climber. Or as Marjorie's remorselessly philosophical husband puts it in his pidgin (or shall we say turkey) English: "I venture to assert that when the gadfly's sting is fairly driven in, when this indefeasible urge of the flesh presses them, few men of normal potency prove able to refrain their feet from that path." But then (a) why hasn't Winner had dozens of such affairs instead of only this one—and for that matter, why was Marjorie able to seduce him only that one summer?; and (b) granted that some men do indeed so behave, why Winner? Does an Episcopalian lawyer, a rational, decent family man with no more and no different sexual urges than the normal ones, act like a dead-end kid? Cozzens insists that the best of us do so behave, but if we do, then we aren't the best. There might be some individual quirk in Winner to explain it, but it is not given; on the contrary, Cozzens' point is precisely Winner's lack of such quirks—"few men of normal potency prove able to refrain their feet from that path." This is neither realistic nor imaginative.

It is the shocked revulsion of the adolescent who discovers that papa and mama do it.

The formula for a best-seller now includes a minimum of "outspoken" descriptions of sexual activities, and *By Love Possessed* doesn't skimp here. Its inventory includes rape, seduction, marital and extramarital intercourse, with touches of sadism, lesbianism, onanism, and homosexuality. *By Sex Possessed* would be a more accurate title. There is very little love, which the author presents as at best a confusing and chancey business, to be patiently endured, like the weather. The provincials, for some reason, got the point here much better than their urban leaders did. The Chattanooga *Times* wonderfully summed up the theme as "the situation of rational man beset by passion," adding: "Cozzens regards each form of love as a threat to Arthur Winner's power to reason, to his ability to live life with meaning." It's too bad this acuteness in diagnosis was not accompanied by equal skill in evaluation; Cozzens' notion of love was accepted as valid; but it isn't, since love, even passion, is not an extraneous monkey wrench thrown into the machinery of life, but rather a prime mover which may burst everything apart but which must function if there is to be any motion at all. This is, at any rate, how the makers of our literature, from Homer to Tolstoy, Proust, and James, have treated the theme; Cozzens' efficiency-expert approach (Gumming Up the Works) is echt-American but creatively impoverishing.

"The readers didn't go much for Cozzens," observed the Detroit *Times,* "until he wrote something with some sex in it." This cynicism is not wholly justified. The literary prestige conferred by the reviewers was, I think, the chief factor. One of the consumer's goods to which every American feels he has a right in this age of plenty is Culture, and *By Love Possessed* on the living-room table is a symbol of the owner's exercise of this right. Granted that the reviews may have led many proprietors of living-room tables to think they could combine business with pleasure, so to speak, word must have gotten around fairly soon that the sexual passages were unrewarding.

For even the sex is meager—perhaps the real title should be *By Reason Possessed.* I have the impression that Cozzens is as suspicious of sex as of love. Most of the sexual encounters he conscientiously describes are either fatuous (Winner and his first bride), sordid (Ralph and Veronica), or disgusting (Winner and Marjorie). Far worse—from a sales viewpoint—they are written in his customary turgid and inexpressive style. Take for example the two pages (264-65) on Winner's love-making with his second wife, the most concrete description of the sexual act in the book and also the only place where sex is presented, as one might say, positively. This passage sounds partly like a tongue-tied Dr. Johnson: "the disposings of accustomed practice, the preparations of purpose and consent, the familiar mute motions of furtherance." But mostly like a *Fortune* description of an industrial process: "thrilling thuds of his heart . . . moist manipulative reception . . . the mutual heat of pumped bloods . . . the thoroughgoing, deepening, widening work of their connection; and his then no less than hers, the tempo slowed in concert to engineer a tremulous joint containment and continuance . . . the deep muscle groups, come to their vertex, were in a flash convulsed."*

The reviewers think of Cozzens, as he does himself, as a cool, logical, unsentimental, and implacably deep thinker. "Every character and event is bathed in the glow of a reflective intelligence," puffs *Time,* while Brendan Gill huffs: "The Cozzens intellect, which is of exceptional breadth and toughness, coolly directs the Cozzens heart." In reality, Cozzens is not so much cool as inhibited, not so much unsentimental as frightened by feeling; he is not logical at all, and his mind is shallow and muddy rather than clear and deep. I think Julius Penrose may fairly be taken as Cozzens' beau ideal of an intellectual, as Winner is his notion of a good man. If Penrose is meant to be taken ironically, if his pompous philosophizings are supposed to be burlesques, then the novel collapses at its center—leaving aside the fact they would be tedious as parodies—since it is Penrose who throughout the book guides Winner toward the solution of his problems. There's a Penrose in Homer, but he's not confused with Ulysses. His name is Nestor.

The reviewers, of course, were impressed by this club bore: "a dark, supernal intelligence" (Balliett), "one of the most compelling [what *does* that critical standby mean, I wonder] and memorable figures in recent writing" (Jessamyn West), "the scalded mind of the archskeptic . . . a corrosive nonstop monologuist with a tongue like a poisoned dart" (*Time*). The intellectual climax—more accurately, anti-climax—of the book is a thirty-page conversation between Penrose and Winner—at their club, appropriately enough—about life and love. It reminds me of two grunt-and-groan wrestlers heaving their ponderous bulks around without ever getting a grip on each other. "How could she like these things [sadistic acts by her first husband]?" Penrose rhetorically asks at one point, immediately continuing in the strange patois of Cozzensville: "My considered answer: Marjorie, though all unknowing, could! She could see such a punishment as condign. She had to submit, because in an anguished way, she craved to have done to her what she was persuaded she deserved to have done to her." Having got off this bit of kindergarten Freudianism: "He gazed an instant at Arthur Winner. 'You find this farfetched?' he said. 'Yes, we who are so normal are reluctant to entertain such ideas.' " Ideas are always entertained in Cozzensville, though they are not always

* "The passages having to do with physical love have a surprising lyric power."—Jessamyn West in the N.Y. *Herald Tribune.*

entertaining. After fifteen more lines of elaboration, Penrose again fears he has outstripped his audience: "You consider this too complicated?" To which Winner, manfully: "Perhaps not. But I've often wondered how far anyone can see into what goes on in someone else. I've read somewhere that it would pose the acutest head to draw forth and discover what is lodged in the heart." Now where could he have read *that?*

It is interesting to note that Penrose and Winner, the two "point-of-view" characters, are lawyers, and that the processes of the law occupy a considerable amount of the book. The reviewers marvel that Cozzens has been able to master so much legal know-how, but I think there is more to it than that. We Americans have always had a weakness for the law. Its objectivity reassures our skittish dread of emotion and its emphasis on The Facts suits our pragmatic temper. But above all the law is our substitute for philosophy, which makes us almost as nervous as emotion does. Its complicated, precise formulae have the external qualities of theoretical thinking, lacking only the most essential one—they don't illuminate reality, since what is "given" is not the conditions of life but merely a narrow convention. Dickens, Tolstoy, and other novelists have written law-court scenes showing that truth is too small a fish to be caught in the law's coarse meshes. But to Cozzens a trial is reality while emotional, disorderly life is the illusion. He delights in the tedious complications of lawyer's talk, the sort of thing one skips in reading the court record of even the most sensational trials. On page 344 a clergyman incautiously asks Winner about the property rights of churches in Pennsylvania. "The difference is technical," Winner begins with gusto, and three pages later is still expatiating.

This fascination with the law is perhaps a clue to Cozzens' defects as a novelist. It explains the peculiar aridity of his prose, its needless qualifications, its clumsiness, its defensive qualifications (a lawyer qualifies negatively—so he can't be caught out later; but a novelist qualifies positively—to make his meaning not safer but clearer). And his sensibility is lawyer-like in its lack of both form and feeling, its peculiar combination of a brutal domineering pragmatism ("Just stick to the facts, please!") with abstract fancywork, a kind of Victorian jigsaw decoration that hides more than it reveals. I, too, think the law is interesting, but as an intellectual discipline, like mathematics or crossword puzzles. I feel Cozzens uses it as a defense against emotion ("sentimentality"). Confusing it with philosophy, he makes it bear too heavy a load, so that reality is distorted and even the law's own qualities are destroyed, its logic and precision blurred, its technical elegance coarsened. There's too much emotion in his law and too much law in his emotion.

The three earlier Cozzens novels I've read, *The Last Adam, The Just and the Unjust,* and *Guard of Honor,* were written in a straightforward if commonplace style. But here Cozzens has tried to write Literature, to develop a complicated individual style, to convey deeper meanings than he has up to now attempted. Slimly endowed as either thinker or stylist, he has succeeded only in fuzzing it up, inverting the syntax, dragging in Latin-root polysyllables. Stylistically, *By Love Possessed* is a neo-Victorian cakewalk.* A cakewalk by a singularly awkward contestant. Confusing laboriousness with profundity, the reviewers have for the most part not detected the imposture.

There is some evidence, if one reads closely and also between the lines, that some of the reviewers had their doubts. But they adopted various strategies for muffling them. Messrs. Gill, Fischer, and Balliett, while applauding the style in general, refrained from quoting anything. The last-named, after praising the "compact, baked, fastidious sentences" went into a long, worried paragraph which inferred the opposite. "The unbending intricacies of thought . . . seem to send his sentences into impossible log-jams," he wrote, which is like saying of a girl, "She doesn't seem pretty." Jessamyn West warned, "You may come away with a certain feeling of tiredness," and left it at that. Malcolm Cowley managed to imply the book is a masterpiece without actually saying so—the publishers couldn't extract a single quote. With that cooniness he used to deploy in the 30's when he was confronted with an important work that was on the right (that is, the "left") side but was pretty terrible, Cowley, here also confronted with a conflict between his taste and his sense of the *Zeitgeist,* managed to praise with faint damns. One magisterial sentence, in particular, may be recommended to all ambitious young book reviewers: "His style used to be as clear as a mountain brook; now it has become a little weed-grown and murky, like the brook when it wanders through a meadow." A meadowy brook is pretty *too*—it shows the mature Cozzens now feels, in Cowley's words, that "life is more complicated than he once believed."

A favorite reviewer's gambit was that Cozzens' prose may be involved but so is James's. "One drawback is the style," *Time* admitted, "which is frosted with parenthetical clauses, humpbacked syntax, Jamesian involutions, Faulknerian meanderings." I am myself no foe of the parenthesis, nor do I mind a little syntactical humping at times, but I feel this comparison is absurd. James's involutions are (a) necessary to precisely discriminate his meaning; (b) solid parts of the architecture of the sentence; and (c) controlled by a fine ear for euphony. Faulkner does meander, but there is emotional force, descriptive richness behind his wanderings. They both use words that are not only in the dictionary but also in the living language, and use them in conversational rhythms. Their style is complex because they are saying something complicated, not, as with Coz-

* "CAKEWALK—a form of entertainment among American Negroes in which a prize of a cake was given for the most accomplished steps and figures."—WEBSTER.

zens, because they cannot make words do what they want them to do.

But the main burden of the reviewers was not doubt but affirmation. In reading their praise of Cozzens' prose, I had a uneasy feeling that perhaps we were working with different texts.

"Every sentence has been hammered, filed and tested until it bears precisely the weight it was designed to carry, and does it with clarity and grace," wrote John Fischer. The sentences have been hammered all right:

> Recollected with detachment, these self-contrived quandaries, these piffling dilemmas that young love could invent for itself were comic—too much ado about nothing much! Arthur Winner Junior was entangled laughably in his still-juvenile illogicalities and inconsistencies. Absurdly set on working contradictories and incompatibles, he showed how the world was indeed a comedy for those who think. By his unripe, all-or-nothing-at-all views, he was bound to be self-confounded. By the ridiculous impracticalness of his aspirations, he was inescapably that figure of fun whose lofty professions go with quite other performances. The high endeavor's very moments of true predominance guaranteed the little joke-on-them to follow.

This is not a Horrible Example—we shall have some later—but a typical, run-of-the-mill Cozzens paragraph, chosen at random. It seems to me about as bad as prose can get—what sensitive or even merely competent novelist would write a phrase like "the ridiculous impracticalness of his aspirations"?

"Mr. Cozzens is a master of dialogue," wrote Orville Prescott. On the contrary, he has no ear for speech at all. "You answer well, Arthur!" says one matron. "But, to my very point!" And another: "They're all, or almost all, down at the boathouse, swimming, Arthur." A practicing lawyer, not supposed to be either pompous or balmy, uses the following expressions during a chat: "I merit the reproof no doubt. . . . My unbecoming boasting you must lay to my sad disability. . . . I'm now in a fettle fine. . . . Our colloquy was brief." In short, Cozzens' people tend to talk like Cozzens. They're out for that cake, too.

"He has always written with complete clarity," wrote Granville Hicks, *"but here, without forsaking clarity and correctness, he achieves great eloquence and even poetic power."* On the contrary, malphony exfoliates, as our author might put it. As:

> The succussive, earthquake-like throwing-over of a counted-on years-old stable state of things had opened fissures. Through one of them, Arthur Winner stared a giddying, horrifying moment down unplumbed, nameless abysses in himself. He might later

> deny the cognition, put thoughts of the undiscovered country away, seek to lose the memory; yet the heart's mute halt at every occasional, accidental recollection of those gulfs admitted their existence, confessed his fearful close shave.

"Succussive" is cake-walking, since it means "violently shaking . . . as of earthquakes" and so merely duplicates the next word; a good writer wouldn't use four hyphenated expressions in a row; he would also avoid the "occasional, accidental" rhyme, and the reference to unplumbed abysses; he would ask himself what a mute halt is (as versus a noisy halt?); and he would sense that "close shave" is stylistically an anticlimax to so solemnly elevated a passage. It's all very puzzling. Here's Richard Ellmann of Northwestern University, who has been perceptive about Joyce's prose, finding *By Love Possessed* "so pleasant to read," while I find almost every sentence grates.*

"Its author has become the most technically accomplished American novelist alive," wrote Whitney Balliett. Let us say rather: the least technically accomplished. To list a few defects of style:

(1) *Melodramatics.* "Deaf as yesterday to all representations of right, he purposed further perfidy, once more pawning his honor to obtain his lust. Deaf as yesterday to all remonstrances of reason, he purposed to sell himself over again to buy venery's disappearing dross." (Haven't seen "dross" in print since *East Lynne.*)

(2) *Confucius Say.* A queer strangled sententiousness often seizes upon our author. "In real life, effects of such disappointment are observed to be unenduring." "The resolve to rise permitted no intermissions; ambition was never sated." Like shot in game or sand in clams, such gritty nuggets are strewn through the book to set on edge the teeth of the reader—though not, apparently, of the reviewer.

(3) *Pointless Inversion.* As Wolcott Gibbs once wrote of *Time:* "Backward ran sentences till reeled the mind." Examples: "Unintelligible to them would be the law." "Owned and operated by Noah's father was a busy grist mill." "Behind these slowminded peerings of sullen anxiety did dumb unreasonable surges of love swell." "For that night, untied

* As: "Thinking last night of Ralph's 'Joanie,' those Moores, all unsuspecting; whose 'shame' or 'disgrace" of the same kind (if more decent in degree) stood accomplished, waiting merely to be discovered to them, Arthur Winner had felt able to pre-figure, following the first horrified anger, the distraught recriminations, the general fury of family woe, a bitter necessary acceptance." I find such prose almost impossible to read, partly because of an inexpressive, clumsy use of words, partly because the thought is both abstract and unclear, but chiefly because the rhythms are all wrong. Instead of carrying one forward, they drop one flat, and one must begin anew with each phrase. An artist creates a world, bit added to bit; each addition of Cozzens destroys what has gone before.

Hope still her virgin knot will keep." The last is interesting. He must mean "tied," since the "still" implies a possible later change, and a virgin knot, once untied, must ever remain so. I think the "un-" was added automatically, because Cozzens makes a dead style even deader by an obsessive use of negative constructions, often doubled, as: "unkilled," "unhasty," "not-unhelped," "not-uneducated," "not-unmoving," "a not-unsturdy frame," "a not-unhandsome profile." May we take it the profile is handsome, the frame sturdy, or do they exist in some limbo betwixt and between?

(4) *Toujours le Mot Injuste*. If there's an inexpressive word, Cozzens will find it. He specially favors: (a) five-dollar words where five-centers would do; (b) pedantic Latinisms, strange beasts that are usually kept behind the zoo bars of Webster's Unabridged.

(a) Multisonous, incommutable, phantasmogenesis (having to do with the origin of dreams), stupefacients (narcotics), encasement ("snug encasement of his neck" for "tight collar"), explicative ("one of his characteristically explicative observations"), solemnization ("wedding" becomes "the solemnization's scene"), eventuated ("acts of eventuated guilt," a phrase undecipherable even with the Unabridged), and condign ("Condign punishment"—means "deserved p.").

(b) I must admit that reading Cozzens has enriched my vocabulary, or, more accurately, added to it. My favorite, on the whole, is "presbyopic," which of course means "long-sighted because of old age." I also like the sound of "viridity" and "mucid," though it's disappointing to learn they mean simply "greenness" and "slimy." But I see no reason for such grotesques as qualmish, scrutinous, vulnerary ("wound-healing"), pudency, revulsively, and vellications, which is Latin for twitchings.

Perhaps the supreme triumph of Late Cozzenesque occurs on page 128, where, agonizedly entoiled in the entracement of a bridegroom's mazed tergiversations, as our author might put it, he manages twice to use the phrase "piacular pollution." The second time is specially impressive: "That concept of piacular pollution, much diminished as the idea of undressing Hope was entertained, received, with the autoptic fact of the undressed Hope, its *coup de grace*." "Autoptic" is simple—an adjective made from "autopsy" or "personal inspection." "Piacular" is more complicated. It means either (a) "of the nature of an expiation; expiatory," or (b) "requiring expiation." If it's (a), then the pollution is an expiation, an atonement for some sin, which is absurd since the pollution itself is a sin; but if it's (b), we are presented, by inference, with the interesting notion of a pollution that does not require expiation, that is, a so-to-speak pure pollution.

Cozzens' style is a throwback to the palmiest days of 19th-century rhetoric, when a big Latin-root word was considered more elegant than a small Anglo-Saxon word. The long, patient uphill struggle of the last fifty years to bring the diction and rhythms of prose closer to those of the spoken language might never have existed so far as Cozzens is concerned. He doesn't even revert to the *central* tradition (Scott, Cooper, Bulwer-Lytton) but rather to the eccentric mode of the half-rebels against it (Carlyle, Meredith), who broke up the orderly platoons of gold-laced Latinisms into whimsically arranged squads, uniformed with equal artificiality but marching every which way as the author's wayward spirit moved them. Carlyle and Meredith are even less readable today than Scott and Cooper, whose prose at least inherited from the 18th century some structural backbone.

That a contemporary writer should spend eight years fabricating a pastiche in the manner of George Meredith could only happen in America, where isolation produces oddity. The American novelist is sustained and disciplined by neither a literary tradition nor an intellectual community. He doesn't see other writers much; he probably doesn't live in New York, which like Paris and London unfortunately has almost a monopoly of the national cultural life, because the pace is too fast, the daily life too ugly, the interruptions too great; and even if he does, there are no cafés or pubs where he can foregather with his colleagues; he doesn't read the literary press, which anyway is much less developed than in London or Paris; he normally thinks of himself as a non-intellectual, even an anti-intellectual (Faulkner, Hemingway, Fitzgerald, Anderson). It is a pattern of cultural isolation that brings out a writer's eccentric, even his grotesque side.

In the case of Cozzens, things have gone about as far as they can. At his country place in Lambertville, New Jersey, he leads a life compared to which Thoreau's on Walden Pond was gregarious. "I am a hermit and I have no friends," he understates. According to *Time,* "Years elapse between dinner guests" and he hasn't been to a play, a concert, or an art gallery in twenty years. (He did go to a movie in 1940). To those who wonder how he can write novels when he has so little contact with people, he says: "The thing you have to know about is yourself: you are people." But he seems signally lacking in self-knowledge. He fancies himself as a stylist, for instance. "My own literary preferences are for writers who write well," he says, pleasantly adding: "This necessarily excludes most of my contemporaries." The level of his taste may be inferred from the fact that he sneers at Faulkner ("falsifies life for dramatic effect"), Hemingway ("under the rough exterior, he's just a great big bleeding heart"), and Lewis ("a crypto-sentimentalist"), but admires—W. Somerset Maugham.

He is similarly deceived about himself. He thinks he is a true-blue conservative of the old school: "I am more or less illiberal and strongly antipathetic to all political and social movements. I was brought up an Episcopalian, and where I live, the landed gentry are Republican." He is proud of his Tory ancestors, who had to flee to Canada during the Revolution: "To tell the truth, I feel I'm better than other people." But this statement itself seems to me not that of an aristocrat, who would take it for granted, but rather of an uneasy *arriviste*. Nor does illiberalism make a conservative, as we learned in the days of McCarthy. Cozzens, like some of his sympathetically intended heroes—Dr. Bull in *The Last Adam* is an example—goes in for Plain Speaking, but it comes out somehow a little bumptious and unpleasant: "I like anybody if he's a nice guy, but I've never met many Negroes who were nice guys." His notion of a nice guy Negro is Alfred Revere in *By Love Possessed,* the colored verger of the local Episcopalian church, which is otherwise Whites Only. Tactfully, Mr. Revere always takes Communion last: "The good, the just man had consideration for others. By delaying he took care that members of the congregation need never hesitate to receive the blood of our Lord Jesus Christ because a cup from which a Negro had drunk contained it." This is not ironical, it is perfectly serious, and is followed by a page of contorted dialectic about God's love.

Years ago Cozzens married Bernice Baumgarten, a well-known literary agent. Although apparently it is a successful marriage, his remarks to the press about it have been rather boorish, even for him: "I suppose sex entered into it. After all, what's a woman for? . . . Mother almost died when I married a Jew, but later when she saw I was being decently cared for, she realized that it was the best thing that could have happened to me." Up to *By Love Possessed,* Cozzens was largely supported by his wife. "It could have been a humiliating situation, but I guess I had a certain native conceit [those Tory ancestors] and felt that her time was well spent," he says with his usual delicacy. Perhaps Cozzens is as inept with the spoken as with the written word. Probably he didn't mean to define quite so narrowly and explicitly his wife's role in his life, just as probably the slick, pushing, crafty Jewish lawyer, Mr. Woolf—he has even had the nerve to turn Episcopalian, to Winner's contemptuous amusement—is not meant to stand for Jews in general, any more than the odious Mrs. Pratt is meant to stand for all Catholics. One only wishes that Cozzens' mouthpiece weren't quite so explicit: "Glimpsing Mr. Woolf's face in the mirror again, Arthur Winner could see his lips form a smile, deprecatory, intentionally ingratiating. Was something there of the patient shrug, something of the bated breath and whispering humbleness? . . . Did you forget at your peril the ancient grudge that might be fed if Mr. Woolf could catch you once upon the hip?"

How did it happen? Why did such a book impress the reviewers? We know whodunit, but what was the motive? Like other crimes, this one was a product of Conditions. The failure of literary judgment and of simple common sense shown in *l'affaire Cozzens* indicates a general lowering of standards. If this were all, if our reviewers just didn't know any better, then one would have to conclude we had quite lost our bearings. Luckily, there were other factors. It is disturbing it could have happened at all: *By Love Possessed* is the Sputnik-Vanguard of the literary world. But there were also specific reasons for the reviewers' misjudgment, some of them also rather disturbing but at least limited in their implications.

The two most important, I think, were related: a general feeling that Cozzens had hitherto been neglected and that he "had it coming to him." And consequently a willingness, indeed an eagerness to take at face value his novel's pretensions. It is difficult for American reviewers to resist a long, ambitious novel; they are betrayed by the American admiration of size and scope, also by the American sense of good fellowship; they find it hard to say to the author, after all his work: "Sorry, but it's terrible." In Cozzens' case, it would have been especially hard because he had been writing serious novels for thirty years without ever having had a major success, either popular or *d'estime*. It was now or never. The second alternative would have meant that a lifetime of hard work in a good cause had ended in failure, which would have been un-American. So it had to be now.

The other factor in the book's success is historical. It is the latest episode in The Middlebrow Counter-Revolution. In the 20's and 30's, the avant-garde intellectuals had it pretty much their way. In 1940, the counter-revolution was launched with Archibald MacLeish's essay, "The Irresponsibles," and Van Wyck Brooks's Hunter College talk, "On Literature Today," followed a year later by his "Primary Literature and Coterie Literature." The Brooks-MacLeish thesis was that the avant-garde had lost contact with the normal life of humanity and had become frozen in an attitude of destructive superiority; the moral consequences were perversity and snobbishness, the cultural consequences were negativism, eccentricity, and solipsism.* The thesis was launched at the right moment. By 1940 the avant-garde had run out of gas—unfortunately no rear-guard filling stations have been opened up, either—while the country had become engaged in a world struggle for survival that made any radically dissident, skeptical-attitude a luxury. Both conditions still persist, and so the counter-revolution has been on ever since.

* Brooks and MacLeish assumed it was good for writers to identify themselves with their society, which in turn assumed the society was good. If it wasn't, then the avant-garde was justified in isolating itself. Empirically, this would seem to be the case—at least most of the memorable art in every field produced between about 1890 and 1930 was done by artists like Joyce, Eliot, Picasso, Stravinsky, and others who had rejected bourgeois society. But there's no space to argue the question here. Those interested might look at my "Kulturbolshewismus—the Brooks-MacLeish Thesis" in *Partisan Review,* November-December 1941, reprinted in *Memoirs of a Revolutionist* (1957).

Perhaps the first to see Cozzens as a rallying point was the late Bernard De Voto, who had a wonderfully acute instinct in these matters. De Voto was Cozzens' Ezra Pound. "He is not a literary man, he is a writer," he observed, a little obscurely but I see what he means. "There are a handful like him in every age. Later on it turns out they were the ones who wrote that age's literature." The wheel has comically come full circle: it used to be those odd, isolated, brilliant writers who were *in advance* of their times—the Stendhals, the Melvilles, the Joyces, and Rimbauds—who later on were discovered to be "the ones who wrote that age's literature"; but now it is the sober, conscientious plodders, who have a hard time just keeping up with the procession, whose true worth is temporarily obscured by their modish avant-garde competitors. This note is struck by the reviewers of *By Love Possessed*. "Critics and the kind of readers who start fashionable cults have been markedly cool toward him," writes Gill, while John Fischer complains that Cozzens, unlike "some other novelists of stature," has hitherto been denied "the reverence—indeed the adulation—of the magisterial critics whose encyclicals appear in the literary quarterlies and academic journals. Aside from a Pulitzer Prize in 1949, no such laurels have lighted on Cozzens' head, and the fashionable critics have passed him by in contemptuous silence."

A highbrow conspiracy of paranoiac dimensions, it seems, is behind it all. Cozzens just won't play our game. "It may be that his refusal to become a public figure—no TV or P.E.N. appearances, no commencement addresses at Sarah Lawrence, no night-club pronouncements recorded by Leonard Lyons—has put them [us] off. By devoting himself to writing, he has made himself invisible to the world of letters." So, Mr. Gill.

And Mr. Fischer: "Even his private life is, for a writer, unconventional. He attends no cocktail parties, makes no speeches, signs no manifestoes, writes no reviews, appears on no television shows, scratches no backs, shuns women's clubs. . . . Few people in the so-called literary world have ever set eyes on him." But doesn't all this precisely describe Faulkner and Hemingway when they were making their reputations? Is the P.E.N. Club—have I ever met a member?—so powerful? Did Fitzgerald sign any manifestoes? Are we highbrows really so impressed by TV appearances, talks before women's clubs, mention in gossip columns? Could it be simply that Cozzens really isn't very good?

Another hypothesis was advanced by *Time:* "The interior decorators of U.S. letters—the little-magazine critics whose favorite furniture is the pigeonhole—find that Cozzens fits no recent fictional compartments, and usually pretend that he does not exist." But there is, in fact, a recent pigeonhole for Cozzens: the Novel of Resignation. *By Love Possessed* is, philosophically, an inversion, almost a parody of a kind of story Tolstoy and other 19th-century Russian novelists used to tell: of a successful, self-satisfied hero who is led by experiences in "extreme situations" to see how artificial his life has been and who then rejects the conventional world and either dies or begins a new, more meaningful life. In the Novel of Resignation, the highest reach of enlightenment is to realize how awful the System is and yet to accept it *on its own terms.* Because otherwise there wouldn't be any System. Marquand invented the genre, Sloan Wilson carried it on in *The Man in the Gray Flannel Suit,* and Herman Wouk formulated it most unmistakably in *The Caine Mutiny*. Wouk's moral is that it is better to obey a lunatic, cowardly Captain Queeg, even if the result is disaster, than to follow the sensible advice of an officer of lower grade (who is pictured as a smooth-talking, destructive, cynical, irresponsible conniver—in short, an intellectual) and save the ship. Because otherwise there wouldn't be any U.S. navy. In short, the conventional world, the System, is confused with Life. And since Life is Like That, it is childish if not worse to insist on something better. This is typically American: either juvenile revolt or the immature acceptance of everything; there is no modulation, no development, merely the blank confrontation of untenable extremes; "maturity" means simply to replace wholesale revolt with wholesale acceptance.

It is as if Tolstoy's *The Death of Ivan Ilyitch* ended with the hero, after his atrocious sufferings, concluding that, as a high official of the Court of Justice, it was in the nature of things that he should die horribly of cancer, and that he must therefore bear his torment like a man for the good of the service. On the contrary, he is driven by his "extreme situation" to reject his whole past way of life. Only when he is finally able to give up "the claim that his life had been good" can he experience anything significant: love—the young servant's gentle care of him—and then death.

The ending of *By Love Possessed* strikes rather a different note. From Winner's climactic six-page interior monologue that ends the book we can take three formulations that sum it up: (1) "Freedom is the knowledge of necessity." (2) "We are not children. In this life we cannot have everything for ourselves we might like to have." (3) "Victory is not in reaching certainties or solving mysteries; victory is in making do with uncertainties, in supporting mysteries."

But what is the reality behind these unexceptional bits of philosophy? It is that Winner, for complicated pragmatic-sentimental reasons, decides to cover up an embezzlement he has just discovered, an embezzlement of trust funds by his venerable law partner, Noah Tuttle, and that he has been eased of his guilt toward his other partner, Julius Penrose, about his old affair with Marjorie, Penrose's wife. In both cases, it is Penrose who gives him the line: exposing Tuttle would not only ruin Winner—who would be equally responsible for his partner's defalcations—but would also mean the disgrace of Tuttle, who is after all paying the money back slowly. As for Winner's liaison with Marjorie, Penrose has known about it all along and has never blamed Winner, considering that "indefeasible urge of the flesh." In fact, Penrose is actually obliged to Winner for *not* telling him: "I've always thanked you for . . . trying in every way to keep it from me."

In short, Ivan Ilyitch feels free because he is compelled to reject his past as "not the right thing," Arthur Winner because he is allowed to accept his past, is even thanked by his best friend for having concealed from him the fact that he had cuckolded him. The last words of the book are Winner's, as he returns home: "I'm here." It's all right, nothing has to be changed: "I have the strength, the strength to, to—to endure more miseries," thinks Winner, gratefully.

August 1960

Henry Roth

THE DUN DAKOTAS

There was something ruinous about the time, or fatal to creative gusto, or so I feel.* I have my inklings about its nature, my brief illumination, but just what it was I leave to others more competent at defining abstractions or rendering something definitive out of the multitude of eddies and appearances. The same sort of thing, we know, has happened before, also in a kind of revolutionary age, or one of rapid transition—the Romantics of the 19th century who either died physically, or figuratively, on the stump.

I have spent a great deal of time wondering about it; I don't spend so much now. By now, I console myself with the thought that my creative powers, such as they were, even though fully employed, would be on the decline anyway, and by now I would have met myself perhaps with certain volumes published, and conscious of a certain modicum of acclaim, and in possession of certain emoluments, to be sure. What difference does it make? The years would have been over in any event. Poor solace, I know. The mind shuttles and reminds. We go this way only once; and shuttles again and rejoins: once is enough.

I think it's been a tough time for writers, as it is. But on the other hand, when hasn't it been? And yet I know that there are periods of greater and lesser ferment, and inevitably those artists are luckier who have as a booster, so to speak, a dynamic time. We, at least those of my generation whom I knew, had it for a time, so I think, the fag end of it. But enough, you know, to get a sense of heady pioneering, stir, viable horizons. What's done's done, undone's undone; take it or leave it.

* After the original publication in 1935 of his first and only novel, *Call It Sleep,* Mr. Roth retired from literature altogether to become a waterfowl farmer in Maine. A few years after this piece was written at the invitation of *Commentary,* a paperback edition of *Call It Sleep* was issued, and the book finally achieved the recognition with a wide public which it had previously enjoyed only with a small group of literary critics.—Ed.

I'll tell you. In the whole range of my thoughts on the subject—and who hasn't his private continuum—right now it's morning. The sun is over the stable, and before me, between the house and stable lies the framed bit of snow-covered countryside in the state of Maine. You can see this could be the origin of a great many things that I could say about my life since *C.I.S.* was published. I can hear the geese bickering behind the stable, and anything I would mention would represent some phase of my present existence—and of course would have its trail all the way back to New York City, the slum childhood, the awareness of some talent, the creative period and the débâcle, and so forth. One has to put a term to things—fill it in as you like. I was a writer once, just as I was an eager East Side kid before that, and a mopey Harlem youth in the interim, who am now a waterfowl farmer. I don't know—now—how long I'll continue to be that. For one thing, one boy is already at college, and the other soon to go. Who will help around the place, lug in geese to be processed, help pluck, shovel the long driveway, chuck cord wood down the cellar bulkhead, and do the hundred chores of arms and legs. And at fifty-four, one's back begins to feel at times as if the plates had been welded.

I'd like to tell you a story, a yarn. It's sort of importunate at the back of my mind, though I'm not sure it's appropriate. And yet I find that these importunings are somehow more apt to be better guides of my destination than my reasoning.

It concerns an expedition into the Dakotas, and more particularly concerns a prologue that I was engaged in writing for the second novel—this, after I had already written a sizeable section. I haven't the prologue with me any more, and won't even attempt to reconstruct it as it was. The inevitable mule team, the soldiers trudging alongside, led by a Captain and a Scout, were crossing from the Bad Lands to the Black Hills. They had been commissioned to do a topographical study of their part of the country, and this was during the 70's of the last century. You can imagine the gnarled terrain, or consult an encyclopedia, or consult Mr. Eliot—the wrenched and contorted land, the lopped pillars and the grinning gulleys—the Scout reined in his horse: "Captain," he said, "did you ever see red cabbage a'growin'?"

The Captain reflected: "I've seen red cabbage. I don't know as I ever saw it a'growin'."

"You'll see it now," said the Scout. "Look around you."

And the Captain looked. And on every ridge surrounding them, there were Redskins mounted on their ponies, their eagle feathers against the sky, a veritable paling of feather-crested men.

"Well," said the Captain, "what do we do now?"

"We gamble," said the Scout. "That's all we can do." He urged his horse ahead a few steps, and raised his arm in signal for parley. And down one of the nearby slopes clattered the bonneted Chief and some of his Braves. "How." No doubt, they said, "How." And perhaps, how kola.

"White man on my people hunting ground," said the Chief.

"Chief," said the Scout, "we're just passin' through. White Father in Washington send us to make picture."

"Picture?"

"Picture of the land. So all white settler stay out. Keep peace."

"Ugh!" the Chief relaxed.

"Chief gamble?" said the Scout, producing a deck of cards. "Chief savvy cards?"

"Savvy poker," said the Chief.

"Good." They placed a blanket on the ground, and the two men gambled. They gambled for silver dollars, there between the Black Hills and the Bad Lands, among the stupendous shapes, under the stupendous sky. And the Chief's luck was extraordinary, and the Scout's bad luck equally so. He lost hand after hand, stake after stake, and his pile of silver dollars dwindled. "Never see such luck," said the Scout.

"Ugh," said the Chief. "Chief heap lucky. Heap strong."

And when his last silver dollar had changed hands, the Scout rose. "Chief," he said, "you won all our money. You let us pass now?"

The Chief folded his arms across his chest and dreamed a long dream or a long thought—whether of bison, or the bright tepees of childhood, or the game birds of youth I do not know.

But that was as far as I got for over twenty-five years, waiting for the decision of the Chief who had turned into stone or into legend, waiting for a man to decide what history was in the dun Dakotas, waiting for a sanction; and oddly enough it would have to be the victim who would provide it, though none could say who was the victim, who the victor. And only now can I tell you, and perhaps it's a good sign—at least for my generation, who waited with me—though perhaps it's too late.

"Will the Chief let us pass?" the Scout repeated. "Always remember Great Chief."

And the Chief unfolded his arms and motioned them the way of their journey. "Go now," he said.

October 1960

Irving Howe

A YIDDISH "MODERNIST"

Isaac Bashevis Singer is the only living Yiddish writer whose translated work has caught the imagination of the American literary public. Though his brilliant stories and novels are crowded with grotesque happenings, though they often seem to comprise an alien sub-world of imps, devils, whores, spirits in seizure, charlatans, and false messiahs, the contemporary reader—for whom the determination not to be shocked has become a point of honor—is likely to feel closer to Singer than to any, or most, of the other Yiddish writers. Offhand this may be surprising, for Singer's subjects are decidedly remote: in *Satan in Goray,* the orgiastic consequences of the false messianism of 17th-century East European Jews; in his book of stories *Gimpel the Fool,* a range of demonic, apocalyptic, and perversely sacred moments of *shtetl* life; and now in his new novel *The Magician of Lublin,* a portrait of a Jewish acrobat-magician-Don Juan in late 19th-century Poland who exhausts himself in sensuality and ends his life as a penitent ascetic. Yet one feels that, unlike many of the Yiddish writers who treat more familiar and up-to-date subjects, Singer commands a distinctively "modern" sensibility.

Now this is partly true—in the sense that Singer, though a master of Yiddish prose, has cut himself off from some of the traditional assumptions of Yiddish literature. But it is also not true—in the sense that any effort to assimilate Singer to literary "modernism" without registering how deeply involved he is with Jewish history and faith, is certain to distort the meanings of his work.

Those meanings, one might as well admit, are often enigmatic and hard to come by. It must be a common experience among Singer's readers to find a quick pleasure in the caustic surfaces of his prose, the nervous tokens of his virtuosity—for simply as a literary *performer* he has few peers among living writers—but then to acknowledge themselves baffled when they inquire into the point or purpose of his fictions. That these do have an insistent point and stringent purpose no one can doubt; Singer is too ruthlessly single-minded a writer to content himself with mere slices of representation or displays of the bizarre. His grotesquerie must be taken seriously, perhaps as a recoil from his perception of how ugly—how gratuitously ugly—human life can be. He is a writer completely absorbed by the demands of his vision, a vision gnomic and compulsive but with moments of high exaltation; so that while reading his stories one feels as if one were overhearing bits and snatches of a monologue, the impact of which is both notable and disturbing, but the meaning withheld.

Now these are precisely the qualities that the sophisticated reader, trained to docility before the exactions of "modernism," has come to applaud. Singer's stories work, or prey, upon the nerves. They leave one unsettled and anxious, the way a rationalist might feel if, walking at night in the woods, he suddenly found himself afraid of bats. Unlike most Yiddish fiction, Singer's stories neither round out the cycle of their intentions nor posit a coherent and ordered universe. They can be seen as paradigms of the arbitrariness, the grating injustice, at the heart of life. They offer instances of pointless suffering, dead-end exhaustion, inexplicable grace. And sometimes, as in Singer's masterpiece "Gimpel the Fool," they turn about, refusing to rest with the familiar discomforts of the problematic, and drive toward a prospect of salvation on the other side of despair. But this prospect does not depend on any belief in the comeliness or lawfulness of the universe: whether or not God is there, surely He is no protector. Things happen, the probable bad and improbable good, both of them subject to the whim of the fortuitous—and the sacred fools, like Gimpel, learn to roll with the punch, finding the value of their life in a total passivity and openness to suffering.

It is hardly a secret that in the Yiddish literary world Singer is regarded with a certain suspicion or at least reserve. His powers of evocation, his resources as a stylist are acknowledged, yet many Yiddish literary people, including serious ones, seem to be uneasy about him. One reason is that "modernism"—which, as these people regard Singer, means a heavy stress upon sexuality, a concern for the irrational, expressionist distortions of character, and an apparent indifference to the more conventional aspects of Jewish life—has never won so strong a hold in Yiddish writing as it has in most Western literatures. For the Yiddish writers, "modernism" has often been a mere adornment of manner upon a subject inescapably traditional, or a means of intensifying a sense of estrangement from collective values to which they nevertheless remain bound.

The truly "modern" writer, however, is not quite trustworthy in his relation to his culture; he is a shifty character by choice and need, unable to settle into that representative solidity which would permit him to serve as a cultural "spokesman." And to the extent that Singer shares in the modernist outlook he will be regarded with distrust by Yiddish readers brought up on such "spokesmen" as Peretz, Abraham Reisen, and H. Leivick. There is, to be sure, no lack of admiration among Yiddish readers for Singer's work: anyone with half an ear must respond to the marvelously taut and subtle rhythms of his prose. Still, it is a qualified admiration. Singer's moral outlook, which seems to move equally toward the sensational and the ascetic, and his assumption that in fiction grotesquerie can be made to serve almost as a mode of knowledge, are hardly traits calculated to put Yiddish readers at their ease.

I must confess that my first response to *The Magician of Lublin* was somewhat like the one I have been attributing here to Yiddish readers. The book is not quite so dazzling as *Satan in Goray,* but it does represent Singer at fairly close to his best, particularly in his gifts for evoking the textures of sensuous life and for driving straight to those moments of tension and inner division which reveal the souls of his characters. But while there is no difficulty in making out what happens in the book, there is a real question as to what it all signifies.

The Magician of Lublin centers on the figure of Yasha Mazur, a Jewish acrobat-magician who travels through the towns of Poland, giving performances and entangling himself with women. Like other figures in Singer's work, Yasha is "half Jew, half Gentile—neither Jew nor Gentile. He had worked out his own religion. There was a Creator, but He revealed Himself to no one, gave no indications of what was permitted or forbidden." The theme is recurrent in Singer: even the acknowledgment of God yields no moral assurance, and with or without Him men lose their way.

At the beginning, Yasha is seen during one of his rare visits home, basking in his prosperity and enjoying a good and faithful wife. But he is a restless creature, always driven to test his powers of performance and persuasion, to try out his gifts in still another place, with still another woman. These gifts constitute his curse, and his pleasure in observing his impact upon other people, his undoing.

Yasha moves on, leaving home, visiting his Gentile assistant, who is also a worshipful mistress, having a lively time with a Jewish whore, skirting the life of a gang of Jewish thieves, savoring an encounter with some Jewish white slavers, and finally ending in Warsaw with the biggest risk of his life: a scheme to run off, as he pretends to be unmarried, with a middle-class Gentile widow. This woman represents for him—the symbolism is clear but not insistent—the attractions of the outer cultivated world he had never been able to reach or conquer. Yasha undertakes a robbery to get money for his elopement, fails because of the residual power of his

Jewish conscience, and then rapidly falls into flight, pain, collapse. "He had looked on the face of death and lechery and had seen that they were the same. . . . He had seen the hand of God. He had reached the end of the road." In an epilogue Yasha is seen at home again, now living as an ascetic who has locked himself in a hut behind his house, suffering cold, hunger, and sexual fantasies, worshipped by the credulous as a new miracle-worker, but still struggling to find his way to God.

From page to page the story, like anything Singer writes, is remarkably vivid. Everything springs to life, everything trembles with the breath of actuality. Yet, as one reads one grows uneasy and begins to consider the kind of criticism to which Singer is sometimes subjected by Yiddish literary people. Why is this juicy description here, that sensual evocation there? Isn't there an indulgence in sensation for its own sake, a surrender to rather than a use of the grotesque? Does not Singer sometimes come close to the self-imitation which is the writer's greatest curse, that self-imitation which consists in falling back upon familiar devices and inflections?

It would be idle to say that these things never happen, yet once we bring to bear the perspectives of "modernism," it becomes a bit easier to grasp and thereby "justify" *The Magician of Lublin*. The very incongruity in the conception of a Jewish Don Juan has its obvious ironic appeal and significance—particularly a Jewish Don Juan with a record of success who fails at precisely the point where conventional Jewish wisdom would predict that he would: his encounter with Christian gentility. The ending of the novel also allows us to see that Singer is working out a complex pattern of suggestion and not merely indulging in his repertoire of tricks. Yasha becomes a penitent, but so weak in body and faith that he cannot trust himself except under lock and key. Nothing is settled, nothing solved. At the end Yasha retains, embarrassingly, the charismatic powers he had enjoyed as a worldling: life is not so different even after the blessed revelation: the flesh continues to lust, the world remains full of temptations, and the fools who populate it still yearn for easy assuagements.

Between the epilogue and the bulk of the book there is, then, an ironic balance: each cancels out the implications of the other, so that finally, as at the beginning, what Singer offers are questions beyond answer. His particular power rests on this ability to hold such contrary elements as the miraculous and the skeptical, the moral and the exotic, in a delicate tension. At times, his style seems almost *as if* it were the style of a man possessed, so thoroughly does he give himself to the subject; yet Singer also maintains rigorous distance, one is always aware of the *conditional* nature of his involvement.

Having gone this far, we must now turn again. If Singer's work can be understood only on the assumption that in some crucial respects he is a "modernist" writer, one must add that in other ways he is profoundly related to the Jewish tradition. And if the Yiddish reader is inclined to slight the first side of his work, so the American reader is likely to underestimate the strength and persistence of the second.

Singer is related to the Jewish tradition not only in the obvious sense that he enjoys a close knowledge of the Jewish past. More importantly, he is one of the few Yiddish writers whose relation to the Jewish past does not depend on that body of attitudes and values we call Yiddishism. He writes *in* Yiddish, but is often quite apart from the Yiddish tradition. He is, so to say, a writer of the pre-Enlightenment and post-Enlightenment; he would be equally at home with a congregation of medieval Jews and a gathering of modern intellectuals, perhaps more so than at a meeting of the Yiddish P.E.N. Club; he has a strong sense of the mystical and antique, but also a stern awareness of psychoanalytic disenchantment; he has evaded both the religious pieties and the humane rationalism of 19th-century East European Judaism. In his fiction Singer has "skipped over" the ideas of the historical epoch which gave birth to Yiddishism, for the truth is, I suppose, that Yiddish literature, in both its acceptance and denials, its writers of faith and its writers of skepticism, is thoroughly caught up with the Enlightenment. Singer shares very little in the collective aspirations of the *folkshtimmlichkeit* of the Yiddish masters; he does not celebrate *dos klaine menshele* as a paragon of sweetness and goodness; he is impatient with the sensual deprivations involved in the values of *edelkeit;* and above all, he breaks away from a central assumption of both the 19th century and Yiddish literature, the assumption of *tachlis,* an immanent fate or end in human existence.

What remains? The Yiddish critic Shlomo Bickel has perceptively remarked that Singer's dominating principle is "anti-Prometheanism," a disbelief in the efficacy of defiance, striving, and pride, a doubt as to the sufficiency of knowledge or even wisdom. This seems true, but only if one remembers that in a good many of Singer's fictions, particularly in *The Magician of Lublin,* the central action does constitute a sort of Promethean ordeal or straining. Singer makes it abundantly clear that his characters have no choice: they must live out their hungers, their orgiastic yearnings and apocalyptic expectations. "Anti-Prometheanism" thus comes to rest upon a belief in the unavoidable recurrence of the Promethean urge—an urge which, in Singer's view of things, is reduced from ideal to obsession or, perhaps more accurately, makes it impossible to separate ideal from obsession.

In the end, what concerns Singer most of all is the possibilities for life that remain after the exhaustion of human effort, after failure and despair have come and gone. Singer watches his stricken figures from a certain distance, with enigmatic moral intent and no great outpouring of sympathy, almost as if to say that before their collapse neither judgment nor sympathy matters very much. Yet in all of his books the Promethean effort recurs, obsessional, churning with new energy and delusion. In the knowledge of its recurrence there may also lie hidden a kind of pity, for that too we would expect, and can learn to find, in the writer who created Gimpel.

March 1961

Philip Roth

WRITING AMERICAN FICTION

Several winters back, while I was living in Chicago, the city was shocked and mystified by the death of two teen-age girls. So far as I know the populace is mystified still; as for the shock, Chicago is Chicago, and one week's dismemberment fades into the next's. The victims this particular year were sisters. They went off one December night to see an Elvis Presley movie, for the sixth or seventh time we are told, and never came home. Ten days passed and fifteen and twenty, and then the whole bleak city, every street and alley, was being searched for the missing Grimes girls, Pattie and Babs. A girl friend had seen them at the movie, a group of boys had had a glimpse of them afterward getting into a black Buick; another group said a green Chevy, and so on and so forth, until one day the snow melted and the unclothed bodies of the two girls were discovered in a roadside ditch in a forest preserve on the West Side of Chicago. The coroner said he didn't know the cause of death and then the newspapers took over. One paper, I forget which one, ran a drawing of the girls on the back page, in bobby socks and levis and babushkas: Pattie and Babs a foot tall, and in four colors, like Dixie Dugan on Sundays. The mother of the two girls wept herself right into the arms of a local newspaper lady, who apparently set up her typewriter on the Grimes's front porch and turned out a column a day, telling us that these had been good girls, hardworking girls, average girls, churchgoing girls, et cetera. Late in the evening one could watch television interviews featuring schoolmates and friends of the Grimes sisters: the teen-age girls look around, dying to giggle; the boys stiffen in their leather jackets. "Yeah, I knew Babs, yeah she was all right, yeah, she was popular. . . ." On and on until at last comes a confession. A Skid Row bum of thirty-five or so, a dishwasher, a prowler, a no-good named Benny Bedwell, admits to killing both girls, after he and a pal had cohabited with them for several weeks in various flea-bitten hotels. Hearing the news, the mother weeps and cries and tells the newspaper lady that the man is a liar—her girls, she insists now, were murdered the night they went off to the movie. The coroner continues to maintain (with rumblings from the press) that the girls show no signs of having had sexual intercourse. Meanwhile, everybody in Chicago is buying four papers a day, and Benny Bedwell, having supplied the police with an hour-by-hour chronicle of his adventures, is tossed in jail. Two nuns, teachers of the girls at the school they attended, are sought out by the newspapermen. They are surrounded and questioned and finally one of the sisters explains all. "They were not exceptional girls," the sister says, "they had no hobbies." About this time, some good-natured soul digs up Mrs. Bedwell, Benny's mother, and a meeting is arranged between this old woman and the mother of the slain teen-agers. Their picture is taken together, two overweight, overworked American ladies, quite befuddled but sitting up straight for the photographers. Mrs. Bedwell apologizes for her Benny. She says, "I never thought any boy of mine would do a thing like that." Two weeks later, or maybe three, her boy is out on bail, sporting several lawyers and a new one-button roll suit. He is driven in a pink Cadillac to an out-of-town motel where he holds a press conference. Yes—he barely articulates—he is the victim of police brutality. No, he is not a murderer; a degenerate maybe, but even that is going out the window. He is changing his life—he is going to become a carpenter (a carpenter!) for the Salvation Army, his lawyers say. Immediately, Benny is asked to sing (he plays the guitar) in a Chicago night spot for two thousand dollars a week, or is it ten thousand? I forget. What I remember is that suddenly there is a thought that comes flashing into the mind of the spectator, or newspaper reader: is this all Public Relations? But of course not—two girls are dead. At any rate, a song begins to catch on in Chicago, "The Benny Bedwell Blues." Another newspaper launches a weekly contest: "How Do You Think the Grimes Girls Were Murdered?" and a prize is given for the best answer (in the opinion of the judges). And now the money begins; donations, hundreds of them, start pouring in to Mrs. Grimes from all over the city and the state. For what? From whom? Most contributions are anonymous. Just money, thousands and thousands of dollars—the *Sun-Times* keeps us informed of the grand total. Ten thousand, twelve thousand, fifteen thousand. Mrs. Grimes sets about refinishing and redecorating her house. A strange man steps forward, by the name of Shultz or Schwartz—I don't really remember, but he is in the applicance business and he presents Mrs. Grimes with a whole new kitchen. Mrs. Grimes, beside herself with appreciation and joy, turns to her surviving daughter and says, "Imagine me in that kitchen!" Finally, the poor woman goes out and buys two parakeets (or maybe another Mr. Shultz presented them as a gift); one parakeet she calls "Babs," the other, "Pattie." At just about this point, Benny Bedwell, doubtless having barely learned to hammer a nail in straight, is extradited to Florida on the charge of having raped a twelve-year-old girl there. Shortly thereafter I left Chicago myself, and so far as I know, though Mrs. Grimes hasn't her two girls, she has a brand new dishwasher and two small birds.

And what is the moral of so long a story? Simply this: that the American writer in the middle of the 20th century has his hands full in trying to understand, and then describe, and then make *credible* much of the American reality. It stupefies, it sickens, it infuriates, and finally it is even a kind of embarrassment to one's own meager imagination. The actuality is continually outdoing our talents, and the culture tosses up figures almost daily that are the envy of any novelist. Who, for example, could have invented Charles Van Doren? Roy Cohn and David Schine? Sherman Adams and Bernard Goldfine? Dwight David Eisenhower? Several months back most of the country heard one of the candidates for the presidency of the United States, the office of Jefferson, Lincoln, and FDR, say something like, "Now if you feel that Senator Kennedy is right, then I sincerely believe you should vote for Senator Kennedy, and if you feel that I am right, I humbly submit that you vote for me. Now I feel, and this is certainly a personal opinion, that I am right . . ." and so on. Though it did not appear quite this way to some thirty-four million voters, it still seems to me a little easy to pick on Mr. Nixon as someone to ridicule, and it is not for that reason that I have bothered to paraphrase his words here. If one was at first amused by him, one was ultimately astonished. As a literary creation, as some novelist's image of a certain kind of human being, he might have seemed believable, but I myself found that on the TV screen, as a real public image, a political fact, my mind balked at taking him in. Whatever else the television debates produced in me, I should like to point out, as a literary curiosity, that they also produced a type of professional envy. All the machinations over make-up, rebuttal time, all the business over whether Mr. Nixon should look at Mr. Kennedy when he replied, or should look away—all of it was so beside the point, so fantastic, so weird and astonishing, that I found myself beginning to wish I had invented it. That may not, of course, be a literary fact at all, but a simple psychological one—for finally I began to wish that *someone* had invented it, and that it was not real and with us.

The daily newspapers then fill one with wonder and awe: is it possible? is it happening? And of course with sickness and despair. The fixes, the scandals, the insanities, the treacheries, the idiocies, the lies, the pieties, the noise . . . . Recently, in *Commentary,** Benjamin DeMott wrote that the "deeply lodged suspicion of the times [is] namely, that events and individuals are unreal, and that power to alter the course of the age, of my life and your life, is actually vested nowhere." There seems to be, said

* "Looking for Intelligence in Washington" (October 1960).

DeMott, a kind of "universal descent into unreality." The other night—to give a benign example of the descent—my wife turned on the radio and heard the announcer offering a series of cash prizes for the three best television plays of five minutes' duration written by children. At such moments it is difficult to find one's way around the kitchen; certainly few days go by when incidents far less benign fail to remind us of what DeMott is talking about. When Edmund Wilson says that after reading *Life* magazine he feels that he does not belong to the country depicted there, that he does not live in that country, I think I understand what he means.

However, for a writer of fiction to feel that he does not really live in the country in which he lives—as represented by *Life* or by what he experiences when he steps out his front door—must certainly seem a serious occupational impediment. For what will be his subject? His landscape? It is the tug of reality, its mystery and magnetism, that leads one into the writing of fiction—what then when one is not mystified, but stupefied? not drawn but repelled? It would seem that what we might get would be a high proportion of historical novels or contemporary satire—or perhaps just nothing. No books. Yet the fact is that almost weekly one finds on the best-seller list another novel which is set in Mamaroneck or New York City or Washington, with people moving through a world of dishwashers and TV sets and advertising agencies and Senatorial investigations. It all *looks* as though the writers are still turning out books about our world. There is *Cash McCall* and *The Man in the Gray Flannel Suit* and *Marjorie Morningstar* and *The Enemy Camp* and *Advise and Consent,* and so on. But what is crucial, of course, is that these books aren't very good. Not that these writers aren't sufficiently horrified with the landscape to suit me—quite the contrary. They are generally full of concern for the world about them; finally, however, they just don't seem able to imagine the corruptions and vulgarities and treacheries of American public life any more profoundly than they can imagine human character—that is, the country's private life. All issues are generally solvable, which indicates that they are not so much wonder-struck or horror-struck or even plain struck by a state of civilization, as they are provoked by some topical controversy. "Controversial" is a common word in the critical language of this literature as it is, say, in the language of the TV producer. But it is clear that though one may refer to a "problem" as being controversial, one does not usually speak of a state of civilization as controversial, or a state of the soul.

It is hardly news that in best-sellerdom we frequently wind up with the hero coming to terms and settling down in Scarsdale, or wherever, knowing himself. And on Broadway, in the third act, someone says, "Look, why don't you just love each other?" and the protagonist, throwing his hand to his forehead, cries, "Oh God, why didn't *I* think of that!" and before the bulldozing action of love, all else collapses—verisimilitude, truth, and interest. It is like "Dover Beach" ending happily for Matthew Arnold, and for us, because the poet is standing at the window with a woman who understands him. If the investigation of our times and the impact of these times upon human personality were to become the sole property of Wouk, Weidman, Sloan Wilson, Cameron Hawley, and the theatrical *amor-vincit-omnia* boys it would indeed be unfortunate, for it would be somewhat like leaving sex to the pornographers, where again there is more to what is happening than first meets the eye.

And of course the times have not yet been left completely to lesser minds and talents. There is Norman Mailer. And he is an interesting example, I think, of one in whom our era has provoked such a magnificent disgust that dealing with it in fiction has almost come to seem, for him, beside the point. He has become an actor in the cultural drama, the difficulty of which, I should guess, is that it leaves one with considerably less time to be a writer. For instance, to defy the Civil Defense authorities and their H-bomb drills, you have to take off a morning from the typewriter and go down and stand outside of City Hall; then if you're lucky and they toss you in jail, you have to give up an evening at home and your next morning's work as well. To defy Mike Wallace, or challenge his principle-less aggression, or simply use him or straighten him out, you must first go on the program—there's one night shot. Then you may well spend the next two weeks (I am speaking from memory) disliking yourself for having gone, and then two more writing an article (or a confession to a gentle friend) in which you attempt to explain why you did it and what it was like. "It's the age of the slob," says a character in William Styron's new novel. "If we don't watch out they're going to drag us under. . . ." And the dragging under, as we see, takes numerous forms. We get, for instance, from Mailer a book like *Advertisements for Myself,* a chronicle for the most part of why I did it and what it was like—and who I have it in for: life as a substitute for fiction. An infuriating, self-indulgent, boisterous, mean book, not much worse than most advertising we have to put up with, I think—but also, taken as a whole, a curiously moving book, moving in its revelation of the connection between one writer and the times that have given rise to him, in the revelation of a despair so great that the man who bears it, or is borne by it, seems for the time being—out of either choice or necessity—to have given up on making an imaginative assault upon the American experience, and has become instead the champion of a kind of public revenge. Unfortunately, however, what one is champion of one day, one may wind up victim of the next; that is everybody's risk. Once having written *Advertisements for Myself,* I don't see that you can write it again. Mr. Mailer probably now finds himself in the unenviable position of having to put up or shut up. Who knows—maybe it's where he wanted to be. My own feeling is that times are tough for a writer when he takes to writing letters to his newspaper rather than those complicated, disguised letters to himself, which are stories.

The last is not meant to be a sententious, or a condescending remark, or even a generous one. However one suspects Mailer's style or his reasons, one sympathizes with the impulse that leads him to be—or to want to be—a critic, a reporter, a sociologist, a journalist, a figure, or even Mayor of New York. For what is particularly tough about the times is writing about them, as a serious novelist or storyteller. Much has been made, much of it by the writers themselves, of the fact that the American writer has no status and no respect and no audience: the news I wish to bear is of a loss more central to the task itself, a loss of subject; or if not a loss, if to say that is, romantically and inexactly and defensively, an attempt to place most of the responsibility outside the writer for what may finally be nothing more than the absence of genius in our times—then let me say a voluntary withdrawal of interest by the writer of fiction from some of the grander social and political phenomena of our times.

Of course there have been writers who have tried to meet these phenomena head-on. It seems to me I have read several books or stories in the past few years in which one character or another starts to talk about "The Bomb," and the conversation generally leaves me feeling half convinced, and in some extreme instances, even with a certain amount of sympathy for fall-out; it is like people in college novels having long talks about what kind of generation they are. But what then? What can the writer do with so much of the American reality as it is? Is the only other possibility to be Gregory Corso and thumb your nose at the whole thing? The attitude of the Beats (if such a phrase has meaning) is not in certain ways without appeal. The whole thing is a kind of joke. America, ha-ha. The only trouble is that such a position doesn't put very much distance between Beatdom and its sworn enemy, best-sellerdom—not much more, at any rate, than what it takes to get from one side of a nickel to the other: for what is America, ha-ha, but the simple reverse of America, hoo-ray?

It is possible that I have exaggerated both the serious writer's response to our cultural predicament, and his inability or unwillingness to deal with it imaginatively. There seems to me little, in the end, to be used as proof for an assertion having to do with the psychology of a nation's writers, outside, that is, of their books themselves. So, with this particular assertion, the argument may appear to be somewhat compromised in that the evidence to be submitted is not so much the books that have been written, but the ones that have been left unwritten and unfinished, and those that have not even been considered worthy of the attempt. Which is not to say that there have not been certain literary signs, certain obsessions and innovations and concerns, to be found in the novels of our best writers, supporting the notion that the world we have been given, the society and the community, has ceased to be as suitable or as manageable a subject for the novelist as it once may have been.

Let me begin with some words about the man who, by reputation at least, is *the* writer of the age. The response of college students to the works of J. D. Salinger should indicate to us that perhaps he, more than anyone else, has not turned his back on the times, but instead, has managed to put his finger on what is most significant in the struggle going on today between the self (all selves, not just the writer's) and the culture. *The Catcher in the Rye* and the recent stories in the *New Yorker* having to do with the Glass family surely take place in the social here and now. But what about the self, what about the hero? This question seems to me of particular interest here, for in Salinger more than in most of his contemporaries, there has been an increasing desire of late to place the figure of the writer himself directly in the reader's line of vision, so that there is an equation, finally, between the insights of the narrator as, say, brother to Seymour Glass, and as a man who is a writer by profession. And what of Salinger's heroes? Well, Holden Caulfield, we discover, winds up in an expensive sanitarium. And Seymour Glass commits suicide finally, but prior to that he is the apple of his brother's eye—and why? He has learned to live in this world—but how? By not living in it. By kissing the soles of little girls' feet and throwing rocks at the head of his sweetheart. He is a saint, clearly. But since madness is undesirable and sainthood, for most of us, out of the question, the problem of how to live *in* this world is by no means answered; unless the answer is that one cannot. The only advice we seem to get from Salinger is to be charming on the way to the loony bin. Of course, Salinger is under no burden to supply us, writers or readers, with advice, though I must admit that I find myself growing more and more curious about this professional writer, Buddy Glass, and how *he* manages to coast through this particular life in the arms of sanity.

It is not Buddy Glass, though, in whom I do not finally believe, but Seymour himself. Seymour is as unreal to me as his world, in all its endless and marvelous detail, is decidedly credible. I am touched by the lovingness that is attributed to him, as one is touched by so many of the gestures and attitudes in Salinger, but this lovingness, in its totality and otherworldliness, becomes for me in the end an attitude of the writer's, a cry of desperation, even a program, more than an expression of character. If we forgive this lapse, it is, I think, because we understand the depth of the despairing.

There is, too, in Salinger the suggestion that mysticism is a possible road to salvation; at least some of his characters respond well to an intensified, emotional religious belief. Now my own involvement with Zen is slight, but as I understand it in Salinger, the deeper we go into this world, the further we can get away from it. If you contemplate a potato long enough, it stops being a potato in the usual sense; unfortunately, though, it is the usual sense that we have to deal with from day to day. For all the loving handling of the world's objects, for all the reverence of life and feeling, there seems to me, in the Glass family stories as in *The Catcher,* a spurning of life as it is lived in this world, in this reality—this place and time is seen as unworthy of those few precious people who have been set down in it only to be maddened and destroyed.

A spurning of our world—though of a much different order—seems to occur in another of our most talented writers, Bernard Malamud. Even, one recalls, when Malamud writes a book about baseball, a book called *The Natural,* it is not baseball as it is played in Yankee Stadium, but a wild, wacky baseball, where a player who is instructed to knock the cover off the ball promptly steps up to the plate and knocks it off; the batter swings and the inner hard string core of the ball goes looping out to centerfield, where the confused fielder commences to tangle himself in the unwinding sphere; then the shortstop runs out, and with his teeth, bites the center-fielder and the ball free from one another. Though *The Natural* is not Malamud's most successful, nor his most significant book, it is at any rate our introduction to his world, which has a kind of historical relationship to our own, but is by no means a replica of it. By historical I mean that there are really things called baseball players and really things called Jews, but there much of the similarity ends. The Jews of *The Magic Barrel* and the Jews of *The Assistant,* I have reason to suspect, are not the Jews of New York City or Chicago. They are a kind of invention, a metaphor to stand for certain human possibilities and certain human promises, and I find myself further inclined to believe this when I read of a statement attributed to Malamud which goes, "All men are Jews." In fact we know this is not so; even the men who are Jews aren't sure they're Jews. But Malamud, as a writer of fiction, has not shown specific interest in the anxieties and dilemmas and corruptions of the modern American Jew, the Jew we think of as characteristic of our times; rather, his people live in a timeless depression and a placeless Lower East Side; their society is not affluent, their predicament not cultural. I am not saying—one cannot, of Malamud—that he has spurned life or an examination of the difficulties of being human. What it is to be human, to be humane, is his subject: connection, indebtedness, responsibility, these are his moral concerns. What I do mean to point out is that he does not—or has not yet—found the contemporary scene a proper or sufficient backdrop for his tales of heartlessness and heartache, of suffering and regeneration.

Now Malamud and Salinger do not speak, think, or feel for all writers, and yet their fictional response to the world about them—what they choose to mention, what they choose to avoid—is of interest to me on the simple grounds that they are two of our best. Surely there are other writers around, and capable ones too, who have not taken the particular roads that these two have; however, even with some of these others, I wonder if we may not be witnessing a response to the times, perhaps not so dramatic as in Sallinger and Malamud, but a response nevertheless.

Let us take up the matter of prose style. Why is everybody so bouncy all of a sudden? Those who have been reading in the works of Saul Bellow, Herbert Gold, Arthur Granit, Thomas Berger, Grace Paley, and others will know to what I am referring. Writing recently in the *Hudson Review,* Harvey Swados said that he saw developing "a nervous muscular prose perfectly suited to the exigencies of an age which seems at once appalling and ridiculous. These are metropolitan writers, most of them are Jewish, and they are specialists in a kind of prose-poetry that often depends for its effectiveness as much on how it is ordered, or how it looks on the printed page, as it does on what it is expressing. This is risky writing, . . ." Swados added, and perhaps it is in its very riskiness that we can discover some kind of explanation for it. I should like to compare two short descriptive passages, one from Bellow's *The Adventures of Augie March,* the other from Gold's new novel, *Therefore Be Bold,* in the hope that the differences revealed will be educational.

As has been pointed out by numerous people before me, the language of *Augie March* is one that combines a literary complexity with a conversational ease, a language that joins the idiom of the academy with the idiom of the streets (not all streets—certain streets); the style is special, private, and energetic, and though occasionally unwieldly and indulgent, it generally, I believe, serves the narrative, and serves it brilliantly. Here for instance is a description of Grandma Lausch:

> With the [cigarette] holder in her dark little gums between which all her guile, malice, and command issued, she had her best inspirations of strategy. She was as wrinkled as an old paper bag, an autocrat, hard-shelled and jesuitical, a pouncy old hawk of a Bolshevik, her small ribboned gray feet immobile on the shoe-kit and stool Simon had made in the manual-training class, dingy old wool Winnie [the dog] whose bad smell filled the flat on the cushion beside her. If wit and discontent don't necessarily go together, it wasn't from the old woman that I learned it.

Herbert Gold's language has also been special, private, and energetic. One will notice in the following passage from *Therefore Be Bold* that here too the writer begins by recognizing a physical similarity between the character described and some unlikely object, and from there, as in Bellow's Grandma Lausch passage, attempts to move into a deeper, characterological description, to wind up, via the body, making a discovery about the soul. The character described is named Chuck Hastings.

> In some respects he resembled a mummy—the shriveled yellow skin, the hand and head too large for a wasted body, the bottomless eye sockets of thought beyond the Nile. But his agile Adam's apple and point-making finger made him less the Styx-swimmer dog-paddling toward Coptic limbos than a high school intellectual intimidating the navel-eyed little girl.

First I must say that the grammar itself has me baffled: ". . . bottomless eye sockets of thought beyond the Nile." Is the thought beyond the Nile, or are the eye sockets? What does it mean to be beyond the Nile anyway? The a-grammaticality of the sentence has little in common with the ironic inversion with which Bellow's description begins: "With the holder in her dark little gums between which all her guile, malice, and command issued. . . ." Bellow goes on to describe Grandma Lausch as "an autocrat," "hard-shelled," "jesuitical," "a pouncy old hawk of a Bolshevik"—imaginative terms certainly, but toughminded, exact, and not exhibitionistic. Of Gold's Chuck Hastings, however, we learn, "His agile Adam's-apple and point-making finger made him less the Styx-swimmer dog-paddling toward Coptic limbos etc. . . ." Is this language in the service of the narrative, or a kind of literary regression in the service of the ego? In a recent review of *Therefore Be Bold,* Granville Hicks quoted this very paragraph in praise of Gold's style. "This is high-pitched," Mr. Hicks admitted, "but the point is that Gold keeps it up and keeps it up." I take it that Mr. Hicks's sexual pun is not deliberate; nevertheless, it should remind us all that showmanship and passion are not, and never have been, one and the same. What we have here, it seems to me, is not so much stamina or good spirits, but reality taking a backseat to personality—and not the personality of the character described, but of the writer who is doing the describing. Bellow's description seems to arise out of a firm conviction on the part of the writer about the character: Grandma Lausch IS. Behind the description of Chuck Hastings there seems to me the conviction—or the desire for us to be convinced—of something else: Herbert Gold IS. I am! I am! In short: look at me, I'm writing.

Because Gold's work serves my purposes, let me say a word or two more about him. He is surely one of our most productive and most respected novelists, and yet he has begun to seem to me a writer in competition with his own fiction. Which is more interesting—my life or my work? His new book of stories, *Love and Like,* is not over when we have finished reading the last narrative. Instead we go on to read several more pages in which the author explains why and how he came to write each of the preceding stories. At the end of *Therefore Be Bold* we are given a long listing of the various cities in which Gold worked on this book, and the dates during which he was living or visiting in them. It is all very interesting if one is involved in tracing lost mail, but the point to be noted here is that how the fiction has come to be written is supposed to be nearly as interesting as what is written. Don't forget, ladies and gentlemen, that behind each and every story you have read here tonight is—me. For all Gold's delight with the things of this world—and I think that his prose, at its best, is the expression of that delight—there is also a good deal of delight in the work of his own hand. And, I think, with the hand itself.

Using a writer for one's own purposes is of course to be unfair to him (nearly as unfair as the gambit that admits to being unfair); I confess to this, however, and don't intend to hang a man for one crime. Nevertheless, Gold's extravagant prose, his confessional tone (the article about divorce; then the several prefaces and appendices about his own divorce—my exwife says this about me, etc.; then finally the story about divorce)—all of this seems to have meaning to me in terms of this separation I tried to describe earlier, the not-so-friendly relationship between the writer and the culture. In fact, it is paradoxical really, that the very prose style which, I take it, is supposed to jolt and surprise us, and thereby produce a new and sharper vision, turns back upon itself, and the real world is in fact veiled from us by this elaborate and self-conscious language-making. I suppose that in a way one can think of it as a sympathetic, or kinetic, response to the clamor and din of our mass culture, an attempt to beat the vulgar world at its own game. I am even willing to entertain this possibility. But it comes down finally to the same thing: not so much an attempt to understand the self, as to assert it.

I must say that I am not trying to sell selflessness. Rather, I am suggesting that this nervous muscular prose that Swados talks about may perhaps have to do with the unfriendliness between the self of the writer and the realities of the culture. The prose suits the age, Swados suggests, and I wonder if it does not suit it, in part, because it rejects it. The writer pushes before our eyes—it is in the very ordering of our sentences—personality, in all its separateness and specialness. Of course the mystery of personality is nothing less than the writer's ultimate concern; and certainly when the muscular prose is revelatory of character—as in *Augie March*—then it is to be appreciated; at its worst, however, as a form of literary onanism, it seriously curtails the fictional possibilities, and may perhaps be thought of, and sympathetically so, as a symptom of the writer's loss of the community as subject.

True, the bouncy style can be understood in other ways as well. It is not surprising that most of these writers Swados sees as its practitioners are Jewish. When writers who do not feel much of a connection to Lord Chesterfield begin to realize that they are under no real obligation to try and write like that distinguished old stylist, they are quite likely to go out and be bouncy. Also, there is the matter of the spoken language which these writers have heard, as our statesmen might put it, in the schools, in the homes, in the churches and the synagogues; I should even say that when the bouncy style is not an attempt to dazzle the reader, or one's self, but to incorporate into written prose the rhythms, the excitements, the nuances and emphases of urban speech, or immigrant speech, the result can sometimes be a language of new and rich emotional subtleties, with a kind of back-handed grace and irony all its own, as say the language of Mrs. Paley's book of stories, *The Little Disturbances of Man*.

But whether the practitioner is Gold or Bellow or Paley, there is one more point to be made about bounciness, and that is that it is an expression of pleasure. One cannot deny that there is that in it. However, a question arises: if the world is as crooked and unreal as I think it is becoming, day by day; if one feels less and less power in the face of this unreality, day by day; if the inevitable end is destruction, if not of all life, then of much that is valuable and civilized in life—then why in God's name is the writer pleased? Why don't all of our fictional heroes wind up in institutions like Holden Caulfield, or suicides like Seymour Glass? Why is it, in fact, that so many of our fictional heroes—not just the heroes of Wouk and Weidman, but of Bellow, Gold, Styron, and others—wind up affirming life? For surely the air is thick these days with affirmation, and though we shall doubtless get this year our annual editorial from *Life* calling for affirmative novels, the plain and simple fact is that more and more books by serious writers seem to end on a note of celebration. Not just the tone is bouncy, but the moral is bouncy too. In *The Optimist,* another novel of Gold's, the hero, having taken his lumps, cries out at the conclusion, "More. More. More! More! More!" This is the book's last line. Curtis Harnack's novel, *The World of an Ancient Hand,* ends with the hero filled with "rapture and hope" and saying aloud, "I believe in God." And Saul Bellow's *Henderson the Rain King* is a book which is given over to celebrating the regeneration of a man's heart, feelings, blood, and general health. Of course it is of crucial importance, I think, that the regeneration of Henderson takes place in a world that is thoroughly and wholly imagined, *but does not really exist;* that is, it is not a part of that reality which we all read about and worry over—this is not the tumultuous Africa of the newspapers and the United Nations discussions that Eugene Henderson visits. There is nothing here of nationalism or riots or *apartheid*. But then, why should there be? There is the world, but there is also the self. And the self, when the writer turns upon it all his attention and talent, is revealed to be a remarkable thing. First off, it exists, it's real. *I am,* the self cries, and then, taking a nice long look, it adds, *and I am beautiful.*

At the conclusion of Bellow's book, the hero, Eugene Henderson, a big, sloppy millionaire, is returning to America, coming home from a trip to Africa where he has been plague-fighter, lion-tamer, and rainmaker; he is bringing back with him a real lion. Aboard the plane he befriends a small Persian boy, whose language he cannot understand. Still, when the plane lands at Newfoundland, Henderson takes the child in his arms and goes out onto the field. And then:

> Laps and laps I galloped around the shining and riveted body of the plane, behind the fuel trucks. Dark faces were looking from within. The great, beautiful propellers were still, all four of them. I guess I felt it was my turn now to move, and so went running —leaping, leaping, pounding, and tingling over the pure white lining of the gray Arctic silence.

And so we leave Henderson, a very happy man. Where? In the Arctic. This picture has stayed with me since I read the book a year or so ago: of a man who finds energy and joy in an imagined Africa, and celebrates it on an unpeopled, icebound vastness.

Earlier I quoted from Styron's new novel, *Set This House on Fire*. Now Styron's book, like Bellow's, is also the story of the regeneration of a man, and too of an American who leaves his own country and goes abroad for a while to live. But where Henderson's world is removed from our own, not about riots or nationalism, Kinsolving, Styron's hero, inhabits a planet we immediately recognize. The book is drenched in details that twenty years from now will surely require footnotes to be thoroughly understood. The hero of the book is an American painter who has taken his family to live in a small town on the Amalfi coast. Cass Kinsolving detests America, and himself to boot. Throughout most of the book he is taunted and tempted and disgraced by Mason Flagg, a fellow countryman, rich, boyish, naive, licentious, indecent, and finally, cruel and stupid. Kinsolving, by way of his attachment to Flagg, spends most of the book choosing between living and dying, and at one point, in a language and tone that are characteristic, he says this, concerning his expatriation:

> . . . . the man I had come to Europe to escape [why he's] the man in all the car advertisements, you know, the young guy waving there—he looks so beautiful and educated and everything, and he's got it *made,* Penn State and a blonde there, and a smile as big as a billboard. And he's going places. I mean electronics. Politics. What they call communication. Advertising. Saleshood. Outer space. God only knows. And he's as ignorant as an Albanian peasant.

However, at the end of the book, for all his disgust with what the American public life does to a man's private life, Kinsolving, like Henderson, has come back to America, having opted for existence. But the America that we find him in seems to me to be the America of his childhood, and, if only in a metaphoric way, of all our childhoods: he tells his story while he fishes from a boat in a Carolina stream. The affirmation at the conclusion is not as go-getting as Gold's "More! More!" nor as sublime as Harnack's, "I believe in God," nor as joyous as Henderson's romp on the Newfoundland airfield. "I wish I could tell you that I had found some belief, some rock . . ." Kinsolving says, "but to be truthful, you see, I can only tell you this: that as for being and nothingness, the only thing I did know was that to choose between them was simply to chose being . . ." Being. Living. Not where one lives or with whom one lives—but that one lives.

And now, alas, what does all of this add up to? It would certainly be to oversimplify the art of fiction, and the complex relationship between a man and his times, to ignore the crucial matters of individual talent, history, and character, to say that Bellow's book, or Styron's, or even Herbert Gold's prose style, arise naturally out of our distressing cultural and political predicament. However, that our communal predicament is a distressing one, is a fact that weighs upon the writer no less, and perhaps even more, than his neighbor—for to the writer the community is, properly, both his subject and his audience. And it may be that when the predicament produces in the writer not only feelings of disgust, rage, and melancholy, but impotence, too, he is apt to lose heart and finally, like his neighbor, turn to other matters, or to other worlds; or to the self, which may, in a variety of ways, become his subject, or even the impulse for his technique. What I have tried to point out is that the sheer fact of self, the vision of self as inviolable, powerful, and nervy, self as the only real thing in an unreal environment, that that vision has given to some writers joy, solace, and muscle. Certainly to have come through a holocaust in one piece, to have survived, is nothing to be made light of, and it is for that reason, say, that Styron's hero manages to engage our sympathies right down to the end. However, when survival itself becomes one's *raison d'être,* when one cannot choose but be ascetic, when the self can only be celebrated as it is excluded from society, or as it is exercised and admired in a fantastic one, we then, I think, do not have much reason to be cheery. Finally there is for me something hollow and unconvincing about Henderson up there on top of the world dancing around that airplane. Consequently, it is not with this image that I should like to conclude, but instead with the image that Ralph Ellison gives to us of his hero at the end of *Invisible Man*. For here too the hero is left with the simple stark fact of himself. He is as alone as a man can be. Not that he hasn't gone out into the world; he has gone out into it, and out into it, and out into it—but at the end he chooses to go underground, to live there and to wait. And it does not seem to him a cause for celebration either.

January 1963

Marion Magid

THE INNOCENCE OF TENNESSEE WILLIAMS

A European whose knowledge of America was gained entirely from the collected works of Tennessee Williams might garner a composite image of the U.S.: it is a tropical country whose vegetation is largely man-eating; it has an excessive annual rainfall and frequent storms which coincide with its mating periods; it has not yet been converted to Christianity, but continues to observe the myth of the annual death and resurrection of the sun-god, for which purpose it keeps on hand a constant supply of young men to sacrifice. Its young men are for the most part beautiful and fawnlike; an occasional rough customer turns up, but in the end he, too, is revealed as beautiful and fawnlike. Its women are alternately in a state of heat or jitters; otherwise they are Mediterranean. The country does not observe the traditional Western sexual orientation which involves the pursuit of the female by the male; instead, its young men reluctantly allow themselves to be had on those occasions when there is no way of avoiding it and when the act is signaled and underscored by portents of Elizabethan proportions. They are right in general to be of two minds regarding the sexual embrace, for it is as often as not followed by the direst consequences: cannibalism, castration, burning alive, madness, surgery in various forms ranging from lobotomy to hysterectomy, depending on the nature of the offending organ.

Perhaps the European would not be very far wrong. A culture does not consistently pay the price of admission to witness a fable which does not ensnare some part of the truth about it. Perhaps that feverish tropical set by Jo Mielziner is the land of heart's desire for Americans, as Italy has been the land of heart's desire for Englishmen, huddled all winter long around their shilling meters and damp fireplaces. In any case, watching the ladies in flowered hats queuing up for a matinee of *Sweet Bird of Youth* inevitably raises questions: How much do they understand? How much do they suspect? What do all these goings-on mean to them? Do they flock to a new play by Tennessee Williams because it is sensational, because it is "poetic," because it is both at the same time and the one quality redeems the other? Finally, do they find anything of their own experience—of love, marriage, desire, loneliness—reflected in that peculiar mirror which Williams holds up to nature?

Probably they do. Tennessee Williams is not our best, but our only American playwright since O'Neill. His imagination, magnetized though it is by the outlandish and the outré, is a kind of fever chart of our national ailments. There is, for instance, an image which runs obsessively through Williams' plays—the beautiful young man at bay, the quarry ringed by his pursuers. The mind, the sensibilities, the stomach, all recoil from this image when it is served up with obvious relish in a darkened theater, snakily choreographed by Kazan or distended on wide screen in all the glory of MGM technicolor. Yet that image is frighteningly akin to the one emblazoned not so long ago on all the front pages of the land: Meredith ringed by the Mississippi National Guard on the campus at Ole Miss; and in the background, blurred figures with clenched fists. Who knows what goes on behind those flat faces with steel-rimmed eyeglasses and slits for mouths? One has a sense that Williams dwells closer to that knowledge than other dramatists writing about us, for us, today. Though Williams has not, so far as I know, delivered himself of a single pronouncement on the question of integration, though his signature is never to be found on a petition or a full-page ad in the New York *Times,* he seems to have located the trouble spots more precisely than Arthur Miller, for instance, who deals so conscientiously with "social" questions. Williams is American in his passion for absolutes, in his longing for purity, in his absence of ideas, in the extreme discomfort with which he inhabits his own body and soul, in his apocalyptic vision of sex, which like all apocalyptic visions sacrifices mere accuracy for the sake of intensity. Intensity is the crucial quality of Williams' art, and he is perhaps most an American artist in his reliance upon and mastery of surface techniques for achieving this effect.

One result is that Williams' plays cannot be talked about except in their performance. Ever since 1947, when *A Streetcar Named Desire* was produced under the direction of Elia Kazan and starring Marlon Brando, Jessica Tandy, and Kim Hunter, with a stage setting by Jo Mielziner, the pattern for rendition of a Williams play has remained as fixed as a Kabuki dance. Other hands than Kazan's have since dimmed the lights, set the underbrush to quivering, and on occasion gilded the lily, yet the results have always been, when successful—that is, when "like a play by Tennessee Williams"—approximations of that *ur*-Williams production.

There is first of all the matter of lighting. As Eric Bentley observed, Kazan sees the world, especially Williams' world, as phantasmagoria. "Don't turn the lights on," Blanche gasps in *Streetcar* and Kazan passed the word on to the electricians. Nor have they been turned on since. Doing so would dispel the shadows, the evanescence, the sense of undefined shapes and meanings lurking in the foliage. In Hollywood, the word "air" is used to designate atmosphere, the intangible stuff of which dreams are made. Directors in the throes of creation have been known to cry out for "more air"—which means the opposite of what it seems to mean: not clarity nor breathing space nor the light of day, but the baying of bloodhounds, the waving of palm fronds, the lonely clarinet solo, the voices of offstage potion peddlers raised in song. The milieu of Williams' plays lends itself especially well to this hot (Southern) "air" treatment. One suspects that, after *Streetcar,* Williams worked with an image in his mind's eye closer to the South of Broadway than to the actual South.

The second element in timing. Kazan is the virtuoso of a certain kind of tension on stage. His method might be called the technique of unexpected syncopation. The regular to-and-fro buildup of a climactic scene, particularly of an encounter between two actors, is slightly distorted. Pauses are a trifle longer than expected, or a trifle shorter. Long speeches are broken up in eccentric ways, so that unexpected words ring out in the electric silence. No Williams play is complete without the participation of at least one, preferably more, actors who have been trained at the Actors' Studio or temples of the same persuasion, where they have perfected their versions of this curious syncopation.

This mode of diction has become a convention of contemporary American theater in the past two decades. Its components are mainly twofold: since it was originally developed by the Group Theater in its attempt to render "realistically" the rhythms of urban, and especially New York, life, it has more than a trace in it of Yiddish inflection as well as Yiddish phrasing; at the same time it has been updated by hipster gesture and talk. The diction can now be heard nightly on those serious hour-long television dramas which frequently give the impression of being dubbed, so many preparatory lip movements does the actor go through before he works around to the crisis of utterance. This nervous medley acts as an assurance to the spectator that harrowing as the content is of what is spoken, what is unspoken is even worse. What is said is the less important half; the better half is the silence.

Williams writes the ideal "line" for this mode of delivery. It is a long line, which achieves its most striking effects through a Steinian repetitiveness, through the use of unexpected archaisms, and the insertion of unexpected "literary" words and ironically elegant turns of phrase. It is a stylized rendering of Southern diction, which is more self-conscious, more evasive, but also more imaginative than Northern speech. The odd thing is that nearly all of Williams' characters speak this language, regardless of class or place of origin, and it is to be heard even in the grunts of Stanley and Mitch in their more pensive moments.

When a Williams libretto is placed in the hands of an actor whose rendition is tailored to it, the result is an orgy of syncopation just this side of hysteria. It has been remarked that Williams writes great parts for actresses, but only for a certain kind of actress. She must bring to the part a fund of that particular kind of nervous intensity that we associate with Geraldine Page, Maureen Stapleton, or Lois Smith. The champion performance of all time in The Syncopated Mode was the one given by Geraldine Page in *Summer and Smoke* in 1951. It was this performance which brought her stardom and spawned legions of imitations that are still among us—actresses who express emotion by plucking at their forearms and the ever-present brooch at their throats, who issue declarations with an upward inflection and ask questions with a downward one.

The actress who lacks this particular intensity is as fatally out of place as a prima donna singing in English with an Italian opera company. A case in point was that of Shelley Winters, who played the female predator in *The Night of the Iguana*. Miss Winters is not on the brink of hysteria, she does not even seem neurotic, much less bizarre. Dressed in blue jeans and a hastily buttoned man's shirt, she romped through the part of the bitch hotelkeeper looking like nothing so much as a plump athletics counselor at a girl's camp. Common sense as well as the sense of humor rebelled against the idea that she represented that ogre-female, the hideous embodiment of the life force, which is central to Williams' vision of life. Lacking its center, the play slowly fell apart.

All of which are some of the reasons why a successful Williams play in full regalia does not seem written and produced so much as masterminded; it is more like the perfect crime than an artistic undertaking. Williams' vision is not only fulfilled, it is over-fulfilled by Kazan's technique, which is to keep the play in a state of constant explosive motion. Perhaps this is one reason why it does not linger in the mind. Its effect is all in the seeing and quivering at the moment of seeing, a series of shocks to the eye and to the nervous system which renders the viewer captive. Occasionally one has an impulse to shout "Stop!" when some particularly questionable assertion has been made onstage, but it has already flitted away, been swallowed up in the chiaroscuro. It is this shimmering motion that most of the critics praise when they invoke Williams' good qualities —his "elusiveness," his "poeticism." It is as though on Broadway that larger ambiguity which is a characteristic of great art can be achieved merely by a blurring of outline. Dim the lights, provide a clarinet solo or the tinkling of a jukebox, buttress the action with a gathering storm and if possible add a symbol or two which seems to flicker on and off like a neon light, saying: "I may look like an iguana, but what I really am is a symbol." Then all efforts to discern what the playwright is actually saying will be dismissed as pedantry, offensive to the "magical" nature of the theatrical occasion.

Lately, however, Williams has been getting a bad press, though for the wrong reasons. Certain of his motifs have become so insistent and so unmistakable that they no longer quite scurry away unnoticed into the underbrush. Yet Williams' vision has not really changed so much between *Streetcar,* which was hailed as our only American tragedy, and *Sweet Bird of Youth,* which outraged even Kenneth Tynan. It seems unjust of the critics to have taken Williams to their bosoms when he hinted coyly at the unspeakable and to chide him when he speaks a bit more clearly about it.

The total effect of Williams' work has been to plunge ordinary conceptions of the male-female relation into such disorder that the services of a Harry Stack Sullivan seem needed to straighten them out again. The first of these grand subversions was the figure of Stanley Kowalski, which appeared before the American public and before the world in the person of Marlon Brando. Though numerous actors have since played the part, Brando remains forever etched in memory as the embodiment of American malehood, and Kowalski is probably the most famous male figure in modern drama. Doubtless at this moment Brando's Korean counterpart is playing the role in whatever passes at the Seoul Repertory Company for a torn t-shirt.

Kazan, who likes to get down to brass tacks, described Kowalski in his celebrated notes to the production of *Streetcar* as "a walking penis." Whatever that would look like (the imagination is certainly compelled), Brando's rendition of it came out as something more ambivalent. His mincing interpretation of the role may even have struck sophisticated members of the audience as a brilliant example of post-Freudian insight: the walking phallus must necessarily take on some suspicious mannerisms: we all know about overcompensation, and what is brutality but the fear of cowardice and impotence?

Leaving Brando's performance out of it and taking Kowalski at face value, as written by Williams—what are we to make of him? Even forgetting temporarily certain cultural data—that members of the lower middle class are rather more inclined toward the sham genteel in their sexual mores than toward the nobly savage, and that it is primarily college graduates who are as conscientious about their sex life as though it were some humanist obligation—one still wonders how Stella and Stanley ever got together. How did Stella ever get over those initial hurdles—Stanley's table manners, Stanley's preferences in dress, Stanley's recreational interests, Stanley's friends, Stanley's stupidity? If we accept Stanley as ape, the character of Stella ceases to be interesting except clinically. Williams claims allegiance with Lawrence in his philosophy of sex, yet in the creation of

Kowalski he forgets utterly Lawrence's basic lesson—that profound sexual experience civilizes, humanizes, lends grace and delicacy. Lady Chatterley is attracted specifically by the natural aristocracy of the gamekeeper which his skill and power as a lover only confirm. Despite his presence on the stage in satin pajamas and his continued invocation of the "colored lights" we do not really believe in the instinctive animal beauty (purity?) of Stanley in bed because out of it he behaves with such benighted crudity. Did Stanley rape Stella, too, just by way of a how-do-you-do? Do all women burn to be raped? Is this the locker-room fantasy that is Williams' version of animal purity?

"They come together with low, animal moans," the stage directions say. Earlier Stella launches into the first of those hushed sexual confidences which run through all of Williams' plays and ring such an astonishingly false note. "I can hardly stand it when he's away for a night," says Stella. "When he's away for a week I nearly go wild. . . . And when he comes back I cry on his lap like a baby. . . ." It is hard to know what is more unpleasant in this image: the overt sentimentality it expresses, or the latent brutality it masks: a fascination with the image of the helpless creature under the physical domination of another, accepting his favors with tears of gratitude. That the emotion of gratitude is not the predominant one that women feel for their lovers seems to have escaped Williams, fixated as he seems to be upon the delights his heroes must be capable of affording. Later Stella's breathless sexual confidences will be echoed by Serafina delle Rose, describing her husband's prodigious feats in bed, and by Margaret describing the absolute "indifference" of Brick, which makes him the perfect lover. When there is no woman on the scene to give testimony, the heroes themselves oblige with weary chronicles of the services they have rendered scores of women: Val in *Orpheus Descending,* refusing to serve any longer as "stud" to women like the impatient Carol; Chance Wayne in *Sweet Bird of Youth* describing the legions of lonely women whom he has taught about love; Shannon in *Night of the Iguana* confiding his rape at the hands of an adolescent girl. At the center of most of Williams' plays there is the same slightly repellent pas de deux: the man austere, eager to keep his purity; the woman turning to him like Potiphar's wife unto Joseph.

The foregoing belongs, in Williams' world, to the category of "corruption." When he describes "pure" love, one expects hoots from the gallery—but perhaps again the gallery is hungering for any version of that fabled sentiment that Williams can manage to offer. "Pure" love in Williams—which antedates the hero's initiation into "corruption" (spoken darkly, with a faint slurring)—generally takes place in aquatic environs when both the hero and the heroine were very young. The heroine—Val's chance encounter on a houseboat off the Florida coast, Chance Wayne's true love by the Gulf Stream—is generally an exceedingly pale girl with long blond hair—ethereal to the point of incorporeality. In *Sweet Bird,* dramatizing one of those fervid paradoxes that Williams so loves, Heavenly, the "corrupted" pure love, rides at the head of a political caravan, dressed "all in whaat . . . laak a virgin . . ." though she's had that—operation—(spoken darkly and crooningly) "done" on her. . . . How strange to find Williams, the disciple of Lawrence, talking about physical (corrupt) and spiritual (pure) love.

In any event it is difficult to credit those dossiers of sexual achievement that Williams' heroes carry around with them like traveling salesmen with a new fall "line." They seem, when actually confronted with it, to go to great lengths to avoid going to bed with women. They would, in general, prefer to go bowling, to throw each other high forward passes, to wander off in quest of correspondences in the world of nature to their own sense of themselves. When authentic warmth is generated in the plays of Tennessee Williams, it is most often on the occasion of an encounter between two men, and at the expense of their temporarily absent womenfolk—as, for instance, in the moving and very beautiful scene between Brick and Big Daddy in *Cat on a Hot Tin Roof*. It takes Brick three long acts to be persuaded into bed, and it is only the threat of having his liquor supply cut off that finally does it; in the play *Night of the Iguana,* two acts elapse and the hero goes off reluctantly, as to a martyrdom, only when his resistance has been worn down through sheer fatigue; in *Sweet Bird of Youth* the bribe of a checkbook and the use of the Cadillac are necessary before Chance Wayne succumbs to the Princess. The filmed version, recording the moment in closeup and with a directness mercifully lacking in the theater, had Paul Newman's classic features wearing an expression of which the verbal equivalent could only have been "aw shucks!" as Geraldine Page undulated rapidly toward the windows to pull down the blinds. Surely even a gigolo enjoys his job somewhat, and Alexandra del Lago is supposed to be a famous and alluring movie queen; but the feeling communicated is of a child being forced to stay indoors and practice his scales for an hour before he will be released to go out and play with the other kids.

Indeed, Williams' heroes seem more compelled by the mysteries of the nursery and bathroom than by the mysteries of the boudoir, or any more epic battleground. Throughout his plays there is a continuous fascination with the intricacies of bodily processes, the unlovely data of mortality, which suggests a small boy eavesdropping on the talk of a couple of old maid aunts. In almost every Williams play there recurs the clinical-medical set piece, in one version or another; sometimes for comic purposes, as in the detailed evocation of Big Daddy's "spastic colon," which provides a sort of running gag to the play; or for darker purposes, as in the dark references to the imminent demise of Lady's husband in *Orpheus Descending,* or the hushed recitation of what the knife did to the young life of Heavenly Findley. Williams is one of the few dramatists writing who can get a nervous laugh from the audience simply by showing a group of pregnant women on-stage. That shrouded Southern setting becomes a metaphor for an equally threatening landscape—the landscape of the body, interior and exterior, made actual in *Summer and Smoke* when Dr. John, standing before an anatomy chart gives the hypnotized Alma a lesson in reality. (". . . and this is the sex.") This landscape of the body seems as fevered as any acreage on the Mississippi delta plain, with its mysterious shadows and weird foliage—the digestive tract, the reproductive tract, the respiratory tract, the alimentary canal. Stanley, whose colored lights leave something to be desired in the way of characterization, is never so convincing as when he is banging on the bathroom door and screaming about his kidneys. Shannon, the unfrocked priest of *Night of the Iguana,* keeps an all-night vigil with a woman who obviously—as she herself might say—feels more than friendship for him, and whiles away the long hours before dawn regaling her with stories, among which is the episode, observed in his travels, of a destitute beggar eating human offal. And earlier, he has described with similar precision how his moral turpitude stems from the moment his mother discovered him practicing the "little boy's vice."

The effectiveness of the beggar episode in the play—which is intended, it seems, to provide the final documentation of Shannon's and Williams' vision of life as hell—is considerably weakened by the fact that Shannon seems to have told his once devastating story numerous times before, in fact whenever he's had one too many, and its power as a Dantesque hallucination has run out. Earlier, Shannon—are we to take him as a ruined saint?—in a gesture of defiance against the bus-load of ladies who have been tormenting him with sexual or other claims, pees on everyone's luggage to the unbounded glee of the audience and of the two Mexican houseboys onstage who are retained by the management to crouch in feline postures and speak occasional sentences in Spanish. Only after he has accomplished these various demonic acts and been, in addition, lashed to his hammock in the most objectionable exploitation of Christian symbolism since Chance Wayne got castrated on Easter Sunday, does he go off to splash in the waves with Shelley Winters.

What, then, are we to make of the "serious" import of the play—with all this bathroom behavior mixed up with an apparent concern with the themes of the loss of faith and regaining of faith? To be sure, Shannon is provided with one of those incredible biographies that Williams gives his heroes-at-the-end-of-their-rope to explain how they got there. He was once a man of God who sinned in the attempt to find "purity." But when he hurls a challenge at God—"you senile delinquent"—and a perceptible stir goes through the audience, and when he later flings a crucifix to the ground, we are in the presence of nothing more than that most unpleasant of travesties—blasphemy without travail, without the prior justification of the loss of a deeply held faith: in short, a black mass with costumes by *Motley* for the titillation of a sensation-hungry audience. It is hard to judge whether the fraud or the foolishness cries out louder in this play, hailed by critics as Williams' "gentlest" thus far. There is always this distinct unease engendered by Williams' ultimate visions—Sebastian devoured by the street urchins, the castration of Chance Wayne, Val torn to pieces by the rabid mob, the madness of Blanche. It is not only because of their intrinsic unpleasantness. Mutilation and violent death are hardly news in an age whose experience of Gehenna makes even Williams' hallucinations seem pastel-colored. What turns the violent and shocking aspects of Williams' plays into something repellent is the sense one has of a disproportion. His view of life seems in excess of its own ostensible causes —rather as though a man were to do in a series of women because his girl friend had failed to keep an appointment. The plays simply do not seem sufficiently somber or profound to warrant their catastrophes; they do not bear witness that the author has wrestled sufficiently with his own demons to give his vision authority. If he had, Williams might have succeeded in creating something like the tragic hero. Wistful, charming, poignant though his characters are, they lack a certain dignity, a grandeur appropriate to their own tragic ends. Instead of resisting them, shaping them, finally transcending them, Williams seems to welcome all too eagerly the most hectic images that flock to his imagination or come across his path in his various sojourns around the globe—as a very chic decorator welcomes something really new in the way of tropical decorations for the patio. And there is ultimately that particular unease produced by evasion—the feeling one always has that his most gothic revelations are themselves masks for a meaning still further hidden.

Perhaps the best illustration of this last point is provided by *Cat on a Hot Tin Roof*—Williams' best play since *The Glass Menagerie*. Here is Williams' finest writing—blessedly free of that false incantatory note and straining after effect which mark his other plays. It is lyric and authentic in its evocation of the American mythology of brilliant halfbacks, beauty queens, and sports announcers. There is an absence of the conspicuously "Southern" or of the Berlitz Italian or Spanish, that Williams usually depends upon for "earthy" atmosphere. Moreover, it is the last of Williams' important plays to be anchored in reality—that bedrock which the theater deserts at its peril—the reality of houses, families, marriage, children, money. Maggie the Cat is the best in Williams' gallery of jumpy Southern women, a more detailed and psychologically accurate portrait than Blanche, whom she somewhat resembles. In general, Williams seems to have written this play with a control that he has not had before or since. Yet the play is astonishingly flawed at its center. It appears to be an Ibsenian play of unmasking, of revelation, of the stripping away of lies to reveal truth. Yet at the crucial moment, the unmasking is evaded. Williams seems to have toyed with the keys of a locked door, dangling them one by one, only to decide at the end that what is behind the door had best remain hidden.

Cat on a Hot Tin Roof is about a marriage that is falling apart. The husband, Brick, who was once a star athlete and later a sports announcer is now an alcoholic who refuses to sleep with his wife, Margaret. His wife loves him and wants to have a child by him because (among other reasons) the inheritance of the family estate depends on it. But Brick refuses to yield, is interested in nothing but alcohol which gives him peace, that "click" in the head which signifies the end of struggle. Each member of the family has his own version of why Brick drinks and why he will have nothing to do with his wife, but all agree that his behavior is related to the recent death of Skipper, Brick's best friend. The hostile members of the family, Brick's brother and his wife, have hinted darkly that Brick's and Skipper's friendship was "not normal." Margaret knows further details. She believes that though Skipper loved her husband "that" way, her husband did not respond in kind. She feels herself responsible for having alienated her husband, because it was her attempted seduction of Skipper which triggered his collapse and death. Only Brick knows the truth, and he refuses to talk.

Since the play announces its theme to be that of "mendacity," and since the crucial scene is the confrontation between Brick and Big Daddy in which they both agree that final disclosures must now be faced, one expects that this scene will reveal the answer to the question that everyone is asking: is Brick homosexual or isn't he? Astonishingly enough, though the characters circle this question for almost the length of an act in a carefully choreographed minuet of confrontation and confession, the question remains unanswered. Big Daddy succeeds in extracting from Brick only the admission that a final conversation he had with Skipper was the immediate cause of his death. And this admission is made to seem sufficient. Brick in turns tells Big Daddy what everyone has kept from him—that he is dying—and there is a sense of the restoration of balance, a lie exchanged for a lie, a truth for a truth.

But the failure to answer the question of Brick's homosexuality makes the play totally incoherent. Is it a play about a man unjustly accused by a society which is right (yes, homosexuality is evil, but this wasn't it) or a play about a man justly accused by a society which is wrong (no, homosexuality is not evil, it is only wicked tongues that make it out to be so)? In place of what would seem to be Brick's obligatory speech—the one in which he faces the real nature of his feelings for Skipper one way or another—there is an eloquent and finely ironic explanation of how "pure" love is no less "abnormal" than homosexual love, being so rare. In view of the fact, however, that we do not know whether this speech proceeds from the lips of a man who is telling the truth or from the lips of a man who is alternatively either lying or self-deluded, we cannot credit it. If Brick were in fact, homosexual, or were unable to face the fact that he is homosexual, the assertion would be patently false—there would then, indeed, be no such thing as "pure" love between men. If he were, on the other hand, neither lying nor self-deluded, then there might. But the assertion cannot possibly hold for all three cases. It seems moreover crucial to the meaning of the play to know whether Brick is weak and self-deluded or whether he is the last example of the pure in heart. Are we to conclude from the author's ambiguities that he finds the two identical?

Most of the daily newspaper critics were so delighted to spot the old-fashioned well-made revelation scene that they missed the point that nothing was, in fact, revealed, and talked rhapsodically about how Williams had once again probed with his scalpel the most hidden places of the human heart, etc., etc. Only Walter Kerr of the New York *Herald Tribune* seemed to have noticed that the play evaded its own questions—that the love that dare not speak its name, so to speak, was still wearing a pseudonym. Williams answered by saying that ". . . some mystery should be left in the revelation of character in a play just as a great deal of mystery is always left in the revelation of character in life . . ." which is tantamount to saying that *Oedipus Rex* might on the whole have been a more profound tragedy if the rumor that Oedipus was sleeping with his mother had remained unconfirmed.

Why did Williams avoid answering this question in the play? Partly for the sake of expediency, the same expediency that permitted him to allow Kazan to tinker with the third act of the play so that it was sweetened, assuaged, and its real meaning—the bitterness and terror of marriage—somewhat masked. An audience that will accept the unproved allegation of homosexuality, that is even prepared to accept an absent or dead homosexual figuring in someone else's psychic drama, is still not quite prepared to accept a real live red-blooded American husband as homosexual, and one who moreover gets into bed with the heroine at the final curtain. By evading the real nature of Brick's feelings for Maggie—by leaving open the possibility that Brick's aversion for her is on ethical rather than psychological grounds—Williams avoided writing the important American play, the one about the American family and its woe-begone sons, the story of American adolescence which so frequently persists into middle age. But he managed instead neatly to insure the nice lady's comment to her husband when the curtain fell: ". . . how sweet, they've gotten together again. . . ."

Williams does not surrender to his audience; rather he establishes the communion between his myths and theirs. He avoided being specific about Brick's homosexuality not only because it is not "nice" to confront an audience with such home truths, but because he shares that curious American aversion to facts: the view that somehow or other people are different from what they do or say, from what experience has turned them into—that a man is defined by something other than his actions. America is after all the home of the new start, the second chance, and there is a kind of gloomy, adolescent optimism, reflected in the culture, which clings to the possibility that people may change—that with enough love (which means forgiveness) they may one day become beautiful, good, and happy. Williams' failure to pinpoint the character of Brick is a gesture of misguided benignity in his behalf. Like America, Williams lacks ultimately the conviction of his own neurosis.

This same hedging before specifics has always been evident in the critical reception of Williams. There are real and apparent themes in Williams, and the critics have invariably seized upon the apparent ones. They are easier to take, and by now sufficiently orthodox, even sacrosanct, to avoid danger: the failure of communication, the destruction of the dreamers by the practical men, how hellish life can be for the lonelies and the losers. Oddly enough, adumbrating these themes, reviewers frequently congratulate Williams on having once again "affirmed the dignity of the human spirit," the one thing that he has not succeeded in doing. For Williams has never created a character who recovered from the wounds and desolation of childhood.

A play like *Period of Adjustment*—Williams' rather touching attempt to adjust his world view to the comic and the domestic by sheer will power —is particularly revealing in the clarity with which it shows, or shows up, the true nature of his obsessions. It is a banal, ordinary, and even vulgar play about, of all things, how scary the wedding night can be. The play is in effect a mild dirty joke sustained for two acts; but the embarrassment that it occasions is the embarrassment of hearing a dirty joke told by someone fairly prudish. What emerges into the open is that shrinking and fastidious side of Williams which has made him so adept at capturing the ironic self-observations of women who are too smart to believe in their own delusions, but too weak to do anything about them, and who are sustained by a certain delicacy of hope. Though it has the requisite Williams touches, the play offers an entirely conformist, trivial view of love as a kind of soothing ointment. Its burden is that somehow or other human beings—weak, frail, tormented, and uncertain as they are—can offer each other at least the comfort of bodily warmth. The bride in the play is a nurse and the controlling image is that the world is a hospital.

The play is about false and true ideas of manhood, and here we observe a curious thing. Williams has always carried with him, in suspension as it were, the corrective to his own distortions of the masculine. He knows, as do most of us, the truth about the excessive blustering of American malehood—the notorious fear of seeming soft or sissyish, the mistrust of hair worn too long, of demonstrations of affection or tenderness among men, the longing to go off with the boys and all the other apparatus of stag party cameraderie—that all of this is not an expression of authentic masculinity, but of its opposite. Yet this knowledge has never inhibited Williams' more lurid perpetrations of the masculine ideal—the crudities of Stanley Kowalski, the grotesque cavortings of "normalcy" in *Cat* and *Streetcar,* the gratuitous obscenity of Big Daddy when he talks about women. It is as though Williams were aware of the reality, but helpless before the fantasy. Even in *Period of Adjustment,* which amounts to a course of instruction in that very truth, Williams stacks the cards to thwart his own purpose. He offers us two "typical" American couples engaged in working out the ambiguities and problematics of the married state. The first man is married to a woman presented as so incredibly homely that her appearance onstage in a nightgown instantly provokes gales of laughter from the audience; a laughter which is sustained by the author's relish for the details of synthetic correction that she has undergone to make herself bearable. The second man is in such an advanced state of anxiety that he literally has the shakes.

The play ends with an extraordinary scene. The stage is divided in two: on either side of the partition, two beds are invitingly made up, and the two protagonists, with many a backward glance, hop into the sack with their all-too-willing wives. After the first recoil the viewer comes to the astonishing realization that only in America could an entire play be constructed on the question of whether four consenting adults will or will not succeed in making love to one another on a given night. Where one would expect a domestic comedy by a sophisticated modern author in 1960 to begin, Williams' play ends.

And Williams has, one must recall, the reputation for being our sexiest American playwright. What could, in fact, be more innocent? Coprophilia, cannibalism, homosexuality, exhibitionism, fetishism, violation of the Mann Act, turn out in Williams to be masks for some other horror, darker than any of these: the catastrophe of normal adult sexuality. In the end, Williams' vision is revealed as a shocked outcry, a child's refusal to accept the fact of sex that, yes, grownups really do it. Perhaps this ultimately is what the ladies in flowered hats understand about Williams—that beneath the mantle of the swashbuckling libertine, the initiate, the participant in the dark mysteries, there beats a heart as virginal as their own, as their husbands', as America's—that country where the women's magazines on every newsstand carry side by side starry-eyed evocations of the "act of love" and "Eric's strong arms. . ." and the most lurid clinical how-to-do-it manuals of the practice and fulfillment of heterosexual love.

VII
THE AMERICAN PREDICAMENT

August 1951

Leslie A. Fiedler

HISS, CHAMBERS, AND THE AGE OF INNOCENCE

Who Was Guilty—and of What?

> ***You will either aid in moulding history, or history will mould you, and in the case of the latter, you can rest assured that you will be indescribably crushed and maimed in the process. . . . History is not a blind goddess, and does not pardon the blindness of others.***
>
> WHITTAKER CHAMBERS in 1931

Alger Hiss is in jail. The last legal judgments have been passed. The decision of the courts stands: guilty as charged—guilty in fact of treason, though technically accused only of perjury. It is time, many of us feel, to forget the whole business: the prison doors have closed; let us consider the question also closed. But history is not so easily satisfied. Like some monumental bore, it grabs us by the lapels, keeps screaming into our faces the same story over and over again. The case of Judith Coplon, the case of William Remington, the case of Julius and Ethel Rosenberg, the inevitable case of tomorrow's Mr. X—the names change but the meanings are the same, and we protest that we have long since got the point. But have we? Of what was Alger Hiss guilty anyhow?

The statute of limitations protected Hiss against the charge of having passed secret material from State Department files to his accuser Whittaker Chambers, of having placed in the hands of agents of the Soviet Union documents which, whatever their intrinsic value, enabled our present enemies to break some of our most important codes. The transaction had taken place in 1936 and 1937—a war away, in years we ourselves find it difficult to remember, in years some of us don't want to remember. It is a painful thing to be asked to live again through events ten years gone, to admit one's identity with the person who bore one's name in a by now incredible past. It is hardest of all to confess that one is responsible for the acts of that past, especially when such acts are now placed in a new and unforeseen context that changes their meaning entirely. "Not guilty!" one wants to cry, "that is not what I meant at all!"

And yet the qualifying act of moral adulthood is precisely this admission of responsibility for the past and its consequences, however undesired or unforeseen. Such a recognition Hiss was called upon to make. Had he been willing to say, "Yes, I did these things—things it is now possible to call 'treason'—not for money or prestige, but out of a higher allegiance than patriotism—"; had he only confessed in the name of any of the loftier platitudes for which men are prepared publicly to admit the breaking of lesser laws, he need not even have gone to prison. Why did he lie?

Had Hiss told the truth, the whole meaning of the case might have been different, might have attained that dignity of tragedy for which Alistair Cooke looks through its dossiers in vain. The defenders of Hiss, and of the generation they take him to represent, would have been delivered from the intolerable plight that prompted them, during the trials, to declare at one and the same time that (a) Hiss was innocent of the charges, the victim of a malevolent psychopath and (b) even if he was technically guilty, he had the moral right, in those years of betrayal leading to Munich, to give his primary loyalty to the Soviet Union. Why did he lie, and lying, lose the whole point of the case in a maze of irrelevant data: the signature on the transfer of ownership of a car, the date a typewriter was repaired . . . ?

The lie, it is necessary to see, was no mere accident, but was of the essence of the case, a clue to the deepest significance of what was done and to the moral atmosphere that made the deed possible. We can see Hiss's lie now in a larger context, beside William Remington's even more vain denials of Elizabeth Bentley's charges, and the fantastic affirmations of innocence by Julius and Ethel Rosenberg. These were not, after all, common criminals, who plead innocent mechanically on the advice of counsel; these were believers in a new society, for whose sake they had already deceived their closest friends and endangered the security of their country. In the past (and even yet in the present—the Puerto Rican nationalists, for instance) such political idealists welcomed their trials as forums, opportunities to declare to the world the high principles behind their actions, the loyalty to the march of history and the eventual triumph of socialism that had brought them to the bar. They might have been, in some eyes at least, spectacular martyrs; they chose to behave instead, before the eyes of all, like blustering petty thieves.

Not that the avowals of innocence, especially in the case of Hiss, were not affecting. Despite the absurdity of his maunderings about "forgery by typewriter," there was something moving—for a generation brought up on stories of Dreyfus and Tom Mooney, and growing to social awareness through the Sacco-Vanzetti trial and the campaigns to free the Scottsboro boys—in Hiss's final courtroom pose as The Victim. Even now, it is hard to realize how little claim he has to the title. For here was no confessed revolutionary, marked by his avowed principles, his foreign accent, his skin color, as fair game for the frame-up; here was a supereminently respectable civil servant from the better schools, accused by the obvious outsider, the self-declared rebel and renegade, Whittaker Chambers. Hiss seemed to desire both the pathos of the persecuted and the aura of unblemished respectability. His is, as we shall see, the Popular Front mind at bay, incapable of honesty even when there is no hope in anything else.

After the hung jury, the second trial, the reams of evidence that frittered away the drama in boredom, one thing is quite clear. Twenty of twenty-four jurors, presumably twenty of twenty-four of us, believed that Alger Hiss was guilty of the perjury with which he was charged, of the treason with which he could not be charged.

For many, that verdict may be sufficient; for some, it is not enough. These cannot help feeling that the total issue of the guilt or innocence of Alger Hiss remains still to be solved. The verdict of the courts applies only to the "facts" as defined by precedent and law, a few fragments torn from their rich human contexts and presented to a group of men deliberately chosen for their relative ignorance of those contexts, and for the likelihood of their not being sympathetically involved with the passions and motives which underlay them.

Is there any sense in which Hiss is *symbolically* innocent—in which he may, indeed, have made the mistake of having passed certain papers via Chambers to the Russian agent, Colonel Bykov, but out of such naive devotion to the Good that it is a travesty of justice to find him on merely technical grounds "guilty"? It sometimes seems possible that when a Remington or a Rosenberg or a Hiss speaks publicly of his "innocence," he is merely using a convenient shorthand for an account of motives and actions too complex to set before an ordinary juryman without completely reeducating him. One of the distinctive features of the recent series of "spy" trials has been that the accused and the chief accusers have been intellectuals, whereas the jury, the lawyers on both sides, even the judges, were not. And since in this country the intellectuals have been notoriously set apart from the general public, living, especially since the Russian Revolution, by different values and speaking a different language, communication is difficult. How can people who do not read the same books, and whose only relationship is one of distrust, arrive at a common definition of innocence and guilt?

One might argue on these grounds that what a jury could have meant by voting "guilty" is ridiculously far from the truth; that Hiss is not what the average mind, brought up on E. Phillips Oppenheim and pulp fiction, means by a "traitor"; that he can surely feel himself neither venal nor skulking, for he has always been faithful in intent to his true fatherland, Humanity; that if in fact he has ended up by helping the interests of just another imperialist power, the Soviet Union, it is not his crime but that of the Soviet Union, which he took in good faith to be the deputy of mankind's best interests.

This was Henry Julian Wadleigh's defense: a minor source of information for Chambers in the pre-war years, and a witness at the Hiss trials, he attempted to declare his innocence and guilt at the same time. With no sign of contrition, he admitted passing secret documents to Chambers but insisted that his course had been justified by history; it had not even struck him, he explained condescendingly, as a matter of conscience—though merely joining the Communist party had, and he had finally *not* signed up.

The comic aspects of Wadleigh strike one first—the cartoonist's pink-tea radical, with his thick glasses, disordered hair, and acquired Oxford accent. The articles which he wrote for the New York *Post* are classics of unconscious humor, monuments to smugness and self-pity, and trailers for the novel which (of course!) he was busy writing about his Experience. When Hiss's lawyers found they could not pin on Wadleigh the stealing of the papers Chambers had disconcertingly produced, they were content to make him the butt of their jokes. At several points during his questioning, the judge had to cover his mouth with his hand to preserve the dignity of the court. Wadleigh is the comic version of Alger Hiss.

The clowning of Wadleigh reveals what is not so easily read in Hiss: a moral obtuseness which underlies the whole case. Mr. Cooke tries to make of Wadleigh his tragic figure, but the true protagonist of tragedy suffers and learns. Wadleigh has learned nothing. He cannot conceive of having done anything *really* wrong. He finds in his own earlier activities only a certain excessive zeal, overbalanced by good will, and all excused by—Munich. Was he not a better man for having tried to counter, however ineptly, the shameful appeasement of Hitler? That the irony of events had made him, just insofar as he was more idealistic and committed, more helplessly the tool of evil, he cannot conceive. In the end, his "confession" is almost as crass a lie as the denial of Hiss—a disguise for self-congratulation, a device for clinging to the dream of innocence. He cannot, even in the dock, believe that a man of liberal persuasion is capable of wrong.

It was this belief that was the implicit dogma of American liberalism during the past decades, piling up a terrible burden of self-righteousness and self-deceit to be paid for on the day when it would become impossible any longer to believe that the man of good will is identical with the righteous man, and that the liberal is, *per se,* the hero. That day came at different times to different people: for some it was the Moscow Trials, for others the Soviet-Nazi pact, and for a good many—including a large number who had, during the war, regained lost illusions—it came on August 17, 1948, when Hiss and Chambers were brought face to face before the House Committee on Un-American Activities.

The facts were clear from the moment of confrontation, but for many the facts did not matter. Chambers stated flatly that Hiss had been a Communist, his associate in the "underground"; Hiss as flatly denied it. Simply to ask *cui bono* would have been enough: which one of the men stood to gain by lying? But somehow such a common-sense appgroach seemed excluded. The most fantastic psychological explanations were dredged up. One heard via the intellectual underground the unlikeliest, proto-Dostoevskian stories to suggest reasons for Chambers' self-vilifying testimony. *Psychopathia Sexualis* was hauled out, and Freud quoted glibly by the same skeptics who had laughed at the psychologizing explanations of the Moscow Trials.

But there remained still the detailed circumstantiality of Chambers' memories, the documents stolen from the office in which Hiss had worked, the microfilms taken from the dusty dumbwaiter in Brooklyn and hidden in the famous pumpkin on Chambers' Maryland farm. For all the theatrical instincts of Chambers, who seemed to possess a flair for adding one artistic touch too many to any situation, out of God knows what compulsion, the documents were there—the undeniable goods.

An unbiased look at the proceedings of the House Committee reveals that from the start Hiss quite apparently lied, or more precisely, half lied and equivocated with the canniness of the trained lawyer. During the trials his version of the events was delivered with great aplomb, but before the Committee one can see him uncertainly feeling his way into the situation, cautiously finding out at each point how much he will have to admit to escape entrapment.

At first, he said simply that to the best of his knowledge (the qualifying phrase hardly seemed significant, a lawyer's habit), he had never met the man Chambers who had named him as one of a Washington cell of infiltrators. There was no mention of espionage, it must be remembered, until Hiss had forced Chambers' hand. Then, advised perhaps of the convincing nature of Chambers' testimony, he began slowly to shift ground, first, however, taking the initiative and charging with increasing surliness that the Committee had been leaking back to Chambers everything he said. At this point the Committee, which had handled him until then with more than normal sympathy, began to press him hard. He could not say for sure, Hiss now testified, but he thought that certainly he had known no one who called himself "Chambers," or anyone who looked very like the photographs he had been shown. They were, however, not very good pictures, so he could not be positive. Indeed, the face on the photograph before him might be that of the chairman of the Committee. It was his last joke.

Finally, he admitted that he had, after all, known the man in question, under a name he had written down on a pad in front of him. It was "George Crosley" (Chambers was later to say that, although he had used many names, he was quite sure he had never used that one), a dead-beat writer whom he had known casually, and with whom he had occasionally talked over possible story material, though he had really found the man despicable. As a matter of fact, he had even once, for certain obscure reasons, let the dead-beat move into his apartment for a couple of days, or was it weeks; and when Crosley had welshed on the rent, Hiss, for reasons even more obscure, had given him a car—just a little old car, it must be understood, with a "sassy" rumble seat, though one, Hiss admitted, to which he had been sentimentally attached. It is a fantastic story, enough to send anyone less well placed to jail without further ado. Later, there was to be a good deal of trouble over the dates of this strange transaction—and records were to turn up proving that the car had never been presented to Crosley-Chambers at all, but apparently to the Communist party!

All the while this amazing farrago was being served up by Hiss, Chambers was patiently building up the story of their actual relationship, born in intrigue and common devotion to an ideal, and destined to end in bitterness and mutual accusation. They had been comrades and close friends, Chambers said, he and the promising young lawyer, whom he was still able to describe as "of a great gentleness and sweetness of character." At first, their dealings were concerned only with dues and reports, but they had quickly grown closer together, in the sort of relationship hard to parallel outside the party, the two of them utterly dependent on each other's loyalty, and both betting their self-esteem on the truth of the Marxist-Leninist dream.

They are men who could never have met outside the Communist movement, and even as Communists they were utterly different: Chambers the romantic recruit of the 20's, hating a world that had rebuffed him at every encounter, and choosing the movement as an alternative to suicide; Hiss, universally respected, and by nature an opportunist, but with a streak of social conscience (personified in his earnest wife, who could not even let a casual visitor call the day "fine" without reminding her of the plight of the sharecroppers), choosing the party to protect himself from a merely selfish kind of success. Different as they were, Chambers had found Hiss a "real Bolshevik," perhaps sensing in him a kind of hardness to which he himself could only aspire, and had defended him against the sneers of their Russian boss, Bykov, who always referred to Hiss condescendingly as "our dear lawyer."

The quality of the feeling that must have existed between the two men is revealed by Chambers' last-minute attempt to draw Hiss with him out of the party, after he himself had become convinced that the Soviet Union was serving not justice but her own selfish national interests. Feeling that he might well be killed by party agents after his desertion (such political murders have occurred even in America), Chambers, nevertheless, risked exposing himself by a final visit to Hiss's home. But Hiss had stood firm, scarcely listening to the arguments of Chambers, though he had finally wept a little (the scene stays in the imagination, the completely unexpected, uncharacteristic tears), and had given to Chambers a trivial Christmas present for his daughter—"a little rolling pin."

Perhaps, even before the break, Hiss was already tired of Chambers as a person, a little ashamed of his admiration for the shabby writer who wrote nothing, and who had a tendency to remake his experience as he told about it, retouching and bringing up the highlights here and there. Mrs. Hiss had distrusted him from the first, finding him, with a strange inconsistency for a genteel internationalist, "too foreign." They had pretended finally, Alger and "Crosley," that "Crosley" was a Russian, which made him all right, of course; and Chambers had played up to it with all his love of subterfuge.

Whatever the status of their personal relations, when Chambers had come to Hiss with his talk about the Moscow Trials and the betrayal of the revolution, Hiss already could not afford to listen to him. He had by then too much to lose; for, without ceasing to be a Bolshevik, he had become a "success," a respectable citizen. To acknowledge that Russia could be fundamentally wrong would have changed the whole meaning of his own life, turned what had perhaps seemed to him his most unselfish and devoted acts, the stealing of State Department documents, into shameful crimes—into "treason"! Only the conviction that there was no final contradiction between his activities, public and private, could have made Hiss's life tolerable. He must have felt that what he had done as a New Deal lawyer, helping to expose the "munitions makers" in the Nye Committee, or working for the AAA in the Department of Agriculture, did not contradict what he tried to do as a member of a left-wing faction in the State Department, urging certain attitudes toward Chiang Kai-shek; and that what he had sought in both these capacities was merely completed by his "secret" work as a purveyor of information to warn the Soviet Union—his Soviet Union, mankind's Soviet Union—of the forces that worked for and against her in the inner world of diplomacy.

He was not a "traitor"! What the Un-American Activities Committee could not understand, what the two juries were certainly not able to comprehend, is that to Hiss, his service to the party and the Soviet Union is an expression of "loyalty," not "treason." Before consenting to marry him, Remington's former wife had made him solemnly pledge "not to succeed"; to so many of the generation of Remington and Hiss, the bourgeois success of the American Dream was the final treachery, and each step forward in their personal careers had to be justified in terms of opportunities provided for infiltration. Hiss offered his "espionage" as an earnest to the inner few whose opinion mattered to him (in those days chiefly Chambers, and always himself) that he had not "sold out" to the bourgeois world in which he was making a splendid career.

No wonder Hiss was inaccessible to Chambers' arguments against the party! No wonder he seemed scarcely willing to admit his existence, refusing him his very name! It was as if Hiss had wanted to shrug off his accuser, not like a real being in the outside world but like a nightmare. Indeed, the persistent voice of the man he had once admired must have seemed to him to possess the quality of a nightmare, speaking in its characteristic half-whisper the doubts, thrust down in himself, that could destroy his self-esteem.

And so Hiss had spoken out over the condemning voice, protesting his innocence with a vigor that contrasted oddly with Chambers' quiet tone. All the accounts speak of the voice of the accuser as one that, symbolically enough, could scarcely be heard. There is, even in the printed testimony, a sense of a counter-desire not to be heard along with the resolve to speak out. Far from seeming the vindictive persecutor of some accounts, Chambers strikes us as oddly reluctant, willing for a long time to risk perjury rather than reveal the full guilt of his former comrade. What Chambers really seems to be after is a confession of the truth from Hiss; he does not feel he can hide forever what Hiss has done, but he would prefer him to speak out himself.

Hiss, on the other hand, baits Chambers furiously, daring him to become the complete "rat," as if knowing Chambers will suffer in speaking out, as if wanting to shame and punish him. He seems to have felt sure that Chambers could not really harm him. A man does not unflaggingly succeed from high school days to early middle age without losing something of humility, and forgetting that a single failure of the most superb luck is enough for destruction. When the end comes, when the threat of a suit for defamation against Chambers leads to the disclosure of the damning papers, to the trials of Hiss for perjury, and to the final conviction, one has the sense that both of the men are surprised.

Some of the commentators on the case have spoken of the anti-Red "hysteria" that prevailed at the time of the case, as if in such an atmosphere the cards were hopelessly stacked against Alger Hiss. But precisely the opposite is the case. He is just the type that does not normally get caught in the indiscriminate "witch hunt," which tends to pick out those who look like "witches," the visible outsiders. A woman like Assistant Secretary of Defense Anna M. Rosenberg, for instance, foreign-born and a Jew, is much more likely to be haled up without any evidence against her, while a man like Hiss can slip past the ordinary Congressman, to whom Red really means loud-mouth or foreigner or Jew (Rankin, who was on the Committee that examined Hiss, apparently spent his spare time thumbing through *Who's Who in American Jewry,* and turned all his fire on—Chambers!).

The Committee did not want to believe Chambers. They were convinced by his, and his wife's, astonishingly specific memories: though some members of the Committee had been eager to "get the goods" on the New Deal, to catch out the State Department at last, they had apparently found it difficult to put much faith in Chambers. It was impossible to like him, as one instinctively liked Hiss for the boyish charm we think of as peculiarly American. Chambers seems to have worn his unprepossessing air (he is the sort of person of whom one believes immediately quite unfounded stories of insanity and depravity) deliberately, as if he had acquired in his revolutionary days the habit of rebuffing all admiration based on anything but his role in the party.

Every word he spoke declared him an ex-traitor, a present turncoat and squealer, and Hiss, sensing his inestimable advantage in a society whose values are largely set in boyhood when snitching is the ultimate sin, had traded on his role as the honest man confronted by the "rat." Really, Hiss kept insisting, they'd have to call the Harvard Club, say he'd be a few minutes late to dinner—after taking care of this unpleasantness. For a while it came off quite successfully, coming from one who visibly belonged, whose clothes beautifully fitted, whose manners were adequate to all occasions.

We learned later, of course, how much the genteel aspect of Hiss was itself a mask, imposed on a background of disorder and uncertainty not unlike Chambers': the suicide of his father and sister, the undefined psychological difficulties of his stepson, into whose allowance from his actual father, we remember, the Hisses sometimes dipped for contributions to the party. It was as if Alger Hiss had dedicated himself to fulfilling, along with his dream of a New Humanity, the other dream his father had passed on to him with his first name—from rags to riches. How strangely the Marxist ideal and the dream of Horatio Alger blended into the motives of his treason. . . .

Any good bourgeois bristles when confronted with Whittaker Chambers. His years as an editor on *Time* (he is "brilliant," of course, but the adjective is itself ambivalent), his present role as a small farmer, cannot conceal his real identity as the outsider: the "butterball who could not even learn to play marbles," the writer of poetry for little magazines, the obnoxious young radical expelled from college, the uncomfortable spirit that either blasphemes or is too religious for respectability. At one point, Chambers is asked by a Committee member how he spent his time during a week-long period when he had borrowed Hiss's apartment; and when he says, "reading . . ." one feels the troubled silence. How could anyone read so long? It is the suspicious vagary of the kind of man who once believed in Stalin and now believes in the Devil.

After his years in the "underground," he still seems ill at ease in our daylight world; and beneath the guise of the magazine executive, assumed only, we remember, to establish an "identity" for himself as a protection against being murdered by the GPU, the old Chambers persists. Everyone who had known him in his revolutionary days—except Hiss, of course—had no difficulty in recognizing Chambers at the time of the trial.

The jowls and the new teeth do not fundamentally change the face we can still see on the inside back cover of the Communist literary magazine, the *New Masses,* for July 1931. After twenty years, the young Chambers looks up at us still with the sullen certainty of one who has discovered in the revolution an answer to the insecurity and doubt which had brought his brother to suicide, him to months of despair and near paralysis. In the movement he had found a way out of immobility, a way to join with the other insulted and injured of the earth to change the world which excluded them. To appear in the *New Masses* in those days was not merely to be a writer, but to subscribe to a new myth of the writer, summed up in the blurb under the photograph: "Youth as a periodically vagrant laborer in Deep South, Plains, Northwest. Brief Columbia College experience ending with atheist publication. . . . Joined revolutionary movement 1925. . . ."

Hiss, who really knew Chambers, of course, better than anyone else except Chambers' wife, put his finger on the sources of this myth when he told the Committee that Chambers thought of himself as a kind of Jim Tully or Jack London. To understand Chambers, one must understand the concept of the literary bum as hero that came out of Tully and London, a special Marxist class-angling of the old bohemian ideal. Chambers' once living in the same quarters with an old whore, and his stealing of library books of which Hiss's lawyers and psychiatrists were to make so much during the trials, his name-changing and wandering, were all standard procedure for the rebel-intellectual in those days.

The life-style he adopted was perfected in the Communist "Third Period," in the years before 1935, and it is the Third Period we must first of all understand. The term is Lenin's, invented to describe that last stage of imperialism, the age of cataclysmic wars and revolutions, but it comes also to describe the way of life of those who believed themselves the sole carriers of the future in those final days. To the young comrades in their blue work shirts or flat-heeled shoes, there was no need to come to terms with the dying bourgeois world; Marx had told them that the point was to change it. They lived in a fine apocalyptic fury, issuing leaflets to ROTC units in Midwestern agricultural colleges, urging the "peasants and soldiers" to turn their guns the other way; they cried for an autonomous Negro republic to be carved out of the Deep South; and in the few cities where they had sufficient numbers, they were forever rushing "into the streets" to shout their resolve to "Defend the Soviet Union" against their own bourgeoisie in case of war. The only reality in their paranoid world was the Workers' Fatherland, still encircled and unrecognized by our own government. Here is a typical passage from an editorial that appeared in the *New Masses* in 1931, and which may actually have been written by Chambers:

> It is only a question of time until all the imperialist powers mobilize their manpower and hurl its bleeding masses in a rain of steel across the frontiers, to destroy the first Socialist Republic. In this situation what are the intellectuals to do? . . . They realize, however imperfectly, that the Union of Soviet Socialist Republics represents the advance guard, the hope of human progress and civilization. . . . And they desire, the most advanced of them, to employ their minds as weapons in the fight to save the Soviet Union from its reactionary enemies.

Reread in the pages of the old magazine, in the heavy black format that seems to shriek at us across the years, and surrounded by the pen and ink drawings with their incredibly depraved bosses and their unbelievably noble workers, the banal paragraph seems merely unconscionably funny, like a bad silent film. But when we remember the universal loss of faith in those years of mass unemployment and of seemingly endless depression, we can appreciate the attractiveness of the Marxist answer, guaranteed by the miraculous existence of the Soviet Union, the last best hope of human culture. We sense, too, the appeal of violence in a world of words—an instant of bloodshed and the whole golden future unfolds!

No Third Perioder could have become, like a later type of Communist, really a "traitor" as distinguished from a mere "spy." How could they betray a world they publicly disavowed? Romantic and ridiculous, they were still revolutionaries, their allegiance single and unconcealed. When such Communists went underground they hid, but they never pretended to be good bourgeois. When the call came in 1932 from Max Bedacht, asking Chambers to disappear as the individual he had been in order to take on "special" work, Chambers seems to have welcomed the chance. He had already sacrificed his will to party discipline, his fate to history. He had little more to offer up beyond his name and the small fame that had become attached to it in the movement: the praise he had received in the Russian press for his stories of Communist life, the popularity of the play *Can You Hear Their Voices,* based on one of his works, already presented at Vassar and about to be produced in Russia.

Something in his temperament seems to have greeted the prospect of self-immolation; even before he entered what the Communists mean by the "underground," he had been, in the Dostoevskian sense, an underground man, his own enemy. It had apparently pleased him to take the final step, to become one whose death it would be forbidden to notice. What did Mundt or Rankin or Dixon know of Dostoevsky, or those twenty-four jurors of the kind of alienated life that conditioned Chambers? What trick of history brought them and him into the same room, pushed them toward an uneasy alliance?

It was Hiss—the embodiment of the subsequent Popular Front era, as Chambers was the embodiment of the Third Period—who provided the common link: Hiss who had as desperately to look respectable as Chambers had not to. The New Deal had moved American politics left, and had opened the doors of the trade unions and the Washington bureaus to the university intelligentsia at the very moment when that intelligentsia had been penetrated by the Communists, and Communism had undergone two decisive changes: first, the national Communist parties had lost all initiative and internal democracy, coming under the absolute control of the Russian bureaucracy; and second, world Stalinism had adopted the Popular Front line of collaboration with the bourgeoisie.

No longer was the ideal Bolshevik the open rebel, the poet-bum chanting songs of protest, but the principled government worker with the pressed suit and the clean-cut look. It was the day of "fronts" and "mass organizations," of infiltrating and "capturing" and "boring from within." As the headlines in the *Daily Worker* declared peace-with-capitalism, a new kind of underground Communist moved into Washington unnoticed among the purer, pragmatic New Dealers.

Hiss is the prototype of the new-model Bolshevik (Lee Pressman and Henry Collins and John Abt, Noel Field and George Silverman were others) who was the more valuable as he seemed less radical. Far from being urged to sell the party press, he was even discouraged from reading it. These new secret workers had never been open members of the party; they did not merely hide, but pretended to be what they were not. For the first time, a corps of Communists existed for whom "treason," in the sense of real deceit, was possible. These were not revolutionaries but Machiavellians, men with a double allegiance, making the best of two worlds and often, like Hiss, profiting immensely within the society they worked so hard to destroy.

Doubtless some of these new Bolsheviks were able to deceive themselves into believing that there was no actual contradiction between their real allegeiance and their pretended one. What helped the self-deception was the rise of Nazi Germany as the chief threat on the world scene, and the changing role of the Soviet Union in international affairs. The blanket phrase "anti-fascism" covered over conflicts as deep as life itself. On the one hand, the New Deal had finally recognized the new Russian regime; and on the other hand, Communist Russia had joined the fellowship of nations. In the League of Nations (which Lenin had long before called "a den of thieves"), Litvinov was calling for the unity of the anti-fascist world. The watchword was no longer "Defend the Soviet Union!" but "Establish Collective Security!" The Communists insisted that the interests of Russia and the United States were forever identical, and the majority of liberals collaborated in the hoax—which was to crash with the signing of the Nazi-Soviet pact, be ridiculously revived during the war when we were "allies," and collapse once more at the foot of the Iron Curtain. Here are the words of Earl Browder, written in the first flush of the Popular Front honeymoon:

> In this world movement, there stand out before the peace-loving peoples of the world two centers of resistance to the fascist flood, two points from which leadership and inspiration can be given to the majority of mankind struggling for democracy and peace, two rallying grounds for the hard-pressed forces of progress and culture—the Soviet Union and the United States. . . . The Soviet Union and the United States have common problems, common interests and common enemies. That is a central fact in the new world situation.

The platitudes, read in their context of rallies-for-Spain sponsored by the "big names" from Hollywood and Broadway, seem only a little less old-fashioned and absurd than those of 1931, but we must read them with attention, remembering that they made treason easy. The bureaucrat, busy making himself a niche in the government service while transmitting secret material to the Russians, didn't even have to pose to himself a moral "either-or"; in both his roles, he could consider himself serving what Browder liked to call "the spirit of Jefferson, Jackson and Lincoln."

Before the Popular Front Communist the ordinary Congressman is helpless, unless there is a "renegade" willing to make revelations. The average legislator pursues ordinarily one of two policies in regard to Communists, springing from his profound inability or unwillingness to tell a Stalinist from a liberal. Either he lumps together as "Reds" everybody left-of-center (and even an occasional right-winger by mistake), or he refuses to recognize as a Communist anyone who denies it. The one kind of Communist likely to be missed by both approaches is the genteel Bolshevik who keeps his nose clean and never even reads the *New Republic*.

That is why the Committee was at first so completely buffaloed by Hiss. When he thundered righteously, "I am sorry but I cannot but feel to such an extent that it is difficult for me to control myself that you can sit there, Mr. Hébert, and say to me casually that you have heard that man [Chambers] and you have heard me, and that you just have no basis for judging which one is telling the truth," Hébert could only stutter lamely something about the degrading necessity of using low "stool pigeons" like Chambers and Miss Bentley.

It is easy enough to understand the shouts of "red herring!" raised in the earlier days of the case by certain old-line Democrats led by President Truman. They did not dissent on principle, but merely on party lines. If a venture sparked by Republicans is admitted to have succeeded, the Democrats stand to lose votes; and one denies anything that might lose votes. But the real liberals, in and out of the Democratic party, from whose ranks most of the actual believers in the innocence of Hiss are drawn, are a different matter. They had not even listened to the earlier testimony, out of a feeling that paying any heed to the House Committee on Un-American Activities was playing into the hands of the enemy, and that, in any event, the personnel and procedures of that Committee made it impossible for it to arrive at the truth. During the trials they paid attention for the first time.

Chambers' documentary evidence was still there, of course, and his circumstantial story was told again; but by this time Hiss was able to make a better showing than he had, taken unawares, before the Committee. He was imperturbable and glib in his testimony; and his lawyers were able to make Chambers seem more than ever a "moral leper," turning his very virtues (the lies and half-revelations by which he had attempted to protect Hiss) against him, and mocking his new-found religion. All the world distrusts a convert, but no part of it does so more heartily than the liberals. Finally, there were the psychiatrists, prepared on the basis of courtroom observation to call Chambers seriously unbalanced.

But most important of all, there arose to stand beside Hiss, one by one, a series of respectable character witnesses, an elite corps, as it were, of the New Deal, distinguished civil servants and honored judges, until it seemed as if the whole movement that from 1932 on had swept the country out of fear and toward prosperity was staking its very reputation on the innocence of this single man. We know the character witnesses did not deliberately lie. But if they were not liars—as they certainly were *not*—they were, in some sense, fools. It is not an easy admission, certainly not for them, but not even for those (among whom I include myself) who have admired in them a vision of national life that still appears worth striving for.

Even the wisdom of Franklin Roosevelt, the final culture hero of our liberal era, is brought into question. For he seems personally to have pooh-poohed the suspicions, relayed to him in 1940 by Ambassador Bullitt, about the reliability of Hiss. How could he have done otherwise? Was not Hiss one of those young men, mocked by the reactionary press as "brain-trusters," it had been his special pride to bring into political life? The big-city bosses, the unprincipled "experts," and the party hacks, he had been forced to carry with him for expediency's sake; but these young idealists he had supported for the sake of principle. Superficially, the history of Hiss is the prototypical history of the New Dealer at his best: the distinguished years at Harvard Law School, the secretaryship to the almost mythical Justice Holmes, the brilliant career that began in the Nye Committee and culminated at Teheran.

Certainly, a generation was on trial with Hiss, on trial not, it must be noticed, for having struggled toward a better world, but for having substituted sentimentality for intelligence in that struggle, for having failed to understand the moral conditions that must determine its outcome. What is involved is not any question of all or most of the younger New Dealers having been, like Hiss, secret agents of the GPU, but of their having been so busy denying that there was a GPU or that it mattered, that they could not identify an enemy of all the values in which they most profoundly believed.

They cannot even flatter themselves on having been fooled by master tricksters. Hiss was, perhaps, an extraordinarily accomplished dissembler, but what of the Pressmans, the Wadleighs, and the Remingtons, more obvious in their intended deviousness? Lest the New Dealers seem "Red-baiters," they preferred to be fools. Even in the case of Hiss, disquieting reports were transmitted to his superiors from time to time, and it was noticed, on at least one occasion, that information which passed through his hands had an odd way of leaking out. At one point A. A. Berle, after a conversation with Chambers, had gone to Dean Acheson, then Hiss's immediate superior, to report the rumor that "the Hiss boys" were members of a secret Communist group, and Acheson called in Donald Hiss to ask him if he and his brother were really Reds.

The naivety of the thing is monumental! He asked Donald Hiss, and when Hiss said no, Acheson was "satisfied." After all, he had known "the Hiss boys" since they were children; they had gone to the same schools, belonged to the same clubs, could speak man to man. Dean Acheson simply could not bring himself to believe that if the Hisses, who were gentlemen, were also Communists, they would as a matter of course lie. One thinks of Mrs. Roosevelt, under somewhat similar circumstances, calling the leaders of the American Student Union into her drawing room, asking them please to tell her the real truth: were they Communists?

In part, the lack of realism shared by Acheson and Mrs. Roosevelt came from belonging to a world in which liberals and conservatives (and even radicals) are assumed to share the same moral values, the values of the old Judeo-Christian ethical system, however secularized; but in another sense, it arises from long conditioning of the public mind by the "front organizations" of the late 30's, through which the bulk of the liberals learned to maintain the paradox that (a) there were really no Communists, just the hallucinations of witch hunters and (b) if there were Communists, they were, despite their shrillness and bad manners, fundamentally on the side of justice. After all, the Communists are "left," and everyone knows that only the "right" is bad. This absurd metaphor of "leftness" managed to conceal from men of good will and some intelligence the essential fact that the Communists had ceased to subscribe to a political morality universally shared, whatever its abuses, until 1917. How many victims of this confusion were able to spend years moving in and out of Communist fronts and say blandly in the end, "To the best of my knowledge, I have never known an actual Communist"!

Seen in this larger context, the half-deliberate blindness of so many decent people, which is a vital part of the total Hiss case, explains itself. The erstwhile defenders of Hiss's innocence show a growing tendency to remain silent, but their silence does not mean, alas, that they are finally convinced. Looking through Carey McWilliams' recent *Witch Hunt,* for instance, one is startled to discover in a study of the rising tide of accusations of Communism, no mention of the name of Alger Hiss—nor, indeed, of Klaus Fuchs. So significant an oversight must mean, if not active skepticism about Hiss's guilt, a feeling that his case is somehow less relevant than those in which charges of Communism have not been substantiated.

We must clearly understand that the failure of Hiss to confess, far from casting doubt on his guilt, merely helps to define its nature. If Hiss's guilt is of the sort I have tried to indicate, it is clear that, without some change of heart or values, he could not possibly have confessed. One has only to think of the recent trial of the twelve members of the national committee of the Communist party. Even these avowed and open leaders of the movement, whom one had perhaps expected to cry out their faith proudly before the tribunal, could only plead—so ingrained had the Popular Front lie become—in the teeth of the evidence of their own early writings, that (a) they had never advocated revolution and (b) by God, it was their inalienable right as American citizens to do so. What could one expect from Hiss?

If there is a note of tragedy in the case, it is provided by Chambers, the informer driven to mortify himself and to harm those he still loves. The Third Perioder, still pursuing the absolute, makes a tragic final appearance as the scorned squealer; the Popular Fronter can only exit in the role of the hopeless liar. It is difficult to say what factor is most decisive in cutting Hiss off finally from the great privilege of confession; opportunism or perverted idealism, moral obtuseness or the habit of Machiavellianism; they are all inextricably intermingled.

In the end he failed all liberals, all who had, in some sense and at some time, shared his illusions (and who that calls himself a liberal is exempt?), all who demanded of him that he speak aloud a common recognition of complicity. And yet, perhaps they did not really want him to utter a confession; it would have been enough had he admitted a mistake rather than confessed a positive evil. Maybe, at the bottom of their hearts, they did not finally want him to admit anything, but preferred the chance he gave them to say: he is, we are, innocent.

American liberalism has been reluctant to leave the garden of its illusion; but it can dally no longer: the age of innocence is dead. The Hiss case marks the death of an era, but it also promises a rebirth if we are willing to learn its lessons. We who would still like to think of ourselves as liberals must be willing to declare that mere liberal principle is not in itself a guarantee against evil; that the wrongdoer is not always the other—"they" and not "us"; that there is no magic in the words "left" or "progressive" or "socialist" that can prevent deceit and the abuse of power.

It is not necessary that we liberals be self-flagellants. We have desired good, and we have done some; but we have also done great evil. The confession in itself is nothing, but without the confession there can be no understanding, and without the understanding of what the Hiss case tries desperately to declare, we will not be able to move forward from a liberalism of innocence to a liberalism of responsibility.

November 1953

Robert Warshow

THE "IDEALISM" OF JULIUS AND ETHEL ROSENBERG

"The Kind of People We Are"

Julius and Ethel Rosenberg were not put to death for their opinions, but from their side, clearly, they died for their opinions nevertheless. And not only did they choose to give up their lives: each sacrificed the other, and both together sacrificed their two young children. Yet they must have loved the children; it is true that they permitted them to be exploited outrageously in the service of propaganda, but from their side, again, this would not have appeared to be exploitation. And obviously they loved each other; there is no hint of disharmony between them, and only a gross want of imagination could lead one to think they were not being spontaneous when, for instance, they stood holding hands to hear their sentence. It would be hard to overstate the immensity of their fortitude, which seems never to have come close to failure, or the weight of their suffering.

For the two years in the death cells they lived within about a hundred feet of each other but could be together only during brief weekly visits or when their lawyer came to confer with them (apparently, if they had been brothers instead of man and wife they might have had adjoining cells). They therefore had to communicate frequently in letters. A selection of their letters to each other, together with some letters to their lawyer, Emanuel Bloch, has been brought out by the "Jero Publishing Company." The selection goes up to the middle of March of this year, and the book itself went to press shortly before the Rosenbergs' execution, which took place on June 19. The volume includes also an outline of the chronology of the case and an appendix containing excerpts from the Rosenbergs' petition for clemency and statements from various people who either believed that the Rosenbergs were innocent or felt that their sentence was too severe. Proceeds from the sale of the book are supposed to go into a fund for the Rosenbergs' two children, Michael and Robert, who are ten years and six years old. In Europe these letters, like all the propaganda in the Rosenberg case, have been received with great excitement. Here, they appear to be making little impact, though there seems to be no inclination on the part of the Communists to let the propaganda campaign subside. (The weekend edition of the *Daily Worker* has been running a series of biographical articles about the Rosenbergs under the title "Two Immortals." Meetings and rallies continue to be held, and the National Committee to Secure Justice in the Rosenberg Case plans to distribute "throughout the world" the "Rosenberg Dedication Book," a slick-paper booklet offering an extremely skillful compendium of demagogy.)

The children came to visit, and the father and mother, like any anxious and intelligent parents, discuss in their letters how best to "approach" the situation, how to give "the impression that we are not unduly upset" and thus evoke a "proper reaction." In advance of the first visit, Ethel considers that she will say something like this: "Of course, it's not easy to know about the death penalty and not worry about it sometimes, but let's look at it this way. We know that a car could strike us and kill us, but that doesn't mean we spend every minute being fearful about cars. . . ." There is even a note of serene understanding about the "people who solved their own problems by lying about us," and she plans to assure the children that "it's all right to feel any way you like about those people, so long as your feelings don't give you pain and make you unhappy—" "Oh, yes," she adds in another letter, "if Michael neglects to question me as to the form of the death penalty, this job will fall to you. . . . Answer briefly that it is painless electrocution, which we believe will never come to pass, of course." After a second visit, Julius reports that Michael did indeed ask how the death penalty is carried out and whether there was an electric chair in the building; Julius answered straightforwardly. Michael said also, "Daddy, maybe I'll study to be a lawyer and help you in your case." "The fact is," Julius writes, "both children are disturbed."

Much of the correspondence deals with plans for the care of the children. "I fully understand and share your anguish," Julius writes, "but we are very well qualified to organize the proper program of rehabilitation for our children. . . . The entire home, play and materials situation needs a radical change. . . . Mind you, I'm not alarmed, as I feel the necessary conditions exist to do a good job. . . . I'm counting on your analytical mind and sense of detail to help carry the ball for us." As Christmas approaches, he consults the *National Guardian* for a list of suitable books for the boys.

Ethel is often more rhetorical: "I . . . experience such a stab of longing for my boy that I could howl like a she-animal who has had its young forcibly torn from her! How dared they, how dared they, the low, vile creatures, lay unclean hands upon our sacred family? And tell me, oh my sister Americans, how long shall any of your own husbands and children be safe if by your silence you permit this deed to go unchallenged!"

The fact that Julius Rosenberg can speak of a lack of toys as the "materials situation" does not in the least permit us to assume he did not suffer for his children just as much as anyone else would have suffered. Nor does the impudence of Ethel's appeal to her "sister Americans"—whose lives she had been willing to put in danger—diminish in any way the reality of the "stab of longing for my boy." On the whole, the Rosenbergs in dealing with their children sound the authentic tone of parental love in the educated and conscientious middle class, facing each "problem" boldly and without displaying undue emotion, though "of course" not denying the existence of emotion either ("Of course it's not easy to know about the death penalty and not worry about it sometimes. . . ."). This is how we all deal with our children, and surely we are right to do so. If it happens that you must "prepare" the children for their parents' death in the electric chair instead of for having their tonsils out, then doubtless something better is required. But what, for God's sake? Some unique inspiration, perhaps, and the truth. But we cannot blame the Rosenbergs for their failure to achieve an inspiration, and the commitment for which they died—and by which, we must assume, they somehow fulfilled themselves—was precisely that the truth was not to be spoken.

Not spoken, not whispered, not approached in the merest hint. These letters were undoubtedly written, or revised, for publication; in any case, they were subject to examination by prison officials. Under the circumstances, they could not have been truthful. But there is something uncanny nevertheless in the way this husband and wife felt compelled to write to each other, never evading the issue but, on the contrary, coming back to it continually in order to repeat continually what was not true. "We are innocent"—again and again Julius tells this to Ethel and Ethel tells it back to Julius. "What have we done to deserve such unhappiness? All our years we lived decent, constructive lives." "I firmly believe that we are better people because we stood up with courage through a very grueling trial and a most brutal sentence, all because we are innocent." "I'm certain we will beat this frame-up. . . ." The word "Communist" never appears except in quotation marks; when Julius seeks to define the faith for which he is prepared to die, he can say only that he is "a progressive individual"—this after a fragment of autobiography, addressed to his lawyer, which makes it especially clear that he was a Communist. He is even forced to speak of espionage—to him, surely, the very crown of the "decent, constructive" life of "a progressive individual"—as a "crime": "Can I deny the principles that are so much part of me? This I can never do. I cannot live a lie nor can I be like the Greenglasses and the Bentleys. My entire life and philosophy negates this and it is obvious that I could never commit the crime I stand convicted of."

No doubt there is a certain covert truth-telling in all this, with "we are innocent" standing for "my resolve is unshaken; I will not confess." But one is forced to wonder whether the literal truth had not in some way ceased to exist for these people. It is now about seventeen years since Communists told the truth about themselves—the "popular front" was inaugurated during Julius Rosenberg's student days at City College—and enough time has passed for the symbolic language of Communism to have taken on an independent existence. On July 4, 1951, Julius clipped a copy of the Declaration of Independence from the New York *Times* and taped it to the wall of his cell. "It is interesting," he writes to Ethel, "to read these words concerning free speech, freedom of the press and of religion in this setting. These rights our country's patriots died for can't be taken from the people even by Congress or the courts." Does it matter that the Declaration of Independence says nothing about free speech, freedom of the press, or freedom of religion, and that Julius therefore could not have found it "interesting" to read "these words" in that particular document? It does not matter. Julius knew that America is supposed to have freedom of expression and that the Declaration of Independence "stands for" America. Since, therefore, he already "knew" the Declaration, there was no need for him to actually read it in order to find it "interesting," and it could not have occurred to him that he was being untruthful in implying that he had just been reading it when he had not. He could "see himself" reading it, so to speak, and this dramatic image became reality: he *did not know* that he had not read it.

Similarly, when he says "it is obvious that I could never commit the crime I stand convicted of," we cannot assume that he is simply lying. More probably, what he means is something like this: If it were a crime, I could not have done it. Since in the language of the unenlightened what I did is called a crime, and I am forced to speak in that language, the only truthful thing to say is that I did not do it.

It is as if these two had no internal sense of their own being but could see themselves only from the outside, in whatever postures their "case" seemed to demand—as if, one might say, they were only the most devoted of their thousands of "sympathizers."

"We didn't ask for this; we only wanted to be left alone, but framed we were—and with every ounce of life in our bodies we will fight until we are free."

"Together we hunted down the answers to all the seemingly insoluble riddles which a complex and callous society presented. . . . For the sake of these answers, for the sake of American democracy, justice and brotherhood, for the sake of peace and bread and roses, and children's laughter, we shall continue to sit here in dignity and in pride. . . ."

"At stake here are the rights, security and very lives of all brave people of all shades of opinions."

"The world is watching our government's action in this case and the conscience of men of good will is outraged by the brutal sentence and the miscarriage of justice in the Rosenberg case."

"The Rosenbergs' calm prediction [it is Ethel Rosenberg who writes this!] that the people would refuse to acquiesce in legal murder has been borne out a thousand times over."

"Is it worth forfeiting two warm, young lives [this too is Ethel], about whose guilt the world says there is reasonable doubt, to save the face of the United States?"

"By our conduct in this case, when our lives are at stake, we are illustrating the fundamental tenets of our democracy."

The tone is no different, really, when they write of the more personal furniture of their lives:

"For about an hour beginning at about 9:00 P.M. I walk and sing songs, mostly folk music, workers' songs, peoples' songs, popular tunes and excerpts from operas and symphonies. I sing Peat Bog Soldiers, Kevin Barry, United Nations, Tennessee Waltz, Irene, Down in the Valley, Beethoven's Ninth Choral Symphony. . . . In all frankness, I feel good and strong while I sing."

"I am reading *Science and Politics in the Ancient World,* by Benjamin Farrington. He gives documentary proof that the enemy of scientific growth was superstition imposed on the people by the nobles of the state and heads of the church for the purpose of maintaining the status quo and their preferred class position."

". . . After a while, some of the pain gripping me eased. It needed only a radio program, and 'Ballad for Americans,' for the finishing touch. With Frank Sinatra's recording of 'House I Live In,' I had a tremendous upsurge of 'courage, confidence and perspective'!"

"Did you ever notice the comfortable feeling one gets reading and listening to rain? I thought, what a wonderful world we live in, and how much man could do with full utilization of his creative ability."

". . . the Dodgers [have] made me bite off every last confounded nail; 10-0, what a trouncing! It's that indomitable spirit that has endeared them to so many. But it is chiefly in their outstanding contribution to the eradication of racial prejudice that they have covered themselves with glory."

"I have been reading again *Gentleman's Agreement,* and it made me realize how starved I was for intellectual exchange. . . ."

"I'm simply carried away, enthralled, enraptured! You can't guess.

Well, I've been listening to 'Old Man Tosc' conducting the NBC summer symphony. What a magnificence of sound that guy can call forth; it's positively incredible."

It would be heartless to multiply these quotations merely in order to make a display of the awkwardness and falsity of the Rosenbergs' relations to culture, to sports, and to themselves. But it is important to observe the dimensions of their failure, how almost nothing really belonged to them, not even their own experience; they filled their lives with the second-hand, never so much as suspecting that anything else was possible. Communism itself—the vehicle of whatever self-realization they achieved—had disappeared for them, becoming only a word to be written in quotation marks as if it represented a hallucination, and they faced death armed not even with the clichés of the proletarian revolution but only with the spiritless echoes of a few fellow-traveling newspapers and the memory of City College in 1934.

We need not doubt that Julius was strengthened by singing "Kevin Barry" or "United Nations" and that Ethel was cheered by hearing "Ballad for Americans," or, making allowance for her language, that she was "enraptured" by the NBC summer symphony. It is even possible to believe that Ethel was actually excited at the "trouncing" administered by the Dodgers to the Giants (it was the second game of the 1951 pennant playoff), and that her excitement was related to her appreciation of the Dodgers' "outstanding contribution to the eradication of racial prejudice." We know how easily those responses could have been changed: if "Old Man Tosc" had slighted Paul Robeson, if the Dodgers had fired one of their Negro players, if *Gentleman's Agreement* had been unfavorably reviewed in the *National Guardian*. But the initial responses and their contradictories would have been equally real, and equally unreal.

There is something in this more profound than insincerity. The ideal Communist responds only to the universal—to Revolution, to Progress, or, in Julius Rosenberg's revealing phrase, to "the kind of people we are." *Gentleman's Agreement* or "Ballad for Americans" are merely particular objects in which the universal happens at the moment to embody itself, and it is all the same if these objects disappear so long as new ones take their place. Whether he cheers the Yankees or the Dodgers, whether he damns Franklin Roosevelt as a warmonger or adores him as the champion of human rights, the Communist is always celebrating the same thing: the great empty Idea which has taken on the outlines of his personality. Communists are still "idealists"—perhaps all the more so because their "idealism" is by now almost entirely without content—and the surprising degree of sympathy and even respect that they can command among liberals is partly to be explained by the liberal belief that "idealism" in itself is a virtue.

Consider the continual display of Judaism and Jewishness in these letters:

"Our upbringing, the full meaning of our lives, based on a true amalgamation of our American and Jewish heritage, which to us means freedom, culture and human decency, has made us the people we are."

"In a couple of days the Passover celebration of our people's search for freedom will be here. This cultural heritage has added meaning for us, who are imprisoned . . . by the modern Pharaohs."

". . . our fellow Jewish expression summarizes my feelings for [Emanuel Bloch]. *Ich shep nachuss und quell fun ihm.*"

"At Hebrew school . . . I absorbed quite naturally the culture of my people, their struggle for freedom from slavery in Egypt. I found the same great traditions in American history."

"The Jewish services were impressive. . . ."

"What solace to hear your voice during the Jewish services. . . ."

"It is amazing how intellectually stimulating Jewish services can be. . . ."

"I'd appreciate it if you would give the question of the Jewish holidays and their special significance for us, as part of a prison congregation, your serious consideration between now and our next talk."

"This holiday [Chanukah], signifying the victory of our forefathers in a struggle for freedom from oppression and tyranny, is a firm part of our heritage and buttresses our will to win our own freedom."

"The heritage of our Hebrew culture has served our people throughout the ages and we have learned its lesson well."

Except for the crudely calculated introduction of the word "Jewish" in places where it could not have been necessary in communication between a man and his wife, most of these sentences merely repeat the worn platitudes of a thousand sermons about the Jewish tradition. Since the propaganda built up around the case emphasized the fact that the Rosenbergs were Jewish, they simply adopted the role that was demanded of them.* If something else had been needed, they could as easily have taken up the pose of Protestantism or Catholicism or Gandhiism, and for any one of these roles they would have made use of the available platitudes (Communists are of course not alone in their predilection for the second-hand).

But is there any difference between the patently disingenuous passages about Judaism and the occasional passages where the Rosenbergs might be

* It is striking that the Rosenbergs' letters make no reference to the claim that they were "framed" because of anti-Semitism; this would seem to indicate that that particular line of propaganda has not paid off. Julius speaks in one of his letters of the possibility that the "frame-up" might stimulate anti-Semitism by encouraging the belief that all Jews are Communists. In another letter he refers to the "smear campaign" attributing anti-Semitism to the Soviet Union.

thought to be expressing sentiments closer to their hearts? Supposing even that they had been ready to confess their espionage and proclaim it defiantly as the service to humanity they must have believed it to be, can it be thought they would have expressed themselves any less falsely than they have done in their claims of innocence or their pious espousals of "our people's heritage"?

The point is that all beliefs, all ideas, all "heritages" were really the same to them, and they were equally incapable of truth and of falsehood. What they stood for was not Communism as a certain form of social organization, not progress as a belief in the possibility of human improvement, but only their own identity *as* Communists or "progressives," and they were perfectly "sincere" in making use of whatever catchwords seemed at any moment to assert that identity—just as one who seeks to establish his identity as a person of culture might try to do so either by praising abstract painting or by damning it. The Rosenbergs thought and felt whatever their political commitment required them to think and to feel. But if they had not had the political commitment could they have thought and felt at all?

Well, we cannot dispose of them quite so easily. They did suffer, for themselves and for their children, and though they seem never to have questioned the necessity of their "martyrdom" or the absolute rightness of all they had ever done (". . . when [the children] are older, they will know that all the way through, we . . . were right . . ."), they wept like anyone else at the approach of death; if it were not for that, one might wonder whether they had any real sense of what they were giving up when they chose to give up their lives.

For the final image is still their glassy serenity of conscience. It has been reported that when the United States Marshal came to tell Ethel Rosenberg that the final stay had been rescinded and the execution would take place in a few hours, she said simply, "Well, the Rosenbergs will be the first victims of American fascism." (The "Rosenberg Dedication Book" prints a brief note from Julius to Emanuel Bloch, dated on the day of execution, which also attributes these words to Ethel.) For her, this was a sufficient definition of what was about to happen to her. Perhaps the fact that she could say this, externalizing even her own death—not she was about to die, but a "victim of fascism"—should be for us a sufficient definition of what she had made of herself.

Inevitably it has been suggested that the Rosenbergs did not write these letters. Yet there is nothing in the quality of the letters to make one believe they could not have written them; they were people of no eloquence and little imagination, and their letters display none. (The "Rosenberg Dedication Book" demonstrates that there were writers available who could have done better.) Unquestionably there has been heavy editing, but again there is no reason to suppose that the Rosenbergs themselves may not have done the editing, both after the letters were written and in the process of writing them. In any case, the question is of no importance. The letters, if they were not written by the Rosenbergs, are what the Rosenbergs would have written. In their crudity and emptiness, in their absolute and dedicated alienation from truth and experience, these letters adequately express the Communism of 1953.

March 1955

James Baldwin

EQUAL IN PARIS

An Autobiographical Story

On the 19th of December, in 1949, when I had been living in Paris for a little over a year, I was arrested as a receiver of stolen goods and spent eight days in prison. My arrest came about through an American tourist whom I had met twice in New York, who had been given my name and address and told to look me up. I was then living on the top floor of a ludicrously grim hotel on the rue du Bac, one of those enormous dark, cold, and hideous establishments in which Paris abounds that seem to breathe forth, in their airless, humid, stone-cold halls, the weak light, scurrying chambermaids, and creaking stairs, an odor of gentility long long dead. The place was run by an ancient Frenchman dressed in an elegant black suit which was green with age, who cannot properly be described as bewildered or even as being in a state of shock, since he had really stopped breathing around 1910. There he sat at his desk in the weirdly lit, fantastically furnished lobby, day in and day out, greeting each one of his extremely impoverished and *louche* lodgers with a stately inclination of the head that he had no doubt been taught in some impossibly remote time was the proper way for a *propriétaire* to greet his guests. If it had not been for his daughter, an extremely hard-headed *tricoteuse*—the inclination of *her* head was chilling and abrupt, like the downbeat of an axe—the hotel would certainly have gone bankrupt long before. It was said that this old man had not gone farther than the door of his hotel for thirty years, which was not at all difficult to believe. He looked as though the daylight would have killed him.

I did not, of course, spend much of my time in this palace. The moment I began living in French hotels I understood the necessity of French cafés. This made it rather difficult to look me up, for as soon as I was out of bed I hopefully took notebook and fountain pen off to the upstairs room of the Flore, where I consumed rather a lot of coffee and, as evening approached, rather a lot of alcohol, but did not get much writing done.

But one night, in one of the cafés of St. Germain des Prés, I was discovered by this New Yorker and only because we found ourselves in Paris we immediately established the illusion that we had been fast friends back in the good old U.S.A. This illusion proved itself too thin to support an evening's drinking, but by that time it was too late. I had committed myself to getting him a room in my hotel the next day, for he was living in one of the nest of hotels near the Gare St. Lazare, where, he said, the *propriétaire* was a thief, his wife a repressed nymphomaniac, the chambermaids "pigs," and the rent a crime. Americans are always talking this way about the French and so it did not occur to me that he meant what he said or that he would take into his own hands the means of avenging himself on the French Republic. It did not occur to me, either, that the means which he *did* take could possibly have brought about such dire results, results which were not less dire for being also comic-opera.

It came as the last of a series of disasters which had perhaps been made inevitable by the fact that I had come to Paris originally with a little over forty dollars in my pockets, nothing in the bank, and no grasp whatever of the French language. It developed, shortly, that I had no grasp of the French character either. I considered the French an ancient, intelligent, and cultured race, which indeed they are. I did not know, however, that ancient glories imply, at least in the middle of the present century, present fatigue and, quite probably, paranoia; that there is a limit to the role of the intelligence in human affairs; and that no people come into possession of a culture without having paid a heavy price for it. This price they cannot, of course, assess, but it is revealed in their personalities and in their institutions. The very word "institutions," from my side of the ocean, where, it seemed to me, we suffered so cruelly from the lack of them, had a pleasant ring, as of safety and order and common sense; one had to come into contact with these institutions in order to understand that they were also outmoded, exasperating, completely impersonal, and very often cruel. Similarly, the personality which had seemed from a distance to be so large and free had to be dealt with before one could see that, if it was large, it was also inflexible and, for the foreigner, full of strange, high, dusty rooms which could not be inhabited. One had, in short, to come into contact with an alien culture in order to understand that a culture was not a community basket-weaving project, nor yet an act of God; was something neither desirable nor undesirable in itself, being inevitable, being nothing more or less than the recorded and visible effects on a body of people of the vicissitudes with which they had been forced to deal. And their great men are revealed as simply another of these vicissitudes, even if, quite against their will, the brief battle of their great men with them has left them richer.

When my American friend left his hotel to move to mine, he took with him, out of pique, a bedsheet belonging to the hotel and put it in his suitcase. When he arrived at my hotel I borrowed the sheet, since my own were filthy and the chambermaid showed no sign of bringing me any clean ones, and put it on my bed. The sheets belonging to *my* hotel I put out in the hall, congratulating myself on having thus forced on the attention of the Grand Hôtel du Bac the unpleasant state of its linen. Thereafter, since, as it turned out, we kept very different hours—I got up at noon, when, as I gathered by meeting him on the stairs one day, he was only just getting in—my new-found friend and I saw very little of each other.

On the evening of the 19th I was sitting thinking melancholy thoughts about Christmas and staring at the walls of my room. I imagine that I had sold something or that someone had sent me a Christmas present, for I remember that I had a little money. In those days in Paris, though I floated, so to speak, on a sea of acquaintances, I knew almost no one. Many people were eliminated from my orbit by virtue of the fact that they had more money than I did, which placed me, in my own eyes, in the humiliating role of a free-loader; and other people were eliminated by virtue of the fact that they enjoyed their poverty, shrilly insisting that this wretched round of hotel rooms, bad food, humiliating concierges, and unpaid bills was the Great Adventure. It couldn't, however, for me, end soon enough, this Great Adventure; there was a real question in my mind as to which would end soonest, the Great Adventure or me. This meant, however, that there were many evenings when I sat in my room, knowing that I couldn't work there, and not knowing what to do, or whom to see. On this particular evening I went down and knocked on the American's door.

There were two Frenchmen standing in the room, who immediately introduced themselves to me as policemen; which did not worry me. I had got used to policemen in Paris bobbing up at the most improbable times and places, asking to see one's *carte d'identité*. These policemen, however, showed very little interest in my papers. They were looking for something else. I could not imagine what this would be and, since I knew I certainly didn't have it, I scarcely followed the conversation they were having with my friend. I gathered that they were looking for some kind of gangster and since I wasn't a gangster and knew that gangsterism was not, insofar as he had one, my friend's style, I was sure that the two policemen would presently bow and say *Merci, messieurs,* and leave. For by this time, I remember very clearly, I was dying to have a drink and go to dinner.

I did not have a drink or go to dinner for many days after this, and when I did my outraged stomach promptly heaved everything up again. For now one of the policemen began to exhibit the most vivid interest in me and asked, very politely, if he might see my room. To which we mounted, making, I remember, the most civilized small talk on the way and even continuing it for some moments after we were in the room in which there was certainly nothing to be seen but the familiar poverty and disorder of that precarious group of people of whatever age, race, country, calling, or intention which Paris recognizes as *les étudiants* and sometimes, more ironically and precisely, as *les nonconformistes*. Then he moved to my bed, and in a terrible flash, not quite an instant before he lifted the bedspread, I understood what he was looking for. We looked at the sheet, on which I read, for the first time, lettered in the most brilliant scarlet I have ever seen, the name of the hotel from which it had been stolen. It was the first time the word *stolen* entered my mind. I had certainly seen the hotel monogram the day I put the sheet on the bed. It had simply meant nothing to me. In New York I had seen hotel monograms on everything from silver to soap and towels. Taking things from New York hotels was practically a custom, though, I suddenly realized, I had never known anyone to take a *sheet*. Sadly, and without a word to me, the inspector took the sheet from the bed, folded it under his arm, and we started back downstairs. I understood that I was under arrest.

And so we passed through the lobby, four of us, two of us very clearly criminal, under the eyes of the old man and his daughter, neither of whom said a word, into the streets where a light rain was falling. And I asked, in French, "But is this very serious?"

For I was thinking, it is, after all, only a sheet, not even new.

"No," said one of them. "It's not serious."

"It's nothing at all," said the other.

I took this to mean that we would receive a reprimand at the police station and be allowed to go to dinner. Later on I concluded that they were not being hypocritical or even trying to comfort us. They meant exactly what they said. It was only that they spoke another language.

In Paris everything is very slow. Also, when dealing with the bureaucracy, the man you are talking to is never the man you have to see. The man you have to see has just gone off to Belgium, or is busy with his family, or has just discovered that he is a cuckold; he will be in next Tuesday at three o'clock, or sometime in the course of the afternoon, or possibly tomorrow, or, possibly, in the next five minutes. But if he is coming in the next five minutes he will be far too busy to be able to see you today. So that I suppose I was not really astonished to learn at the commissariat that nothing could possibly be done about us before The Man arrived in the morning. But no, we could not go off and have dinner and come back in the morning. Of course he knew that we *would* come back—that was not the question. Indeed, there was no question: we would simply have to stay there for the night. We were placed in a cell which rather resembled a chicken coop. It was now about seven in the evening and I relinquished the thought of dinner and began to think of lunch.

I discouraged the chatter of my New York friend and this left me alone with my thoughts. I was beginning to be frightened and I bent all my energies, therefore, to keeping my panic under control. I began to realize that I was in a country I knew nothing about, in the hands of a people I did not understand at all. In a similar situation in New York I would have had some idea of what to do because I would have had some idea of what to expect. I am not speaking now of legality which, like most of the poor, I had never for an instant trusted, but of the temperament of the people with whom I had to deal. I had become very accomplished in New York at guessing and, therefore, to a limited extent manipulating to my advantage the reactions of the white world. But this was not New York. None of my old weapons could serve me here. I did not know what they saw when they looked at me. I knew very well what Americans saw when they looked at me and this allowed me to play endless and sinister variations on the role which they had assigned me; since I knew that it was, for them, of the utmost importance that they never be confronted with what, in their own personalities, made this role so necessary and gratifying to them, I knew that they could never call my hand or, indeed, afford to know what I was doing; so that I moved into every crucial situation with the deadly and rather desperate advantages of bitterly accumulated perception, of pride and contempt. This is an awful sword and shield to carry through the world, and the discovery that, in the game I was playing, I did myself a violence of which the world, at its most ferocious, would scarcely have been capable, was what had driven me out of New York. It was a strange feeling, in this situation, after a year in Paris, to discover that my weapons would never again serve me as they had.

It was quite clear to me that the Frenchmen in whose hands I found myself were no better or worse than their American counterparts. Certainly their uniforms frightened me quite as much, and their impersonality. And the threat, always very keenly felt by the poor, of violence, was as present in that commissariat as it had ever been for me in any police station. And I had seen, for example, what Paris policemen could do to Arab peanut vendors. The only difference here was that I did not understand these people, did not know what techniques their cruelty took, did not know enough about their personalities to see danger coming, to ward it off, did not know on what ground to meet it. That evening in the commissariat I was not a despised black man. They would simply have laughed at me if I had behaved like one. For them, I was an American. And here it was they who had the advantage, for that word, *Américain,* gave them some idea, far from inaccurate, of what to expect from me. In order to corroborate none of their ironical expectations I said nothing and did nothing—which was not the way any Frenchman, white or black, would have reacted. The question thrusting up from the bottom of my mind was not *what* I was, but *who*. And this question, since a *what* can get by with skill but a *who* demands resources, was my first real intimation of what humility must mean.

In the morning it was still raining. Between nine and ten o'clock a black Citroën took us off to the Ile de la Cité, to the great, gray Préfecture. I realize now that the questions I put to the various policemen who escorted us were always answered in such a way as to corroborate what I wished to hear. This was not out of politeness, but simply out of indifference—or, possibly, an ironical pity—since each of the policemen knew very well that nothing would speed or halt the machine in which I had become entangled. They knew I did not know this and there was cretainly no point in their telling me. In one way or another I would certainly come out at the other side—for they also knew that being found with a stolen bedsheet in one's possession was not a crime punishable by the guillotine. (They had the advantage over me there, too, for there were certainly moments later on when I was not so sure.) If I did *not* come out at the other side—well, that was just too bad. So, to my question, put while we were in the Citroën—"Will it be over today?"—I received a *"Oui, bien sûr."* He was not lying. As it turned out, the *procès-verbal* was over that day. Trying to be realistic, I dismissed, in the Citroën, all thoughts of lunch and pushed my mind ahead to dinner.

At the Préfecture we were first placed in a tiny cell, in which it was almost impossible either to sit or to lie down. After a couple of hours of this we were taken down to an office, where, for the first time, I encountered the owner of the bedsheet and where the *procès-verbal* took place. This was simply an interrogation, quite chillingly clipped and efficient (so that there was, shortly, no doubt in one's own mind that one *should* be treated as a criminal), which was recorded by a secretary. When it was over, this report was given to us to sign. One had, of course, no choice but to sign it, even though my mastery of written French was very far from certain. We were being held, according to the law in France, incommunicado, and all my angry demands to be allowed to speak to my embassy or to see a lawyer met with a stony *"Oui, oui. Plus tard."* The *procès-verbal* over we were taken back to the cell, before which, shortly, passed the owner of the bedsheet. He said he hoped we had slept well, gave a vindictive wink, and disappeared.

By this time there was only one thing clear: that we had no way of controlling the sequence of events and could not possibly guess what this sequence would be. It seemed to me, since what I regarded as the high point—the *procès-verbal*—had been passed and since the hotelkeeper was once again in possession of his sheet, that we might reasonably expect to be released from police custody in a matter of hours. We had been detained now for what would soon be twenty-four hours, during which time I had learned only that the official charge against me was *receleur*. My mental shifting, between lunch and dinner, to say nothing of the physical lack of either of these delights, was beginning to make me dizzy. The steady chatter of my friend from New York, who was determined to keep my spirits up, made me feel murderous; I was praying that some power would release us from this freezing pile of stone before the impulse became the act. And I was beginning to wonder what was happening in that beautiful city, Paris, which lived outside these walls. I wondered how long it would take before anyone casually asked, "But where's Jimmy? He hasn't been around"—and realized, knowing the people I knew, that it would take several days.

Quite late in the afternoon we were taken from our cells; handcuffed, each to a separate officer, led through a maze of steps and corridors to the top of the building; fingerprinted, photographed. As in movies I had seen, I was placed against a wall, facing an old-fashioned camera, behind which stood one of the most completely cruel and indifferent faces I had ever seen, while someone next to me and, therefore, just outside my line of vision, read off in a voice from which all human feeling, even feeling of the most base description, had long since fled, what must be called my public characteristics—which, at that time and in that place, seemed anything but that. He might have been roaring to the hostile world secrets which I could barely, in the privacy of midnight, utter to myself. But he was only reading off my height, my features, my approximate weight, my color—that color which, in the United States, had often, odd as it may sound, been my salvation—the color of my hair, my age, my nationality. A light then flashed, the photographer and I staring at each other as though there was murder in our hearts, and then it was over. Handcuffed again, I was led downstairs to the bottom of the building, into a great enclosed shed in which had been gathered the very scrapings off the Paris streets. Old, old men, so ruined and old that life in them seemed really to prove the miracle of the quickening power of the Holy Ghost—for clearly their life was no longer their affair, it was no longer even their burden, they were simply the clay which had once been touched. And men not so old, with faces the color of lead and the consistency of oatmeal, eyes that made me think of stale *café-au-lait* spiked with arsenic, bodies which could take in food and water—any food and water—and pass it out, but which could not do anything more, except possibly, at midnight, along the riverbank where rats scurried, rape. And young men, harder and crueler than the Paris stones, older by far than I, their chronological senior by some five to seven years. And North Africans, old and young, who seemed the only living people in this place because they yet retained the grace to be bewildered. But they were not bewildered by being in this shed: they were simply bewildered because they were no longer in North Africa. There was a great hole in the center of this shed, which was the common toilet.

Near it, though it was impossible to get very far from it, stood an old man with white hair, eating a piece of camembert. It was at this point, probably, that thought, for me, stopped, that physiology, if one may say so, took over. I found myself incapable of saying a word, not because I was afraid I would cry but because I was afraid I would vomit. And I did not think any longer of the city of Paris but my mind flew back to that home from which I had fled. I was sure that I would never see it anymore. And it must have seemed to me that my flight from home was the cruelest trick I had ever played on myself, since it had led me here, down to a lower point than any I could ever in my life have imagined—lower, far, than anything I had seen in that Harlem which I had so hated and so loved, the escape from which had soon become the greatest direction of my life. After we had been here an hour or so a functionary came and opened the door and called out our names. And I was sure that *this* was my release. But I was handcuffed again and led out of the Préfecture into the streets—it was dark now, it was still raining—and before the steps of the Préfecture stood the great police wagon, doors facing me, wide open. The handcuffs were taken off, I entered the wagon, which was peculiarly constructed. It was divided by a narrow aisle, and on each side of the aisle was a series of narrow doors. These doors opened on a narrow cubicle, beyond which was a door which opened onto another narrow cubicle: three or four cubicles, each private, with a locking door. I was placed in one of them; I remember there was a small vent just above my head which let in a little light. The door of my cubicle was locked from the outside. I had no idea where this wagon was taking me and, as it began to move, I began to cry. I suppose I cried all the way to prison, the prison called Fresnes, which is twelve kilometers outside of Paris.

For reasons I have no way at all of understanding, prisoners whose last initial is A, B, or C are always sent to Fresnes; everybody else is sent to a prison called, rather cynically it seemed to me, La Santé. I will, obviously, never be allowed to enter La Santé, but I was told by people who certainly seemed to know that it was infinitely more unbearable than Fresnes. This arouses in me, until today, a positive storm of curiosity concerning what I promptly began to think of as The Other Prison. My colleague in crime, occurring lower in the alphabet, had been sent there and I confess that the minute he was gone I missed him. I missed him because he was not French and because he was the only person in the world who knew that the story I told was true.

For, once locked in, divested of shoelaces, belt, watch, money, papers, nailfile, in a freezing cell in which both the window and the toilet were broken, with six other adventurers, the story I told of *l'affaire du drap de lit* elicited only the wildest amusement or the most suspicious disbelief. Among the people who shared my cell the first three days no one, it is true, had been arrested for anything much more serious—or, at least, not serious in my eyes. I remember that there was a boy who had stolen a knitted sweater from a *monoprix,* who would probably, it was agreed, receive a six-month sentence. There was an older man there who had been arrested for some kind of petty larceny. There were two North Africans, vivid, brutish, and beautiful, who alternated between gaiety and fury, not at the fact of their arrest but at the state of the cell. None poured as much emotional energy into the fact of their arrest as I did; they took it, as I would have liked to take it, as simply another unlucky happening in a very dirty world. For, though I had grown accustomed to thinking of myself as looking upon the world with a hard, penetrating eye, the truth was that they were far more realistic about the world than I, and more nearly right about it. The gap between us, which only a gesture I made could have bridged, grew steadily, during thirty-six hours, wider. I could not make any gesture simply because they frightened me. I was unable to accept my imprisonment as a fact, even as a temporary fact. I could not, even for a moment, accept my present companions as *my* companions. And they, of course, felt this and put it down, with perfect justice, to the fact that I was an American.

There was nothing to do all day long. It appeared that we would one day come to trial but no one knew when. We were awakened at seven-thirty by a rapping on what I believe is called the Judas, that small opening in the door of the cell which allows the guards to survey the prisoners. At this rapping we rose from the floor—we slept on straw pallets and each of us was covered with one thin blanket—and moved to the door of the cell. We peered through the opening into the center of the prison, which was, as I remember, three tiers high, all gray stone and gunmetal steel, precisely that prison I had seen in movies, except that, in the movies, I had not known that it was cold in prison. I had not known that when one's shoelaces and belt have been removed one is, in the strangest way, demoralized. The necessity of shuffling and the necessity of holding up one's trousers with one hand turn one into a rag doll. And the movies fail, of course, to give one any idea of what prison food is like. Along the corridor, at seven-thirty, came three men, each pushing before him a great garbage can, mounted on wheels. In the garbage can of the first was the bread—this was passed to one through the small opening in the door. In the can of the second was the coffee. In the can of the third was what was always called *la soupe,* a pallid paste of potatoes which had certainly been bubbling on the back of the prison stove long before that first, so momentous revolution. Naturally, it was cold by this time and, starving as I was, I could not eat it. I drank the coffee—which was not coffee—because it was hot, and spent the rest of the day, huddled in my blanket, munching on the bread. It was not the French bread one bought in bakeries. In the evening the same procession returned. At ten-thirty the lights went out. I had a recurring dream, each night, a nightmare which always involved my mother's fried chicken. At the moment I was about to eat it came the rapping at the door. Silence is really all I remember of those first three days, silence and the color gray.

I am not sure now whether it was on the third or the fourth day that I was taken to trial for the first time. The days had nothing, obviously, to distinguish them from one another. I remember that I was very much aware that Christmas Day was approaching and I wondered if I was really going to spend Christmas Day in prison. And I remember that the first trial came the day before Christmas Eve.

On the morning of the first trial I was awakened by hearing my name called. I was told, hanging in a kind of void between my mother's fried chicken and the cold prison floor, *"Vous préparez. Vous êtes extrait"*—which simply terrified me, since I did not know what interpretation to put on the word *"extrait,"* and since my cellmates had been amusing themselves with me by telling terrible stories about the inefficiency of French prisons, an inefficiency so extreme that it had often happened that someone who was supposed to be taken out and tried found himself on the wrong line and was guillotined instead. The best way of putting my reaction to this is to say that, though I knew they were teasing me, it was simply not possible for me to totally *dis*believe them. As far as I was concerned, once in the hands of the law in France, anything could happen. I shuffled along with the others who were *extrait* to the center of the prison, trying, rather, to linger in the office, which seemed the only warm spot in the whole world, and found myself again in that dreadful wagon, and was carried again to the Ile de la Cité, this time to the Palais de Justice. The entire day, except for ten minutes, was spent in one of the cells, first waiting to be tried, then waiting to be taken back to prison.

For I was *not* tried that day. By and by I was handcuffed and led through the halls, upstairs to the courtroom where I found my New York friend. We were placed together, both stage-whisperingly certain that this was the end of our ordeal. Nevertheless, while I waited for our case to be called, my eyes searched the courtroom, looking for a face I knew, hoping, anyway, that there was someone there who knew *me,* who would carry to someone outside the news that I was in trouble. But there was no one I knew there and I had had time to realize that there was probably only one man in Paris who could help me, an American patent attorney for whom I had worked as an office boy. He could have helped me because he had a quite solid position and some prestige and would have testified that, while working for him, I had handled large sums of money regularly, which made it rather unlikely that I would stoop to trafficking in bedsheets. However, he was somewhere in Paris, probably at this very moment enjoying a snack and a glass of wine and as far as the possibility of reaching him was concerned, he might as well have been on Mars. I tried to watch the proceedings and to make my mind a blank. But the proceedings were not reassuring. The boy, for example, who had stolen the sweater *did* receive a six-month sentence. It seemed to me that all the sentences meted out that day were excessive; though, again, it seemed that all the people who were sentenced that day had made, or clearly were going to make, crime their career. This seemed to be the opinion of the judge, who scarcely looked at the prisoners or listened to them; it seemed to be the opinion of the prisoners, who scarcely bothered to speak in their own behalf; it seemed to be the opinion of the lawyers, state lawyers for the most part, who were defending them. The great impulse of the courtroom seemed to be to put these people where they could not be seen—and not because they were offended at their crimes, unless, indeed, they were offended that the crimes were so petty, but because they did not wish to know that their society could be counted on to produce, probably in greater and greater numbers, a whole body of people for whom crime was the only possible career. Any society inevitably produces its criminals, but a society at once rigid and unstable can do nothing whatever to alleviate the poverty of its lowest members, cannot present to the hypothetical young man at the crucial moment that so-well-advertised right path. And the fact, perhaps, that the French are the earth's least sentimental people and must also be numbered among the most proud aggravates the plight of their lowest, youngest, and unluckiest members, for it means that the idea of rehabilitation is scarcely real to them. I confess that this attitude on their part raises in me sentiments of exasperation, admiration, and despair, revealing as it does, in both the best and the worst sense, their renowned and spectacular hard-headedness.

Finally our case was called and we rose. We gave our names. At the point that it developed that we were American the proceedings ceased, a hurried consultation took place between the judge and what I took to be several lawyers. Someone called out for an interpreter. The arresting officer had forgotten to mention our nationalities and there was, therefore, no interpreter in the court. Even if our French had been better than it was we would not have been allowed to stand trial without an interpreter. Before I clearly understood what was happening, I was handcuffed again and led out of the courtroom. The trial had been set back for the 27th of December.

I have sometimes wondered if I would *ever* have got out of prison if it had not been for the older man who had been arrested for the mysterious petty larceny. He was acquitted that day and when he returned to the cell—for he could not be released until morning—he found me sitting numbly on the floor, having just been prevented, by the sight of a man, all blood, being carried back to *his* cell on a stretcher, from seizing the bars and screaming until they let me out. The sight of the man on the stretcher proved, however, that screaming would not do much for me. The petty-larceny man went around asking if he could do anything in the world outside for those he was leaving behind. When he came to me I, at first, responded, "No, nothing"—for I suppose I had by now retreated into the attitude, the earliest I remember, that of my father, which was simply (since I had lost his God) that nothing could help me. And I suppose I will remember with gratitude until I die the fact that the man now insisted: *"Mais, êtes-vous sûr?"* Then it swept over me that he was going *outside* and he instantly became my first contact since the Lord alone knew how long with the outside world. At the same time, I remember, I did not really believe that he would help me. There was no reason why he should. But I gave him the phone number of my attorney friend and my own name.

So, in the middle of the next day, Christmas Eve, I shuffled downstairs again, to meet my visitor. He looked extremely well fed and sane and clean. He told me I had nothing to worry about any more. Only not even he could do anything to make the mill of justice grind any faster. He would, however, send me a lawyer of his acquaintance who would defend me on the 27th, and he would himself, along with several other people, appear as a character witness. He gave me a package of Lucky Strikes (which the turnkey took from me on the way upstairs) and said that, though it was doubtful that there would be any celebration in the prison, he would see to it that I got a fine Christmas dinner when I got out. And this, somehow, seemed very funny. I remember being astonished at the discovery that I was actually laughing. I was, too, I imagine, also rather disappointed that my hair had not turned white, that my face was clearly not going to bear any marks of tragedy, disappointed at bottom, no doubt, to realize, facing him in that room, that far worse things had happened to most people and that, indeed, to paraphrase my mother, if this was the worst thing that ever happened to me I could consider myself among the luckiest people ever to be born. He injected—my visitor—into my solitary nightmare common sense, the world, and the hint of blacker things to come.

The next day, Christmas, unable to endure my cell, and feeling that, after all, the day demanded a gesture, I asked to be allowed to go to Mass, hoping to hear some music. But I found myself, for a freezing hour and a half, locked in exactly the same kind of cubicle as in the wagon which had first brought me to prison, peering through a slot placed at the level of the eye at an old Frenchman, hatted, overcoated, muffled, and gloved, preaching in this language which I did not understand, to this row of wooden boxes, the story of Jesus Christ's love for men.

The next day, the 26th, I spent learning a peculiar kind of game, played with matchsticks, with my cellmates. For, since I no longer felt that I would stay in this cell forever, I was beginning to be able to make peace with it for a time. On the 27th I went again to trial and, as had been predicted, the case against us was dismissed. The story of the *drap de lit,* finally told, caused great merriment in the courtroom, whereupon my friend decided that the French were "great." I was chilled by their merriment, even though it was meant to warm me. It could only remind me of the laughter I had often heard at home, laughter which I had sometimes deliberately elicited. This laughter is the laughter of those who considered themselves to be at a safe remove from all the wretched, for whom the pain of the living is not real. I had heard it so often in my native land that I had resolved to find a place where I would never hear it any more. In some deep, black, stony, and liberating way, my life, in my own eyes, began during that first year in Paris, when it was borne in on me that this laughter is universal and never can be stilled.

June 1957

Isaac Rosenfeld

LIFE IN CHICAGO

The Land and the Lake

All faces, coins, and questions have two sides, there is concave and convex, and what man isn't a Janus head? This being topology it holds good of all things: so also of cities with their inside and out. I was born well inside Chicago, four miles from the Lake. Public transportation being what it was—I might just as well say *is,* but in those days no poor man had a car—and since the only practical measure of distance from the Lake was distance from a beach, all residents of the Jewish West Side, around Roosevelt and Kedzie, were dry-docked. To see water, you had to stand long, sweaty streetcar rides (the red and buff streetcars, reeking of ozone, with their clanging bells and screeching wheels, the wire-mesh window guards and the air compressors going *diga-diga-diga-diga* at each stop, the dust, the confetti of transfer punches, mashed cigarette butts and soiled newspapers, hot rattan seats on the sunny side, green shades)—how long those rides were! You might have been living in the heart of some central land mass, for all the difference it made, your proximity to water. Herewith, a theory on the matter.

All cities hug water, but it's available, accessible, visible, sensible water that counts. You wouldn't have known it, living inland in Chicago—and you won't, I am sure, to this day—that the city sprawls for miles along a great lake that is capable of oceanic moods when the right weather takes it, of biologic odors when its meadows bloom and its fauna spawn and crawl; you wouldn't have known that this lake makes sea-waves, and in winter, ice cliffs, under a wild-flying spray. Thales never walked these streets, or he would have held earth to be the source of all creation, the peculiar, cracked, ashy, mineral-gray Chicago earth with its derivative dust, grit, and grime that rise swirling when the wind blows. We had sun-pictures in those days: you held a glass negative to the light, backed by a piece of photo-sensitive paper—images of Tom Mix, Jack Holt, Hoot Gibson straddling their lover-horses, or Rin-Tin-Tin in an earlier incarnation, but never of ships, not even a tub or a barge, let alone ocean liners. Locomotives there were aplenty—the Twentieth Century, which runs to New York.

So we were land-locked, and the mind was parched for moisture. Call it Gobi Desert, we were in Central Asia, and even when the rain poured, as it did, from hoses, the sewers would gurgle, the baked earth would crack open again, and only a little mud remained in the depressions we had pocked out with our heels to play killer-in-the-hole. Such is the source of isolationism in the Midwest: it is an ignorance and fear of water.

It took estrangement to make this clear to me. I had to move away and come back a visitor, and at last, as I am now, a residential stranger, to discover the Lake front and its implications. I had to approach the city from the outside, to throw off the heavy, bitter birth-burden and the natural piety by which I held this place dear, to see it under an aspect external to both my love and hate: to peer down its streets and not see myself at the end of them.

The visitor who approaches Chicago by plane from the East gets the preferential view: granite and white marble skyscrapers and museums, bordered by park, bordered by water. Then more of the same by car for some twenty miles along the lake, over the Outer Drive. Lake, lake, lake, but not really lake, for there is no opposite shore, only water-cribs, tankers, lighthouses, sails—and on the land side, tall apartment buildings, a continuous façade. One way, look as far as you like and let the horizon float you into space. The other way, blind and abrupt, no peeking. Chicago is trying to hide something. Walk about and you will see what—not north and south along the Lake—east, let us say, of Broadway, Clark, and State, for there you will see only that which Chicago wants seen, its Gold Coast and Magnificent Mile of Fifth Avenue and occasionally then-some shop windows, stores, hotels, hospitals, restaurants, cocktail lounges, and fashion centers which furnish the home and the mind. Go west, cross State, proceed out on North Avenue or Division, where the hog-butcher lives. Architecture is frozen music, but this is cut-throat screaming. Here are the hidden poor in outhouses with inside plumbing—what did the Great Chicago Fire burn that these hutches and coops should still stand? Not picturesque South Halsted Street with strings of garlic and garlands of fig, an atmosphere burning bright of Mediterranean ports and Polish ghettos, but Stashu-plain West Division Street with the blond, brutal, crew-cut hair, or Germantown North Avenue with the saloons and Deutsches Kino, the hardware stores, bakeries, the shiny furniture stores, the railroad yards, the factories, smokestacks, gas tanks. Mile after mile of vanished Nile culture reconstructed out of archaeological debris, but no people, the crowds in the street rendered invisible through incongruity: an inhuman landscape (does anyone *live* here?)—hence, no inhabitants. These are some species of nomad on the move, fellaheen taking off after the Israelitities, they, too, fleeing a smitten Egypt. The pyramids are plainly labeled, Butcher Shop, Auto Parts, Wrecking. It goes on forever, the hidden Chicago, not to be seen from the outside. The point of it all is its pointlessness.

Let me say it by birthright. Natural piety revolts, I would not have it spoken by an outsider, to bray it aloud like A. J. Liebling and publish it in Gath. But if Chicago is one of the Seven Wonders, then the eighth is that a city should be so pointlessly huge. You can take down the statement in a mile or two, you get the drift soon enough, of landscape burdened by industry, but it goes on and on, over and over and over, a Walt Whitman storehouse of democracy come alive, a Sears catalogue of people and occupations endlessly varied in repetitive similitudes cracking Leibniz on the numskull conk, identity of indiscernibles, indeed! Why so much, so many, so indiscernibly all-alike-and-different, who needs all these dry goods stores, groceries, factories, railroads yards, sidings, lampposts, funeral parlors? Would the world collapse if there were just one less?

No fiery riddles, this is all very plain. I mean to say, Chicago produces practically nothing that it does not manufacture. Between the work of hand and mind a balance must be kept. This balance was never established in the wonder days when Chicago rose from nothing to the nation's fourth largest city in the first generation of its incorporated existence, and our schools, churches, museums, libraries, universities, art galleries, theaters, and concert halls have not yet righted the balance, though we are second in the land.

Come back to the Lake. We have a saying in Chicago; when we want to dispose of someone we tell him to walk east—till his hat floats. The Lake is the city's eastern boundary, and all along this boundary for some twenty miles but seldom more than a mile deep, the East has, you might say, established a beachhead. Chicago can't keep its eye off New York; not only La Salle vs. Wall Street, the whole city is shot through and has been over most of its history, with rivalrous attitudes. State and Madison is "the world's busiest corner," the Chicago *Tribune* is "the world's greatest newspaper," the Merchandise Mart is "the world's largest office building," Midway Airport is "the world's busiest," etc, etc.

Some of these boasts are well founded, Chicago does rank first in shipping, packing, railroading, its commercial traffic is second to none; but consider for a moment, not the truth but the *direction* of our claims—they are aimed at New York. One by one Chicago has overtaken its earlier rivals, St. Louis, Boston, Philadelphia, San Francisco; we are ahead of them in size, productivity, and importance (whatever we mean by that). But New York stays stubbornly in first place. All sorts of happy statements float about town; now that the St. Lawrence seaway is opening up and Chicago is building port facilities at Lake Calumet (at the southeastern extremity of the city), it will outstrip New York and become the country's number one port. It is so many miles nearer Liverpool than New York is, it has no many natural advantages, not the least considerable of which is the fact that the city is farther from the peak of its climb than New York. Now we are going to make it!

In five years the Port of Chicago may well become what the city's optimists predict, but it will take more than five years, at least a generation, more likely fifty, for the real issue in Chicago's rivalry with New York to be settled. This will require an elemental transformation. Chicago must move from earth to water. Such are the implications of the narrow strip along the Lake.

Such are the implications of the long narrow strip of Lake-culture, and its three points of concentration, off the North Shore at Evanston, where Northwestern stands (not properly in Chicago, but its culture necessarily bound fast to it), off the Near North Side and the Loop in the middle, and to the south, off the Midway which is spanned by the University of Chicago. The water-culture as opposed to the land means internationalism, an openness to interchange, a hospitality to ideas. The massive land-culture means heavy production, but no city can be truly great that does not reach out to water. It need not be nearby. Paris is no sea-coast town, neither is Rome, but the Seine and the Tiber are revered, and there men have at least built lovely embankments. The Chicago River, in the heart of town, runs dirty and neglected. It was a great engineering feat to make it reverse its course (in 1900, to draw sewage and foul odors away), but having done that, we were for years unable to think what else to do. Only in the last two years has a strip of embankment off Randolph Street been planted to grass, but so much remains to be done, this hardly counts as a beginning.

There is the matter of bridges, for one. A bridge must be a beautiful thing to symbolize intercourse, joining, but the Chicago River is spanned by no graceful rise of arch. Heavy, girdered, bridges flat as a Dutchman's foot join the Loop to its northern and western environs, and the union between the shores is not even a permanent thing, for the bridges must split open in the middle, stalling the land traffic, when a ship sails by. You can imagine how this will snarl an already congested traffic when enlarged port facilities bring an even greater amount of activity to the Chicago River, as they will inevitably do. Not until stairways, benches, and walks sprout among the still unplanted trees and gardens at the riverbanks will the Chicago become a proper place for loafing and dreaming, as are the Seine and the Tiber, even the commercial Thames and Hudson (where you dream of different things, all, however, touched by water). Not until then will water become a property of the city as a whole.

Look to fishing for our true progress. It is easy enough to sit and fish along the Lake, and hundreds of fishermen do so daily. But the heart of the city must find a place for them, they must not be required to sit at the edge. Only then will commerce once more come to mean intercourse—when one need not turn his back upon it, but can lean back, at ease among busy things, resting against stone and brick, activity wedded to inactivity, action to contemplation, and natural piety blessing all things—bird call and policeman's whistle—as it has done in Paris for centuries.

The beachhead is in a perilous position: it is so narrow, so precious and *précieux;* and it makes up such a small porportion of the total land mass of Chicago. When there has been a particularly violent crime, or when the chronic racial tension in Chicago flares up, I am sometimes taken with fear and I see this vulnerable area, in which the city's cultural life is concentrated, invaded by the land forces, come to smash the records and the art objects and trample the Swedish-blond or Danish walnut furniture of the style centers under hobnail boots.

Violence, not precisely of this kind, has been going on in Hyde Park for years, where the streets are rude by day and unsafe by night, with robberies, burglaries, and assault quite common. To grasp the full meaning of these events, you must know that Hyde Park, for more than fifty years, has been the city's chief seat of culture—a South Side neighborhood of about two square miles in which the famous Midway, left over from the Exposition of 1893, the University of Chicago, the Museum of Science and Industry, the homes and apartments of University personnel, and fine parks, bathing beaches, shops, and hotels are located.

Hyde Park is bordered, on the west, by the terribly overcrowded Black Belt, which slipped its buckle during the war years; the resulting spillover, plus migrations, still going on, of Puerto Ricans and of poor whites and Negroes from the South, converted the area into one of the city's worst trouble spots, full of crimes, juvenile and adult, and racial incidents. Some of the violence has been checked by arc lights and increased police patrols, which were granted by the city administration, rather belatedly, after the residents of the area held many protest meetings and circulated endless petitions. Conditions are much better now, but the meaning of these incidents persists; at work here are not racial tension, poverty, the maladjustments of uprooted populations, and resentment of the underprivileged alone, but the revolt of the masses, in Ortega's sense, the execration of quality and of things of the mind. It is hard to say how much damage has been done along these lines to the neighborhood and its institutions, and to what extent a recovery can be marked; but in the nature of the case, such blows to the security and ease of a city's cultural life may cause considerable and even permanent harm.

The University of Chicago, faced by the prospect of complete isolation in a rough-neck slum, is at last "doing someting about it"—together with the Southeast Chicago Commission, the Chicago Housing Authority, and the Hyde Park-Kenwood Community Conference, it is sponsoring conversion of its immediate environs into a high-cost rental and shopping area, which should eliminate "undesirables" regardless of racial lines and enable the "better class of people" to live at ease. But this is hardly a fundamental solution, and it does not affect all of Hyde Park. Tenements, traps, and slums between the Midway and the south side of 55th Street will be torn down, but the area immediately north of 55th Street and within striking distance of the University and its precincts will only become more congested, and deteriorate all the more rapidly; the same may be expected across the southern boundary line, and one cannot suppose that forced removals will turn the gangs and hoods toward benevolence.

But the psychological aspects of this solution stand a somewhat better chance of working out. The strain on liberal conscience (Hyde Park is highly liberal) of opposing racial prejudice while complaining about "the neighborhood" and supporting block organizations to "keep up the standards," may shortly be removed, if the redevelopment of Hyde Park produces an interracial area of relatively equal economic, social, and cultural standards. The way one white liberal put it, "We don't care what color our neighbors are, but when they play their radios too loud, we'd rather hear Vivaldi than pops." But a conversation between two Negroes of the upper class, reported to me by Rolf Meyersohn, a University of Chicago sociologist, and his wife Mary Lea, puts the entire redevelopment project under a different light. "What self-respecting Negro would *want* to live in Hyde Park!" I don't know to what extent this sentiment is general among the colored; but the first may be taken to be universal among liberal whites.

Community life in Hyde Park is dominated by the University, its students, faculty, and administrative personnel. I am willing to risk a few generalizations on the University culture—as anthropologists use the word—with the understanding, of course, that no generalizations are as sound as they are attractive.

Not so long ago, under the chancellorship of Robert M. Hutchins, the students at the University—I shall restrict myself throughout to undergraduates—made up a fairly uniform body. Football was out, and with it went the usual rah-rah accessories of collegiate and fraternity life. Raccoon coat, pennants, beanies, megaphones, and sloganized flivvers may have flourished in the 20's; but the 30's and 40's, under Hutchins, were lean and studious years, with the students forming a self-conscious intellectual elite, newly introduced to Aristotle, Aquinas, and a revolutionary college program which gave great advantages to the bright and more industrious. In the postwar years, when enrollment dropped and the University found itself with a critical shortage of funds, a number of changes began to take place, the influence of which is still being felt. Chief among the changes was the succession to the chancellorship of Lawrence A. Kimpton, who views the return of football as a prime educational necessity, and who, a few years ago, shocked the campus by declaring that the University was no place for "queer" students. By queer, Chancellor Kimpton meant intellectuals—a position there is no reason to suspect him of having abandoned.

Kimpton's policies have gone over with the trustees, improved the University's financial position, and attracted a larger and more apple-cheeked student body. The "queers" to be sure, still persist, and always will, so long as the University retains its present scholastic standards, but among the students may now be found a considerable number of the "yaks"—as they are called in derision—more or less healthy and well-adjusted young men and women of rather inflexible mind, who regard life not as an adventure but an investment. In an argument with one of them —we were debating the relative merits of the Hutchins and Kimpton administrations—I found myself routed by my interlocutor, an Ivy Leaguish graduate in law, who declared, "Do you realize that until I came to the University I did not know how to play golf!" As we say, *"Darf men gehn tsu college?"*

Indirectly and by default, the intellectuals are also promoting the return of football. (I trust that the term "intellectuals" may be applied, without too much stretch, to students who are not "yaks" and who may, conceivably, leave the University without learning how to play golf—in short the "queers." These equivocations are made in good faith, and are necessitated by an extraordinary shift in perspective among the students, which I hope to make clear in a moment. Let us call them the "serious" students, with the understanding that here, too, the term requires qualification.)

The outstanding change in student life, over the last decade or so, is the disappearance of politics as an active interest. Chicago, which was once considered a "hot bed of radicalism" by the *Tribune* and the local Hearst press and is still held in suspicion by the state legislature, has gone the way of all other American universities, with revolutionary groups passing into desuetude. In the old days (I would call them good; it is my own conviction that politics furnishes the best of all bases for secular culture) the political interest colored practically every student activity on campus, with the major division drawn between Stalinists (who dominated the American Student Union) and Trotskyites (who worked through the local chapter of the Young People's Socialist League.)* The two Marxist groups, with their symps and associates, spoke bitterly about, but never to, each other and avoided all contact, except to heckle, and occasionally strong-arm, each other's meetings. Politics was everywhere, in a measure, one ate and drank it; and sleep gave no escape, for it furnished terror to

* I am speaking of an avant-garde, the pace-setters and conscious students, and also the ones who were out of it in a special way.

our dreams: Hitler, Mussolini, the Moscow Trials, the Spanish Civil War, the plaguey bill of Stalinism, the stop-gaps of NRA, WPA, and the New Deal, and the approach of inevitable war. We lived in the shadow of annihilation, drawing on the pattern of Guernica and Ethiopia, to imagine what bombings would be like. Liaisons, marriages and divorces, let alone friendships, were sometimes contracted on no other basis than these issues, and dominated, in a way that might seem incomprehensible to the present generation, by events of the world order. Even students who were *hors de combat* were involved, for everyone called upon them to justify their disinterest, and they had hard work convincing even themselves. Politics was form and substance, accident and modification, the metaphor of all things.

Now this has vanished like Villon's snows. The metaphor is no longer political; it is not even social, but anti-social, and anti-social in a special sense, for the word, as older generations understand it, carries connotations that have become obsolete. Insofar as there is a metaphor governing the attitudes of life, it seems to be derived from the world of jazz, with the avant-garde leading the way in speech, manners, and dress. A few alliances exist with the pipestem, narrow-shouldered Ivy League tradition, and there is a sprouting of striped and buckled caps, but the University, as a whole, has not plunged. This is due to the fact that the University of Chicago is still dominated by intellectual tradition, and no definite tradition comes along with the suit and extra slacks.

But the dominant intellectual tradition is hardly recognizable as one. Tag ends of Aristotelianism and of Hutchins still stick to it, but they are as confused as they are confusing to the undergraduates, who take quite a rocking in the College, while new administrative policies are under hot debate. For the last several years everyone has been predicting the complete disappearance of the College, as Hutchins organized it, in a year or two; the predictions have not yet come true, but slow changes are in process, hard to make out on the surface, which, everyone supposes, are preparing the way for the University with a strapping enrollment and buzzing with the wholesome athletic activities that Kimpton desires. Meanwhile the students have retreated from the more pressing local issues as they have from international ones, and have taken to calling one another "man." This key-word of bop talk is highly significant, expressing, as it does, the least common biological denominator, to which all things are reduced by the universal solvent of jazz.

The South Side is dominated by the University, but the University, in turn, is dominated by the South Side. The neighborhood life of the students, their favorite bars and hangouts (Jimmie's, the Compass Tavern, the University Tavern, Stineway's on 57th Street) have developed an interracial clientele of mixed types. Besides the recognizable students (many are no longer so), there are bohemians, workers, white-collar men, hangers-on, moochers, delinquents, and near-delinquents. From the last four groups, some require a new category for proper classification; I would call them *retired students*—young men, and some women, who need not actually have attended the University; they are no longer active as students, but still follow the student pattern, by habit or imitation, maintain contact with the students, and have a considerable following and reputation among them as "characters." The retired student, a sort of recently discovered missing link, is but one of the many new forces blurring the distinction between town and gown. One meets types in the varied off-campus dives whom one would mistakenly warrant as students, and students on campus who would seem, by nature, to belong on a motorcycle or behind a counter, tending bar. The shrinking of the distance between extremes has produced a student culture typical, as a particular, and lower, social level, of the amalgamations taking place all over society in our conservative time.

Phenomenologically, the student-complex consists in bop-talk (with its basic expressions, such as *crazy, cool, gas, stoned,* etc., etc., deriving from insanity, narcosis, and death; very often the vocabulary is dated as, in a larger sense, the practice is—the avant-garde leadership in New York, for example, has begun to drop bop), narcotics-mythology (marijuana and main-line drugs, as part of the folkways of jazz musicians; very little indulgence, however), rudeness ("man," "cat," and "chick" being the major human designations, they call for none of the amenities that accompany the recognition of human beings as individual souls), Hi-Fi, short haircuts, jeans, cotton-twill slacks, zipper-jackets, and occasionally fashionable but always dirty or neglected clothes, and sports cars parked along the curb.

The ideal is to lead a passionless, "cool" life, exposed, but uncommitted, to many worlds and to be *au courant* in them all: to be able to chatter —actually, drone—of drama, books, art, jazz, Hi-Fi, recordings, liquors, mixed drinks, Aristotle and other philosophers, events about town, the underworld and its leading characters, as well as the leading personalities in the entertainment worlds; to avoid extremes of romanticism in sexuality or love, and all extremes of feeling, which extremes (actually normal emotion) are held in bad taste and called "frantic." (It is of course obvious that this anti-romanticism is one of the most romantic of all cults.) One undergraduate I know calls the composite *formo-frigidist,* an excellent description, as it unifies the standards of taste over the entire range, including furniture and literary criticism. The whole is a masquerade. Intellectuality is cultivated as mindlessness, is required to confine itself to the crippling, limited vocabulary noted above, and to endorse guitars, Calypso, and other folk music; the rich students act and dress poor; and the poor students, within their means, rich; racial equality, though often genuinely believed in, sometimes seeks hostile expression, the whites calling their colored friends *spooks,* and the colored (who often refer to themselves by the same term) returning the favor through the use of the word *ofay,* so that it is more than a little puzzling, at times, to tell the dancer from the dance. The dead-pan Afro-Cuban mask, though optional, is worn on all occasions.

The foregoing is not, of course, true of all students, not does the entire complex necessarily occur in students who do fit the pattern, but to a degree almost all of them are growing on this compost. There remain, of course, purer types, now as at all times, students without nonsense whose culture heroes might be some great poet, novelist, painter, philosopher, or composer, rather than the jazz musician. Their fate is inseparable from that of the series throughout Chicago's beachhead—and similar beachheads all over the world.

I don't know to what extent the phenomena of student life, and the Hyde Park crime rate, may be attributable to the invasion of the beachhead by land forces. Surely, some such process is involved, but the process must be an extremely complex one, since very often the predator upon the cultural, as well as the material, wealth of the beachhead is himself of the beachhead. (Nor do I mean to imply that all land forces are vicious; most of them, on the contrary, are associated with the prime middle-class virtues of stability, security, and respect for law and order. But the distinction between the lake and the land still holds true in terms of culture.)

I should judge that we are dealing, in Hyde Park, not so much with an invasion of the beachhead, as with the absence, on the beachhead, of an adequate idea of what the cultural life in and around a university should be. In part, the University is also to blame for this; in recent years it has begun to show that it, too, lacks a clear idea of itself.* Its own unclarity is

* In one small part, the University has passed undamaged through its own turmoil. I am speaking of the Basic Program of Liberal Education for Adults. Classes are held, most of them, off campus, downtown, at the University's Downtown Center; they are devoted to a four-year seminar and tutorial course in reading the great books from Plato and Aristotle through Dostoevsky and Freud—the original Hutchins-Adler idea, somewhat modified and elaborated, and absolutely proof against the educational imperatives of football, folk music, and golf. Sports cars, if any, are parked inconspicuously in the welter of downtown traffic, and *steel-bon* and Calypso do not penetrate to the ears of the adult students. We tie ourselves nightly to the mast (there are also forenoon and early afternoon classes, attended mostly by housewives, and 7:30 A.M. "early-bird" classes, attended, I should imagine, by grackles) and have thus far resisted destruction, though enrollment is sometimes precarious. Staff meetings, which occur almost weekly during the academic year, and several times a week during the summer, take on a salutary violence, and the interchange of ideas and criticism reaches an intensity unequaled since the old political days on questions of curriculum, policy, and interpretation of the various readings. For a reason I have not yet discovered, this program, which is quite severe in its demands

reflected among the students, not only yaks, but non-yaks. In time, the latter may well become a subspecies of yak, also capable of attributing their "education" to the University—e.g., "Man, do you realize that until I came to the U, I didn't dig folk songs!" It is in this way that they support their opposite numbers from the frats and football claques: by letting their "queerness" become something other than conspicuous intellectuality.

An entirely different culture is exhibited by the faculty, administrative personnel, and older graduate students—but here, too, the distinction between academic and non-academic life cannot always be clearly drawn; many professional men, strangers to the University, inhabit the area, and in its broader features life in Hyde Park follows a neighborhood pattern rather than a strictly academic one.

This pattern, which my sociologist friend Meyersohn calls the Hyde Park syndrome, shows some remarkable uniformities. First of all, the members of this group are married; and while marriage and family life predominate in nearly all neighborhoods, in Hyde Park people marry, furnish apartments, and raise children in a unique way. The children are all out of Spock and Gesell, with an assist from Bruno Bettelheim of the University's Orthogenic School. The furniture is from Bordelon's or aspires to be (Bordelon's is a modern furnishings center; it has recently closed out its Hyde Park store and moved to the wealthier Near North Side) and a few modern *objets,* such as chairs or tables with wire legs, are sure to be found in every house. Marriage has a youthful, cheerful, share-and-share-alike tone to it, with the young couples doing their shopping together at the Co-op, drawing on the services of the same (or the same kinds of) baby-sitters and pediatricians, encountering the same kinds of problems, and solving them in similar ways. Infidelities are rare—such, at least, is the impression; this is my riskiest generalization—and one of the few differentiae between Hyde Park's academic and non-academic professionals may be drawn along this line, with the incidence of infidelity and divorce higher among the latter. (I suspect that nearly all differentiae between these highly similar groups are reducible to income, and that the differences in culture-pattern become greater, the higher one climbs the income-gradient.)

Other things being equal, one sure way of telling whether you are visiting an academic or non-academic household is by the behavior of the children, and the extent to which you can make yourself heard above their clatter. If it is still possible to conduct a conversation, you are in a non-academic household. The men and women form groups of their own for tennis, handball, gymnaisum workouts, or buggy-pushing, shopping in the

---

of both faculty and students, is unbeatable for sheer serious fun. Everybody loves it, and there is nothing quite like it in Chicago or any other city.

neighborhood or downtown, but by and large the couples are always together; pub-crawling and other single-handed pursuits are rare (at least when it comes to conducting them in the neighborhood).

The Goths may be sacking this Rome, but many of the Romans go on leading the established life, making the big time in their middle-class villas. I call Romans the ones whom it will take fire or other catastrophe to push out of Hyde Park; they are entrenched in their love of place and firm in their liberal convictions; an interracial atmosphere, if not entirely congenial to them, is still a cheerful price. It is not hard to see what they find lovable in Hyde Park. Nowhere else in a city of comparable size is there quite the same "small town " feeling as in this community. It has a relatively rooted, peaceful look, and in some sections, an aged dignity far beyond its years. The residential streets are all planted to lawns and trees (mostly cottonwoods, elms, and catalpas) with hedges, shrubs, and flowers not uncommon. The University's bell tower booms out quarter-hour intervals in shivery tones and sends the strokes of the hour floating over the neighborhood, never on time; the red-tile roofs and crew-cut Gothic of the University buildings shine through the trees like the City of Oz, and when in the right frame of mind you can convince yourself that the outlying houses and streets are a village snuggling up to a castle. (In its administrative complexities, the castle, I might add, is much like Kafka's, but let's not spoil a pretty picture.)

But the key to the small-townishness of Hyde Park is provided by bulletin boards. These, of course, are all over the University, and it was but a short step to carry them off campus, yet the bulletin-board culture began on a tree trunk outside a bookstore on 57th Street. Hundreds of signs, slips, chits, and notices hang pinned to this tree, all around the trunk, sometimes overlapping, several layers deep, from as high as a man can reach to sidewalk level, advertising rooms and apartments to rent and sublet, baby buggies and cars for sale, beds, armchairs, scrabble sets, English bicycles for both sexes, baby-sitters, potted plants, tropical fish, Hi-Fi apparatus and repairs, rides to points east and west, recorders from soprano to bass—and the corresponding notices of goods and services wanted. (Recently the tree offered for sale a pair of ladies' straw sandals, worn only once, and a hermaphroditic hamster.)

Similar notices are to be found on the bulletin board of the Hyde Park Co-op, and lost and found signs are posted on tree trunks all over the neighborhood. Telephone numbers and addresses are freely stated, in spite of the degeneration of the neighborhood, on a patent assumption of cultural homogeneity, as though it were inconceivable for burglars to consult the tree for leads. And yet, in all likelihood, they may never do so; at any rate, the assumption of homogeneity is fully justified, for the notices are often worded in such a way as to be unintelligible to outsiders.

There is a compact, solid, middle-class "what-I-shall-assume-you-shall-assume" feeling about these signs, a sense of shared life and values, we are all friends. I don't know of any studies of the subject, but I am sure they would reveal a striking uniformity in outlook and habits among the people who post and read these advertisements, and I venture to say it would go somewhat as follows. For some reason I imagine that they are solidly for Stevenson (I can't imagine a Republican rubber-necking the tree trunk) and yet for Stevenson in a special sense, by way of Independent Voters of Illinois (a special chapter of the ADA), or out of conviction that he is intellectual and not, say, as the hill-billies in the neighborhood are for him. (Hill-billies are also unimaginable at the tree trunk.) Many of our tree-trunkers (let's call them Druids for convenience) work for the IVI and IVI-endorsed candidates, and give of their time to ring doorbells, circulate petitions, and relieve the watch at headquarters during election campaigns. They read the *New Yorker* and the *Reporter,* and buy the New York Sunday *Times* for the Book Review. On clement days in summer they go out to the Point, a recreation area and rocky projection into the Lake off 55th Street; there some of them go skin-diving. Though the rocks are slippery, sharp, and often slammed by strong waves, our types prefer them to the sand beach at 57th Street; the Point is town pump and tabernacle, for all Hyde Park, and if faculty is not as well represented there as are the students this is not for cultural reasons. (Many of them have children, for whom the rocks and deep water are unsafe; and besides, as many of them as are able to, go to the country in the summer. Besides, the tree is one of the chief points where the faculty and student cultures intersect, and the typology I am developing round the tree is meant to hold good for the University culture as a whole, and not for faculty alone.)

There is a complex pattern here, somewhat mystifying in its principle of cohesion. It is easy enough to see why there should be a division among the faculty, student, and bohemian aspects of the University culture, but not why or how each group acquires its own particular pattern, or why the culture as a whole should be composed of such various elements as sports cars, bop-talk, gin-and-tonic, Station WFMT, cottage-cheese-and-garlic, paper-bound books, short haircuts, IVI, foreign movies, Bordelon's furniture, copper jewelry and earrings, a painfully ambiguous attitude toward the color question, guitars, folk music, skin-diving, Dr. Spock, recorder-playing, Hi-Fi, open sandals, and hamsters as standard zoological equipment for introducing the children to the facts of life. Just what is the secret affinity between Hi-Fi and short haircuts, for example, that they should so often be found together, or between Bela Bartók and the IVI, or wall-to-wall carpeting and a subscription to *Harper's?* This, to be sure, is not a question for Hyde Park alone to answer; one might very well ask it of urban culture as a whole. The cohesiveness seems to lie in the cohesion;

essence lags scandalously far behind existence—and yet, I am sure it is no hodge-podge, some principle must be present.

There is more of the same on the Near North Side. This is Chicago's "New York" neighborhood—but much cleaner, more concentrated, and in some respects more like New York than the original. It combines Fifth Avenue (a number of Fifth Avenue shops, such as Bonwit's and Saks, have branches on North Michigan) with Central Park West and Riverside Drive, but this is only a manner of speaking. Oddly enough, it is the manner spoken here. Actually, this section has a quality and beauty all its own, with the Lake providing the distinctive atmosphere. Again, there is a complex in evidence, a mixture of elements and types, not so oddly assorted as in Hyde Park, but still of considerable range.

One immediately apparent difference is the concentration of homosexuals, and their attendant culture. Some of the shops and night spots have an exclusively homosexual clientele; others are mixed. Even some of the corner drug stores, whose fountains and lunch counters are patronized by cab drivers and local merchants, give preference, in the magazine racks, to jock-strap and body-beautiful cheesecake; the girlie magazines are often hidden behind several layers of brightly oiled young men.

This neighborhood also has its contrasts, the tracks on North State Street distinguishing the right from the wrong side. East of State, there is considerable elegance; west of State, decline sets in, running rapidly to the squalor that begins at Clark. (The Lake culture also begins to peter out at State.) The sharp division between east and west moderates the clash somewhat, and you don't encounter the startling juxtapositions of hotels and hovels so frequently as you do in New York, but the neighborhood is still pre-eminent in contrast. There are mean pigeon-fouled rooming houses, and flops, missions, employment agencies, pigeon-fouled on the outside and cluttered with lithos and bric-a-brac within, the skyscraper apartments with liveried doormen and snipped hedges, barber shops that serve coffee and barber shops where you can place a bet, dinky Spanish groceries for the Puerto Rican colony and greasy-spoons, second-hand automobile lots and second-hand clothing stores, and some of the better known night clubs, key clubs, and restaurants that play progressive jazz—all within a few blocks of one another.

Rush Street, the cabaret center, is brightly lit and fairly crowded all hours of the night. (Night crowds are a rarity in Chicago; of the downtown streets, only Randolph, the amusement center, stays awake after the shops close, and then mostly on week-ends.) Coffeehouses, that double as art galleries, and serve atmosphere and *espresso* (which most of them spell *expresso*), abound in the neighborhood, and put some three or four ice cream tables out-of-doors, if space permits, for that continental touch (Ricardo's, one of the largest restaurants, even surrounds you with travel posters). There is a rash of key clubs, with sedate or moderne façades, where you may enjoy the dubious privilege of entree by card or key only. These are unknown on the South Side.

The people round about are of several kinds. In addition to the obvious homosexuals, there are office workers and stenos from the nearby Loop, advertising executives and publicity men, students, painters, musicians, con men, chorus girls, call girls, entertainers, wrigglers, peelers, transients, bohemians, creeps, and hardy old ladies who carry shopping bags. The conspicuous difference between the Near North Side and Hyde Park is the absence of faculty. The University facilities in or near the neighborhood are mostly for evening students and the staff of the University of Illinois College at Navy Pier either live on the South Side or the Far North or the North suburbs. At any rate, professors and their wives are not in evidence, the young-liberal complex is quite diluted, and bulletin boards and notices on trees are virtually unknown.

The Near North Side is not as homogeneous as Hyde Park; it does not have a large, homogeneous middle-class group that lends its character to the streets and gathering places. It is an anonymous neighborhood, transient and big town. Puerto Ricans and Negroes inhabit the outskirts, but racial tensions are insignificant or very well concealed. Crime in the area a few blocks off the Lake is confined to burglary and traffic violations, and street incidents are uncommon. Bug House Square, facing the Newberry Library, does not draw the crowds of the 30's, and there are fewer *nudniks* and spielers.

Nevertheless the syndrome, with a few modifications, is similar to Hyde Park, and a purer formation of upper-class taste and life patterns is in evidence. Bordelon's has a huge furniture and fashion center on Walton Street, and next door Max Siegel, the bookseller, manages to achieve the same effects with birthday cards and books that Bordelon's does in the slip covers—he carries a fair number of books, but they are so carefully loaded on light, airy shelves, as to appear purely decorative. The concentrated, foxed, browsy, and intellectually-brown atmosphere of traditional bookstores is gone; with a few minor changes the place would do well as a first-class airline waiting room. All is glass and steel, doors that open electronically, and pastel colorcombos.

There are plenty of sports cars here, but their significance as indices of wealth is much more frankly admitted, and since the drivers are seldom students, they can afford to go all the way in accessories of costume, or feel under no pressure to pretend that they can't. Hi-Fi also flourishes more openly in the money-culture. There are more dogs on the Near North Side than in Hyde Park, but they cannot as yet touch the pigeons for making a mess. The syndrome, then, is Hi-Fi, modern furniture, Ivy League fashions, exclusive women's shops, and millineries, with politics, faculty life, and bulletin boards significantly absent.

The bohemians are much like their counterparts to the south, and also lisp of the drug and jazz mythology in dated bop-talk, but there are fewer or none of the retired-student types among them, and the quasi-criminal and delinquent motorcycle characters are scarce. The only pure bohemian hangout is the College of Complexes (the sign is misspelled, perhaps not deliberately) at the site of the old Dill Pickle Club. It offers a variety of lectures and debates on topics in the news, and on off nights the clientele can pursue edification by reading the slogans scrawled in chalk on the blackboard that makes up one wall: "Bed wetters of the world unite," "2 + 2 = 4," etc., etc. Other hangouts, such as the Gate of Horn, feature folk songs, American and foreign.

Many of these streets are a joy for their cleanliness, which persists in spite of choked traffic and a great variety of life and activity, and for the harmony between the rooming houses—once highly fashionable houses—and the apartment buildings and hotels. Bellevue Place, at the foot of which stands the former Mrs. Adlai Stevenson's famous 1020 Club, is downright beautiful: quiet, reserved—it seems miles away from everything—big town, modest, harmonious, with well-kept lawns, hedges, and trees.

The quiet life—pace it as you please—is still possible in Chicago. You can live in neighborhoods which have retained a distinctive character, and among middle-class types who have moved with the time into outer space, acquiring tastes and habits unknown a decade ago, but have retained their traditional integrity. Among some of them, in their homes, say, on Fullerton of the mid-North Side, or on Hyde Park Boulevard, you encounter an attractive mixture of respectable vocation and artistic avocation (mostly painting and writing), with a laudable bourgeois sense of responsibility toward civic and national issues, and a well-cultivated middlebrow obligation to keep up with the right books and magazines.

Among some of these good people you get the sense that discord and neurosis are mild afflictions, that homes are permanent and children a tie which is not resented. These, to be sure, are land virtues, but they are borne without too much incongruity by people of the Lake front. Perhaps they live in the strip for the sake of the breeze—I am not speaking meteorologically—but it is a sure thing they will not be blown away by it. An evening in their homes—they often form "drama circles," in which plays, but more often magazine articles, are read aloud, and followed by cake and coffee—gives one assurance of the abiding virtues, of group solidarity, and the abundance of the good, quiet, effortless things of life. These are the people who are relatively free of the syndrome. The appearance of well-being is fully developed. The principle of cohesion is the traditional one, the home.

My proposition, then, is this. The culture strip along the Lake is not strong or rich enough to defend itself against invasion or internal corruption. There are too few plays for one—theater has long been dead in Chicago—and the recent attempts to found a local repertory group, outstanding among which were the excellent Chicago Playwrights Theater Club, died for lack of support. Another such attempt is being launched in October (1956) in the long-defunct Studebaker Theater, by Bernard Sahlins and Co. (good luck!). Opera came alive with the Lyric Theater but—good old Chicago!—administrative squabbles are now threatening the whole enterprise. The press is disgraceful—not because the individual newspapers are so bad; some of them compare quite favorably with their counterparts in New York, e.g., the *Sun-Times* with the *Post,* but because none is excellent.

Criticism is atrocious, and a worse blight than any slum. Music, dance, and drama get by, considering what small call there is for discrimination and close judgment; but books are butchered like pig meat in the *Tribune* and *Sun-Times*—the only papers which run reviews (on Sundays). Anyone who wants to read competent reviewing must consult the *New Yorker* or the New York *Times Book Review*. The other magazines, with the exception of mass circulators and the middle-class standbys such as *Harper's* and the *Atlantic,* make little impression. No one seems to read *Partisan Review* any more, and few of the bookshops carry it. (*Commentary* is virtually by subscription only.) There has been some talk of starting a quality review, fortnightly or monthly, but nothing has as yet come of it. (Interested parties please get in touch with me.) *Poetry Magazine* continues to come out, leaning heavily on local endowment, but it makes rather small difference in the city's life.

The art world is kicking up a stir, locally, with the All-Chicago show at the Art Institute (recently concluded) drawing the usual derision from the press, and housewives, patrons, and collectors putting in their tuppence: it ran, for some surprising reason, almost exclusively to abstract expressionism. Considerable quantity, mediocre quality.

In addition to the Institute shows, Chicago has two annual spring outdoor shows, one for the South Side painters, and one for the North Side. Here the styles are various, and run the whole range of modern painting but usually by way of clichés. Both shows are vastly superior to the Greenwich Village outdoor exhibit, but only because the better painters do not shun outdoor exhibits as they do in New York. The best painters, however, do; most of them are affiliated with Momentum, which runs its own exhibit. This is better than the outdoor stuff, but not by terribly much and my own feeling is that the paintings benefit from being hung indoors, away from the pitiless sun. The only painter of genuine merit with this group is, I think, Edith Smith.

In the last few years the feeling has been running high in Chicago that the town is waking up and beginning to produce. The clearest evidence, for the city as a whole, is in building. New office buildings and apartment houses are going up, and the newly completed skyscraper of the Prudential Insurance Company, at Randolph off the Lake, whatever its merits as architecture, stands in commitment on this score. It will take a lot more building, cleaning, sweeping, and improving to shake off the lethargy that has dogged Chicago for the last two decades. Chicago's new Mayor, Richard J. Daley, a Democratic machine man, has surprised everyone, and pleased most, by seeming to be wholeheartedly devoted to this task. Plans are being made to rescue the Near North and South Sides from blight and indignity by erecting administrative, civic, and art centers in these areas.

But the big job is not, of course, a work for mayors and city officials to accomplish. It is for the Chicagoans who do not run off, and for the small-towners who are drawn here to stay, to accomplish of their own volition and capacity. Above all, it is a matter of defending, preserving, and extending the precious crust of culture along the Lake; of overcoming its terrible disproportion to the rest of the city, and of watering the desert reaches of our industrial moon. We are forever at rivalry with New York, but our laudable ambition to outstrip New York (I suppose it is laudable) will get nowhere until we discover the principle of New York and of all great cities.

As I see it, this principle is very simple (but then, I am a *luftmensch:* with a thirst for water). It is to give the city something to lose. And this is done by producing without manufacturing, consuming without eating (or wearing or using), enjoying without belching, and finding the everlasting in the ephemeral things: not in iron, stone, brick, concrete, steel, and chrome, but in paper, ink, pigment, sound, voice, gesture and graceful leaping, for it is of such things that the ultimate realities, of the mind and the heart, are made.

August 1957

Norman Stein

A SECOND CHANCE FOR SAMSON

A Story

> *"Mirrors are pools where the soul bathes its wounds. See there! I have a salve and poultice to heal that one. Take them. Allow me, in return, to set the gods an example of mercy and a modest profit."*
>
> KESSLER

Danny had known for weeks that it would come to this and yet he had no sense of decision; instead, of further concession. He knocked on the door.

A muffled voice invited him to enter. He pushed the door open and stepped into a long shadow-draped hallway. Danny pitched his voice to the end of the hallway. "Mr. Kessler?"

"I'm taking a bath."

Danny traced the answer to a closed door deeper in the hallway. "Oh, I'm sorry. Do you want me to wait?"

"You should have called for an appointment." There was a short period of busy splashing before, "Tell me, my man, when did you start losing your hair?"

Danny was embarrassed. He moved closer to the door. "About three months ago."

"It's too soon. Much too soon. You are practically newborn. You must wait a while longer before Kessler can help you. Come back again, sometime."

Danny wanted to know when to return but Kessler went on, "When you decide please telephone for an appointment. You'll know when it's time to come again. Make sure the door is closed behind you, please."

Too surprised to feel anything Danny obeyed and closed the door to the dim hallway.

An hour later Danny stood before another door, this on the sixth floor of a midtown office building, reading and rereading its legend, Suite 606: THE BARTON SYSTEM.

His deliberation about entering versus not, shame versus modesty, skepticism versus faith was nullified by the laughing chatter of two approaching office girls. Danny opened the door to Suite 606 and found himself in a comfortably furnished office with pine panels and soft indirect lighting. Across the room a young man dressed like an intern smiled and motioned him to a chair beside his desk. While taking the few steps to the chair Danny cautioned himself to resist believing too easily; he planned to keep mental debit and credit entries on the sales talk.

The man in the white uniform said, "My name is Dave Lapp."

"I'm Danny Foxe."

They shook hands. Dave Lapp straightened the papers on his desk and looked at Danny as if to say, What can I do for you? Rather than explain, Danny removed his hat.

"When did you start losing your hair?"

Exactly the question Kessler asked and Danny repeated his answer, "About three months ago," and he added, "it began to fall in handfuls."

Dave Lapp nodded thoughtfully, inviting Danny to continue. "I was shaving and all of a sudden . . . I saw my hair all over the sink." The words were out and he wiped his lips as though his speech had stained.

"Just relax. I know how you feel. Have one." He offered Danny a cigarette and lit it for him. He beamed a friendly smile while Danny stared at his hair. It was a mane of brown-blackish color grown long enough for a woman; combed high on top, straight back on the sides making it appear like a turban. Danny felt that he couldn't possibly understand—a debit entry.

"For thirty-seven years," Dave Lapp said with a tinge of rote, "the Barton System has been a citadel for men with alopecia. That's the technical term, it's our business to know."

Danny inhaled his cigarette and exhaled a smile in return for Dave Lapp's.

"Usually, I don't explain this to everyone," a pause, then, with slight emphasis, "but I think you'll understand. As the Barton System is a scientific method we had a well-known psychologist study our clients, discreetly of course, so that we could understand them better. He found a majority of men with alopecia react in a definite way. They lose confidence in their potency, they tend to be overly sensitive, overly polite. They exhibit a pervasive deference. Generally, they feel unworthy or guilty." He studied Danny. "From my experience I'd say these findings apply to you," he qualified, "though not entirely."

Danny replied that he thought there was a great deal of truth in the findings of the well-known psychologist—a credit entry. He had become apologetic and deferential while he admitted, to himself, that Kessler came closer to an explanation when he described Danny, through the bathroom door, as "newborn." It was a self he lacked. The quarrel between the memory of who he was and the face he saw in the mirror left him without a someone to be.

"Why'd you wait until now to see us?"

"I don't know. When it began I didn't know what to do."

"Well, I can't say definitely, but those three months may count against you."

Danny was about to ask what kind of handicap his hesitation would be when his thought was complicated by a comparison; to Kessler three months were brief and indifferent to his case, and here that time might be punitively long.

In a serious tone Dave Lapp digressed, "Do you believe we can help you?"

The question, unanticipated, pleased Danny by the honesty it implied—a credit entry. "To tell the truth, I'm a little doubtful but I'd like to believe you can."

"I'm quite sure you'll be convinced. Now, there's some information we must have." Dave Lapp took a yellow card from a drawer and plucked one of three pens offered by a white marble desk set. "Full name?"

"Danny Foxe. I spell it F-O-X-E."

"I see. Age?"

"Twenty-eight."

"Place of business?"

"I'm an auditor for the Munroe Furniture Company. We're at eight, eight, one, Columbus Avenue."

"Salary?"

Misgiving, Danny asked, "What do you need that for?" preparing a large debit entry.

Dave Lapp smiled indulgently, "We must know beforehand whether a client can manage the prescribed treatment."

It seemed like an honest explanation. "I average a hundred and ten with overtime."

"Did either of your grandfathers have alopecia?" He restated in a softer voice, "Were they bald?"

"My grandfathers?"

Another indulgent smile, "These questions will help us to make a profile of the hereditary forces involved in your condition."

"It sounded funny, that's all. Only one was. My mother's father."

"Your father?"

"He died when I was a kid. He had all his hair."

"Have you been sick recently?"

"No. Just a cold once in a while."

"Last question. How did you learn about the Barton System?"

"I've seen your ads in the paper."

Dave Lapp returned the pen to its holder. "Now, our examination. Over here, please." Danny moved to a white-enameled chair to his right. Dave Lapp prepared himself by dusting his hands with a white powder. "It's antiseptic," he said; from a green glass jar standing on a corner of his desk he took a translucent plastic comb packaged in cellophane. Unwrapping the comb he said, "We keep all our instruments sterilized, you see." He touched a switch on his desk and a bright white fluorescent light stuttered to life above Danny's head. Dave Lapp used the sterile comb to push aside the wiry tufts of hair carefully arranged to cover as much of Danny's scalp as possible. He combed down the middle of Danny's head, starting each stroke at the back and ending high on the forehead. At the end of each stroke he murmured either a confirming, "Hmmm," or a quizzically inflected "Hmmm?"

Back at his desk Dave Lapp snapped the comb in two; dropping the pieces into a wastebasket he sloganed under his breath, "Expensive but preventive." He picked up Danny's information form and slowly summed the items; he leaned back and said, "Mr. Foxe, there are only two causes of alopecia, regardless of what you've heard. One is illness and that doesn't concern us. The other does. Take the common phrase 'inherited baldness.' It simply means an inherited tendency to have a poor blood supply to the scalp. An efficient blood supply is the secret of life and health." He paused and looked at Danny to indicate that he could ask a question. Danny had none so he asked, "Are you in the habit of brushing your hair, daily?"

"Yes, almost every day."

Dave Lapp pounced on Danny's answer, "Vigorously?"

"No. Not too hard."

"I thought so." Dave Lapp smiled a justified smile. "You see, Mr. Foxe, the scalp is like the skin all over the body. It grows a top layer, what's technically called the epidermis. This layer is dead tissue and must be removed so blood can circulate freely and provide the tissue underneath with nourishment. Vigorous brushing is one way to remove the epidermis. Now, if it isn't removed the hair roots, technically called follicles, get clogged up." A preface of silence as he leaned forward, "In other words, the roots get buried alive and die." An epilogue of silence as he leaned back. "When you pinch a healthy scalp it becomes red. That means a good blood supply. Your scalp is pale. A healthy scalp is loose, permitting efficient circulation. Yours is very tight."

"Sounds hopeless," Danny said softly.

Dave Lapp encouraged, "Not entirely. Your scalp shows years of neglect. There's a great accumulation of dead tissue. However, I think that underneath your follicles are in good condition. The Barton System aims to rescue suffocating follicles and restore them to their fullest capacity."

Cautiously, Danny asked, "What are the chances of my hair growing back?"

"Remember, I said," he raised a finger as if pointing back to the word, " 'restore.' Not grow. We'd be frauds if we promised to 'grow' hair. For thirty-seven years the Barton System has been the only scientific method available to rescue man from alopecia. We can prove, with unsolicited testimonials, that we've restored hair to eighty-five per cent of our clients. They can see this restoration after a few months. This is because we treat only those we know we can help."

Danny succeeded in asking matter of factly, "Do you think I fit into that eighty-five per cent?"

"From my examination," a pause for suspense, "I feel there's an excellent chance."

Reprieved, Danny sighed, "Well, okay. I'm a client."

"Congratulations. I'm doubly glad because I always like to meet a man with an open mind. Would you like to begin treatment today?"

"Sure. I guess I've wasted enough time."

"Fine. I'll arrange for an operator. Excuse me." Dave Lapp rose and went through a doorway on the other side of the room.

Danny got up and moved to a wall, on his left, that held a mirror. Assuring himself that he was still alone he looked into it and was shocked to see his scant hair standing on end from Dave Lapp's combing, dry and twisted; surrounding the ruined crown was thick, very black hair that had recently covered it all. Danny checked and examined his impulse to smooth it down and felt it to be dishonest. There was no need to pretend here; here he was merely data on a yellow card. Data eligible for a system, a scientific equation which didn't include the self he was or the one he'd lost. He gladly accepted the privilege offered by the system, the privilege of a convalescent, to suspend volition and personality until the chemistry was finished.

Dave Lapp returned. "I have an operator for you. Our treatment has three parts. First, our special formula shampoo. Then, the Barton solution. It will burn a little but we have to get rid of that dead tissue. Lastly, the most pleasant part, our special massage. The treatment takes an hour and there's no tipping allowed. When you're through I'll be here and we can arrange your schedule. I prescribe three treatments per week. Each treatment is four dollars. Four for fifteen if paid in advance."

Another young man stood in the doorway Dave Lapp had gone and come through. He directed Danny's attention to him, "Mr. Foxe, this is Carl. He'll take good care of you."

Danny followed Carl—who was also dressed like an intern and had an abundance of hair exceeding Dave Lapp's—into a dressing room where he recalled and dismissed his debit and credit entries. He hoped enough for it to pass as belief. From the dressing room they went into a large windowless room. "This is the clinic. It's completely air conditioned. That keeps the air pure and bacteria free." The floor was covered with immaculate white tile. A ribbon of mirror a yard wide circled the room and was bordered by more white tile which ran up to the ceiling and down to the floor. White fluorescent lights were almost invisible against the white ceiling. Ten white-enameled chairs faced the mirror on one side of the clinic. Behind each chair was a tripod supporting a chrome-plated cone. Carl explained, "They're humidifiers. We use them with the Barton solution, you'll see." He pointed to a row of sinks, "Over here, first."

Danny sat down and was tipped back until his neck rested in a groove in the sink and his head in Carl's hands. The shampoo was accomplished quickly and pleasantly, three soapings and rinsings. After his head was dried with a ". . . sterile towel," Carl offered, pointing to the white-enameled chairs and chrome apparatus, "Take your pick. Most of the treatments are given after seven. That's when it gets busy."

Choosing a chair at one end of the row, Carl draped another sterile towel around Danny's shoulders. From somewhere in his uniform he produced a small corked bottle of clear liquid. "This is the Barton solution."

Danny felt that it was right for it to be colorless and pure.

Uncorking the bottle Carl sprinkled a few drops of the solution on Danny's head and with his free hand massaged it into the scalp. "You'll feel it burn a little but that's the only way to get rid of the dead tissue. Here's the humidifier. It steams your scalp and opens the pores. That lets the solution penetrate."

Danny's scalp began to sting. Carl slipped the cone over his head; a switch clicked and the cone started to hum. A mist filtered from the cone around Danny's face. "That's fine," Carl said reassuringly; "if you want me, press this button on the arm." Danny watched Carl, in the mirror, leave; he was alone in the white clinic.

The wispy strands of mist knit themselves into a fog and obscured the mirror. The burning feeling grew more intense, and gave Danny a sense of being purged. He was no longer a victim. It was a struggle now. He had an enemy, "the accumulation of dead tissue," and a weapon, "the Barton System."

The cone hummed diligently and thickened the vapor into a cloud. The steam was white before it was nothing, blending into the white of the room, enveloping Danny in an illuminated darkness. He gave in, his senses relented, he had a feeling of peace despite the assault of the Barton solution.

He heard footsteps and brushed a peephole into his cloud. It was Carl with another client. They passed to the sinks before he could see their faces in the mirror. The cone repaired the damage and Danny thought about the other client. He thought with the word "we," forming or joining a community with the nine empty chairs on his left. According to Dave Lapp a little better than eight of the ten chairs would be rescued; that left fifteen per cent, a chair and a half, beyond salvage. He straightened up in his chair, pushing his head deeper into the cone to speed penetration of the solution.

Carl turned the humidifier off and the cloud disappeared. He toweled Danny's head again and connected a vibrator to the humidifier. He pressed the electric pulse to Danny's head until Danny felt his own heart rhythm throb through his scalp. When the vibrator was turned off, Danny had finished his first Barton treatment; he was stranded with an excitement that had no content. As he left the white clinic Danny counted seven sad knights wearing chrome helmets and vapor visors.

Danny returned to the office; Dave Lapp asked, "Feels good, huh?"

Touching his forehead, Danny answered, "It feels alive."

"Now, your schedule. How about Monday, Wednesday, and Friday? Same time. You can pay for each treatment separately or take four for fifteen dollars. In advance, you save a dollar this way."

"I'll take the four for fifteen."

Danny stopped counting treatments after the tenth. From that point he used weeks to measure the Barton System. Three times each week he met Carl or another hirsute, uniformed young man and was shampooed, humidified, and vibrated in the white clinic.

During the eighth week Dave Lapp came into the clinic to examine Danny. He inspected his scalp and took Carl off to a corner for a ". . . consultation." Dave Lapp's prognosis, "You should be flaking soon. That means the first strata of dead tissue is coming off."

Danny flaked the following week. His scalp snowed dandruff. He was ecstatic; the Barton System applied to him. He was safe from the vagaries of a unique case, he was normal and predictable. Danny suggested an increase in his schedule of treatment to five each week.

Dave Lapp agreed but cautioned, "We can't rush nature and undo years of neglect, overnight."

Danny agreed but his mind went ahead and put a tune to the words, "eighty-five per cent." He became addicted to the daily applications of the Barton solution. Danny needed the regular jolts of pain to attend his feelings of regeneration.

In the second week after the third month Dave Lapp predicted another flaking. Two days later Danny reported that it had begun. Dave Lapp asked him to the enameled chair near his desk and switched on the overhead light. Uncellophaning a comb he raked the dandruff from Danny's scalp. "Just a minute," Dave Lapp said. He took two small mirrors from a desk drawer. He held one above Danny's head and fixed the other in Danny's hands, at eye level, to catch the reflection of his head. "See? Here!" He traced the perimeter of Danny's hairline with the comb. "We've done it!" Meaning a patch of blond, downy fuzz.

In a panic Danny turned and asked Dave Lapp's satisfied face, "What do you mean 'done it'? My hair's black."

"Take it easy, Mr. Foxe." Dave Lapp sat down behind his desk. "I mean we've reached your active follicles." He hinted a smile.

"This isn't what you promised me."

"Please," in a firmer tone, "we never promised anything except to restore those follicles that are still alive and I called you in so you could see for yourself that the Barton System does work."

Danny's voice squealed out of control, "But, this isn't my hair."

"I thought your attitude was excellent but now I can see that you've misunderstood a great deal. We've restored those follicles that are still alive. We may be able to rescue others deeper in your scalp. It all depends on how much life you have there."

"Will they be black hair?"

"I can't say. I think your disappointment is due to what you wished for rather than the actual results. Basically, what you want is magic, we deal in facts, science. One's reality and the other isn't."

Danny tried a compromise, "How long will it take to reach the deeper follicles?"

"I can't guarantee there are any. You've responded to treatment very nicely and there may be further improvement. I sincerely recommend you continue. If I were you I'd consider it the only practical thing to do."

Danny lit a cigarette and was silent.

To prod a response Dave Lapp said, "Those are the facts."

"I'll call you Monday."

"What about your treatment today?"

"No. I'll let you know Monday."

Danny spent the weekend in bed with the blinds drawn against light and sound. Hermetically sealed from time, the scene of his injury, it was painless for him to think about his hair. He recalled his last exchange with Dave Lapp and abstracted, ". . . you want magic, we deal in facts, science . . . you want magic, we deal in facts, science . . . one's reality and the other isn't." Danny itemized the facts in Dave Lapp's reality; the white clinic, the Barton solution, humidification collaborating to produce a blond fuzz. But there were other facts, predicates to Dave Lapp's.

Getting up, he turned on a lamp. He went to his bureau and pulled out the bottom drawer. Carrying it to his bed, he inhaled a confusion of perfume. It was his souvenir drawer and he emptied it on his bed; a handful of unmatched earrings, lipstick tubes, a few pieces of lingerie, make-up compacts, and cigarette lighters.

One by one he replaced them, recalling a circumstance and name for each. He found himself estranged from these memoirs. They were, now, apocryphal biography, taken on faith, relics, belonging to him now as much as the stories told him about his infancy.

Last was a cigarette lighter, Barbara's, a brunette, one of four Barbaras he'd known. Danny held it over the drawer recognizing it as the last. He had a sudden thought of death and the sorting out and storing away that follows. Unwilling to have an end, he spilled his souvenirs back on the bed; there'd be no end.

He picked up the phone book and searched for the pages labeled "hair." There were four pages of ads with pictures and slogans, all preferring the large type for the term "transformation" to the smaller for "wig" and "toupee." For the second time Danny found the austere square inch which stated, "Kessler, an artist," an address and phone number. Danny copied the numbers down, he'd call Monday after work.

The phone was picked up after seven rings and a voice inquired, "Yes?"

"Mr. Kessler? I don't know if you remember me. I came to see you a few months ago and. . . ."

"Your name?"

"I didn't tell you them. You were taking a bath. Remember?"

"I'm home now. Come over." The receiver was replaced.

Danny walked down the dim hallway following Kessler's instructions. "Come all the way. I'm in the kitchen."

Kessler sat at a table littered with movie magazines. He was middle-aged, of medium height, and almost fat. He had a pale round face, light blue eyes, and a small flat nose. Danny was disappointed by his hair. He'd expected him to have either a thick crop or none at all. Kessler's was sandy colored and thin, showing his scalp.

They looked at each other for a moment and Kessler said, holding up a magazine, "Research." He dropped it, "To business. I'll provide answers without troubling you for the questions. First, it will not fall off. Second, no one will know you are wearing one. Right?"

Danny began a response to the gratuitous answers when Kessler continued, "Also, you want to know if Kessler really is an artist as he advertises." Danny staggered back as Kessler ripped his thin sandy hair off and revealed a thick, shiny black crew cut. "Do you doubt?"

"Christ! I never thought you had one."

"Thank you, my boy. I remember when you first came I sent you away to ripen. There's more to this than buying and selling. It concerns the soul."

"I think I'm ready." Impressed with the style of Kessler's speech, he tried to imitate. "You were correct in sending me away. Now, I see my situation . . . in terms of science and magic."

"You don't say?" Kessler said, his eyes wide in mock surprise. "They are more extravagant components than I usually deal with. Please, go on."

Flustered, Danny lit a cigarette slowly to mask the assembling of a redeeming interpretation. "Well, truthfully, I was glad when you sent me away. I guess I still had some hope left. I mean that my hair'd grow back. So then, I went to the Barton System. If you've read their ads . . . they're so easy to believe. They're logical, I mean scientific. There's something to them but it didn't work for me. What I meant before was that the science didn't work for me so now I'm ready for what I called magic, a pretense."

Kessler shook his head doubtfully. "You are mistaken, my boy. Kessler does not traffic in magic or pretense. Kessler will give you something you can feel and see. Something real to the world. What you call science is simply sophisticated magic. It's the manipulation of matter plus dull ritual that cancels out mystery and joy by a high rate of probability. It's reality for those of meager faith, for those who take definitions seriously instead of appearances. Kessler will give you all the reality you can endure, he will give you illusion." More doubtful shaking of the head. "There is a chance you expect too much," he smiled, "but Kessler will gamble on his power to prepare you."

"I guess I got my story a little tangled. I should have just said 'I need it.' "

"Yes, but we shall assume you require instruction. To business. I take three orders each month. I cannot rush. Since I have my quota this month you shall return next Thursday and bring a picture of yourself. As you were before. Price depends on the work. Minimum, two hundred, cash."

Danny nodded.

"I won't do this to you." He picked up a magazine with a handsome movie star on the cover. "They disguise. Kessler consults the soul."

Danny left the apartment still shaken by the picture of Kessler crumpling his sandy-haired wig into a ball and tossing it on the table.

On Thursday Kessler examined the photograph Danny brought. It was taken at a cousin's wedding and showed Danny in a tuxedo. "Yes, yes, you were noble, you were royal, my boy. Kessler will give you the sign again. You will have another coronet. Today, I only require this." He snipped a lock of hair from the side of Danny's head. "For color, texture. Come back Monday."

"Is that all there is to it?"

"Too abrupt? Oh, I know. You've graduated from the Barton people. You should have a procedure. Kessler can be efficient. We will have an interview."

"I didn't mean that. I just thought there'd be more." He really did want to stay and talk.

"I have a questionnaire especially for my customers. It's brief and about love. It demands that you reveal your most secret secret. The one you promised never to tell."

Danny knew he was being teased and he knew he'd tell; first he stalled, "I don't have any."

"Why else would you be here? Except for love. Don't be coy. It's a part of the procedure."

Pleased, attempting nonchalance, "I don't know if you'd call this a secret. It's more of a thing I know to meet women. The best time is Monday and Tuesday nights. Late at night. The whole town goes to bed early because the weekend is too far away to postpone sleep against it. So, you meet people who are a little reckless."

He wanted to be coaxed for details but Kessler was satisfied. "A valuable city secret. Another question, tell me how you please women?"

"I don't know. I guess I wasn't too bad looking, before."

"Was that your most special quality?"

"It's the most important thing to women," Danny said seriously. "They talk a lot about personality and things but there's no substitute."

Kessler's broad smile introduced laughter. "Enough. You are pure. Pure enough to discontent Kessler with his power."

"I didn't mean . . ." Danny defended against the laughter.

"Please, don't be offended. I meant that there are limits and rules to art, even mine. They separate art from the divine and for you Kessler would like to be a god. To raise you up again. I've weaved many bonnets for many humiliated Samsons but never one so perfect. Never one so. . . ."

A growing anxiety made Danny interrupt, "What makes me . . . different?"

"You know Samson's story, don't you see any similarity?"

Danny shook his head to mean yes and to mean no.

"Again, don't be offended. We're being didactic you and I, not personal. Also, I must remind you about the instruction I'd furnish. Understood? Good. Samson was a man with one quality, one special quality that released him from life as it is to men. He was exempt from fear. Life for him was a mirror of applause. He took every morsel . . . pride. A god will not mouth a petty word like 'ingratitude,' they prefer 'pride.' Ergo, Delilah. Here is the irony. After Samson was contrite and forgiven, his strength returned and he redestroyed himself. He never did understand. Now, to the analogy. In our time the gods do not employ Delilahs. . . ." Kessler broke off as Danny rose from his chair.

Danny looked at his watch and lied about having an appointment. He hadn't followed the last part of Kessler's speech. It seemed that the texture of Kessler's voice had changed from the bantering questions of a few moments ago, giving Danny a premonition that imminently it would shape something unpleasant, something he shouldn't hear.

"I'm sorry to make you late by talking so much. Come tomorrow. Same time here in Gaza and we begin to measure."

The kitchen table was covered by a neat arrangement of compasses, paper, and pencils. Danny sat in a chair close to it while Kessler made his calculations and spoke on, "My life's work. The falsification of nature's intentions. That, my boy, is what accounts for the human condition. Fools will tell you that to be human is to be conscious or that we are unique because we alone have a foreknowledge of our death. Nonsense. Besides, they can't prove either. But, to falsify! To prove it, ask yourself what use any beast would have for a mirror? Done, proved. We paint, perfume, pad, and suffer the agony of discovery. That's the proper business for a priest." He repeated his premises and conclusions before coming to specific examples. "Those Shakespearean actors, in tights. You watch the women in front. You'll see where they're looking. There's never been an actor who didn't pad his part."

On his next appointment, the day for fitting the scalp, Kessler opened the door for Danny. He was gleeful at Danny's astonishment. Instead of the sandy-haired wig or his real crew cut, Kessler's face was haloed by bright red curls. "Do you like it? My lady friend complains of a lack of variety. Tonight, I shall be varied for her."

The scalp was pronounced, ". . . perfect, a perfect fit and it won't shrink. It will take a few days to festoon. Your penance is three hundred and fifty. Ten-dollar notes, if you can."

Danny gave Kessler a white envelope. Kessler asked, "Ten-dollar notes?"

"Thirty-five."

"Good." Kessler left the room and returned with a small gray box. "Here is your reprieve." He shook the box, "Hear it?"

Danny heard a little crush of tissue paper.

"We should have a ceremony. First, a blessing." He tapped Danny on the forehead with his index finger. "I bless you. However, you will have to anoint yourself. In the box are two tubes, a paste and a cosmetic. There is a paper with instructions. My lady friend types them for me. Kessler has given you the sign and you will know how to wear it better than he. All he asks is that you come and show him."

"Thanks." He gestured with his hand to indicate that that was all he could say.

"Come and show me. We'll have another talk."

At home, Danny removed his wig from the box and placed it on his dresser. It seemed to him that Kessler had collected every hair he'd lost. He examined the tubes and read the typewritten instruction sheet. It had two sections. The first was titled CARE OF THE ARTIFICE and had five conditions: (1) Spread modest film of paste on clean scalp. (2) Press artifice down evenly. (3) Use cosmetic to blend hairline into forehead. (4) Do not sleep with artifice. (5) When not in use place on object that will preserve contour.

The second section was titled ADJUSTMENT TO ARTIFICE, with three conditions: (1) Wear artifice in privacy. (2) Wear artifice under hat on walks. (3) Wear artifice openly in the movies.

At the bottom of the page was the single line, "Kessler is always available."

After two readings Danny had memorized all the conditions. He decided to fulfill them over the weekend and see Kessler on Monday night. Danny washed his head and applied a modest film of paste. He pressed the artifice down, it slipped a bit before holding firm, and he blended the hairline into his forehead with the cosmetic.

The mirror verified the word "transformation" used in the phone book ads. The thick black wavy hair, a few locks casually tasseling his forehead, transformed Danny's face from thin to delicate. The shadows around his eyes were anchored, softening them; the straight line of his nose took a hint of grace, his mouth was defined as full and strong. This face was the sign of who he used to be.

Tonight he'd wear it in his apartment, tomorrow under his hat on a walk, and Sunday openly in the movies. Using a grapefuit to preserve its contour overnight, until he got something better, Danny dispatched the final condition.

Kessler opened the door for Danny. "Yes, I remember, you had a penchant for Monday and Tuesday nights. Let me see you. Come into the kitchen where the light is better."

He turned Danny's head from side to side. "I'm proud, very proud. Sit down, we'll have our talk."

"Sure." Danny forced a smile.

"You know, my boy, that Kessler works close to the brain," he showed Danny his hands, "and he can feel things that are left unsaid. I talk to my customers without a word. Can you imagine what my fingers hear?"

Danny made what he thought was a reflective face to hold Kessler's attention. He felt the same urge to escape from Kessler's tone of voice as he had when Kessler spoke about Samson. Unable to answer or maintain the pretense of thought, he shrugged his shoulders.

Kessler continued.

"At times, my fingers hear hate. Hate for their luck or me. Others admit the deception as a necessity and others are satisfied that they can suffer more. They always have a conclusion. Except you. You haven't spoken to Kessler's fingers. I felt your brain say, 'Hush, hide, he's listening.' You haven't told yourself about the artifice."

Danny was right about Kessler's voice. He had to escape. He looked at his watch to re-play the lie of having an appointment and then at Kessler to tell it, when he caught his reflection in the window. He'd forgotten, he'd been restored, there was no reason for fright. "You've been trying to draw me out since I came here. I don't know about your fingers but I do know you're overestimating me. You are overestimating the whole thing. I only want to believe in myself. I couldn't be the same without my hair."

"Are you the same?"

Danny slumped back in his chair.

With a deep sigh, almost an apology, Kessler rose and went to the window. He said, his back turned on Danny, "I'm justified in calling you an exhibit of mine. . . "

"I'm not that," Danny said weakly. "I'm almost what . . . I was. All I want is to go back. To have my life again."

Still looking through the window, as though respecting modesty, Kessler said, "You see, you said, 'almost what I was.' And how much of your life is left?" Kessler spoke slowly to allow interruption, "After all, I have a right to ask these questions for it was I who . . ." Kessler broke off as he saw a handsome young man leave his building and cross the street. He got into a car and drove away.

Danny paid for the last round of drinks. For the last hour he, the bartender, and the pretty blonde had been talking. During the three-cornered conversation Danny and the blonde caught each other's eyes and exchanged looks of more significance than the conversation warranted. Danny finished his drink and said goodbye.

His car was parked a short way from the bar. He got into the back seat to get a better view of the bar. Trembling with excitement, he knew if she came she'd take at least five minutes. He promised himself that he'd only wait ten minutes. It was only two or three minutes since he left.

The door to the bar opened and the blonde came out. She lit a cigarette, looked right and left, up and down the block.

Danny's heart abandoned its rhythm and beat single, powerful strokes that shook his body.

She walked to the curb and looked across the street, again right and left, up and down the block.

Danny's heart was in riot.

The blonde took a pair of glasses from her purse and put them on, stepped into the gutter and looked right and left, up and down the block. She returned the glasses to her purse and walked away.

Danny lay across the back seat. He wanted to smoke but couldn't manage to get his cigarettes. After a while he climbed over to the front seat, pleasantly tired and hungry. He started the car and at the first red light switched on the radio. He dialed until he found music that suited his mood, dreamy and relaxing, and hummed along.

March 1960

Daniel Bell

THE SUBVERSION OF COLLECTIVE BARGAINING

Unhappy is a society that has run out of words to describe what is going on. So Thurman Arnold observed in connection with the language of private property—the myths and folklore of capitalism—which even thirty years ago was hopelessly out of date. How to find real words to describe the recent strike in the steel industry, or the consequences of the wage-price negotiations of the past decade? Two parties are locked in struggle, each seeking to articulate its claims over the other, while from the sidelines arise the moralistic alarms of spectators worrying about damage to the innocent public. But the desiccated language of collective bargaining is a trap; its syntax too constricting, its images too mechanical. The complex fact? The combat is a mimetic one, painfully real in the sense that emotions are aroused, but unreal because no economic loss can occur; in fact, each party, knowing in advance the price it will have to pay, pretty much gets what it sets out to get, and both end up with a profit—the corporation, usually, the greater gainer.

I am not suggesting that all this, like wrestling, is "fixed." Far from it. The antagonism between the contenders is quite genuine. But a highly intricate mechanism is at work in the game, and by now each side knows the unwritten rules. Sociologists have a phrase, "the unanticipated consequences of purposive actions," to suggest that things don't always work out as planned; and this is often the way of the world. As far as the corporations are concerned, the pattern of collective bargaining in this country follows an opposite principle which can be called "the utilized consequences of non-purposive action," meaning that even if you didn't plan it that way, you can turn it to your advantage.

Over the past decade, the corporations have precisely learned how to turn the collective bargaining process—and the strikes—to their advantage. The powerful unions gain impressive wage increases; the powerful corporations gain an excuse for impressive price increases—which, in the case of steel and auto, have in almost every instance been more than proportional to the jump in wages. Who loses? Unorganized workers (e.g., textiles), workers in marginal industries, *rentiers,* pensioners, and the like. Is this just? It is hard to define an equitable standard. A deflationary situation would benefit the *rentiers* and pensioners. But why should this group gain rather than another? The present situation reflects existing market power, which in turn shapes the rules of the game. The first thing to be determined is not who wins and who loses, but the nature of the game itself, and whether it ought to be revised. The following, therefore, tries to sketch some basic characteristics of the current wage-price situation, to puncture some myths, to delineate some consequences, and to present some alternatives.

The single most important fact about contemporary corporate capitalism is that expansion comes about through "self-financing," through retained earnings derived from high, protected prices. In formal theory—the mythical language of private property—a firm went to the capital market for financing. It floated stock, people "risked" their money and got a share of the enterprise as their equity. Later, corporations went in for institutional borrowing; insurance companies or banks would lend large sums of money to a firm, taking debentures or preferred stock in return. In either case, some outside control theoretically existed; a legal equity was always exchanged for the money raised. The actual situation is vastly different. Few firms today, except for utilities, go to the capital market for funds. Tax laws make it costly to distribute all retained earnings as dividends and then "recoup" the capital, by the investors' fiat, through new stock. The managerial decision to utilize retained earnings for expansion allows the managers to reinforce their social power and gives them independence from outside control; their ideas become the decisive factor in determining the social use of capital surplus.

But it is equally important to understand that when expansion is financed through high protected prices, it is the *consumer* who does the financing, and he neither receives equity in the firm (not even the promise of future price reductions) nor has any say about how his money should be used. In effect, the whole process depends upon what I shall call a "hidden tax mechanism" through which corporations can raise huge sums of money without giving away anything in return. Public taxation is openly and hotly debated in Congress and in the legislatures; bills involving the raising or spending of money are subject to all kinds of pressure and become the cause of great political divisions. Yet under the banner of "free enterprise," a corporation can, through a protected price policy, "tax" consumers for its own purposes and do whatever it wishes with the money. In consequence of the recent expansion of steel capacity, for example, the industry—*at present demand under protected prices*—can supply all the steel the country uses in nine months rather than twelve. This means that the industry can "take" a three-month strike almost without reducing the average profit it would have made had no strike been provoked. In short, the strike is—that is to say, *was*—financed by the consumers.

The key term in the above argument, of course, is the concept of "protected price." A firm is interested primarily in its profit margins. If sales fall, the firm cuts production—and employment—rather than price. Firms with some degree of market control can do this. The chief complaint of the farmers is that, being unorganized—other than through government crop reduction programs—they cannot adjust production to demand, but have to let prices fall.

To anyone who has read with care the Kefauver Committee reports of 1958 on "administered prices" in the steel and auto industries, it will be clear that these industries exercise an extraordinary degree of market control and thus have been able to place themselves in a protected position. We can best understand how such control is exercised by looking at the "standard volume" system for setting prices used by the auto industry. This system, which was developed by Donaldson Brown for General Motors in 1924, is based on an equation of three variables—price, estimated average rate of plant operation calculated in terms of a percentage of total annual capacity, and net return on investment. The price set for a single car is thus a function of the other two variables. But how are these variables determined? Net return on investment is simple: General Motors has decided that it must get roughly 20 per cent a year after taxes every year. "Estimated average rate of plant operation" is more complicated, however. The company figures in its best year on reaching only 80 per cent of its theoretical maximum operating capacity because of seasonal and other fluctuations in sales; in an *average* year, it figures on reaching 80 per cent of the production that can be achieved in its best year: thus it figures, theoretically, on using 64 per cent of its capacity in any normal year. But in actual practice, the "standard volume" has generally been calculated on a 55 per cent capacity. That is, General Motors so sets its prices as to plan for a return of about 20 per cent after taxes on the assumption that its plants will operate through the year for a total of only 180 days, or 36 weeks. (General Motors could "take" a four-month strike and still come out at its predetermined margin by operating for the rest of the year at full capacity.)

The long-range target of "standard volume" is to make it possible for General Motors to recoup its net investment in five years, but this goal has been surpassed by a phenomenal margin. In 1955, for example, net earnings (after interest and income taxes) were sufficient for the company to recoup its *entire* net plant investment in only two years. The American

Institute of Management, which made this calculation, pointed out that such a record was not exceptional for General Motors, but was, "in fact, a continuing characteristic of the enterprise being equaled or bettered in 12 of the preceding 20 years."

From 1950 to 1957, for every year except the last, General Motors' actual sales were, on the average, about 30 per cent higher than the "standard volume" on which the company set its prices.* When asked whether some of these gains from the large volume should not have been passed along to consumers through lower prices, Harlow Curtice, then head of General Motors, told the Kefauver Committee: "[Our prices] are as low as they can be and still produce the indicated return on the net worth at the standard volume." Even, it would seem, when actual output was 50 per cent greater than the "standard volume." As the Kefauver Committee said rather stodgily in its report: "It is clear that the use of standard volume as the basis of pro-rating expected costs and the desired aggregate profit in order to establish prices adds a considerable element of rigidity to these prices."

What this has meant in terms of the price power of General Motors can be grasped by tracing the company's net worth. In 1947, General Motors had a net worth of $1,428,000,000—on which it made a return, before taxes, of 38.8 per cent. A decade later, General Motors' net worth was $4,582,000,000—on which it made a return of 35.6 per cent before taxes. Of this increase in net worth of more than 3 billion dollars (or 221 per cent), all but $395 million came from profits which were ploughed back into the company. In short, the increase came from consumers who were making an "involuntary investment" in General Motors.

One important clue to the efficiency of a company and its ability to reduce prices is "the break-even point"—a measure that is based on the relationship between costs (divided into fixed and variable) and sales—and that gives us the figure at which the company begins turning a profit. Computations by Mr. Fred Gardner, a prominent management consultant, indicated that, including a high allowance for depreciation, General Motors' "break-even point" in 1956 was 48.8 per cent of sales. Sales, of course, do not represent full capacity; if one took full capacity into account, General Motors' "break-even point" would probably come to somewhere between 40 and 45 per cent of capacity.

These figures become even more significant in the light of the fact that

* Thus, in 1950, General Motors estimated its "standard volume" at 2,250,000 units, in order to give it a 20 per cent net return, and sold 3,812,000 units, or a 69 per cent margin of safety. In 1955, "standard volume" was 3,000,000 units, and factory sales were 4,368,000, or 54 per cent above target. In 1957, when "standard volume" was estimated at 3,470,000, sales were a shade under (3,418,000)—the only year of the eight in which the target was not exceeded.

Ford's "break-even point" in 1956 was 64.7 per cent and Chrysler's 87.4. Clearly General Motors has little to fear in the way of real price competition from the other automobile companies. In a serious price war, General Motors, with its superior efficiency, could probably run Ford and Chrysler into the ground. It doesn't do so, first, because a position as a single auto monopolist would simply invite public regulation, and second, because Chrysler and Ford, as the marginal firms, hold up a neat "price umbrella" for General Motors.

Since the products of the steel industry are more diversified than those of the auto companies, the steel companies do not use any such simple measure as "standard volume" for setting prices. In general, the industry figures on making a 15 per cent net return on investment when operating at 100 per cent of capacity. U.S. Steel argues that every dollar's worth of increase in employment costs will lead to an increase of more than $2 in total costs of production, and sets its prices accordingly. How does this claim square with U.S. Steel's "break-even point"?

In its presentation to a government commission investigating monopoly in 1937 (the Temporary National Economic Commission), U.S. Steel estimated that its "break-even point" then was 63.3 per cent of sales. In 1956, an analysis by management consultant Gardner for the Kefauver Committee showed the "break-even point" to be 44.3 per cent of sales. After the price increases in 1957—which had followed a large union wage increase—the "break-even point" went *down* to 38.6 per cent of sales, or (since sales are lower than capacity) about 32 per cent of capacity. In other words, by working less than two full days a week, U.S. Steel could move out of the "red" and make money.

How low should a "break-even point" be? The average "break-even point" of all U.S. industry is roughly 50 per cent of capacity. A "break-even point" between 50 and 60 per cent of capacity is considered "sound" since it gives most companies a margin wide enough to cover their fixed costs if sales fall sharply. In twenty-five years of computing "break-even points" for 1500 companies, Mr. Gardner testified, the lowest he ever encountered was that of U.S. Steel. The Corporation, he said, could cut its prices by 10 per cent, and still end up with a "break-even point" of 50 per cent of capacity.

The nub of the analysis, as applied specifically to the wage-price situation of 1957 (the last major wage-price increase in steel), is that when wages went up, prices—and profits—went up *even higher*. After the new contract with the union had been put into practice, a correlational technique showed a higher rate of profit at a lower rate of operating costs than in the previous year, and a decline in the "break-even point" as well. In brief, it was quite clear that the steel companies had used the negotiations as an excuse for boosting prices, in order to jack up their profit margins.

As the Kefauver Committee concluded, "U.S. Steel [can] cover its costs at an operating rate below 40 per cent of capacity and make very satisfactory profits while a substantial part of its capacity lies idle."

The point of all this (to return to the role of collective bargaining) is that the net effect of union pressure—apart from the gains which have been won for the small group of highly organized workers—has been to help install a mechanism whereby the large corporation is able to strengthen its price position in the market. In the past, price protection was achieved by "basing point" systems (now outlawed), price umbrellas (in which U.S. Steel set the lead), or informal collusion. Today the union serves as the vehicle. (According to Walter Reuther, for *every* dollar of increased labor costs since 1947, General Motors by 1956 imposed about $3.75 in cumulative price increases on the American car buyer. In effect, the United Auto Workers, taking a small share of the increased profits, has become, albeit unwillingly, the "junior partner" of General Motors.) The companies can truthfully say that they do not like the union negotiations, since other than wage demands are often involved (work rules, fringe benefits, etc.). And the companies are usually inclined to resist the union's demands strenuously. But it invariably turns out that the union negotiation offers a lovely opportunity to increase prices—and, with exquisite irony, to blame the union for inflation.

Are the unions responsible for inflation? Industry's argument is that they are, because by raising costs, they set off a wage-price spiral. But simple economic logic exposes the patent falsity of this charge. To determine the true effect of union wage pressure, one has first to make a distinction between the *structure of wages* (i.e., the relative spread between industries—say, steel and textiles), and the *level of wages,* which is the total wage bill in relation to other economic factors. What union pressure may do is to affect the *structure* of wages: that is, it can increase the gap between one group of workers (who have a strong union) and another (which does not). It is quite possible that wage and subsequent price increases in one area of the economy *may* have a linked effect on others—though with all the propaganda about the wage-price spiral, the actual spread of this effect has *never* been traced, and even so eminent a conservative economist as Milton Friedman of the University of Chicago doubts that it can go very far.*

For actually the degree of impact of a wage increase in one area on the rest of the economy depends, simply, upon the stock of money in circula-

* The steel companies themselves were in a wonderfully quixotic position. On the one hand, they claimed that steel wages, by rising faster than productivity, were inflationary; on the other hand, they protested vehemently that the effect of the increase of steel prices—which should reflect the steel wage inflationary pressure—was "negligible" on the cost of living.

tion. If this stock were held constant, then an increase in wages and prices in one sector could only cause a shift in the share of money to that particular sector—provided it were strong enough to impose its increases (i.e., provided that people needed the products of that sector more than they needed other products; or, in technical terms, the demand was relatively inelastic). Thus, there would be a change in the *structure,* but no effect upon the general *level* of wages and prices.

In practice, however, money supply is not held constant, but goes up (theoretically about 4 per cent a year, or slightly ahead of the growth pace of the economy). This increase in the supply of money, which is the result of political decisions by the monetary controllers, has a far greater effect on the general price level than wage pressure could ever possibly have. The current inflationary situation is due in large measure to the $13 billion budgetary deficit that the government ran in meeting the 1957-1958 recession. Although the administration refused to use direct government spending to counter the recession, it achieved the same effect by indirect methods (accelerated spending on committed programs, lower tax receipts, and the like). If any single factor can be held responsible for the inflation-deflation seesaw of recent years, it is the erratic timing of the Federal Reserve Board, which has either stepped a little too hard on the gas or jerked the brake a little too abruptly (as it is doing now). While the business community contradicts the basic precepts of economic theory in ascribing inflation to union wage pressure, conservative economists who know better have kept shamefully quiet.

But there is another argument which holds that union wage pressure can put a particular firm or a particular industry in a difficult competitive position vis-à-vis other firms or products—it can "price them out of the market." This argument is plausible in theory, except that if it were true, production would fall and unemployment would mount—which does not seem to be the case in the relevant sectors of the economy. Actually, the one element in the whole wage-price picture which has been almost completely ignored—the emergence of a large class of non-production workers within the manufacturing firms, and the consequent rise in salary costs—is a more likely candidate, if any single one is to be cast, for the role of "villain" than the unions.

By now it is commonplace that in the last decade the white-collar force has been expanding rapidly while the blue-collar force has remained virtually stable. This increase in white-collar force, however, has taken place not only in the so-called "tertiary" area (insurance, banks, real estate, services, education, recreation, and the like), but—through the proliferation of administrative services (personnel, marketing, merchandising, etc.), of research, and of automation—within the area of manufacturing itself. From 1947 to 1957, the number of non-production workers in manufacturing increased by 60 per cent (from 2,400,000 to 3,900,000) while the blue-collar force remained almost stationary (a little under 13,000,000). In 1947, salaries (the mode of payment to white-collar workers) were one-fourth of the labor costs in manufacturing; by 1957 they had gone up to one-third.

There are two important consequences to this change in the composition of the work force. One relates to productivity, the other to unit labor costs. In all their propaganda on the effect of wage increases, the corporations have talked of the rise in *employment* costs—but this is never broken down into unit *wage* costs (usually the unionized sector) and unit *salary* costs. Given the nature of industrial organization, direct production costs (wage costs) are more immediately subject to control than white-collar costs (salary costs). In other words, if productivity is broken down on a man-hour per production worker basis, and on a man-hour per salaried worker basis, the corporation can recoup its costs more easily in the first sector, where it can achieve economies and technological savings by substituting machines or tightening production schedules. The rise in the proportion of the salaried worker has acted as a drag on productivity, and on unit costs.

In sum, the argument I am making is that a significant share of the rise in manufacturing costs in the last decade has been due not to direct wage costs, but to an extraordinarily large increase in salary costs, which usually become an added fixed cost.

The Federal Reserve data available before the recession of 1957-58 show this shift in cost burdens quite clearly. Between 1947 and 1957, *unit* payroll costs (total wages and salaries) rose 26 per cent, while unit *wage* costs increased by only 16 per cent.* Much of the payroll rise was a consequence of the rise in unit *salary* costs which in 1957 were almost *30 per cent* higher than in 1953.

This burden becomes even greater during a recession, for when production falls the large corporations cut down their blue-collar force while the white-collar force is maintained whole.

The picture within the steel industry is instructive. Table I shows the steadily rising slope of salary employment and the fluctuating course of blue-collar employment.†

But even more instructive when we consider the effect on costs of this new balance between production and non-production workers is a comparison of what happens to each class during a recession (Table II).

* In the period from 1953 to 1957, when the greatest increase in non-production workers took place, salary payments rose by 37 per cent while wage payments to the blue-collar force rose by only 7 per cent.

† Source: Background statistics bearing on the steel dispute, Tables 3a. and 3b. U.S. Department of Labor.

TABLE I: STEEL EMPLOYMENT (in thousands)

	Production Workers	*Administrative, Professional & Clerical*
1950	532.9	78.1
1951	560.2	83.3
1952	486.5	84.2
1953	559.6	93.7
1954	492.5	88.3
1955	544.6	90.7
1956	532.6	97.6
1957	537.0	105.7

TABLE II: STEEL EMPLOYMENT

	Mid-1956	Autumn 1958	Drop
Semi-skilled workers	250,000	200,000	20%
Skilled workers and foremen	175,000	155,000	11%
Laborers, helpers, misc.	120,000	90,000	25%
Clerical and sales	75,000	75,000	None
Professional and technical	30,000	30,000	None
Administrative	10,000	10,000	None

Two other items from the Kefauver data round out the picture. When the steelworkers (or other such unions) win wage increases, the companies usually give "tandem" increases to the unorganized non-union workers. When U.S. Steel submitted cost data to the Kefauver Committee on the effects of the 1957 negotiations, it indicated that its employment costs had gone up 21 cents an hour, against a union claim that wage costs had only increased 16.4 cents. "Supplementary information provided by the corporation disclosed that the 21-cent figure is a weighted average of benefits extended to 161,500 members of the United Steelworkers, estimated at 19.4 cents per hour, *and simultaneous increases granted to 47,600 other* employees, estimated at 26.6 cents per hour." The union in its data had estimated that non-union employees (principally white collar) would receive the same cents-per-hour adjustment as union members. *Instead, nonmembers received increases which on the average were 37 per cent higher than the increase called for in the union contract.* As the Kefauver Committee said primly: "This may be excellent personnel policy, but there is some question as to the propriety of charging the cost of such a policy to the union agreement."

It should also be observed that in calculating the "break-even point" for the steel industry, the Kefauver Committee analyst used the generous concept of "standby cost" rather than "fixed cost." Fixed cost includes the conventional items of overhead, interest payments, depreciation, and the like. Standby cost covers all these plus management salaries, payments to supervisory and maintenance employees and to the sales and office personnel who are usually retained even though sales and production may fall. This is obviously a more realistic concept than fixed cost since such salaries do become a "fixed" charge for the corporation. Nevertheless it is a fact that the "break-even point" kept falling steadily after every union agreement *even though standby costs went up*—which indicates how little the corporation actually suffered from these agreements.

What, then, does the argument add up to? Because the steel companies refuse to give breakdowns on unit costs, one cannot fix the relative weights accurately, but the inference is warranted that a large portion of their increased employment costs—and those of other major manufacturing enterprises—is the consequence not of union pressure but of the rise of a salary sector which has become an added fixed expense.

This would seem to give the unions a powerful bargaining point. They could say, in effect, that the production workers, by raising productivity, are pulling their weight in a situation of increased costs, while the white-collar workers are not. But the unions can't. For they are desperately trying to organize the growing white-collar sector within the manufacturing industries, which makes it impossible for them to "blame" these groups for benefiting unduly from wage increases and pushing up employment costs.

The recent steel strike will not change the basic pattern I have been sketching here. If anything it will tend to reinforce the power of the corporations. Despite the "shotgun settlement," the terms show clearly that the industry was the economic victor, though the union may have gained a certain "symbolic satisfaction" in having avoided an even greater disaster.

From a *rational* point of view, there was little ground for a strike. The union knew that this was not "its year." It had no new radical demands to make. It also knew that its wage levels, because of previous victories, were higher than those of auto, with which it has been linked in historic tandem. Privately it was willing to settle for modest wage increases. It certainly was not going to challenge the industry on prices. Financially, the steel companies could easily afford a wage increase *without* raising their prices. The profit figures for the first half of 1959 were spectacular and even embarrassing. Profit as per cent of stockholders' equity, after taxes, was 14.2 per cent, *the highest in twelve years;* profit as per cent of sales, after taxes, was 7.6 per cent, *the highest since 1950*. That some of this was due to stepped-up production because of inventory buying by customers who were anticipating a strike merely proves that the strike was not caused by economics. Everybody knew, in fact, that the companies had decided to force a strike no matter what the union did.

For years the industry has been spoiling for a strike, and this time the situation was favorable; the companies recognized that they could afford a long one. Technological development has been so great that at present levels of demand the industry can fill virtually all the orders it gets by operating for only nine months of the year. (In 1958, the industry operated at 60.6 per cent of capacity; in the fiscal year ending June 1959, it was at 77.5 per cent of capacity.) The rest of the time can be absorbed in short work weeks, lay-offs, or a strike. The effects are the same, and the economic loss minimal.* And the industry wanted a strike.

For years the industry has smarted at the union's power. During World War II, the union had forced through a wage rationalization program to even out rates between jobs and end the discriminatory practices by which supervisors could practice favoritism. In the Inland Steel case, in 1949, which went to the Supreme Court, the union won a break-through on pensions. And fortuitous timing on contract expirations had allowed the steel union to come in on the upswing of the business cycles and come out with larger wage gains than other unions. But even though the corporations had learned how to take advantage of the wage pattern for price increases, there were important psychological and symbolic issues at stake. This was particularly true at U.S. Steel, where in 1958 a new management team, composed of Roger Blough as chairman of the Board and Conrad Cooper as industrial relations vice-president, had taken over. Blough is a lawyer with no experience in production; his forte is finance. Cooper is an engineer, with little feel for the human give-and-take of a bargaining situation. These two had replaced the old team of Ben Fairless, a production man who had come up through the mills, and John Stephens, whose background was in personnel. Fairless and Stephens had been pragmatic operators, tough-minded but not rigid, inclined to make a "deal" whenever it seemed necessary. Recognizing the vanity and weakness of Dave McDonald, the union chief, they had adopted the tactic of "sweet-talking" him, boosting his ego, making him feel like an equal, arranging for joint trips to the steel plants, where Fairless and McDonald—the two symbols of Management and Labor—would stride the floor together. And McDonald, pipe in mouth, chest puffed out, and distinguishing himself from that red-

* The steel industry, then, has to some extent begun to approach the situation that existed in coal when John L. Lewis would order staggered strikes that created a three-day work week in the industry. Newspaper editorialists screamed about the loss of production, but as a detailed analysis later showed, there were, given the level of demand, roughly 165 workdays in the industry anyway, so that it made no difference whatever whether the miners struck or were laid off. Lewis had called the strikes in part as a service to the industry since the anti-trust laws forbade collusion of companies to limit production and maintain prices.

haired, radical fellow Walter Reuther, would talk in orotund tones of the "mutual trusteeship" concept of management and labor, the equal responsibility of union and industry to free enterprise.

But Blough and Cooper would have none of this charade. Both were men of principle, ideologists, and their main principle was that labor should be put in its proper place. In an age of growing managerial power, when the corporate manager was taking credit for the remarkable performance of American industry, when managing itself was deemed a great new complex skill involving the administration of salesmen, production men, finance men, merchandising men, public relations men, engineers, and personnel men, there was no reason to assume that union leaders should be treated as equals—for labor, after all, was only one of a large number of "coordinates of production." Labor was to be reduced to its proper dimensions as a small problem, to be handled by the labor relations department.

Equally, the legal mind and the engineering brain wanted to tie up the ragged ends of the work rules issue. The steel companies have always had the right to introduce new machines or any other technological changes without interference from the union. But existing practices were another matter. In many plants, informal work rules or traditional ways of doing things had become the norm, arising, as is common in any human situation, out of custom and habit. To the engineer, such practices may be "irrational." To the worker it is his "way." The two are bound to clash. In 1945, when the wage rationalization analysis of U.S. Steel was completed, Cooper, who had been brought into the company to implement the program, insisted that the new contract contain a pledge by the workers to do a "fair day's work." Like the verbiage of loyalty oaths, this phrase is mere mumbo-jumbo; everyone accepts the idea of "a fair day's work for a fair day's pay"—but how is a fair day's work to be measured? To the surprise of all parties, Mr. Cooper had a measure. A "fair day's work"—and this was written into the contract negotiated on May 8, 1946—is "that amount of work that can be produced by a qualified employee when working at a normal pace. . . . A normal pace is equivalent to a man walking, without load, on smooth level ground at a rate of three miles per hour." Presumably, therefore, the energy that would be used to walk 24 miles a day should go into a fair day's work. Cooper began applying this visceratonic definition to every job in U.S. Steel. The following year Phil Murray gave the corporation an ultimatum. The definition might remain, but all existing work rules were to be preserved or the union would refuse to sign any contract—and the companies capitulated. Thus the so-called 2-B clause was frozen into the contract. U.S. Steel has never forgiven that ultimatum. They regarded it as a violation of the previous contract. Technically it was, since Lee Pressman, then the union counsel, had, without realizing the consequences, accepted the company's authority to change work rules, and the following year Murray had repudiated the agreement negotiated by Pressman. A more flexible management would have understood that the program was inherently unworkable anyway. Men are not automatons, and despite time-study rules and all the paraphernalia of "scientific" work analysis, they will go on their own, stubborn ways. But U.S. Steel has rarely been known for its flexibility.

The fact is that the 2-B rule was primarily a symbolic test of authority. There was no vital economic issue at stake. The corporations talked of the losses in efficiency, but when pressed by George Taylor (the head of the government fact-finding board) to document their case, they could only come up with one example—the "man in the air-conditioned crane cab," which was entirely irrelevant. And the same symbolic issues of authority and power were the crucial factors in the recent steel strike; real economic questions were again non-existent.

In the end, the industry lost the symbolic fight. It was quite clear that the work rules issue could not be translated into any terms capable of enlisting public support. Moreover, management's stubborn insistence on this point served to solidify the union ranks. At the start of the strike, the company had made some headway among the steelworkers by raising the spectre of inflation. And a strike conducted solely to increase wages would not have spurred enthusiasm among the workers. But the work rules issue gave the union a rallying cry meaningful to every steelworker in the form of a threatened speed-up, or a cut in piece-rate for certain specific jobs.

And yet, in economic terms, the steel companies did uncommonly well in the negotiations. For one thing, they have virtually succeeded in knocking the cost-of-living clause out of the contract, thus putting a fixed ceiling on wage increases. Under the new arrangement the steelworkers can get a maximum of six more cents an hour over a thirty-month period, but at the same time the companies can deduct rising insurance costs from the cost-of-living increment—which will in effect wipe the latter out altogether as an expense. Furthermore, since the contract is not retroactive, the steel companies also get a two-months' free ride on wages. In straight wage terms, the steelworkers will receive an increase of 8.2 cents an hour *in December 1960,* more than a year after the strike, and a second, 7.6 cents, increase in October 1961. In straight cost terms, the increase will come to 3.75 per cent an hour, as against gains by the steel union of 4.5 per cent an hour in the can industry, and of 5 per cent an hour in aluminum.

Meanwhile, prices are already beginning to shoot up, and, to paraphrase an old remark, "before they hurt." A story in the *Wall Street Journal* recently carried the headline: "Steel Pact Triggers Factory Price Boosts." The lead paragraph quoted a furniture manufacturer as saying: "Two weeks ago, I was considering raising prices a little in March or

April but since the steel settlement I've decided to increase them at least 3 per cent and do it as soon as possible." One retailer remarked: "This type of settlement makes it easier . . . to bring my markup back up. Most of my customers work at Crucible Steel Co., and they know that the more they make the more they will have to pay for most products, including furniture. I started buying more furniture here as soon as I heard about the steel settlement." The fact that furniture has little to do with steel, and that furniture costs have not yet really gone up is, of course, irrelevant in such a conditioned atmosphere. The price spiral is already under way.

And at some point during the year, when much of the publicity has died down, the steel industry will quietly raise its prices. Where then, does the whole situation leave the union, and the country?

No dogmatic or simple answers are possible. The Joint Economic Committee of the Congress, headed by Senator Douglas, in warning of the power of the large corporations "to raise the price of their goods or services in the absence of excess demand pressure," suggests the need for "government participation in the price-wage setting process . . . [at least] for a fact-finding procedure . . . on the justification and desirability of such proposed increases." The economist Abba Lerner has proposed that where capacity lies idle, corporations be forbidden to raise prices, and when pockets of unemployment in an industry persist, unions be barred from asking for wage increases. Such yardsticks are important to have, though it is hard to see how Lerner's proposal could be carried out administratively without becoming overly bureaucratic and cumbersome.

But surely more is involved than the question of price increases. What is really at stake is the question of the "legitimacy of power" of the managerial groups. Who gives the manager his mandate? The traditional theory of private property has little legal or social validity in the age of the large corporation. A more plausible justification of managerial power is the argument that it allows for multiple, decentralized decision-centers to counter the dangers of arbitrary bureaucratic planning. But what checks exist on the enormous market power of the large corporation itself? Certainly not the market. As I have already tried to show, the corporations have been able to create a "hidden tax mechanism" which allows them to manipulate the market and to raise large sums of money for private expansion. Is such a thing socially desirable? For the situation amounts to this: in response to their own drives for status and power, the large automobile and oil companies have created a huge productive capacity, which in turn forces them to wage large coercive campaigns in order to stimulate consumption of their products—not only through advertising, but through political lobbying as well. One consequence is that Congress can pass a 12 billion dollar road-building program more easily than it can appropriate a billion dollars for schools. And we have the ludicrous spectacle, in New

York and Los Angeles, of fantastic sums being levied for expressways—with houses torn down, views blocked, and open spaces cluttered—while public transport, which is faster and more economical, goes hang. Except for a few books by people like A. A. Berle, there has been little critical study in recent years of the social power of the corporations, and the questions of limits to that power.

As for collective bargaining, the other term in the general situation, we can say with some degree of truth that it has almost reached the end of its long career as an instrumentality for economic and social justice. The fact that in the major industries the big corporations have been able to subvert negotiations with unions by utilizing them as a device for masking a protected price policy calls the social utility of collective bargaining into deep question.

Collective bargaining has always been regarded as the chief means of achieving the traditional goals of unionism. These goals can be listed as follows:

a) to raise sub-standard wages;

b) to eliminate wages as a lever for comparative advantage between firms;

c) to eliminate discrimination and favoritism in the treatment of workers and to establish the worker's conception of equitable standards: e.g., the principle of seniority in lay-offs and promotions;

d) to provide a juridical mechanism for grievances outside the arbitrary decisions of management;

e) to provide basic security and welfare for the individual worker through "fringe" benefits like medical care, pensions, and supplementary unemployment benefits;

f) to obtain a "fair share" of the profits of a firm;

g) to redistribute income in favor of the lower class groups;

h) to maintain consumer purchasing power, particularly during recessions.

Considering that the modern American trade union movement is only twenty-five years old, the unions have been remarkably successful in achieving most of their goals. But where does the labor movement go from here? The answer depends upon one's conception of the social role of the trade union. If a union's aim is simply to get a higher wage for its own members—the attitude of the building trades union, par excellence—it can then only become a partner in a collusive enterprise which strong-arms the rest of the community. This is what has happened—albeit unwillingly—to the auto and steel unions. But if the union has a wider view of its role in society—and seeks to enlist liberal and intellectual support for its claims—then it may have to begin reorienting itself and to think of collective bargaining in a new and different light.

Of the eight objectives outlined above, the unions have been able to achieve the first four, and most of the fifth. But the three strictly economic aims, which form the heart of present-day collective bargaining, have gone by the board. There has been little redistribution of shares between profits and wages, either as proportion of the national income or within firms. Nor has collective bargaining been the agency for maintaining purchasing power. The chief result of bargaining has been to favor strong unions at the expense of weak ones, to strengthen the monopoly positions of highly organized industries, and in consequence, to affect the *structure* of wages, but not the level (i.e., comparative shares). And the added fact that wage increases now run close to the ceiling levels of increases in productivity sets strong outer limits on the ability of unions to have *any* salutary effect on the economy through bargaining.

A simpler mechanism than collective bargaining for raising the standard of living of low-income groups, or maintaining purchasing power during recessions, or creating relative equity between different groups of wage workers, is government fiscal policy. The unions could use their influence to win a tax reduction for the lower-income classes of the country; this would be more equitable than pressing for the advantage of a particular group of workers, for it would be "across the board." Another thing the unions might do is exert pressure on the corporations to reduce prices, which would provide for a more equitable distribution of savings in productivity. Admittedly this is difficult. A union, its leaders say, exists to serve its own members; and the best way to do this is to fight for wage increases. As for other workers, let them go and do the same. But if union leaders adopt such a completely parochial view, they then forfeit the claims unionism has to the sympathies and allegiances of the liberal middle class and intellectuals. To help other workers—especially during recessions—it may be necessary to forgo direct wage increases and rely on government tax policy as the economic gyroscope. To engage in such action, however, the labor movement would have to become more political and begin thinking in broader social terms than it has grown accustomed to doing.

But is there no further innovating role for collective bargaining? I think that there is, that one last historic step remains to be taken—a true annual wage. Sociologically, this is the most revolutionary step the unions can take, but they will have to take it if they wish to consummate their long effort to give workers a legitimate place in society.

Historically, the worker has been treated as a commodity, to be paid by the piece or by the hour for his labor. However much one may declare (formally, as in the Clayton Act, or piously in Labor Day addresses) that labor is not a commodity, the existing system of wage payment shows that that is exactly how the worker is regarded. General Motors still pays its blue-collar force on the basis of every tenth-of-an-hour worked, and despite some union-imposed restrictions, such as "call-in" pay (which guarantees a man at least four hours pay if he is called to work that day), wages are still determined by time or piece, as with any other commodity. The most bitter complaint of auto workers is that they have no way of knowing, from one week to the next, how many hours they will work in any given week; through the year, a man may get as many as twenty "short work weeks."

All this emphasizes the distinction between the production worker (who is regarded simply as "labor") and the salaried worker who is paid by the week, month, or the year. Salaried workers (usually of the white-collar class) are laid off less often (they are carried as part of standby, or fixed, costs), they are entitled to sick leave, excused for jury duty, and given a whole host of amenities often denied to the production worker. Why? Such practices are in part a carryover from the old notion of the production worker as an "interchangeable hand," and in part simply a status distinction enforced by traditional cultural attitudes toward manual labor. But is there any reason of an economic, sociological, or moral character for this "double standard" to continue? Increased costs, says management. Yet what of the gain in status that would accrue to the worker—the gain in psychological as well as economic security—if the double standard were abolished.*

In March 1958, the International Business Machines Corporation made the unprecedented move of placing its 20,000 regular production workers on a weekly salary basis—a move which, surprisingly, received little public attention. Like most blue-collar workers, the IBM production men had been paid on an hourly rate. As salaried employees they became entitled to full pay during absences due to illness or accident, as well as to paid time off for authorized personal reasons (jury duty, death in the family, etc.) IBM is not, of course, in a "seasonal" industry, and has therefore been able to take this step with comparative ease; but few industries in the U.S. today are seasonal—even auto is not wholly so—and those who are can use counter-seasonal pricing devices to even out demand.

It is unlikely that American industry will eliminate piece work and hourly rates voluntarily; union pressure is needed through collective bargaining. But it is also unlikely that the unions, psychologically dispirited or with aging fat-cat leaders, will launch the necessary campaign in the

* Increased costs has been the cry of employers against every innovating device from shorter hours to pensions. Fifty years ago, corporations resisted workmen's compensation for accidents and the installation of safety devices on the grounds of increased costs. Yet today, in the changed climate of public opinion, what corporation would object to installing safety devices on the grounds of cost? On the grounds of mental health, one can justify the increased costs of reducing the pace of work, or the extreme division of labor. On the grounds of justice, one can argue for the elimination of the treatment of labor as a commodity.

near future. Nevertheless, such a move would be the most important means the unions could find for reducing the "status barrier" between blue-collar and white-collar work—the very barrier in the way of organizing the white-collar workers. And without organizing the white-collar worker, American unionism, in the long run, cannot survive.

Theodore Solotaroff

THE GRADUATE STUDENT: A PROFILE

Now that college education is becoming a commonplace in American life, the graduate student seems to have preempted what novelty and prestige remain in being a student. In some ways he resembles that young intellectual hero of pre-World War II days, the boy who was working his way through college. Like him, the graduate student—particularly the Ph.D. candidate—is viewed by many people, including the more scholarly undergraduates, as a man of opportunities and purpose. He spends his days and nights on the frontiers of nuclear physics, or of learning theory, or of logical positivism. Sacrificing the opportunity to earn a good living for the sake of continuing his education, he works in a community of scholars and lives in the stimulating graduate student enclave, where young people are cheerfully poor together and one keeps up with the Joneses by reading Samuel Beckett. If the student is married, as he usually is, it is to a woman who shares in his purpose as she shares in his sacrifices; in some respects, she is a modern version of the American female pioneer —a young woman of enterprise and pluck, who types her husband's term papers while her infant naps, her cake bakes, and her laundry goes through the community washing machine. Or, advanced woman that she also is, she may be off taking a seminar of her own, while her husband rocks the bassinet with one hand and turns the pages of a Russian grammar with the other.

These images have been circulating ever since the veterans of World War II returned to "revolutionize" university life. One principal change that did occur was in the displacement of the formerly staid and monastic atmosphere of graduate school by a more robust intellectual, domestic, and egalitarian spirit, as large numbers of bright and irreverent ex-GI's—many of them the first members of their families to go to college at all—went on to work for advanced degrees while raising families in converted service barracks.

The new social pattern of graduate student life continued to prevail after the veterans had left campus. Increasing numbers of students now took advanced work as a matter of course,* either to improve their chances in an increasingly crowded and specialized job market or to prepare for careers in the academy itself. For the gifted children of families on the social or economic margins of the society, graduate school became one of the best ways to move up, and the names of the top departments became familiar and magical, like the names of the medical schools. Meanwhile the campus continued to be a domicile of early marriage and parenthood. Thus, when one of the national weeklies took its readers into university seminars and student housing, they would find an alert-looking cross-section of American facial types preparing to meet the challenges to the free world, and serious young couples gazing thoughtfully into the future at the end of an evening. Furthermore, the new intellectual spirit that the veterans had produced was presumably being sustained by the much-discussed influx of writers, artists, and other non-academic types who were finding their way to university careers, and by the more open relationship generally between the academy and the society.

Recently the image of the graduate student's favorable situation—a seemingly normal life-style joined to an aura of heightened possibilities—has received a good deal of support from a leading sociologist, Bernard Berelson. In his book, *Graduate Education in the United States,* he concludes that the students themselves believe both their academic and private lives to be gratifying. Who should know better? Questioning his sample of recent Ph.D.'s, Berelson found that "on the whole they were quite satisfied with their social life as graduate students," that most of them had completed their degrees out of "academic" rather than "practical" motives, that the five or six years or more spent earning the degree was not too long, that their dissertations were worth the time and labor they put into them, and so forth. In sum, 35 per cent of the group reported they were "very satisfied" with their experience generally, and 53 per cent said they were "satisfied." Of the handful of malcontents—about one out of ten—Berelson judged that their grievances were probably related to their dissatisfaction with the academic posts they had been given for their labors.

Now the popular attitudes I have been caricaturing do not penetrate very deeply into the actualities that seem to me to characterize the world of the graduate student today; and like Lewis A. Coser, who reviewed Berelson's book in *Commentary* (March 1961), I have a distinct sense of unreality when Berelson describes and evaluates this world largely by

* According to Bernard Berelson's *Graduate Education in the United States* (1960) there were some 105,700 graduate students in 1940 and over 250,000 during the 1950's, nearly half of whom were doctoral candidates.

means of the responses of people who have successfully completed their graduate work. This is rather like describing how Americans feel about military service on the basis of what the members of a veterans' organization might say about life in the army. In both cases there is a vested interest in expressing satisfaction and a summary sense of personal history. At the veterans' club it takes the form, "I went in a boy, I came out a man"; at the faculty club, it is likely to be phrased, "As an undergraduate I was a dewy-eyed impressionist, but when I took my doctorate I had a disciplined mind."

At the same time my own years in graduate school* lead me to believe that the dissatisfaction which Coser (a professor of sociology at Brandeis) finds among his students and the "strong vote of approval" which Berelson's all-rightniks give to the institution are not irreconcilable. Rather, these opposing reactions often represent stages in a subtle process by which even the fiercely critical students slowly and ambiguously sign on with the system in order to fight their way through it. For all the talk about the revolution in university life, about its new role as a creative center in the society, this painful conforming to academic attitudes and scholarly methods, with resulting gains and losses, still characterizes, it seems to me, graduate ecucation in America; and underlying the process, is often the quiet and deep desperation of the student's private life.

To understand the experience of graduate school, it is useful to begin with the contrasts ordinarily encountered between undergraduate and graduate training. For the sake of the argument, let's take a bright, if somewhat wayward, student in a good liberal arts college; after two desultory years of general education he is still undecided about his vocation, and in his junior year drifts into an honors program. What he will probably find is that there is no longer any "horsing around": work is piled on, the standards are rigorous and professional. For a while he resents the tougher demands made on him, but in time begins to respond to the challenges—to the note of seriousness in his class lectures and discussions, and to the

* Most of the following is based on an awareness of what life is like in three graduate schools usually listed among the top five in the country. What I have to say is perhaps less true of the less prestigious and high-pressured schools, though many of these schools are currently expanding in size and ambition, and their models are likely to be the more famous universities. Also the kind of graduate student I have in mind is someone in the humanities or social sciences, rather than in the natural sciences, which tends to be a world of its own, though not very different in respect to the student's relation to his work and to his private life from what I shall describe. It should, finally, be noted that I shall be describing only one type of student, though one whose progress has, I believe, a good deal of general reference. For an excellent typology of contemporary graduate students, as well as a remarkably sensitive treatment of their problems, see Edgar Z. Friedenberg and Julius A. Roth, *Self-Perception in the University*. Supplementary Educational Monographs, No. 80 (University of Chicago Press, 1954).

illuminations of his instructors, who are likely to be top men, dedicated to their program and unwilling to suffer fools gladly. Under their influence, the student begins training himself to read, to write, and to think. As part of a strict but rational program, taught by men with a stake in teaching, he finds himself engaged in his work, and sees that most of his fellow-students are similarly engaged. A strong sense of community almost inevitably develops. Faculty supervision is apt to become more benign and informal as the student demonstrates his seriousness, and friendships often follow, especially with the younger teachers in the program. Under the direction of one of these young teachers the student starts reading for his honors essay, having been led to a subject that really interests him—let's say, "The Modern City as Viewed by Dickens and Marx." During his final months of intensive reading and writing, he begins to feel at home in the library and more comfortable with scholarly method. His stubborn prejudice for contemporaneity dissolves, as he finds himself living in the Victorian London of his imagination as excitingly and perceptively as in his courses and in his conversations on campus. The campus has by now become a very satisfying place to be. The charm of research and of the past, together with a sense of vocation settle upon the student. After receiving his B.A. he moves on to a famous university to do graduate work, bearing with him his fantasy of becoming an erudite teacher and writer.

On the face of it, the graduate school might be expected to be similar enough to the honors program our student has just left. His new group of M.A. candidates is presumably a select one; his program is demanding but again rational; his teachers are members of the graduate school faculty of a top-ranking institution, men of long experience and high standing in their fields. But the student, from the first day on, feels himself living in a radically changed atmosphere: any resemblances to his past situation seem mainly coincidental.

Undergraduate education is still largely "liberal education"; it provides, at its best, a curriculum and instruction proper to the training of the free man, that is, the man capable of thinking independently and critically about himself and the world; further, by its program of general and specialized education, it envisages the intellectual development of the whole man. Graduate education likes to say that its main purpose is the "training of teachers and scholars," but in practice, the "teaching function," as it is called, gets lost in the "research function." The most satisfying vision of the graduate school is full production of functioning scholars. Indeed, were graduate schools to take seriously their own announced purpose, and prepare teachers fit for their own undergraduate colleges, they would be very different institutions.

Thus, while the undergraduate in a good college has the sense of being directed toward realizing his best intellectual possibilities, the graduate student finds himself part of an impersonal and often rigid orientation. The department's techniques, values, and needs of research are quickly placed between the student and his passion for the larger reaches of the subject matter. Other than that, he is left to fend for himself.* The student who was interested in Dickens *and* Marx *and* the modern city finds himself forced to choose one of the three and prepare himself to study Dickens or Marx or the modern city by the methods which conform to his department's canon of acceptable research.

The men who formulate these canons, and teach the three-year program of graduate courses, are likely to be the senior men of the department. Most of their professional attitudes naturally tend to have settled on the fixed base of their special academic interests, their annual offering of the same courses to more or less unresisting students, and their role in the department hierarchy. In general, as Paul Lazarsfeld and Wagner Thielens, Jr., have suggested in *The Academic Mind* (1958), these older men are the conservative members of the department, inclined to exercise "a dampening effect on the innovating spirit" of their junior colleagues and certainly of their students. Members of the academic elite, they maintain the traditions and values summed up in the phrase "respectable research." The ideal of the advancement of scholarship, inherited originally from the German universities, still sets for them their standard of prestige and their purpose as educators. In practice, this can mean little more than working the treadmill of "scholarly opinion" in their specialty, and training students—when they think of the matter of graduate education at all—to do likewise. Now and then, one of them happens to be a wise and civilizing figure, even a powerful and provocative thinker or a rebel who has won his unconventional way—often through his prestige outside the academy. But the spirit of most graduate departments remains reductive and restrictive, and our entering student soon begins to feel that the large, benign world of his undergraduate honors program has given way to a system which in effect operates directly against the open and inward attitude toward learning that he had been encouraged to cultivate.

One way and another, he discovers that his attainments as an undergraduate are discounted. The courses he is now required to take may even seem designed for the express purpose of disabusing him of any pretensions toward creativity or sophistication; they work also to disabuse him of his enthusiasm and confidence. A key course, often titled "Principles and Methods of Research," will immediately lay upon his spirit the wet blanket of pious procedures and apparatus. Otherwise, the atmosphere is perfunctory and amorphous: the famous scholar he has come to study under

* Or as the late Dean Woodbridge of Columbia is reported by Berelson to have once put the matter: "Interest in the students (rather than the subjects) is the great temptation which tries the graduate school and the great obstacle to its success."

turns out to be a supernaturally remote figure whose lectures are drawn from his books; the course that looked so fascinating in the bulletin he pored over all summer turns out to be taught by a cranky old man, who has been treading the same shallow waters for thirty years, or by a very intense young scholar, who conducts impressive monologues in a strange new jargon. Gone is the relaxed and inspiriting communication that our student once had with his undergraduate teachers; he moves, now, in a world where such relations seem to him more like those between the townspeople and the officials in *The Castle*.

His first semester is likely to drag itself out in a succession of gray realizations. He may, at first, attribute his initial sinking feeling to being uprooted and lonely, but he soon perceives that some other students are as apathetic and resentful as he. With a shock, he sees himself in a mechanical process by which some fifty students are being run through the assembly line of an M.A. program. Classes seem divided—about evenly—between those who madly take notes during the hour and then hustle back to the library, and those who doodle or look vacantly out the window and then wander off into one of the coffee shops. He himself alternates between feeling intimidated and feeling contemptuous. Sometimes he envies the "stacks rats"—those fellow students who seem to have a consuming passion for bibliography and the language of "the learned journals." He becomes dull and disconsolate, wearing a path from his desk in one of the graduate reading rooms to his classes and back to his desk again. He begins to wonder if he should drop out.

But his situation does improve by the second semester. With a somewhat freer selection and with a knowledge of the faculty, he can line up one or two engaging courses. He discovers a few fellow students who manage to be intellectually independent and yet efficient in the ways of the department, and he takes heart. His social life picks up as he runs into some of the less stuffy manners and morals that exist on the margins of the university community. He goes to parties, meets girls, enters a circle of friends. He is more at home—and less hobbled to his role as a graduate student. But his relation to this role is likely to remain no less problematic. He still feels intellectually curbed. He comes upon a vital and provocative teacher but notices that, even so, there is little passion or controversy in the classroom discussions, and that a brilliant lecturer can speak for weeks without being asked a question. He himself is, to be sure, better able to imitate the attitudes and jargon that prevail in his field, but wonders what purpose they serve to anyone outside the academy. Now and then he pauses in the stacks of the library to thumb through a Ph.D. dissertation and thinks that some day he will have to write one. Reading the dreary learned journals in his field, he thinks that some day he will be forced to write for them—his career will depend on it.

Many students who are working for a Ph.D. give up at least once along the way. Often as not, the break comes at the end of the M.A. year. Some of the men go into the army; some journey out into the word to see what the other possibilities are, often in the belief that they will find there a healthy dose of "reality." What the ex-student usually discovers is that the universities these days have no priority on dullness or conformity. After the regimentation of the army or the corporation or the public agency, the venality of publishing or advertising, the intellectual inertia of teaching in a secondary school or a fourth-rate college, the graduate school can begin to loom in one's mind again as a place of meaningful effort. Such phrases as the "academic community," "intellectual honesty," "a meaningful way of life," begin to drift through the ex-student's mind and eventually he may surprise himself in the act of writing away for bulletins and enthusiastically making plans to go beyond his Master's, to get his Ph.D.

Let us then pick up our student who after a few years has decided to go back to graduate school again. And let us give him the additional typicality of having acquired a wife and a child or two.

Certain things now work to help him adjust. Having been once through the graduate school mill, he has few illusions to trip over. He is better able to accept the hard, gray facts of the Ph.D. program as part of the hard, gray facts of life, having seen that imagination or independence or intellectual ambition count even less outside the academy. The less extreme examples of academic triviality leave him indifferent—or cynical—rather than rebellious. Also, the responsibilities of marriage and parenthood make him less self-indulgent, more determined. The amorphousness, the uncertainty, of the first year of graduate work is replaced by a more definite set of norms—the alternatives, in line with the need to specialize, are fewer; and the department's standards of competence are more strictly imposed. Among the better students there is a more uniformly accepting spirit, a more committed academic stance.* Our student now sees before him a straight and narrow path and with whatever self-irony prepares to climb it. The major demand for accommodation, however, will come from outside his classes—from the daily struggle to meet the requirements for the Ph.D. as quickly and as successfully as possible, for behind the married student's academic situation usually lie the much more intense pressures of his private life.

* Thus Friedenberg and Roth find that in their group of successful graduate students in the social sciences at the University of Chicago, "there is a remarkable correspondence between the officially stated purposes of the University" and those of the group, "between the consciously held attitudes and those deemed by the division to be appropriate." The authors find also that "only one of the nine individuals whose perceptions of the scholarly life were unique was declared by his department counselor to be successful. . . ."

The graduate student is typically self-supporting (unlike the student in a professional school like law or medicine who—as Berelson points out—generally receives financial assistance from his family). Unless he has a fellowship, he will have to devote half his time to some sort of job—usually either research or teaching. Most such positions that I am aware of range from $1,500 to $3,000 a year, which is also the customary range of fellowships in the humanities and social sciences. With the help of the GI Bill and later the Korean War Veterans Bill, some students could manage, but otherwise the economics that govern the world of the married student community are grim.

At the state universities the student loses a smaller portion of his stipend in tuition but also finds that his job opportunities are more or less restricted to campus and to its exploitative wage scale. The main purpose of graduate student teaching is not to offer training and experience but simply to cut costs. Where there is a large freshman population, as at the state universities, the graduate student is used to provide instruction at one-half to one-third the cost. Similarly, smaller schools in a university area such as Chicago are able to hire a graduate student to teach four courses at a salary of $2,400 a year. Thus the usual teaching stipend will pay the graduate student only about $50 a week for nine months and leave him without any resources during the summer. At the private city-based universities such as Harvard, Columbia, and Chicago the student may find more lucrative part-time teaching at the other schools in the area (or may simply be free to teach more courses at the slave-labor rates), but this advantage is undercut by higher tuition costs and living expenses. Consequently, whether he has a teaching or research job or a fellowship, he is likely to end up at the same financial impasse.

The student can, of course, live on his $50 a week for several years; he can even support a wife and have another child and drive a used-up car. But a root-canal, a siege of flu, a burnt-out clutch, can precipitate a crisis and drive the student further into debt, and a major financial set-back can mean leaving school for a year. The expense of spirit is severe. The young couple's eager will to "make do" fades into the daily sense of slogging through a mire of difficulties. The "compact" or "cute" little flat in married student housing becomes a cramped, tense, depressing scene. Savings run out, and in time the look of the veteran graduate student family shows—the male, drawn, tense, frayed at the cuffs; his wife, lean and a bit haggard in her uniform of blue jeans; and even the children looking the worse for wear.

Aside from financial problems, other pressures of the student's situation multiply as he advances through successive stages of course work, qualifying examinations, thesis. During the first two or three years his teaching or research job can be fitted into a more or less manageable schedule, depending on how skillful he is in cutting corners at each end. Also the rhythm of the academic semester helps to carry him along, and the vacations between give him a chance to regroup his forces and settle down with his family for a stretch of relatively normal living. Then, too, he is apt to find that his teaching or research job offers a welcome release from the regimen of his courses.

Once he finishes his course requirements, however, or concurrently begins to prepare for his examinations or "prelims," he loses the support of his clear, limited program; and has to provide his own momentum in order to get over vast amounts of material. Now he pushes himself harder, partly in response to the demands of the examination which will comprehend most, if not all, of his general field, and partly in response to the accumulated tensions of his private life—the increasingly pressing need to do well or at least to get done. He holes up much more in the library, and at home is at it farther into the night. His working day can run to sixteen hours and carry over into entire weekends and vacations. The closer the examination date, the more he resists the contending claims of his job and his home life. A batch of student themes or tests now get pushed aside to the last moment; his teaching itself is done more *ad lib,* in varying degrees of cynicism and recklessness. And as the concentration, nervousness, and fatigue of his days undermine his powers of patience and consideration, his marriage tends to suffer in more marked ways. His wife's needs become a distraction, to be dealt with as summarily as possible; communication between them declines—so too, likely as not, does sexual interest. The children get on his nerves altogether. During these months before "prelims," if not earlier, the special desperation of the married graduate student has set in.

After six months, perhaps, he takes his examinations and—if he has been sufficiently systematic and sufficiently ruthless in his preparations—passes them. The siege is over, a few weeks follow of relaxation, of straightening out the private dislocations and disorders, of looking briefly at what had been swept under the rug. He paints the flat and takes walks with the children. Meanwhile, the financial problems, the little deprivations of mean, cramped living, go on. He sees how the other students are already looking for dissertation topics, and begins to grow restless. Thus, if he chooses to stay on campus and write his dissertation, the climb to the top of the last, roughest mountain begins.

All this is not to say that the world of the graduate student is one long unrelieved ordeal. There are the particularly deep friendships that develop —the close ties between students dependent on each other's ideas and irony to keep the channels of personal intellectual communication open. Then, too, there are the close ties between couples who need each other for ballast and cheer as well as for baby-sitting, and who have little to protect or begrudge. There is the concert, the lecture, the foreign film series that give university life its pleasant cultural style. There are the livelier graduate student parties in which couples can come alive again and let go. There come periods of satisfaction when the course has been completed, the qualifying exam passed, the dissertation chapter approved, or simply when the student's work is going well and he accepts his own efforts and the impersonal discipline of the system and the whole vast, intricate web of tradition and endeavor with which a great university transcends its academic vices and follies and keeps the spirit of learning alive. The graduate student has his moments of illumination, of achievement, and of peace, and I have no wish to gainsay them, for they can be very intense.

At the risk of repeating myself, what I do wish to say is that the daily existence which goes on in the cramped quarters of the graduate student enclave, is neither cosy nor simple, and that it exerts a powerful influence on the student's relation to his work. At best, it provides a steady push from behind to make him climb the long trail upward to the degree. At worst, it may drive him right out of graduate school once and for all; or, as often happens, it may drive him to leave the campus before he has completed his dissertation, in order to teach at a smaller school. Here he can double his income as a regular faculty member and provide a better life for his family. This he does at the hazard of trying to write a dissertation, as it were, by mail and at a more intermittent pace—which in the long run can create graver problems than pushing on to the end.

In terms of his intellectual development, the peculiar circumstances of the graduate student's private life foster the process by which even the intellectually ambitious and independent student eventually fits himself into the mold of the efficient, unobjectionable young scholar. The daily price that not only he but his wife (and children) are paying for him to remain in school impels him to steer a prudential course. The man who is struggling to keep his head above water is not likely to try diving for pearls. The student may even come to prefer the routine but manageable course to the challenging but difficult one; the low-pressured, humane, sensible professor to the brilliant but unreliable man; the trivial but safe dissertation topic to the adventurous and problematic one.* He learns to go along with the acceptable style of scholarly thinking, in which "originality" means mainly finding a problem, or segment of one, that is still to

* One reason that the interdisciplinary programs such as "American Studies" or "History of Ideas" have not attracted the students they should is that they are felt to involve risks, both in obtaining a degree and a satisfactory position afterward. It is doubtful whether these risks are, in fact, any greater than those involved in the conventional Ph.D., but with all of the compulsion to view the doctoral program as a straight and narrow and prudential path, the student even becomes suspicious of the opportunities for breadth and freedom that are available.

be explored, "pertinence" means mainly the amount of fresh factual documentation that can be accumulated, and "soundness" means mainly working within the existing body of "scholarly opinion." Moreover, he begins to find satisfaction in the close, skeptical examination of evidence, in the thoroughness of research, in accumulating a great deal of knowledge about a particular question. He develops a respect for factuality and for careful arguments that remain within clearly defined terms. He discovers that in many cases it is both easier and more satisfying to do the research and ride with the evidence than it is to spin a position out of a few hunches. He realizes that competent scholarship does temper the mind, that to suspend value judgments can contribute to understanding, that small discoveries have their own excitement. In short, he reaches the stage where he is able to write an acceptable dissertation, possibly even a valuable one.

Some dissertations are done in one frantic year, the majority in two or three, some stretch out over ten. But the pattern is usually much the same: a prolonged period of submerged anxiety followed by a growing momentum of nervous energy, as the student begins to see glimpses of the summit of the mountain. The typical intellectual quality of the experience itself is perhaps best suggested by the description which an urbane professor once gave to a class: "First you find a little desk in the stacks where most of the books you will need are shelved. Then, one by one, you take down a book, read it, and transfer its contents in cryptic, quotable form to little white cards. After you have gone through all the books, you take the cards and put them in an order. Then, one by one, you transfer their information to your manuscript. When you are all finished, the manuscript is bound, and one day a librarian carries it back to your place in the stacks and puts it on the shelf." Of course, not all dissertations are done this way but few escape the common fate of being mainly a complicated, exhausting, and expensive form of exercise. For one thing, it is increasingly difficult to find a meaningful research problem which the legions of doctoral students and scholars combing the field each year in search of the same thing have managed to overlook. Besides, the more comprehensive and illuminating the thesis, the more prolonged and uncertain the research and writing will be. The wise dissertation adviser tells the student to get his degree and then worry about doing a definitive piece of work, and if he is as desperate to get done as he usually is, the student tells himself the same.

William James said that by the time a man is thirty his character has set like plaster. However rebellious he may have been at the outset, the man who emerges from graduate school at about that age has inevitably moved in the direction of accepting the scholarly image. Exploited by a research or teaching job, subjected to the dislocation of his inner and family life, disarmed by the genteel authoritarianism of the academic will, he has become habituated to the feeling that the deeper questions of personal purpose are not worth asking and that the risks of intellectual freedom, passion, and non-conformity are not worth taking. The intellectual virtues which he has learned to emulate are pretty much those that Leo Marx, recently in *Commentary,* associated with modern documentary scholarship—"precise, neutral, and impersonal." * He has become more narrow, diligent, and cautious in his ideas, more respectable in his style of thinking and writing, more politic in his behavior. He worries more about being "sound" than being stimulating; he finds it more natural to adopt a middle position rather than an extreme one, an analytic line of inquiry rather than an evaluative one, an academically fashionable stance rather than a personal one. He is likely to be more in touch with "scholarly opinion" about his subject than with his own feelings, intuitions, and sense of relevance, and thus to find himself having as much difficulty thinking and writing about history or literature or politics or society in direct, open, nontechnical terms as he once had in disciplining his personal demands on his field to the methods and vocabulary of research. The gain in his ability to contribute to the learned journals can involve the loss of the intellectual energy or confidence to communicate beyond them. Five or six years is a long time. The graduate student who once cynically put on the mask of the conventional scholar, planning in his heart to remove it as soon as he has his degree, finds often enough that his face—as George Orwell remarked in another connection—has grown to fit it. Even—judging by Berelson's Ph.D.'s—to grin through it. By then our graduate student, perforce, will have joined the community of scholars. Whether he will still possess a capacity for breadth, inwardness, and risk-taking, a grasp of the time and the culture to which he belongs, whether he will be fit for the intellectual community without which (as Leo Marx wrote at the end of the essay I have cited) "the culture dies"—all of this is another question. One that lies outside the scope of the present discussion, as they say in graduate school.

* "The American Scholar Today" (July 1961).

May 1962

Edgar Z. Friedenberg

THE GIFTED STUDENT AND HIS ENEMIES

One of the most heavily emphasized themes in current discussions of education in the United States is the search for potential excellence. In the past we have tended to equate academic promise with high intelligence, and to infer that the most serious wastage of young people in school resulted from the school's failure to recognize and reward high academic aptitude in lower-status youngsters. The search for excellence, on these terms, became an extension of the traditional American quest for equality of opportunity, which served as its moral justification. But this defines the issue far too narrowly. Of perhaps more fundamental importance is the effect of the school on kinds of giftedness that may be useless or even disadvantageous in earning good grades and high recommendations in a typical high school milieu. High IQ and diligence do not exhaust the possibilities of superior capacity. Originality and insight, disciplined but impassioned sensitivity, and a highly personal and unique quality of mind contribute as indispensably to human achievement.

In the school, as in much of our society, creative youngsters seem usually to arouse a specific animus. Teachers dislike them, and the students learn quite early that the spontaneity and subjectivity they prize in themselves cannot be expected to lead to success in school or in later life.

What is the source of the animus, and why is the creative student so likely to encounter it? Particularly useful in answering these questions is a concept which, though explicitly introduced by Friedrich Nietzsche, has only recently had much impact on American social thought. This is the concept of *Ressentiment*.* The word sounds like a French translation of "resentment," and this does approximate the meaning. But only imprecisely. *Ressentiment* is less completely conscious than resentment, and less focused on the particular real experiences that are its actual causes. In contrast, it is usually rationalized, covert, diffuse, and largely unconscious.

* Max Scheler's *Ressentiment* (Lewis A. Coser, ed., 1961) is the authoritative statement and exegesis of the meaning of *ressentiment*.

Just as one may legitimately refer to "free-floating anxiety" as a decisive element in certain kinds of personality, *ressentiment* is a kind of free-floating ill-temper. It is the syndrome produced by intense hostility intensely repressed over long periods of time. As such, it is familiar enough. Why then is it worth discussing as a *social,* rather than a psychological, disorder? Because of the peculiar and devastating ways in which *ressentiment* has become institutionalized in 20th-century mass culture.

The conditions of contemporary life have reified *ressentiment* into a massive social and political reality. The operation of democratic political institutions—and especially their underlying egalitarian value assumptions—has greatly increased the political influence of the most *ressentient* social groups while weakening the will of more affirmative individuals to resist them.

Public education is one of the social institutions most strongly affected by *ressentiment.* The public schools attract, as teachers, administrators, and counselors, individuals from groups in the population that are particularly subject to it, and for reasons which are likely to influence the selection of the more *ressentient* from among such groups. The school is the traditional avenue—and arena—for social mobility, which many of its clientele appear to conceive as its sole *raison d'être;* one goes to school in order to get ahead, or one drops out; few youngsters are held in school by any real commitment to the cultural values represented by education, and few public schools in fact represent those values adequately. But those who are most anxious about social mobility are also most likely to be *ressentient.*

Those social groups are most prone to *ressentiment* whose members are especially subjected to frustration in their position in life, but who feel so impotent that they do not dare to get consciously angry and rebel and hit back, or strike out for themselves against the actual source of their frustration. Generally, they dare not even recognize it. Instead they identify with and accommodate to the very individuals or social forces undermining their position, and whose strength they tend to admire and exaggerate. By thus exercising their impotence, they increase it; what a less threatened individual would have felt as rage becomes resentment, then a kind of small-shopkeeper's fearful and self-pitying distrust, and finally, perhaps, merely an unconscious predisposition to sanctimonious spitefulness.

Ressentiment therefore ravages most seriously the rootless lower-middle or white-collar classes who give up most in order to be respectable and get least real deference and security in return. The threat to them is much more serious now that Western life permits its lower-level personnel to develop so few real skills. Yet, they cannot attack the system that has made their lives meaningless, for they are in collusion with it and want to rise within it.

It is not merely the economic threat that leads to *ressentiment,* for *ressentiment* is not simply anxiety. The *ressentient,* rather, are those who have given up important human potentialities in making deals with the system, and are now faced with mounting evidence that this is not going to pay off. Thus the German inflation of the 20's, wiping out the savings of millions of petty bourgeois who for a lifetime had slaved to confuse thrift and order with decency, helped pave the way to Nazism, which epitomized *ressentiment* in its Eichmannesque combination of sadism and alienation. The essence of the Nazi position, after all, is that its motives were worthy of the highest traditions of the civil service; one likes to think that the executioners of Joan of Arc, by comparison, at least felt that there was something cheerful about a nice fire. Even hatred is too strong an emotion for the highly authoritarian, who can handle feeling only by bureaucratizing it, so that it emerges as prejudice against classes of individuals rather than open hostility. Good authoritarians never get personal.

But the rigidity, hostility, and alienation that reveal the authoritarian personality in face-to-face relationships are not peculiar to adherents of the political far right. In the presence of the doctrinaire young liberal, the professional Negro or Zionist, the militant opponent of atomic warfare, one often senses the existence of the same animus, however strongly one may agree with their views. It does not seem to matter very much—it does matter somewhat—whether humanitarian issues are themselves a central part of the ideology. The aggressively poor young college instructor, flaunting his radical views, minority status, and undisciplined children as explanations of his lack of recognition and status, is no fascist. But he does seem to run on the same fuel. Such a person, feeling helpless to begin with, becomes frightened lest his resentment provoke further punishment, and rationalizes it as a more positive emotion: Christian love, the desire to protect the weak, or to secure social justice. All these are perfectly real emotions that may and do arise as spontaneous responses to real human experiences. It is perfectly possible to wish, through love or compassion, to help a suffering fellow being, whether the cause of his misery be poverty, disease, sheer misfortune, or any combination of evils. It is likewise possible to be moved by his plight to genuine and fierce anger at the persons or circumstances that have brought it about, and to commit oneself wholeheartedly to fight the good fight on his behalf. But this is a very different attitude, and expresses a very different character, from that represented by *ressentiment*—which prizes the victim *because* he is a victim, and loves the suffering while covertly exploiting the sufferer.

No one has expressed this difference more clearly, or evaluated it more precisely, than Thoreau in the following passage from *Walden:*

> I would not subtract anything from the praise that is due to philanthropy, but merely demand justice for all who by their lives

> and works are a blessing to mankind . . . I want the flower and fruit of a man; that some fragrance be wafted over from him to me, and some ripeness flavour our intercourse. His goodness must not be a partial and transitory act, but a constant superfluity, which costs him nothing and of which he is unconscious. This is a charity that hides a multitude of sins. The philanthropist too often surrounds mankind with the remembrance of his own cast-off griefs as an atmosphere, and calls it sympathy. We should impart our courage, and not our despair, our health and ease, and not our disease, and take care that this does not spread by contagion. From what southern plains comes up the voice of wailing? Under what latitudes reside the heathen to whom we would send light? Who is that intemperate and brutal man whom we would redeem? . . .
>
> I believe that what so saddens the reformer is not his sympathy with his fellows in distress, but, though he be the holiest son of God, his private ail. Let this be righted, let the spring come to him, the morning rise over his couch, and he will forsake his generous companions without apology. . . . There is nowhere recorded a simple and irrepressible satisfaction with the gift of life, any memorable praise of God. . . . All health and success does me good, however far off and withdrawn it may appear; all disease and failure helps to make me sad and does me evil, however much sympathy it may have with me or I with it. . . . Do not stay to be an overseer of the poor, but endeavour to become one of the worthies of the world.

In the contemporary American high school, *ressentiment* is much more effectively institutionalized in its "philanthropic" than in its authoritarian form. Individual teachers and administrators representing either tendency are common, but one way of expressing a major change in the climate of American education over the past half-century is by saying that authoritarianism has been placed in a thoroughly defensive position, while the "philanthropic" attitude has become dominant.*

Teachers and administrative officials of schools come primarily from lower-middle class backgrounds. Many come from families of somewhat higher status, but the folkways of the schools are lower-middle class folkways: the official language, the customs and regulations governing dress—

* The shift from "traditional" to "emergent" values in the schools discussed by George P. Spindler in his classic paper, "Education in a Transforming American Culture" (*Harvard Educational Review,* Summer 1955), might be expressed with equal validity as a shift from the dominance of authoritarian to "philanthropic" modes of *ressentiment.*

even the food in the school cafeteria. All these tend to be shabby-genteel. They are not forthright expressions of the actual limitations of the schools' financial, intellectual, and social resources, such as peasant life and art express, but cheap reproductions of corporate or academic life, as imperfectly conceived. Schoolteachers by and large have likewise notably resisted, even more than most white-collar workers, identifying with the working class in their own financial interests, as by unionization. One may, of course, dislike joining a union and refuse to do so on a variety of grounds from social ideology to personal taste. But the actual circumstances of the public school teacher's background and vocational life make union membership a promising device for achieving his legitimate economic aspirations. The difficulty seems to be that teachers' economic aspirations are regularly subordinated by their middle-class identifications. Unionization is inconsistent with their insistence that they practice a profession. Fully established professions, like medicine and law, have of course evolved militant organizations to advance and safeguard their economic interests, though these are not called unions. But teachers have not so far created any organization suited to the purpose of direct economic action on their behalf.* The life-style of the public high school teacher remains, characteristically, that of the dutiful subordinate awaiting preferment in a niggardly bureaucratic structure.

Such a life is the very breeding ground of *ressentiment*. The teacher is linked to his principal, his superintendent, and his peers by a pretense of professional equality that prevents him from either demanding the perquisites of status or the liberty to scoff at it. Within a bureaucratic structure in which one depends not merely for advancement but for personal gratification as well on the endorsement of one's peers and subordinates, open conflict generates intolerable anxiety. Frustration and anger degenerate into malicious gossip, and are absorbed into the general ambience of wariness and cynicism. Ultimately, the consequence is alienation; in such people there is no longer direct connection between their actual experiences, their feelings, and their actions.

Nothing about this is peculiar to the career of teachers in contemporary America; this is rather the familiar catalogue of complaint about life in the organized system. *Ressentiment* probably is less prominent among teachers than among many social groups like waiters or cab drivers, whose work keeps them in constant contact with people visibly enjoying a higher standard of life than they can achieve in a culture that makes it impossible to take pride in performing personal service well—or like social workers, whose "philanthropic" enterprise puts them in a position of unparalleled opportunity to intervene in the lives of other people whose poverty and

* See Myron Lieberman, *Education as a Profession* (1956), especially chapters 9 and 10. A teachers' union, of course, is again very much in controversy.

tendency to act out conflicts make them both particularly tempting and particularly vulnerable to the *ressentient.* And there are many other social groups in which *ressentiment* has become institutionalized under somewhat different conditions: yellow journalism and the pornography of violence, for example. But there are further reasons that are peculiar to the education establishment why the public high school should be the locus of strong *ressentiment.*

The official function of the schoolteacher is still defined in academic and intellectual terms, however irrelevant the definition may be to the daily work a teacher in a slum school actually does. And in academic and intellectual terms, the public secondary school teacher is inferior. This, moreover, is a fact he must consciously face. The elementary school teacher can avoid facing it—if indeed it is a relevant judgment to apply to her—because she is not graded in her professional training in direct competition with people who are going into other work. In other words, she is likely to be—in many states she virtually has to be—an "ed major." High school teachers are not; they are math majors or English majors or history majors and, generally speaking, they are the ones who made poorer grades than those who head into industry, the professions, or higher education on the basis of their specialized study. In graduate school such direct comparisons are again inapplicable, but the norms for graduate students in education on standardized intelligence tests (like the Miller analogies) are substantially lower than those for graduate students in other academic disciplines.

Students are forced into secondary school teaching because they are not able to make the grade in a specialized or scholarly discipline. Finding themselves comparatively impotent academically, they are unwilling to relinquish respectable intellectual pretensions altogether, and settle for something that, in their own view, is decidedly second-rate. It is perfectly possible, of course, to define the function of a high school teacher as an honorable and extremely significant specialty in its own right; and it is also perfectly possible that, if it were so defined, it would have a rather low correlation with conventional academic and intellectual achievement. If high school teaching *were* so defined, the people who go into it would not have a sense of partial failure, and there would be no reason for their academic situation to lead to *ressentiment.* Certainly, neither the early-childhood nor the primary grade school teacher seems so prone to it. The public image of such a teacher as a constricted and punitive spinster has disappeared—though, as usual, more slowly than the reality—to be replaced by the image of the young woman who thinks of herself as, and very often really is, a professional emissary to the private world of childhood. She may not be especially scholarly or analytical-minded, but she knows her job and does it well. The children know that she does; and there is a good deal of mutual respect and affection.

In the later grades and in junior high and high schools the situation is much worse.* Subject matter has begun to matter, and so has the fact that the teacher is often incompetent to handle it. There is more to this incompetence than relative ignorance or stupidity. There is also the fact that the school has begun to deal with controversial content and controversial purposes. High school civics, social studies, and biology courses are no place for people who do not know their history, economics, or biology. But they are also not the place for timid or insecure people, for people who are especially anxious to make a good impression on the community or to keep out of trouble. These are, of course, exactly the kinds of people that a principal or superintendent who is timid or insecure himself will try to keep there.

Again, in this context, the feeble persistence of identification with academic norms contributes to the high school teacher's *ressentiment.* The identification is not strong enough to make him a hero.† But it is strong enough to make him ashamed of himself, and to add to his feeling of impotence. His impotence is real enough; he generally just does not *know* enough to defend an unpopular position on scholarly grounds even if he had the courage. But until he abandons the professional stance, or ceases to link it to academic competence, he cannot accept himself as a part of the local propaganda apparatus either. The statement "You shall know the truth, and the truth shall make you free" is quite false; knowledge can be a dreadful burden. But like pregnancy, knowledge to a teacher is a form of commitment no longer subject to voluntary abridgment without a sense of catastrophic guilt, and to have only a little is no help at all.

I have stated that the most serious consequence of *ressentiment* is alienation. The *ressentient* individual loses the connection between his feelings and the situation in which he is actually living. His emotions, and even his perceptions of reality, are channeled in the directions that cause least anxiety rather than toward the experiences that actually arouse them, either in the past or in the immediate present. All neurosis, of course, has this effect, but *ressentiment* is especially effective because it is the emotion itself—anger, rage, impotence, and fear of retribution—that is the source of anxiety and that must be repressed. So *ressentient* individuals are especially clumsy and insensitive, in contrast to those with other sorts of neurotic

* See Martin Mayer, *The Schools* (1961) for an excellent treatment of observations dealing with this point.

† Not, to be sure, that college and university people, in the social sciences at least, behaved particularly heroically under pressure. See Paul Lazarsfeld and W. Thielens, *The Academic Mind* (1958) for a canny account of the extent of accommodation, from widespread self-censorship to occasional outright betrayal of colleagues, that occurred during McCarthy's dreadful reign.

difficulty, in using their feelings to help them understand the meaning of their lives and to discipline their moral conduct. This is why they become sentimental; they prefer fake experiences that decorate the actual situation to symbolic evocations of its actuality. This kind of sentimentality has become a negative status symbol, evoking the atmosphere of lower-middle class life as surely as a whiff of H_2S brings back freshman chemistry: the plastic flowers in the apartment house lobby, which insist that this is a place in the sun; the conventional cuteness of the mass-produced, mock-hostile office signs and mock-boastful chef's aprons. The worst thing that could happen, obviously, is that a genius really should be at work.

What happens when one is—even an embryonic one? The essential quality of the creative student, as he is beginning to be defined in the literature, is that his thought is divergent. He doesn't arrive at right answers by deducing them from established premises, but by an intuitive understanding of how the problem he is dealing with really works, of what actually goes into it, and the right answers he arrives at may not be right in the textbook; they will not be, if the textbook has been carefully edited to make it as widely acceptable as possible. He works hard when the problem requires it, and respects facts as a part of reality. But for the creative student, facts are not right answers but tools and components for building original solutions.

How will the high school teacher react to this? If he is a high school teacher because the job gives him joy, and is competent intellectually, with astonished delight. But to the degree that he is *ressentient,* with defensive hostility. Consider the poor mathematician who manages to salvage enough math to become a high school teacher, or the ninth-grade teacher who hates mathematics and never meant to have any traffic with it at all. Such teachers manage by knowing a set of answers, and a conventional procedure for arriving at them. They maintain their self-esteem by convincing themselves that this is really enough; and the student who really understands mathematics puts them in a dilemma. On the one hand, he may show them up as incompetent. On the other, they don't know but that he may be cheating somehow, and laughing at them for being taken in. They dare not commit themselves either way. If they are authoritarian, they bully him into solving the problems "the way I show you as long as you are in my class." If they are "philanthropic," they respond with studied tolerance and amusement to Johnny's "attention-getting behavior." But in either case they try to make sure that he doesn't embarrass them again by actually getting up and doing mathematics in front of the whole class.

In the humanities the creative student is both more threatening and more vulnerable. He is more vulnerable because there aren't any right answers to support him. He is more threatening because the humanities, if truthfully handled, are themselves threatening to the *ressentient*. It is the job of the humanities to get to the root of human experience, which at best means hewing austere beauty out of some very ugly blocks in such a way that their real character is revealed. This is just what the alienated cannot tolerate. What happens to the adolescent boy or girl who writes a theme about an experience that had deep meaning for him—at this age it will probably be in part a sexual experience—as it really was? For that matter, how does the well-indoctrinated professional educator, suffused with the benign values underlying his course in child development and his belief in the wholesomeness of family living, handle either Medea or Salome?

The position of the social science teacher is more ambiguous. *Ressentiment* is not always such a handicap in the social sciences, which provide a superb eminence from which to look down on one's neighbors while discharging one's scholarly obligations. The convention of objectivity keeps the *ressentient* social scientist from having to face the full responsibility for his hostility and destructiveness; after all, he is just doing his job. The creative student in social studies may therefore get an additional chance. Besides the possibility common to all fields of encountering a superior, *ressentiment*-free instructor, there is the possibility in social studies of finding an instructor who does not clobber the creative even though he is *ressentient,* but identifies with their undisciplined or rebellious disjunctivity and accepts and encourages it as an expression of his own *ressentiment* —taking refuge in academic freedom and his obligation to the truth if detected.

But such teachers are inevitably rare; they are selected out in the process of teacher-training, which requires the candidate to suffer a great deal of nonsense without protest; and administrators get rid of them if they find them out in time as likely to get the school in trouble with intransigent groups in the community. The creative student is far less likely to encounter a social critic on the high school staff than he is teachers with whom he will quickly establish a mutual loathing and who are continually reminded by his freshness of perception that they have consented to devote their lives to teaching what they know to be false or irrelevant; to denying in class that the fundamental experiences of his life can even have occurred. Hundreds of high school teachers can, and do, spend several hours a day trying to teach slum children in civics courses the official syllabus on the American Way of Life. If the children are creative, the questions they raise are difficult to answer, especially after they have given up trying to ask them verbally, and express them directly through their attitudes and behavior in class. One gets used to it, in time, and learns to maintain order. But the job of an assistant warden in a custodial institution is a long step down from earlier expectations.

Overlying the special influence of *ressentiment* on instruction in the separate fields of knowledge and reinforcing its effects is the "philanthropic" ideology of the school. Students, by definition, are subordinate in status to their schoolmasters; they are in a partially dependent position, and the function of the school is to nurture them. It is appropriate that the school devote itself to their needs and attend to and utilize their interests. Its primary purpose is to serve them.

But an institution designed to nurture the relatively weak and dependent presumably does so because it cherishes their potential strength and autonomy. There would be good reason for it to value most highly those youngsters who show most intellectual vigor and originality in the disciplined handling of ideas; as, in some cultures, a father will love his strongest and most virile sons most even though he fears them a little. The *ressentient,* identifying with impotence and resentful of strength, respond very differently. The school, strongly influenced by *ressentiment,* is rather inclined to cherish the weakness of the weak.

Thus one notion that even very poor students of educational sociology grasp eagerly is that schools are generally biased against lower-class students. They certainly are, and this is an important truth. But when the proposition is explored, what it seems to mean in the professional curriculum of education is that middle-class students "have advantages" which they ought to be forced to share more generously. The remedy is to insure that the lower-status students get their share of good grades, scholarships, opportunity for social leadership, and so on.

But these are still conceived almost wholly in middle-class terms. There is no corresponding respect for the lower-status child's own experience of life, his language, and the forms of social organization he spontaneously adopts. It is true enough that the school faces a difficult dilemma; lower-class behavior creates real difficulties in running a formal social organization like a school, quite apart from any question of bias; yet the bias is real and harmful. But professional education both in its curriculum and in its practice tends to respond to the bias as if the chief objection to it was that it gave the privileged too many privileges, rather than with a real, imaginative concern for the quality of life of lower-status youngsters.

This is a major reason why the bias is hard to eliminate. Its most important consequences do not occur in the schools, but in the long run. Giving the children of Southern Negro migrants more high grades even if they don't read or do arithmetic very well is not really going to help them much in getting into medical school. What is needed is something like the original conception of progressive education, which combined an extremely flexible conception of both educational content and instructional technique with a rather rigid adherence to standards of achievement. This is *genuine* acceptance of the meaning of underprivileged life, and real help

It is possible that students respect an elite of athletes because good athletes are encouraged to be proud of themselves for being as good as they can, and that these are the only people left on campus with anything in particular to be proud of.

Among the most important educational consequences of *ressentiment,* then, are failure to recognize the gifted, or to nurture their gifts when discovered; differential drop-out rates among students from different social classes; and fundamental difficulties in curriculum construction that vitiate earnest and costly efforts to adapt the curriculum to the needs of divergent individuals or social groups. *Ressentiment* also influences the total experience of education in ways that are so general that they can hardly even be recognized as problems: the flavor of education itself; whether students will come to think of it as opening their understanding to a wider and deeper range of experiences or as constricting and limiting their range of possible emotional and intellectual response; whether, in the long run, the school tends more to liberate than to alienate. The total social function of education is intimately involved with *ressentiment;* for the secondary school has both a cautionary and a mithridatic function. It is here that one learns to avoid the expression of noble or heroic aspirations in noble or heroic terms, so as not to destroy at the outset the chance that they may be realized. Conversely, it is here that one learns to tolerate without surrender the demands of guilt and humility; to retain, in some measure, the power to continue to enjoy privileges and personal achievements without being disconcerted by the envy they arouse. Now that the differences are neither clearly indicated nor morally defended, many Americans devote their lives to an effort to steal into the first-class compartment without awakening the tourist passengers; and the school is where one first learns how numerous and vigilant they are. The school is where you learn to be an American; and an important part of Americanism is to learn the prevailing norms and limits of achievement and self-assertion and how to maintain them against the encroachments of a mass society that the moral support of a strong egalitarian tradition has made extremely aggressive.

June 1962

Paul Goodman

THE INEFFECTUALITY OF SOME INTELLIGENT PEOPLE

When we treat man as he is, we make him worse than he is. When we treat him as if he already were what he potentially could be, we make him what he should be.

GOETHE

At their meeting in 1960, the American Association for the Advancement of Science resolved that it was the duty of scientists to inform the public of the dangers of bomb-testing and heard C. P. Snow predict as a matter of statistical certainty that some of the bombs would go off within ten years. I asked Margaret Mead—I think she was their president at that time—if this meant that scientists working to produce these deadly products should quit their jobs. "Certainly not," she said, "it is their duty as scientists to inform the public." But what simple soul would then believe them? Or, if one believed them, how to regard them except as monsters? Professor Mead's theory, apparently, was that the public, if informed, would exert pressure on the governments; but the scientists did not exert the pressure that *they* had. "Why don't the American and Russian scientists, who are so friendly," I asked, "strike, exert their power, put a stop to it?" "That would be conspiracy," said Professor Mead tartly. So it would.

I am again and again baffled how persons of intellect, of good intention, of strong conviction, reason in a way that must logically lead to an action, and yet do not act. This seems to me to be profoundly pathological, yet how to cure it? Such people are not hypocritical, so one cannot expose and shame them. I do not believe that they are merely timid and afraid of losing their jobs. They do not seem to suffer from the despairing idea that nothing can be done, since they speak up and urge us to do this and that.

But they themselves seem to have lost the spring of initiative, the ability of moving themselves, which Aristotle singled out as a chief property of living animals.

I. Unitarians, etc.

To explore this pathology of professors and scientists, let us first consider a (perhaps) simpler group of well-intentioned, intelligent, solid citizens, whose ineffectuality seems to be explicable on more familiar social grounds. This group we may loosely identify as Unitarians, Universalists, Humanists, members of the Ethical Culture Society, many Quakers. They are more than a hundred thousand, educated far above the average, richer than the average, with considerable moral courage and high ideals of life. Why do they throw so little weight? We can think of half a dozen reasons.

In the first place, they have the defect of their virtues: they are decent and observe the rules of the game, even when the rules are manipulated against them. Suppose, for instance, they have been vehemently opposed to the bomb-shelter, following Mrs. Roosevelt, whom many of them respect as a leader. Nevertheless, when the government, by its characteristic arts of crash publicity and scientific quackery, manages to set a shelter program moving with popular acquiescence, soon our friends—again following Mrs. Roosevelt (and Margaret Mead)—bow to the "democracy" and agree to the bomb-shelters if they are *community,* rather than private, shelters. But contrast with this the behavior of certain high school youngsters in the New York City schools. A couple of years ago, to protest the shelter drills, these students wore blue arm bands, although that was forbidden; and in one school a few were suspended. By the next semester, the youngsters refused to participate in the drills altogether, and the principal of one school now *asked* them to wear blue arm bands to register their protest. But the students persisted in boycotting the drills and again a few were suspended. Now the principal has agreed for them not to take part in the drills, if only they do not obstruct the others. By this time the drills have become a farce and are so treated by the teachers who do not mark down the delinquents' names. There has been a change of the rules not against the dissenters but for them.

Our Unitarians, etc. are balked also by their false Realism and Practicality. They remain in a framework of action even when it offers no possibilities for *their* kind of action. This occurs at every election. Our friends have an obsessional inability to refrain from marking a ballot, though they are offered no relevant candidates. They will not vote for a minor candidate because they do not want to throw away the vote; and they reason that not to vote at all is a futile protest. But the practical alternative is to *actively* not vote, to campaign against voting with an ad in the press and on TV, and picket a hundred feet from the polls crying "DON'T vote, till we get a candidate representing what we believe." This would, of course, be scandalous—but not so scandalous as having to choose between a Kennedy and a Nixon.

False Practicality is sometimes the bathetic illusion of exerting possible influence if one "works within the system," and naturally the major political parties use window-dressing to attract this kind of support. (Certainly conceited identification with the powerful works mightily in some of our academics and scientists.) In describing the American Communists of the 30's, Harold Rosenberg has scathingly exposed their lust to be on the governing board, no matter what. But in general in America—perhaps because of the methods by which people get office—it is almost out of the question for anyone indignantly to resign; and our intellectuals agree that it would be imprudent for one to give up one's chance of exerting influence! But of course one's *not* resigning is what exerts a discouraging influence, for it means that no issue is really earnest.

The general class of falsely practical behavior is choosing the lesser of two evils; and there is current an abominable doctrine that *only* such choices indicate that a man is tough-minded and serious, rather than utopian and dilettantish. (To do them credit, I do not think that the Unitarians, etc. accept this abomination of Dr. Niebuhr and the *New Leader*.) Let us be clear on what is involved here. Choosing the Lesser Evil does not mean accepting half a loaf, or one slice, or even the promise of a crumb tomorrow; it means swallowing a milder rat poison rather than a more virulent rat poison. But to be stuck with such a choice also means that we have long neglected our duty and interest; there are terrible unfinished situations which prevent the emergence of new possibilities. Then it is to this unfinished business that we must address ourselves, and not choose still another evil to avoid unfinished business. We cannot hope, after long neglect, to escape without suffering. Surely the history of colonialism and its breakdown has taught nothing else but this. Only penitence and magnanimity in making amends can now shorten the time of travail. Gimmicks, gradualism, puppet-rulers cannot avail. Since the French must quit Algeria in 1962, it would have helped them magnanimously to begin to do so in 1954. I will merely mention Cuba and South America. But of course the *ne plus ultra* of Choosing the Lesser Evil is accepting Deterrence as a policy, even though this policy is likely to produce the maximum calamity, and even though the first stroke of unfinished business in this area would be to call for a national and world-wide mourning for Hiroshima.

The False Realism of the better educated often amounts to a contempt for plain people and a pessimistic notion of democracy. It is thought that the "mass" of people are not up to ideal or magnanimous behavior; they must be won or pacified in terms of surface prejudices and venal interests; and our real aims must be concealed and debauched by Public Relations. Inevitably such behavior has caused a continual further debasement and confusion of the electorate. The result is that by now it is almost unknown for any genuine issue—an issue that could be decided by real evidence and real differences of interest—to be debated in an electoral campaign. But if there are no real issues, there is no possibility for an inventive or statesmanlike resolution of them. Yet these people who must be cajoled and tricked are no others than our neighbors who, individually or especially in small groups, are not morons if directly confronted. (In great numbers, to be sure, the whole is less than the sum of its parts.) One of the very few honest public figures whom I know, Congressman Kastenmeier of Wisconsin, has told me that the chief virtue is to be willing to lose; then if one finally wins, one is free and clean. In his opinion, his constituents do not agree with everything he speaks for, but there is mutual respect and they return him.

Finally, our Unitarians, etc. are saddled with their bourgeois and churchly respectability. They are embarrassed, for instance, to give themselves personally to a cause, to carry a sign on the street, rather than sending a telegram or contributing money for an ad. Therefore they do not get the moral and psychological support of solidarity, which comes only from commitment of one's person with one's fellows. Middle-class respectability is also squeamish about who its fellows are; it finds it hard to associate with young beards, jeans, and sandals. Nevertheless, it is a mistake for peace actions to discipline themselves to "respectability" in order to win bourgeois support. (Both SANE and the Committee for Non-Violent Action are susceptible to this temptation.) Discipline for such a motive takes the heart out of any committed behavior, which one must perform as one is, not as one wishes to appear for public relations. Let the others learn that peace is more important than proper clothes. Indeed, one of the most salutary effects of the movements for peace and for civil rights has been just to acquaint respectable people with rough facts; in many a middle-class family these days there has suddenly come to be a member in the common jail or out on bail.

Also, it is hard for respectable people to associate themselves with burning but "disreputable" causes. Peace and racial integration are now quite respectable; the repeal of the irrational sex and drug laws is much less so. Yet unfortunately, it is only if the respectable, the professionally competent, and the churches speak up on these laws that we will ever get rid of them.

II. *Professors and Social Scientists*

In part, well-intentioned and radical professors are kept from decisive action by these same decencies, gullibilities, petty ambitions, and embarrassments. Their futility often has a similar middle-class background. To be more precise, I think that, as stronger-minded scholars, they are less hampered by moral respectability and mere appearances; but on the other hand, as organization men often working close to the disputed areas, they are more timid about losing their jobs. And as experts, as I have said, they are even peculiarly liable to fall into the trap of being "influential" though they do not determine policy, because they are exploited for their brains and not merely as prestigious names. An academic is likely to take enormous pride in seeing his brain child become great in the world, even as a monster.

Yet the professors are peculiarly puzzling. Their very energy of intellect drives them to make sense, and their ineffectuality is mysterious. Take, roughly as a group, the Committees of Correspondence, writers of newsletters that we circulate to put whatever intellect we have into relaxing the cold war and preventing the nuclear war. (The ambitious American Revolutionary title was chosen to fit the gravity of the task, but it is certainly pompous considering the activity of the members.) Pretty unanimously these correspondents agree that war is not thinkable as a policy; that deterrence is suicidal; that the garrison-state is undermining liberty and morality; that the American administration is not bona fide in its peace talks—it does nothing to reconvert the economy, it lies to us, etc.; and indeed, that national sovereignty must go. Nevertheless, whenever there is an actual event—a "crisis" in Berlin, a resumption of testing—at once the professors start over as if they had not made up their minds, and they bat it around in the terms of the front page of the *Times*. They argue the technical pros and cons; they sympathize with Jack Kennedy's difficulties; they advise the government. They even go so far as to indulge in the speculations of war-game theory, their difference from the Rand Corporation being that the Rand people think we can win whereas our people prove that we must lose. In the New York Committee, of which I am a laggard member, the watchword is research. This means research not on how to make our wishes prevail, but on the inaccuracies of Herman Kahn!

Of course, professors are academics and suffer the moral hazards of that situation, the disconnection of thought and practice, the check-rein of administrators who make the important decisions, immurement with adolescents whom they can neither lead nor mix with, the vanity of classroom authority, and battles of book reviews. Also, there is little community of the faculty in American universities, and we suffer from the disastrous

German rule of "academic freedom" that forbids faculty pronouncements in politics. As we have it in America, the academic environment is not calculated to produce commitment and engagement as a climax of intellectual conviction. (Under other circumstances, of course, academic society has been admirably apt for intellectual engagement.) Just as in their schools where the administration sets up the syllabus and the classes, the professors seem to require somebody else's framework in order to act; they can think and criticize but they cannot initiate policy out of their own convictions. They demonstrate that the official position will ruin us, but they panic at any unofficial alternative.

Yet the pathology goes deeper than this environmental conditioning. There is a political pathology in the essence of contemporary social theory that makes revolutionary alternatives inconceivable to the social scientists. With the best will in the world they cannot see any source of power outside the established power, so there is no point in wishing or talking in other terms, even though the established power has no other *raison d'être* than to wage the cold war! The social scientists are balked by the narrowness of what they regard as admissible evidence. Contemporary social theory consists in analyzing the arrangement and possible rearrangement of units that are defined as entirely socialized to the system of society, or as deviant. The theory omits animal nature, which cannot be entirely socialized; it omits history, which tells us that men have been very different from those they are dealing with; it omits political philosophy, which tells what men ought to be if life is to be worth living; it omits poetic literature, which imagines other ways of being men. But if we omit these approaches and deal only with "men as they are," we are soon left with the world of the front page and of TV, as if this were the real world. In that world there is no other power than the established power, of force, publicity, status, vested holdings, protocol, and the market. Of these, only the market offers free choices, of course powerfully manipulated; the rest are systematically imposed. On the other hand, there are no conceivable viable alternatives that might newly spring from desire, community, compassion, productive function, jealous freedom, simple justice, utility, common sense, scholarship, tradition, etc. Such things are hardly mentioned on the front page, but sometimes in obituaries or as human interest.

Once, at a conference on disarmament at Columbia, I tried to introduce sexual and animal factors as relevant to the discussion of a psychotic system of theorizing. The response was merriment. This mirth was partly, of course, produced by the school-girlish embarrassment of professors and statesmen at the mention of copulation; but it was mainly that such factors do not occur, and perhaps cannot occur, in the discussions of the cold war in the New York *Times* or the *Studies in Deterrence* distributed by Naval Ordnance.

In my opinion, the political pathology of the present social scientific method is of high importance, so let me give a few random examples of it. Here are some "Psychological Observations on the Student Sit-in Movement," by Drs. Jacob Fishman and Fredric Solomon. The gist is that the Negro sit-ins are a "pro-social acting out," like delinquency acting out deprivation, unconscious parental wishes, aggression and rebellion, but consciously based on moral imperatives, "the goals of conscience representing traditional Christian morality and the highest principles of traditional American democracy." In brief, for these Negro students, "Public action toward social goals is their way of at least temporarily resolving problems of identity, super-ego formation, and aggression." (In like manner, a more assertive behavior of the professors would betoken an unfinished neurotic situation.) In this analysis there is no mention of simple justice—that is, whether traditional Christian morality and American democracy are true or good. There is no mention of human indignation at being insulted; nor of the ingenuous political effort of youth to make a safer and happier world. I doubt that identity can be merely the resolution of an "inner" problem rather than also something to be discovered-and-created, in a community, by a man.

Sometimes the method is almost ludicrous. Criticizing a commodity-oriented suburb, Maurice Stein points out that "The accumulation of appliances can never render cooking permanently meaningful as long as the woman is unsure of its relation to her feminine identity"—and he proceeds to borrow from Erik Erikson the thought that "Identity depends on the accessibility of roles in which acceptance by significant others is assured." This has merit, but oddly, at no point in the discussion does Professor Stein once mention food, feeding, or good cooking, although in the end it must be these that make cooking meaningful and guarantee acceptance, and make the cook proudly feel that she is somebody. It is characteristic of our social scientists never to mention the function, the satisfaction (or danger), the process, the product, or the utility. This leaves out most of the things by which we could actively *change* anybody's "acceptance" or "rejection." There is no factual criterion outside the system of roles to justify liquidating some of the roles.

Let me give another example along the same lines. In our economic and industrial relations a workman has no say in the utility of the product or the technique of the process; *therefore* his foreground criterion for a job is "security." But under normal conditions, a workman is secure if what he makes is necessary, so that his work is wanted; and if the process employs his aptitudes, so that it is he who is wanted. Yet in management and labor unions both, our social engineers do not think in these terms. Rather, they take the secondary sentiment of "security" as the ultimate desire of the man, and make no effort to cope with the real irk of the job. Men socialized to an unsatisfactory situation are mistaken for "men as they are."

(We utopians are said to want the ideal, which is unrealistic, for society can never provide more than the tolerable. The charge is false. We would be quite content with the tolerable, which would allow individuals to make something of themselves if they have it in them. But it is the way of the present democracy-by-consent to settle for the not-intolerable, for the system to oppress as far as it can without arousing a squawk. Inevitably, as we see in our urbanism, people become inured and resigned to a greater and greater degree of the not-intolerable. Yet none of this will seem important to a sociologist until there is a fantastic explosion.)

In an essay on Vassar, Theodore Newcomb points out that "Students and faculty are two societies occupying the same territory." So Professors Jencks and Riesman of Harvard: "Professors and students know one another as ambassadors from mutually fearful cultures." Pursuing this notion of the colleges "as they are," the social scientists then try to devise a system of education in terms of acculturation of the alien tribes. But by so doing they neglect the possibility of making a good university, one founded on a more correct anthropology, namely that the students and teachers are one society, the students growing up and learning from the teachers as veterans. In the analysis of the professors, the youth sub-culture is taken as irreducible, whereas this sub-culture is in fact their reaction to being balked by adult society. And the teachers are relegated to being forever academics, but it is their embarrassment, timidity, and lack of function in the world that make them so.

Thus, neglecting history, animal and social nature, political philosophy, and poetry, the social scientists are left with a closed society in which nothing is possible but a better arrangement of the same forces. People's opinions, prejudices, neuroses, and fears as revealed by questionnaires and depth-questionnaires will fairly reflect the same structure of society—what else would they reflect? But indeed the questions themselves usually offer only the usual choices. Only the "No Opinion" gets outside the box. Tests of personality are not used for therapy, as they were designed, to open new possibilities for removing personality blocks, but are used precisely for social engineering, to facilitate a more painless and "efficient" adjustment of the same personalities to the same system. Not surprisingly people increasingly do not adjust—the most recent study says that 80 per cent of persons in midtown Manhattan are nutty—but this is again taken not as a defect in our way of life but as a defect in our way of socializing people to that way of life.

Then suddenly some of the professors notice that the *system as a whole* is drifting toward disaster. The cold war is "escalating." They cry out in alarm. They underwrite ads in the *Times*. They form Committees of Correspondence. All this is earnest, courageous, non-conforming. But they do not, apparently they cannot, think, or step, outside the framework of the drifting system. The cold war escalates further, but their response does *not* escalate further. They do not say "I won't." They do not invent.

III. Practical Syllogism

To explain all this, we must explore ahead. The professors are balked more by their habits of thought than by their middle-class and academic habits of life. They are intellectuals; inquiry is their existential commitment; if they could habitually think differently, they would eventually live differently. What is the background of their frustrating kind of thought?

The problem can be defined pretty sharply: they reason practically but do not come to a conclusion of practice. Consider a practical syllogism of a simple form: "I want an X," "Here is an X," then the conclusion from these premises is *not* another proposition, but an action—to take the X and use it. (So negatively: "This behavior is disadvantageous," "I could stop it," then the conclusion is in fact to stop.) Psychosomatically, the meaning of this simple logic is clear. Where does the energy of action come from? The desire expressed in the first premise is the energy of the action of the conclusion. The second premise, that gathers information about the environment, is also selected and attended to because of the desire in the major. And finally, the act, the climax of practical reasoning, is the release to activity of the motoric system that has been held in check during the verbal part. Now let us consider this verbal part. Why does the man verbalize his experience at all? Presumably the speaker *says* "I want" as a request or a demand on another, and meanwhile holds his own motor behavior in check, waiting for a response. "Here is, etc." is seeking orientation: to ascertain the availability, permissibility, location which must be determined for action. Since there is a problem, there is a delay called "thinking"; since there is a useful interpersonal context, there is speech; but the solution of the problem is a feelingful and appropriate action. On the whole, practical reasoning, like any other normal act, is an integration of feeling, sensation, and motor behavior, usually in a community.

In recent models of practical reasoning, however, there is an extraordinary emphasis on a stage called "deciding" or "decision-making." To quote one of the writers on administration, John Corson: "Decision-making is the central and continual business of every human enterprise." What is implied in this astonishing proposition? Normally, apart from obsessionals, deciding is not a major part of practice.

There is, in the present economic and social arrangements, a high concentration of control of capital, a large (and usually excessive) component of frozen capital regarded as an investment that must pay off, a top-down management of the machinery, long-chain bureaucracy, considerable ignorance and indifference of most workers as to what the enterprise is about, and almost total ignorance of everybody as to what they as persons are about. The style of the products is largely built into the machinery; the style of life into the relations of production; and the style of thought is predetermined by the system itself. Indeed, the limits of choice, of deciding, are narrowly set by what the predetermined thought and style of the system can allow as alternatives. The choice of one or another of the limited alternatives is called "decision-making" and it seems to be vastly important because it "influences" so vast a machine; but of course the influence is slight, because nothing can be decided that differs from what the machine will accept as a program to operate with. The machine itself cannot be much altered because it is so heavily capitalized and must pay off. And the system of relations as a whole is so tightly controlled and so complicated that it "goes by itself." Little is really decided, but deciding stands out as an act peculiarly potent, important, and free simply because it is so isolated from the matrix of immediate desire, concrete perception, inventive thought, motoric strength and rhythm that constitutes ordinary practical and intellectual life. Managers are prestigious because they are the remnants of men, whereas the others are not men at all.

But the decision-maker, the administrator, is only a remnant. He has little personal desire or concern for the goal; he knows little about the information that comes to him in a form so highly processed that it has often lost the essence of the reality; nor is it he who implements the decision, so that he does not grow by practice. In brief, our present style of big practical judgment—corporate, mechanical, managerial—is, psychosomatically, a trivial remnant of normal practice; but it does satisfy the illusory conceit of being a big wheel.

Return now to our professors. My guess is that they, whose private lives are usually pretty restricted, have become so mesmerized by this big style that they no longer remember what it feels like simply to reason and act. Secondarily they rationalize their avoidance of important life-choices by saying that only "big" decision-making has public consequences. In my opinion, even this rationalization is an error, because straightforward reasonable practice has great rhetorical force (especially by contrast), whereas corporate, managerial, and public-relations decisions are rightly taken whence they come, as making little significant difference.

(By the way, I do not believe that an advanced technology necessarily involves what I have been describing: concentrated management, bureaucracy, alienation of labor, and the emasculation of practical reasoning to decision-making. Quite the contrary, these are by and large inefficient, unexperimental, uncritical, and discouraging to invention. I write this paragraph because I have learned from experience that to point out structural defects of the present social arrangements is at once to be called a machine-breaker who wants to return to something called the Middle Ages. This is again an example of mesmerized superstition.)

Another important factor in the professors' behavior is their disposition to verbalize experience and keep it verbalized, rather than to use speech as an action upon others. They shun any argument *ad hominem*. "Communication" comes to mean the exchange of ideas from one head to another with each person's character-defense left intact and his pattern of behavior unaltered. Speakers put only their formulation at stake, not their lives, their fortunes, or their sacred honor. When they come to share a common idea, it is with the same detachment. Since they have staked nothing and have not committed their persons in their speech, their agreement gives them no strength of solidarity, and there is no engagement in the action that would normally follow on agreement.

This is, of course, what is meant by an argument being academic; since nothing is changed by it, it is always possible to reverse positions and argue the contrary. (It is a good teaching method for the freshman and sophomore years.) Faculty meetings, with their departmental courtesy, are a training-ground: one is supposed to excel in speech in one's field, but it is bad form to insist on anything, for the sake of action, that would invade somebody else's preserve. Scholarly detachment is necessary for intellectual consideration, but finally the flow of words must come home to oneself, in action or character-change; otherwise we have mere conversation-pieces and ping-pong, a speech-game designed for ceremony, or to show off, or at best to one-up and establish a pecking order.

Effective speech, however, is a personal contact and the grounds of personal contact, whether affectionate or aggressive, are psychosexual and communal. Until our mores become sexier, dirtier, friendlier, and angrier, we cannot expect intellectual speech to be *ad hominem*. Yet if argument is not at least potentially *ad hominem,* the speaker's lurking motivations and deep-grained habits are never brought into the foreground, challenged, and tested. And without felt motivation and felt attitude, new reasoning cannot pass into new practice.

To think and then act requires faith. A man must believe that he and his peers, correcting one another's reasoning, and making it common and public, have finally as good a sampling of reality as there is. And they are as adequate judges of it as there are, for any other judgments are merely made by other groups of men who, one has reason to suspect, might be more ignorant or fraudulent. And most important, a man must believe that the world is a world *for* him; if he exercises initiative and takes a step, his action will have an effect, however small, in the same real world. He will not suddenly be without ground underfoot. Faith is animal faith, as Santayana said, but it is also a ground of poetry, according to philosophy, in the stream of history. It is humane. A man has faith that if he is well-intentioned, rational, not fanatical, he is not alone; there is a human community that is thinking the same thoughts as himself and his friends, and ready to act in concert. Of course I do not know where such faith in the nature of things and in the human community comes from, nor how it can be infused. It is faith. It seems to me to be the most proximate cause of initiative. It is not very helpful of me to end these reflections with a confidence that I cannot transfer from my breast to yours. But at least I have tried to show how the conditions of our society discourage it, my hope being that we can then learn to stand out of the way.

October 1962

William Phillips

WHAT HAPPENED IN THE 30's

For the last two decades almost everyone has been trying to forget what happened in the 30's; now, suddenly, everyone is trying to remember. Ideas that had been written off are back in circulation again, and commitments that for years had been dismissed as "irresponsible" are once more taken seriously. The explanation is not so hard to find, but it is sticky and takes us into problems we do not like to face. For the new turn means that temperate solutions having failed, people are looking again for radical ones.

In this see-saw of beliefs and commitments lies the main story of our time. And to ask what happened in the 30's is only a way of asking what is happening today.

The going version of the story is that the radical spirit ruled the 30's while the 40's and 50's were dedicated to conservatism, philistinism, chauvinism, and that now the pendulum is swinging once more to the left. This picture is really too simple, and comes out of the sentimental association of radicalism with purity. It ignores the unsavory side of the radical movement, brought mostly by the Communists, just as it leaves out the legitimate distaste for party-line thinking that originally led many people to break with ideas and organizations linked to the Communists. Still, the going version of the story does contain a certain amount of truth. The fact is that despite all the illusions and duplicities of the 30's, it was a time when human aims seemed more attractive than national goals and when articulate people talked more about the hope for an ideal society than the benefits of the existing one. It was a time when responsibility meant responsibility to ideas and convictions, justice seemed more important than expediency, the greater good meant more than the lesser evil, dreams seemed more cogent than reality.

Mostly, the 30's was a period of contradictions. It was a time of sense and nonsense, idealism and cynicism, morality and immorality, disinterestedness and power drive, and it was a time when it was possible to believe simultaneously in democracy and dictatorship, in an anti-human abstraction called History and in a moral idea of man usually regarded as unhistorical. It seemed possible to believe in everything and its opposite; and a theory of dialectics along with a politics of expediency were used to rationalize the untenable and justify the reprehensible.

If we are content to itemize these pluses and minuses and to reiterate that they add up to a state of contradiction, it is not so difficult to say what happened in the 30's, and what has happened since then. The trouble starts when we try to figure out the exact relation of sense to nonsense, of right to wrong both in the radical tradition and in the swing away from it toward the center and the right. For this means we must decide whether the radicalism of the 30's was an aberration or a movement in the main line of history, or both, and whether the anti-radical mood that followed was a reaction against being taken in or a reconciliation with things as they are. What we think of these periods has to do as much with the future as with the past.

One could deal with such problems systematically. But I have been struck, from the beginning, by a question that gets to the heart of the subject: how the radical movement in this country—which included not only the Communists but all the splinter groups on the left—could at the same time be so marginal, so parochial, so mindless, and also so relevant and so central. I am thinking mostly of the literary and intellectual side of the radical movement—which could take Mike Gold, Jack Conroy, and Edwin Seaver as important writers—though I am not exempting completely its politics, which resembled most of the other great radical movements of the past in everything except the level and subtlety of its thinking. Despite the sweep of its ideas, despite the fact that the radical movement—rightly or wrongly, it does not matter—addressed itself to the major issues of modern life, in America it always seemed alien and off-beat, like some avant-garde tendency that had not yet become respectable. There was an enormous incongruity between the claims of the left to relevance, centrality, universality, and the sectarian crudity of almost everything it said and did. People who spoke for the future had the most shaky relation to the present.

An example of this incongruity is the John Reed Clubs. The John Reed Clubs were supposed to be organizations of left-wing writers and artists, scattered throughout the country. But they were made up mostly of aspiring writers and artists, part of the army of magazine rejectees, and of cultural functionaries who tried to overcome their creative frustrations by attending endless meetings and making passionate speeches about such unreal subjects as the "culture" of the working class. Yet most accounts of the 30's miss this peculiar, almost pathetic, combination of deception and self-deception, this perpetual activity which not only furthered the doctrines of the Communists but also filled the lives of people who found their way to art through politics, by all kinds of cultural bustling. Richard Wright's account in *The God That Failed* of the convention of the John Reed Clubs in Chicago is an instance of the failure to convey the tone of the organization. As Wright tells it, the story of the convention sounds like an epic of soul-searchings and heroic statements about art and society. The truth is that the result of the meeting, the disbanding of the John Reed Clubs, was decided in advance; and most of the speeches one after another either advocated dissolution or recited the non-existent achievements of each club.

One wonders—one even wondered then—whether or how such people change the world: and for the better?

Incongruities of this sort crop up constantly both in politics and in art. Revolutionary movements usually begin in the wings, in an intellectual ghetto and the transfer from the marginal to the central is a matter of shifting the balance of power. In art, too, particularly in modern times, the familiar course is from the fringe to the center. It is not simply that a new work gets praised often enough until it becomes a classic; frequently, as in Joyce and Kafka, works that lie solidly in the middle of the tradition were regarded as alien and aberrated when they first appeared. It is as though the main stream must periodically have the look of a creek.

Thus, there would seem to be precedents for the incongruities of the 30's. Yet this was not just another instance of the typical disguised as the marginal, of the sage in the role of the outcast. It was not only the novelty and originality of the left, its genuinely radical quality, that gave it an alien look. The fact is there was something alien, something inauthentic, in the crude and sectarian form into which Marxist ideas had been squeezed by the official Communists. This is not to say that the movement was entirely inauthentic; it means that it was not free to make its own mistakes.

In this combination of authentic and inauthentic elements lies the key not only to the 30's but to what is going on today. The mixed character of the left is of course not a secret, but for polemical reasons one or the other part of the mixture usually has been ignored. The right, for example, constantly plays down the authentic side, the legitimacy of revolt; the left, on the other hand, often glosses over breaches of democracy. (A good current example is Cuba: conservatives deny the just goals of the revolution; radicals tend to close their eyes to the injustices.) In the 30's we saw the first, traumatic eruption of these contradictory forces, which insofar as they are free are revolutionary and insofar as they are tied to Soviet interests serve bureaucratic and dictatorial ends. The situation is further complicated by the fact that this country has seceded, more than is commonly assumed, from European thinking. Hence Marxism, which grew out of the European mind, was not able to take on a native accent and thus seemed all the more alien.

For a time the true character of the 30's was obscured by political bias. Now it is blurred by the opposite tendency: the failure to make distinctions. Today anything in the past, sense and nonsense, of all political shades, is filed away under History, and what with the new interest in the 30's, the machinery of scholarship has been put to work full-time to set the record straight. But frequently those chosen for this task have been scholars whose main qualification is that they know nothing of the period or the subject, and are thus through ignorance endowed with objectivity. (Objectivity, so far as I can tell, means an inability to make discriminating judgments.) The turn against revolutionary theory, having become a turn against theory, works to idealize raw facts and to break down the distinctions not only between theories but between different kinds of facts. For you can distinguish between facts as well as theories only on the basis of some theories, some assumptions, some idea of the past and of the future. Hence the native suspicion of theory in this country has combined with the reaction against left ideology and with the new academicism to produce bland, homogenized histories of radicalism that sound like retroactive tape-recordings.

Daniel Aaron's recent *Writers on the Left* is freer of these faults than most other histories of the period. I suppose Aaron would be the best choice if one were looking for an intelligent and open-minded historian. His book is a remarkably balanced and fair account of a period that was made up mostly of intellectual infighting. On the theoretical side, Aaron's sober treatment of the question of why so many writers went left, part or all the way, should serve as an antidote to the notion of Communism as nothing but a "conspiracy," bandied about by reactionaries and obsessive anti-Communists—a notion which absolves people from thinking about history. On the factual side, the book is bound to be most valuable as a reference work, particularly to supply the facts for those who want to argue about the meaning of the period.

But the pile-up of the facts gave me the feeling of re-living rather than re-examining or re-thinking the period. What I mean is that in reading the book one is carried back to the feeling of being engaged in a day-to-day way in the hum of things, and one loses one's sense of perspective. This is particularly disturbing to one who, like myself, lived through these events. For, by being thrown back, I was constantly reminded of the claustrophobic excitement and absurdity of the 30's and of my own feeling of wanting to escape the breathless activity that twisted almost everything that counted, without losing the idea of oneself as a radical.

What comes through strongly in Aaron's book is the vulgarity and the idiocy, much more strongly than the idealism, which is taken for granted;

and when the idealism does appear in the statements of the leading figures, like Mike Gold or Granville Hicks, it is so loaded with a militant philistinism of the left, almost inevitably so, that one wonders how it could ever have existed in any other form. And since Aaron is committed to a scholarly neutrality, it is difficult for him to separate independent ideas from orthodoxies or from free-lance nonsense that was officially tolerated, and all these things are given equal importance as they are paraded before one in a procession of dates, documents, meetings, arguments. For example, the mixture of native populism and imported Marxism, vulgarized for organizational purposes, that gave Communist rhetoric its characteristic flavor, is put on the same plane as efforts by people like Edmund Wilson and those who wrote for *Partisan Review* to work out a position on their own. Also all kinds of statements, even those made retroactively for purposes of self-justification, like those of Joseph Freeman, are given equal weight. Aaron's seeming lack of bias actually produces a biased view of the 30's, the bias coming from the assumption that something called the "record" is identical with the history.

But there is also an explicit bias—a conventional one—in the assumption that breaking was better than staying in the fold. If there are any heroes and villains, then the villains are those who stuck with the party and the heroes those who eventually saw the light. Hence figures like Max Eastman, Joseph Freeman, Granville Hicks, Dos Passos, come off pretty well, though the fact that none of them had much to say at that time that might be interesting today is glossed over by Aaron. Actually Aaron's idea of the 30's is currently the most enlightened, liberal view: like an indulgent parent, it sees the 30's as a stage of wildness which one outgrows. Thus by making the frivolous and the serious sides of the 30's indistinguishable from each other, both of them are played down. And by playing down its serious side, its revolutionary side, the failures of the 30's are made to look like lapses in intellectual history.

Since we cannot come intellectually unarmed to these questions we must begin with one or another bias. And, paradoxically, we can reach some kind of objectivity only through the power and depth of our bias. My own bias amounts to a polemical position developed in the 30's and one which I am still more or less committed to. This position, shared mostly by a group of young writers associated at that time with *Partisan Review,* was for purity in politics and impurity in literature. Politically, this meant a stand for morality in politics. In literature, it meant a radicalism rooted in tradition and open to experiment, and an awareness that the imagination could not be contained within any orthodoxy. It meant that one could not rule out any literary beliefs or forms as incompatible with socialist aims. For example, T. S. Eliot's ideological conservatism automatically made him taboo in official leftist circles, but to the group around

Partisan Review he was a major poet, and a revolutionary one, who—as Edmund Wilson put it in *Axel's Castle*—had accomplished in the area of sensibility a breakthrough analogous to Marxism in political thought.

Such a position really amounted to a complete break with the Communists, though this was not perhaps so clear at the beginning because the conflict was muffled by practical pressures and by the illusion that the Communists were educable. Generally, we were aware of the party's effects on thinking and writing before we understood what was wrong politically. As I now see it, it was the inauthenticity of the radical movement that many of us who youthfully were drawn to it turned against. The accepted view of the 30's, and one that Aaron shares, is that Marxist—or Communist—doctrine was grafted on to native radicalism. But what is usually overlooked is that American radicalism was of a very special kind. It was essentially populist, insular, anti-intellectual; and most of its standard-bearers had a characteristically rough-and-ready American style.

The earlier figures, like Eugene Debs, Upton Sinclair, Jack London, Max Haywood, Floyd Dell, were particularly homegrown in their outlook and their tone. But it is most significant that even later writers, like John Reed, Mike Gold, Max Eastman, and Joseph Freeman, did not break with the grass-roots tradition, and some of them—Mike Gold, for example—actively promoted it. In effect, then, the radical movement in the 30's, particularly in the arts, got its accent from the more primitive, egalitarian, plain-speaking strains in American culture.

Now we know that there have been two dominant strains in American culture, and in choosing the "folk" tradition while repudiating the "intellectual" one, the radical movement was taking a political as well as a literary stand. And why, one must ask, did it take that stand? After all, the Marxist movement was nothing if not ideological, full of historical portents and meanings and connections. It actually was a haven for people who preferred theories to facts; and much of the resistance to Marxism in this country came from the native empirical, anti-ideological temper. It seems to me, therefore, that if the radical movement had been permitted to follow its natural course it would never have become entangled with the free-wheeling, grass-roots tradition. It would have been urban, intellectual, and critical, as it was in the writings of Marx and Engels, and even later in Plekhanov and Lukacs. And I think left-wing writers on their own would have come to terms with literary tradition instead of rejecting it outright or latching on to its crudest expressions. They would at least have tried to relate themselves to the most advanced, the most "radical" (in a literary sense) figures and currents: to Joyce and to Kafka rather than to Jack London and Upton Sinclair, to the School of Paris and not to our domestic naturalists. Who knows?—we might have been spared all those proletarian novels and pictures of workers that made a principle of amateurism and banality. But the movement was not a free one; and in the end it must be said that the needs of the Communist party determined the literary course of American radicalism.

Why this was so is not entirely clear. But it does seem natural for a bureaucracy to celebrate the "culture" of the common man, partly as a compensation for control and also as a means of creating the illusion of freedom. An undemocratic organization favors the rise to power of bureaucratic types who out of ignorance or envy encourage a contempt for intellectual traditions. As one re-reads some of the salutes to illiteracy quoted in Aaron's book, all in the name of democracy, one is struck by the fact that this was really an assault on the "establishment." Personal and party interests came together in this alliance of functionaries with writers who were not successful and amateurs who became writers by joining literary clubs and parading as spokesmen for the working class. Behind the crude aesthetics lay the question of power.

Power meant organizational control and manipulation of people and ideas. But it also took a negative form: the resistance tended to be expressed in literary dissidence. For dissidence made itself felt through a criticism of crude, agitational, populist slogans—like the idea of art as a weapon, or that of proletarian art—and in an insistence that art be separated from party politics. Most dissidents did not go along with the rejection of past culture as "bourgeois" culture, nor did they accept the orthodox notion that "tradition" was the baggage of reactionaries. Of course, their idea of tradition was a selective one, but only the academy thinks of tradition as the sum of all the values and works of the past, to be taken over intact by new periods and writers. Each new work and each new idea is subversive, but instead of destroying all links with the past it creates new links. "Tradition" is an ever-changing sense of the past, a retroactive revolution.

In this respect, all radical literary movements are alike, whether or not they are tied to a radical politics. And one need hardly point out again that most of the literature of the last hundred years was rooted in a criticism of society or in some idea of revolt, or in some utopian principle. Sometimes, as in a writer like Zola, for example, the connections were explicit; in someone like Rimbaud, the legendary *revolté,* the radical break is expressed through a derangement of reality. In any case the assertion of the new rearranges but does not deny the past. And within the Communist movement it was the arch-dissident, Trotsky, who came out for this principle of radical continuity. He not only dismissed the whole idea of proletarian art as a bureaucractic myth, but he also said he believed, in opposition to official doctrine, that all radical literary movements in this period were bound to be bohemian and avant-garde.

As I see it, this was the conflict on the left in the 30's: the conflict between a free-floating radical spirit and a historical force that both channeled it and throttled it. But this was not only the literary conflict; it was also the heart of the political one. For the Communist movement killed the *idea* of socialism for western intellectuals at the same time that it planted it in masses of people throughout the world. Hence to be a revolutionary socialist in America or Europe meant being a utopian and having nothing to do with power, while to be a socialist in Latin America, for example, meant being related to power and dissociated from any traditional—or utopian—ideals of the free mind. It is much easier to be an authentic radical when one is not tempted by power. What ultimately compromised the idea of socialism was the possibility of putting it into practice, and almost immediately the question raised by the character of the Soviet Union was whether the lack of democracy was accidental or inevitable.

If much of the history of the left has been obscured, it has been because many beliefs held in the 30's were abandoned without being refuted. They were simply assumed to be false though no one bothered to cite the proof. The proof was in the air, and the new generations just inhaled it, along with all the other advanced ideas that were taken for granted. This is one reason why the revival of left-wing attitudes today has brought confusion.

Actually, the enthusiasm for socialism that flourished in the 30's waned quite slowly, as we went through several stages of skepticism and disaffection. The first shock came with the discovery that the new utopia was a dictatorship. The disillusionment reached its peak during the purges and the Moscow Trials. But for some years the disaffection was with the Russian variety rather than with the principle of socialism. The question whether this was the natural form a socialist movement must take once it seizes power was simply never resolved. What happened instead was that the anti-Communist recoil was so strong and the possibility of creating a free socialist movement so weak that the concern with socialism began to wither away. After a time it was just assumed that the verdict of history was in—against socialism. And, as we can now see, the anti-Communist mood merged with a growing acceptance of the life of this country, and of the West, as a whole. Content does not usually stimulate radical feelings; and any discontent that could not be repressed was diffused into concern with the human condition, as in existentialism, or transformed into sexual revolt, which has become the rebellious mode of our time. Socialism—indeed any form of radicalism—was assumed to be a doctrine for those romantics who were either too young to remember the past or too old to forget it.

This, as we know, is the way things stood until just a few years ago, when suddenly the intellectual mood became a radical one again. The moderates and conservatives were brushed aside. The thinkers who had presided over the return to the fold were abruptly dismissed as having nothing to say to this period: having played out their role as apologists they could now be installed as the elder statesmen of the status quo. The campuses were teeming with meetings, and marches, and protests, first on the issue of civil rights and then on the issue of nuclear war. And writers began to exhibit again the radical badges of their profession. It looked as though we were back in the 30's.

But there was a big difference: the left was no longer political in the old sense, in the sense of having a vision of a new society, and a theory to support it. The left was concerned not with society but with humanity, or rather with the threat of its annihilation by a nuclear war. The radical movement became a peace movement. There were many reasons for this shift, some having to do with the exhaustion of the old radical tradition and the failure to create a new one, but mostly it was because the spectre of total destruction had made the ordinary problems of social change look academic. This is our paradox. A radical politics requires a sense of stability and continuity, a span of time, and, ironically, this is precisely what the new weapons have destroyed. You can no longer transform society in time of war—in the time, that is, between the launching and landing of a missile, nor can you transform it in time of peace, for then you might risk the possibility of war, without disturbing the delicate balance of terror on which peace depends.

History has a remarkable way of providing—in a Hegelian sense—the necessary (though not always the right) force for the moment. And the peace movement looks like just such an inevitable force. It seems almost as though all the bottled up feelings of wide-eyed hope and fear in the era of the missile have exploded into the "peace movement"; and through its very chaos, its spontaneity, its amateurism, the peace movement as a whole expresses the unusual combination of utopianism and practicality so typical of political idealism today.

In another way, however, the 60's do mark a return to the problem of the 30's, but turned inside out. For the 60's, like the 30's, are concerned with the revolutionary assault on existing society promoted by the Soviet Union, but this time the assault relies as much on military power as on political manipulation. As in the 30's, the prescription for change is in the Marxist critique of capitalism, and in an ideology for liberation and technological fulfillment for backward societies. But the important difference is that in the 30's choices presented themselves in organizational forms; and Western intellectuals felt they had to define themselves in relation to parties and movements, to organized zealots who talked in the name of history. Today, however, it might be said that we face history directly. For one thing, the power of the Soviet Union is such that the ideology of the state has taken the place of the ideology of the party. But more important is the fact that revolutionary change throughout the world is a reality, not just a threat, that haunts the West. And if there should be no war, the so-called peaceful competition between West and East is really very little more than an enactment on a global scale of the intellectual arguments of the 30's. One is dazzled to see in official form what used to be the problems of an intellectual underground: today, for example, the American government must actually cope in Latin America with the old factional, intramural questions of whether a backward country could solve its problems under an enlightened capitalism, and if not, whether a revolutionary regime could preserve democratic forms.

The avante-garde questions of the 30's have become the mass questions of today, and, as has happened frequently in matters of culture, Western intellectuals have lost their particular stake in them. The politics of the intellectuals has become the politics of governments, which means the intellectuals today have no independent politics. Practical intellectuals are busy telling the government how to use its power; impractical ones are trying to get the government to give up its power—by disarmament.

But, whatever the continuity of radical politics, there seems to be no continuity in literature. For the unnatural situation of the 30's cannot be duplicated; and even the Communist countries, particularly Poland, are having difficulty holding on to the notion that art is a branch of politics. If the literary radicalism of the 30's had any lasting effect in this country, it was mainly to reinforce the populist, egalitarian, anti-intellectual attitudes so deeply rooted in American history. Most of all what the left did was to make intellectually respectable popular attitudes that literature in the past had either attacked or ignored. In the 20's, we recall, writing found most of its excitement in being alienated, advanced, experimental. There were exceptions, of course, but most writing was anti-social, anti-philistine, unpolitical; much of it was by liberal standards reactionary; and it carried the elan of a minority, as it snubbed the idea of audience and was impatient with the idea that literature was along with politics, civil liberties, and housing, part of a general good.

If we think of the era before the left took over as being dominated or expressed by such writers as Proust, Joyce, Mann, Lawrence, it becomes evident that, beginning with the 30's, there has been a major shift of sensibility. All of these figures, now dangling like classics, created large unified visions, of the kind no longer sought after by writers; and the reason, I think, is that the opposition of contemporary writing to contemporary life takes place within the accepted world, while the writers of the earlier period were really creating another, self-contained system. Of Lawrence or Joyce or Kafka, for example, it can be said that each in his own way was constructing some ideal consciousness, some pure vision that was not only revolutionary but also messianic, and was rooted in the assumption of a moral and intellectual elite. In a Nietzschean sense, literature was conceived as an act of breaking through the accepted categories: which is why so much writing of the 20's was anti-naturalist, mythic, obsessive, and ultimately moral in its search for a new kind of wholeness and authenticity. If we compare Gide's or Proust's handling of a perverse theme with that of Nabokov, what strikes us most is that Proust, by transforming the theme, treated it as part of the human condition, and Gide turned it into a moral conflict between one's nature and one's responsibilities. Nabokov, on the other hand, handles a morally subversive theme as though it were odd but not unacceptable, and he gives it an air of normality by using a picaresque form and a prose so smooth and facile that it makes *Lolita* sound like another funny story. Similarly, most new fiction—and many of the new movies—give the impression of having broken through the sexual taboos. But here, too, the point is that both the fiction and the movies are simply reflecting free-wheeling habits already taken for granted in more advanced circles.

It is difficult—and risky—to generalize about these trends. But I do think it can be said that after the 30's writing took to greater realism in style and theme, to smaller subjects, to more recognizable worlds. Quality aside, an important difference is that writing now is continuous with a common experience while in the past it might almost be said that writing competed with experience. There have been, of course, exceptions like Faulkner, who out of detachment wrote as though nothing had changed, or someone like E. M. Forster, who links the past with the present. Then, too, of contemporary Americans, Saul Bellow's fiction has its own boundaries, and writers like Norman Mailer, Bernard Malamud, or Mary McCarthy are by no means the naturalists they are sometimes taken to be. Recently, too, the trend has shown signs of reversal: Beckett and Genet (in their plays) remind us of the earlier generalizations of experience which could be at once true and unreal, and whose energy lay in a kind of warped idealism. The new novelists in France, whom I do not find very exciting, also are attempting to break with common assumptions through a new style of observation, a so-called higher objectivity.

What I am suggesting is that the radical movement of the 30's broke the radical spirit of literature by lowering its sights and making it more palatable for popular consumption. And, in this country, at least, the process of intellectual domestication fits in with the growing middle-class market for culture. The new audience for books and magazines, which was earnest, progressive, freed from moral and sexual taboos, overcivilized and undereducated—this new monster of consumption required the most serious and the best writing so long as it did not go beyond the limits of its experience and imagination. This is the tyranny of the enlightened audience. But it was not simply a commercial alliance between producer and consumer: the idea of the audience is an old standby of populists, reformers, and educators, and it was given a stamp of approval by the forces of the left in the 30's. One is, of course, tempted to say that this tyranny of the audience got its political impetus from the perversions of the left, and is not inherent in socialist doctrine. Still, the modern idea of progress does contain a belief in cultural improvement, and this means cultural servicing which, in turn, creates the shape and power of the audience.

One must conclude that radical literature reaches for an ideal rather than a *real* audience, for the *real* audience whether commercially or, as in Russia, politically manipulated, or simply formed by the inertia of the culture, tends to housebreak writers and preserve the illusion that the culture is all of a piece. The ideal audience, on the other hand, is constantly being recreated, and is continuous not with itself but with the history of new writing and new ideas. This is why the darlings of a kept audience rarely survive.

It now looks as though a radical literature and a radical politics must be kept apart. For radical politics of the modern variety has really served as an antidote to literature. The moral hygiene, the puritanism, the benevolence, the rationalism—all the virtues that sprout on the left—work like a cure for the perverse and morbid idealism of the modern writer. If writing is to be thought of as radical it must be in a deeper sense, in the sense not simply of cutting across the grain of contemporary life but also of reaching for the connections between the real and the forbidden and the fantastic. The classic example is Dostoevski, who, by connecting human with historical logic, found a moral thread running through the psychology of crime and the politics of revolution.

Maybe the lesson of the 30's is that radical politics has not been able to escape the dilemma of being distorted by power or left hanging without power, while literature to be radical need not—perhaps cannot—be tied to radical politics.

NORMAN PODHORETZ

Born in New York City in 1930, Norman Podhoretz has degrees from Columbia University, the Jewish Theological Seminary and Cambridge University. A member of the Phi Beta Kappa Society, Mr. Podhoretz has received Kellett and Fulbright fellowships. After teaching English literature and English moral philosophy at Clare College, Cambridge, in 1952 and 1953, he served in the U.S. Army with the Army Security Agency. From 1955 until 1958 he was associate editor of *Commentary*. During the next year he was editor-in-chief of Looking Glass Library, reprinters of children's classics. Since 1960 he has been editor-in-chief of *Commentary*. Mr. Podhoretz's articles and reviews have appeared in *The New Yorker, Show, Commentary, Harper's, Partisan Review, Esquire, The New York Times, New York Herald Tribune, Scrutiny, Midstream, The New Leader, The New Republic, Essays in Criticism* and *The Reporter,* and many have been reprinted in anthologies. He is the author of *Doings and Undoings: The Fifties and After in American Writing,* published in 1964.